Amarāvatī

Amarāvatī

Art and Buddhism in Ancient India

Jaś Elsner

With best wishes

Jaś

REAKTION BOOKS

For three good friends: Nai B.P., P.A.D., and in memory of L.S.C.

Published by Reaktion Books Ltd
Unit 32, Waterside
44–48 Wharf Road
London N1 7UX, UK
www.reaktionbooks.co.uk

First published 2024

Printed and bound in India by Replika Press Pvt. Ltd

A catalogue record for this book is available from the British Library

ISBN 978 1 78914 869 5

Contents

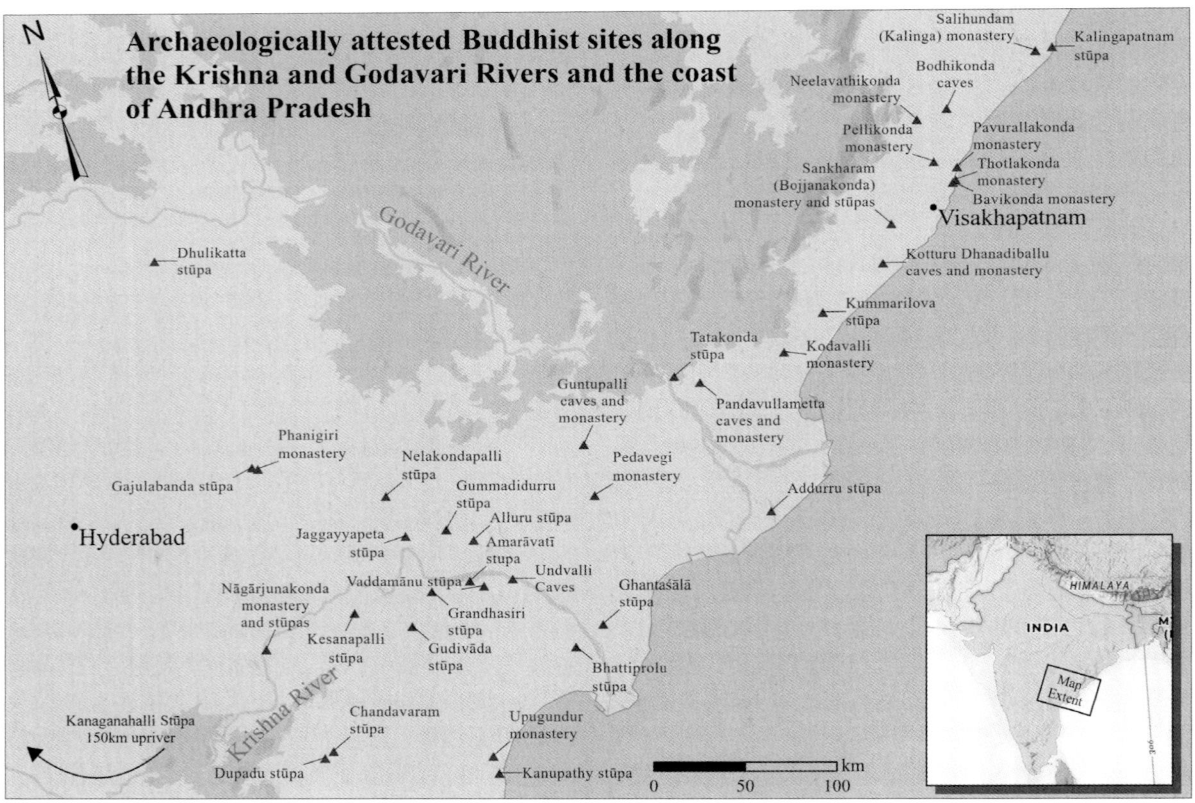

Archaeologically attested Buddhist sites along the Krishna and Godavari Rivers and the coast of Andhra Pradesh
N
Salihundam (Kalinga) monastery
Kalingapatnam stūpa
Bodhikonda caves
Neelavathikonda monastery
Pellikonda monastery
Pavurallakonda monastery
Thotlakonda monastery
Bavikonda monastery
Sankharam (Bojjanakonda) monastery and stūpas
Visakhapatnam
Godavari River
Dhulikatta stūpa
Kotturu Dhanadiballu caves and monastery
Kummarilova stūpa
Tatakonda stūpa
Kodavalli monastery
Guntupalli caves and monastery
Pandavullametta caves and monastery
Phanigiri monastery
Gajulabanda stūpa
Nelakondapalli stūpa
Pedavegi monastery
Gummadidurru stūpa
Addurru stūpa
Alluru stūpa
Hyderabad
Jaggayyapeta stūpa
Amarāvatī stūpa
Undvalli Caves
Vaddamānu stūpa
Nāgārjunakonda monastery and stūpas
Grandhasiri stūpa
Ghantaśālā stūpa
Kesanapalli stūpa
Gudivāda stūpa
Bhattiprolu stūpa
Krishna River
Kanaganahalli Stūpa 150km upriver
Chandavaram stūpa
Upugundur monastery
Dupadu stūpa
Kanupathy stūpa
km
0
50
100
HIMALAYA
INDIA
Map Extent

Preface

The aim of this book is to reconstruct (insofar as is possible) one of the most significant monuments of the late ancient world, the great stūpa of Amarāvatī, from the fragments, drawings and archaeological reports that have come down to us. It seeks to put the visual culture of the stūpa into a series of historical contexts: the history and geography of the area of its production and principal appeal (the Krishna River delta of Andhra Pradesh on the eastern coast of southern India) during the Sada, Sātavāhana and Ikṣvāku dynasties between the first century BCE and the early fourth century CE; the artistic and architectural environment of the creation of Buddhist art, especially stūpas across the Indian subcontinent; the ritual, religious and conceptual culture of Indian Buddhism at this time, a period of unprecedented creativity; and the larger intellectual macrocosm of Indian literary, philosophical and rhetorical culture beyond Buddhism – including Jain, Brahmanic and Vedic spiritualities – with which the arts created under Buddhist patronage inevitably engaged. These varied interconnections take us beyond Andhra, not only across the subcontinent and Sri Lanka but to trade routes via the Indian Ocean as far as the Roman Mediterranean.

It is hard to find a rival to the quality and quantity of sculptural decoration of the Amarāvatī stūpa at any time or place across the ancient or modern world. The monument is a superlative example of the religious and artistic vision of its makers, but it also made a significant material contribution in its own time to the culture's thinking about the meanings and doctrines of the religion that inspired it and arguably to their development in a particularly rich period of creativity in Indian Buddhism. There has hardly been any attempt to read Indian Buddhist art as a contribution to the vibrant scriptural and commentarial culture of the many schools of teaching and monasticism that developed across the subcontinent between the third century BCE and the sixth century CE, and were ultimately exported north and east to China, Tibet, Indonesia and Thailand, and west into Iran and Central Asia. I will argue here that the sculptures of Amarāvatī – even in their current damaged and debilitated state – are outstanding evidence of the theological (or we should rather say Buddhological) thoughtfulness of the stūpa's planners, patrons and sculptors, and this evidence works in dialogue with oral and written narratives and formulations of their religion.

Since its firm establishment as a respectable academic discipline at the end of the nineteenth century, the history of art has been and remains pulled in two directions: the formal appreciation and stylistic analysis of its objects of focus, and the attempt to set them in historical context. The first is an act of loving – the careful embrace of things, their materiality, textures, colour, iconography and internal structure, a form of empathy and imaginative affection that attempts to enter the mind of the maker through the things they have made. The second is a cooler and more distanced assessment of where the thing sits by comparison and in context; it is more generalizing and dispassionate, attempting to enter the spirit of a place or period through the objects made there. In the wake of great theoretical arguments in the early and mid-twentieth century about formalism and meaning, about historicism and generalization, the discipline of art history has stood firmly, but creatively, crucified between these approaches.

The study of Indian Buddhist art is particularly challenging and problematic in relation to both of these practices. This is because the historical data by which we establish any kind of chronology in relation to formalism – for instance, the reigns of monarchs as given through inscriptions – is sparse and difficult to place. Chronologies and typologies can be established through stylistic examination, but what do they mean when there are so few external hooks on which to hang a handful of disputed facts? And when the possible comparisons – the art of other stūpas, for example, in the case of my subject here – are no more or less secure than the object in question? Moreover, broader contextual historicism – the reflex pursued by most of art history in order to supply explanation for the nature of our objects – is made extremely difficult in the case of India, since so much of the external evidence is quite as uncertain chronologically as the material culture that we are trying to place. In the case of Indian Buddhism, we can hardly date with surety any of our texts (early Buddhist or Mahāyāna), situate them geographically or even place them in an order where one certainly preceded or influenced the next. The same issues apply to non-Buddhist texts such as the *Nāṭyaśāstra*, the ancient Indian treatise on dance and drama, which I have used in this book, especially given that the recensions and developments of all these writings include later and earlier phases in addition to commentaries, the literary archaeology of which has not been fully explicated. Nor in many cases do we have a more than general sense of the political and cultural developments of the local history of Andhra, or the larger history of central and southern India in the period of the Amarāvatī stūpa's making.

So, writing about Amarāvatī is like playing a sort of multidimensional, fantastical chess game in which the rules are broadly as obscure as the board on which you play. But you *do* have the pieces: absolutely tangible blocks of stone, exquisitely carved. They survive in a high enough quantity and quality of preservation for us to tell a story, even if they represent a very sad gathering of what once was – significantly less than 10 per cent, and most of it deprived of its final finish, colour and outer skin. This is a worse empirical situation than that of the equivalent period in the Mediterranean, but this epistemological problem should not be allowed to obscure the extraordinary excellence of the artistic materials and ambition of the monuments in this period of Indian culture, second to none in the history of human artistic creativity.

The Introduction to this book surveys the many difficulties involved in this project – especially around empirical evidence and historical specificity – but it also places the stones of Amarāvatī within the contextual complex through which they must be understood. Part I is a presentation of the stūpa, insofar as we can reconstruct it, building its argument from the elements of material culture of the Amarāvatī stūpa that have survived varieties of nineteenth-century trophy excavation, transportation around various depots and museums in India, conveyance to Europe for a substantial number of the finest pieces and, in certain cases, damage from subsequent travels for exhibition. Chapter One examines what a stūpa is and focuses on decorated stone blocks from the perimeter railing and sculptural veneer of the main monument. It offers a reconstruction of its form, building on the great archaeological and museological investigations of a series of fine scholars and excavators from the nineteenth and twentieth centuries. It presents that form by means of a 'phenomenological' account of how the monument was laid out in relation to the approach of its visitors – pilgrims, devotees, tourists – who were certainly both Buddhist and non-Buddhist, male and female, lay and monastic and of a wide social range. The form of the building and its many remarkable (and exceptional) decorative choices are themselves a claim to monumental authority within and a contribution to Indian Buddhist culture, established at a site of substantial monastic and sacred significance. Chapter Two examines the Brahmi inscriptions, mainly in the Prakrit language, carved on many of the surviving blocks, drawing on a venerable history of scholarship, especially in German and English, to explore what they mean for understanding the patterns of patronage and donation that enabled the stūpa's construction as well as the ideology of generosity, *dāna*, which was fundamental to early Buddhism.

Part II investigates the ways narrative imagery – and especially the superb sculptures for which Amarāvatī is most famous – is developed into a grand vision of time, cause and karma in relation to the multiple lives and development of perfection in the being who would become Gautama Buddha in his final lifetime. This represents a visual celebration of the Bodhisattva and his path, with many parallels in early Buddhist texts (including in proto-Mahāyāna writings), which is in certain respects distinctive. Chapter Three, the single chapter in this part, draws on both oral and written traditions of Buddhist mythology, hagiography and lore. It attempts to place the stūpa's narrative content in the context of devotee expectations and practices, insofar as these can be reconstructed, and in relation to exegetic understandings of how the multiple stories told within Buddhism functioned in commentaries to explicate Buddhist teaching and doctrine. The stūpa is, as it were, a monumental artistic commentary on the Buddha's teachings, offered as an object of both meditative contemplation (especially using the practices of recollection of the Buddha) and philosophical instruction.

Part III explores the relation of the stūpa's visual culture to that of the non-Buddhist environment (especially Brahmanic). In two chapters, this section explores themes in which specifically Buddhist takes sit within a much larger cultural frame of Indian thinking and aesthetics. Chapter Four looks at its artistic uses of theatricality and the imagery of dance, which extend deep into Indian aesthetics and well beyond Buddhism. Ancient Indian traditions of theatre and dance provide a significant strand of the stūpa's surviving imagery but are used in certain ways to distance the monument from traditional Brahmanic culture so as to establish aspects of Buddhist cultural identity. Chapter Five contemplates the stūpa's attempts at cosmography, and the way it conveys a cosmological vision that is both in accord with Buddhism and in dialogue with the rich cosmographic models of Indian culture more broadly in this period.

Part IV looks at more philosophical questions in relation to the problems of representing beings whose comprehension lies beyond normal human capacities. The art of Amarāvatī is strikingly thoughtful and reflective on such issues, which are themselves embedded in the conception of the Buddhist path presented by the monument. Effectively problems of representation as raised by the stūpa's artistic remains are themselves theologically charged investigations of a number of underlying issues in Buddhist philosophy. Chapter Six focuses on the creation of an icon of the Buddha's footprints, the *buddhapāda*, which is much repeated not only at the site (including in large slabs of grand size) but throughout the roughly contemporary Buddhist art of Andhra Pradesh. This is an object that uses but also defies naturalistic depiction to create the vision of a being at once human and superhuman, capable of presentation within a human body and impossible to conceive within the means available to human beings: the mind and hands. Yet the supra-mundane marks of the great man, an ancient tradition on which the *buddhapāda* imagery draws, nonetheless allow such a person to assume a form that can interact with normal beings and at the same time indicate his special status. Chapter Seven turns to the multiple Buddha bodies found in the art of the site, from emblematic agglomerations of schematic symbols to naturalistic and embodied human forms. It explores how the stūpa's sculpture effortlessly exploits the visual means available to it in order to establish models of replication, as well as multiple two-dimensional reflections on a variety of three-dimensional forms (including Buddha statues), in order to evoke a thrilling world of multiple levels of reality, self-reflection and emptiness. The art of Amarāvatī is extraordinarily sensitive and thoughtful about all these matters, reflecting on its own limitations in envisaging or depicting the Perfect One and exploring multiple discursive strategies, both anthropomorphic and aniconic, for evoking aspects of the Buddha's being.

The aim of the book as a whole is to evoke the ways the intimate detail of carved imagery in a great Buddhist monument could bring to mind, comment on and make philosophical contributions to the vibrant debates about the nature of Buddhism in the cultural contexts of its making and devotional significance. Despite all the empirical and archaeological difficulties, the arts of ancient Andhra Pradesh have compelling insights to offer to the modern student, whether of art history or of ancient Buddhism.

Introduction

The great monument at Amarāvatī was the first Buddhist stūpa to be discovered in the modern period.[1] Traditionally regarded as founded by the Maurya king Aśoka (*c.* 268–232 BCE) in about 250 BCE, it was enlarged and richly ornamented with spectacular reliefs between about 50 BCE and 300 CE.[2] The stūpa has rightly been described as 'the finest monument of the Buddhist world in the second century of the Common Era', the compositions of its narrative arts exhibiting 'an unparalleled confidence and . . . a maturity rarely surpassed'.[3] Terms applied to the sculptures from the monument include 'fluid', 'dynamic', 'exuberance and extravagance' and 'unrestrained activity'.[4] Their very first excavator wrote in 1823:

> Upon a minute inspection of the several sculptures, in many a story is completely told, with clearness and precision, and the characters accurately defined. The passions also are naturally exhibited and strongly marked; and exactness of outline in the representation, as well as in the air and carriage of animals, is happily delineated, and the festoons, foliage and flowers, and an infinite variety of other decorations, which adorn these carvings, are altogether excellent. The artists appear to have been skilled in perspective also; upon the whole, neither taste nor elegance are wanting, and in the article of neat and delicate finishing, the carvings and sculptures . . . are far superior to any ancient or modern Hindoo production.[5]

These responses are in part the result of tremendous creativity in solving sculptural problems of spatial representation – notably the use of low-relief carving, but so deeply undercut as to make the figures stand away from their backgrounds, leaving deep pools of shadow against which the figural groups emerge.[6] While some aspects of the Amarāvatī style remained local to the site, most of the decorative and compositional solutions were exported widely across Andhra Pradesh, for instance to the great stūpa complex at Nāgārjunakonda, which is usually dated a little after that at Amarāvatī.[7] The subject-matter depicted includes a rich range of narratives from the Buddha's life and from his previous lives as a Bodhisattva;[8] a series of repeated symbolic images evoking fertility and well-being (such as vases overflowing with flowers, or garlands on the rail coping) as well as signalling major events in the Buddha's spiritual path (such as the *dharmacakra*, or 'wheel above a column', implying the First Sermon and the turning of the wheel of dharma); icons for worship as discrete tablets in frames (such as the Buddha's footprints, or *buddhapāda*); sensual and even erotic imagery of *mithuna* couples;[9] strikingly self-reflexive imagery evoking a stūpa, the forms of which are very like the monument they decorate. This book will attempt to explore the significance of these subjects within the context of Buddhism in Andhra Pradesh.[10]

The great stūpa, normally called in its inscriptions *mahācaitiya*,[11] stands on the plain between the ancient city of Dharanikota (or Dhānyakataka) and the nearby hills. It is surrounded by a number of smaller, probably mortuary, stūpas (decorated with relief sculpture in the Amarāvatī style).[12] Very little is known about the monastery and monastic complex (including living quarters and temples) of which the stūpa was a major part and the principal attraction;[13] but clearly the monument and its satellite stūpas were both central to the monastery and part of its cultural life. It is likely that monks were involved in its building.[14] The *mahācaitiya* was one of a series of characteristic architectural creations associated with the spread and establishment of Buddhist monasticism in southern India. Other elements of construction include monastic accommodation, dining and cooking facilities and shrine halls (as at Thotlakonda and Bavikonda, a little way north along the coast from the Krishna delta). But they also include rock-cut cave monasteries (as at Undavalli, downriver from Amarāvatī, or Nasik and Karla on the southwestern coast of India, which were sponsored by the Satavāhana kings who ruled at Amarāvatī in the same period) that may themselves have included shrine halls and stūpas, as at Karla and Nasik. A major monument like Amarāvatī, however, was intended for and supported by a much larger community than just the local monastery.

As a key centre of pilgrimage and the 'living presence' of the Buddha,[15] the stūpa sits in a network of sites across the Indian subcontinent, including Sri Lanka, and up the eastern coast of India, as well as locally in Andhra Pradesh and along the Krishna River going far to the west. Beyond being a major monument, a stūpa like that which stands at Amarāvatī is a representation of the Buddha, housing him through his relics and maintaining his presence as if alive.[16] In their multiplicity of subjects, narratives and symbolic types, the stūpa's images represent the Buddha and his various earlier lives; they thus comment on the monument that they adorn. That double process of decoration and commentary, culminating in remarkable levels of self-reflection in the slabs with reliefs of stūpas that are carved to look like the one they decorate, which made up the main facing of the drum, is an exceptional quality of the art of Amarāvatī.

I will argue that the nature of the stūpa's commentary on Buddhist tradition was deeply informed by the creativity of Buddhist theory, storytelling and teaching of the period during which the monastery and stūpa were built; and that, vice versa, it is quite possible that the inventiveness of Buddhist thought in late antiquity was itself modulated by that of the visual culture. In particular, Buddhist art draws on models of teaching that are inflected in ways different from the canonical traditions of *Vinaya* (the monastic rules), *sutta*s (the written-down versions of the memorized teachings of the Buddha) and the *Abhidhamma* (the technical systematization of doctrine including philosophy, psychology and ethics). It emphasizes stories, legends, events and miracles of the Buddha's life and previous lives rather than these more discursive or analytical forms of exposition most familiar to current accounts of Buddhism. Such narratives, much more susceptible than the *sutta*s to visual evocation, may be said to instantiate and demonstrate through example various forms of Buddhist doctrine, such as causality, suffering and liberation, the attainment of perfections and so forth. But they do so (in the case of the Amarāvatī stūpa) in non-discursive and non-propositional ways, through imagery, symbol and repetition.

This approach is a deliberate gesture against the long history of a perhaps largely unconscious 'Protestant' bias in the scholarship on Buddhism that has generally valued only doctrinal or philosophical texts and scriptures as a guide to the religion, downplaying such 'Catholic' horrors as art, material culture, storytelling, commentary and devotion (ubiquitous themes in the visual culture of the stūpas, as we shall see[17]), and in relation to art obsessing on the question of aniconism in the representation of the Buddha.[18] In general, and particularly in the study of ancient Indian Buddhism, the place of material culture in constructing the religion's self-conception and self-presentation has been underplayed in a largely Western scholarly tradition committed to the priority of texts.[19] The Christianizing frame as a problem in scholarly assumptions extends well beyond a disdain for material culture.[20] Notably the use of terms such as 'sect', 'schism' and heresy', which we find frequently in the literature on the early Buddhist schools,[21] is drawn straight out of the playbook and conceptual framework of Christian theological polemic. A more Indologically appropriate model might be to see the development of schools, plural positions, debate and disagreements in relation to the third-century edicts promulgated by the Buddhist emperor Aśoka, which formulate an ideal of pluralism and the toleration of views between different cults.[22] (They do, however, warn against dissent in the Buddhist *saṅgha*, a topic with some traction in the *Vinaya* texts of the Pāli canon.[23]) Even if it may be objected that Aśoka's model of pluralist toleration is an ideal imposed from above in the face of a likely much more aggressive and intolerant reality, the fact is that it existed and had significant authority in India, in contrast to the contemporaneous West, where no such standard was ever entertained (let alone imagined) by Christianity, whether in relation to its polytheistic religious predecessors, its heterodox internal alternatives or religions that arose after it (such as Manichaeism or Islam).

At the risk of generalization, it is important to clarify some issues about Indian Buddhism in the period. Today we think of two main forms of Buddhism: Theravāda ('the doctrine of the Elders', disparagingly described by its Buddhist opponents as the Hīnayāna, or 'lesser vehicle') in Sri Lanka and Southeast Asia; and Mahāyāna ('the great vehicle') in Tibet, Mongolia, China, Korea and Japan,[24] within which forms of Esoteric or Tantric Buddhism (so called Vajrayāna, or 'the diamond vehicle') subsequently developed. Theravāda has its original scriptures in Pāli; Mahāyāna – which comprises a large range of types of Buddhism including Zen, Tibetan and so forth – has its scriptures in translations into local languages from Sanskrit and other Prakrit originals (many of which are lost) and in some new compositions without Indic predecessors.[25] But in ancient India, for some centuries after the Buddha's death and in the time during which the stūpa at Amarāvatī was constructed, there were many schools of Buddhism (traditionally numbered as eighteen, although their numbers and identities varied at different times) that may collectively be called Nikāya, meaning schools connected to particular monastic lineages.[26] These developed not only different philosophical traditions, often in conflict with each other, but somewhat different scriptural canons and monastic rules, some in Sanskrit, some in Gāndhāri and some in Pāli.[27] Theravāda Buddhism is a descendant of one of these lineages, the Thera school (known as Sthavira in Sanskrit), itself defined in relation to an early differentiation from the group known as Mahāsāṃghikas.[28] Within the rich range of positions and practices developed among these schools came the rise of what would ultimately become a new interpretation of Buddhism, founded on the philosophy of emptiness and the notion of the Bodhisattva path as one available to all beings and not just to the Buddha or previous Buddhas: the Mahāyāna.[29]

Current scholarly consensus is relatively sure that before the fifth century CE we cannot speak of any Mahāyāna dominance or strength of position in the Buddhist culture of India, which contrasts with what was happening in China from the third century. In the words of Gregory Schopen: 'In India it appears more and more certain that the Mahāyāna was not institutionally, culturally, or art-historically significant until after the fifth century, and not until then did Mahāyāna doctrine have any significant visible impact on the intentions of Buddhist donors.'[30]

This position has been extended and accepted by many, but it has also been refined in recent discussion.[31] Its definition of Mahāyāna is quite specific (namely a universal aspiration to the nature of Buddhahood) and correlates to terminologies for supposed adherents of Mahāyāna that may not be secure.[32] The likelihood of numerous proto-Mahāyānist positions (the cultivation of the perfections (*pāramitās*), the significance of compassion, the philosophical emphasis on emptiness) is not to be excluded;[33] and the possibility that various pre-Mahāyāna developments may have been in regular conversation with (and mutual influence in relation to) mainstream positions has been proposed.[34] It is true that one does not *need* to make reference to the classic Mahāyāna sūtras, or commentaries, to explain the arts of South Indian Buddhism. But we need to remember that in this field we are dealing with probabilistic, rather than positivistic, 'facts', which are reliant on a model of less unlikely or least unlikely as opposed to certain when it comes to historical assertion. Proto-Mahāyāna positions undoubtedly existed in the monastic mix of South India (from precisely when, we cannot determine) and were part of a vibrant, often contested, religious and scholarly conversation. In referring to such positions, I affirm here only the possibility that they had a part to play in the lives of those who decorated the stūpa; I do not intend to make even an implicit claim for the certainty of their influence.

Where exactly in the vast Indian subcontinent particular developments took place and when are very difficult issues to pin down, because the framing devices of sūtras are concerned with religion and doctrinal or philosophical positions, as opposed to placing their authorship in a given temporal moment or geographical region, while the (later) hagiographical traditions of great teachers are legendary rather than historical in genre. That is our problem in asking historical questions of the sort cultivated by Western scholarship; but it was not a problem for a religion concerned with understanding reality and the path to freedom, in both abstract theory and meditational practice, on its own terms, without caring much about issues of chronology or provenance.[35] However, it does mean that, while many great Buddhist teachers lived in South India, and the development of a number of key positions – in both the rise of Mahāyāna Buddhism and the Nikāya responses to it – likely took place in Andhra, it is not easy to be precise about matters of place or time. While inscriptional evidence makes it impossible to identify Buddhist dedications as unambiguously Mahāyāna before the fifth century at the earliest,[36] even then, the divide may not have been firm.

In this sense, the range of uncertainties about the textual and theoretical (Buddhological) traditions relevant to the arts of Amarāvatī are as indeterminate as the precise dating of the stūpa's sculptures is. However, we can say that a number of different Nikāya lineages flourished in Andhra in the period of the stūpa's making (notably the Mahāsāṃghikas, of which several subsects are attested in the region,[37] as well as the Sthaviras). Some aspects of what would become characteristic of Mahāyāna thinking were known and possibly developed in South India, notably in Andhra Pradesh,[38] and partly founded on a series of positions held by the Mahāsāṃghikas,[39] even if the view that the Mahāyāna originated there from developments in Mahāsāṃghika thinking is now thought to be exaggerated.[40] But my point is that there was great theoretical, philosophical and contemplative creativity in the dialogue of multiple forms of Buddhism in Andhra in the period of Amarāvatī, and this is part of the context in which the stūpa's art was generated.

In any case, we have to be subtle and cautious about connecting images to doctrinal positions. The long attempts to identify works of art with theological positions adumbrated with some clarity and much polemic in early Christianity (from, say, the fourth to sixth century CE) have been strikingly unsuccessful.[41] We may say that, in that context (but also, as I will argue, in Indian Buddhism), images, inherently inclusivist of multiple positions and heterodoxies, offer a much more open and flexible discourse for advancing propositions about religion than do texts whose composition is often apologetic or polemical, especially when hoping to maintain a doctrinal posture. The difficulties of determining whether the Buddhist imagery of ancient India firmly adhered to Mahāyāna or earlier positions have been acknowledged, and rightly so.[42] But it may be that such positions were less mutually exclusive than scholarship has traditionally supposed.[43] My approach is not to argue for particular positions (Nikāya, Mahāyāna and so on) in relation to the visual culture of Amarāvatī, but rather to make the case for the evolution of a complex artistic discourse capable of exploring, by visual as opposed to literary means, the deeper philosophical and soteriological issues at the heart of Indian Buddhism in the period. I will suggest that many creative developments in Buddhist theory find parallels in the visual explorations of the sculptures at the stūpa, and that they may potentially have anticipated the mature formulations of various theological positions that have come down to us. I will be led by the visual evidence, as is proper to an art-historical investigation, and will adduce what seem to me to be relevant textual accounts drawn from a range of Buddhist traditions all potentially available in Andhra and certainly related to the kinds of texts produced in and used by Buddhism there. But we must be aware that none of the texts that survive to us now actually belonged to the precise *Vinaya*, sūtra, *jātaka* or *abhidhamma* traditions of the site (whatever these were precisely).

If we ask *why* so major a monument as the Amarāvatī stūpa should have been built at this particular site, one answer – not discussed at all in the literature on the stūpa – is that in Buddhist legend, aeons ago, Amarāvatī was the birthplace of an important former incarnation of the Buddha, the brahmin Sumedha (also named Megha in the northern traditions).[44] The story goes that Sumedha assumed the ascetic life and then journeyed north to the Himalayas. There he heard that the Buddha of that time, Dīpaṅkara, was passing by; he lay down on the road, spreading his hair before Dīpaṅkara so that the Buddha tread on him rather than the dust and mud of the road itself. But when he beheld Dīpaṅkara, instead of making the resolution to follow him and attain enlightenment as his student, he considered:

> It does not serve my purpose merely to extirpate the defilements and attain Nibbāna [Nirvana] as a man of no consequence. I would rather, like Dīpaṅkara, the Lord of ten powers, attain the highest enlightenment, and taking mankind aboard the ship of Dhamma, ford them across the ocean of Samsāra, and afterwards enter into the perfect Nibbāna.[45]

At this point Sumedha made the resolution to become a buddha, that is – in what would become a crucial stage in the Mahāyāna traditions – he took the Bodhisattva vow to attain enlightenment only for the sake of all beings.[46] Upon seeing him, Dīpaṅkara understood that in the distant future (technically 'four countless aeons and one hundred thousand kalpas') he would become Gautama Buddha, and prophesied to his retinue: 'See ye this very austere hermit with matted hair? Countless ages hence he will become a Buddha in this world.'[47]

If one were to trace the origin of origins for Gautama's path to Buddhahood, then this moment – Sumedha's vow and thus his embarkation on the process of lifetimes that would culminate in Buddhahood – is the key moment, the moment of inner resolve and the Bodhisattva vow. The site of Amarāvatī effectively celebrates the origin of that life, the birthplace of the man Sumedha who would through countless lifetimes become Buddha.[48] In this sense it was an obvious site of pilgrimage, and hence monumental celebration.[49] That the start of Gautama's journey to enlightenment at the feet of Dīpaṅkara mattered to the Mahāsāṃghika tradition prevalent in Andhra is proven by its repetition in the opening to one of the few surviving texts from this school, the *Mahāvastu*, a vast compilation of stories that purports to be the introduction to the *Vinaya* of the Lokattaravāda branch of Mahāsāṃghikas.[50] We shall see that the link with the Bodhisattva vow makes sense of a number of key themes in both the visual culture of the monument (whose narratives insistently focus on the Buddha and his former lives) and the interests of Andhra Buddhism (whether Nikāya or Mahāyāna) in elucidating the Bodhisattva path. As it happens, there are no depictions of the meeting of Sumedha and Dīpaṅkara that survive from Amarāvatī, although of course we only have evidence of significantly less than 10 per cent of the original sculpture.[51] But there are examples of the theme (which was popular in Gandhara[52]) from a slightly later stūpa, further up the Krishna River, made in a similar style and by the same school of artists at Nāgārjunakonda.[53]

In an intriguing story, repeated twice in the Sanskrit *Divyāvadāna*, which was perhaps composed in the second century CE, the Buddha comes to the site of Toyikā, where the 'undisturbed skeleton of the perfectly awakened Kāśapa [a previous Buddha]' lies buried and unmarked.[54] Seated at the spot of Kāśapa's interment, the Buddha causes *nāgas* (semi-divine serpents) to raise the remains of Kāśapa so that two perfectly awakened beings can be venerated together at the same place and time; when the *nāgas* disappear, others continue to worship at the spot by circumambulating it. This notion of a sacred reliquary shrine that encompasses or alludes to more holy figures than one (in the case of Amarāvatī, Dīpaṅkara and Sumedha/Gautama) is fundamental to the major stūpas, which were imagined to evoke multiple sacred beings, and whose relics included not only those of the Buddha but his senior disciples. The Mahāyāna tradition developed this model of double buddhas in the famous eleventh chapter of the *Lotus Sūtra* (*Saddharmapuṇḍarīka Sūtra*), which circulated widely in India in the early centuries CE before becoming extremely important in China and Japan.[55] In it, the jewelled stūpa of the Buddha Prabhūtaratna floats above the Earth and is revealed to contain his living presence.[56] Śākyamuni Gautama, the living buddha who is preaching the sūtra, and Prabhūtaratna, the living presence of a buddha from the distant past, then proceed to conduct their teaching together.[57]

THE PROBLEMS OF STUDYING THE ARTS OF AMARĀVATĪ

The difficulties of working on Amarāvatī are many. The archaeology of the monument in the nineteenth century, despite the high quality of much of the scholarship on the stūpa by the 1870s and '80s, was essentially a treasure hunt, its excavation largely a destructive disaster for both the site as a whole and our understanding of it.[58] In 1914, Alfred Foucher evoked the lamentations of Jeremiah in his consideration of the 'ruine des ruines' of the site;[59] but I hope to show that such despair (while understandable) is excessive. However, the results of the mess of the archaeology reverberate in a number of areas, for instance the reconstruction of the whole monument (which must be done almost entirely from materials extracted from their original contexts and kept in museums[60]) and the understanding of how its sculptural remains fitted together. Poor preservation of some objects and the disappearance of many that were excavated at the beginning of the nineteenth century are partially mitigated by the remarkable collection of drawings made by draughtsmen working for Colin Mackenzie (1754–1821, India's first British surveyor general and Amarāvatī's first excavator) between 1816 and 1819, now in an album housed in the British Library, and the photographs of objects gathered in the courtyard of the museum in Madras (now Chennai) made by Linnaeus Tripe in 1858.[61] The site in its current condition – at least the bottom part of the mound has been reconstructed to give the visitor a sense of its size (illus. 1) – is a bit of a sad backwater across the road from the site museum, in a small enclosure administered by the Archaeological Survey of India, though by no means as near-impossible to find as other local stūpas such as Bhattiprolu or Ghantaśālā. A few remnants of panels from the railing and drum have been arranged at the side facing the current entrance.[62]

In the case of the monument as a whole in its original context, there is agreement that the stūpa – like those to the north in Bharhut and Sāñcī, for instance – comprised a rubble-filled mound with a brick casing to form a cylindrical drum that was covered by a veneer of carved limestone slabs surmounted by a dome finished in a mixture of plaster and carved limestone cladding. The entire monument was then surrounded by a railing.[63] The railing was pierced at the four cardinal points by entrances that jutted outwards in four gateways that projected from the railing (illus. 2). The height of the stūpa's drum has proved controversial: most scholars have now agreed it was a low cylindrical platform 48.75 metres (162½ ft) in diameter and about 1.8 metres (6 ft) high.[64] (Others have argued for a much higher drum of more than 6 metres/20 ft.[65]) Much of the difficulty is that the archaeological records are sparse and speculative, meaning that arguments turn on visual comparison with supposed representations of the stūpa on the drum slabs (always a very difficult model for making rigorous or positivist inferences) and comparison with other stūpas in Andhra, which were certainly less complex.[66] An outer retaining wall around the drum, 1.2 metres thick,[67] formed the base of a wide platform (about 3.5 metres[68]) from within which the dome sprang. At each cardinal point opposite the gate, the drum platform extended to a squared *āyaka* platform measuring about 9.75 metres × 1.8 metres (32 × 6 ft).[69] The height of this platform must have been the same as the rest of the drum, so reconstruction depends on the height at which this latter is conjectured to be (which, as we have seen, is moot). Each *āyaka* platform had five pillars, a peculiar feature of the stūpas of Andhra Pradesh,[70] with rectangular bases and octagonal shafts that stood 3–4 metres (10–14 ft) high. If we believe the visual evidence of the drum slabs, the central pillar (if not all five) was often crowned with a depiction of a stūpa, while all had reliefs carved at their bases – either tree, wheel, stūpa, tree, wheel (in that order), or five stūpas. They could also feature five standing Buddhas, but these might conceivably have been free-standing statues in front of the columns.[71] It has been suggested that the drum platform featured a raised ambulatory, presumably accessible by stairs, although there is no proof of this and the proposition has been contested.[72] The platform may have been used for votive offerings and to exhibit free-standing statuary.[73] The dome rose from this drum platform, but nothing of it has survived for modern archaeology to explore, so all assumptions are wholly conjectural. It is unclear,

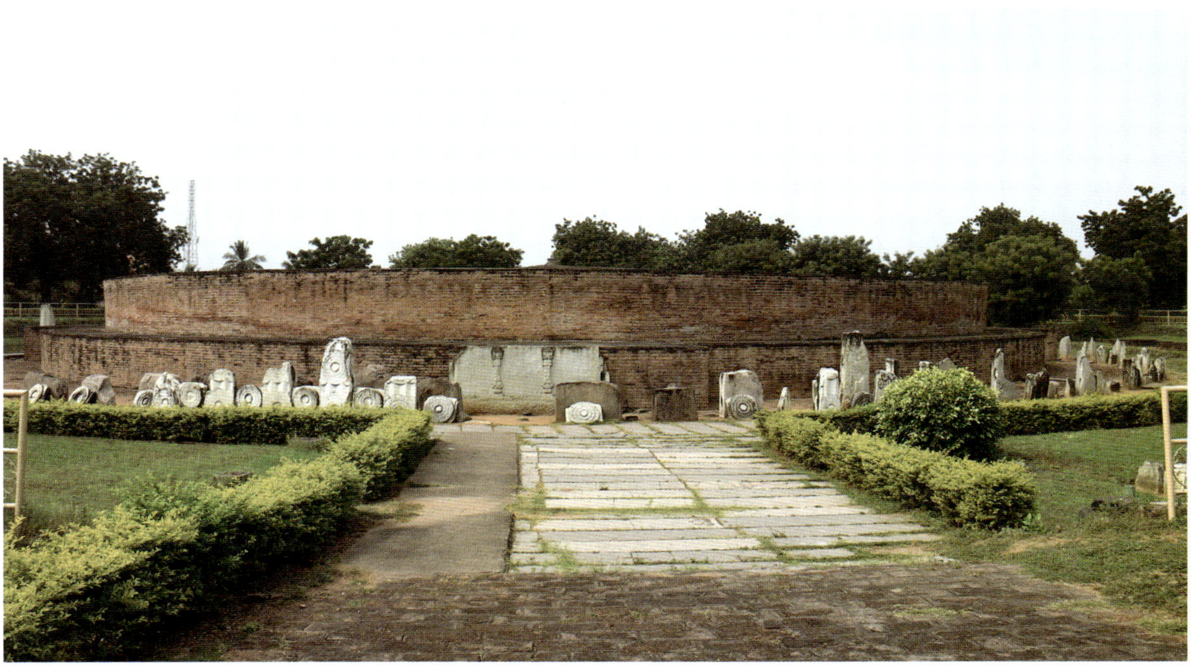

1 View from the east of the reconstructed lower parts of the drum of the great stūpa at Amarāvatī, 2022.

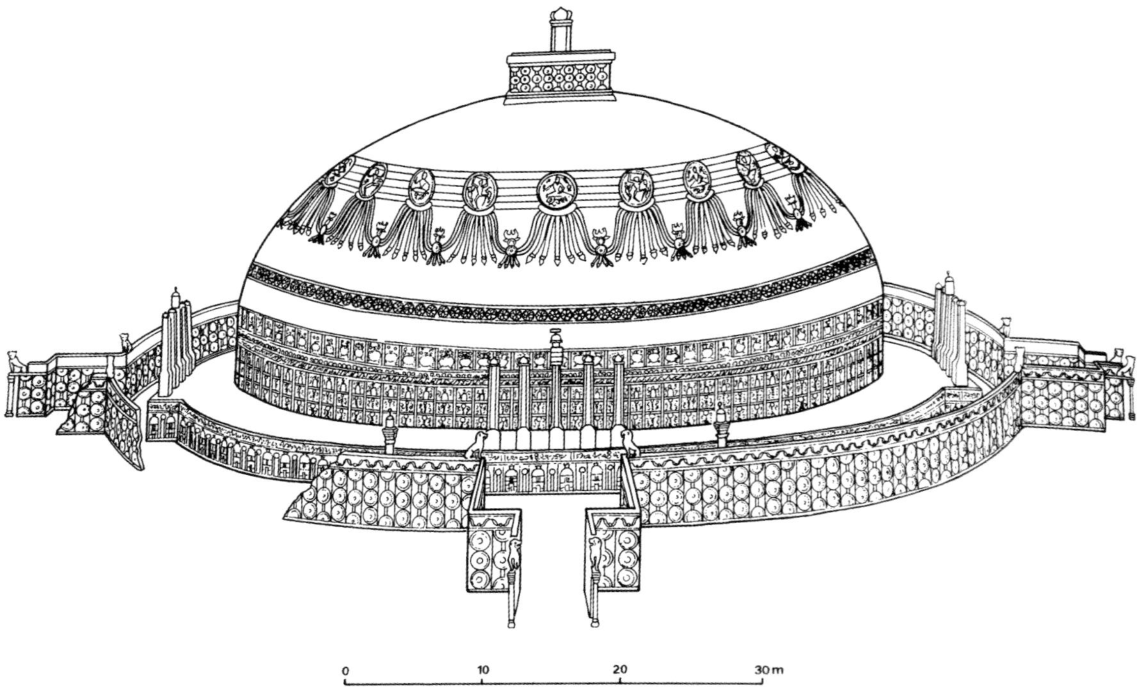

2 Reconstruction of the great stūpa at Amarāvatī after D. Barratt, *Sculpture from Amaravati in the British Museum* (1954).

for instance, whether the dome was built of solid brick (as in the stūpas at Bhattiprōlu and Gudivāda) or hollow and filled with earth.[74]

Considering the surviving dome slabs, which are not curved, it appears that the dome rose vertically to a height of about 4.5 metres (15 ft) above the drum, before curving upwards to a height of about 18 metres (60 ft) above the ground.[75] Above the dome was the *harmikā*, a square platform with a low railing,[76] at the centre of which stood a short octagonal pillar surmounted by a stone umbrella,[77] and small pillars to which may have been attached cloth banners, ribbons and flags.[78] Much of this is the result of best guesses and conjecture, inferences and entailments from an inadequate and fragmentary evidential base. But the architectural form of the smaller and much better preserved Kanaganahalli stūpa in Karnataka – about 500 kilometres (310 mi.) to the west of Amarāvatī but situated along the Bhima River, a branch of the Krishna River on whose banks Amarāvatī is located – which was only discovered in the 1980s, confirms these inferences about its architectural appearance.[79]

The Amarāvatī or Elliot 'Marbles' (so called to echo the Elgin Marbles, although the stone is local Palnad limestone, characteristically of a whitish-green hue[80]), excavated in the late eighteenth and nineteenth centuries, were essentially piled up and distributed between museums in India and England (the majority landing in the Madras Government Museum, in what is now Chennai, and the British Museum). The products of twentieth-century colonial and post-Independence excavation largely found their way into the Amarāvatī Archaeological Museum at the site. The blocks (especially of the railing) were created to fit into each other, like an ancient, prefabricated form of Lego, and feature carvings with uncertain thematic or narrative continuity from block to block. What we cannot do now (except in very rare circumstances) is to ascertain with certainty how any one stone fitted with or against any other. Nor have we much sense (except in the most general way) of where on the site any given item was excavated. Thus there is minimal stratigraphy and almost no archaeological context. But a large number of architectural elements and carved stone sculptures, both three-dimensional pieces and panels with relief decoration, have survived. These give an excellent sense of the compositional elements of the stūpa's structure and decoration, even if we can only very rarely join one slab to another with any degree of certainty,[81] or know where it originally sat.

These archaeological materials have never been collected or published in a single volume or series. There exist publications of each of the major museum collections individually, but none uses the same scheme of object denomination as the others.[82] The only complete accounts are of the British Museum's collection (in its own published and online catalogues), and only the British Museum has published photographs of all the Amarāvatī objects in its care. The materials scattered in other collections around the world are much more haphazardly published. The important collection of 85 drawings from 1816–19, made at the behest of Colin Mackenzie, of the earliest finds (many now lost), and some representing the earlier condition of known reliefs – now in the British Library – has never been fully published in print and is only relatively recently available online.[83] The eccentricities of publication

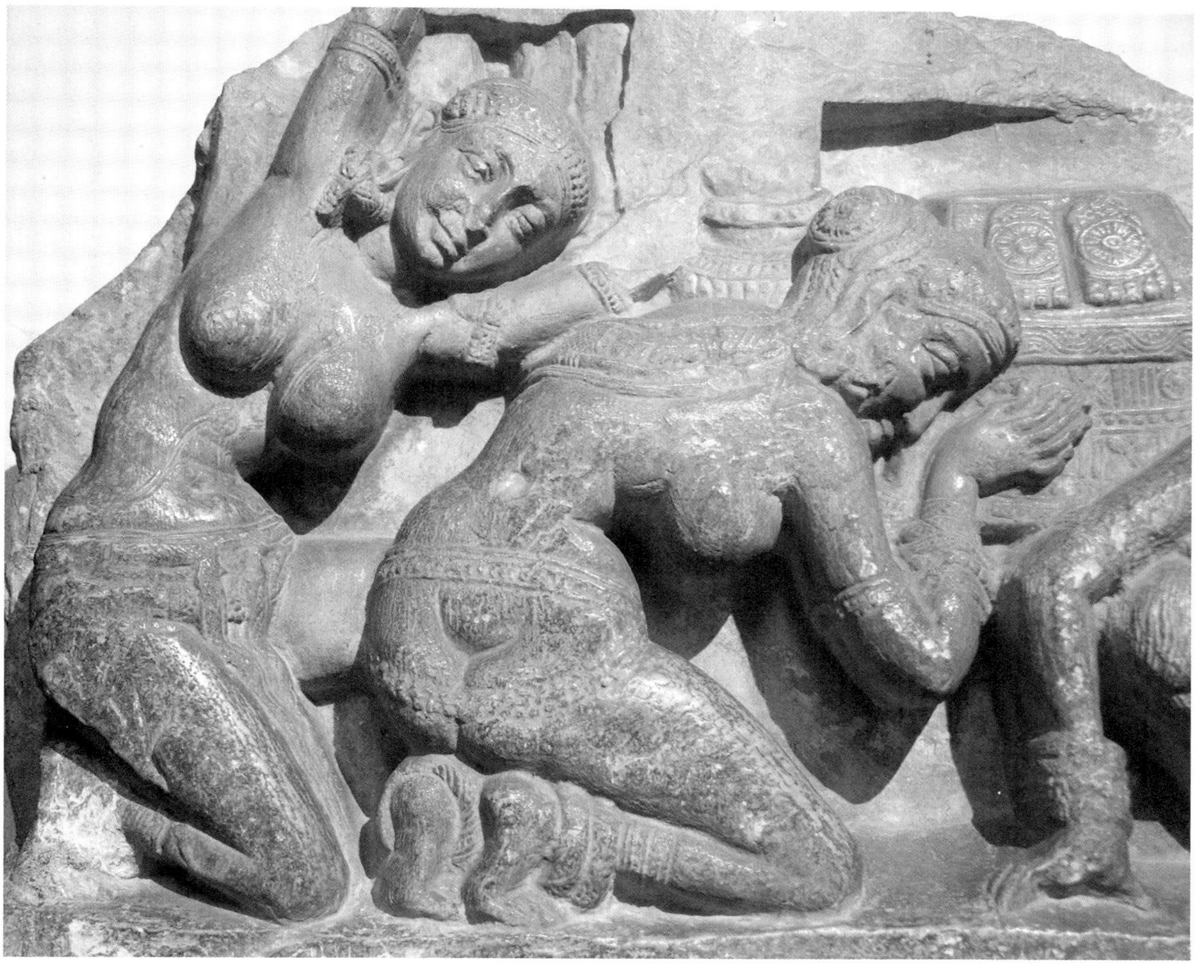

3 Two women prostrating before the *buddhapāda* on a footstool beneath a throne. Broken fragment of a lost larger panel, detail of illus. 116.

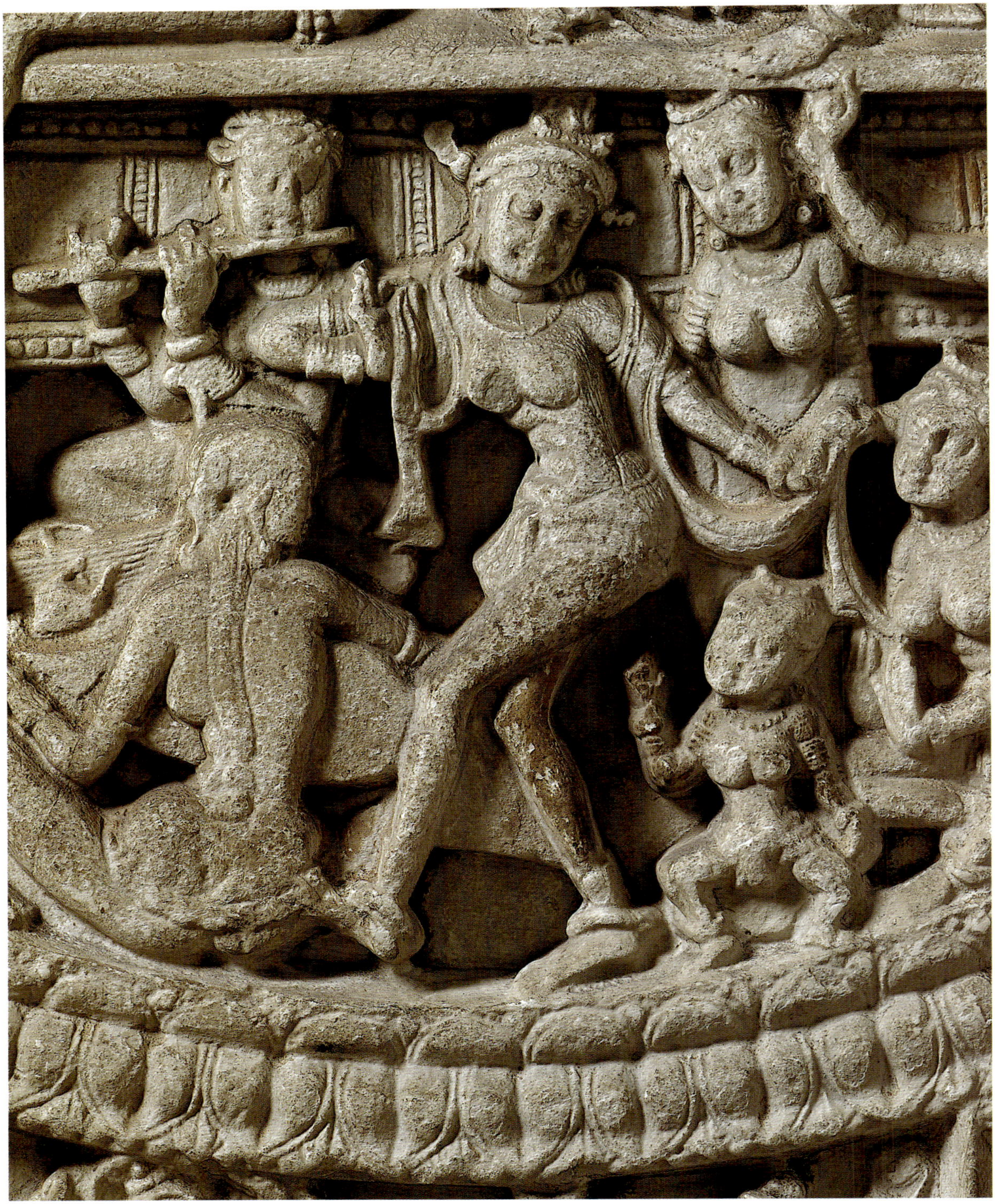

4 Female dancer and dancing dwarf among musicians, from a court scene in the central medallion on the interior side of a railing pillar, detail of illus. 74.

and the fact that other Andhra stūpas were stylistically and iconographically influenced by Amarāvatī means that occasionally objects from elsewhere are wrongly discussed as if from the site.[84]

It is worth making a few technical observations about the surviving sculptures. The limestone of which they are made is relatively easily carved, but it is also friable, and in many examples has lost its surface finish.[85] Most of the surviving sculptures have lost their outer surface layers at least, but the exquisite nature of the final finish (without any layers of paint that may have been added) is evident from the few examples that are in the best condition. Take, for instance, a fragment with two women prostrating before what was probably the empty throne with *buddhapāda* (or the Buddha's footprints) in the footstool beneath, now in Chennai Government Museum. The figures are near intact, so the execution, the turn of the bodies and the sculptor's representation of what is simultaneously the gracious charm of the human body and a sense of devotion is commanding (illus. 3). Or one might cite the exquisite dancing figure among female musicians depicted on what remains of a railing pillar medallion, now in the British Museum (illus. 4).[86] This is simply superb workmanship delivering virtuoso narrative naturalism, impressive depth of relief and undercutting of the stone and a wonderful, sensuous range of postures including frontal, three-quarter and back views, the figures crisp, individual and varied. Likewise, parts of an exceptionally well-preserved pilaster from the sculptures of the drum still give evidence of the red coating (probably lead vanadate) that Mackenzie noted on some of the carvings in 1823, and which appears to have been part of the original polychromy (illus. 5).[87] Especially in relation to the railings, designed on a characteristic tongue-and-groove model of construction, it has been surmised that the artists of stūpas (and this applies across India from the Swat Valley of Gandhāra to the far north via Bharhut and Sāñcī, and to Amarāvatī in the south) were adapting in stone models of building derived from woodwork.[88]

As was recognized very early, one of the distinctive features of the Amarāvatī sculptures is their rich inclusion of inscriptions, most contemporary with the erection and embellishment of the stūpa, composed in Prakrit and written in the Brahmi script.[89] These provide immensely valuable information about many aspects of patronage and devotion, although the majority are notably unexplicit about matters of dating, and the range of arguments regarding the relative dating of Brahmi palaeography does not lend much succour to those hoping that the material appearance of an epigraph would give us a clear date.[90] They also provide some information about artists – a topic that has hardly been studied in the long history of scholarship on the Buddhist arts of India.[91] While all the inscriptions in the Chennai Government Museum and most in the Amarāvatī Archaeological Museum appear to have been transcribed, translated and published, this is unfortunately not the case with those that feature on objects now in the British Museum.[92] Thus no complete collection of the inscriptions exists.[93] There is currently

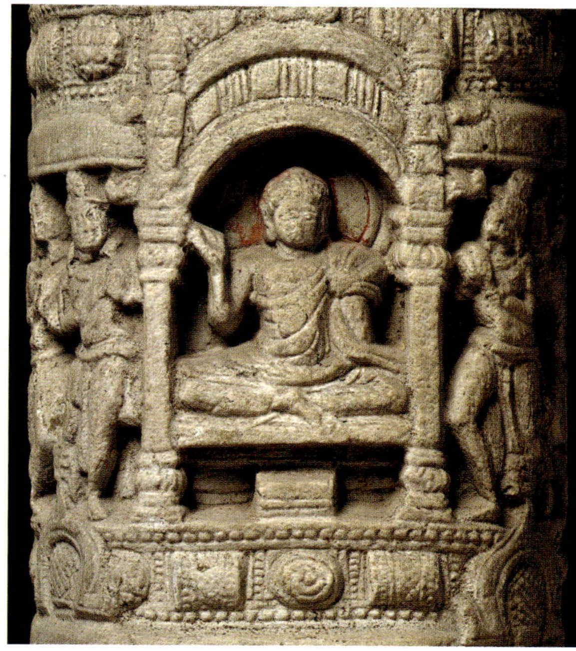

5 Pilaster from the drum with the Buddha enthroned in the *abhāya mudrā* under an arched gateway flanked by male worshippers. Traces of red pigment remain on the Buddha's halo.

a project being conducted under the auspices of the École française d'Extrême-Orient to create a complete online database of the inscriptions with translations and commentary, although when it will be finished remains to be seen.[94] Since the inscriptions were often collected and published separately from discussion of the slabs on which they were carved (and from discussion of the sculptural decoration of those slabs), it is not easy, and in some cases it is impossible, to tie a specific inscription down to a specific object, and vice versa.[95] It is unfortunate also that the most authoritative list of Amarāvatī inscriptions, made by a great philologist of early Indian epigraphy, Heinrich Lüders, fails to give full transliterations or more than summaries of the content.[96] We may say, as with the other early Buddhist inscriptions of Andhra, that even after nearly two centuries of work – some of it of excellent quality – the inscriptions of Amarāvatī (including definitive readings, comprehensive publication and full collection) remain something of a mess and a significant desideratum.[97]

The absence of objective or independent criteria by which to construct a dating system for the monument – that is, the failure of the inscriptions to offer dates, and the failure of the archaeology to establish a firm stratigraphy – has reduced the field to attempting to establish a chronology, dependent entirely on the relative evaluation of evidence from the site, on the basis of the sculptural styles of the blocks and to some extent the epigraphical forms of their inscriptions.[98] The problems of this are apparent when we consider the two inscriptions that have been considered 'historical' in the literature, in the sense of offering reference to potentially (but not certainly) datable reigns.[99] These are both on objects in the Chennai Museum. The first is a rectangular slab, without sculptural decoration, cut in three steps in descending order from the top of a pillar by one of the gates, which formed the base for a lion statue. Its inscription names the Sātavāhana dynasty king Śri Pulumāvi.[100] The second is a segment of coping from the top of the railing with garlands on the outer side and the narrative of Kavikumara, one of the *jātaka* tales of the Bodhisattva's previous lives, on the interior; the inscription, naming King Siri Sivamaka Sada, is on the inner face.[101] On stylistic grounds the slabs were dated, on relative terms, in the order I have introduced them (Pulumāvi before Sada), which is how Calambur Sivaramamurti presented them in his catalogue of the Chennai Amarāvatī collection, first published in 1942. Unfortunately, the dates of both kings are uncertain. In 1954 the British Museum curator Douglas Barrett, tying what was then known of these kings to the numismatic evidence available to him, dated Pulumāvi to 130–59 CE and Sada, whom he identified with a king called Śivaskanda Sātakarni, to 167–74 CE.[102] Since the coping stone was sculpted in what Burgess called the 'Middle Phase' of the 'mature style', this enabled Barrett to date the establishment of that phase and style to the third quarter of the second century.

However, fast-forward to the early twenty-first century and we find that the dates and identifications of monarchs have changed.[103] The current consensus on Pulumāvi places him in the later first, or late first and early second, century CE, pushing his reign to at least fifty years earlier than posited in previous discussions (with an accession date after 85 CE).[104] Sivamaka Sada, identified with a different monarch from that chosen by Barrett, was probably the last king of the Sadas, the dynasty preceding the Sātavāhanas, which would put his reign in the last years of the first century CE, say around 75 CE.[105] In other words, the chronology is extremely difficult to establish. But in this case, it plays havoc with the stylistic analysis by which both Sivaramamurti and Barrett placed the Sivamaka coping stone *later* than the Pulumāvi slab; modern chronology reverses this, placing the dates of both kings significantly earlier. Because specific datings that would ground stylistic analysis of the sculptures in external referents are, at best, tentative, and in any case extremely rare, we must beware the temptation of excessive precision: any instance is based purely on the connoisseurial eye combined with speculative chronology. And even with questions of relative chronology and assuming one style is earlier than another, we may find (as in this case) that it is deeply unreliable. One of the problems here is that over a long period, and with the likelihood of restoration within that time frame, it is perfectly possible that competent artists (and in the case of Amarāvatī, they were much more than just competent) worked in earlier styles for the purposes of aesthetic consistency. But the fundamental art-historical problem is that the chronological model for dating the sculptures in the available catalogues, including those produced most recently, still broadly follows the parameters set by Sivaramamurti and Barrett, despite the overturning of the tie between style and date assumed by them.[106]

The attempt to create a chronology and root it in external dates has been a major focus of the literature (far more than the monument's functions or meanings) for about a century.[107] It is, as we have seen, a notoriously subjective process, dependent, in addition to the stylistic analysis of the surviving sculptures, on comparison with material from monuments like the stūpas at Bharhut, Sāñcī and elsewhere in India, which are of equal uncertainty when it comes to precise dating and just as subject to certain idealist drives (such as the urge to establish a date of foundation for the stūpa in Aśoka's reign).[108] Suffice it to say here that within a relatively firm dating of circa 200 BCE to 300 CE (an extraordinarily long period) we can place the major development of the monument and its many refurbishments, with some earlier elements kept in place in later phases and quite a lot of re-carving and spoliation of earlier pieces for new purposes within that time. This is, in contrast to some fields in archaeology or art history, a very imprecise chronological spectrum – but it is not by any means out of kilter with the difficulties of chronology and precise dating in early Buddhist art in India.

It is worth adding that Buddhist chronology is not a problem solely for archaeology. The very date of the historical Buddha is contested, and we know surprisingly little about when the major developments in the Buddhist traditions (such as the rise of the Mahāyāna) began or took root.[109] One issue is that apparently late texts like the Pāli commentaries – or rather, texts written down and made systematic as late as the fifth century CE, but not all of them yet translated into non-ancient languages – may in fact contain rich material, some of it going as far back as the time of the Buddha himself.[110]

A further problem, specific to the interpretative issues around the sculptures' themes and especially their rich narrative content, is the complete loss of the literary traditions, including the specific versions of the Buddhist canon and its commentaries, that were prevalent in Andhra Pradesh.[111] Likewise, we have no complete account of the philosophical and doctrinal positions of what was probably (with a number of internal factions) the dominant Buddhist tradition in Andhra, the Mahāsāṃghika school.[112] This means that we cannot identify with certainty many of the narratives on the Amarāvatī reliefs because they follow traditions (potentially including commentarial variations) different from the surviving Pāli texts or the northern Buddhist Sanskrit tradition, much of which survives only in Chinese or Tibetan translation.[113] The loss of the actual scriptures and commentaries used in the context of Amarāvatī is compounded by much complexity (and no little uncertainty) regarding the range of doctrinal affiliations of the monastic culture of the site and in the broader region. The monastery at Amarāvatī in the period of the stūpa's construction has been seen as a focus for more than one school of early Buddhism, to judge from the inscriptional evidence (although what this actually tells us, when it does so at all, is the stated allegiance of a given donor[114]), while a large multiplicity of schools flourished in other connected sites along the Krishna River and elsewhere in Andhra Pradesh.[115] But much is uncertain – not least the range of Mahāyāna and Nikāya adherences in the monastic culture of the region as well as the specific texts, commentarial traditions and scholarly positions that developed in the flourishing Andhra Buddhism, which continued into the eighth century CE. The number of famous Buddhist teachers who either came from the region or thrived there, in all the main Mahāyāna traditions (including Tantra), as well as in Theravāda, is striking.[116] It reflects not only the richness and creativity of Andhra Buddhism (to which I would add its artistic culture) but the nature of the region's commercial life: an easy centre of maritime and land communications south to Sri Lanka, north to the rest of India, east towards Indonesia and wider afield across the Indian Ocean to Africa and Europe.

Finally, beyond the loss of so many early Buddhist written traditions, a great deal of what does survive has not yet been fully edited in modern critical editions, let alone translated into European languages for the benefit of those (like the present author) who do not command Sanskrit or Pāli, never mind Tibetan or Chinese. For example, it is excellent that the entire Pāli canon exists in a number of reliable translations; but the incredibly important commentarial tradition that goes hand in hand with the canon and was codified in the fifth century (especially by the great South Indian and Ceylonese commentators Buddhaghosa and Buddhadatta, followed by Mahānāma, Upasena and Dhammapāla) has hardly been translated, be it the bulk of the principal discussions of the *Vinaya*, suttas or *Abhidhamma*, or the numerous sub-commentaries produced to supplement them.[117] This commentarial tradition – packed with stories and legends that may go back to the earliest Buddhism and were certainly current in the period of the stūpa's making – provides essential information that will only become generally accessible when the great project of its full translation has been accomplished.

HISTORICAL CONTEXT

The reconstruction of the political history and chronology of the Deccan plateau and Andhra Pradesh in the years when the stūpa was constructed is hardly less fraught than any of the other historical questions surrounding it. From roughly the middle of the first century BCE to the end of the first century CE – according to modern accounts based on epigraphy and numismatics, with some help from ancient Greek itineraries and geographical texts – the region was ruled by a local dynasty, the Sadas, which gave way to the Sātavāhana dynasty, who appear to have ruled the whole Deccan until about 250 CE.[118] The specific involvement of each of these royal houses with Buddhism and the rich range of Buddhist sites in Andhra is not easy to assess, but it is clear that they did not resist or impede the patronage of religious establishments by individuals and communities in a very wide social range from merchants to civil servants to monastics within their kingdom.[119] Despite this openness to patronizing diverse arenas, as a dynasty the Sātavāhanas were unequivocal adherents of a Vedic worldview with explicit Brahmanic self-identification.[120] The Ikṣvāku dynasty, which succeeded the Sātavāhanas, appears to have devoted more official patronage to monastic sites (notably Nāgārjunakonda) than its predecessors.[121] There is no evidence of direct royal support at Amarāvatī.[122] But royal power and the provision of order in the domain certainly made possible the spread of monumental Buddhist sites across Andhra and far up the Krishna River to Kanaganahalli in the west, which itself had direct royal patronage.[123]

More significant than rulers perhaps is the relation of the stūpa and monastery to the urban context of the local capital city at Dhānyakataka (Dharanikota).[124] The stūpa, like many others in its time, was placed close to a city, but just outside, conforming to a peripheral pattern that has been identified for pilgrimage centres.[125] The question of urban proximity is not unrelated to the wealth accumulated in the Andhra region through trade, and the significant place of merchants in the patronage structure of donation to the major stūpa sites along the Krishna River. Much work still needs to be done to refine the issues and offer precision regarding the relation of varied social classes, both rural and urban, to different religions (varieties of Brahmanism and perhaps some Jainism as well as Buddhism) and to monumental patronage.[126] But the broad picture is of relative political and economic stability, enough wealth to generate a significant surplus that could sustain the building of so many monuments and the maintenance of so many artisans and sculptors of a particularly high level of proficiency.[127]

The upshot of these issues is that there is much we can do, nonetheless. We can have a sense of the incredible visual and material culture of the site and the ways this worked in relation to the religious culture of Indian Buddhism. The connections are not as precise as they would be if we certainly knew what the links were between Andhra Buddhism and the religion in other areas of the subcontinent, between the arts of Andhra and other parts of India, between the monastic communities of the region and its government or urban centres. Likewise, if we knew for certain the origins of the many Buddhist texts and teachers that we have an inkling were from Andhra, we could more securely grasp the intellectual contexts in which the highly thoughtful and conceptually sophisticated arts of Amarāvatī came into being. Yet, informed and considered 'best-guesswork' can get us somewhere in the process of grasping how the stūpa appeared to, and how its forms elicited meanings in, the many people who contributed to its making or came to worship at the site. Some questions are likely never to be answered (for instance, it is hard to conceive we will recover the Mahāsāṃghika canon of scriptures and commentaries that we suspect were principally used in Andhra Pradesh), but others – like a full reading of all the relevant inscriptions – remain within the arena of the doable and the possible.

GOVERNING ASSUMPTIONS ABOUT THE ARTS OF AMARĀVATĪ

The Great Stūpa, like the others of Andhra, was made of discrete prefabricated architectural elements (railing pillars, crossbars and coping slabs, *āyaka* columns and other pillars, and so forth) that were embellished with exceptional sculpture before being assembled. The same process took place with the elements of the stone veneering that covered most of the monument's surface from large drum panels, narrow horizontal drum friezes and narrow vertical drum pilasters to tall, oblong dome friezes, all again carved in relief, and all found not only at Amarāvatī but at other great stūpa sites such as Nāgārjunakonda. Similarly, the monument's forms employ an iteration of shapes and designs – medallions, railing motifs and framing devices such as animal, floral or garland friezes – but they also use a relatively restricted repertoire of repeated visual motifs, for example wheels, stūpas, *buddhapāda*s, lotus flowers, *pūrṇaghaṭa*s, *triratna*s, *dharmacakra*s and so forth, and iconographies (many complex, representing varieties of Buddhist narratives and icons), all of which were employed at other stūpa sites in Andhra Pradesh. The result of this kind of prefabrication and assemblage, as far as the monument's visual narratives are concerned, is that meaning could be in the artist's design and the placement of sequential blocks adjacent to each other, or it could be created for and by viewers in the happenstance of the contiguity of different narratives between juxtaposed slabs. This model of 'happenstance' is not outside the intent of the cultural system because the narratives are all either about the Buddha's own final lifetime or about the multiple earlier lives of the same being – in which, according to Buddhist understandings of karma, there is an infinite patterning of potential connections. I will explore some of these issues in Chapter Three.

Underlying this specific and to some extent local model of construction – both practical and conceptual – was a larger culture of connections. The visual arts of early Buddhism in general follow an eclectic pattern whereby artists borrowed forms, motifs and styles from a wide range of earlier and external influences to create works of art that suited particular rhetorical and narrative needs in given contexts. Although the distances are huge, and although the local artistic traditions in any given part of the Indian subcontinent or along the Silk Road to the northwest were substantially different, and subject to very different influences, there is likely to be greater interconnection than might otherwise be expected because monks travelled and transmitted Buddhism across this area, translating texts, carrying objects and bringing teachings in ways that are difficult to evidence empirically today – but were clearly parallel to the well-recorded and remarkable Chinese ventures into India attested to in the fourth to the eighth century.[128] Xuanzang (*c.* 602–664), for instance, a Chinese Buddhist monk from the Tang capital Chang'an (modern Xi'an), made a sixteen-year-long journey to India in search of sacred texts, to see the sacred sites and to study with Indian masters (629–45 CE).[129] In his *Record of the Western Regions* (Book 10, 928c–32a), Xuanzang visits eastern and southern India. Highly sensitive to doctrinal issues, he remarks on a range of Buddhist sects

– Sthavira, Mahāyāna, Mahāsāṃghika, and 'numerous heretics'.[130] He describes the country of Andhra, where he mentions a number of stone stūpas, before coming to Dhānyakataka, the ancient capital close to Amarāvatī.[131] There he remarks that most of the monasteries are in ruin, but twenty are still occupied by about 1,000 monks, whom he identifies as adherents of the Mahāsāṃghika school. In Amarāvatī itself (which he calls 'Avaraśilā'), however, Xuanzang claims there have been no monks left for a hundred years.[132] The interconnections between prestige monastic sites of artistic significance at the time of their construction are made explicit in a remarkable inscription on a pair of drum slabs found at Amarāvatī itself. This avers that a number of gifts to the stūpa were donated by a family group who also donated materials to 'the great *caitya* at Rajagīri' (illus. 68 and 69).[133] This was the ancient capital of the kingdom of Magadha, 11 kilometres (7 mi.) from the great monastery–university of Nālandā, in what is now Bihar, northeast India (some 1,500 kilometres/930 mi. north of the Krishna River).

I will make the assumption that the Buddhist arts of ancient India follow a pattern not entirely dissimilar from that which in Roman art has been described as a visual system across a huge geographic and multicultural territory (in that case spanning the entire Mediterranean). Existing visual vocabularies could be continually repurposed in a variety of eclectic and creative manners to enable a cohesive visual language of both power and religion (categories not easy to separate at any period in antiquity).[134] In the case of India, while there may not have been a single imperial system lasting as long as the Roman Empire, the rise of religions supported by various monarchs who affirmed themselves visually, and acquired some model of identity through visual and material culture, operated in something at least akin to this manner within their own cultural contexts and in relation to the multiple other religions of the region. This means that, although my focus is on Amarāvatī, I will take account of, and make some comparison to, the major contemporary visual monuments of Indian Buddhism from across the subcontinent.

At the same time, the necessary resistance to Eurocentrism in writing the history of the arts of South Asia should not blind us to the fact that not only north of India, where the Silk Road ran, but throughout the subcontinent – and especially on the coasts, where the Indian Ocean trade routes operated – the culture was visually receptive to artistic influences from everywhere, and immensely creative in refashioning them for its own purposes,[135] as well as highly successful in exporting its products and styles.[136] There were certainly artistic forms and styles from the Persian, Hellenistic and Roman worlds to the west of India that had a significant impact on the development of Buddhist art.[137] There has been a series of recent interventions to show at least the availability of some Roman models, through coins and Indian Ocean trade, and to suggest the possibility that a range of Mediterranean influences were available for appropriation by Amarāvatī sculptors.[138] My assumption will be that just as the Buddhism of Andhra appears to have been creatively and discursively receptive to Buddhist ideas from across India and to have made a series of major theoretical and philosophical moves in the definitions and understandings of positions within what would become both the Nikāya and Mahāyāna traditions, the artists of Andhra (working in the same sites and monastic contexts as the scholar monks) were equally receptive and creative. They repurposed any visual models that seemed useful to create a distinctive visual language that was designed to make a case about what Buddhism and the monuments of Andhra meant in their context of construction.

My purpose here is not the study of the origins of motifs and styles or the developments of iconography. Instead – following the lead of some of the more interesting recent writing on Graeco-Roman religion[139] – I want to explore the way images offered acute reflections on the nature of religious life through their use of the visual discourses they appropriated in relation to the literary traditions in which they flourished. While most study of theology has been resolutely textual – not surprisingly, when considering the scriptural nature of the world religions – the impetus for looking at images to construct theology is particularly motivated in the ancient Mediterranean world, because it did not have scriptural religions (with the exception of Judaism) until the emergence of Christianity.[140] One of the problems with the study of Buddhism in India has been the separation of the necessarily philological field of Buddhology (with its need to command not only the Indian languages but those such as Tibetan and Chinese into which lost Sanskrit sources were translated, and those such as Japanese and Korean that have produced substantial secondary literature in the course of the last century) and the material-cultural and art-historical field of Buddhist archaeology. My point will be that the Buddhist arts of Andhra Pradesh from the second century BCE to the third century CE, exemplified by Amarāvatī, were extraordinarily creative and that this creativity went hand in hand with the creativity of Andhra Buddhist theory (both Nikāya and Mahāyāna) both in the same period and after. Moreover, although it is traditional to assume that all religious innovation and thinking is by means of texts, this assumption simply need not be true – even of religions that had a written and canonical scripture. It is quite possible that a number of theological ideas were in part worked out by visual means on the kinds of great monuments that inspired pilgrimage and devotion, such as Amarāvatī.

THE BUDDHISM OF ANDHRA IN THE PERIOD OF THE MAKING OF THE AMARĀVATĪ STŪPA

We know a surprisingly small amount, in specific, positivist terms, about where the great developments of early Buddhist thinking took place and to whom they should be ascribed. Given the richness of the surviving scriptural traditions of both early and Mahāyāna Buddhism, it is striking how many of the various schools and traditions of Indian Buddhism are now almost entirely unrepresented by surviving texts; how many, even of famous Mahāyāna sūtras, do not survive in the original Sanskrit but rather the later Tibetan or Chinese translation (and perhaps elaboration). This is, as has already been mentioned, unfortunately the case with the Mahāsāṃghika school, within the early or Nikāya traditions, which is likely to have been predominant – but not exclusively so – in Andhra. I divide the discussion in this section into two questions: first, what are the most likely schools, teachers and texts that we can place in southern India, and therefore in the context of the makers of the Amarāvatī stupa? And second, what positions held or developed by these parties seem to resonate most directly with aspects of the stūpa's visual discourses and arguments? My proposal is that we cannot separate the extraordinary monuments of Indian Buddhist art from the extraordinary exegetic, commentarial and philosophical developments of Indian Buddhist thought, especially when both are likely to have been formulated in close proximity within monastic or monastic-influenced contexts. The weakness of this approach historically is that precision on either side of this equation – the dates and construction, the patronage structures of the making of a stūpa like that at Amarāvatī, and the history of Buddhism and its many writings in the period of the stūpa's making and early flourishing – is impossible to achieve given the current nature of the available empirical evidence. But since, I would contend, we would not have the incredible art of these monuments without the remarkable developments of the faith that they celebrate, in themselves the difficulties of finding positivistic answers do not make the investigation a foolish one.

Most significantly, stūpas were Buddhological interventions at the level of actual devotional practice (including ritual and pilgrimage), religious storytelling and narrative as well as philosophical understanding, beyond being material interruptions in the landscape and significant statements of architecture and art, patronage and finance. As has been well said,

> the interpretation and symbolism of the Buddhist stupa . . . reflect variant teachings about the Buddha's identity and about his real or enigmatic presence in the realm of *saṃsāra*. The Buddha's presence in stūpas is a recurrent subject of Buddhist deliberations and debates, but essentially all such deliberations and debates

> form an integral part of a much larger spectrum of Buddhist speculations and theories which are concerned with the Buddha's identity, presence and activities in the world after his *parinirvāna*.[141]

That is, the visual culture of stūpas stands – through the metonymic and indeed synecdochic link of actual relics to the Buddha himself – for his living presence in the world that the pilgrim or devotee inhabits. Beyond this, it offers a range of exegetic meanings within the immense complexity of debates regarding how that living presence offered salvation – the path to freedom – to the living worshipper, debates that ramified in terms of the different Nikāya schools and the rise of positions that later came to be associated with the Mahāyāna, and the live conversations between and within these communities that took place at the very time, place and context in which the Amarāvatī monument was created. I hope that by the end of this book, the reader will have a sense of the ways the visual culture of the site was itself a vibrant contribution to the deliberations and debates of early Indian Buddhology.

Much of the difficulty in academic terms has been the fierce argument between modern scholars as to whether the origins of the Mahāyāna are based in southeast India or the north, and when.[142] But at issue in the question of the creativity of Buddhism in Andhra, Mahāyāna origins are much less important than the potential existence of a pre- and proto-Mahāyāna culture in the south, very likely in dialogue with both early Mahāyāna theorists from the north and Nikāya positions (as adopted by numerous sects, but particularly the Mahāsāṃghikas) in the locale. That Andhra was the site of significant contributions to the origins of Mahāyāna thought is not in doubt, and it is striking that in the mythological origins attributed by later Tibetan and Chinese culture to a series of key sūtras and tantras, southeast India has pride of place. Even if we assume this is pure fiction (not always the right response to mythical, legendary or folkloric traditions), it proves the esteem of Andhra in later fantasy. In the Chinese version of the *Mahāmega Sūtra*, the Buddha prophesies that seven hundred years after his Nirvana there will be a fruitful moment for Buddhism under the patronage of a king named Sātavāhana and his daughter, Srīvrddhi, in the kingdom of Andhra and specifically the city of Dhānyakataka on the Krishna River.[143] Notably, the Kālacakra Tantra is said in Tibetan tradition to have been first delivered in Amarāvatī itself, preached by the Buddha at the stūpa.[144] Likewise, Sudhana, the pilgrim-hero of the *Gaṇḍavyūha Sūtra*, which comprises the 39th and culminating chapter of the huge *Avataṃsaka Sūtra*, is said to come from Dhanyakara, which most scholars identify as Dhānyakataka, the town adjoining Amarāvatī.[145] Indeed Sudhana takes the Bodhisattva vow at Amarāvatī itself.[146] In light of the story of Sumedha, these may well be mythological moves to tie Mahāyāna developments to a key site of the origin of origins; but they may simultaneously preserve a memory that the earliest Indian origins of some Mahāyāna and Tantric texts were linked to Andhra. Certainly, much Tibetan Tantric tradition credits the great founders of the Mahāyāna, notably Nāgārjuna and Āryadeva, who are both associated with South India, with being founders of Tantra.[147]

Historically, much of the problem is that we can only certainly identify inscriptions with Mahāyāna substance from no earlier than the fifth century CE, although we know that Mahāyāna texts, or texts with significant Mahāyāna tendencies, were circulating from the first century BCE and were already being translated into Chinese by the third century. How much do we extrapolate backwards? Our best evidence of early Mahāyāna is now the range of textual materials written on birchbark in Gāndhāri, discovered in the north of the Indian subcontinent. Does this mean that we should decide Mahāyāna really flourished there and was at best incidental in the south of India, just because the specific evidence does not survive (in climatic conditions where, for instance, birchbark manuscripts would have rotted not so long after their making)? Likewise, much of what we know about the Pāli tradition is given by commentaries made in the fifth and sixth centuries that claim to preserve and relate much earlier material.

How much should we believe these, since we cannot tell what positions are very old and what may be the invention of the commentator? But if we decide to accept the commentarial evidence of the fifth century on the Pāli side, on what grounds do we (for instance) reject the reading back of certain Mahāyāna positions from later texts into, say, the second or third century CE in Andhra? How consistent should we be in the context of all these doubts?

There is no doubt that a number of major teachers appear to have been based in southeast India according to varieties of more or less legendary tradition, impossible to verify by the standards of Western scholarship but nonetheless not all certainly dismissible or wrong for that reason, and some, as in the case of the great Madhyamaka scholar Nāgārjuna, perhaps correctly placed there following a 'least unlikely' probabilistic process of the annihilation of still less likely alternatives.[148] Likewise, Nāgārjuna's student Āryadeva has been located in the south.[149] In the first half of the seventh century, Xuanzang's description of the east and south of India is notable for the famous Buddhist masters whom he mentions (as Bodhisattvas) and of whom he offers anecdotes: Nāgārjuna, Dignāga (*c.* 480–540), Bhāviveka (or Bhāvaviveka, *c.* 490–570) and Dharmapāla of Nalanda (*c.* 530–561).[150] Others we might add to this list include Harivarman (third to fourth century), Buddhapālita (*c.* 470–550), Sthiramati (sixth century), Candrakīrti (600–650) and Dharmakīrti (sixth or seventh century).[151] Likewise the three major Theravāda commentators of the fifth century and after, Buddhaghosa, Buddhadatta and Dhammapāla, all spent time in southern India, notably Kāverippūmpattinam in Tamil Nadu, as well as in Sri Lanka.[152] None of this proves what the artists, patrons or viewers of the stūpa knew or thought, but it indicates traditions that placed many of the most creative thinking in both the Nikāya and the Mahāyāna approaches to Buddhism in the broad region around and including Andhra Pradesh.

While it is still more difficult to place ancient Buddhist texts in the locale of their creation than it is to place at least the legendary seats or origins of individual teachers and writers, there are several instances of major early Mahāyāna scriptures for which the case has been made (admittedly on evidence that is tenuous but better than any other existing information) that Andhra is the least unlikely site of their creation. The *Srimālāsimhanāda Sūtra*, or the *Lion's Roar of Queen Srimālā*, survives now in Tibetan, Chinese and Japanese, with some original Sanskrit fragments (preserved as quotations in other texts, since this was a popular and influential sūtra in later Mahāyāna traditions). A combination of internal hints within the text and inscriptional evidence from Nāgārjunakonda (near Amarāvatī) makes a case for the recipient of the sūtra being Queen Cāṃtisiri, who is attested as a patron of Nāgārjunakonda in the third century CE.[153] On the basis of its similarities with the *Lion's Roar*, recent scholarship has placed the perhaps slightly earlier *Tathāgatagarbha Sūtra* also in Andhra;[154] while the most current position on the origins of the Tathāgatagarbha tradition (in the *Mahāparinirvāṇa-mahāsūtra*, which survives mainly in Chinese and Tibetan with some Sanskrit fragments) again sees Andhra as the least unlikely location.[155] Likewise, the *Gaṇḍavyūha Sūtra*, probably datable in its original form between the second and third centuries CE (it was later much expanded and incorporated into larger texts), has been placed by its most recent commentators in the arena of Andhra.[156] This is a spectacular and imaginative text, as we shall see later, with an emphasis on the positive role of female lay teachers (in line with the celebration of Queen Srimālā in the *Srimālāsimhanāda Sūtra*), a strong devotional content and some proto-Tantric elements.[157]

The evidence provided by these texts, tentatively associated with the Buddhist centres of the Krishna River, offers the possibility of vibrant, innovative thinking within the intellectual context that gave rise to the art of the stūpa. It also supports the likelihood that significant proto-Mahāyāna writings were produced in monastic contexts that we think were probably dominated by Mahāsāṃghika monks operating within a Nikāya tradition.[158] This indicates open conversation and much greater interconnectedness and debate regarding different doctrinal positions and assumptions in the general context of Amarāvatī than Buddhology has sometimes allowed in the past. Note that the evidence tying each of these traditions or teachers specifically to Andhra is tenuous, and there is no single clinching or compelling piece of data or argument. Moreover, the traditions whose creative early thinking might be connected to the environment of the stūpa are anything but consistent: Nāgārjuna's anti-essentialist philosophy of emptiness has little in common with the argument for Buddha nature as an essential seed in every sentient being of the Tathāgatagarbha traditions, and neither is obviously interconnected with the florescence of imaginative reflections and multiple worlds of the *Gaṇḍavyūha Sūtra*. But all could be seen as different speculative models of presenting the dharma, and developing key Buddhist ideas in a variety of directions that would ultimately become characteristic of the Mahāyāna.

The many schools of Nikāya Buddhism differed on a series of issues (such as monastic rules or *Vinaya*) but significantly in terms of different attitudes regarding how to conceive of the Buddha. This – like the parallel Christian concern with the natures of Christ (human and divine) – is not abstract theorizing, but a key problem in understanding the status of the being who brought salvation, and therefore of the possibilities and potential of the path to salvation for the followers and devotees of the religion. It affected every adherent of Buddhism personally. Not all the positions of all the schools are fully understood given our current level of evidence. But notably the Sarvāstivādins, the principal group in northern India, appear to have held a two-body theory of the Buddha: a duality of his physical form as a human being (*rūpakāya*), which was subject to the defilements of the world, being impure and imperfect, and of his perfect body (*dharmakāya*), which was the ground of his true or essential being.[159] The Theravādins, who had a significant presence in South India, including Andhra, and especially in Sri Lanka, appear to have largely shared this position.[160] The Mahāsāṃghikas (prevalent in Andhra), by contrast, along with the Vibhajyavādins, appear to have developed a transcendental model of an omniscient and omnipotent Buddha who manifested in numerous forms (one of which was Śākyamuni), with a special emphasis on his compassion.[161] An entailment of this was that the *rūpakāya*, the physical body of Gautama, was pure, unsullied, perfect.[162]

In the context of Buddhist art, and especially the variety of embodied and 'aniconic' or 'emblematic' forms for the Buddha that appear side by side at Amarāvatī,[163] these developing and competing positions regarding multiple Buddha bodies appear to be mapped out and conceptually developed through different formal solutions for the representation of the founder of Buddhism, an issue we will examine in due course. These different forms (including, for instance, the repeated symbols employing the *buddhapāda* – such as the *dharmacakra*, a wheel on a column over an empty throne and *buddhapāda* beneath; or the Bodhi tree with empty throne and footprints; or a flaming column crowned by a *triratna* (a ω-shaped symbol over a circle, representing the triple gem) above a throne with the *buddhapāda* beneath – as well as the embodied figure of the Buddha, whether seated or standing, and the multiple forms of the Buddha in earlier lives as a Bodhisattva) are all reiterated and juxtaposed in the imagery of the stūpa. It is impossible, in the absence of textual evidence, to identify any one of these forms with a given Buddhological position as upheld by one school or another; but it is by no means fanciful to see such artistic experimentation as the visual equivalent of the kinds of thinking that explored and developed the theoretical positions on the Buddha's bodies among the Buddhist schools of southern India. Those multiple positions themselves developed in a variety of Mahāyāna engagements into a three-body (*trikāya*) theory of the *dharmakāya* (truth or essential body of the Buddha), the *nirmāṇakāya* (manifestation body) and the *saṃbhogakāya* (enjoyment body or the body of compassion).[164] It is possible that some of the earliest Mahāyāna 'takes' on these issues were formulated by Nāgārjuna, who towards the end of his life may have been based in Andhra,[165] and the duality of *rūpakāya* and *dharmakāya* is central to the *Gaṇḍavyūha Sūtra*,[166] perhaps composed in Andhra Pradesh. It is again not impossible that the stūpa's visual thinking is in dialogue with all this.

Beyond the discussion of the Buddha's bodies, Nikāya schools argued about the number of buddhas and the different levels of enlightenment or attainment on the path. Different schools held differing views, but many accepted that there had been huge, perhaps limitless, numbers of buddhas.[167] This raised the issue of the numbers of future buddhas, and of whether there could be many simultaneously.[168] The open plurality of past and future buddhas in the earliest Theravāda texts, for instance, certainly implies an infinity of Buddhas without beginning or end, to respond to the open infinity of *saṃsāra*.[169] That in turn implies an open plurality or infinity of Bodhisattvas, on the path to becoming a Buddha – all of them with multiple lives that may overlap. Clearly these concerns – with the past lives of the Buddha, with a multiplicity of Buddhas and with the Bodhisattva career as a path to Buddhahood – are very close to what would become the Mahāyāna commitment to the Bodhisattva path as a response to and a result of speculation on these issues.[170] What we can say in relation to this is that the stūpa's imagery is relentlessly focused on the life of the Buddha and his previous lives as a Bodhisattva, exploring parallels through visual juxtaposition of narratives. In the *Mahāpadāna Sutta* in the *Dīgha Nikāya*, or collection of longer discourses, the Buddha tells the story of Vipassī Buddha – one of his predecessors as a Buddha (and hence not an account of a previous life).[171] Strikingly, this is a very similar story to the one that the tradition has presented as his own, with a number of precise variations – coming into his last human rebirth out of the Tuṣita Heaven, born as the son of a king who might have become a wheel-turning monarch in his own right, being protected from all sight of suffering in his youth, seeing examples of old age, sickness and death as a young man and prompted by them to leave his life in the palace and enter the path to awakening, enlightened under a tree, and so forth. So, implicitly, the imagery that describes the Buddha's past as a Bodhisattva in his final lifetime turns out to be a formulation of the multiple paths of all the other Buddhas, past and future (and vice versa).[172]

The arts of Amarāvatī sit within, and stand out as, a monumental artistic contribution to the rich speculative culture on the Bodhisattva path to Buddhahood, which was the most vibrant driving focus of intellectual life in all the Buddhist traditions in India from the Nikāyas to the rise of Mahāyāna in the last century BCE and the first few centuries CE.

Part I
The Great Stūpa at Amarāvatī

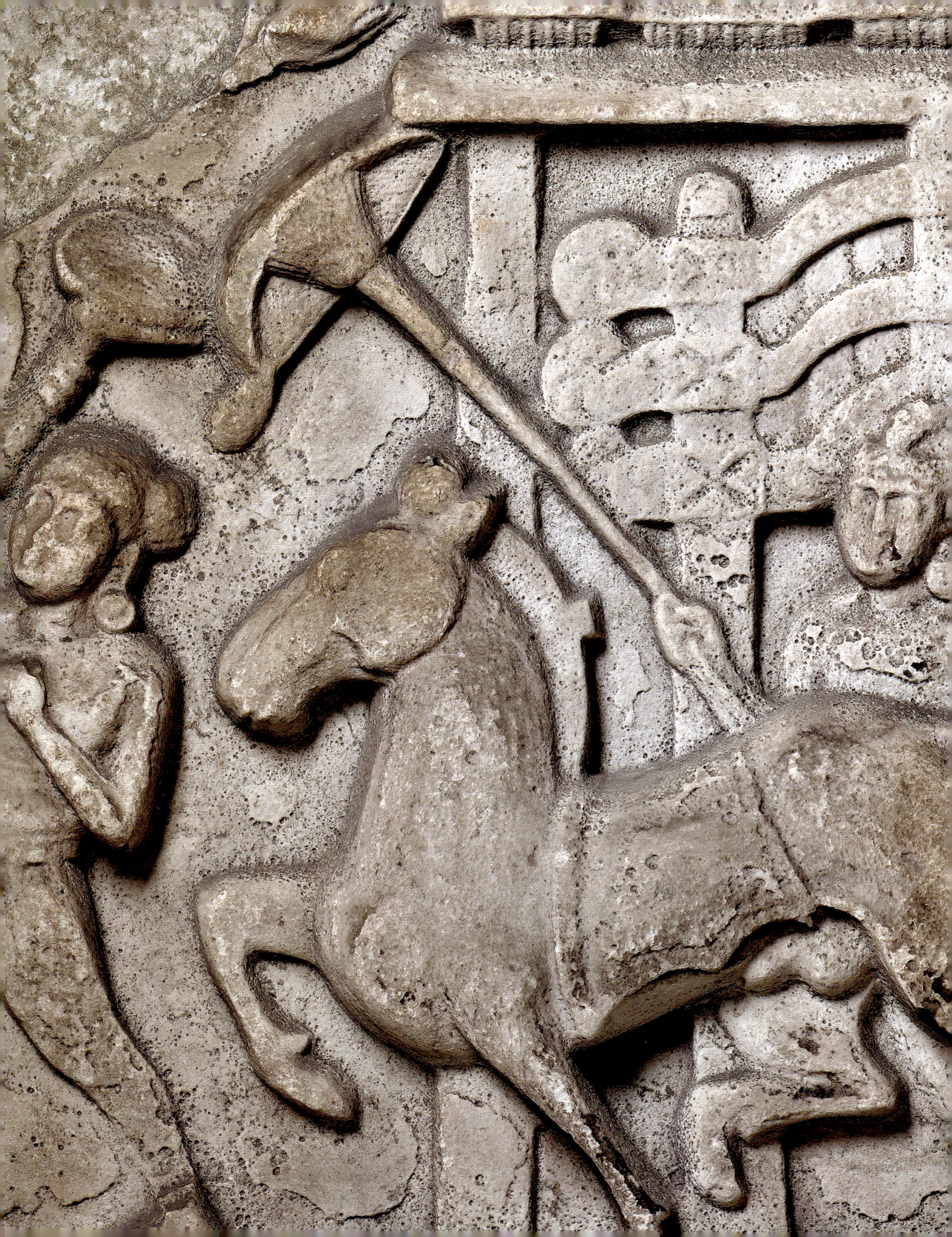

one

Approach and Circumambulation

Having made a funeral-pyre of all manner of perfumes they cremate the king's body, and they raise a stūpa at the crossroads. That, Ānanda, is what they do with the remains of a wheel-turning monarch, and they should deal with the Tathāgata's body in the same way. A stūpa should be erected at the crossroads for the Tathāgata. And whoever lays wreaths or puts sweet perfumes and colours there with a devout heart, will reap benefit and happiness for a long time. Ānanda, there are four persons worthy of a stūpa. Who are they? A Tathāgata, Arahat, fully enlightened Buddha is one, a Pacceka Buddha is one, a disciple of the Tathāgata is one and a wheel-turning monarch is one. And why is each of these worthy of a stūpa? Because, Ānanda, at the thought, 'this is the stūpa of a Tathāgata, of a Pacceka Buddha, of a disciple of the Tathāgata, of a wheel-turning monarch', people's hearts are made peaceful, and then, at the breaking-up of the body, they go to a good destiny and rearise in a heavenly world. That is the reason, and those are the four who are worthy of a stūpa.
Mahāparinibbāna Sutta 5.11–12, *Dīgha Nikāya Sutta* 16, II.142–3.

Thus, eight stūpas were built for the relics, a ninth for the urn and a tenth for the embers. That is how it was in the old days.
Mahāparinibbāna Sutta 6.27, *Dīgha Nikāya Sutta* 16, II.167.[1]

6 Detail of illus. 12: fragment of a monumental dome slab depicting the Bodhisattva's departure from the palace in aniconic form (that is, his presence shielded by the parasol to be imagined riding the horse).

MONUMENTAL RELIQUARY

According to the earliest Buddhist tradition, a stūpa is a mound, often made of earth and rubble, which contains a relic (or several relics[2]) of a fully enlightened buddha, a *paccekabuddha* (one who has achieved full enlightenment but cannot teach the path), a disciple of the Buddha or a wheel-turning monarch inside one or more reliquaries.[3] These reliquaries may sit one within the other, like a Russian doll, or they may be laid out in a variety of places within the stūpa's structure.[4] The fact that in early Buddhist India many of these reliquaries – perhaps the majority of surviving examples – were shaped like a stūpa supports the sense that the stūpa is itself a vast outer reliquary, the exterior skin of a closed container (or series of containers) of a holy presence.

In the complex at Amarāvatī, a number of such reliquaries, along with their contents, have been discovered over the course of its excavation history (illus. 7).[5] These were made in a variety of materials ranging from what were probably stone or clay outer caskets to rock crystal, gold, silver, copper and ivory inner reliquaries. Some were in the shape of a stūpa, and their contents include bone fragments and gold flowers as well as pearl, coral, lapis lazuli, beryl and crystal beads.[6] The relics contained in these boxes and hence within stūpas have been described in early inscriptions as 'living entities' and 'endowed with life'.[7] The Sāncī stūpa, a monumental reliquary, is described in one inscription as 'the house of the teacher', as if the teacher were still living inside.[8] This attitude seems to have gone hand in hand with a second, even more animating, conception, in which stūpas were regarded as legal entities with rights of property ownership – effectively living persons[9] – and hence (through the collection of relics they contained) as equivalent to the Buddha's living presence.[10]

Buddhism undoubtedly inherited the tradition of stūpa mounds as sites of devotion from much earlier Indian Brahmanic practice, adapting them to new reliquary uses.[11] Stūpas may indeed owe something to prehistoric megalithic culture, whose monuments survived throughout India, notably in the south.[12] Other non-normative Indian religious groups, such as the

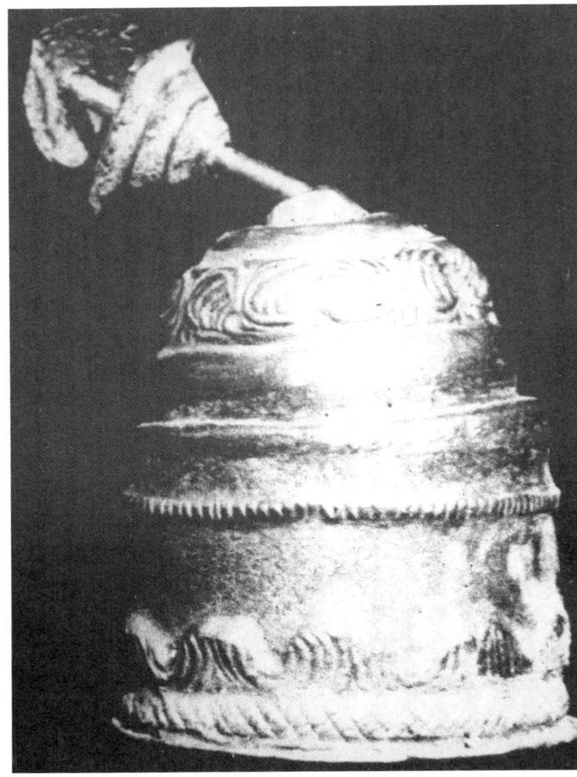

7 Gold reliquary in the form of a stūpa discovered in the excavations of 1888–9 in the small votive stūpa found beyond the east side of the southern gate (shown in illus. 24). From the (poor-quality) photograph published in A. Rea, *Annual Reports, Archaeological Survey of India, 1908–9*.

Jains, also appear to have used the form and embellished their stūpas with stone sculpture.[13]

The relic tradition is not only central to the understanding of stūpas historically, as material and cultural monuments, but to the extended thinking around them that developed in the Buddhist tradition. In the Pāli introduction to the *jātakas*, written by the great commentator Buddhaghosa in the fifth century CE, who drew on earlier oral and written accounts, the Bodhisattva's presence in his mother's womb is compared to the relic inside a stūpa.[14] This led to later traditions that present the relic as an embryo inside the relic casket, which was itself a womb within the stūpa,[15] and to the development of the concept of Buddha-nature (*Buddhadhātu*) as a quality essential to all sentient beings, being parallel to the presence of the Buddha in his relics within stūpas.[16] Interestingly, the most likely origin within India for this line of thinking – the so-called Tathāgatagarbha approach to the presentation of Buddhism, which ultimately became a powerful element of Mahāyānist thought – is currently thought to be Andhra Pradesh, in the vicinity of Amarāvatī, in roughly the early centuries of the common era, when the stūpa was constructed.[17]

Stūpa mounds themselves could not be entered: they were closed spaces, indeed simply piles of earth, rubble and brick over buried relics, dressed in a stone veneer. They were recipients of worship in the form of circumambulation by individuals and groups, both during festivals or mass celebrations and on a more ad hoc, informal basis. Among those visitors, in addition to affirmed Buddhists (both lay and monastic, and of both genders, as richly attested in the inscriptional culture of the stūpa), it is likely there were adherents of other cults (Brahmanic, Jain) within a broadly inclusive Indian religious culture that would ultimately find ways of incorporating the Buddha within Hinduism. The reliquaries from the main stūpa at Amarāvatī, found beneath the *āyaka* platforms at the four cardinal points,[18] include bone fragments. The *Manjuśriyamūlakalpa*, a Tantric text translated into Chinese in 702 CE and perhaps of the previous century,[19] claims that the stūpa contained relics of the Buddha himself.[20] The inner structure of the mound, not visible after construction was finished, likely had symbolic significance. A number of stūpas in Andhra Pradesh were built on foundations constructed in the form of a ground plan that simulates a wheel with concentric walls at the hub and the rim, and joined by spokes in the form of walls, the spaces between which were filled with rubble and mud; others had walls formed in the shape of a *svastika* at the hub of the wheel; others again were made of concentric wall circles filled with rubble.[21]

This model of a hidden structure within the mound is also found in the Jain stūpa of Kankālī-Tīla at Mathurā, where the foundation is a wheel made of brick.[22] A finished stūpa was often surrounded by a perimeter wall and a stone railing, with four ceremonial gateways at the cardinal points. This is largely the case in both Jain and Buddhist examples (including the famous instances at Bharhut and Sāñcī, as well as Amarāvatī[23]), but many did not have a railing (or at least one made in permanent material like stone[24]), particularly in Gandhāra, where railings are rare and appear to have largely been replaced with raised square bases.[25] In Buddhist stūpas, the gateways signalled the 'crossroads' where the Buddha himself stipulated stūpas be set up in the *Mahāparinibbāna Sutta*, the great discourse that recounts the last days of his life on earth and his passing into Nibbāna.[26]

The stūpas of Andhra differed in form and conception from those in the north. Notably Sāñcī offers cylindrical mounds topped with domes, which appear to have been rendered with concrete, then covered with plaster and minimal stucco decoration; no sculpture survives from drum or dome.[27] In the case of the circular stūpa at Bharhut, not enough survived from the core of the monument for its excavator, Alexander Cunningham, to

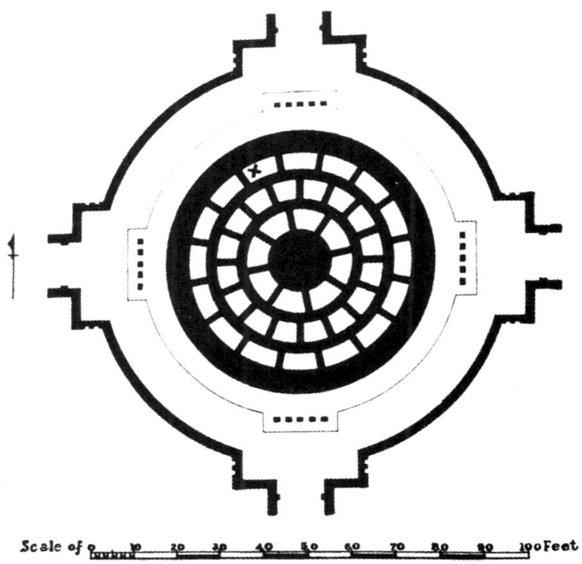

8 Three-wheel-based plan of the great stūpa at Nāgārjunakonda, made in brick and filled with earth and rubble. A cross marks the findspot of the reliquary at the northwest. The plan is based on A. H. Longhurst, *The Buddhist Antiquities of Nāgājunakonda* (1938).

draw conclusions, but certainly no sculpture from the drum or dome was excavated.[28] By contrast, the stūpa at Amarāvatī, as well as a number of major stūpas in its orbit (notably Nāgārjunakonda and Kanaganahalli), were richly veneered in sculptural relief. In Gandhāra it appears that domes were coated in coarse stucco and finished with coats of limewash;[29] this means that, given the relatively poor survival of plaster in contrast to stone, we have little evidence of decorative schemes on the dome.

The stūpas of Andhra were not circular, by contrast with Bharhut and a few examples in Gandhāra,[30] but instead had *āyaka* platforms (crowned with columns and perhaps statuary) projecting from the drum at the cardinal points facing the gateways to the precinct, creating a marginally cruciform plan.[31] In the case of the great stūpa at Sāncī, as well as stūpas 2 and 3 there, the circular form of the monument was augmented with a single projecting platform ascended by two flights of steps facing one of the cardinal points (the south in the case of the great stūpa and stūpa 3, the east in the case of stūpa 2).[32] Such steps to an upper walkway or platform are not attested at all at Andhra Pradesh.

Most significantly, in Amarāvatī the sightlines through the four gateways at the four cardinal points that pierced the railing that formed the exterior barrier to the precinct allowed direct visual access to the stūpa mound (illus. 9). By contrast, the entrances to the stūpa precincts at both Sāncī and Bharhut were oblique to the monument, allowing no penetrative gaze. At Bharhut (illus. 10) and stūpas 2 and 3 in Sāncī, the railing plan formed a *svastika*, funnelling the visitor through an entryway initially with their right-hand side to the outer railing of the monument and then making them turn

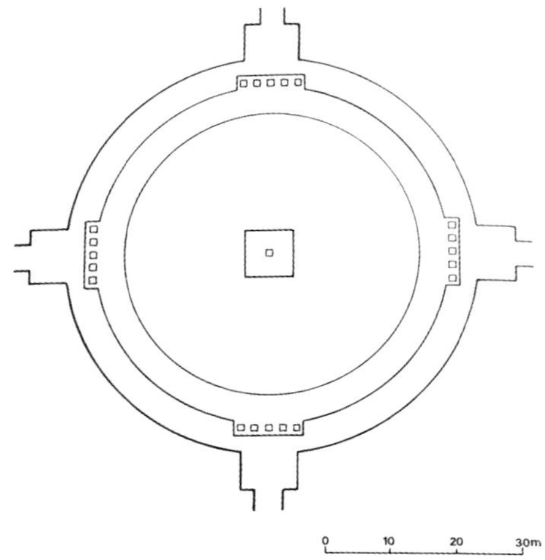

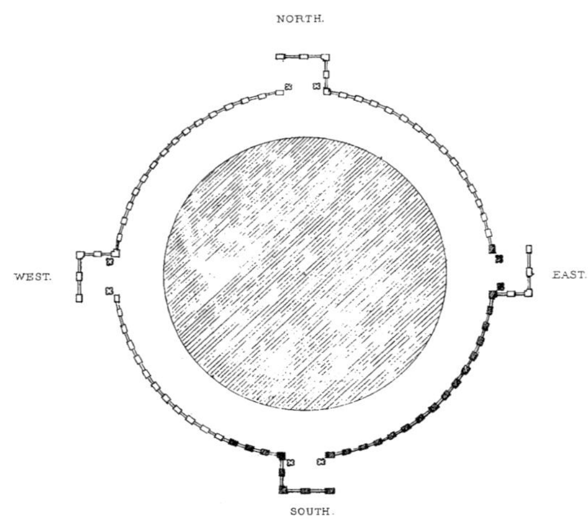

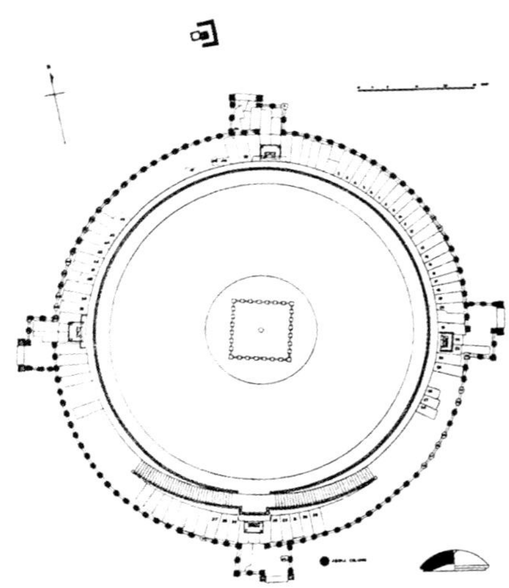

9 Plan of the great stūpa at Amarāvatī, after D. Barratt, *Sculpture from Amaravati in the British Museum* (1954).

10 Plan of the stūpa at Bharhut, after A. Cunningham, *The Stūpa of Bharhut* (1879).

11 Plan of the great stūpa at Sāncī, after J. Marshall, A. Foucher and N. Majumdar, *The Monuments of Sanchi* (1940).

right, through the railing, in order to gain access to the processional path.[33] At Bharhut, *toraṇa*s (ceremonial gateways) were erected at the point of entrance into the precinct, directly facing the stūpa (only the remains of the eastern *toraṇa* survive), but they were shielded by the return of the railing in front of them, and the means of approach was from the right.[34] The entrances to the great stūpa and the southern entrance of stūpa 3 at Sāñcī, all of which had elaborately carved (and justly famous) *toraṇa*s, show a more complex variation of the *svastika* form of entry plan: the outer railing to the left of the entry extends away to the right from the entrance of the precinct and then swings at a right angle to the right, in order to cover the entry and close any sightlines (illus. 11). The left pier of the *toraṇa* looking towards the monument adjoins this extension, standing to face the stūpa but slightly to the right of the entry. A further segment of railing extended from the perimeter rail at the right to join the right-hand pier of the *toraṇa*, which ensured that there was only one entrance to the monument on each side (through the *toraṇa*). In all these cases, in fundamental contrast to Amarāvatī (and the stūpas of Andhra Pradesh generally), the purpose, apart from offering a great space for display sculpture on the *toraṇa*, was to prevent direct visual access and straight penetration into the precinct without the visitor turning. It was also effectively to pause the viewer at the entrance, which is also the most spectacular part of the monument in terms of sculptural decoration and the visual programme of Buddhology extended through it. In Gandhāra, the raised square platform, which had to be climbed to give access to the main monument, meant that the visitor's gaze was likewise denied direct access to the stūpa mound and its decor.[35] At Amarāvatī, despite the lavish decoration of both inner and outer railings, the pull was a direct and unimpeded passage to the stūpa mound at the heart of the precinct, and its equally spectacular relief sculpture.

Within the railing at Amarāvatī – that is, the space between its inner-facing wall and the stūpa itself – was a paved passageway where devotees could conduct the principal act of ritual obeisance associated with stūpas, namely the circumambulation of their perimeter in a clockwise direction, with the worshipper's body keeping the mound to the right. The railing established both an external arena of ritual approach – outside the perimeter wall – and an internal sacred space or processional way for devotional circumambulation, as well as enhancing the cut-off nature of the mound itself through architectural gestures towards liminality. The fact that in all the stūpas with railing walls, including those at Andhra, the rail could be partially penetrated by glimpses through the gaps between its pillars and crossbars enabled a logic of anticipation and fulfilment in the approaching devotee akin to a pilgrimage.

Spectacular entranceways though the *toraṇa*s of northern India are,[36] and magnificent structures for sculptural decoration, these gates further impede the sense of visual access to the stūpa, the characteristic three bars of its upper structure certainly blocking a full view of the mound within.[37] Amarāvatī, alongside the other stūpas of Andhra, eschewed the *toraṇa* form,[38] employing for its gateways a model of railings that narrowed to an entrance width of just under 4 metres (13 ft), projecting outwards from the main perimeter rail. As pilgrims entered, the impression was of the railing walls on either side widening as they progressed towards the main monument: a funnel effect, with the great domed cylindrical space of the stūpa mound itself growing ever wider as one approached. This meant that from the entrance there was no impediment to the view of the stūpa, except for the perimeter railing itself, at ground level. The processional path between the railing and the main drum of the stūpa was between 3 and 4 metres in width, paved in rectangular flat slabs of different lengths.[39] Within the walkway, at either side of each gateway opening, there may have been placed pillars surmounted by stūpas carved in the round.[40]

However, the imagery of the stūpa's relief sculpture included numerous images of *toraṇa*s representing palace or city gates, and thus alluding obliquely to the architectural norm for stūpas in the north (for example, illus. 12, also illus. 5).[41] Self-reflexive commentary in the imagery of the stūpa's reliefs on what the monument as a

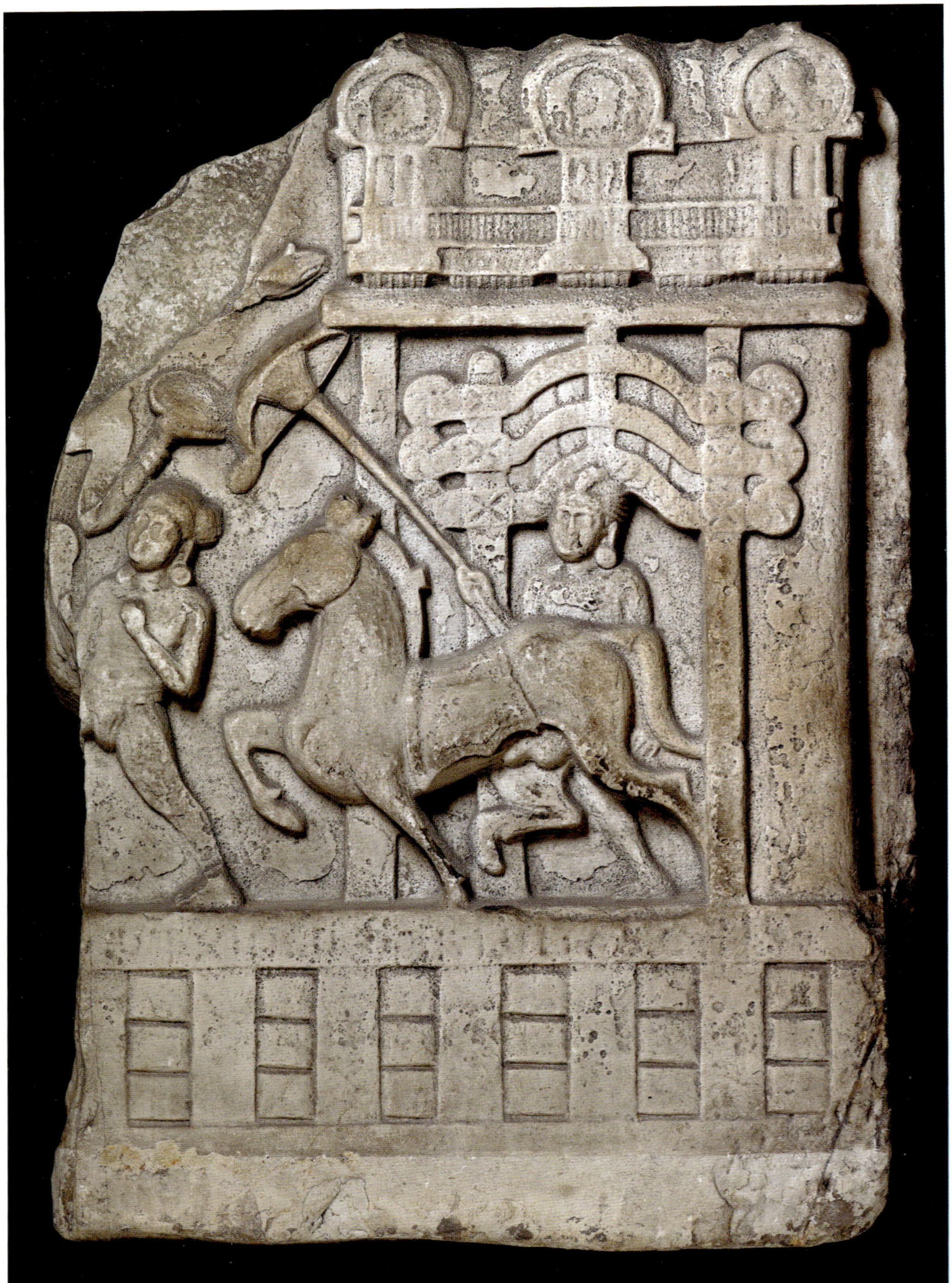

12 Fragment of a monumental dome slab depicting the Bodhisattva's departure from the palace in aniconic form (that is, his presence shielded by the parasol to be imagined riding the horse). He leaves through a fine *toraṇa* before a city gate with elaborate entablature.

whole looked like is a characteristic aspect of the arts of Amarāvatī, and in this case it represents a complex game of reflecting on what the monument is not. One might cite the fine dome slab showing the Great Departure, now in the British Museum, where the horse Kaṁṭhaka followed by a groom with a turban holding an umbrella over its head (and no image of Prince Siddhārtha, the future Buddha) leaves the great gates of Kapilavastu.[42] The gate is a grand *toraṇa*, with three crossbars and scroll terminals, very like those at Bharhut and Sāñcī, but more arched in the centre. Such *toraṇa*s appear in the narrative imagery of the coping friezes of the inner railing (see illus. 37), in the historiated scenes of the medallions of the inner railing crossbars, in the railing uprights, and in the dome slabs (see illus. 128).[43] Their pictorial function is effectively to enrich the narratives with the illusion of architecture, but they consistently mark an absence – an affirmation of what the Amarāvatī stūpa is not.

In the case of the most spectacular and developed examples of the hallowed architectural genre of the stūpa – usually occupying sites where stūpas had long existed, either since the immediate aftermath of the Buddha's own life or in the wake of the emperor Aśoka's redivision of his relics and his building of 84,000 stūpas across India (a legendary number, of course[44]) – many of the external parts of these structures came to be elaborated with extensive and exquisite sculptural embellishment. In contrast to Bharhut, where the sculptural elaboration is all focused on the *toraṇa*s and the railings, the great stūpa at Sāñcī, where the sculpture is principally on the gateways,[45] or Sāñcī stūpa 2, which had no *toraṇa* but rather finely sculpted railings, in Andhra the railings were the prelude to further and extensive sculptural decoration of the stūpa mound itself. Arguably the logic of the visual embellishment of the stūpa in India reached its high point in the richness and proliferation of imagery in Amarāvatī. The point of embellishment that would have arrested the beholder's eye and the provision of opportunities for worship through sculpted icons are made implicit in the *Mahāparinibbāna Sutta*'s emphasis on the effect of a stūpa in bringing peace to the viewer's heart and offering the occasion for laying wreaths, and putting out 'sweet perfumes and colours', as quoted in the epigraph to this chapter. Arguably, the sculptural decoration and its thematic insistence on the great themes of the Buddha's mission and on acts of devotion to him were devised to evoke wonder at the former and imitation of the latter.

There has been a traditional view that stūpa devotion was a lay form of ritual, and rather discouraged for monks and nuns.[46] But in the *Mahāparinibbāna Sutta*, referring specifically to 'the four places the sight of which should arouse a sense of spiritual urgency [*saṃvega*] in the faithful' (the sites of the Buddha's birth, enlightenment, turning of the wheel and passing away, all repeatedly celebrated in the visual culture of the Amarāvatī stūpa), the Buddha brings *saṅgha* and lay worshippers together in pilgrimage. He says: 'The faithful monks and nuns, male and female lay followers will visit those places. And any who die while making pilgrimage to these shrines with a devout heart will, at the breaking up of the body after death, be reborn in a heavenly world.'[47]

Certainly, the inscriptions of Amarāvatī – like those at Kanaganahalli, on the stūpa at Bharhut and many at Sāñcī[48] – give a rich sense of the men and women, both lay and in monastic orders, who were pilgrims and donors. It has indeed been argued that the act of *dāna*, or giving, was the principal ritual context in early Buddhist India that brought lay and monastic communities together.[49]

In this chapter, I follow a phenomenological trajectory of exploring the stūpa through a viewer's experience as she or he enters the gate and performs the devotional ritual of circumambulating the monument in a clockwise direction along the processional path with the main stūpa and its imagery on the right and the richly decorated inner wall of the precinct railing to the left. The sad history of the site's depredation over time, as well as early archaeology and too much clearance, means that we cannot reconstruct with certainty the contiguity and juxtaposition of any specific surviving stone blocks or their iconographies. But since so much has survived, the broad parameters of imagery, iconography and programme are ascertainable.

THE APPROACH

The stūpa at Amarāvatī was surrounded by a circular perimeter limestone wall with a circumference of about 185 metres (607 ft), pierced by four gateways at the cardinal points.[50] This was constructed as a railing consisting of tall pillars, 2.7 metres (9 ft) high and about 85 centimetres (33 in.) in width.[51] Between the pillars were three tiers of crossbars consisting of large circular bosses sculpted on the exterior into exquisite lotuses with three, four or five rows of petals radiating around the central circle, and projecting tenons from either side that fitted into vertical, lenticular-shaped mortises cut at three levels into the sides of the pillars (illus. 13).[52] The model was a stone imitation of a wooden railing of piers and crossbeams,[53] and is similar in its construction model to the stone railings at both Bharhut and Sāñcī. The whole was topped with a coping frieze some 80–90 centimetres (30–35 in.) in height, which ran along the entire railing; thus the height of the whole wall was about 3.5 metres, or roughly double the span of a human being. The total extent, including the projections of the railing to create the gateways, has been calculated as 136 pillars, 348 crossbars and 240 metres (787 ft) of continuous coping.[54] Most pillars, crossbars and coping slabs were carved on both the exterior and the interior sides (the latter being much more elaborate, as we shall see).

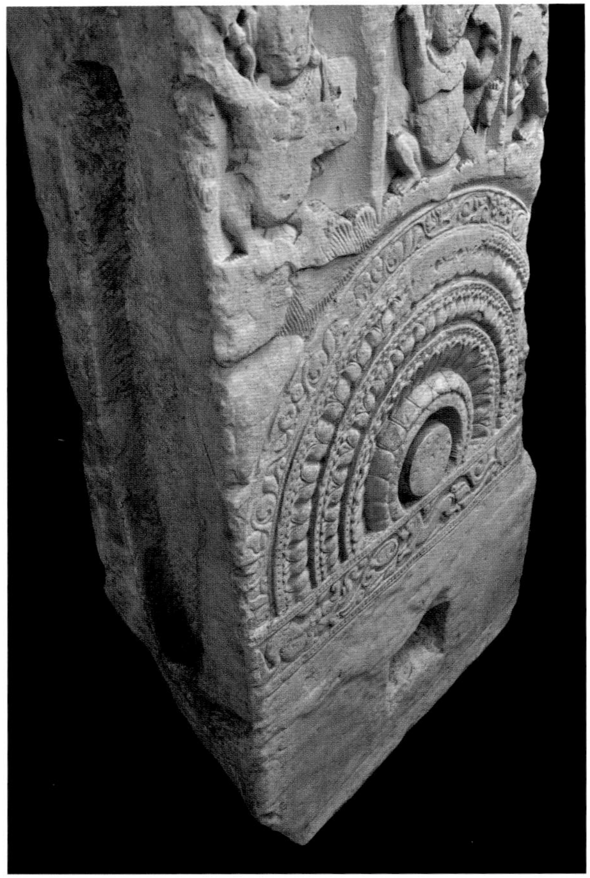

13 The lower section of a fragmentary railing pillar showing the socket on the left side into which the tenons for a crossbar were inserted. The entire interior view of the pillar is in illus. 74.

The appearance of the exterior railing was broadly speaking a wall of flowering lotus blossoms, no two exactly alike.[55] Each pillar had a large central lotus roundel cut in deep relief, often with many rows of petals and a finely carved outer rim with floral patterns, vegetation and sometimes animals (illus. 14 and 15). At the top and the bottom were half-lotuses, also with rows of petals, and a fine frieze rim with a half-open lotus and stem filling in the corners of the semicircles that make up the upper and lower blossoms. Some, like the example in illustration 14, have significant historiation in the fluting between the lotuses and in the framing borders at top and bottom; others – like that in illustration 15 – are likely to have offered simpler models of fluting between the lotus medallions, over which inscriptions could be carved.[56] Between the pillars, the crossbars (each consisting of a full lotus medallion) were laid out in three tiers in dialogue with the pillars to either side (illus. 16).[57] Above and below the half-lotuses, each pillar is framed with friezes marking its borders, often richly carved with vegetation emanating from the mouths of *makaras*, legendary sea creatures in Indian folklore, at the bottom and with a stūpa or Bodhi tree at the top centre, to which elephants and mythical winged animals pay homage (for example, illus. 14). The lower sections of pillars survive in the best condition, and the bas-relief friezes, incised in contrast to the deeper relief of the half-lotuses, reflect remarkable variation and creativity in ornamental design (illus. 17 and 18). In the spaces

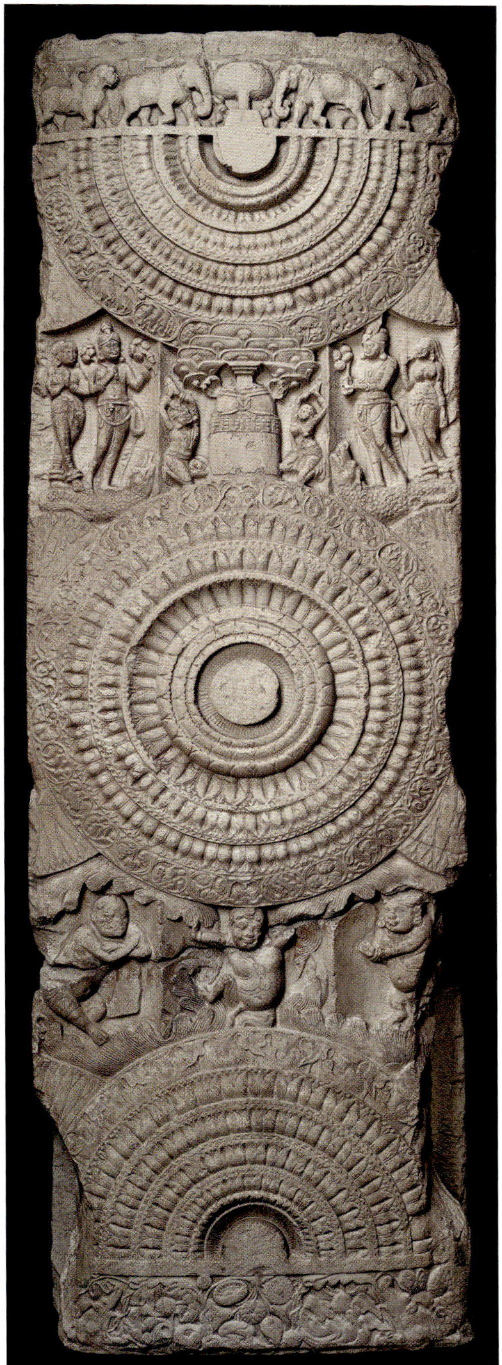

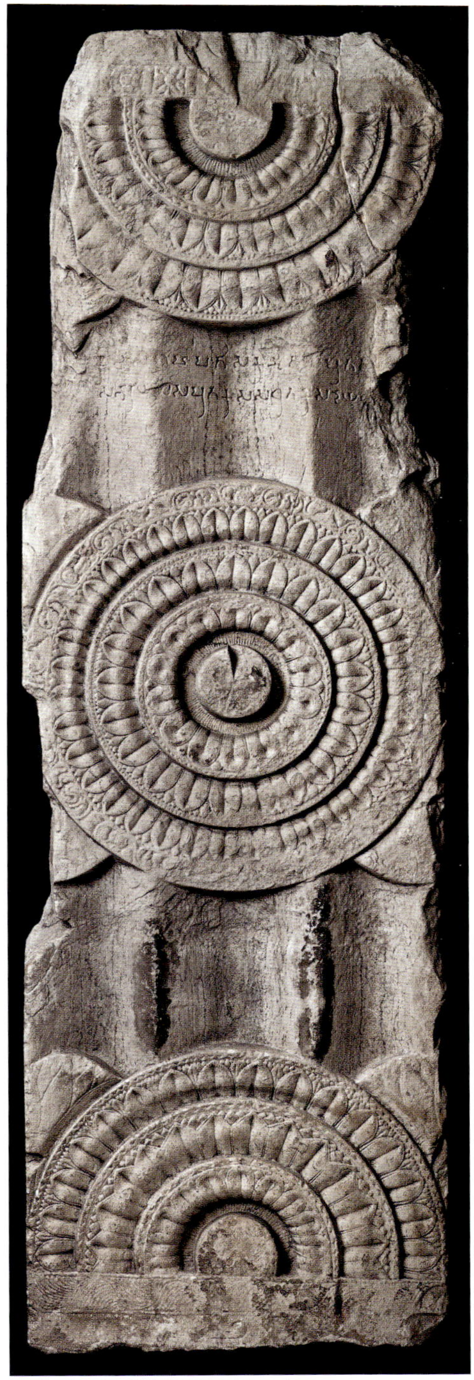

14 Complete surviving railing pillar, exterior face, elaborately carved with much figural historiation in all elements and in exceptional condition (2.66 × 0.86 m). The interior is illus. 112.

15 Complete surviving railing pillar, interior face, with purely vegetal motifs consisting of deep-cut lotus petals in three rows (2.74 × 0.73 m).

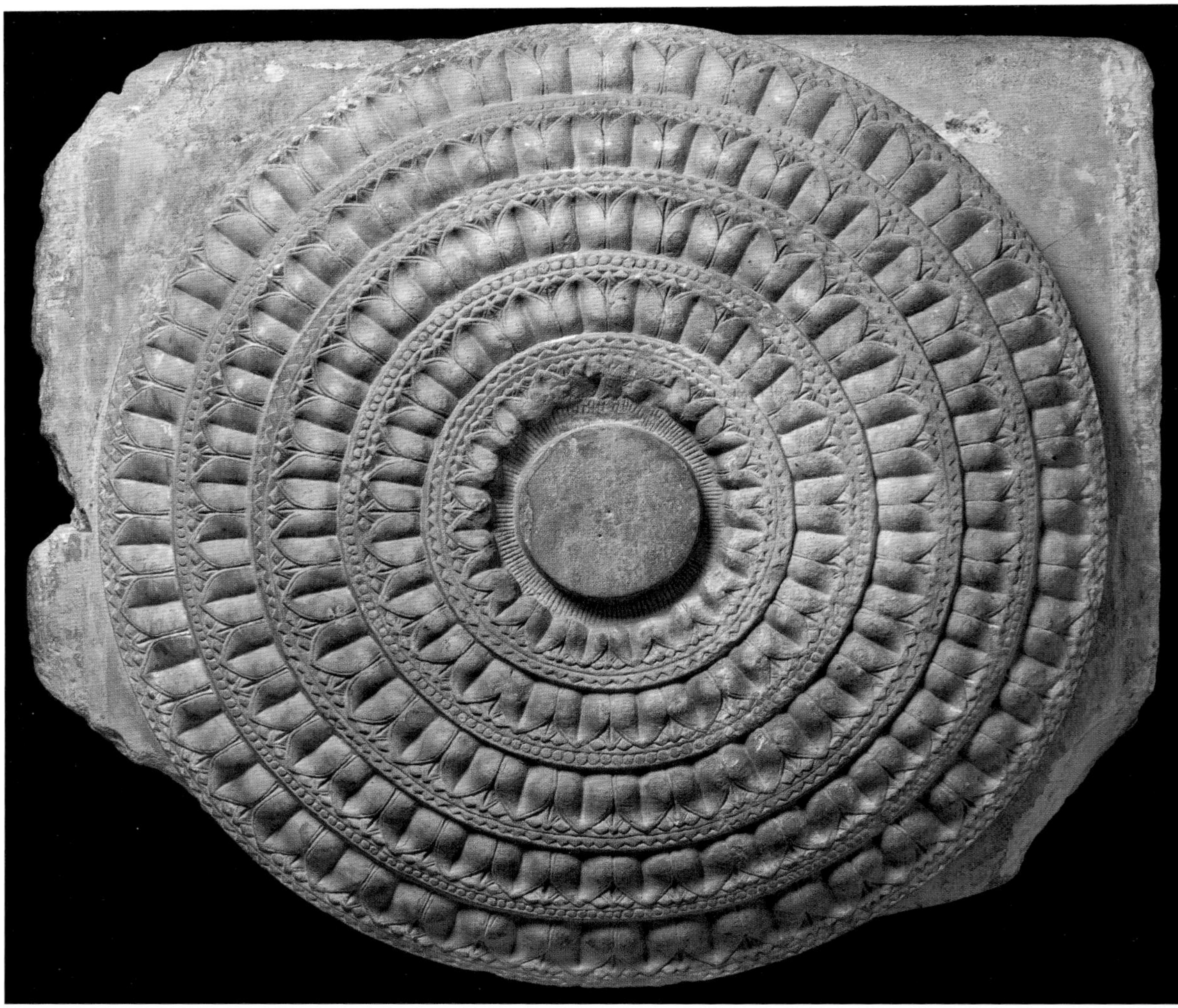

16 Lotus crossbar, exterior side, with five rims of petals all outward-pointing and preserved tenons for insertion into the railing pillars.

between the central lotus roundel and the two half-lotuses at top and bottom, there are a variety of sculptural solutions. In some of the earlier examples these spaces appear to have been marked by simple – that is, deep and clean-cut – fluting, probably on both the interior and exterior of the railing.[58] But within the characteristic lozenge shape with concave curves (created by the framing of this space with two large semicircles and two smaller part-circles), the fluting was often carved with further decoration. This ranged from striated foliate waves envisaged as emerging from the lotuses,[59] to dancing dwarfs in the lower fluted lozenge and figures worshipping a central sacred object in the upper lozenge – a stūpa or a *nāga* serpent, as in illustration 14. (This is the case in the two surviving examples where the top of the outer face of the railing pillar survives, but the iconographic range is likely to have been much greater.[60])

The effect would have been of a wreath of lotus blossoms garlanding the entire stūpa, from within and above which the main monument arose, since the image of the Buddha is sometimes represented seated or

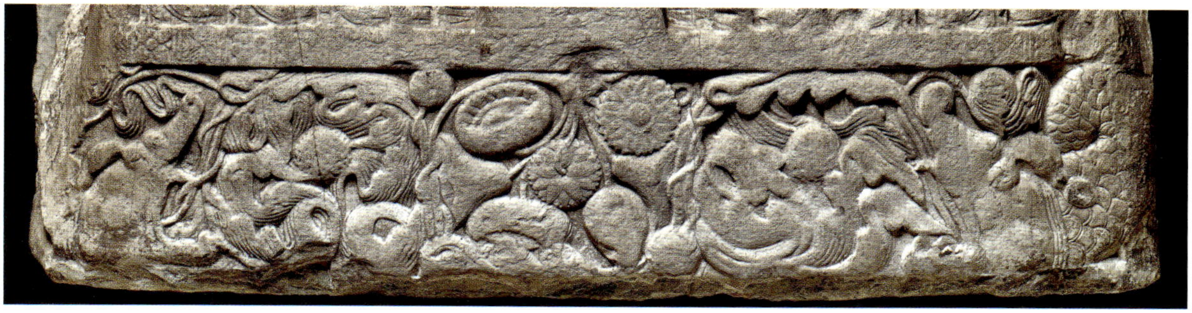

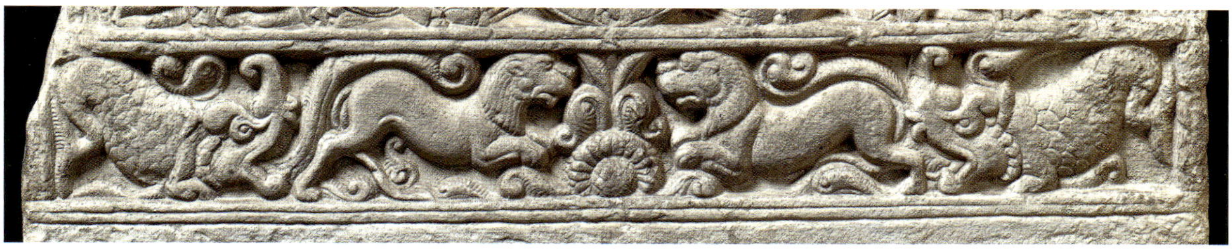

17 Lower rim of the exterior face of illus. 14: superb bas-relief border of vines, lotus buds and flowers mixed with waves and entwined stems emanating from the mouths of fish-tailed scaly *makaras*.

18 Lower rim of a railing pillar, exterior face. Fish-tailed *makaras* flank a pair of lions facing a flower head in the centre.

standing on a lotus.[61] This kind of wreath is precisely what the Buddha prescribes as the appropriate offering to a stūpa in the passage quoted at the opening of this chapter; and in the very early group of the Buddha's sayings collected in the *Dhammapāda*, one who walks the Buddha's path is compared to an expert garland maker,[62] while the making of garlands from a heap of flowers is a metaphor for good deeds done in the mortal life. At the same time, the hints of sculptural elaboration peeping out from between and behind the lotuses (through the gaps between the crossbars and in the fluted lozenges) point to the immense richness of visual magnificence within. The elaboration of the lotus motif in a series of variations on the exterior of the railing is striking. In addition to the full-blossomed flowering roundels in both pillars and crossbars, seen as if from above, and the lotus buds (seen from the side) in the corners of the central medallions and half-lotuses of most pillars, friezes of joined lotus flowers in flat relief make up the wide outer borders of the roundels and half-roundels of the pillars and crossbars (for example, illus. 14, 35, 54, 118, 136).[63] At the base of the pillars, lower border bands feature with lotus blossoms and sometimes animals issuing from the mouths of *makaras* (for example, illus. 14, 17, 18);[64] upper and lower lotus border bands in low relief frame the coping that capped the railing wall (for example, illus. 19, 20, 22, 23);[65] and in one instance, in a section normally undecorated and thought to be set below ground, there are vases of plenty (*pūrṇaghaṭas*) from which lotus buds and flowers issue, as well as an almost invisible light engraving of lotuses growing downwards from the lower border.[66] Insofar as lotus blossoms may have been gifts to the stūpa, as seems to be shown in some of the better-preserved drum slabs of the main stūpa (for example, illus. 49, 61, 71, 90, 95),[67] the railing as giant garland is a supreme offering, draped around the sacred mound and eternalized in stone. The repeated imagery of those who carry and bring the garland – gods or human beings – enriches the reference to ritual in mimicking the presence and activity of pilgrims bringing garlands.

The lotus itself had deep symbolism in early Buddhism, which arises from a series of scriptural texts. In a Pāli poem by the Elder Udayin from the *Theragāthā*, or verses of the elder monks, the lotus serves as a symbol of the Buddha himself:

> As the flower of a lotus,
> Arisen in water, blossoms,
> Pure-scented and pleasing the mind,
> Yet is not drenched by the water,
> In the same way, born in the world,
> The Buddha abides in the world;
> And like the lotus by water,
> He does not get drenched by the world.[68]

This develops an image used by the Buddha himself in the *Doṇa Sutta*, to which we will return in due course: 'Just as a blue, red or white lotus flower, though born in the water and grown up in the water, rises above the water and stands unsoiled by the water, even so, though born in the world and grown up in the world, I have overcome the world and dwell unsoiled by the world.'[69]

In the *Dhammapāda*, the Buddha directly compares his followers to lotus blossoms:

> Upon a heap of rubbish in the roadside ditch
> blooms a lotus, fragrant and pleasing.
> Even so, on the rubbish heap of blinded mortals,
> the disciple of the supremely Enlightened one
> shines resplendent in wisdom.[70]

In the *Buddhavaṃsa*'s version of the meeting of Sumedha and the Buddha Dīpaṅkara, quoted in the Introduction to this book, lotuses and flowers fall upon the two from heaven and earth.[71] In the versions (originally in Sanskrit) that were taken up by the Mahāyāna tradition, Sumedha purchases lotus blossoms that he throws over the Buddha's head before he prostrates himself.[72] These lotuses magically turn into a stūpa-like pavilion crowning Dīpaṅkara as the Amarāvatī stūpa itself crowns the relics it contains. If the lost Mahāsāṃghika canon of scriptures and *jātakas* included this version of the story, as is quite possible, then it may be that the lotuses of the lotus-born stūpa at Amarāvatī were also designed to evoke this moment, and by implication the taking of the Bodhisattva vow.

The garland theme, created by the lotuses of the external face of the stūpa's railing, is extended by the deep-cut continuous frieze that runs along the coping (illus. 19). Not all coping stones were carved on the exterior side, although it is only a group of stylistically close examples, which scholars have dated to early in the stūpa's making, that are carved on the interior alone.[73] But the majority are carved on both sides. It may be added that while we can imagine most of the stūpa's carved blocks to have been sculpted before being set up, the fact is that the coping frieze with continuous decoration across slabs on each of these sides is much more likely to have been carved *in situ* once it was erected.

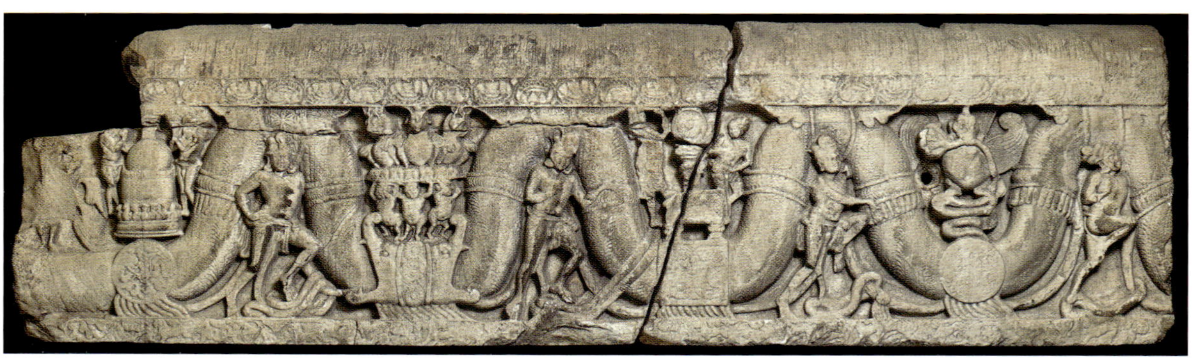

19 Damaged and somewhat abraded but intact coping slab (2.76 m in length), exterior face (of illus. 79) with thick garland, turbaned bearers and, in the undulations of the garland, images of stūpa worship, fantastic animals supported by dwarfs, worship of the *dharmacakra* and a *garuḍaḥ* with a *nāga* in its beak. This deep-cut frieze is bordered by bas-relief rims of alternately inverted lotus heads at the top and vegetation with fabulous animals below.

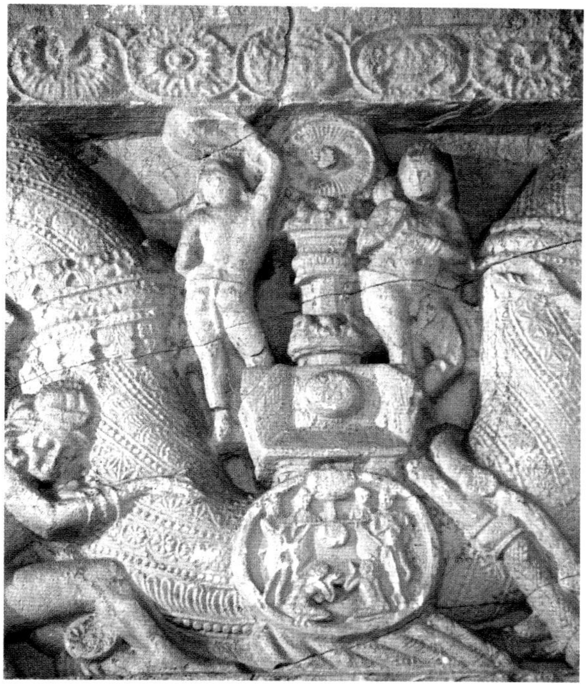

20 Detail of worship of the Bodhi tree in a roundel with that of the *dharmacakra* above, coping exterior.

The exteriors show a thick, undulating garland of undetermined flowers,[74] which at least on one example seems to include lotuses,[75] carried by a series of young men in turbans,[76] occasionally accompanied by females.[77] The garland is held together by encircling bands decorated with fluting at roughly the shoulder height of its bearers. Where the garland touches the upper border it may have been adorned by a pair of striated foliate leaves; where it touches the lower border, it is as if the garland's thread runs through a large bead with hanging tassels in the form of a *makara* with two mouths, or a medallion or square incised with finely detailed miniature decoration,[78] for instance showing the *dharmacakra*, or the empty throne with a Bodhi tree (illus. 20),[79] lotus flowers,[80] figural scenes[81] or abstract decoration.[82] The upper spaces left above the garlands' U-shape are filled with iconic motifs such as stūpas, *dharmacakras* (illus. 20) and Bodhi trees, as well as animals and dwarfs, *garuḍaḥs* (legendary winged creatures) and *nāgas*.[83] This main coping frieze is framed by upper and lower borders in fine low relief, much of it with lotus heads or lotus flowers, vegetation and animals (some fabulous).[84] The bearers are exuberantly carved in a range of postures – take, for instance, the figure seen from behind straining to hold up the garland in a fragment with detail surviving in fine condition from the site museum at Amarāvatī (illus. 21). The ends of this thick garland, presumably at the exterior end points of the railing at each of the four gateways, are in the hands of fat, seated dwarfs, who may hold it (as in illus. 85) or have it thrust into their mouths (as possibly in illus. 22).[85] Likewise, the ends may emerge from the mouths of *makaras* (as in illus. 23).[86]

The coping garland is a riff on the main visual impression of the railings' pillars and crossbars, whose lattice form, founded on a wooden model, nonetheless performs the interlacing of a floral garland to brilliant effect. This double vision of garlands – as something constituted by the railing itself and represented on its coping as well as on some of the dome decoration (illus. 42) – is typical of the arts of Amarāvatī, where an object seen in one dimension, such as a flowering lotus blossom in the pillar or crossbar bosses, is shown from numerous other angles and dimensions in the surrounding imagery, and at other moments in its lifecycle (as a half-open bud, for instance, as in illus. 136). In the slabs of the stūpa's drum with reliefs showing mini stūpas, the coping of the outer railing is frequently depicted with a tiny version of the garland coping described here, effectively repeating the double vision of lotus rails and garlands in miniature (for example, illus. 25, 70, 143).[87]

Metaphorically, the garland (*mālā* in Pāli and Sanskrit) is, in India as in Greece, a term used for the collection of stories or poems. The third-century CE *Kalpanāmaṇḍitīkā Dṛṣṭāntapaṅkti* (Collection of Examples Adorned by Poetic Fancy), written by the Gandhāran monk Kumāralāta, or the fine collection of *jātakas* in Āryaśūra's *Jātakamālā*, conceivably from the fourth century but perhaps later, both written in Sanskrit in a mix of verse and prose, are fine early examples of the genre – dealing with Buddhist material in an elevated literary style, and close in date to the making of the

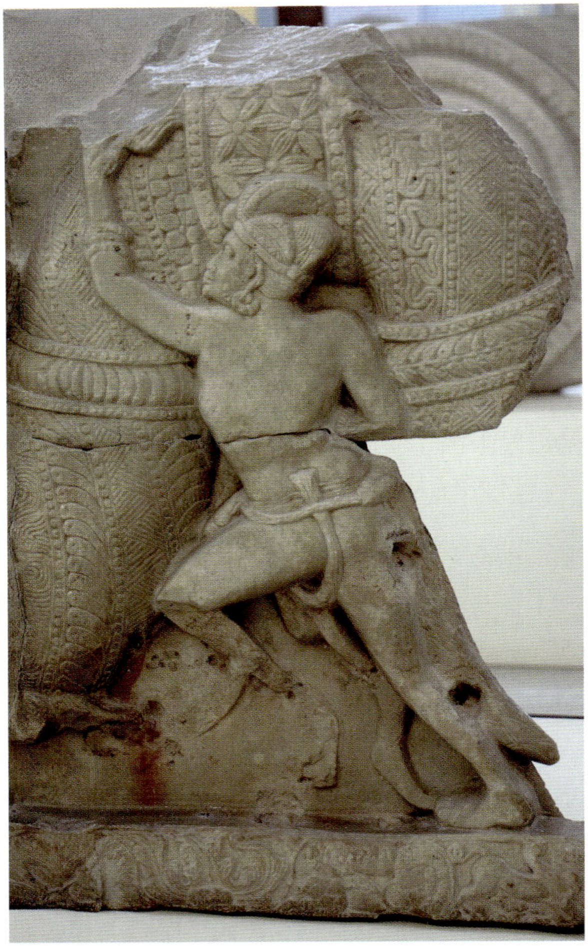

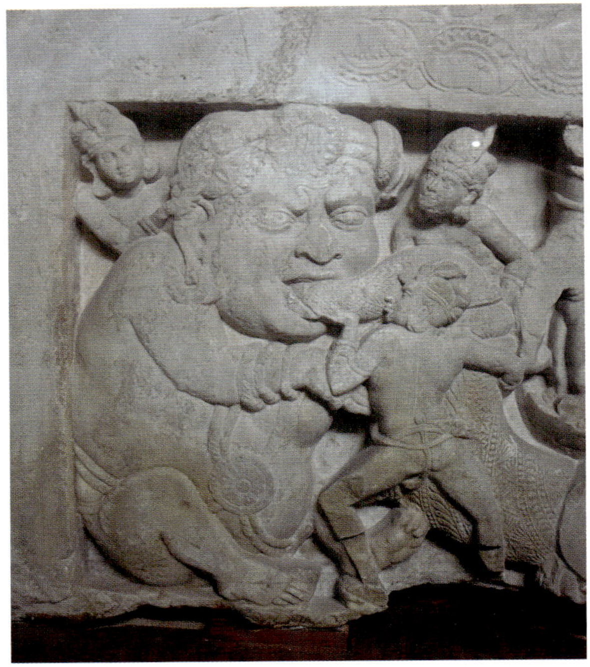

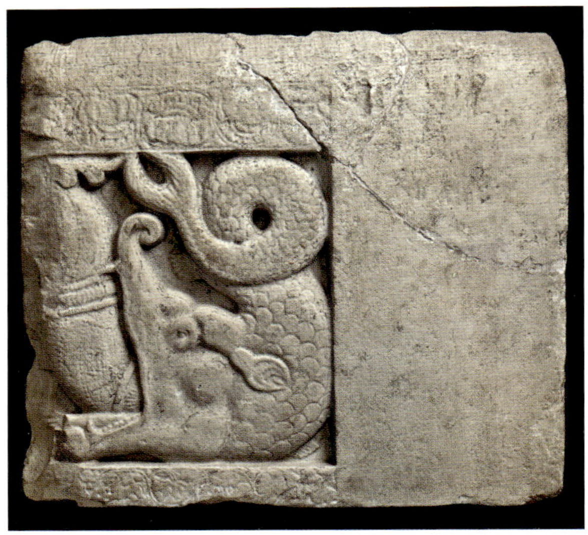

21 Fragment with garland bearer taking the weight, coping exterior.

22 Rail coping exterior face, endpiece at one of the four gateways with large dwarf and garland bearers either pushing the garland into his mouth or carefully extracting it.

23 Rail coping exterior face, endpiece at one of the four gateways, with scaly fish-tailed *makara* disgorging thick garland.

stūpa.[88] The imagery of floral garlands at Amarāvatī is a complement to and a visual instantiation of the way that the many *jātaka* and *avadāna* stories presented through images – especially on the railing but also perhaps on the sculpture of the main monument – form a garland of narratives around the body of the stūpa. These narratives are also an offering to it: a celebration of the long biography of its principal honorific figure, the Buddha himself, and an ideological presentation of the Bodhisattva path to enlightenment as a model for the stūpa's devotees. But we may certainly say that the art of the stūpa presents its own version of a garland of stories, parallel to the literary compositions of Buddhist writers of the time, with many of its finest sculptures presented rimmed in petals, in the medallion form of its lotus bosses on both crossbars and railing uprights, as if the flowers bloom into narrative.

ENTRY

The visitor, approaching the stūpa and looking to enter, would need to walk around the external railing to one of the four gates. If we believe the implications of some of the imagery of the stūpa reliefs set around the drum, and imagine that these refer to the actual conditions of pilgrimage to the monument, then the outer railing would have been a space abutted by numerous vendors with offerings for purchase by pilgrims (as in so many pilgrimage sites in all religions around the world).[89] At each gateway, from whichever side one approached, the perimeter railing turned a sharp right angle, projecting outwards from the gentle curve of the monument's circumference for 4.8 metres (16 ft).[90] It then turned inwards at a second right angle for 1.95 metres (6½ ft), before projecting out in the same direction as before for a further 2.4 metres (8 ft) to the actual opening. This meant that the entrance to the inner precinct extended 7.2 metres (24 ft) from the perimeter rail and was marked at the entry point by a pair of three-dimensional stone lions on pillars (for example, illus. 150 and 151), signalling the terminal of the railing and the front face of the gate. The opening itself at this point was relatively narrow, 3.9 metres (13 ft), but offered an unimpeded view of the entire monument, which widened as the pilgrim walked through past the outer neck of the gateway into the much wider section of the projecting entryway (7.8 metres/25½ ft), which was again marked, at the points where the railing turned from circumference to gate, by statues of lions seated on pillars. As mentioned above, we might imagine the approach as creating a kind of funnel effect with the gateway widening on both sides as the visitor moved towards the stūpa, while the monument itself appeared to move forward towards the viewer from the main circumference of its drum through the projecting *āyaka* platforms with their five columns. Barrett's excellent reconstruction drawings give a sense of both the effect for a person entering a gateway and the plan of the entire monument on this model (see illus. 2 and 9).[91]

The interior decoration of the perimeter railing in the gateway areas cannot be differentiated from that in the processional path, since we do not have enough evidence of the findspots of coping, crossbars and rail pillars. It may be that the richest sculptural embellishment was reserved for these sections; or that it was relatively plain, and the most elaborate sculpture faced the stūpa's drum as the railing encircled it; or that there was no differentiation in the railing embellishment between entrances and processional path. The drum slabs with stūpa reliefs that show the gateways usually make their view of the inner railing of these gateways a simple design of lotus-boss crossbars and fluted columns with lotuses, but this may be artistic convention in a visual world where no imitation need be rigidly dependent on material reality. The archaeological record of actual findspots for elements of the railing is very poor. But elaborate historiated crossbar, coping and rail-pillar stones were found around the circumference periphery,[92] some perhaps in secondary locations,[93] as well as many in the vicinity of the gates.[94] Since some of the Amarāvatī inscriptions do stress objects given to adorn the gateway areas – a *dharmacakra* at the western gate, a pillar for lamps (*divathabha*) at the southern gate and a pillar with a relic at the southern gate, as well as other gifts, the identities of which have now been lost[95] – we may assume that these entrance spaces accumulated much by way of impressive votive statements in stone and sculpture. One may add that a number of the icon-like *buddhapāda* slabs from the site were excavated at the eastern and western entrances and may well have been part of their additional embellishment.[96]

THE STŪPA MOUND: THE DRUM

The drum, a vast cylindrical platform covering an area of about 1,850 square metres (19,900 sq. ft), stood 1.8 metres high and 48.75 metres in diameter (6 × 160 ft); from it sprang the great dome, the height of which is understood to be about 18 metres (60 ft).[97] In the case of Amarāvatī, the sculptural decoration of the stūpa in the last phase of decoration in this period is marked by an extraordinary level of self-reflexive imagery. One striking aspect of this is the visualization of images of stūpas within its iconography.[98] We find fine imagery of stūpas receiving devotion (as suggested by the *Mahāparinibbāna Sutta*) on the external railing pillars (for example, illus. 14 and 142),[99] on the external coping interwoven among garlands (visual versions, as we have seen, of the wreaths stipulated in the sutta, for example, illus. 19, 85)[100] and on the inner face of the railing in some of the sculpted tondi.[101] But we also find it on the friezes of the inner coping (for example, illus. 79),[102] the friezes that decorated the main stūpa's drum,[103] a series of drum pilasters[104] and a range of dome slabs (for example, illus. 38, 39, 128, 141),[105] not to speak of free-standing columns on both the *āyaka* platform and the processional path between railing and mound, whose bases boasted carved reliefs of stūpas and which may have been topped by three-dimensional stūpas (for example, illus. 45).[106] Most striking of all are the remarkable relief panels, on average about 120–50 centimetres (47–60 in.) high, that made up the principal decoration of the drum, which displayed the repeated, intensely detailed, imagery of stūpas looking much like the great monument they adorned (for example, illus. 25, 34, 61, 70, 71, 90, 94). The representation of stūpas is by no means an unusual motif in Indian Buddhist art,[107] but it is exceptionally developed, and with remarkable complexity, at Amarāvatī.

This phenomenon has been described as the provision of 'meta-stūpas', meaning the use of images of stūpas to reflect upon the significance of the stūpa as a whole, as well as its ritual setting and practices.[108] The effect on the viewer of the proliferation of these relief stūpas, carved in precise and loving detail, one per slab in the outer face of the drum, has been called the creation of a multiverse, in visual emulation of, or perhaps in response to, the kinds of worlds evoked by Buddhist texts, notably the *Gaṇḍavyūha Sūtra*.[109] One may add that just as the stūpa itself is the final reliquary containing a series of other stūpa-shaped reliquaries, each effectively a reflection of the others, so in the two-dimensional dispensation of the relief decoration of its exterior face it replicates endless stūpas, evoking the 84,000 stūpas said to have been erected by the third-century BCE Indian king Aśoka.[110] We know from excavation photographs that the smaller stūpas around the site were adorned with the same kinds of reliefs, evoking the large monument of which they were part (for example, illus. 24), the main stūpa of the site and perhaps an ideal space that the stūpa represents.[111] I want here to explore the ways these reliefs – similar to each other but each distinctive – comment upon the monument and, in particular, on the spatial logic of its perimeter walls and entrances, so crucial to the architectural dispensation of devotional experience.

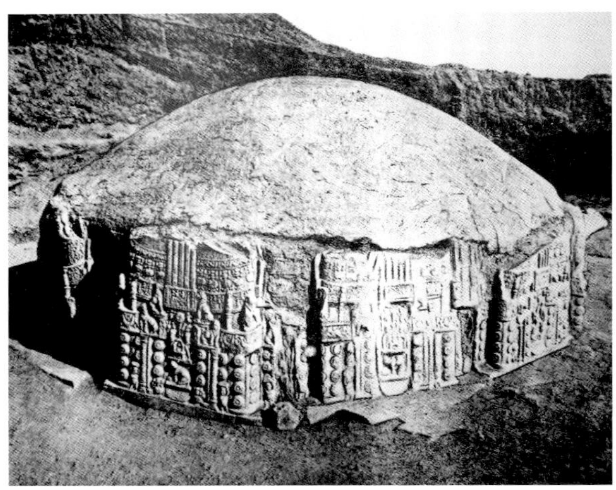

24 Small votive stūpa (3.3 m in diameter) found beyond the east side of the southern gate in Rea's excavations of 1888–9 (published in 1905–6). It survived to three-quarters of the height of the drum, which was faced with ten drum slabs depicting miniature stūpas without pilasters between them.

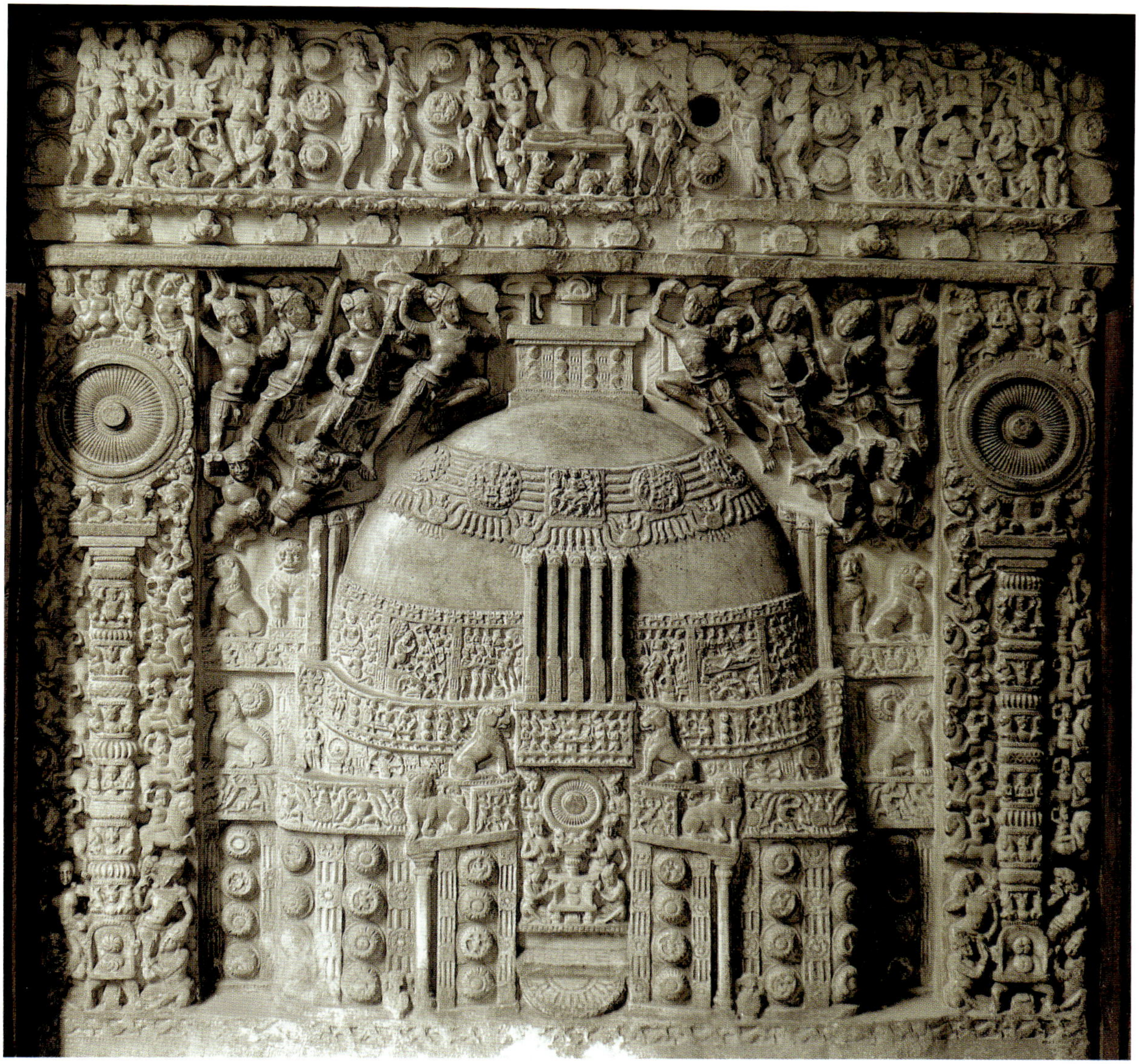

25 The best-preserved drum slab showing a view of a stūpa through a gateway and from outside its railings. Exceptionally, this slab includes flanking pilasters with *dharmacakra*s and upper frieze with scenes of veneration (1.95 × 2.15 m).

Let us begin with a detailed account of one of these slabs, which is currently housed in the Chennai Government Museum in India (illus. 25).[112] There is no information as to where on the monument it was once placed, beyond being one of about a hundred such panels that sat around the drum at roughly eye level. The entire slab is 195 centimetres (76 in.) in height and 216 centimetres (85 in.) wide.[113] It survives in exceptionally good condition, and hence enables a full account of form and iconography, much of which is relevant to all the other drum slabs of its type.[114] The panel depicts a stūpa front-on, seen with the perimeter railing before it. The railing is constructed of narrow fluted pillars, each with four roundels depicting lotuses in low relief, and four lotus crossbars, of which the lotuses are carved in high relief, like bosses (all of this strongly reminiscent of the actual outer railing of the Amarāvatī stūpa itself). The railing is high, and topped by a coping with a relief frieze of running figures and garlands interspersed with roundels, which in turn have stūpas or *dharmacakras* over columns above them.[115] It covers almost the entire drum of the stūpa, which means the stūpa's elaborate miniature decoration does not show the relief slabs of the drum that occupied the position of this slab and would perhaps have replicated its iconography, although glimpsed on the upper drum, above the point where the railing obscures the view, are slabs with *dharmacakras* and *nāgas*.[116] At the centre is one of the four great gateways leading to the stūpa, topped by two sets of paired seated lion figures, the front pair seated on a platform resting on the stepped capital of a pillar.

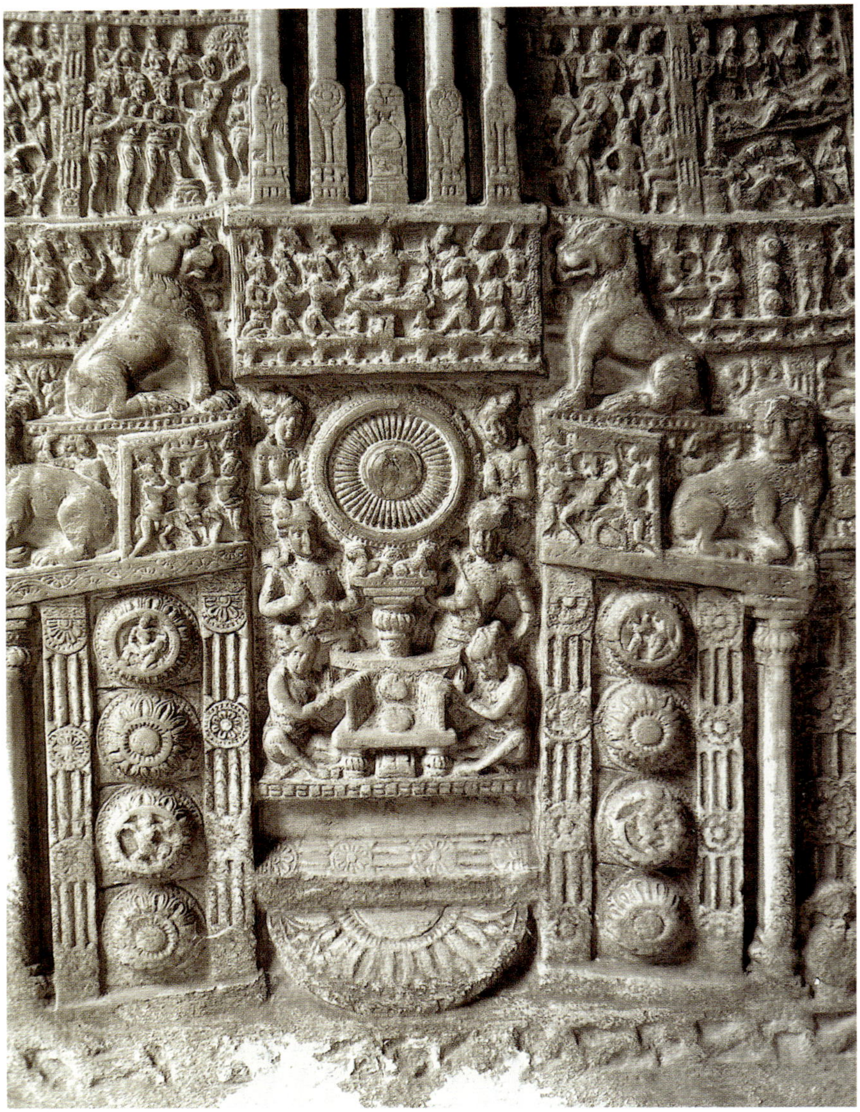

26 Detail of the gateway of illus. 25 with *dharmacakra* flanked by six worshippers inside, *āyaka* platform and columns, all with well-preserved miniature sculpture whether carved or incised.

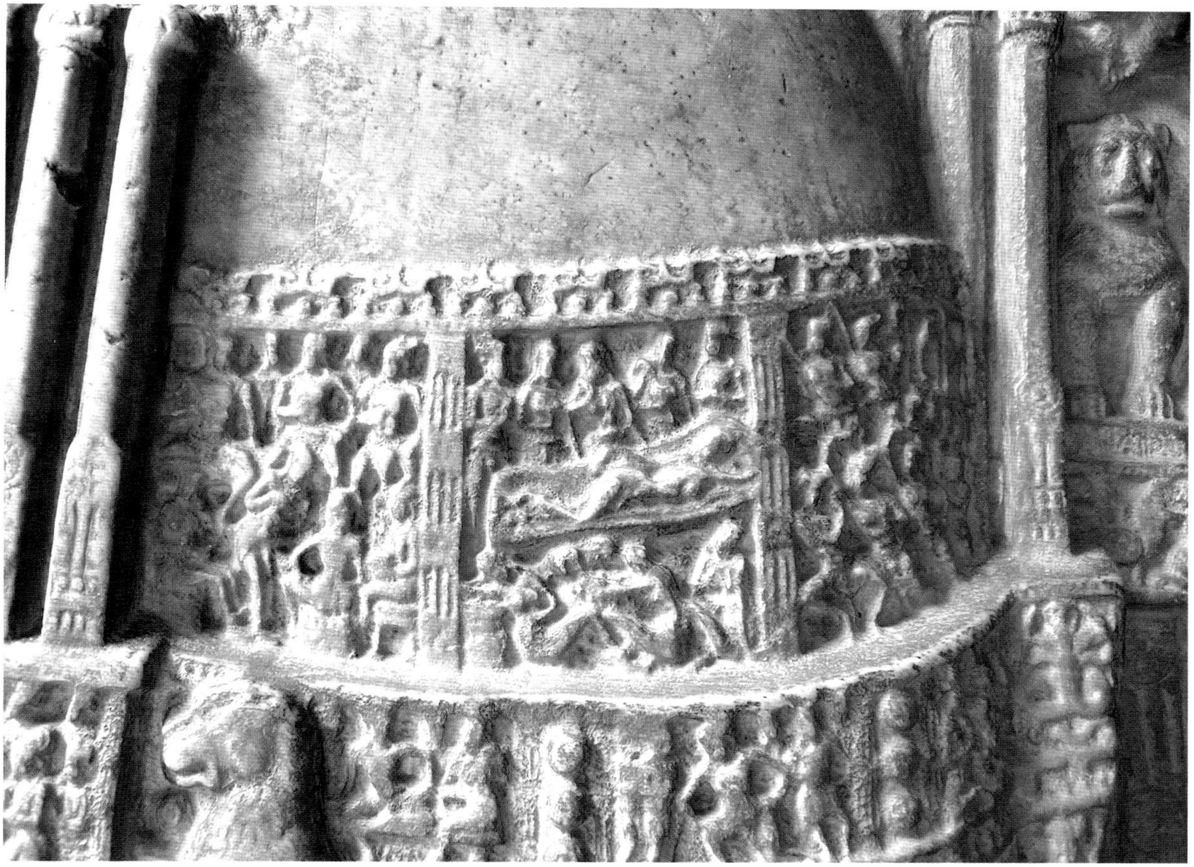

27 Detail of the right-hand side of the miniature sculptures in the dome of illus. 25 depicting three scenes from the narrative of the Bodhisattva's conception.

The perspective has been modified so that the two segments of railing at either side of the entrance, which should project straight forwards, are opened out sufficiently to show the internal sculpture of their railing walls and copings. Lion figures like those depicted certainly adorned the gateways of the entire monument, and several survive (for example, illus. 150 and 151),[117] as do fragments of the pillars attached to these gateways (for example, illus. 44).[118] To the left and right of the stūpa are images of two of the other gateways in the railing, each 90 degrees around the circumference from the gate at the front. These are likewise topped with seated lions in profile, and each also shows one of the lions on the platform supported by a column, facing head-on. Each of the gates at the side is accompanied by an image of the *āyaka* platform, which juts out of the main stūpa and faces the gate, and its five pillars, depicted head-on in the centre of the panel.

The stūpa and its decorations are rendered in exquisite detail in sharp low relief. The drum is largely obscured by the railing, but its visible imagery includes *nāga* serpents and *dharmacakras*.[119] Above, completing the drum, is a frieze perhaps with scenes from the *jātaka* tales of the Buddha's many previous lifetimes as a Bodhisattva.[120] At the same level, on the *āyaka* platform, is a scene of the Bodhisattva enthroned among worshippers, perhaps teaching in the Tuṣita Heaven, his right leg descending to the ground rather than cross-legged (illus. 26). At the base of each of the five *āyaka* pillars, engraved in very fine relief into the stone, are images

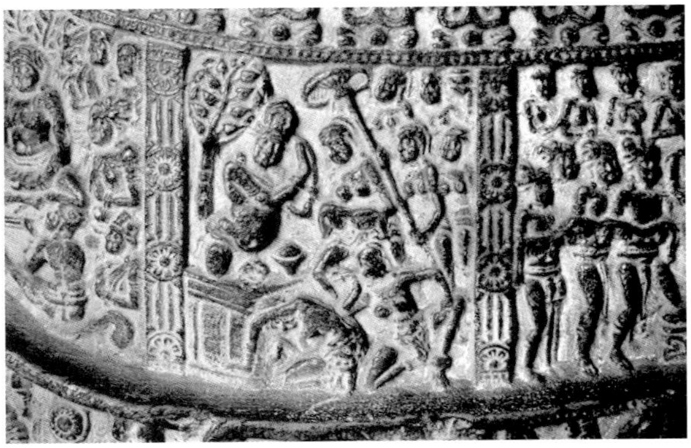

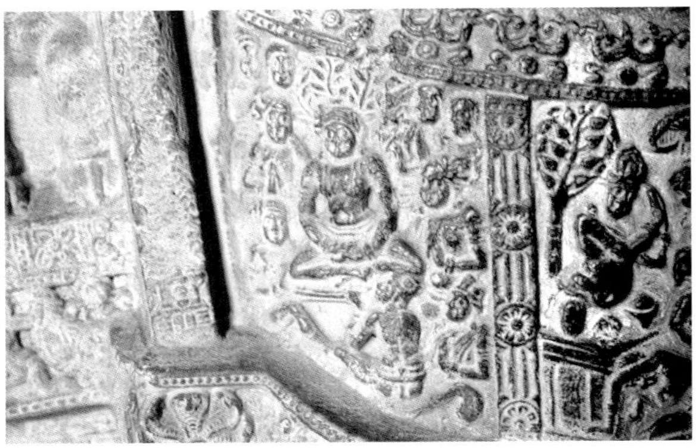

28 Detail of the miniature scene of the presentation of the infant Bodhisattva to a tree spirit, left-hand side of the dome of illus. 25.

29 Detail of the miniature scene to the far left of the dome sequence of illus. 25, showing the Bodhisattva's first meditation beneath the rose-apple tree.

of the Bodhi tree to the far left and right (symbolizing the enlightenment), the *dharmacakra* to the near left and right (symbolizing the Buddha's First Sermon), and a stūpa in the centre pillar (symbolizing the Buddha's death and *parinibbāna* (final passing away)).[121] Above the drum frieze the dome springs, with a further series of larger friezes at its base; in this slab, they represent narratives of the Buddha's birth and early life, starting from the right (the direction in which a viewer, circumambulating the stūpa, would have come upon the panel).[122] At the far right the Bodhisattva, in the form of an elephant in a palanquin, descends from the Tuṣita Heaven; next the Buddha's mother, Queen Māyā, conceives while lying on her couch, dreaming of the elephant. In the panel to the right of the *āyaka* pillars, she reveals her dream to the king and his soothsayers (these three scenes can be seen in illus. 27). Most easily identifiable is the panel to the immediate left of the *āyaka* pillars, which shows the birth of Prince Siddhārtha at Lumbinī, with the standing figure of his mother and the Bodhisattva invisible but imagined as walking along the cloth held by the queen's attendants (illus. 26 upper left). Further left is a scene of presenting the newborn (imagined again as invisible above the cloth held by a woman, perhaps his mother, with a parasol above it) to the local tree deity Śākyavardhana, who predicts that the child will become a Buddha (illus. 28).[123] The final scene, to the far left, shows the miracle of the rose-apple tree whose shade did not move but protected the Bodhisattva when he spontaneously entered meditation for the first time, attaining the first *jhāna* or absorption during the ploughing festival (illus. 29).[124] It is worth noting that the same scenes, in the same order and with the same iconography, including the *āyaka* platform and the *dharmacakra* in the gateway, appear on a drum slab with a miniature stūpa, perhaps from the small stūpa excavated by Alexander Rea in 1909, now in the site museum at Amarāvatī (illus. 30).[125]

The upper part of the dome, festooned with sculpted garlands and swags, has five large sculpted panels, the central one a square and the others tondi. From right to left these represent the Great Departure, where Siddhārtha left the palace on his white horse Kaṁṭhaka,[126] led by his groom, an image perhaps representing the elevation of the Buddha's turban or his begging bowl in the second roundel, the Bodhisattva in the Tuṣita Heaven in the square panel,[127] the enlightenment in the form of the Bodhi tree over an empty throne with the *buddhapāda* beneath it in the fourth roundel, and the First Sermon in the form of a *dharmacakra* in the fifth (illus. 31).

This effectively continues the narrative of the Bodhisattva's life in sequential form, moving from his conception in the tier below to the inauguration of his teaching mission (with the exception of the square panel with the scene in the Tuṣita Heaven, emulating that on

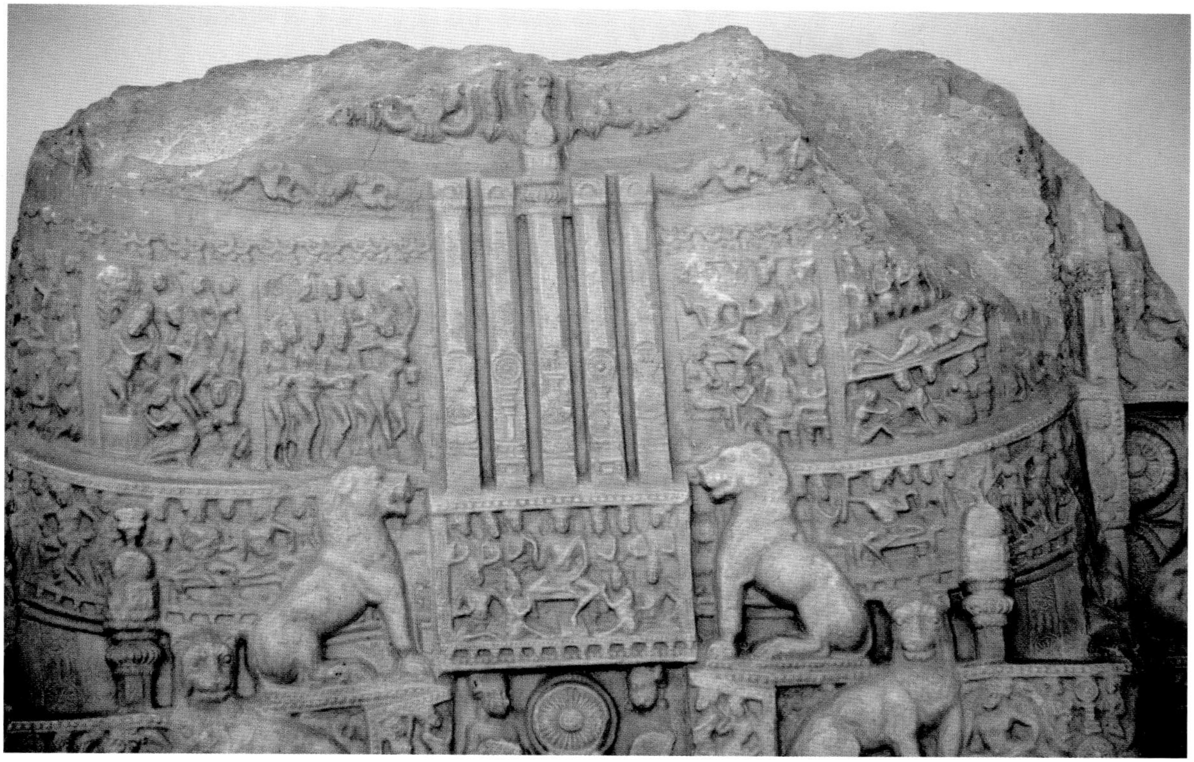

30 The upper section of a drum slab from the small stūpa shown in illus. 24 with the same sequence and iconography of scenes as in the slab in illus. 25–9.

the *āyaka* platform beneath it, which both represent the moment of the Bodhisattva's determination to take his final rebirth). The dome is crowned with a *harmikā*, or railed area, at the top of the summit (the railing emulating that which surrounds the stūpa as a whole, with three rows of lotuses in both the pillars and the crossbars) surmounted by an octagonal pillar, with a *gavākṣha*, or horseshoe arch, at the peak, and featuring two ceremonial umbrellas with swags (illus. 32). Over and around the dome, divine figures carved in high relief hover in the air, presumably celebrating the Buddha, the relics inside the stūpa and the narratives depicted.[128]

The panel depicting the stūpa is flanked by two *dharmacakra* pilasters rising from behind the empty throne of the Buddha, beneath which is a *buddhapāda* (illus. 25 and 131). The scene implied is the First Sermon, with the great wheel of dharma at the peak sitting atop a stepped capital with seated lions back-to-back. Human worshippers stand and kneel beside the throne while a variety of divine beings (dwarfs) hover on animals to either side of the column, the shaft of which is itself made up of fluted cushions interspersed with (or upheld by) dwarfs and groups of animals. The frieze above the main stūpa image shows three scenes: from right to left, these are the adoration of the empty throne, perhaps with a reliquary in front of it; in the centre, the seated figure of the Bodhisattva defeating the armies of Māra (represented as warring dwarfs and seductive ladies) immediately before his enlightenment, between a trio of stacked roundels of which the central one has a miniature figural scene and the upper and lower ones have lotuses in relief; to the left, the adoration of the throne beneath the Bodhi tree.[129] Along the border between this frieze and the top of the stūpa dome is a partially damaged inscription. This reads 'Adoration to Siddhartha. Gift of a coping-stone (*unisa*) to the great stūpa of the

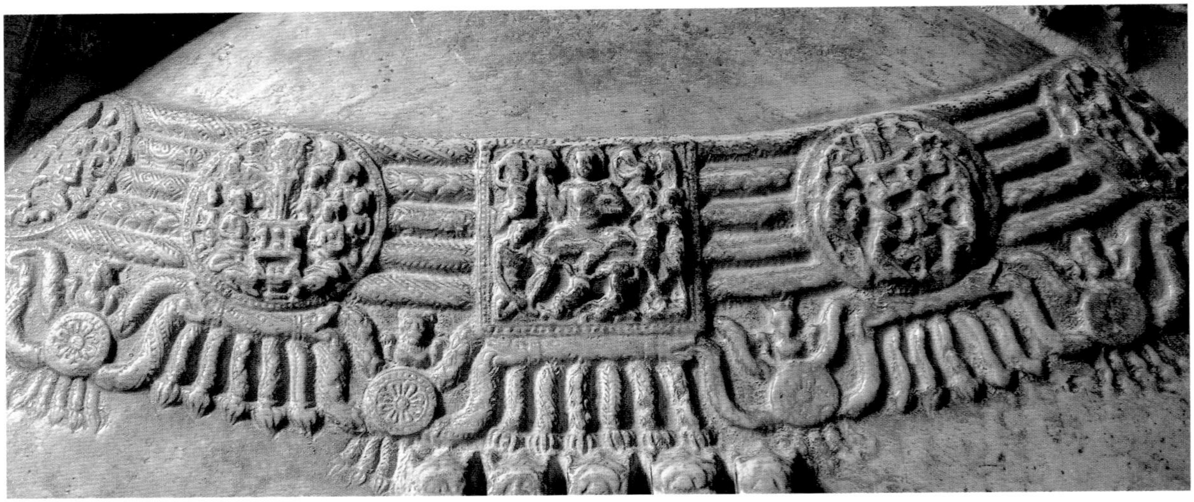

31 The upper dome of illus. 25.

Lord by the wife of the merchant Samuda, son of the householder Hamgha, who lived in the chief city of the Puki district, and by the . . . householder Kotacandi, for the welfare and happiness of the whole world.'[130] The inscription is interesting in part because the gift commemorated on this drum slab is not the slab itself but another piece of the stūpa's decoration: a coping stone, presumably from the railing.

At the lower centre of the panel is the open gateway, the scene inside it framed by the open railing panels with lions above (showing, right, the elevation of the Buddha's bowl and, left, that of the Bodhisattva's topknot) and the *āyaka* platform with the seated Bodhisattva and its five pillars. Inside that entrance is the Buddha's empty throne, with *buddhapāda* beneath and the *dharmacakra* pillar surmounted by a stepped lion capital and the Wheel, signalling the First Sermon and the turning of the wheel of dharma (illus. 26). It is not clear whether this is meant to represent a large slab carved on the drum (the only one we are able to see in full through the opening, but set alongside similar slabs of which we can see the top of the Bodhi tree, the upper parts of *nāga*s and further *dharmacakra*s around the drum poking above the railing) or whether it is intended to be the miraculous real presence of the turning of the Wheel, enacted through aniconic representation and 'activated' by the relics at the heart of the depicted stūpa. The scene plays upon the two flanking pilasters, the second and fourth *āyaka* pillars above it, the first medallion to the far left of the dome, the *dharmacakra* columns on the drum and coping of the railing, and a number of other miniature occurrences of the theme in the rich decoration of the panel, for they all repeat it. Clearly there is also a play in the vertical dimension between this 'aniconic' scene of the Buddha, the embodied image of the Bodhisattva in the *āyaka* platform immediately above and the central relief with the embodied teaching scene in the upper dome.

Narratologically, there is a series of references to episodes around the passage from Bodhisattva to Buddha: the pre-incarnate Bodhisattva in the Tuṣita Heaven, the story of the early life from conception to the first meditation, the Departure, the defeat of Māra, the enlightenment beneath the Bodhi tree and ultimately the First Sermon, when the enlightened being becomes universal teacher and turns the wheel of dharma (which forms both the focus and the frame for this relief panel).

In most respects, this panel is typical of the many drum slabs that survive (most in rather worse condition), with the same characteristic image of a highly decorated stūpa and railing, and divine beings above the dome. In two respects, however, it is unusual. First, it preserves within the same stone block the two side pilasters (depicting *dharmacakra* columns) and the frieze above the inscription. In all other cases, these are separate pieces of stone. Second, it does not have any divine or human figures approaching the entrance of the stūpa at the bottom (as in illus. 34 and 70), as are frequent in the surviving drum slabs (for example, illus. 49, 61, 71, 90, 94, 95). Nonetheless, the exceptional inclusion of the framing devices used for all the drum slabs within this one is useful in illustrating the way its iconography bleeds across and beyond the panel – both in the replication of *dharmacakras* and in the embodied versus aniconic Buddha/Bodhisattva figures on the central vertical axis. Aspects that may be considered typical, in addition to the form and iconography of the slab, are the immense richness of coherent decoration (certainly identifiable at the time of making, even if some of it is obscure to us now, or too abraded to be certainly determined). This extends to tiny miniatures, such as the historiated roundels in the *harmikā* railing at the top or in the stūpa railing alongside the lotus bosses (for example, illus. 33), or the symbols carved in the *āyaka* pillars (illus. 26). If the image as a whole replicates the stūpa on which it was placed, then all its elements replicate elements on either it or other stūpas. The narrative and symbolic models for conveying meaning, by means of signs like the Tree, *dharmacakra* or indeed stūpa form itself, or by means of visual storytelling across miniature friezes, medallions and panels, replicate the larger and more extensive narrative structures of the whole monument.[131] These strategies of replication in the miniature as well as the monumental – repetitions of structural and decorative forms, such as tondi, railings, friezes, pillars and stūpas, and of iconographies, such as the narrative types of the major events of the Buddha's life, and symbols – enforce the sense of a multiverse in both the exquisite miniature of a single panel and the large scale of the stūpa as a whole crammed with such panels, and in relation to other smaller stūpas at the site, let alone the many other stūpas in the Krishna River basin.

One final and particular feature of the Chennai panel is the fact that it repurposed a piece of fine, already dressed stone on the other side of which a pilaster has been carved.[132] The reuse of earlier materials, while not

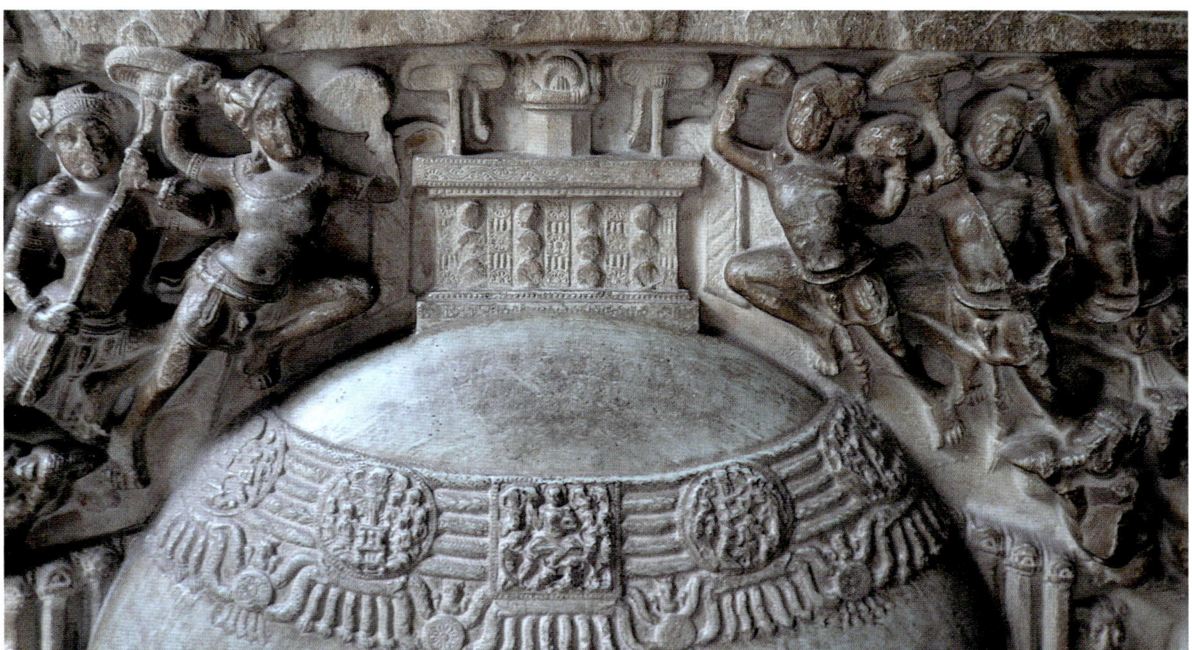

32 The *harmikā*, umbrellas and hovering divinities at the top of the stūpa panel in illus. 25.

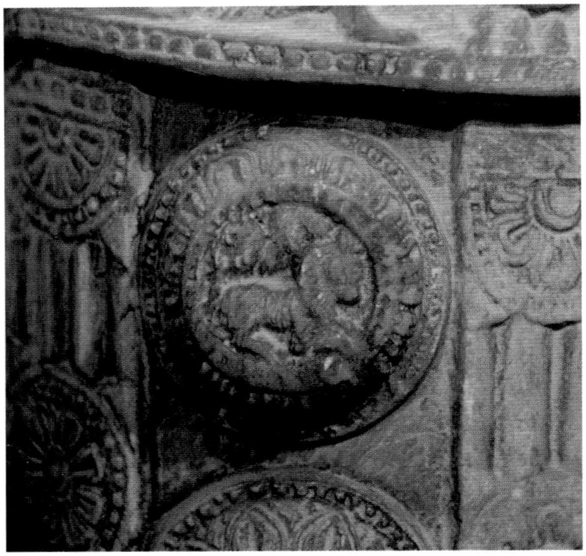

33 Detail of miniature historiated lotus roundel on the left side of the outer railing of illus. 25, showing the horse Kaṁṭhaka and hence representing the Bodhisattva's departure from the palace.

common, is found in two other drum panels with images of stūpas – one now in the British Museum and the other in the Museum of Fine Arts in Boston.[133] This form of spoliation is found infrequently, but certainly in other instances in the sculptural decoration of the Amarāvatī stūpa,[134] not perhaps surprisingly given the longevity of the monument's phases of enlargement, redesign and redecoration.[135]

Let us move beyond this panel to the many others on the drum (for example, illus. 34, 49, 61, 70, 71, 90, 94, 95). The diameter of the stūpa was 48.75 metres,[136] making a circumference of about 153 metres (500 ft). The rough measurement of each slab was 120–50 centimetres (47–60 in.) in height and 80–115 centimetres (31–45 in.) in width.[137] Assuming an average width of 150 centimetres (59 in.) for both slab and side pilasters, we may reconstruct the number of panels like the one just discussed as something over a hundred (in a circumference of circa 15,300 centimetres/6,000 in.). It may be some of these did not portray stūpas, and certainly reliefs identified as drum sculpture from Amarāvatī do survive with narrative historiated themes.[138] This is generally assumed to be from an earlier phase of decoration, and some of it was perhaps preserved in the phase where the majority of stūpa panels were carved. But the principal issue is that once beholders had gone through any of the gates and found themselves in the processional path between railing and monument, the principal decoration in the visual field at roughly eye level (though archaeology cannot determine heights with as much accuracy as it can diameters and circumferences) was the series of exquisitely carved stūpas, with their intense miniature detail.

Much may be said about the play between a monument whose totality can only be grasped by a gaze from a great distance – so great that the detailed decoration is invisible – and these slabs that give a partial view of a single face of what they present as a voluminous whole, but nonetheless offer themselves in rich elaboration to full spectatorship with the naked eye. The visual game is of the monument both offering itself to the devotee's gaze and denying complete access, even as it enables that access through its open gateways and fully available sculptural detail. The process is parallel to the way a reliquary can be held as a whole, but its contents cannot be accessed unless it is opened. But it is also about the way a three-dimensional monument cannot be grasped in its entirety by a human viewer from any specific point, although the illusion of such a grasp can be offered by the two-dimensional perspective created in the stūpa slabs.

Again, as with the replication of stūpa imagery across the monument as a whole, these miniature stūpas are adorned with images that include stūpas, notably on the tops of the columns rising within the perimeter railing to either side of the gateway, and on top of the central pillar of the *āyaka* platform, in multiple surviving examples. In many cases, echoing the actual exterior friezes of the coping on the railing, the miniature friezes figure garland swags with stūpas.[139] Likewise, emulating some actual drum friezes, those friezes of the miniature stūpas may show fluted columns with lotuses, framing the worship of the stūpa.[140]

The entrance as it approached the sacred precinct gave way not to interiority but to endlessly repeated imagery of microcosms of whole stūpas, centred on gateways that themselves framed scenes that may have been intended to be sculptural, or to represent the 'real presence' of a divine person or event. Scholarship has usually taken the pedestrian option (following the intensity of detail with which these miniature stūpas replicate elements of the main monument) of supposing these figures in the gateways to represent panels carved into the *āyaka* platform.[141] This may be so; indeed, this option is always open. But the relief stūpas usually have human worshippers (male and female, akin to the viewer) approaching the gate alongside possibly nonhuman beings, such as the dwarfs, carrying offering plates, although these latter may have been intended to depict statues.[142] (For a fragment with an exceptionally detailed example in the British Museum, see illus. 49.[143])

The air above the dome is thronged with celestial worshippers, musicians, gods and dwarfs. That these may be invisible to real beholders as they pass through a gate or along the processional walkway does not mean they are not there in the *imaginaire* of late ancient Indian culture; the sense of a site pulsating with the supernatural is essential to the viewing process. So what is visible in the gateway may be the carved image of a relief, or it may be an image of the real thing: the Buddha in dynamic, magical action in the contemporary world.[144] The relief stūpas thus offer themselves on a series of levels: as pure decoration; as highly self-reflexive representation of the monument that they adorn (including a variety of details down to miniature precision in symbolism and iconography); as microcosms of the stūpa ideal as sacred monument at the crossroads designed to elevate the devout heart; as windows onto, or visualizations of, the full divine world of beings visible and invisible that congregate around a stūpa; as meta-commentary on the monument and its ritual processes; as multiverse of stūpas each reflecting and being reflections of the others; and so on.

If we turn to the iconography inside the gateway, there is much variation in the surviving panels. Several, like the example in Chennai, show the *dharmacakra* over the throne with *buddhapāda* beneath and a series of four or six worshippers.[145] In three of these cases, as with the Chennai relief, in the *āyaka* platform panel above the entrance is the Bodhisattva in the Tuṣita Heaven, his last abode before his final human rebirth as a Buddha, being exhorted to teach the dharma by the surrounding gods.[146] In the two other cases where it survives, the *āyaka* relief offers a courtly scene involving a king and his consort, signalling perhaps a cakravartin (wheel-turning monarch), such as the Buddha might have become, or was in several former lifetimes.[147] The other most frequent scene within the gateway, in contrast to the aniconic rendering of the *dharmacakra*, is the embodied Buddha himself. In several cases he appears seated in the *abhāya mudrā* (his right hand raised to banish fear) – for instance, before the great curling body of the *nāga* serpent Mucalinda (see illus. 94 and 95), whose hooded heads arise behind the Buddha and protect him,[148] or on a throne amid devotees.[149] In other instances, he is standing in the same gesture (for example, illus. 50 and 61).[150]

The *āyaka* platform relief above – always in dialogue with the internal scene – is varied; examples include the Bodhisattva in the Tuṣita Heaven,[151] sometimes the seated Buddha in the *abhāya* posture[152] or in meditation,[153] or teaching,[154] or as Bodhisattva receiving the gift of grain from the girl Sujātā.[155] Other figures inside the central entrance include the *nāga* with five hooded heads (perhaps an aniconic rendering of the Buddha, invisibly seated beneath the serpent, illus. 70),[156] the worship of the Bodhi tree (perhaps meaning the enlightenment and perhaps referring to the tree as memorial relic of the Buddha's Awakening, illus. 143),[157] certain episodes from the Buddha's life (illus. 71),[158] the veneration of relics in a stūpa-shaped reliquary by humans or *nāga*s (illus. 90),[159] the veneration of the *buddhapāda* by *nāga*s, protected by the coils of the *nāga* Mucilinda,[160] a scene with *nāga* kings,[161] the *Vessantara-Jātaka* (the story of the Buddha's penultimate reincarnation[162]), in which the Bodhisattva perfects generosity by giving away all his possessions and ultimately his two children to a Brahman (for example, illus. 49). The *āyaka* panels for this more varied range of gateway subjects most frequently show the

Tuṣita Heaven scene, the seated Buddha or imagery from his life.[163]

All these instances are ambivalent as to whether the beholder is seeing through the doorway the thing itself – be it Buddha, Bodhisattva, an event from his previous lives or magical beings such as *nāga*s worshipping his remains – or a miniature relief representation of sculptural images of these things. That ambivalence is pushed further by the symbolic renderings of the wheel-turning First Sermon as *dharmacakra* and the enlightenment as Bodhi tree. The symbolic presentation of these events enables an interesting and potent ambiguity as to whether these images represent the enlightenment and First Sermon as such (in their cosmological aspects, with many divine beings present and celebrating their significance) or whether they show devotion to a memorial of the event (such as a wheel or tree, or the image of these things, whether at the original site or elsewhere). The function of these images as living memorial is, of course, closely related to the stūpa's own function as reliquary, the commemorative imagery of which is activated by the presence of relics, and where devotional wonder on the part of worshippers may activate the combination of relic and image into real presence.

In a number of other stūpa panels, two roundels resembling the sculpted medallion reliefs shown in the domes of the miniature stūpas and in the inner side of the perimeter railing of the actual stūpa are carved one above the other in the gateway opening (illus. 34).[164] These appear to represent sculptures rather than real presence, but in the context of the other gateway imagery, this only heightens the possibility that the entranceway sculpture is meant to imply that all the sculptural imagery at Amarāvatī offers the option of real presence alongside representation. Interestingly, the three surviving examples of this type have identical iconography in a series of elements: the two scenes represented in the roundels are always the Great Departure at the top (shown through the horse Kaṁṭhaka, without figural imagery of the Bodhisattva) and the Bodhisattva in the Tuṣita Heaven with worshippers below, or possibly the Bodhisattva's first meditation, which precipitates his departure from the palace.[165] To the sides of the upper panel, framing the Departure, the inner coping of the gateway is turned outwards to reveal scenes of the elevation of the Buddha's begging bowl and the elevation of his knot of hair the Bodhisattva cut off after escape from the palace, which affirmed his adoption of an ascetic life.[166] Above the gateway, framing the opening and the Departure image, the relief of the *āyaka* railing depicts the embodied Buddha seated among female devotees, perhaps receiving grain as still a Bodhisattva from Sujātā.

In each of these stūpa reliefs with two medallions in the gateway, the roundels have a pair of small lotus medallions placed at their junction and pillars with cushion capitals flanking them within the gateway. None of these panels has human devotees approaching the stūpa, although they do have dwarfs with trays for offerings outside the railing, a vase of plenty at each side of the gateway opening and a moonstone engraved with a half-lotus at the threshold beneath a fluted bar with lotus roundels at the upper side. Again, in each of these there are *buddhapāda* slabs beneath a parasol in the upper dome decoration. These examples use the central scenes at the stūpa entrance to stage a mini narrative of the Buddha's progress from his previous abode in the Tuṣita Heaven, or his experiments with meditation in the palace, via his renunciation of the sense world (implied by his departure and the elevation of his princely topknot in the headdress scene) to his embodied self just before enlightenment in the *āyaka* platform panel, accepting a meal and then throwing away the bowl in which he ate (the scenes of deities adoring the bowl and the hair-knot to left and right also hint at relic adoration).[167]

The majority of the drum relief stūpas, however, have devotees outside the railing, approaching the gateway entrance from both sides. These figures, in addition to the dwarfs with offering trays, include male and female worshippers,[168] and often also seated vendors (presumably selling offerings[169]). Clearly, this imagery has rich allusion to the devotional culture of the Amarāvatī stūpa as a sacred monument.[170] That devotion, in certain cases, may extend to kneeling figures close to the ground line of the gateways, although it is

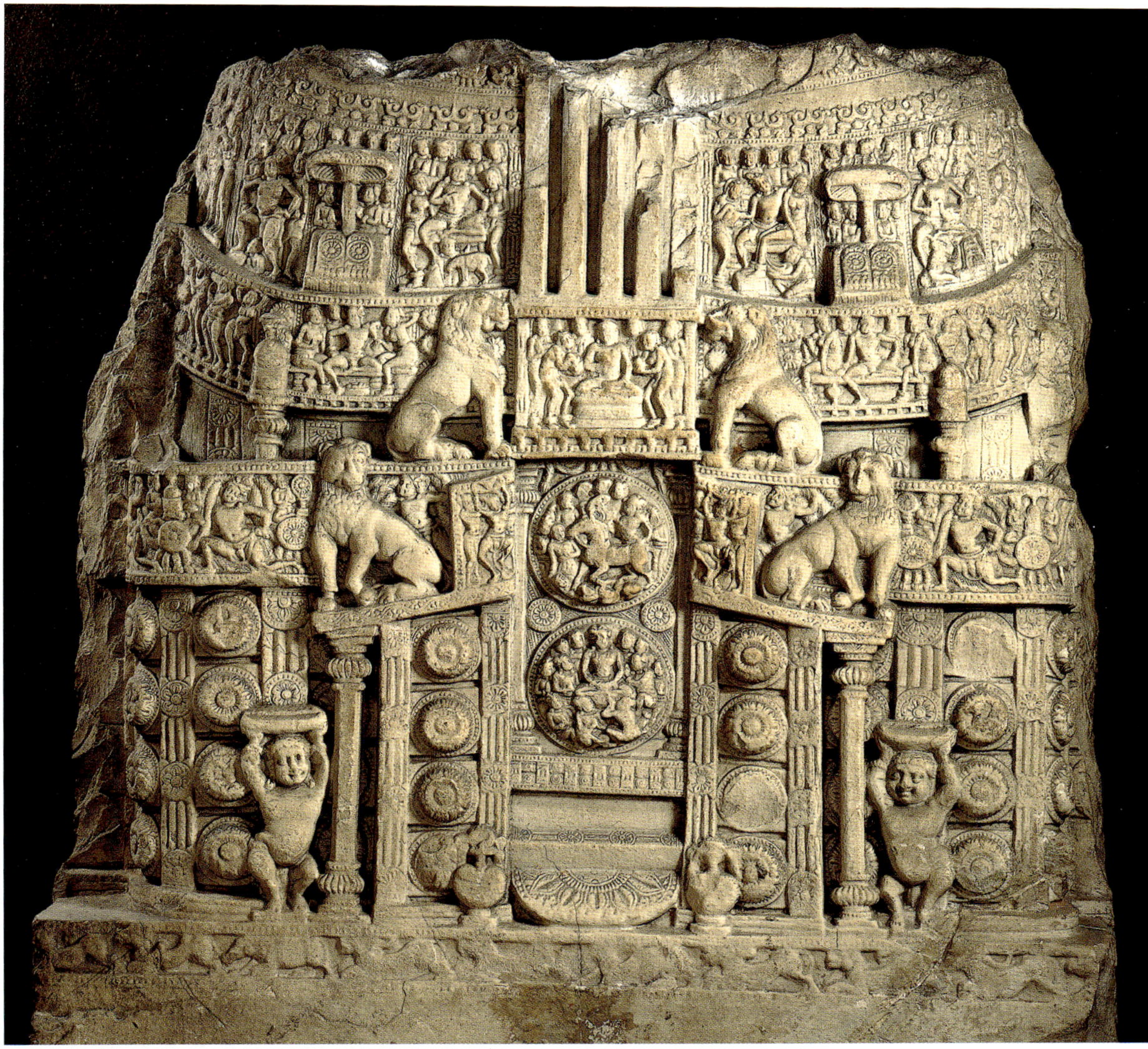

34 Remains of a drum slab with a view of a stūpa through a gateway and from outside its railings.

impossible to be sure whether these figures are not in fact meant to be part of the inner scene (whether an image of a relief or of the actual presence of the subject or main figure).[171] So, once again, the imagery within the gateway offers a liminal negotiation between representation and real presence, a calculated ambiguity between figures of actual devotees as intended on the exterior of the precinct railing and what are presented as either carved or real human and divine figures in the presence of the Buddha or Bodhisattva.

One of the ways that the miniature relief stūpas from the drum differ (surely deliberately) from the actual stūpa they adorned is that, on the outer perimeter wall, they show fluted railing pillars with four lotuses and four crossbars, each with a lotus boss in high relief between the pillars.[172] The actual stūpa, as we have seen, had pillars with a single lotus in the centre and half-lotuses at top and bottom, and three crossbars.[173] The actual railing was penetrable by the viewer's gaze from the exterior through the gaps between the crossbars, not an impermeable mass, like the bulk of the stūpa itself, or a fully open space to be bodily transgressed, as were the gateways. These gaps within the railing are occasionally staged in the mini stūpas.[174] None of the slabs shows what the viewer might see through such gaps, but in two cases it is possible to make out a panel of the enlightenment on the lower dome in the form of a *dharmacakra* over a throne incised behind the five *āyaka* pillars (for example, illus. 94 and 95).[175] This ultra-detailed motif might be said to signal the possibility for the gaze to penetrate between and beyond other barriers, such as the railing crossbars. So only at the gateway, at the centre of the stūpa image, is the gaze of the carved pilgrim and the actual pilgrim visiting the site able to penetrate the interior at ground level; and the gaze is met with a vision that relentlessly complicates the boundaries between its status as relief representation of sculpture and image of actual presence, in respect of both the miraculous events depicted and the figures shown performing devotions to them.

It is clear that the perimeter gateways at Amarāvatī are potential crossing points across worlds. The liminal space on the ground as the devotee crosses the threshold into the processional path for circumambulation is presented and re-presented – repeatedly, one might even say endlessly – in the art of the site as a space where image cannot be separated from real, where human beings can meet with divine beings of all kinds, where the Buddha himself and the miraculous events of his life, and even those of previous lives, confront the visitor who enters in present time. In this respect, it is striking that the art of Amarāvatī uses imagery that evokes both the figural and the invisible presence of the Buddha, as symbolized by the throne and the *buddhapāda* in the *dharmacakra* reliefs, or Kaṁṭhaka, with unseen rider, led by the groom Chandaka in the Great Departure. Invisible beings are no less present than visible ones in the sacred space of the precinct. In the *Mahāparinibbāna Sutta*, shortly after the instruction to build a stūpa for his remains, the Buddha passes away (6.9), and his death is accompanied by earthquake, thunder and turmoil among the *devas* (divine beings, 6.10–11).[176] After his First Sermon, the turning of the wheel of dharma,

> the earth gods raised the cry: 'At Benares, in the Deer Park at Isipatana, the matchless Wheel of truth has been set rolling by the Blessed One, not to be stopped by monk or divine or god or death-angel or high divinity or anyone in the world.'
>
> On hearing the earth-gods' cry, all the gods in turn in the six paradises of the sensual sphere took up the cry till it reached beyond the Retinue of High Divinity in the sphere of pure form. And so indeed in that hour, at that moment, the cry soared up to the World of High Divinity, and this ten-thousandfold world-element shook and rocked and quaked, and a great measureless radiance surpassing the very nature of the gods was displayed in the world.
> (*Dhammacakkappavattana Sutta*, *Saṃyutta Nikāya* 56.11, v.423–4).[177]

The Amarāvatī stūpa insists on the presence of these beings, visible and invisible, in the space of its perimeter railings.

While the majority of the gateways focus their imagery on the Buddha or his aniconic form (in the *dharmacakra* First Sermon scene, for instance), usually in the presence of disciples, at least one represents his former life as a Bodhisattva, and a number refer to *nāga*s and other beings venerating his remains after his passing away (for example, illus. 90).[178] If the imagery of Amarāvatī-school drum reliefs from other stūpas in the Krishna River basin emulates lost subjects from the main site, then the gateway themes may have included the Bodhisattva,[179] and perhaps also wheel-turning monarchs.[180] This imagery has the potential to evoke, beyond the Buddha himself, some of the other kinds of beings for whom a stūpa is prescribed by the *Mahāparinibbāna Sutta* – notably a wheel-turning monarch and disciples of the Buddha. That range of reference is extended if we include the elaborate framing scenes around the gateway. One thinks of the many disciples around the imagery of the Buddha teaching (such as the First Sermon and on many *āyaka* platform panels) or courtly scenes involving king and consort in several *āyaka* reliefs. The stūpa is not only a multiverse but a time machine, evoking multiple instances and incarnations and referring beyond the Buddha himself to the other figures celebrated at the sacred devotional space at the crossroads: to deities, to his disciples, to the devotee as contemporary visitor to the site and even to the vendors seated outside.

CIRCUMAMBULATION

On proceeding through the gateway to the stūpa mound itself, the principal devotional act was circumambulation (*pradakṣiṇa* in Sanskrit), with the implication of turning in the same direction as the sun: clockwise, or with the object of veneration to one's right.[181] Thus, worshippers turned left at the entrance through which they had come and proceeded to walk around the monument, perhaps pausing for prayer or prostration at given points (including particular images or statues, which might include contemplation of the spectacular imagery on the interior of the railing or on the stūpa drum). This clockwise direction is in keeping with the veneration of the Buddha in his lifetime, as described by the sūtras.[182] The act of circumambulation, whether of a Buddha or a stūpa, might have been enacted once or perhaps three times (both are attested in early texts[183]), or more.[184] The processional path along which the devotional process took place, paved with grey limestone slabs, appears to have been punctuated by pillars at either side of the gateway opening, and crowned with stūpas.[185] To the viewers' right would have been the great series of relief slabs on the drum depicting stūpas like the one they were visiting; to the left would have been the inner railing.

Some of the railing uprights were decorated like those of the exterior: a large central lotus roundel, cut in deep relief, with rows of petals; a finely carved outer rim with vegetation and sometimes animals; and half-lotuses at the top and the bottom, with a half-open lotus filling in the corners of the upper and lower semicircles

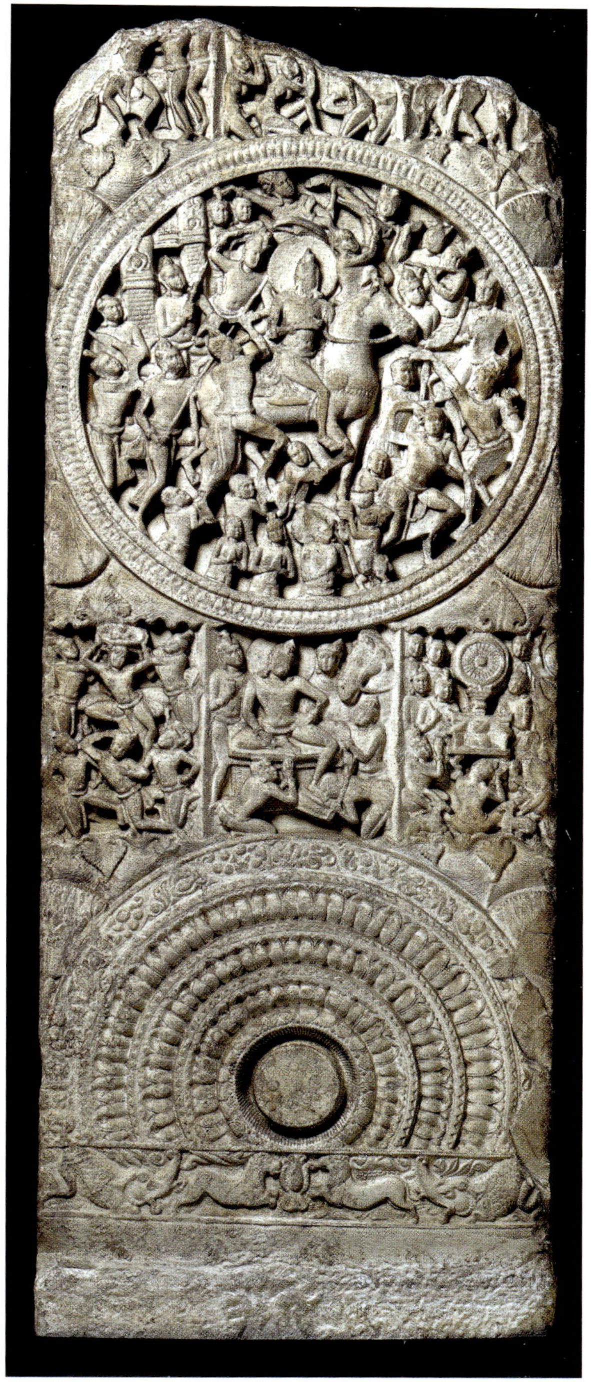

35 Surviving fragment of a railing pillar, interior view with scenes from the Buddha's life.

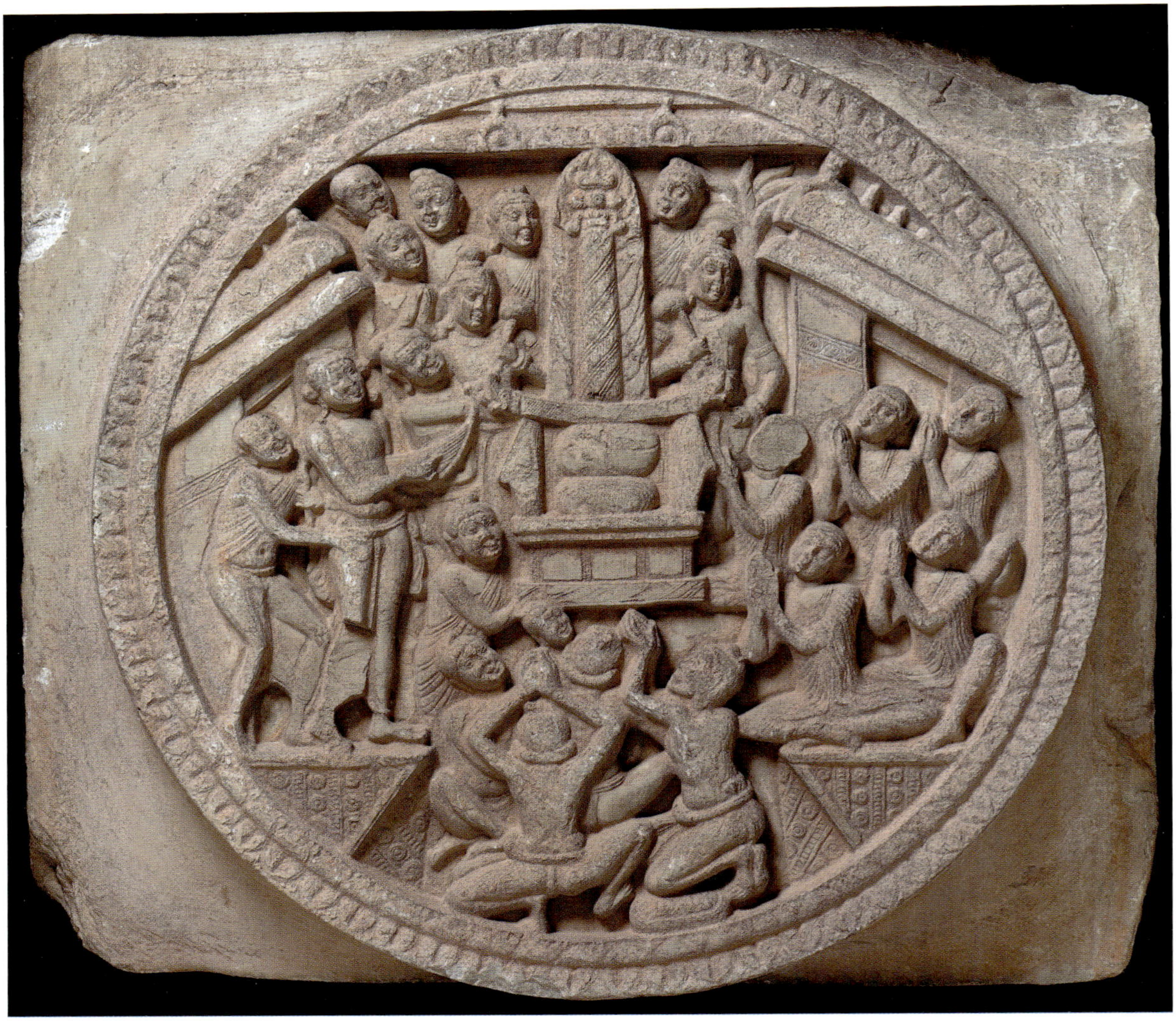

36 Crossbar tondo from the railing interior with tenons intact, showing brahmans and monks worshipping a flaming pillar crowned by a *triratna* over an empty throne. Found near the middle of the southwest quadrant of the railing.

and concave fluting in the lozenge space between the roundels.[186] (There would also sometimes be figures encroaching on the fluting.[187]) Occasionally the central bosses of these lotuses and half-lotuses are themselves carved.[188] In all cases, border friezes at top and bottom, as on the exterior, framed the pillar. Most uprights of the interior railing, however, replace the central lotus medallion with a circular historiated scene, itself framed with outer lotus petals and the usual floral frieze (illus. 35).[189] This creates a rich surface for sculptural narrative with a unique form in that it offers a central narrative medallion framed above and below by lozenges, also richly carved.[190] In the partially damaged example illustrated, it is clear that there were historiated scenes in the upper fluted area that are now largely lost. The central roundel with a simple lotus-petal rim has the Great Departure of the Bodhisattva from his palace – this time shown in figural form – apparently a solitary escape in the company of his horse, Kaṁṭhaka, and his groom, Chandaka, but here surrounded by celebrating deities. The lower fluting reads from left to right in the direction a viewer would have walked in relation to the inner railing on her left-hand side. To the left it shows the elevation by deities of the prince's hair-knot, which he cast away as a mark of entering the ascetic life; at the centre, the prince takes leave of his horse and groom at the end of the Departure; and to the right, in a vignette that skips to the end of the narrative pattern initiated by his leaving the palace, a scene of the wheel of dharma over an empty throne, representing the First Sermon and Siddhārtha's attainment of full Buddhahood as teacher.

The three tiers of crossbars to either side of each railing pillar all held medallions, the same blocks as are carved with lotuses on the exterior, but in the inner railing a significant number were sculpted in the same kinds of rich narratives as the central roundels of the uprights,[191] while others were lotus blossoms.[192] All the historiated tondi were framed with a floral frieze in low relief or with lotus petals (illus. 36). It is not clear how these were arranged (for instance, if the central medallion of each tier was historiated and the others floriate, or if the structure and placement of the figural roundels were more fluid). The coping that ran along the top of the rail was also richly historiated with narratives (illus. 37).

Detailed discussion of the narrative imagery will come in a later chapter, but suffice it to say here that, in contrast to the iconic rendering of stūpas (that is, sacred architecture animated by images and divine beings) on the viewer's right, the imagery on the left would have been a riot of figures and stories. It was structured both vertically, especially with linked scenes along the three main historiated panels of the uprights (two lozenges and a central medallion),[193] and horizontally through the continuous friezes in the coping and the potential relationships of the scenes in the crossbar roundels with those within the uprights on either side,[194] although such crossbars may also offer monoscenic narratives focused entirely on the roundel itself.[195] The coping friezes are complex, since narrative patterns move both left to right (that is, in the direction the pilgrim would have walked) and right to left,[196] which might conceivably imply placement in the inner railings of gateways, out of which pilgrims would have also exited the monument. Most commonly, the coping uses imagery of architectural or natural features to create boundaries between discrete scenes and sequential narratives that are structured out of a sequence of such scenes (for example, illus. 37, 52, 86).[197] The important issue is subject-matter. The largest number of themes in the reliefs of the railing's interior are either stories associated with the Buddha's life or *jātaka* narratives of his previous lives as a Bodhisattva.[198] It is important to note, however, that some identifications are at best provisional, and many scenes cannot be identified.[199] But the point is that to the viewer's left there would have been a profound and multiple visualization of the narrative frames of Buddhahood and the

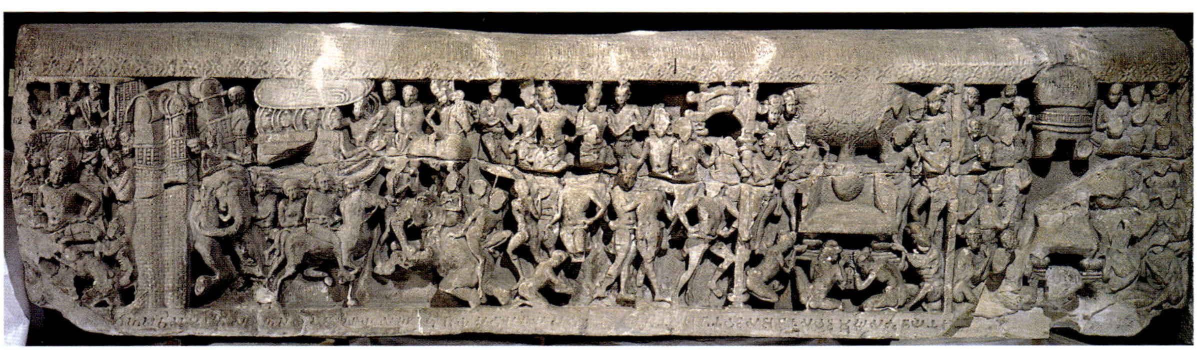

37 Damaged but intact coping slab (2.25 m in length), interior face. This has four scenes: a prince with a halo to the far left, a procession including horses and elephants in the long scene, an empty throne beneath the Bodhi tree surrounded by worshippers and on the far right a throne apparently topped by a stūpa surrounded by worshippers.

Bodhisattva's path of multiple reincarnations, while to the right would have been the monument containing the Buddha's living presence through his relics, its liveness configured in the central entrance images of each of the drum slab reliefs, and its supramundane implications in the present moment evoked through the many divine beings represented there.

However, the stūpa slabs, placed at a level visible to the naked eye, also contain rich and extensive narratives in miniature relief, as we have seen.[200] These adorned the *āyaka* platform and drum friezes of the relief stūpas, a tier of large square panels on the lower dome and the great roundels of the upper dome in a series of examples.[201] These miniature scenes, some now in much abraded condition, have proved difficult to identify, but there is little doubt that the pattern of narrative emphases, on the Buddha's life and his former lives as Bodhisattva, emulates that of the inner railing. For discussion of the narrative issues, see the account of a miniature stūpa slab in Chapter Three.

It is only by appreciating the play between the imagery of the drum panels, with their stūpa reliefs, and that on the interior of the railing – which ran around them, sandwiching the viewer, as it were – that one can grasp the full brilliance of the multiverse conception underlying the arts of Amarāvatī. The broad subject-matter of the historiated imagery of both railing and stūpa-panel narratives is the same – *jātaka* stories and the range of events of the Buddha's life. But they are not configured in the same way. The railings offer large-scale reliefs – historiated roundels with a diameter of between 50 and 85 centimetres (20–33 in.), and coping friezes with a height of between 70 and 80 centimetres (27–31 in.) – while the mini stūpas offer miniatures of these narrative panels. Just as the epigraphy of the site has a tendency towards what I will describe as 'referential transference' in Chapter Two – that is, allusion to a donation other than the particular stone on which a given inscription has been cut[202] – so there is a reflective transference of themes between miniature stūpa panels and imagery of the monumental railing. This offers not only a reflective parallelism in form and theme but a dissonance in function and structural placement between the two sets of imagery. The stūpa reliefs create a microcosm that both includes the railing imagery and denies or absconds it through these panels' visual form, just as they avoid representation of themselves, hidden behind the perimeter railing. The stūpa reliefs do, of course, figure the railing itself – not the hyper-historiated interior to which the viewer has direct access, but the lotus-rich exterior and its copings. They may be said to include the rail behind the viewer as she looks at them, but to occlude representation of its interior (available in any case if the viewer were to turn around). The result is a multifarious vision of repeated but different stūpas, in repeated but differently configured narratives (in both stūpas and railing panels), that *includes* its pilgrim-viewers within its texture, representing them outside the exterior perimeter and enclosing them within the immensely sophisticated visual play of its processional pathway.

THE DOME

The dome, the sculptures of which survive in the least number, must be reconstructed from comparison with the mini stūpa relief panels more than any other part of the monument – a methodologically fraught and problematic procedure. It would have towered over the viewer inside the processional path, visually accessible at a highly acute angle and with a different order of visibility from the drum and railing friezes, which could be seen close at hand with the naked eye. Arguably, the dome was more clearly visible from afar, both on approach to the stūpa and after exit from the devotional walkway within, but in that case its imagery was hardly conducive to minute detailed examination.

Following the indications of the surviving slabs, the majority of which are flat,[203] the dome would have risen vertically from the drum platform for some 4.5 metres

38 Abraded but intact dome frieze upright panel (2.35 m high) with the worship of a stūpa, the *dharmacakra* and the Bodhi tree respectively from top to bottom with dividing friezes of foliage and running animals and bordered to the right by the imitation of a fluted pillar with lotus bosses.

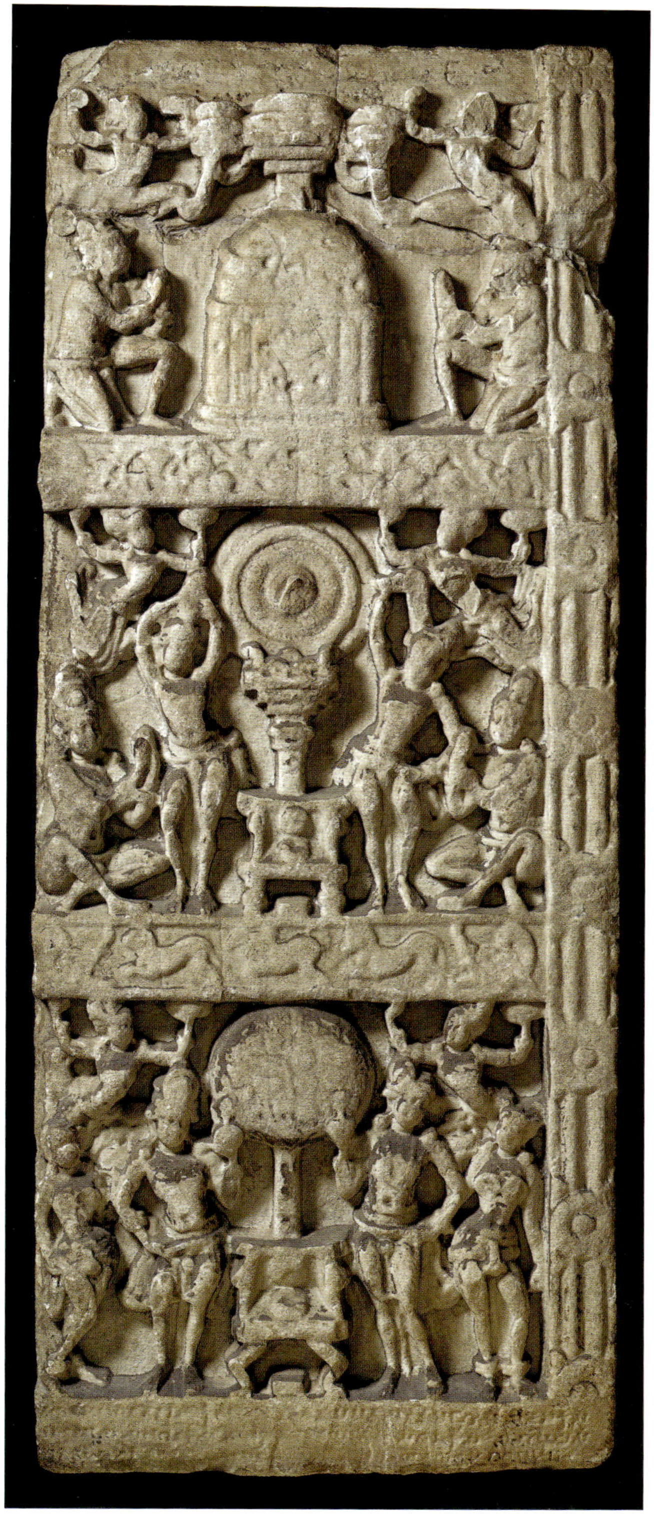

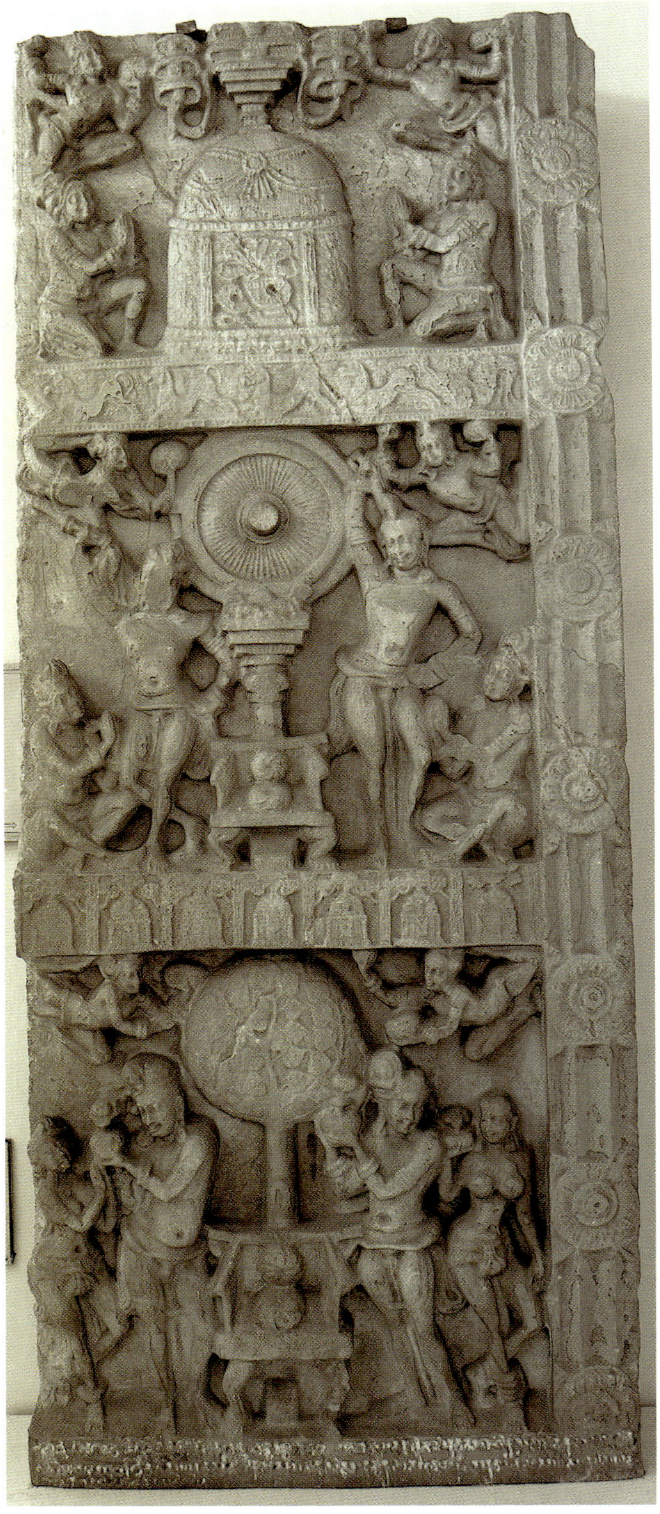

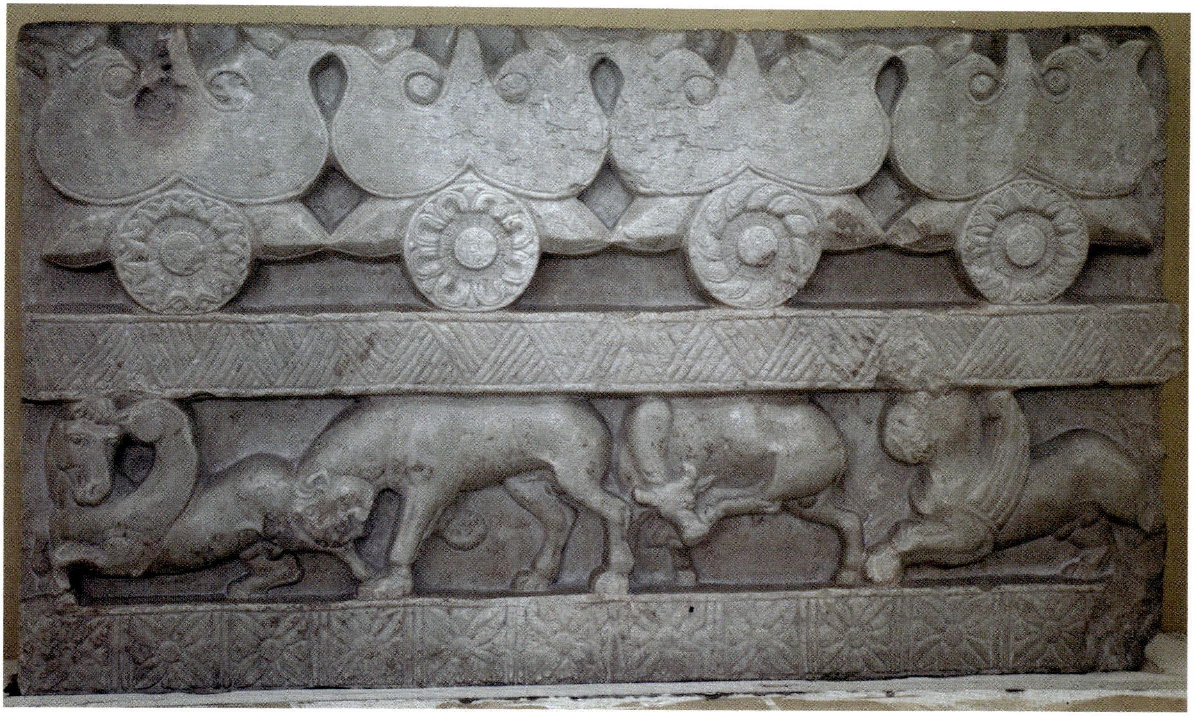

40 Dome upright topper with animals and *triratnas* in excellent condition.

(15 ft) before curving towards the *harmikā* platform at the top.[204] These slabs consisted of tall panels (about 2.8 metres (9 ft) in height, although none survives entirely complete) in three levels of imagery showing iconic events from the Buddha's life: the Great Departure;[205] the enlightenment as Bodhi tree and empty throne,[206] or the seated form of the embodied Buddha beneath the Bodhi tree in the *abhāya mudrā* at the bottom tier;[207] the First Sermon as *dharmacakra* and empty throne in the middle;[208] and, at the top, a stūpa (perhaps indicating the *parinirvāṇa*, or reflecting on the monument itself[209]) framed by thin borders with fluting and lotus roundels (illus. 38 and 39) and topped by a frieze of running animals and a row of *triratnas* (illus. 40).[210] The exceptionally well-preserved topper fragment from the Amarāvatī site museum in illustration 40 shows the high level of creativity and finish in these sculptures, which would not have been visible to the naked eye, such as the highly differentiated postures and kinds of (mainly) mythical beasts in the frieze, and the different designs of the lotus blossoms with wheel-like spokes that sit beneath the *triratnas*.

39 Intact dome frieze upright panel (2.32 m high) with the worship of a stūpa, the *dharmacakra* and the Bodhi tree respectively from top to bottom with dividing friezes of running animals and stūpas and bordered to the right by the imitation of a fluted pillar with lotus bosses.

It has been astutely pointed out that each of these tiered slabs without the Buddha at the bottom may be related to the themes of enlightenment, First Sermon and *parinirvāṇa*, but represents the absence of the Buddha, perhaps implying the sites of those events but after his death. There is a deliberate interplay or contrast with those images that embody him in human form.[211] Above these, still with a vertical profile, were large slabs about 1.4 metres (4½ ft) in height with *pūrṇaghaṭas*, or vases of plenty, overflowing with lotus blossoms (illus. 41).[212]

In a number of the drum panels with reliefs depicting stūpas, animals, *triratnas* and *pūrṇaghaṭas* – that is, the three rows of friezes – are depicted in that order at

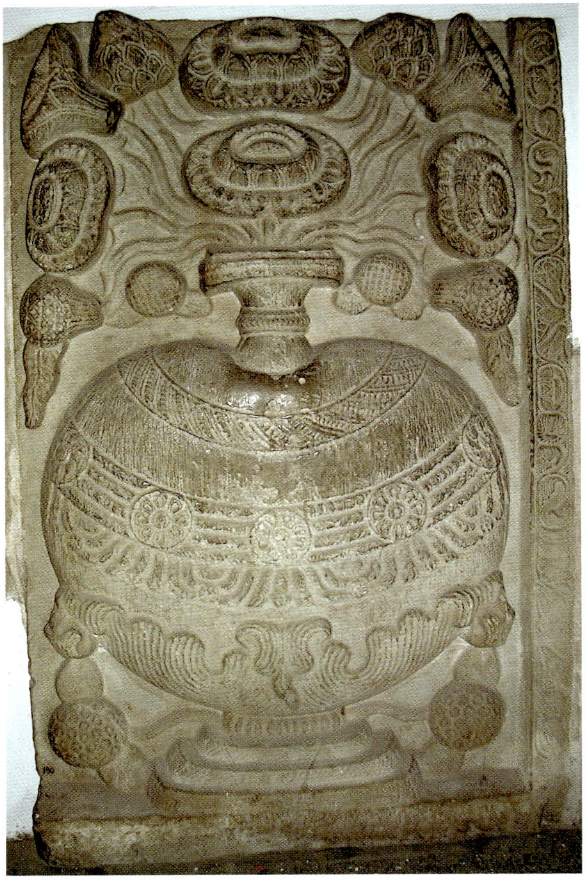

41 Large dome slab (1.33 × 0.82 m) with *pūrṇaghaṭa*, vase of plenty and lotus blossoms.

the point just before the dome curves, above the large dome panels with narratives and at roughly the summit of the *āyaka* pillars (for example, illus. 61, 90, 94, 95).[213] At the same time, all these drum reliefs with stūpas offer miniature panels with narrative themes in the vertical portion of the dome below the trio of friezes – something quite unlike the actual surviving slabs of the stūpa, with their iconic tiers of three scenes of the Buddha's life (always ending in stūpas). This is a good example of the closeness to a 'realistic' version of the stūpa in its miniature sculptures and the simultaneous distance of them from the reality, choosing narrative elaboration in a coherent form when it suits, which has no necessary imitative relation to the dome but may play against, say, the railing, as we have seen. It is another instance of referential transference: using the techniques of imitation and parallel imagery to refer to different aspects of the whole within the single monument.

Very little sculpture from higher up on the dome now survives. Many of the relief stūpas show a frieze of heavy garlands carried by running figures or dwarfs above the *pūrṇaghaṭa*s.[214] Interestingly, there do exist a few fragments of such a frieze, which certainly adorned the dome at the point where it began to curve, since the profiles of these slabs are concave.[215] Iconographically, the dome sculpture as shown on the relief stūpas is very similar to the garland frieze of the coping of the outer rail, including the bands around the garland near the shoulders of the garland-bearers and the beads in the form of *makara*s or as historiated medallions with tassels at the bottom of the garland's curve (illus. 42). This repetition of a distinctive frieze motif around the stūpa – at the top of the outer railing, at the point where the dome curves towards its one-pointed centre and in miniature in the relief stūpas at both rail-coping and dome levels – marks the way the votive dedication of lotus wreaths, enjoined by the *Mahāparinibbāna Sutta*, becomes a reiterated theme in the stūpa's visual injunctions to its viewers. But, alongside the *pūrṇaghaṭa*s, running animals and *triratna*s, it also defines a visual rhythm of large-scale repetition across the entire circumference – played out likewise in the lotus blossoms of the railing crossbars and uprights, or in the stūpa reliefs of the drum – and in the repeated iconic themes such as *dharmacakra*, the Bodhi tree and *buddhapāda*. This model of replicative imagery, all hand-carved and of the highest order, so never precisely the same and sometimes distinctively differentiated in small but probably significant ways, goes hand in hand with the remarkable one-off schemes of many of the narrative images.

No fragment has survived of any of the great circular panels shown on the dome of the stūpa in the stūpa reliefs of the drum.[216] Did they exist in that form or are they a conceit of the miniatures, playing off against the rich dynamic of medallion sculpture on the railing? Some fragments of what appear to be larger-scale historiated

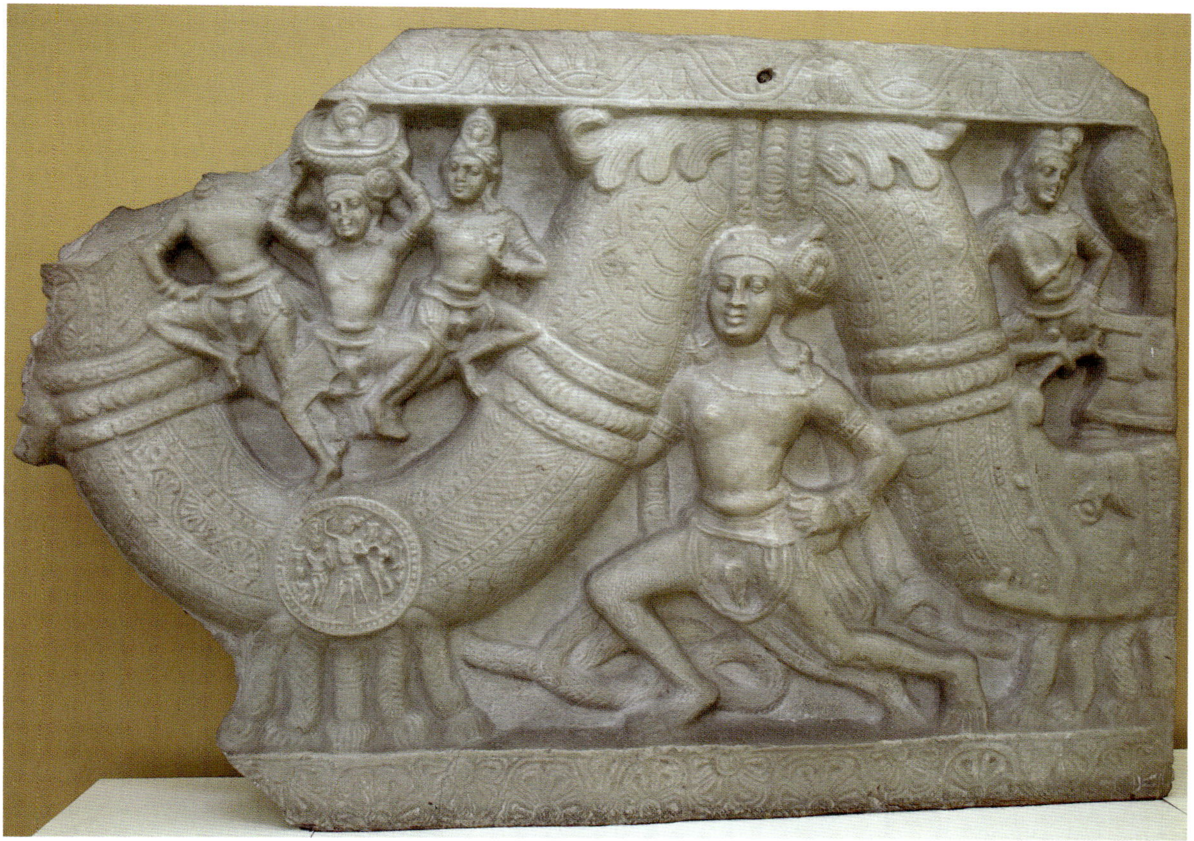

42 Dome frieze segment, curved at the back, with thick floral wreath, garland-bearer, the elevation of the Bodhisattva's turban and worship of the Bodhi tree in the undulations, and a rimmed medallion perhaps showing a universal monarch.

dome sculptures than those of the three-tier panels, with different motifs, do survive.[217] These do not seem to have been curved at the back, but could nonetheless have been mounted as panels on the dome, or behind the *āyaka* pillars,[218] although there is no evidence of any of this. While most of the stūpa reliefs show rich sculpture on the dome, a few imply much greater simplicity, closer to a whitewash.[219] It has been suggested that the dome embellishment (rich in imagery or more restrained) was done in stucco, perhaps painted and gilded against the dazzling white of the plastered dome,[220] but nothing survives of such plaster work from the site. The issue of colour is itself moot. Colin Mackenzie observed from his studies of 1816–17: 'All the carvings appear to have been originally painted red and varnished; and so fine was the composition used, that the stones still retain part of the ancient colouring, which from the length of time they have lain underground, is now somewhat faded, inclining to a copperish red.'[221]

In 1914, Alfred Foucher suggested that the sculptures were gilded, on the basis that red colouring was often the ground for gilding in Gandharan sculpture,[222] but no one has found traces of gold leaf on any sculptures at the site. Conservation work done on the sculptures in the British Museum has been inconclusive regarding the origins of the orange-brown and red coatings that are now visible under a microscope; but the balance of probability is that the sculptures were painted (although at what point in their existence as decorations of the stūpa can of course never be determined).[223] The two lion sculptures in the British Museum, from the tops of columns at the gateways,[224] certainly seem to have been painted red, while there is a thick and distinctly reddish coating on a slab from the external coping frieze.[225] At any rate, the likelihood of colour, both in the dome and in the many sculptures of the drum and railing, is an important variable in assessing the stūpa's impact on viewers and devotees.

REFLECTION AND ILLUSION

> In a single atom,
> There are worlds equal in number to atoms.[226]

The experience of entering the Amarāvatī stūpa and contemplating its visionary palatial glory is reminiscent of many Buddhist texts,[227] and its rich, self-reflexive imagery has been described as a multiverse.[228] This model may be fleshed out in a terminological and conceptual frame vibrant within the local Buddhist culture of the Krishna River, by reference to a number of surviving Mahāyāna texts either composed in Andhra or known and commented upon there. The play of two-dimensional representations of stūpas as illusory forms in relation to the architectural and three-dimensional substance of the great stūpa and the smaller ones around the site, is like that of the many two-dimensional reliefs of Buddhas in relation to the full Buddha statues in the round from the site,[229] which will be discussed in Chapter Seven. It evokes what has been called the 'doctrine of illusionism' that underlies some Nikāya thinking, as well as Mahāyāna Buddhist imagery, especially in the *Prajñāpāramitā* (Perfection of Wisdom) sūtras.[230]

The model of the world as illusion goes back deep into the earliest Buddhism. The Buddha himself said:

> Suppose, monks, that a magician or a magician's apprentice should display a magical illusion at a crossroads. A man with good eyesight would inspect it, ponder it, and carefully investigate it; and it would appear to him to be void, hollow and insubstantial. For what substance could there be in a magical illusion?

He went on to define the five mental and material *skhandhas* (literally 'heaps' or 'aggregates') that determine a person in terms of their voidness:

> Form is like a lump of foam,
> Feeling like a water bubble;
> Perception is like a mirage,
> Volitions like a plantain trunk,
> And consciousness is like an illusion.[231]

This model of the world (subject and object, mind and matter) as a play of illusions, magic, mirage and dreams is taken up by later traditions. Buddhaghosa, the famous fifth-century Pāli commentator, uses it to summarize the development of insight (*vipassanā*) in his great manual of meditation practice, the *Visuddhimagga* (Path of Purification).[232] Perhaps influenced by the *Prajñāpāramitā* tradition,[233] it was employed by Nāgārjuna, the great philosopher of emptiness. Nāgārjuna probably lived in Andhra around the time that the stūpa of Amarāvatī was being built,[234] and his work was the subject of a vibrant commentarial tradition – notably conducted in South India – by a series of Buddhist philosophers in the following centuries.[235] Nāgārjuna specifically quotes the sutta where these verses are found.[236] For instance, he writes:

> Just as the teacher, by magic,
> Makes a magical illusion, and
> By that illusion
> Another illusion is created,
> In that way are an agent and his action:
> The agent is like the illusion.
> The action
> Is like the illusion's illusion.
> Afflictions, actions, bodies,
> Agents and fruits are
> Like a city of *Gandharvas* and
> Like a mirage or a dream.[237]

Here we may imagine the stūpa (located, as we saw at the epigraph of this chapter, 'at the crossroads') as one kind of illusion while the reliefs with images of stūpas are illusions of that illusion.

While these texts have resonance in a monument that plays relentlessly on the self-reflexive mirroring of three-dimensional objects in two-dimensional images that appear to represent them, the multiple reflectivity in the arts of the stūpa brings to mind one of the most powerful and extended Mahāyāna developments of the doctrine of illusion, the *Gaṇḍavyūha Sūtra*. This remarkable text survives in Sanskrit as well as in a range of early Chinese and Tibetan translations.[238] Its original composition, however, has been placed in Andhra Pradesh in the second to third centuries CE.[239] The sūtra was incorporated as the 39th and culminating section of the *Avataṃsaka Sūtra*, which became the key canonical text for the later Hua Yen school of Buddhism in China.[240] A famous literary masterpiece, the *Gaṇḍavyūha* has been described as 'perhaps the grandest drama of the Buddhist canon'.[241]

The text tells the story of the pilgrimage of a man called Sudhana through India in search of enlightenment. It begins, however, with the Buddha in his celestial form as Vairocana,[242] seated in a pavilion among his retinue.[243] There he enters the concentration called the 'lion's yawn',[244] and we are presented with a vision of the world from the Buddha's own point of view. The pavilion in which he sits becomes boundless in a majestic account of a multiverse of endlessly interpenetrating reflections.[245] These represent 'the mutual interpenetration of all worlds . . . the interpenetration of minute objects and immense lands'.[246] This vision is not available to his immediate disciples, who are not on the Bodhisattva path.[247] It is, however, presented to the sūtra's reader, effectively inviting them onto that path through the pilgrimage upon which the text embarks. This kind of vision resonates with the visual world of the Amarāvatī stūpa and its extraordinarily self-conscious game of miniature stūpa reliefs reflecting the monument as a whole:

> They were in a realm of showing the reflections of all worlds and one world contained in each other in a single atom . . . They attained the knowledge that all realms of beings are like illusions . . . all buddhas are like reflections . . . all existences, states of being and births are like dreams . . . all developments of actions are like images in a mirror . . . all becoming is like a mirage . . .[248]

Crucially, one of the Buddha's attendant Bodhisattvas, Mañjuśrī, decides to leave the Buddha's presence to 'go south on a journey in the human realm'.[249] He arrives at a great city in the south named Dhanyakara, where he stays with his retinue in a forest

> to the east of the city, at a shrine where past buddhas had dwelt, established by buddhas for the sake of perfecting sentient beings, a place where the Buddha, in the past, carrying out the practice of an enlightened being, relinquished many things that are difficult to relinquish, a place where gods, dragons, goblins, nymphs, titans, birds, centaurs, serpents, humans, and nonhumans always presented offerings . . .[250]

Since the Amarāvatī stūpa is to the east of Dhānyakataka,[251] this is potentially a reference to the site, if we allow the identification of Dhanyakara with Dhānyakataka (following the current scholarly assumption), which would richly resonate with all the beings, supernatural and human, represented in its images.

The people in the city hear of Mañjuśrī's presence and many come to see him, including Sudhana, 'an outstanding boy'.[252] After hearing the wonderful qualities of the Buddha from Mañjuśrī, Sudhana takes the Bodhisattva vow – 'I am set on enlightenment for the good of all beings' – and is commanded to begin his pilgrimage by visiting a spiritual friend, Meghaśrī, for initial instruction.[253] Thus, in the *Gaṇḍavyūha Sūtra*, the hero's taking of the Bodhisattva vow is placed in Amarāvatī itself, emulating the vow taken by Sumedha (a man also from Amarāvatī) before the Buddha Dīpaṅkara, which transformed Sumedha into the Bodhisattva who eventually became Gautama. A fundamental difference between Sumedha and Sudhana is that the latter's vow will be fulfilled through the attainment of Buddhahood (in the course of the text) within a single lifetime, following the promise of this in the Mahāyāna, rather than over aeons of lifetimes, including the lives of a number of other Buddhas.[254]

In response to Sudhana's vow, Mañjuśrī sends him on a pilgrimage around India and Sri Lanka, visiting one spiritual teacher after another (some monastic, some lay, some apparently non-Buddhist,[255] some ascetic and some wealthy, and including many women) from whom he learns different meditative attainments, absorptions and insights. Eventually, after many meetings (the sūtra says 110 spiritual benefactors[256]), Sudhana comes to the 'great tower of the chamber of adornments of Vairocana', and meets Maitreya, the Buddha of the future, at the foot of the tower.[257] If the tower equates to a stūpa, then the implications for the monument at Amarāvatī as a material instantiation for the famous account of the miraculous tower that follows are significant. Maitreya invites Sudhana into the tower, which is vast, measureless and resplendent:[258]

> Inside the great tower he saw hundreds of thousands of towers, similarly arrayed; he saw those towers as infinitely vast as space, evenly arrayed in all directions, yet these towers were not mixed up with one another, being each mutually distinct, while appearing reflected in each and every object of all the other towers . . . Sudhana perceived himself in all of those towers.[259]

He sees the entire cycle of Maitreya's Bodhisattva path, his lives and his movement towards his enlightenment as Buddha-to-be, that which has not yet happened and yet is eternally present.[260] There is a particular emphasis on Maitreya's *dāna*, in giving away everything – head, heart, limbs, body, wife, sons, daughters, all his possessions.[261]

Resonant for the art of Amarāvatī is the vision of infinite towers, each distinct, each mutually reflected in the others and in the objects within them, in which the perceiver is himself envisioned.[262] If we imagine entry to the stūpa as a kind of pilgrimage, like Sudhana's, then once the devotee arrives at the mound itself within the railing, they are confronted at eye level on the drum with a multiverse of over a hundred carved relief reflections of the whole taking in the entire circumference – each one mutually distinct and each containing reflections of other aspects of the stūpa down to very fine detail, as has been discussed. That logic of reflectivity, a kind of interpenetration of visual motifs across the entire material articulation of the stūpa, applies in every part of the decoration. One might notice the *dharmacakra* columns over empty thrones and the *buddhapāda* that appear between the swags of the outer rail coping, on friezes and dome slabs, as drum pilasters, and – within the relief stūpas of the drum – in the central gateway, on the *āyaka* pillars, on dome panels and medallions, as well as on free-standing pillars (in a range of scales from monumental to miniature). The logic of reflectivity applies particularly to the exquisitely carved lotuses ubiquitous in all railings and crossbars, and miniature images of railings and crossbars, which recall the jewelled lotuses of the multi-turreted mansion of the laywoman Asha, whom Sudhana visits as one of his spiritual friends:

> Calyxes of lotuses, luminous jewel lotuses, radiant jewel lotuses, world-illuminating jewel lotuses, lotuses of various treasures, lotuses of pure jewels, lotuses inlaid with jewels, lotuses of multifaceted jewels, lotuses of jewels with auras of light, lotuses of jewels shining with the radiant lights of arrays of pure jewels of the ocean, jewel lotuses covered with diamond lions.[263]

The model of vision whereby 'all things interpenetrate unimpededly, and the microcosm and macrocosm become co-extensive', applies perhaps above all to the Amarāvatī stūpa's imagery of stūpas.[264] Apart from the macrocosm of the three-dimensional monument itself and the multiplicity of its reflections in the drum panels representing stūpas, as we have seen, the monument offers images of stūpas in miniature scattered across the entirety of its structure: at the crowns of the outer faces of railing pillars;[265] in the lozenges between lotuses on the outer railing;[266] between the swags of the exterior coping;[267] in the inner hubs of the lotus bosses of cross-bars;[268] on the bases for lion-statues at the entrances;[269] in some of the historiated medallions of the inner rail;[270] in the copings of the inner rail;[271] on the friezes of the drum;[272] in the many large slabs of the drum, as we have seen (and within those slabs, on top of *āyaka* pillars, inscribed on *āyaka* pillars, on columns within the processional path, as reliefs within copings); in pilasters from the drum;[273] and on dome slabs (effectively constituting a frieze around the circumference).[274] For some examples, see illus. 19, 30, 38, 39, 45, 46, 60, 79, 85, 88, 91, 92, 94, 97, 128, 141, 142. This plethora of microcosmic mirrorings of the macrocosm of the monument itself, and the reflections within some of these of further mini-images of stūpas, enable a discourse of interpenetration by visual means no less potent or poetic than that of the *Gaṇḍavyūha Sūtra*'s presentation of the multiverse of towers in Maitreya's tower.

The sūtra culminates with Sudhana's vision of the Bodhisattva Samantabhadra, as the revelation of an entire universe of beings vouchsafed by compassion:

> Sudhana saw from every single one of Samantabhadra's pores clouds of purified lands completely filled with assembled groups of bodhisattvas who were produced from all buddhas equal in number to the atoms in all buddha lands come forth in every moment of thought and pervade the entire Dharma Realm up to the realm of space, acting for the purification of beings who have a mighty resolution. He saw from every single one of his pores clouds of purified and afflicted lands equal in number to atoms in all Buddha lands come forth in every moment of thought and pervade the entire Dharma Realm up to the realm of space, arising for the purification of afflicted beings. He saw from every single one of his pores, clouds of purified lands and lands containing afflicted minds equal in number to the atoms in all Buddha lands come forth in every moment of thought and pervade the entire Dharma Realm up to the realm of space, arising for the purification of those severely afflicted.[275]

His reward for this vision is 'the ten abodes within the perfection of knowledge' and the blessing of Samantabhadra, who places his right hand on Sudhana's head, enabling the pilgrim to attain 'trances equal in number to the atoms in all buddha lands. Through every single trance he penetrated oceans of world realms equal in number to the atoms in all buddha lands and accumulated previously unseen requisites for omniscience equal in number to the atoms in all buddha lands.'[276] Samantabhadra then recounts his own Bodhisattva path (like Maitreya, focusing on the generosity of giving everything away[277]), inspiring Sudhana in the final section to attain full enlightenment.

Effectively, the sūtra opens with a vision of the world as an enlightened being sees it (specifically not as it is seen by the Buddha's own disciples). That vision operates within a discourse of the interpenetration of all things, the microscopic in the macrocosmic and vice versa, all aspects reflecting each other, and all aspects dwelling in completeness even in the smallest element of each, like the famous image of Indra's cosmic net of gems stretched infinitely across the universe, where a glittering jewel hangs in each eye of the net, the surface of which mirrors the infinity of all the other jewels in an endless process of reflection.[278] The pilgrimage of Sudhana is then portrayed as a path of ever deeper contemplative practice that develops the powers of concentration and wisdom, of compassion and understanding, that enable him to see the world in its interpenetrations, all aspects empty of any intrinsic reality outside the multisphere of reflecting mirrors – the way the world truly is. In entering the stūpa complex at Amarāvatī, at the site of Sudhana's Bodhisattva vow and where the Buddha's own previous incarnation Sumedha was born in the life he took the Bodhisattva vow, the worshipper is offered a material vision of the world as an artistic construct of endless reflections on the body of a mound that is magically and conceptually (even legally) synonymous with the Buddha through the living presence of the relics enshrined in it. The stūpa's visual logic of self-reflexive imagery performs the reflective magic of the gems of Indra's net in evoking the worldview of the *dharmakāya*, or truth body out of which the whole of manifest existence (including Buddhas themselves) arise and dissolve.

The stūpa reliefs of the drum are careful to include images of worshippers approaching the monument, mirroring viewers in the purview of their own vision, as Sudhana sees himself at Maitreya's feet everywhere in the tower of Vairocana, among the 'measureless arrays of reflections in the mirrors'.[279] One of the things that normal perception does not grasp, according to the sūtra, is the numerous supernatural beings pervading every atom of the universe. But when visitors to the stūpa look at the myriad images on its limestone veneer, what they see includes a vision of multiple celestial figures, crowding every space around the action. Like Sudhana in Vairocana's tower (who sees Maitreya in hell worlds, ghost worlds, animal worlds, celestial kingdoms, heaven worlds, among dragons, serpents, goblins, fiends, humans, cherubs, titans, birds, minotaurs[280]), we witness a multiplicity of beings of all kinds in the stūpa's sculpture, themselves the witnesses of the Bodhisattva's path and the recipients of his salvation. Where doctrinally the *Gaṇḍavyūha Sūtra* is undoubtedly Mahāyāna, since its vision of Buddhahood and the Bodhisattva path extends beyond Gautama to infinite other beings, the stūpa anticipates its visionary imagery of an infinitely reflective multiverse within a Nikāya understanding of the Boddhisattva ideal,[281] as focused on the Buddha himself and the placement of scenes of his life against those of his past lives.

The issue that is unassailable here is the reflective and interpenetrative vision that underlies both the visual logic of the stūpa's art and the poetic logic of the *Gaṇḍavyūha Sūtra*. The dates of monument and earliest versions of the sūtra, both placed around the first to third centuries CE, are tentative and provisional, which means that given our current state of knowledge and evidence, we can best adduce that these dates are the most likely (or least unlikely) options on a necessarily probabilistic model of what constitutes fact. The placing of the composition of the *Gaṇḍavyūha Sūtra* in Andhra is likewise tentative and provisional – another instance of the principle of the least unlikely possibility. But if those provisional facts do hold, then there is good evidence that a single and highly poetic model of thinking, dominated by a vision of the liberated mind as an interpenetrating unity with the entire cosmos including all that cannot be seen with normal sensory consciousness, informs both. We cannot say which work of art – sūtra or stūpa – came first or influenced the other (indeed, by the logic of mutual interpenetration, that would be a fallacious operating assumption!). But it is at least possible that the extraordinary artistic decision to turn the stūpa's drum into as many exquisitely shaped self-reflections of the monument's entire form as could be fitted into its circumference may have preceded the developed structure of the *Gaṇḍavyūha Sūtra*. Both sūtra and stūpa depend moreover on the conceptual assumption of vision and visualization as a form of spiritual practice, development and wisdom, although the developed formulations of these issues (in Buddhist Tantra, for instance) are later than either the monument or the text.[282]

The Amarāvatī stūpa's model of a multiverse of meta-stūpas depicted in relief on the drum of the main monument, reflecting it and each other like the jewels of Indra's net, is not replicated by the surviving major stūpas in India outside Andhra Pradesh. It is, in other words, a major innovation of Amarāvatī, likely to have been made in dialogue with the creation of the visionary poetics that gave rise to the *Gaṇḍavyūha Sūtra*, and alongside the much greater openness of the stūpa mound to the visitor's vision by getting rid of the *toraṇa*s and blockages observable at Sāñcī and Bharhut. It is unclear if this phenomenon is part of the efflorescence of a certain collective way of thinking about and communicating dharma shared by writers, scholars and artists, or a case of direct textual–artistic interchange. The meta-stūpas on drum reliefs at sites like Nāgārjunakonda, Gummadidurru, Ghantaśālā and

Alluru are characteristic of the Andhra style developed with greatest sophistication at Amarāvatī and then created by its school of sculptors at other sites in the Krishna River area.[283] Likewise, the small stūpas outside the railing at Amarāvatī are known to have had their drum slabs adorned with meta-stūpas (see illus. 24).[284] In all these cases, the drum slabs – as with those at the main Amarāvatī stūpa – show a railing, but it is likely that the monuments they adorned did not have one, at any rate not one in stone. It is plausible that the meta-stūpas became an established iconographic form that moved from Amarāvatī to other sites in Andhra, and in each site were intended as reflections of the stūpa there (even if they did not reflect the appearance of that stūpa particularly accurately, due to the inclusion of a railing); but it is also not impossible that they were intended as images of the Amarāvatī stūpa, a multiverse of reflections that extended beyond the site and across the Krishna basin.

It may be added that Amarāvatī has no images from the *Gaṇḍavyūha Sūtra*, or of its major figures, such as Maitreya or Mañjuśrī.[285] This is in contrast to the remarkable programme of the great ninth-century stūpa (or, perhaps more accurately, vast architectural mandala) at Borobudur in Java, the rich imagery of which from the *Gaṇḍavyūha Sūtra* is one of the major glories of South Asian art.[286] Images illustrating the sūtra occupy 460 relief panels, more than for any other single text, in the main walls and balustrades of the second, third and fourth galleries. While not being narrative reliefs, unfolding over a chronology, these sculptures nonetheless conceptualize the sūtra's own innumerable visualizations in a panoramic mode.[287] In other words, the relation of the *Gaṇḍavyūha Sūtra* to the stūpa at Amarāvatī is of an entirely different order from its sculptural illustration at Borobudur.[288] Rather, Amarāvatī attempts, through the unique conceit of its self-reflective meta-stūpas and the many other miniatures of its formal replications of its own imagery, to put into dynamic play upon its viewers a version of the self-reflective multiverse that later Mahāyāna culture would characterize through the imagery of Indra's net as well as the evocative poetry and prose of the *Gaṇḍavyūha Sūtra*.

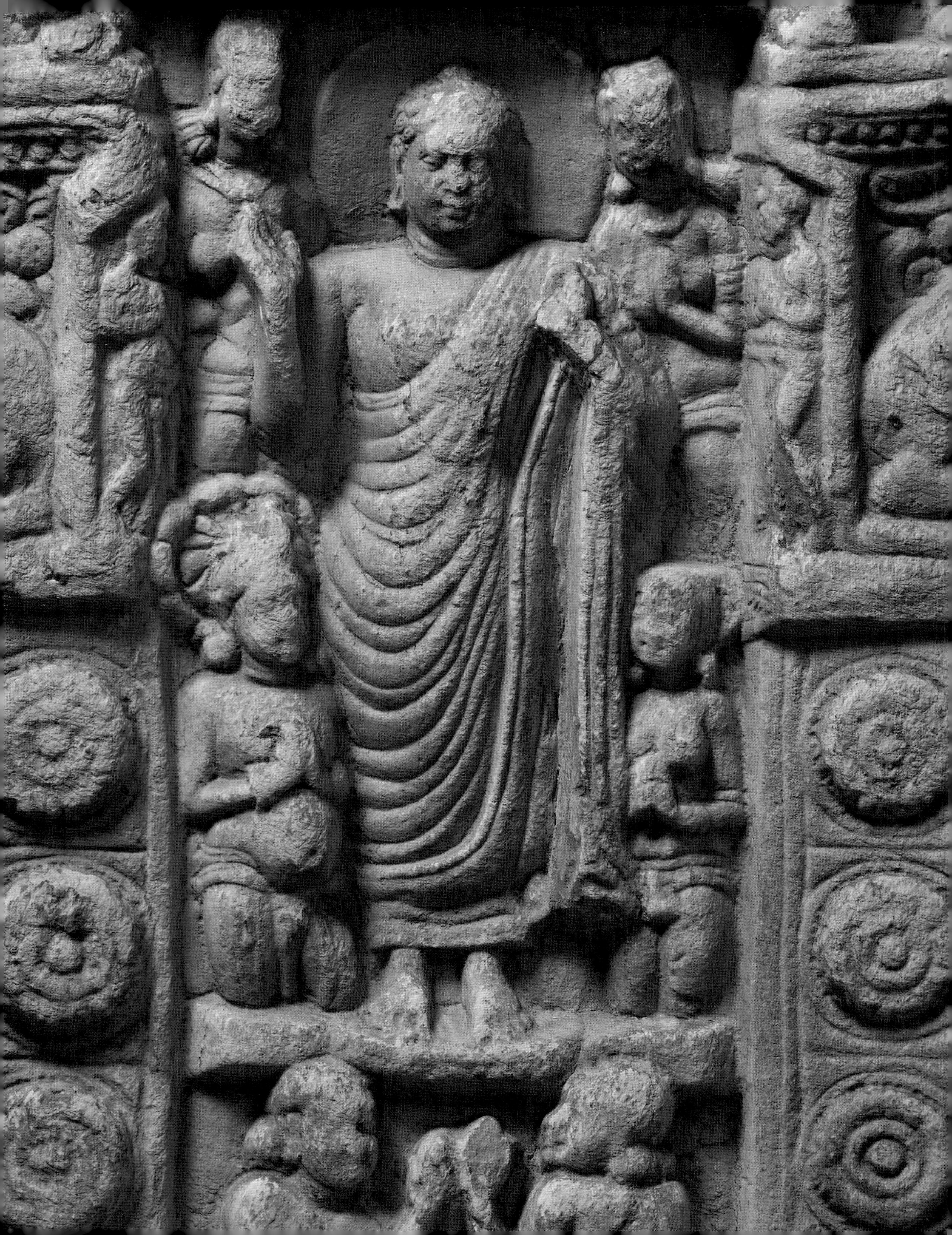

two

The Inscriptions and Their Messages

Since the earliest archaeology at Amarāvatī, the inscriptions have aroused great scholarly fascination for their version of Prakrit in Brahmi script, their guidance in matters of chronology and their immense sociological interest when considering the structures of donation and patronage underlying the site and its devotees.[1] Despite the attention, not all the surviving inscriptions have been read or published (notably many in the British Museum and some in the Archaeological Museum at Amarāvatī),[2] and those that *have* been read were only comprehensively collected in 2016.[3] The intention is that the new online database for all the early Buddhist inscriptions of Andhra Pradesh will ultimately be that complete publication.[4] The Amarāvatī inscriptions belong with a larger class of epigraphy at privileged Buddhist sites, and especially stūpas, in some respects adhering firmly to a genre and yet in others marking a distinct series of differences from further examples within that genre. This chapter explores the specific relations of donative inscriptions to the stones that they are cut into or describe, the sociology of donation they evoke and the ideology of generosity or giving within Indian Buddhism, of which they are a material record and evocation.[5] It will conclude with some comparisons between the epigraphy of Amarāvatī and that of broadly contemporary, comparable sites.

STONE BY STONE

One striking issue, relevant to both art history and the question of patterns of patronage, is the ways that the epigraphy of individual pieces characteristically marks both the specific architectural nature of the slab donated and the relation of donors to the stones for whose dressing and sculpting they had paid. Despite the fragmentary nature of many of the inscriptions (partly due to the broken and scattered condition of

43 Detail of illus. 50 showing a view of a stūpa from outside its railing; the Buddha stands in the *abhāya* posture with kneeling *nāga*s to either side.

many of the surviving stones on which they were carved and partly due to poor preservation of such pieces), a number of phenomena may be discerned.

First, the model of patronage was stone by stone: specific elements of the stūpa's structure (railing pillars, coping and friezes, drum slabs, dome slabs, umbrellas at the top, pillars and elements of pillars such as capitals or statuary) were donated by individual patrons (male and female) or groups (including kin, tribes, townships and villages). The patrons occupy a striking social range from a princess via a general, government officials and professionals (merchants, traders, artisans, perfumers), all often acting with their families, to nuns and monks.[6] Many stones are inscribed simply 'gift of', with the implication that the specific stone with the epigraph is the one given by the named donors.[7] But an interesting model is the formal announcement of the specific item being donated, usually at the end of the inscription, often as its last word, and even when the object exemplifies what the terminology describes.[8] This has proved hugely useful to scholarship for constructing a language for the various items out of which the stūpa or, as the inscriptions name it, the *caitiya*, was constructed.[9] Hence, in the perimeter wall, both railing uprights and free-standing columns are inscribed in the form of 'pillar [*thabha* or *khamba*], gift of'.[10] Likewise, railing crossbars, usually carved with deep-cut lotuses in the medallion on the exterior face and with lotuses or historiated reliefs in the interior side of the roundel, announce themselves as 'crossbar' (*sūci*).[11] Stones in the coping frieze that crowns the railing are inscribed 'gift of coping stone' (*unisa* or *vetika*).[12] In the unique case of one rectangular block, beautifully carved on two sides, which concluded the rail coping at the final opening of one of the four gateways and formed the base for one of the seated lions that framed the gate, the piece is inscribed 'gift of a lion seat' (*sihāthana*, see illus. 44).[13] In the main monument, slabs of all kinds (for the veneer of both dome and drum) are named 'slab' (*pata* or *pendaka*) or 'upright slab' (*udha(m)pata*).[14] Rather wonderfully, we have evidence of one stone parasol or umbrella (*chatta*) that sat on the *harmikā* at the top of a stūpa (perhaps a small stūpa attached to the site) with the inscription 'gift of a parasol (*chatta*)' (see illus. 138).[15]

If we compare this model with the rich epigraphy that has survived from a number of roughly contemporary stūpas, including Sāncī, Bharhut, Nāgārjunakonda and Kanaganahalli, we may say it is broadly parallel. At Sāncī and Bharhut, individual elements of the stone structure are carved with votive inscriptions – notably rail pillars, crossbars and coping stones, as well as the gateways – and (more rarely than at Amarāvatī) the object given is occasionally named.[16] At Kanaganahalli and at Nāgārjunakonda, a number of objects are named, mainly in inscriptions on those objects.[17] As at Amarāvatī, the social range is large, extending from members of royal families to varieties of kinship and local groups, and from merchants and tradesmen to monks and nuns.[18] The donative pattern, which is also to say the patronage and economic base on which Buddhism rested, was effectively the same in these different areas of India.

Clearly the stūpa, like the others from which significant epigraphy survives, was funded by numerous donations from a diverse group of devotees,[19] a significant number of them female,[20] who cover a vast social range.[21] This has justly been described as an effort that both depended on community and created the sense of that community, as a grouping of individuals and collectives that was particularly committed to Buddhism within the larger spectrum of Indian religions in the period.[22] It was, as we have seen, both a collective and popular process, rather than one imposed or underpinned by royalty.[23]

However, in complete contrast to anything that survives from Sāncī or Bharhut, a significant number of the Amarāvatī inscriptions denote gifts other than the stones on which they are carved.[24] It is as if the donative commemoration is transferred from the object or range of objects that were actually offered to some other part of the monument. Examples include (on a drum frieze panel) 'gift of tablets of homage (*yaghapata*) to the great Chaitya of the Blessed One';[25] (on a currently unidentifiable fragment of sculpture) 'gift of a pillar for lamps (*divathabha*) at the southern entrance (*āyaka*) to the great Chaitya';[26] (on a segment of drum frieze) 'gift of a chaitya [that is, a small stūpa], a rail (*vetika*) and a slab (*pata*)';[27] (on the fragment of a relatively elaborate octagonal pillar) 'gift of a chief pavilion (*padhanamadava*) to the *saṅgha*';[28] (on a three-stepped slab for the support of a seated lion at the outer entrance of one of the gates) 'pious gift of a wheel of law (*dhamacaka*) at the western gate';[29] (on a pillar) 'a wheel of law (*dhammacaka*) at the eastern gate';[30] (on a stone fragment) 'a slab (*pata*), railing stone (*sūci*), umbrella (*chatta*) and slab (*pata*)'.[31] A number of gifts of rail coping (*unisa*) are inscribed on drum frieze slabs (unless the term *unisa* means drum or dome frieze – carved on one side of the stone veneer of the stūpa – as well as coping frieze, which is carved on both sides of the stone finish that tops the railing).[32] This is a fascinating structure of referential transference – continuing to celebrate the act of *dāna* and the donors, but removing them from the object donated. It potentially reflects aspects of commissioning and construction. Did donors always specify the object or objects to be given in their name, or were the needs of the building process such that donative commemoration was sometimes assigned to objects after the event, on the receipt of offerings to the Amarāvatī complex? Or did some donors prefer their gifts to be remembered on the main stūpa monument itself, rather than on the railing or pillars? Is it always the case that the inscriptions that name objects other than the one donated were inscribed later than the stone bearing the epigraphy was carved and set up on the site?[33]

A particularly interesting example is the drum frieze panel that announces a large 'gift of two chaitya slabs (*chetiyapata*), three footprints (*patuka*), a coping stone (*unisa*), a slab with a flower vase (*puphaganiyapata*) and other objects to the great Chaitya at Dhamñakata [the city next to Amarāvatī] and the erection of . . . at the great chaitya at Rajagīri [Rājgir] at the northern door' (see illus. 68–9).[34] In this case, the panel not only signals a range of gifts to the stūpa (all elements that can be identified at the site), one of which may indeed have been the stone on which it was carved, but intimates *dāna* made to a major stūpa far away, in Rājgir, the ancient capital of the kingdom of Magadha (in modern Bihar, in the northeast of India).[35] This substantially extends the model of referential transference of *dāna* beyond the citation of other gifts than the object inscribed at Amarāvatī itself, reaching to other sacred sites significant distances away. But it also proves, alongside a number of other donations made by pilgrims from different parts of the subcontinent,[36] the interconnection of major Buddhist monuments across India, raising all kinds of possibilities for the movement of artists and epigraphers as well as patrons and donors, and for the influence and appropriation of artistic solutions from one site to another.

It is worth noting that the kinds of stones mentioned in the inscriptions are usually architectural elements, functionally central to the making of the monument or its decorative structure. These include pillars, whether free-standing columns or railing pillars (*thabha* or *khamba*) as well as pillars for lamps (*divathabha*), railing crossbars (*sūci*), coping stones with carved friezes on both sides (*unisa* or *vetika*), revetment slabs for the drum and dome of the main monument (*pata*, *pendaka* or *udhapata*), a lion seat (*sihāthana*) and an umbrella (*chatta*). It may be that the term *unisa* also describes frieze panels carved on one side, used as revetment on the drum and dome. All these kinds of stones have been identified and studied archaeologically. The range is much richer than at Sāncī and Bharhut, where only pillars (*thabha*), crossbars (*sūci*) and gateways (*toraṇa*) are named.

Much more rarely, and again unlike the inscriptions of Sāncī or Bharhut, mention is made of iconography.[37] Inscriptions specifying imagery include the gift of a slab of Lord Buddha,[38] two slabs with a Wheel (*dharmacakra*),[39] two dome slabs with a vase of plenty (on the slab itself),[40] two slabs with *svastika* and something called an *abātamālā*, which remains obscure to us,[41] and the gift of 'three elephants to the rail (*vetika*)' – meaning presumably three carved elephants and hence referring to iconography.[42] If the Wheel is a *dharmacakra* column, then the term refers to an iconographic theme with symbolic significance ubiquitous at the site. Certainly, the imagery of a *pūrṇaghaṭa* in the shape of a reliquary, with narrow neck and a wide-lipped mouth, filled with lotus blossoms overflowing its sides and often sitting on a stepped plinth, is frequent and may well have occupied a tier of decoration around the entire dome (see illus. 41).[43] If we are to infer correctly from three of the drum reliefs depicting stūpas that seem to play upon the form and decoration of the Amarāvatī monument,[44] it may be that *buddhapāda* reliefs beneath a parasol were used to ornament some parts of the dome (see illus. 34); but it may also be that these panels were set up in some other part of the site, such as the processional path.[45] None of the inscriptions refer to any form of narrative sculpture (of the sort for which Amarāvatī is most famous), or to the most frequent of all the sculpted motifs, the great lotus-flower bosses of the railing. This is in contrast to the inscriptions from Bharhut and Kanaganahalli that briefly label the narrative subjects of historiated panels.[46] It is, however, related to the epigraphic naming of some iconographies at Kanaganahalli.[47]

The tendency to referential transference in the inscriptions has ramifications in relation to two issues: first, the question of *dāna* as the ideological and fiscal model by which the structure was financed and enabled; and second, the persistent and exceptional tendency to iconographic referentiality in the imagery of Amarāvatī. Whether the panels representing stūpas across the decoration at Amarāvatī, and especially on the exquisitely detailed sculpture of the drum slabs, refer to the monument itself or to other monuments of its type, or indeed to a stūpa ideal, is unclear and as we have seen perhaps deliberately so. In the case of *dāna*, while acknowledging the individual source of the gift (often with some precision about family relationships), transferring the commemorative praise from the object donated to a more generalized space among hundreds of other inscriptions marking the Amarāvatī stones enables a sense of collective rather than personal will. Given the striking absence of named royal or state patronage, this not only highlights the wide spread of the stūpa's supporting community but signals defensively its strength in depth in case of potential official opposition, for instance by a monarch who might be cool or even resistant to Buddhism. It takes away a sense of implicit chronology in changing styles of carving or script, by avoiding dates (with hardly any reference to reigns or other externally verifiable temporal markers) in the epigraphy, in order to create a picture of universal harmony among donors, many marked on stones they did not themselves offer or pay for, or on stones already set up and part of the monumental structure. In relation to the repeated iconography of stūpas on the drum, the form of which seems to emulate that of the main monument – including its rich decoration, its railing adorned by pillars and cross-beams decorated with lotus flowers, and its gateways with seated lions – the material logic of referential transference pushes meaning beyond the specific sculpted segment carrying the iconography or script to the larger whole, and beyond that, further still, to the ideal to which the reliquary function, monumental size and imagistic excess of the stūpa seem to point.

It is important to emphasize that the inscriptions become integral to the decoration of the slabs they are carved on. Take the fine block with a mortise hole on both its flat top and bottom that once held a lion on top of a pillar at the outer entrance of one of the main gates (illus. 44).[48] The long face (65 centimetres/25 ½ in. in length) has a pair of elephants with bunches of lotuses in their trunks bowing to a stūpa in the centre, the dome of which is knotted with the bodies of two four-headed *nāga* serpents. The upper border has 22 twelve-petalled lotuses, each in a circle; the side borders consist of two columns made of strips of alternate hatching with beaded borders on either side; the exquisitely cut inscription announces that this is the 'Pious gift of a Lion-pedestal [*sīha-ṭhāna*] by the Elder [*thera*] Bhayata Budhi, the enlarger of the Chaitya, and his sister the Nun Budha'.[49] It is not obvious how legible this inscription would have been – at any rate to the literate viewer with a command of Brahmi script – since we do not know the height of the pillar on which it sat, but its decorative visibility as inscription is not in doubt. The shorter face (42.25 centimetres/17 in. wide) has a fleshy, flat-faced dwarf

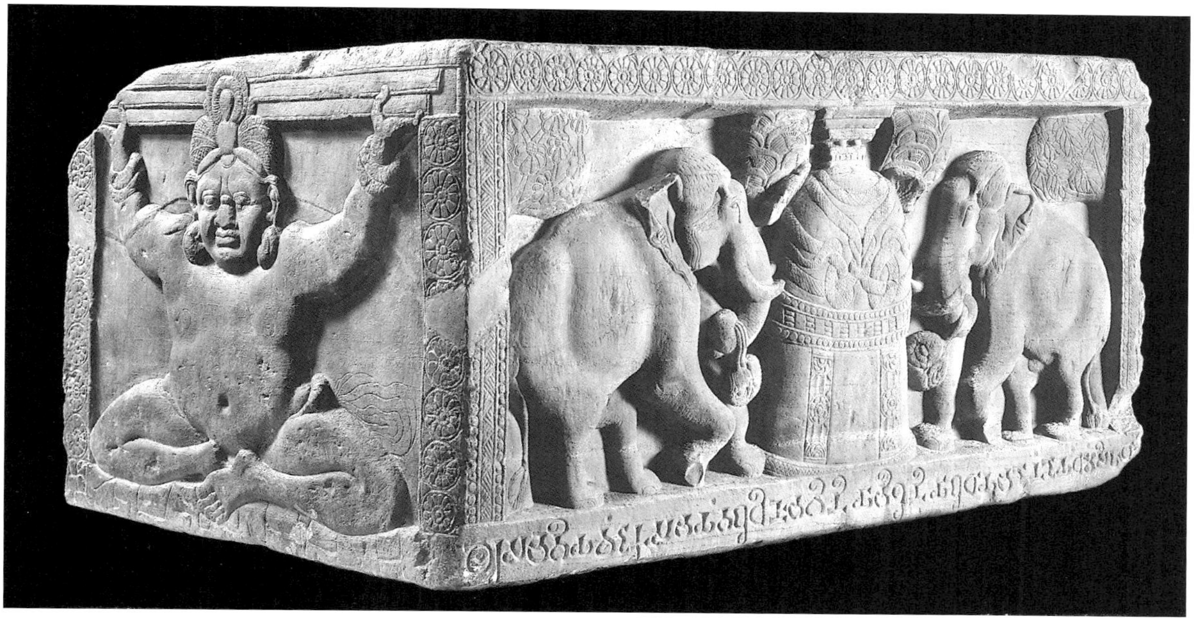

44 Rectangular block from the end of the railing at one of the gates, inscribed 'lion seat', on which one of the lions (as in illus. 150 and 151) were placed. Carved with a flat-faced dwarf bearing the weight of the lion above, and two elephants bowing to a stūpa.

with an elaborate turban and bracelets seated and holding up the three-stepped base for the lion statue that would have been above him. This base forms the upper border, with two rows of eight twelve-petalled lotuses in circles making up the two side borders. The lower border, which the dwarf's seated foot transgresses at the centre, is curved to take the weight of his legs and marked with irregular lines, indicating impressionistically the ground on which he sits. It has been suggested that the style of the carving makes it early (first century CE), while that of the script on the lower rim of the long side is late (second to third century CE).[50] But the careful attention to all the framing borders of both carved faces does imply that the blank space of the lower border on the long side was designed for the inscription to be carved there. The majority of the surviving frieze blocks from Amarāvatī are certainly decorated or inscribed on all their borders.[51] Most of the Amarāvatī inscriptions that survive on large enough blocks to determine their placement in relation to the rest of the decorative surface appear to occupy borders.[52]

By contrast, some railing pillars (usually dated relatively early) with fluting rather than narrative scenes carved between the lotus medallions have inscriptions carved across the upper area of fluting. In one case, this commemorates a gift of a *buddhapāda* by a large family group, implying the possibility that this inscription was added to the pre-existing railing some time after it was set up.[53] In a second case, the inscription appears to imply the pillar itself is the gift of a householder and his family.[54]

Apart from being a different kind of decorative element – that is, script rather than imagery – the inscriptions add the celebration of contemporary humanity within the world evoked by the stūpa's iconography. The bulk of the stūpa's images offer iconic scenes of the Buddha's life – sometimes almost as schematic symbols (such as the empty throne and Bodhi tree for the enlightenment, or the empty throne with *dharmacakra* for the turning of the Wheel), but often peopled in vivid narratives that include a range of devotees, disciples and deities of all kinds, as well as animals and magical beings. A significant range of the imagery appears to refer to the *jātaka* tales of the Bodhisattva's previous lives, many identifiable,[55] but many still unidentified in part because the literary traditions of early Buddhism in Andhra Pradesh have now disappeared,[56] and in part perhaps because of the inventiveness, and hence unusual pictorial solutions, of so much of the Amarāvatī sculpture.[57] To this taxonomy of kinds of beings, with its special emphasis on spiritually developed figures such as the Buddha and the Bodhisattva in his previous lives, the inscriptions add a sociology of humanity in the here-and-now of the stūpa's making and celebration. This extends from the aristocracy across social classes to monks and nuns, with individuals named personally. While most are donor epigraphs dating roughly to the period of the stūpa's construction, some inscriptions are much later. For instance, on the fragment of an octagonal pillar original to the building of the site, a long Sanskrit inscription with palaeography indicating a date of circa 1100 CE celebrates a gift of something (whatever precisely has now been lost) 'worked in gems, gold and silver'.[58] That is, the occasional (if rare) addition of later inscriptions to the great number that made up the casing of the stūpa, alongside its images, was a constant gesture towards modernity's investment in the monument, as long as there were Buddhists left in southern India to worship there.

Like so much of the imagery of the monument, the inscriptions emphasize devotion. Beyond the naming of gifts and donors, they invoke the Blessed One – calling for 'success' (*sidham*,[59] or *nilikam*),[60] and sometimes announcing adoration for the Lord (*namo bhagavato*).[61] This invocation usually opens an inscription (which is one reason it does not survive on many, as they are fragmentary), while the naming of the kind of item donated, especially if it is the slab inscribed, is usually at or near the end alongside the word *dāna(m)* meaning, in the context of a specific donated object, 'gift' in the sense of an act of generosity by the donor. Unfortunately, since some scholars have regarded these invocations as simply repeated formulae, they have often failed to be reported in discussions and translations of the Amarāvatī inscriptions.[62] But this misrepresents the nature of these epigraphs (which may indeed provide *us* with a sociology of patrons and a helpful hand in dating through the palaeography of scripts, but were not intended or designed for either of these purposes!). It also fails to give the inscriptions their properly devotional context as invocations of the Buddha as well as memorials of *dāna*. Moreover, repeated formulae in ritual contexts are anything but meaningless, as is obvious from the repeated nature of much of the iconography and symbolism of the art at the stūpa – that is, wheels, *buddhapādas*, stūpas, empty thrones and *dharmacakras*, vases of plenty, garlands and so forth. In all these respects, the inscriptions, both in content and in replicative form, belong profoundly with the broader material culture of the site. Alongside the imagery of devotion to the Buddha by human beings and gods, and notably the imagery of pilgrims approaching the stūpa in the great panels on the drum (see illus. 49, 61, 71, 90, 94, 95), the inscriptions add the personal testimony of such worshippers – their own voices, as it were – complete with the gifts they have brought in the form of stones for the stūpa's structure and invocations of the Buddha in their own written words.

To take an example of a complete inscription in context:

> *Sidham vāniyasa Kutasa sa*
> *bheriyasa saputakasa saduhu*
> *tukasa sanatukasa dakhināyā*
> *ke cetiyakhabho sadhāduko dānam*
>
> Success! Gift of a *caitya* pillar with a relic at the southern gate by the merchant Kuta with his wife, sons, daughters and grandsons.[63]

Here the family unit and its fine gift, itself presumably commemorated on the base of the actual pillar they gave, is sandwiched between the invocation and the naming of their act as *dāna*.

It happens that the object that this inscription adorns is 'the finest fragment of a pillar recovered', and

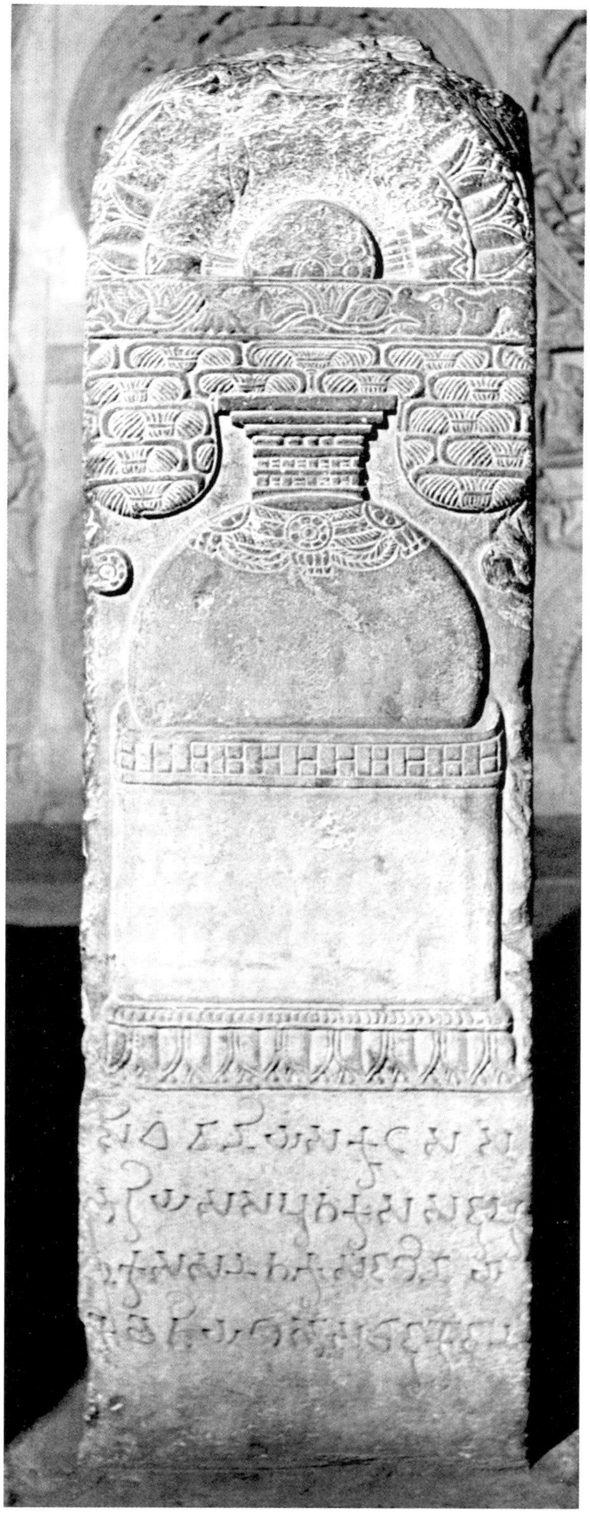

appears to have some excavation context, having been found by James Burgess at the south entrance (as the epigraph tells us, illus. 45).[64] The inscription is beautifully cut on the lower section of the wider side of a four-sided pillar (34 × 28 cm in section, the piece survives to a height of 130 cm).[65] Above, carved in low relief, is a fine stūpa sitting on a row of lotus petals, its dome adorned with swags and roundels with eight-petalled lotuses, and what has been described as 'an army of parasols' issuing from its *harmikā*. Above this flamboyantly crowned stūpa is a narrow border frieze of lotus blossoms issuing from the mouth of a crocodile-headed *makara* on the right and, above this, the now somewhat damaged remains of a half-lotus medallion. The other sides have equally fine decoration. The wider side on the obverse of the pillar has an open pavilion on columns with a dome, the pinnacle of which, resembling a stepped pyramid, cuts into the framing border above with lotuses emerging from a crocodile *makara* to the right (illus. 46). The frieze of the pavilion above the pillars and the dome, which sits on top of it, are decorated with *caitya* windows. Inside the pavilion is a relic casket in the shape of a stūpa on a square base (or perhaps inside a square railing), topped with an umbrella touching a descending canopy above it. Above the border is a half-lotus medallion, as on the opposite face. The reliquary in stūpa form clearly refers to the relics named in the inscription on the opposite side, while the reliquary's form plays against that of the stūpa above the epigraph. The line of connection between the top of the reliquary, the canopy of the pavilion, the pinnacle of the pavilion dome and the border may imply visually the ascending power of the relic, perhaps buried beneath the donated pillar. On the smaller face to the left of the inscription is a great many-spoked wheel on a squat column with stepped capital behind an empty throne and curving *svastika* on the central cushion, with *buddhapāda* beneath (illus. 47). The wheel is topped with an umbrella and floating

45 Lower section of a square pillar found at the south gate. Carved with a fine four-line Brahmi inscription and a stūpa beneath a half-lotus.

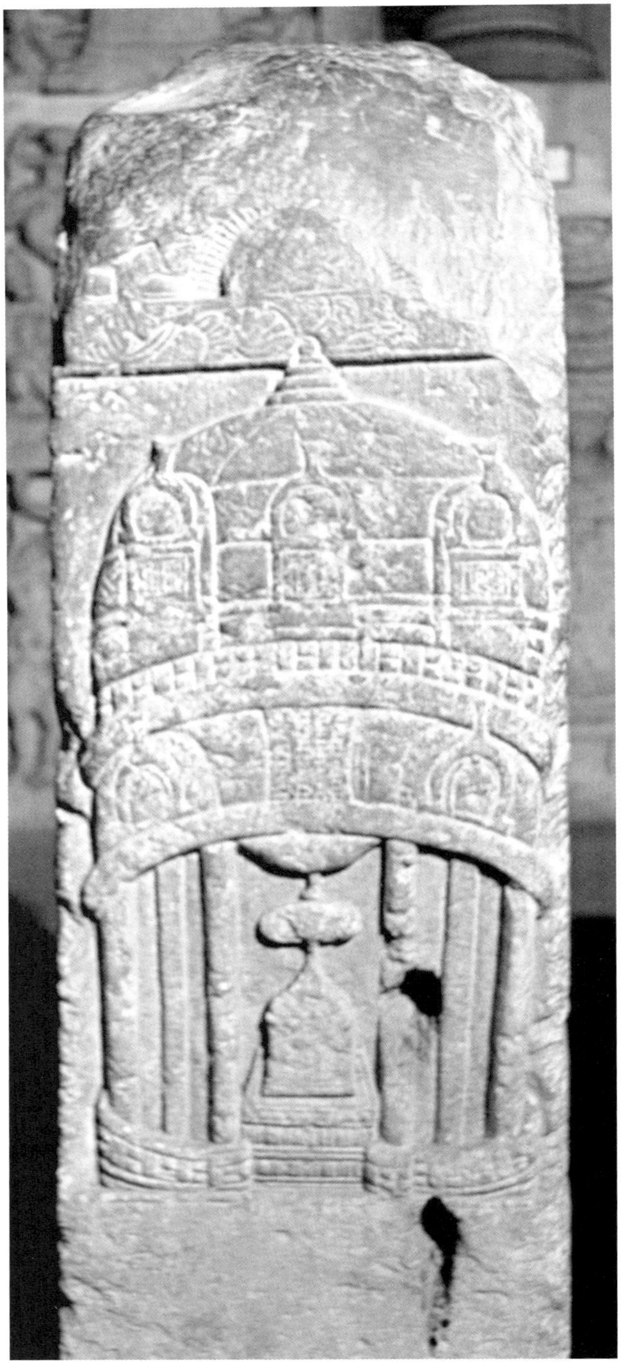

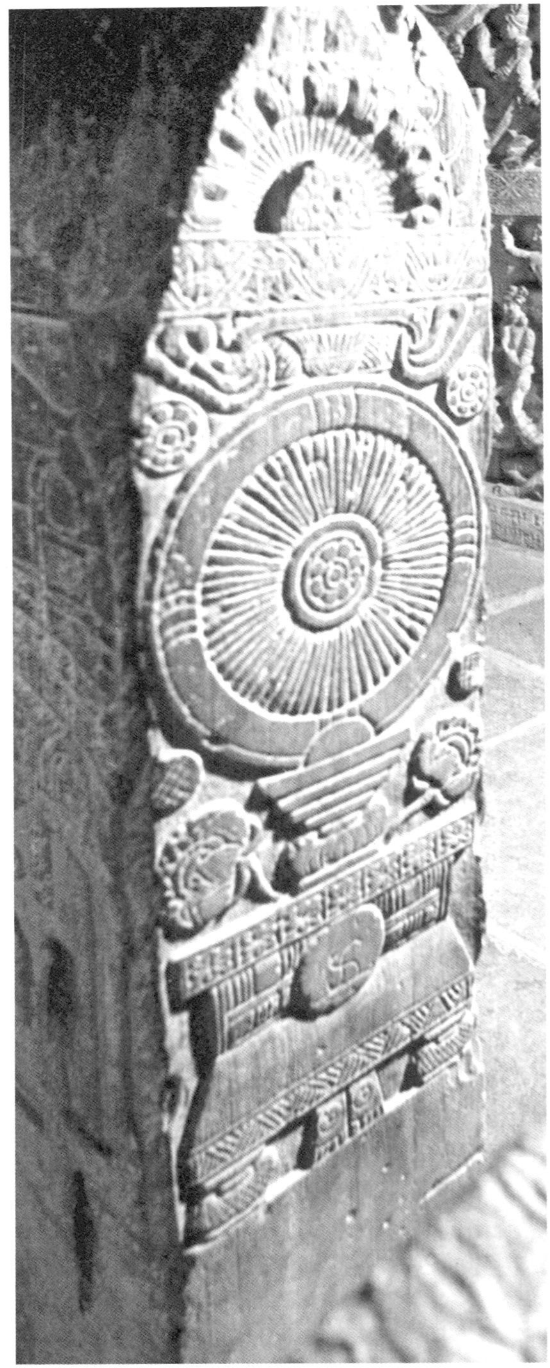

46 Reverse side of the same pillar as illus. 45, with a domed circular pavilion on pillars enclosing a stūpa-shaped reliquary.

47 Side to the left of the inscription on the pillar in illus. 45, with *dharmacakra* over an empty throne beneath a half-lotus.

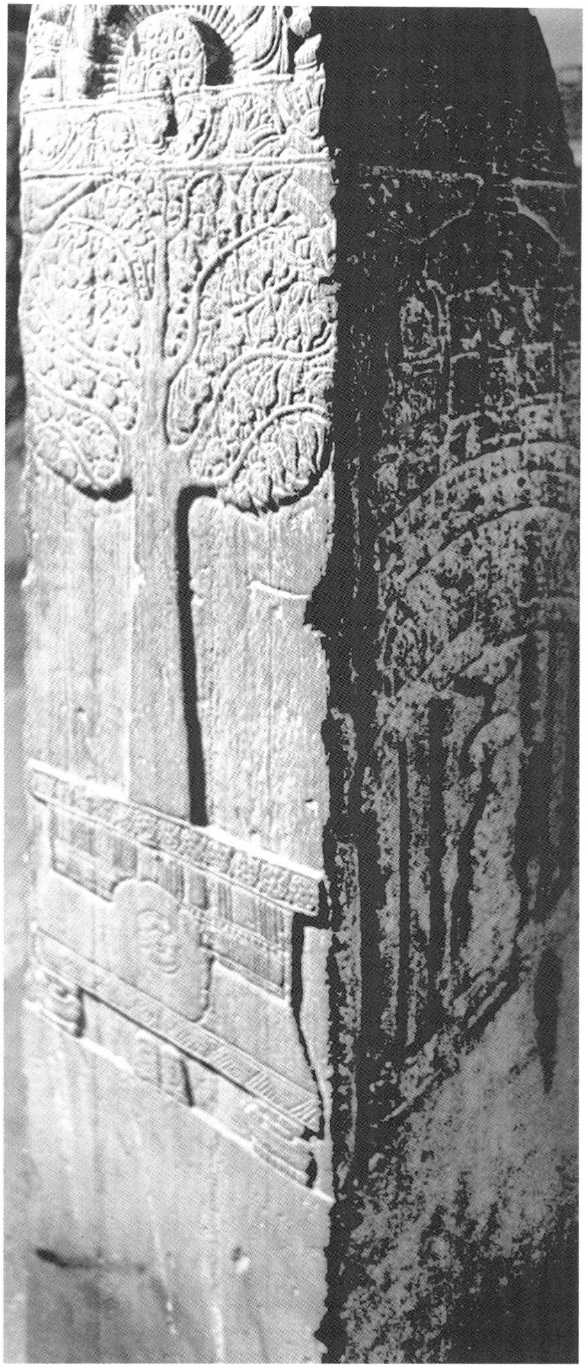

48 Side to the right of the inscription on the pillar in illus. 45, with Bodhi tree over an empty throne beneath a half-lotus.

ribbons and has a lotus with eight petals at its hub. The border above has a frieze of lotuses (with no *makara*), and above that is the half-lotus medallion. On the smaller face to the right of the inscription is the Bodhi tree above a throne with a cushion that is decorated with a lotus and the *buddhapāda* beneath (illus. 48). Again, the border above the tree has lotuses without a *makara*, with a half-lotus medallion above that.

The imagery – Bodhi tree and throne, *dharmacakra* and throne, and stūpa – may be said to symbolize the three key events of the Buddha's life: enlightenment, the turning of the wheel of dharma at the First Sermon and the *parinirvāṇa*, or passing away of the Buddha. The relic scene, with its unusual upwards alignment of images touching or breaking through the borders framing them, takes this dynamic into the present: the gift of relics to go with the pillar made by Kuta and his family; the reliquary context of the Amarāvatī stūpa as a whole, as a monumental embodiment of the Buddha and his teaching; and the outer casket of many interred relics and reliquaries. The inscription uses the normal term for stūpa at Amarāvatī, namely *caitya*, to describe the pillar (*cetiyakhabho*, *caitya* pillar), and the image above it responds with a stūpa, perhaps indicating the monument as a whole (and possibly signalling a now lost stūpa at the top of the column). That stūpa is itself in dialogue with the reliquary stūpa on the reverse side, which cites the relics named in the inscription. The face with the inscription is one of the wider sides of the pillar, the inscription filling space that is elsewhere covered by relief sculpture. Ironically, if there is a blank space it is on the body of the stūpa carved above the epigraph. The inscription is integral to the whole – to its embellishment as surface decoration, its meanings as the gift of Kuta and his clan and its self-consciousness as an object that is labelled in respect of its position and function within the Amarāvatī complex as well as its exceptional reliquary value.

We may say that every part of this object is formulaic. The formulae in the inscription include the invocation for success (*sidham*) at its opening, the naming of the kind of object, the close on the affirmation that it is *dāna* and the terminologies for the donor kinship group (nameless but for the senior member of the family),[66] with only the specific name and occupation to distinguish Kuta. The call for *sidham* and its direct relation to the act of *dāna*, defined in relation to the object donated to the stūpa, is implicated in the ideology and economy of merit, as something accrued to generate good karma as the result of skilful acts.[67] The visual formulae of the block include all the imagery: half-lotus medallions, framing lotus-blossom borders with and without *makaras*, the symbolic clusters on the pillar's faces (stūpa with parasols, *dharmacakra* with throne and Bodhi tree with throne) and the individual elements of those clusters – wheel, stūpa, parasols, throne, *buddhapādas* and so on. These formulae are repeated endlessly across the arts of the site. But they are also executed exquisitely (not least in this example) and in configurations that are never precisely the same, creating the possibilities for originality through the mixing and juxtaposing of types. In this case it is the relic that adds spice to the donation, and its imaging on the face with *caitya* pavilion that creates out of the visual formulae something special to the stūpa as well as to Kuta through his gift. Arguably, there is little difference in the ways the inscription and the imagery function by means of collecting formulae and making something distinctive and personal out of them, while fitting perfectly with the aesthetic, ethical and religious ethos of the monument as a whole. At the same time, the naming of the donors, however formulaically framed, introduces to this – and to every inscription – an element that is both unique and personal.

DĀNA

One of the most frequent ways of ending an inscription at Amarāvatī (in the case of those whose last words have survived) is with the term *dāna(m)*, meaning the act of giving or generosity and hence also the gift that is the result of a generous impulse.[68] But the word occurs also within the main body of several inscriptions.[69] It may occur alongside the naming of the kind of stone given or not.[70] In terms of repeated epigraphic patterns, the naming of the gift that is the occasion of the inscription as an act of *dāna* is the end of a formula that opens with the invocation of the Buddha. In many respects, *dāna* is the most interesting term in the epigraphy of Amarāvatī: it represents something so obvious and unnecessary as to be redundant (the fact that a gift has been made in a context where votive dedications were normative), and at the same time it represents a key concept in Buddhist theory, which serves as the ideological underpinning for the monument, its existence and making, its funding and support. Even more than the movement between the making of a great enterprise like a stūpa and the collective particularities of those who have enabled it, *dāna* unites the universal (a fundamental model for the Bodhisattva path as defined by both Nikāya and Mahāyāna Buddhist savants in South India) and the immensely specific (a gift of a particular stone by a named individual or group).

It is the aim of this section to explore what *dāna* meant, beyond simply a description of patronage and donation, in the ideological context of late ancient Buddhism in Andhra. The concept is a fundamental basis for the development of Mahāyāna Buddhism and the responses to it from the Nikāya traditions in South India, and as such it infuses the underlying expectations of those who came to the site – whether as donors of major elements of its structure or as dedicators of simple and ephemeral offerings, like the implied objects (perhaps flowers) represented as available from offerings by vendors seated outside the main gateways in so many of the drum reliefs that are carved with images of stūpas (illus. 49, 61, 71, 90, 94, 95).[71] The images of dwarfs, or statues of them, holding large trays in so many of these reliefs appear to represent receptacles provided by the site for the deposition of offerings (illus. 26, 34, 49, 61, 71, 90, 94, 95).[72]

Traditionally, following the seminal early twentieth-century theoretical work in anthropology by Marcel Mauss,[73] scholarship has been too eager to see votive offerings within a universal model of reciprocity (that has been frequently assumed to transcend cultural specificities[74]), in which they are offered under obligation as the price of a benefit from a higher power. The 'votive

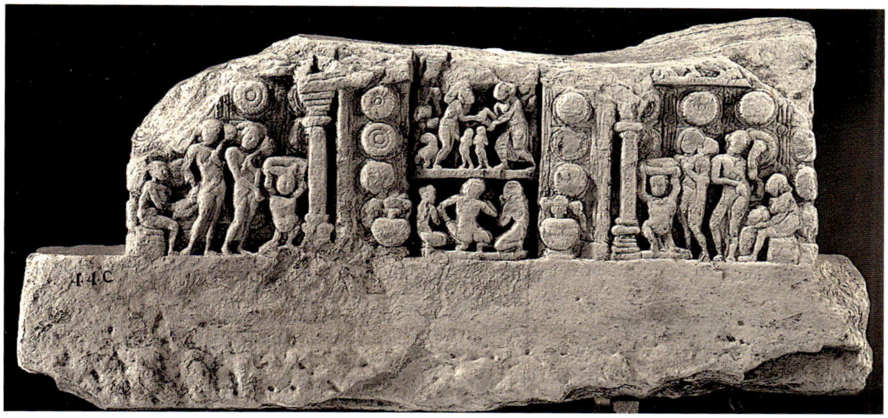

49 Abraded lower fragment of a drum slab showing a view of a stūpa through a gateway. In the central gateway is a scene from the *Vessantara-Jātaka*, where the Bodhisattva in his previous life gives his children to a brahmin. Outside the railing on each side are a seated flower seller, two standing pilgrims each carrying a blossom and a statue of a dwarf with a tray to receive the offerings.

system' or 'scenario' has been seen as a matter of striking a 'bargain',[75] which depends on the 'exchange of material objects for supernatural favours'.[76] This model, although still probably the norm in the discussion of *ex votos*, has rightly been criticized,[77] notably for an excessively transactional and instrumental flavour and its failure effectively to account for the kinds of qualities implied by what Christians might call 'grace'[78] and a variety of Indian religions (Hindu, Jain, Buddhist) call *dāna*.[79] There is no doubt that one aspect or understanding of *dāna* in late ancient Indian Buddhism has transactional qualities – the practice of giving in order to accrue merit.[80] But in relation to a highly theorized concept with many levels, which is fundamental to the Bodhisattva ideal, to see this model as the sole one or even as normative would be grossly reductive.[81]

In early Buddhism, both in the Pāli Nikāyas and in the Āgamas of other schools, summaries of the Buddhist path offer 'the step-by-step discourse' that starts with *dāna* as the first foundation.[82] In relation specifically to the Bodhisattva ideal, both Theravāda and Mahāyāna Buddhism, which means probably also the other Nikāya traditions whose scriptures have not survived (including the Mahāsāṃghikas of Andhra Pradesh), present *dāna* as the first of the perfections (*pāramī* in Pāli and *pāramitā* in Sanskrit).[83] These number ten in the Theravāda system and six in the Mahāyāna, with a further four added in some texts.[84] But the key issue for us is that *dāna* is the foundation in each system.[85] It is significant that as a presentation of Buddhist teaching, the perfections as a group are not mentioned in the early canon of suttas.[86] They are, however, central to the concept of the Bodhisattva as a being in the process of perfecting himself in the *Cāriyāpiṭaka*, *Buddhavaṃsa* and *Apadāna*, a group of late canonical Pāli texts focusing on biography and perhaps dating to the second or first centuries BCE,[87] and to a number of the early Mahāyāna texts such as the *Bodhisattvapitaka*, the *Ugraparipṛcchā* and the *Akṣayamatirnirdeśasūtra*, which are all likely to be from the first or second century CE or earlier,[88] and above all the *Prajñāpāramitā* sūtras,[89] including the earliest that survives, the *Aṣṭasāhasrikā Prajñāpāramitā* (The Perfection of Wisdom in 8,000 Verses), whose probably later verse summary culminates in an account of the six.[90] It is not clear where the Prajñāpāramitā tradition first arose (the two strongest candidates geographically are the Krishna River area and northwestern India/Central Asia), or exactly when (100 BCE is a current best guess for when the *Aṣṭasāhasrikā* was first written down).[91] However, what matters for our purposes is not the origin of these traditions or their dates, but their availability – much increased once the sūtras moved from oral to written form – in southern India, which certainly does coincide with the florescence of Buddhist visual and epigraphic culture in Andhra. Interestingly, in neither the Mahāyāna (by definition) nor the Nikāya schools (at least as represented by the Theravāda) are the perfections unique to the being who would become Gautama, the Buddha-to-be: they are exemplary in the career of any Buddha, but are a model to be followed and perfected by his disciples, family and lay followers (all of whom may in the Nikāya model become *arahat*s, and in the Mahāyāna model become Buddhas).[92]

Dāna is the first of the perfections in the lists – and may stand for all of them, as in the fourth chapter of the *Vajjracchedikā Sūtra* (possibly also one of the earliest of the *Prajñāpāramitā Sūtras*[93]) and in the opening of the exposition of the chronicle of Buddha Gautama in Buddhadatta's fifth-century commentary on the Pāli *Buddhavaṃsa*.[94] Or *dāna* may enable the attainment of all, as in the *Pañcaviṃśatisāhasrikā prajñāpāramitā Sūtra*, the Perfection of Wisdom in 25,000 verses.[95] The Pāli commentary on the *pāramīs* by Dhammapāla, who lived at an uncertain date about 160 kilometres (100 mi.) south of Amarāvatī,[96] implies that the perfection of giving incorporates the others when he presents his analysis of all the perfections by means of the example of *dāna*.[97] Perhaps written in the sixth century or perhaps still later, this commentary draws on earlier tradition. Vasubhandu, the great fourth- to fifth-century Mahāyāna scholar from Gandhāra, broadly agrees, presenting all the perfections through the prism of *dāna* at the end of the fourth chapter of his great *Abhidharma* commentary,[98] in which he follows the presentation of the first- or second-century CE *Ugrapaṛiprcchā* where the lay Bodhisattva's practice of all six perfections is effectively presented through *dāna*.[99] In the *Mahāprajñāpāramitāśāstra*, the major commentary on the Perfection of Wisdom in 25,000 Verses that was translated into (and only survives in) Chinese by Kumārajīva in the first decade of the fifth century and is ascribed by him to Nāgārjuna (probably incorrectly[100]), the section on *dāna* culminates in the way it relates to and enables the other perfections.[101] In the narratives of the Buddha's biography, the priority of *dāna* is well illustrated by an important moment in the enlightenment narrative, when Māra makes his final assault on Gautama to prevent him from awakening. In the fifth-century Pāli *Nidānakathā*, it is the recollection of the perfections that serves as 'my shield as well as my weapon of attack' against Māra, turning the demon's razor-edged discus into a canopy of garlands.[102] But it is the recollection of his *dāna* as Vessantara, in his last life before that in which he attains enlightenment, and his calling of the earth as witness to this great act of *dāna* that overcomes Māra once and for all.[103]

In the *Nidānakathā*, the prose 'biography' of the Buddha from his taking of the Bodhisattva vow as Sumedha in the presence of the Buddha Dīpaṅkara to the foundation of the Jetavana monastery in his final lifetime, which served as the formal introduction to the Theravāda collection of *jātakas* and has been ascribed to the great fifth-century commentator Buddhaghosa, the ten perfections have a significant programmatic role.[104] Immediately following Dīpaṅkara's prophecy that Sumedha will attain Buddhahood, the new Bodhisattva resolves to pursue the perfections (each described at some length in their traditional order in the Theravāda system[105]), at which point, in homage to his mastery of them and in emulation of its action at his enlightenment and the turning of the wheel of dharma, the great earth 'Trembled, shook and quaked, making a mighty roar, like a sheaf of reeds trodden by an elephant, or a sugar mill with pressure applied to it; and it spun round and round like a potter's wheel or the wheel of an oil-mill.'[106] Thereafter, in each of the accounts of the Buddhas succeeding Dīpaṅkara, previous lives of the Bodhisattva at those times are briefly recounted with a summary of the relevant perfections that were developed then.[107]

The period from the third to the seventh centuries gave rise to the writing of an extremely rich commentarial literature on the perfections as a group and individually, in both the Theravāda and Mahāyāna traditions (and one presumes therefore in the lost commentarial texts of the other Nikāya schools), a literature that drew on what were certainly oral and may have been written exegetic teachings in the period when the stūpas of Andhra were created.[108] These commentaries elaborate rich and diverse interpretative explorations that stress different aspects and levels in the practice of *dāna* as a key constituent of the Bodhisattva's path to becoming a Buddha. Each is a compendium of knowledge, not necessarily completely consistent in itself, let alone with other commentaries. I draw on this material freely below, guided by the thematic exposition of *dāna* in the imagery and epigraphy of Amarāvatī.

Of key visual significance is the fact that numerous stories of the previous lives of the Buddha as Bodhisattva (and indeed of other saints and liberated beings), reported in the commentaries and gathered in such collections of narratives as the *jātakas* and *avadānas*,[109] are strongly associated with the development of the different perfections,[110] with a special emphasis on *dāna*.[111] Crucially, the *Cāriyāpiṭaka* lists the series of *jātakas* it retells in verse form by means of the perfection that the story exemplifies, with ten tales under the heading *dāna*,[112] while the later *Nidānakathā* offers a list of eleven as embodying the perfection of *dāna*.[113] Out of the 35 stories in the *Cāriyāpiṭaka*, nine are found in visual form at Amarāvatī, of which two (the narratives of Śaśa and Vessantara[114]) belong to the *dāna* division and a further five (the tales of Bhūridatta, Campeyya, Cūlabodhi, Mātanga and Sankhapāla) to that of *sīla* (morality).[115] It is tempting to speculate that the selection of subjects for the stūpa's *jātaka* representations may have been framed by a text like the *Cāriyāpiṭaka*, but one belonging to the local Mahāsāṃghika tradition, which no longer survives. In the case of one further story that also emphasizes *dāna* at Amarāvatī, the *Sarvamdāda Avādana* is related to the *Śibi Jātaka*, which does appear in the *Cāriyāpiṭaka* (1.8).[116] Of the *jātakas* that have to date been identified in the surviving sculptures (which are probably significantly fewer than were represented, given that their subjects are not inscribed and the Mahāsāṃghika oral and literary cultures from Andhra in which they were embedded are lost), a number of others also emphasize *dāna*. These include the *Khadaringāra* and *Chaddanta jātakas*.[117]

The five narratives that focus on *dāna* give a series of folktale ramifications to the theme – from the giving up of everything (including the donor's family, flesh and life[118]) in the stories of Śaśa, Sarvamdāda and Vessantara, and the giving up of the noble elephant's tusks in the *Chaddanta* tale, to the resolute determination to save a *paccekabuddha* from death by making an offering despite the wiles of the evil demon Māra in the *Khadaringāra Jātaka*. The *Vessantara* (*Viśvantara* in Sanskrit) *Jātaka*, the last story in the *Mahānipāta* or final group of ten tales in the entire *Jātakatthavaṇṇanā*, and the story of the Buddha's last rebirth before the one in which he is enlightened,[119] is not only the supreme celebration of *dāna* in the folktale tradition but one of the most repeated of the visual subjects from the *jātakas* at the stūpa and in Buddhist art generally (illus. 49).[120] This story culminates the entire *jātaka* tradition on the theme of *dāna*, and, as mentioned above, is recollected according to the *Nidānakathā* by the Bodhisattva in his defeat of Māra immediately before his enlightenment. This storytelling focus for *dāna*, apart from its appeal to visual narratives and representations, enabled a staging and exploration of the possibility that *dāna* might be excessive – in effect an internal conversation within Buddhism on whether there were appropriate ethical limits to the perfections. In the *Milindapañha* – a text written between the last century BCE and the second century CE that purports to record the conversations of the Graeco-Bactrian monarch Menander and a Buddhist monk called Nāgasena – the issue of whether Vessantara was right in giving away his wife and children is debated at some length.[121]

Among the Pāli commentators, both Buddhaghosa and Dhammapāla recognize an incremental quality of three levels in each perfection – basic (*pāramī*), intermediate (*upapāramī*) and ultimate (*paramatapāramī*).[122] In the case of *dāna*, Dhammapāla analyses the basic level as 'the relinquishing of one's children, wives and belongings', the intermediate level as 'the relinquishing of one's own limbs' and the highest

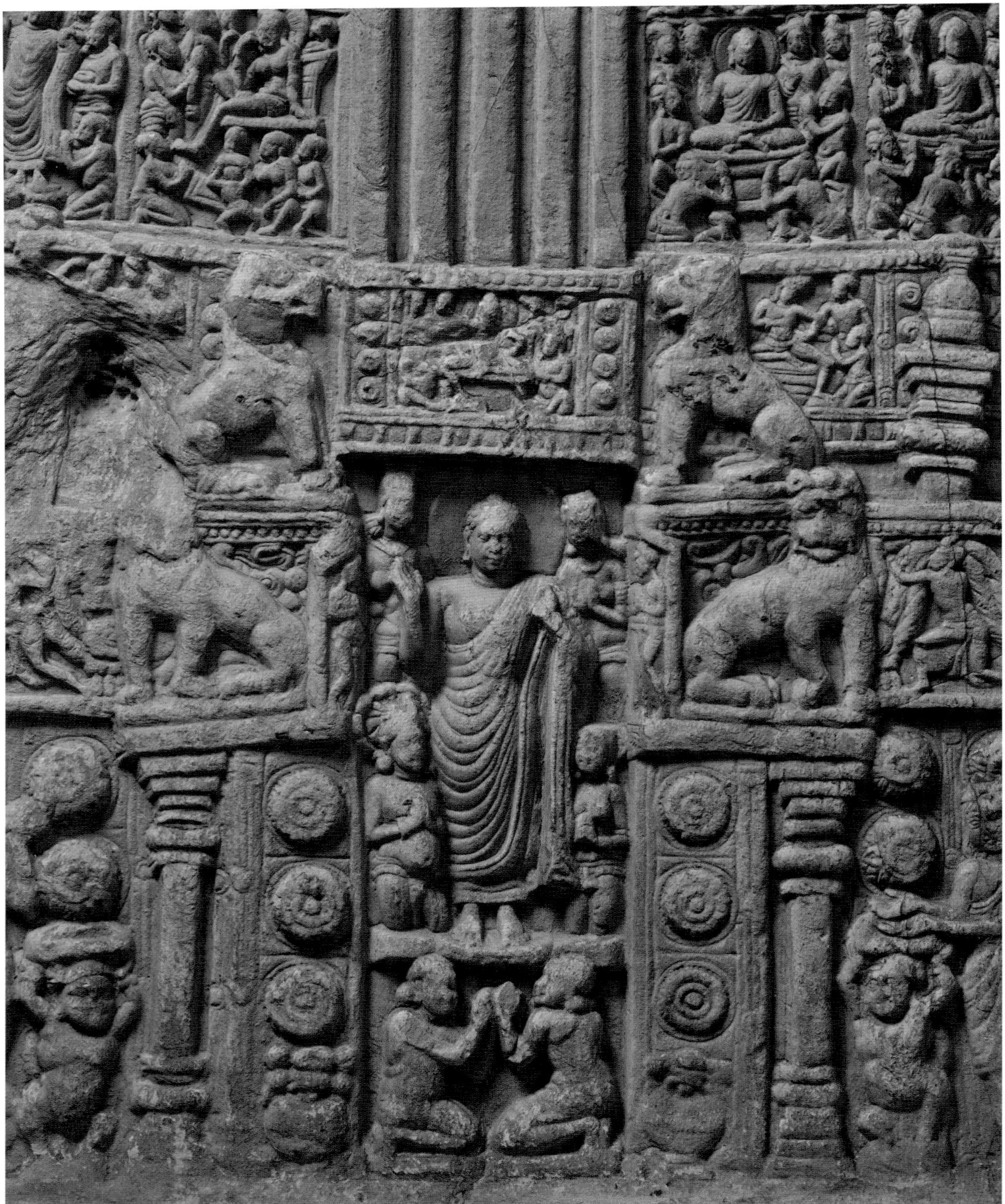

50 Detail of the gateway of a well-preserved drum slab showing a view of a stūpa from outside its railing. The entrance has the Buddha standing in the *abhāya* posture with kneeling *nāga*s to either side and kneeling worshippers in front.

level as 'the relinquishing of one's own life'.[123] He then proceeds to determine the three levels he accords to each of the other perfections in terms of the example set out by *dāna*.[124] In the story pattern, visually performed at the stūpa, this translates directly into the *Vessantara-Jātaka* in which the Bodhisattva gives up his wife, children and all possessions (see illus. 49), the *Sarvamdāda Avadāna* (see illus. 58) where he gives up his flesh to ransom a bird from a hunter (and arguably the *Chaddanta Jātaka*, where the Bodhisattva as a six-tusked elephant gives up his tusks to the hunter who has shot him with a poisoned arrow) and the *Sasa Jātaka* (see illus. 57), where he is a hare who offers his life to feed a brahmin.[125] Effectively the art of the stūpa presents the three levels of *dāna*, as interpreted in the commentarial traditions, through its visual narratives.

In a striking further tripartite division of *dāna*, Dhammapāla agrees with a number of early Mahāyāna presentations that the practice of giving involves three different kinds of objects in a hierarchy – the giving of material things (*āmisadāna*), the giving of fearlessness (*abhayadāna*) and the giving of Dhamma (*dhammadāna*).[126] The implication of this model being present in both Theravāda and Mahāyāna commentaries is that they draw on a common source. Clearly, the endowment of the stūpa and the giving of stones by donors is a case of *āmisadāna*, the first level. Equally, the stūpa as a whole – with its embodiment of the Buddha's presence through relics, stories and monument and as a presentation of the path – is a prime example of *dhammadāna*, the gift of Dhamma itself to its visitors (and indeed to its patrons and donors). The second level, *abhayadāna*, or the gift of fearlessness, is interesting.[127] The commentators are surprisingly reticent about what this might mean, despite relatively lengthy expositions of the two other levels. Dhammapāla says only that 'the giving of fearlessness is the giving of protection to beings when they have become frightened,' while the *Mahāprajñāpāramitāśāstra* places it in the context of the union of the second perfection (*sīla*, or morality) with *dāna* and says only 'the type of morality which refrains from tormenting living beings constitutes generosity which bestows the absence of fear'.[128] However, in the context of the art of the stūpa, the absence of fear is visually ever-present in one significant way.

This is the overwhelming predominance of the *abhāya mudrā*, the 'freedom from fear' gesture where the right hand is raised with the palm towards the viewer,[129] in the imagery of the embodied Buddha and Bodhisattva at Amarāvatī – in reliefs, standing and seated (for example, illus. 50, also 5 and 124),[130] and in the surviving three-dimensional sculpture (illus. 145–9).[131] The same observation about the preference for this *mudrā* has been made about the related site and Buddha statuary from Nāgārjunakonda, of around the same date.[132] While some sites elsewhere in India show a preference for other postures (such as the *bhūmisparśa mudrā*, or 'touching the earth' gesture[133]), the images of the Buddha at Andhra belong to the majority of early Indian Buddhas, including those from Mathurā and many from Gandhāra, in their preference for the fearlessness iconography.[134] This has a number of ramifications directly relevant to the theme of *dāna*. One may consider the stūpa's offer of *abhāya* as a higher-level *dāna* response to the giving of a material offering – whether of elements for the building of the site or of flowers or incense as part of a pilgrim's visit – as if the gift of material things by the worshipper is rewarded by the gift of fearlessness by the stūpa itself. But the state of protection implied by fearlessness is also the state in which the devotee is free and able to receive the teaching of the path, opening her to the third level of *dāna*, *dhammadāna*. The stūpa's emphasis on *dāna* – visually in the *jātaka* and *avadāna* narratives, through repeated epigraphic naming, and through the Buddha's own offering of *abhāya* – is both a picture of how the path operates and a staging of that operation, allowing spiritual development at and through a devotional visit to the site. In this sense, the ideology of *dāna* is related to the stūpa's wider self-referentiality, its imagery and inscriptions acting like an endless chain of mirrors: the worshipper who comes to the stūpa to make an offering is mirrored in the *dāna* embodied in the imagery, inscriptions and very existence of the monument itself.

The emphasis on *dāna*, alongside that on veneration in so many of the reliefs, is designed to bring into being the psychological state of what is called in Pāli *pasāda* and in Sanskrit *prasāda*: a quality of purity and faith or spiritual opening, which the sight of Buddha or stūpa is intended to inspire in the giver.[135] The quality of trust that arises in the worshipper through *prasāda* – enabling the purity of mind necessary for embarking on the path – is precisely what is engendered through *abhāya*, the protection of a beneficent force that disables fear. In the Sanskrit *Divyāvadāna*, a group of 37 stories and other texts mainly drawn from the *Vinaya* tradition of the Mūlasarvastivādin school, which emphasizes previous lives, continuing karmas and implicitly the perfections,[136] the Buddha utters these verses:

> Hundreds of thousands of gold coins or nuggets
> are not equal to one who with *prasāda* in his heart
> circumambulates the shrine of a Buddha . . .
> places a single lump of clay . . .
> places heaps of pearls and lovely flowers . . .
> festoons with garlands . . .
> makes a gift of oil lamps . . .
> sprinkles perfume . . .
> raises umbrellas, flags and banners . . .
> at a shrine of a Buddha.[137]

Clearly, all forms of veneration and gift-offering at the shrine of a Buddha, of which a stūpa with his relics is a perfect example, are precisely appropriate for *prasāda*.

The fundamental point here is that the very idea (including the thought) and especially the sight of a stūpa is meant to bring *prasāda* to mind.[138] This in turn generates the impulse to *dāna* of the material kind,[139] which then gives rise to great potential karmic benefits. Of these the gift of fearlessness, *abhāya*, is one, arising through confrontation with the Buddha images of the stūpa itself and enabling the purity of mind to take in the Buddha's *dhamma* as presented by the monument. This pattern, which needs some extrapolation from a variety of texts and is not expressed directly in the rather terse references to *abhayadāna* in the range of commentators, is essential to the deep structure of the ideology of *dāna*, on which the site's imagery and epigraphy (let alone the material bases for its construction) depend.

The final element in the Mahāyāna exploration of *dāna* is the subjection of the gift, the donor and the beneficiary to a sustained analytic critique from the point of view of emptiness (*sunyata*). The *Mahāprajñāpāramitāśāstra*, appropriately for a text that attributes itself to Nāgārjuna, argues for the non-existence of the donated thing, the donor and the recipient.[140] It follows this with an analysis of the non-existence of self (*ātman*) that cannot certainly be established as permanent or transient, self-dependent or not self-dependent, active or inactive, material or immaterial or having any other characteristics.[141] As the fourth-century treatise *On the Generating of the Bodhi Resolve Sūtra* puts it: 'When the bodhisattva-*mahasattva* cultivates giving, he does not perceive the existence of any material wealth, of any benefactor or of any recipient. This is because they are devoid of any inherently existent characteristic signs.'[142]

Or, in the words of the *Pañcaviṃśatisāhasrikā prajñāpāramitā Sūtra*, the Perfection Wisdom in 25,000 verses: 'A Bodhisattva . . . has with regard to the gift no notion of a gift, with regard to the recipient no notion of a recipient, with regard to the donor no notion of a donor. And why? Because he cognizes all dharmas as empty of own-marks, and sees them as not really existing, not totally real.'[143] Since emptiness of intrinsic or inherent existence is understood by the *Prajñāpāramitā* tradition as the viewpoint of wisdom (*prajñā*), the sixth and final perfection in the Mahāyāna scheme, this is not surprising. The effect of emptying all the grounds of *dāna* as a triangulation of the thing given between donor and beneficiary is to universalize the practice of generosity as it is purified by the other *pāramitās* culminating in enlightenment itself: 'When a gift is given for the sake of attaining the state of a Buddha, and for the benefit of living beings, it is the gift of the Bodhisattvas . . . it is in this manner that generosity engenders the perfection of wisdom . . . The state of omniscience has its roots in generosity.'[144]

It should be said that the quality of universalism is not limited only to Mahāyāna models, since the perfections with *dāna* at their base are about the development of the Bodhisattva's mind and his attainment of Buddhahood in the Nikāya schools too. As Dhammapāla puts it: 'Giving and the other *pāramis*, accompanied by wisdom and compassion, are the requisites for the great enlightenment culminating in the attainment of Buddhahood.'[145] That enlightenment is universal: 'Always engaged in work promoting/ The welfare and happiness of all living beings'.[146] Its fruit is 'The glorious Dhamma-body [*dhammakaya*] radiant with its collection of infinite and boundless meritorious qualities.'[147]

Let us conclude by returning to the Amarāvatī inscriptions. In only a few examples does the expression of an aspiration or purpose of the donation survive, and it is likely such an aspiration was not given verbal form in many. In several cases, there is a reciprocity implication – a request for the accumulation of merit,[148] for the benefit of the donor's family or other persons,[149] or for long life. But in three cases, the aspiration is universal: 'for the benefit and happiness of all the beings in the world';[150] 'for the welfare and happiness of the whole world';[151] and (unfortunately the inscription is very fragmentary) 'for the . . . of all'.[152] These inscribed wishes emulate the range of *dāna* motivations explored by the commentaries, from the personal desire for merit or the benefit of one's kin in return for a dedication to a universal aspiration that eschews issues of instrumental exchange or personal benefit.[153] It is perhaps a cause for reflection that the last two appear on drum reliefs with images of the stūpa on them, themselves evoking a multiverse of mirroring emanations that may well be related to the Mahāyāna imaginary thinking of the *Gaṇḍavyūha Sūtra*. The pattern of aspiration for the well-being and happiness of all beings is repeated in inscriptions from Kanaganahalli, some as early as 120 CE,[154] and is known from a number of other sites in relation to Buddha images, including Mathurā.[155]

The emphasis on *dāna* in so many aspects of the stūpa's monumental presentation – from its very construction stone by donated stone and the inscriptional commemoration of those gifts to its narrative and visual subject-matter – evokes a powerful ideological thrust. It would be a strongly instrumentalist – even a cynical, and surely reductive – interpretation to argue that this is solely the monastic culture's visual and religious reassurance to those who sustained its material existence from the feeding of monks to the building of monastery complexes, including stūpas. Beyond the necessary pragmatics by which giving enabled the existence of a *saṅgha*, and the architectures within which it could flourish, *dāna* stands as the opening to the path of perfection and enlightenment defined by the Bodhisattva ideal across all the schools of early Indian Buddhism but perhaps especially and most universally emphasized in the traditions that ultimately became the Mahāyāna.[156]

In certain respects, the Amarāvatī inscriptions are typical of an epigraphic genre established especially at the monumental stūpas of ancient Buddhist India. The two best surviving monumental complexes of broadly the same period – usually, in fact, dated earlier than the bulk of the Amarāvatī materials, but on the same uncertain grounds – namely the stūpas of Sāncī and that of Bharhut, the remains of which are now in the Indian Museum in Kolkata, have even richer inscriptional remains. In many aspects, the epigraphic cultures of all these stūpas are very similar. Notably the formal model whereby an inscription concludes with the word *dāna(m)* characterizes the vast majority of the votive epigraphy of both Sāncī and Bharhut,[157] and many examples at Kanaganahalli,[158] but none of the relatively longer inscriptions from Nāgārjunakonda. In the great majority of examples where it appears, *dāna(m)* is the last word, closing the inscription as at Amarāvatī. Given the significance of *dāna* in relation to the Bodhisattva ideal, to the interpretative culture of the *jātaka* and *avadāna* traditions, as represented in the imagery of these monuments, and to the economics of Buddhist monasticism as well as stūpa construction, it is not surprising that these monuments advertise a similar ideological pattern to that at Amarāvatī.

On the other hand, the opening devotional invocation often found in the Amarāvatī inscriptions (*sidham* or *sidham namo bhagavato*) is never present in the more than eight hundred examples from Sāncī, or at Bharhut. It does, however, appear at Nāgārjunakonda and Kanaganahalli,[159] both sites within Amarāvatī's Krishna River remit of influence. Perhaps in Andhra Pradesh, the emphasis on devotion caused the act to be emphasized through writing. The sociology of donors is similar across these stūpa sites, with a diverse lay and monastic involvement that included gifts from women as well as men (but with rather more royal patronage at Nāgārjunakonda, especially from royal women, and at Kanaganahalli).[160]

In certain respects, however, the inscriptions of Amarāvatī are systematically and distinctively different from those of the other stūpas from which good epigraphic evidence survives. The differences include the almost complete lack of identifying labels for the subject-matter of the narrative reliefs at Amarāvatī (as at Sāncī), in contrast to rich provision of such materials at Bharhut and the recent find at Kanaganahalli.[161] This implies either that such labels were written in paint, or that there was an expectation of greater visual knowledge on the part of those imagined as the stūpa's principal audience, or that the monastic guardians of the site performed a significant exegetic role in interpreting its narratives and their meanings. Likewise, in contrast to Bharhut or Sāncī, the epigraphy of Amarāvatī (like Kanaganahalli) has an aspirational aspect, naming those to whom merit is to be offered, which may include all beings. Most distinctively – and in deep accord with the referential and reflective aesthetic of a site whose monuments are packed with images of itself or ideal stūpas like it – the Amarāvatī inscriptions reinforce the transferential dynamic whereby the act of *dāna* extends beyond the self to others (whether in a limited or infinite sense), the reflections of the stūpa extend into the kind of limitless multiverse implied by the *Gaṇḍavyūha Sūtra* and the aspirations of giving and the transfer of merit rise from oneself and one's family to 'the benefit and happiness of the whole world'.

Part II
Narrative Sculpture

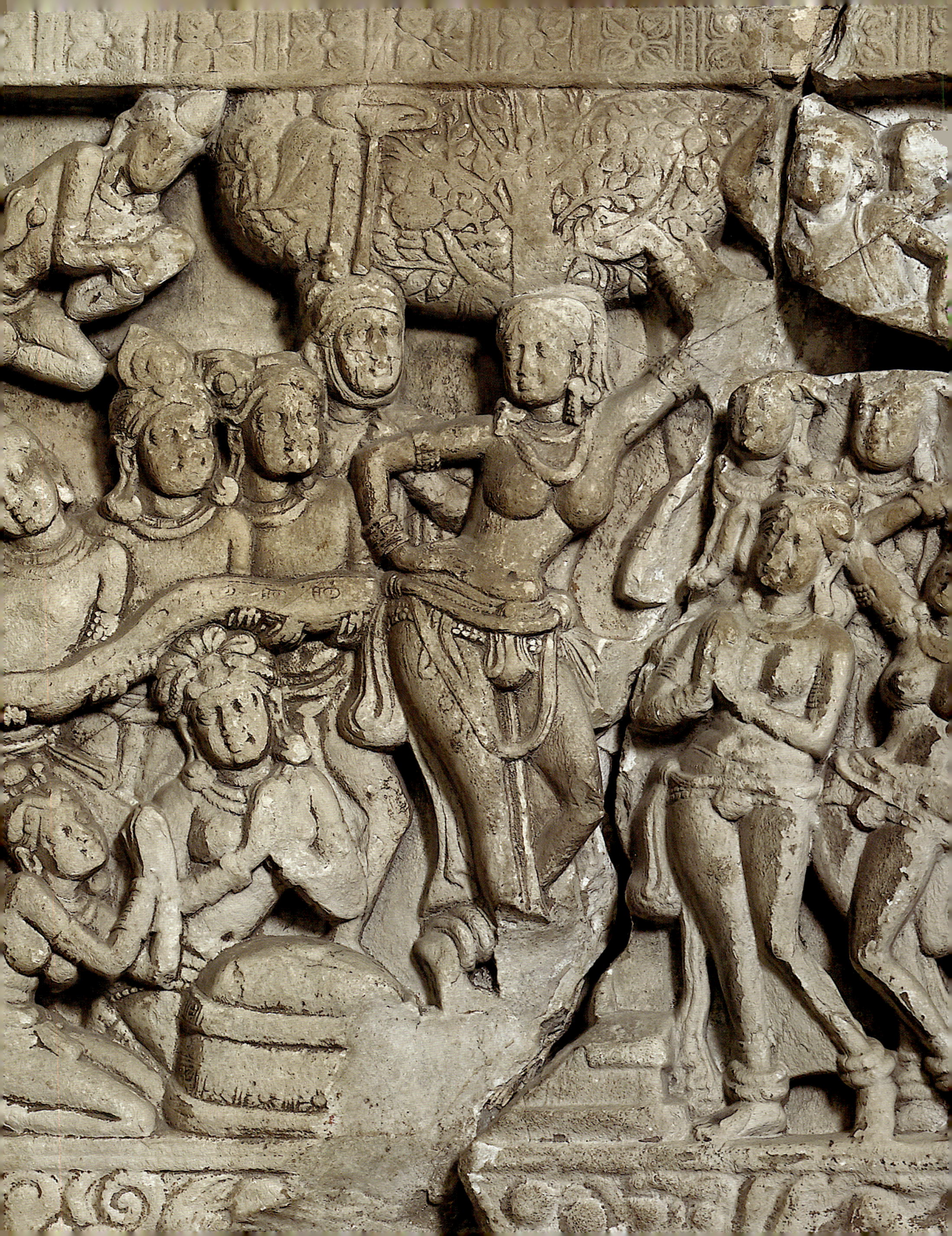

three

Visual Storytelling and the Vision of Karma

Amarāvatī is justly famous for the creativity of its narrative images. I am going to argue that it represents – alongside the range of rich narrative traditions from other sites of early Buddhist art in India – a remarkable employment of visual storytelling within an extraordinarily vibrant Buddhist culture that used stories (from oral retellings to elaborate formulations in written prose and verse to dramatic performance) for a series of explanatory and exegetic purposes. We have already seen something of the place of *jātaka* and *avadāna* models of tales about previous lives – narratives marshalled for all kinds of purposes by Buddhism in various sūtras, texts like the *Vinaya* (or monastic rules), the verses of the Elder monks and nuns (*Theragāthā* and *Therīgāthā*), the *Vimānavatthu* (the sixth book of the canonical Pāli *Khuddaka Nikāya*) and the many commentaries on these books and on others such as the *Dhammapāda*.[1] These traditions were richly exploited, perhaps with slightly varied emphases, in the different Nikāya schools of early Buddhism and also in the early Mahāyāna. They were also employed and developed by the Buddhist literary writers of India such as Aśvaghoṣa (an early exemplar of Kāvya poetics, who probably wrote in the second century CE in Sanskrit[2]), the fourth-century poet Āryaśūra (author of a collection of *jātakas* in verse known as the *Jātakamālā* or *Bodhisattvavadānamālā*[3]) and Cāttanār (the author of the final redaction of the remarkable Tamil verse novel *Manimēkalai*,[4] which perhaps belongs to the sixth century).[5] It is important to note that the visual renditions of these stories in early Buddhist art for the most part precede the textual traditions of their literary collection and retelling in the versions that have come down to us: the visual culture is not dependent on the surviving texts, but both belong within a manifold world of earlier (and now lost) orality, visuality and literacy.

51 Detail of illus. 54: intact coping slab (2.59 m in length), interior face with image of Queen Maya giving birth to the Bodhisattva, who emerges invisible from her side and immediately takes seven steps, indicated by the footprints on the cloth held by her attendants to the left.

My suggestion here is that the visual tradition of the great stūpas – and their particular narrative focus on past lives of the Bodhisattva as a process of development and fruition rising to the perfection of the Buddha's enlightenment – lies entirely within the larger frame of ancient Indian narrativity, using its many conventions (such as 'branch stories', 'comparison stories' and narratives explaining cause and effect) to portray the great process of causality, or karma, that leads to liberation.[6] It is striking that the many adventures of Manimēkalai, with reference to former births and later lives, end with her renunciation of the world as a nun in the last chapter,[7] but look forward to a future (male) life as the senior disciple of the Buddha-to-be.[8] The interplay of past and future, of the multiple causes of skilful action in past lives and their fruition in later ones, is fundamental to the epitomic exemplarity with which the architectural scaffolding of the Amarāvatī stūpa mounted its narrative account of the Bodhisattva path through relief sculpture.[9]

As mentioned in the Introduction, the nightmare of the site's archaeology – alongside that of so many Buddhist sites excavated in the colonial era – means that it is virtually impossible to reconstruct the original place of any one slab alongside another, and thus to do more than give a general evocation of the effect of the whole. The specific arrangement and discursive structure of narrative sequences between slabs cannot be attempted, at least in the frame of current knowledge and scholarly epistemologies,[10] although within single slabs some aspects of narrative discourse and its expectations can be examined. While this makes it impossible to build arguments about narrative construction through visual means in more than exceptional specific cases or to present a total picture of its narrative functions (in the way one might do with Trajan's Column, to cite a remarkable narrative structure of around the same time from a different culture[11]), a number of general issues regarding how Buddhist visual storytelling works at Amarāvatī can at least be clarified.

It is unfortunate that the recognition of narrative richness of the site's imagery has gone side by side with a critical assumption among too many commentators that the correct response to a visual narrative is to identify and retell the story,[12] rather than attempt a deeper or more analytic account of how that story may resonate with the tradition, or how storytelling functions visually (and specifically within the artistic dynamics of the monument). The exceptions here are Vidya Dehejia's deep and detailed account of discourse in early Buddhist art in general, which includes a chapter entitled 'The Maturity of Narrative', devoted to the two most extensively surviving Andhra stūpas, Amarāvatī and Nāgārjunakonda,[13] and Catherine Becker's approach to visuality, devotion and narrative in her readings of reliefs from the same two sites.[14] Becker shows effectively the interest in storytelling in the stūpas of ancient Andhra, as well as their concerns with visual engagement and viewer affect. Dehejia analyses a number of 'modes' of narrative in the ways early Buddhist art renders stories visible (such as 'monoscenic', 'continuous', 'sequential', 'synoptic', 'conflated', as well as 'narrative networks'[15]) and finds most of these exemplified in Amarāvatī.[16] Her emphasis – unlike mine – is on how an existing canonical tradition (whether oral or textual) is visualized and made concrete through formal representation in sculpture or painting; while she is squeamish about granting 'priority, even primacy', to written texts, nonetheless her model assumes 'viewers familiar with the literary prototypes'.[17] For her, the literary traditions for all of early Buddhist art belong to the Nikāya schools of early Buddhism, largely lost for most of these sects (her list includes Sarvāstivādins, Mahāsāṃghikas and Mūlasarvastivādins) but represented richly in the surviving Pāli canon of the Theravāda school.[18] In contrast to this approach, I emphasize the non-canonical commentarial traditions that grew alongside the canon as well as texts within the canon itself. Many of the Theravāda commentaries represent extremely ancient interpretative positions that go back to the earliest Buddhism and were indeed incorporated within canonical texts in other schools. These include famous stories (like that of the mad elephant Nālāgiri) that do not appear in the suttas but are related in the commentaries or the framing narratives within the *jātakas*. Following the thrust of earlier chapters in this book, where I have seen proto-Mahāyāna tendencies in both the visual culture and the Buddhology of the stūpa alongside and not in conflict with Nikāya attitudes, I will look at how narrativity in the visual culture of the site creates a model for imagining and visualizing the Bodhisattva.[19] One issue is the lack of interest among archaeologists and art historians in the Buddhological issues raised by the problems of narrative, which are profound and central to the visual culture.[20]

The reluctance to conduct a proper scholarly enquiry into how narrative works by the majority of those who have written on Amarāvatī is perhaps explained (but not excused) by the hopeless history of the archaeology of the site, as discussed in the Introduction, by which we really cannot tell whether any one surviving carved segment of stone stood side by side with any other. It is as if the monument in, say, the third century CE was a complete jigsaw of many thousands of carefully finished pieces, subsequently shattered and scattered, with only a few hundred (and those largely fragmentary) remaining; we may have collected those shards and have a general sense of their structure (what type went roughly at which bit of the three-dimensional whole) but we have little idea of how to fit them together piece by piece. Only in those cases where a narrative flow of several episodes or stories can be seen in a single block can we begin to tell the story of visual and thematic contiguities. Hence one can see how determining which story is the subject represented on any given slab appears a triumph of analysis; particularly when so many of the subjects of the surviving sculptures remain obscure.[21]

Dehejia is quite right in stating that the discursive system of Buddhist narrative builds on a Nikāya model of *jātakas* and narratives of the Buddha's life – although, of course, we should note that the entire Nikāya tradition was accepted within the Mahāyāna. But what the stūpa does crucially is to emphasize at least two levels or dimensions of narrative: the story of the Buddha's last life (itself divided, as we shall see, by the moment of enlightenment into the 'not-so-remote' and 'proximate' epochs) and the range of stories of his former lives. These are the *jātakas* – the previous lives of the Bodhisattva who became Gautama – rather than other kinds of past lives or former connection narratives of other beings, known as *avadānas* or *pūrvayoga*.[22] By placing these levels of narrative in dialogue and juxtaposition, the stūpa's art weaves a complex and visible picture of the Bodhisattva's journey to being the Buddha he would become, of the Buddha's dependence – despite being in his own right a fully liberated being – on the Bodhisattva path. The interdependence of these narratives, of Gautama's Buddhahood on a process that began with Sumedha's Bodhisattva vow, has a resonance with the visual logic of interdependent reflections in the drum reliefs representing stūpas. As we have seen in Chapter Two, the Bodhisattva path and the multiple *jātaka* tales are themselves demonstrations, indeed proof-texts in folkloristic form, of the acquisition of the perfections (whether the Theravāda's ten *pāramīs* or the Mahāyāna's six *pāramitās*) whose fulfilment *is* Buddhahood. It is true that the visual material focuses only on Gautama and his previous lives, but in its stress on the Bodhisattva path, it opens the way to a potentially proto-Mahāyāna vision and interpretation very much in concert with the sense that many major developments in early Mahāyāna thought and writing took place in the supportive context of Mahāsāṃghika monasteries in Andhra Pradesh.

TIME

I want to begin here by contesting the universal assumption in the scholarly literature on early Buddhist art that the overwhelming narrative thrust of the sculptures at Amarāvatī and other stūpas is in only two directions: the final life of the Buddha (that is, his early existence as Bodhisattva, including his descent from the Tuṣita Heaven, birth and departure from the palace, via his enlightenment and teaching and to his death and the worship of various relics); and his many earlier lives as Bodhisattva.[23] This distinction has been made according to modern models of thought, but it needs to be redefined according to the tripartite pattern offered implicitly by the mainly Sanskrit *Mahāvastu* (compiled between the second century BCE and the sixth century CE), a text belonging to the Mahāsāṃghika school, which is likely to have been predominant in Andhra.[24] It is also offered explicitly in the introduction to the Pāli collection of *jātakas*, the *Nidānakathā*, whose date is uncertain,[25] but is related to other early biographical traditions extant in the exposition of the *Vinaya*.[26] This model of a distant epoch (*dūre-nidāna*), an intermediate epoch (*avidūre-nidāna*) and a proximate epoch (*santike-nidāna*)[27] offers a much more contextually and conceptually appropriate paradigm for understanding narrative and biography as well as the past and issues of causality in early Indian Buddhism. It should be said that the meaning of the Pāli *nidāna* (usually translated as 'epoch' or 'antecedent' in the context of the Buddha's previous lives[28]) is more subtle than just temporal. According to the Pāli dictionary, the word means 'cause, ground; underlying and determining factor; antecedent; occasion' as well as a preamble or introduction that establishes occasion, setting or context.[29] The *Mahānidāna Sutta*, which immediately precedes the *Mahāparinibbāna Sutta* in the *Dīgha Nikāya*,[30] is the great discourse on 'cause'; and clearly the word *nidāna* and the concepts implied by it within early Buddhism have the sense of a complex layering that includes implications not only of temporal progression but of origins, determining factors, causes and underlying karmic processes.[31]

Here is how Buddhadatta's perhaps fifth-century commentary on the *Buddhavaṃsa* (which appears to have been written in southern India[32]), known as the *Madhuratthavilāsinī*, describes the three *nidānas* that structure the *Nidānakathā*:

> The remote antecedent [*dūrenidānam*], the not-so-remote antecedent [*avidūrenidānam*], the proximate antecedent [*santikenidānam*] . . . Herein the demarcation of these antecedents must be understood from the beginning . . . After the Great Being had made his resolve at the feet of Dīpaṅkara of the Ten Powers till the time when he deceased from his individuality as Vessantara and was reborn in the Tuśita-abode, the course of existence is spoken of as the remote antecedent. After his decease from the Tuśita-abode till the attainment of omniscience on the dais round the Tree of Awakening, the course of existence is spoken of as the not-so-remote antecedent. When it is said 'At one time the Lord was staying in Anāthapindika's Park in the Jeta Grove near Sārvatthi', and 'He was staying at the squirrels' feeding-ground in the Bamboo Grove near Rājagaha', and 'He was staying in the Hall of the Gabled House in the Great Grove near Vesālī', in the interval between the enlightenment on the dais round the Tree of Awakening till the time when he was on the couch of the final nibbana, wherever the Lord stayed that is to be understood as the proximate antecedent.[33]

To this trio of antecedents must effectively be added a fourth epoch concerning the world after the *parinibbana*, when the Buddha passed away from this world never again to be reincarnated, including representations of relic worship and later devotion.[34]

The first element of the *Nidānakathā* structure – former lives of the remote antecedent – are recorded in the Pāli tradition in a collection of 547 *jātaka* tales that were edited in the late nineteenth century and translated into English and German in the last years of the nineteenth and the beginning of the twentieth centuries.[35] This has become the standard reference for modern scholarship, but it is profoundly reductive of a genre of what might be called 'past lives and past karmic connections' that includes many other kinds of texts, such as *pubbayoga* (*pūrvayoga* in Sanskrit), *apadāna*, *nidāna* and *bhūtapubbaṃ* narratives as well as *jātakas*, with different recensions in all the Nikāya schools (none that survive in their original other than Theravāda), as well as a vast series of generally less well-known Mahāyāna versions of all these forms, surviving in a series of languages as well as Sanskrit.[36] It is often the case that the visual traditions have earlier versions of these stories than the surviving texts, an issue with significant implications for Buddhology, which has only recently begun to be taken on board.[37] One substantial difference between the visual materials and the *jātaka* texts, for example, is that while the *jātakas* – with their main story situated in the remote epoch and their frame story in the proximate epoch (as a narrative told by the Buddha to illustrate the causes of, or give teaching in relation to, a current issue) – deal only with two of the three epochs, the visual imagery offers a much more complex temporal, commentarial and exegetic interplay between all three, without explicit guidance as to how to interpret the connections made by juxtaposition of stories and a great deal of openness for viewers to create meaning.

Notably, as we saw in the earlier discussion of *dāna*, early commentary on the narratives of the *jātaka* stories in particular associated them with the acquisition of specific qualities or attainments along the Bodhisattva path,[38] especially the *pāramīs* (perfections).[39] Their exemplary juxtaposition through visual epitome in the relief art of the stūpas as well as in painting at Ajanta is a technique that uses allusion to more than one story to evoke a particular take on one or several of these qualities;[40] and this may be described as one of the principal Buddhological functions of Buddhist art. That take is especially subtle given the tripartite range of antecedents in play and the model of developing fruition to spiritual perfection. That is, the stories represent karmic seeds, origins or ripenings that give rise to the development of perfections, or the elimination of defilements, in a being across lifetimes – they are not sequential narratives in the usual sense. Questions of ethics are 'thought through' within the Buddhist tradition (especially in the commentaries and the *Vinaya* as well as in the collections of stories) by using folkloric models of storytelling.[41] Alternation between points of view (depending on the actors within stories, and on the use of first- or third-person narratives) enables a rich presentation of causality, psychology and the complexities of karma.[42] Crucially, such stories serve as models capable of imitation by other human beings beyond the Bodhisattva himself;[43] indeed, they are calls to imitation and hence to the path of self-perfection in the devotee.

The issue of self-perfection ties the ethical and karmic approaches to the antecedents to meditation practices, especially in the group of contemplations known as *Buddhānussati* in Pāli and *Buddhānusmṛti* in Sanskrit, meaning 'recollections of the Buddha'.[44] These typically included contemplation of his image from at least the second century CE,[45] precisely the period of the great Indian stūpas. In Buddhaghosa's extensive account of *Buddhānussati* in his great fifth-century compendium of meditation practices drawing on much earlier traditions, the *Visuddhimagga* (Path of Purification), recollection of the Buddha includes reflection on the Bodhisattva's past lives and notably Sumedha's vow in the presence of Dīpaṅkara. Buddhaghosa writes: 'he has rightly gone from the time of [making his resolution] at the feet of Dīpaṅkara up till the enlightenment session, by working for the welfare and happiness of the whole world through the fulfilling of the thirty perfections and through following the right way without deviating towards either of the two extremes'.[46] The devotee thus visualizes the Bodhisattva's practice over immense periods of time and innumerable lifetimes as striving for the perfections (each of the ten *pāramīs* of the Theravāda in its initial, developed and supreme form) while driven by compassion for living beings and holding to the middle way.

In the earlier compendium known as the *Vimuttimagga* (Path of Freedom), attributed to Upatissa and certainly used by Buddhaghosa, but which now only survives in Chinese and Tibetan translation,[47] reflection on the Bodhisattva's previous lives 'during twenty incalculable aeons from his first aspiration to his last birth' is more extensive and carefully set out. The text specifies recollecting each perfection through a particular exemplary and explicitly named *jātaka* life that embodies that perfection's attainment.[48] That is, bringing the image of that life to mind is a means of evoking the particular *pāramī* in the devotee, effectively of the practitioner developing the perfection themself. For instance, the story of the Bodhisattva as Sasa the hare is invoked for the perfection of *dāna*, a narrative depicted at Amarāvatī and discussed later in this chapter (see illus. 57).[49] Since the *Vimuttimagga* was produced before Buddhaghosa's *Visuddhimagga* – which means at the latest in the fourth century and perhaps around the period that the stūpa was being completed[50] – and since it certainly reflects earlier as well as current attitudes and practices at the time of its writing, its meditative recollections in relation to the *jātaka* narratives are highly resonant with how contemplative practice in relation to the imagery at the site might have worked.[51] Notably, in relation to art, in the *Ekottarāgama* (III.1) – originally a Sanskrit work, translated into Chinese in the fourth century – the practitioner is charged to 'contemplate the image of the Tathāgata without taking his eyes off it'.[52] The effects of such recollection, according to Upatissa (or at least his Chinese translator), are that persons who recollect the Buddha become themselves as 'worthy of contemplation as a Buddha image house'.[53] This obscure formulation allows the possibility of the devotee as being like both a Buddha image and a stūpa, as is explicitly claimed by Buddhaghosa, who writes: 'And his body, due to the recollection of the Buddha's special qualities inhabiting it, becomes as worthy of veneration as a stūpa shrine-house.'[54]

The visual tradition across early Buddhist sculpture from the stūpas of Gandhāra, the north of India and Andhra, and in the cave paintings of Ajanta adds the power of visual contemplation to the meditative culture of recollection. Moreover, it recasts *Buddhānussati* by way of an episodic epitome of exemplary narratives, which brings the chance to create new interpretations and commentaries by juxtaposition – whether of *jātaka* stories from the remote antecedent or of events that appear in different antecedents.[55]

On the one hand, the treble narrative structure of the Buddha's teaching mission, his final life as a Bodhisattva before the enlightenment and the Bodhisattva's many previous lives can be seen as the single biography of one being (the man who, as Sumedha from Amarāvatī, took the Bodhisattva vow aeons ago and, after many lives in many forms ending with that as Prince Vessantara, became Prince Siddhārtha and Śākyamuni Buddha in his last life), down to the distribution and worship of his relics. These antecedents effectively form the decoration of the monumental reliquary in which the continuance of that life through the living presence of his relics within the stūpa is vouchsafed to believers – and it is worth noting here that the *Buddhavaṃsa* text ends with an account of the distribution of Gautama's relics 'out of compassion for breathing things'.[56] On the other hand, that structure may be thought of as the celebration of the living relics through the frame of the triple antecedents – especially the life of the Buddha (whose remains they are) and of the Bodhisattva he was in his last rebirth until he became enlightened. This 'final life' story is told both in the symbolic reiteration of key scenes like the Great Departure, the enlightenment and the First Sermon, and in more extended narrative form (as we saw in Chapter One in relation to the great miniature stūpa slab in the Government Museum in Chennai); with both these visual approaches embedded in a series of vignettes that evoke the multiple earlier lives of the Bodhisattva. In fact, we are hardly offered continuous narratives at all. The various framing forms in which narrative themes are carved (lozenges and medallions in the railing uprights, roundels in the railing crossbars, friezes with architectural features distinguishing one story from the next in copings and drum and dome reliefs) are all discrete panels (as are the square and round slabs depicted on the miniature stūpas in relief from the drum, which are our best guide to any form of programmatic arrangement of the visual narratives). Each such panel points to one of the three antecedents.

SEQUENTIAL AND THEMATIC STORYTELLING: STRATEGIES OF EPISODIC EXEMPLARITY AND VISUAL JUXTAPOSITION

The narrative art of Amarāvatī functions through typical or essentializing episodes that evoke a larger story, and these episodes are strung together in a model of juxtaposition that enables them to reflect on each other.[57] This differs from the continuous narratives found in some early Buddhist sculpture – for example, on some of the gateway architraves at Sāñcī (as in the scenes of the Great Departure on the outer face of the east *toraṇa*).[58] Those

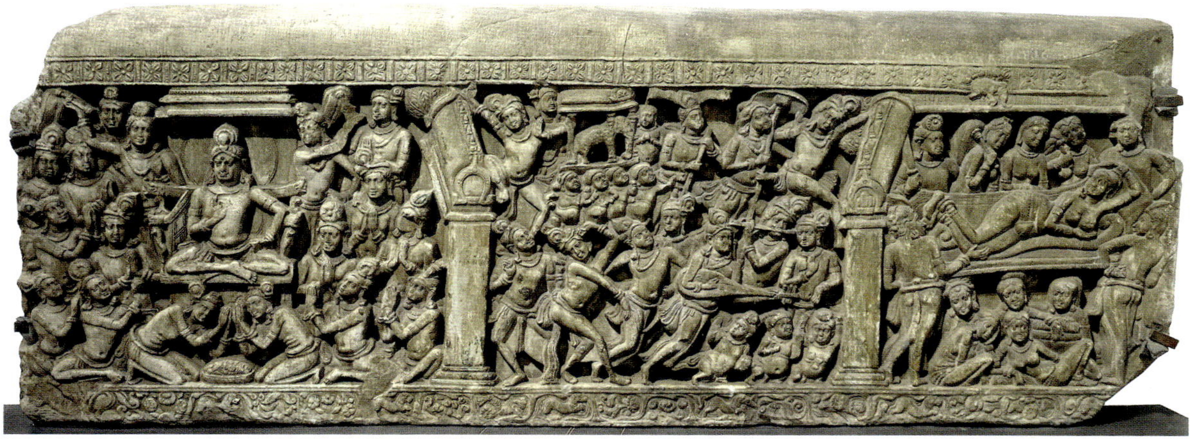

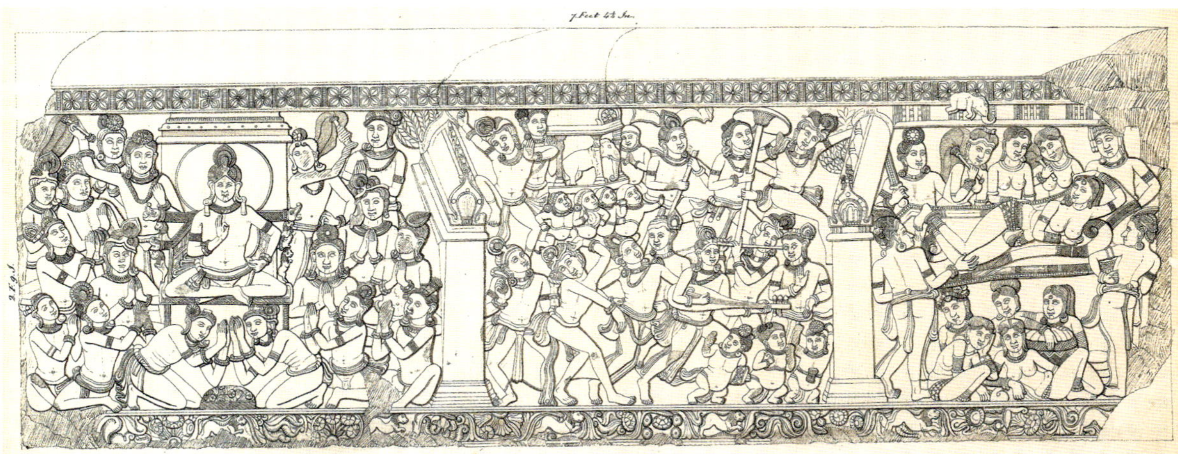

52 Intact coping slab (2.25 m in length), interior face in exceptional condition, with scenes of the Bodhisattva's journey from the Tuśita Heaven to his conception in his final lifetime.

53 Drawing of illus. 52 from MacKenzie's Album WD1061, folio 83. Made by Nujibulla, 22 April 1819.

essentializing vignettes may stress particular facets to focalize a continuous narrative around key images or iconographies, as is the case with the elephant theme in the story of the Buddha and Nālāgiri, discussed later in this chapter (see illus. 56, 59, 60 and 71). Since so much of Buddhist thinking works through similes and metaphors,[59] one way in which the visual impact of a large-scale monument such as a stūpa with multiple images operates on its viewers is to read across stories by means of chosen visual subjects – for instance, the depiction of elephants in a range of narratives beyond that of Nālāgiri (whether specific storylines,[60] or elephants in acts of veneration,[61] as in illus. 14 at the top and 44).[62] These may break down the temporal structure through epochs and antecedents, allowing different interpretative lines to different viewers. So, for example, in Dhammapāla's commentary on the *Udāna*,[63] the suttas making up the third book of the Pāli *Khuddaka Nikāya*, the Bodhisattva's previous relations with elephants in earlier lifetimes are presented as a karmic link to the Nālāgiri story.[64]

But the episodic model also enables sequential segments of narratives to be juxtaposed in order to tell a given and coherent story.[65] If we took the processual movement of the devotee through the stūpa, circumambulating the monument to her right along the processional path, then we would expect the narratives on horizontal friezes to unfold from right to left on the drum but from left to right on the coping of the inner rail. This is indeed the case, some of the time.[66] For example, take the great coping block found by Mackenzie in 1819, drawn by his draughtsmen, and now still in excellent condition in the Indian Museum in Kolkata, with an upper border of four-petalled flowers and a lower border mix of running lions, lotuses and vegetation (illus. 52 and 53). The slab has the story of the descent from the Tuṣita Heaven – the opening of the not-so-remote antecedent – in three episodes, separated by walls capped with arched gables tapered to a point.[67] This is the interior coping of the railing and moves from left to right. The left-hand scene shows the Bodhisattva frontally enthroned in a teaching gesture in the Tuṣita Heaven, with the gods arranged symmetrically around him; this appears to represent the scene described in *Nidānakathā* 47–9 and *Madhuratthavilāsinī* XXVI.25.272–3, where the gods approach the Bodhisattva, now that he has attained the ten perfections, to request that he take final rebirth and become a Buddha.[68]

The central image has a procession of deities including dwarfs, parasol bearers, celestial musicians and dancers bearing him in the form of an elephant on a litter with four pillars. Again, this appears to visualize the passages in *Nidānakathā* 49–50 and *Madhuratthavilāsinī* XXVI.25.273–4 where, having determined that 'it is time to become a Buddha,' the Bodhisattva enters the 'Nandana Gardens in the city of Tuśita in the company of the deities of Tuśita'.[69] The scene to the right shows his mother, Queen Māyā, reclining on her couch and dreaming. In her dream, according to *Nidānakathā* 50, she sees the 'four Guardian deities of the world', the four male figures at each corner of the couch, who take her to a lake in the Himalayas where she is bathed, anointed by female attendants and laid on a heavenly bed with her head to the east.[70] The Bodhisattva 'in the form of a lordly white elephant' comes upon her from the north. In the image, she looks up at the descending elephant, carved into the framing pattern that rims the upper border of the slab. The disposition of the slab, with the queen lying left to right and the elephant above, effectively becomes a topography with Māyā's head at the right to the east and the upper part of the panel as the north. It is striking that the left-hand scene is entirely male, with the Bodhisattva central and upright, while the right-hand scene to which the narrative moves is largely female, with Queen Māyā central and horizontal. In all the scenes, the key figure – the Bodhisattva in human form to the left, the Bodhisattva in elephant form in the middle and the queen on the right – is framed by or elevated on furniture: a throne, a litter, a couch. In the central scene the Bodhisattva travels in a roofed

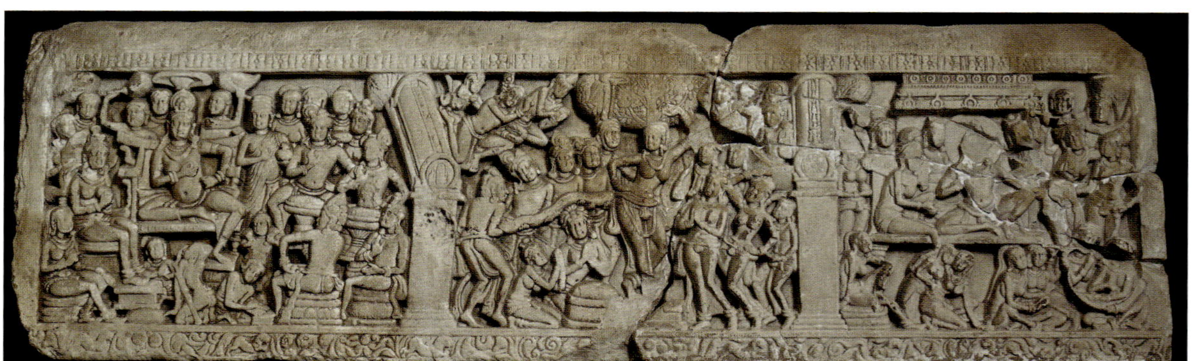

54 Intact coping slab (2.59 m in length), interior face in good condition but with significant damage to the right-hand scene. Images of the queen retelling her dream (left), the Bodhisattva's birth (centre) and Prince Siddhārtha in the royal harem (right). Perhaps originally the slab adjacent to illus. 52.

palanquin, while in the right-hand scene the queen is borne to the mountains on an open bed.

Likewise, one might take the beautifully executed slab in the British Museum with three scenes separated by walls topped by arched gables, which is also bordered with four-petalled flowers at the top and a mix of running lions, lotuses and vegetation at the bottom (illus. 54).[71] Given the formal and stylistic similarities to the Kolkata slab, and the fact that the narrative follows on, it is not impossible that it was originally contiguous and by the same artist.[72] On the left-hand scene, Queen Māyā is seated on a high chair to the left surrounded by attendants recounting her dream of the descent of the white elephant before the Buddha's father, King Śuddhodana, in high turban, enthroned with a parasol above him, and surrounded by his court, or perhaps the 64 brahman soothsayers mentioned in *Nidānakathā* 50, to the right. In the central section, the queen stands in the classic 'three-bends' posture, grasping the *sāl* tree above her as she gives birth to the Bodhisattva from her side, as described in *Nidānakathā* 52 and *Madhuratthavilāsinī* XXVI.25.275. He is invisible except for the seven footsteps he takes immediately after his birth (*Nidānakathā* 53, *Madhuratthavilāsinī* XXVI.25.275), which are represented as footprints on the swaddling cloth held up by her attendants to the left. The final scene, which has suffered significant damage, has the Bodhisattva in the centre, seated on a long throne or bed, in his harem. He is with a female figure, perhaps his chief wife, Yasodharā, beneath a fine three-tiered canopy with arch-shaped gables and lotus blossom roundels (the narrative of how he comes to acquire palaces and wives at the age of sixteen is given at *Nidānakathā* 58 and *Madhuratthavilāsinī* XXVI.25.278–9). The pair are surrounded by musicians to the right and female attendants seated below, their disposition echoing, with variation, that of Śuddhodana and Māyā in the scene to the far left.

It is important to note that in both slabs the visual narratives do not depend on the texts that have come down to us, and may in fact represent an image-tradition independent of textual retellings. For example, in Māyā's famous dream of her conception of the Bodhisattva, he appears as a white elephant in all accounts. But there is no textual presentation of his passage to the Nandana Grove within the Tuṣita Heaven as an elephant, although this is how the visual tradition conceives the movement to his last conception. That iconography is repeated elsewhere at the site, for instance in a fragmentary rail pillar now in the Chennai Museum, where the upper lozenge shows the white elephant in an elaborate litter borne by dwarfs,[73] or in the far-right panel of the frieze decorating the miniature stūpa slab in Chennai discussed in Chapter One (illus. 27).[74]

Other friezes, however, particularly from the drum of the monument (which the viewer would have approached from the right), appear to operate on a centralized model, presenting their narrative from the sides to the middle of a given slab or sequence.[75] It should be emphasized that the subjects of many surviving friezes are not certain, which means we cannot determine the direction of their narrative thrust. But, in contrast to the pattern of sequential narrative just discussed, the model of placing visual episodes in contiguity also allows the juxtaposition of stories from different temporalities in the Bodhisattva's many lifetimes – placing particular *jātaka* traditions alongside each other and juxtaposing these (or events within these) against particular events in the Buddha's life. An excellent example of a drum frieze with a row of worn animal busts in the lower border, now in the British Museum, has three scenes separated by vertical lines of four lotus bosses in high relief (illus. 55).[76] This would have been placed above the drum panels depicting miniature stūpas, a little above eye level but likely quite visible to the naked eye, despite the detailed minutiae of the figures.

The central scene shows the Buddha, standing to the left with halo and robe and probably with Ānanda, his attendant, to the far left, taming the intoxicated elephant Nālāgiri (illus. 56).[77] On the right of the image, the elephant rushes out of the gate of the city of Rājgir, released by associates of the Buddha's evil cousin and enemy, Devadatta, crushing a person beneath its feet in its rampage and scattering a crowd of others who run towards the Buddha. But when it reaches the Buddha's

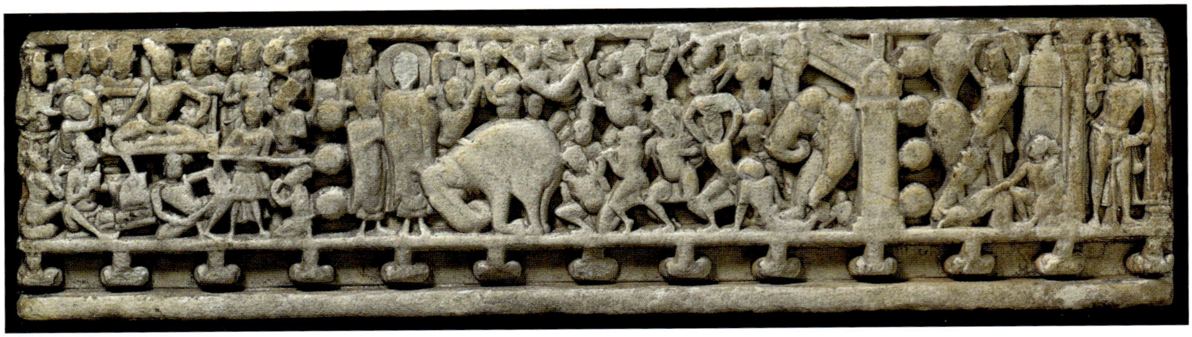

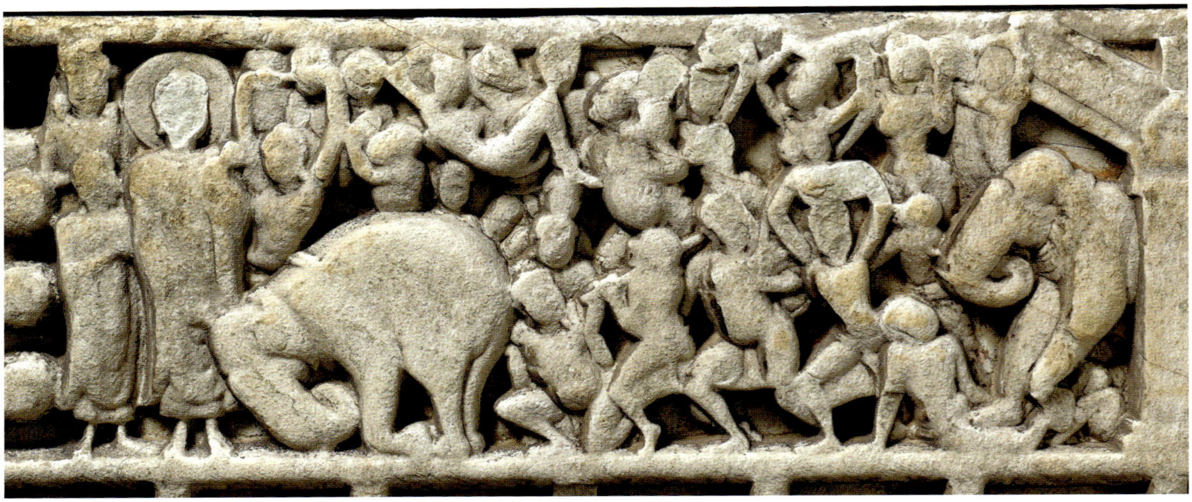

55 Abraded but intact drum frieze slab (1.44 m long) with three scenes.
56 Central scene of illus. 55 with the story of the Buddha and the elephant Nālāgiri.

presence, the elephant is tamed and bows before him. This scene is clearly read from right to left, following the circumambulatory passage of the viewer–devotee. It represents a famous story from a number of non-canonical traditions (that is, not from the suttas given by the Buddha), offers two moments within it – the elephant's charge and the act of taming with the animal depicted twice – but climaxes on a specific episode, namely the Buddha's action in banishing the madness. However, the story has a number of other elements excluded here (such as the malice of Devadatta, who is not shown) and more elements excluded but perhaps implicit when interpreted against its contiguity with the two *jātaka* scenes to either side; for example, the offers made by a number of the Buddha's disciples, including Sāriputta and eighty chief elders, to confront the wild animal, and especially that of Ānanda to sacrifice his life for the Buddha in order to allow him to escape.[78] In other words, what is depicted – and especially in its relation with the images to either side – requires the viewer (or at least some viewers) to know more of the story than is explicitly seen and to use this knowledge exegetically. Beyond the specific story, one might add, the model of elephant training as persistent metaphor for training the mind (in the case of this narrative, the extreme and crazed mind) is deep in the Buddhist tradition.[79]

To either side of Nālāgiri's madness are scenes not from the Buddha's life but from the *jātaka* tales of his former lives as Bodhisattva in the remote antecedent. The versions of these tales perhaps belong to a lost

Mahāsāṃghika tradition of the *jātakas*, which means they differ in a number of details from narratives surviving in either the Pāli Theravāda tradition or the Sanskrit *jātaka* stories later transmitted in Tibetan and Chinese.[80] The subject of the episode on the right is thought to be a representation of the *Sasa Jātaka*, in which the Bodhisattva is a wise hare called Sasa, whose generosity is tested by Sakka, the king of the gods, who disguises himself as a brahmin and asks for food (illus. 57).[81] The Bodhisattva's companions, a monkey, a jackal and an otter, all offer food of their own, but Sasa offers his own flesh to the brahmin. Sakka reveals himself, refuses the gift and honours the hare by painting his shape on the face of the moon. In the much-abraded frieze, it is possible the regal figure standing to the far right between two columns is Sakka observing the action, or it may be that this is intended to be some other subject. To the left of this is a country setting defined by trees and a rustic hut with pointed roof, with the hare at the lower centre leaping up to a seated figure, presumably the brahmin, ahead of the other animals (which are now very difficult to identify). Behind them is a standing figure with arms raised, perhaps Sakka revealing himself.

The subject on the left is a story associated with the Bodhisattva's incarnation as King Śibi in some versions and King Sarvamdāda (meaning 'all-giving') in others (illus. 58).[82] The *Sarvamdāda Avadāna* is not retold at length in the surviving Pāli tradition, but is preserved in the *Bodhisattvāvadānakalpalatā*, a long poem by the eleventh-century (non-Buddhist) Kashmiri

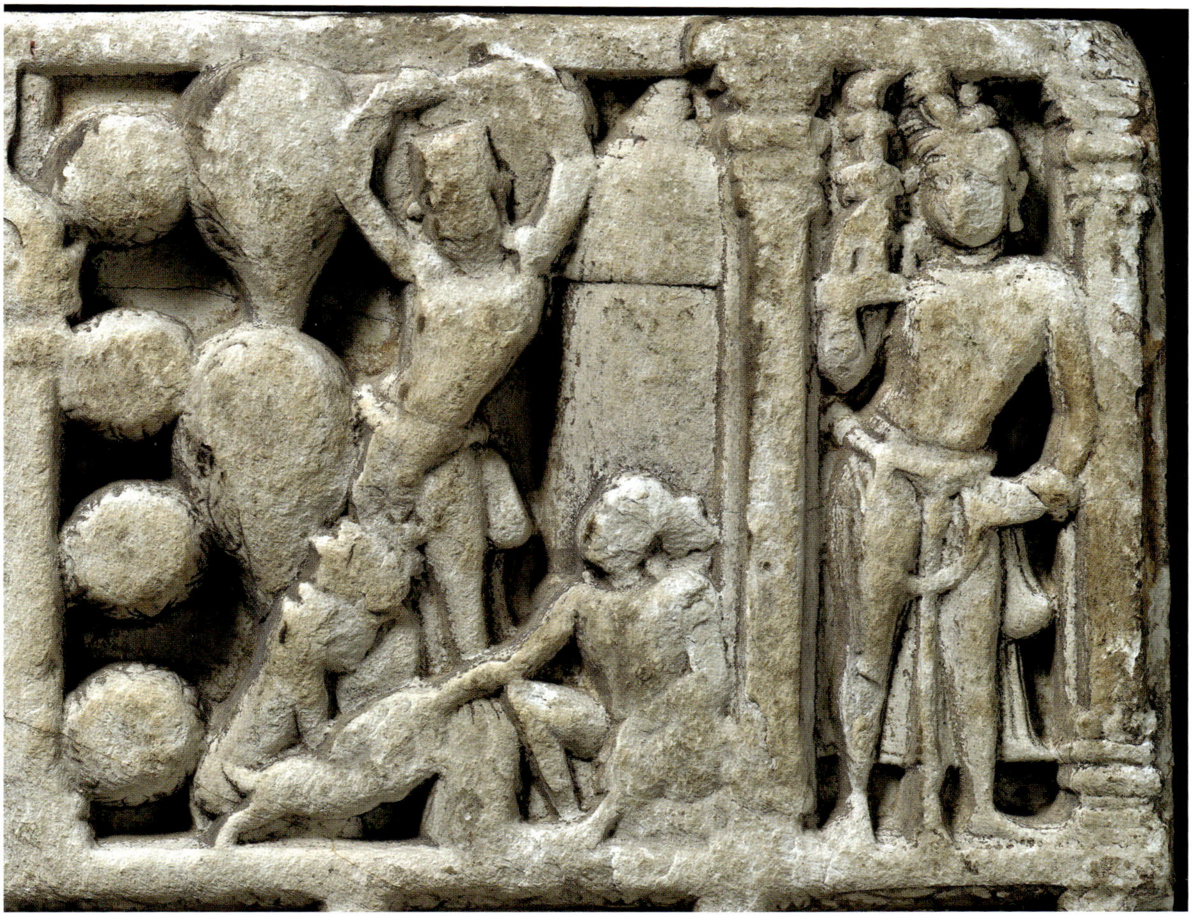

57 Right-hand scene of illus. 55 with the *Sasa Jātaka*.

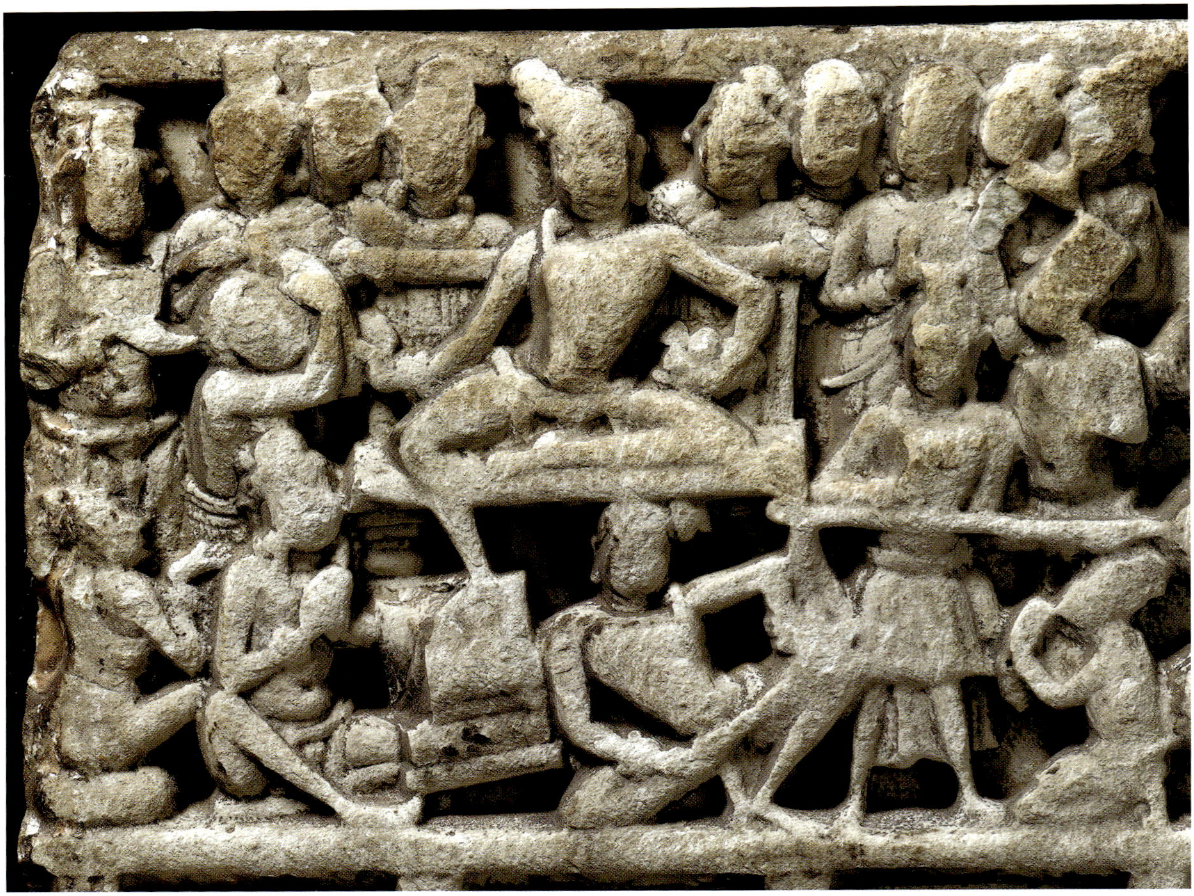

58 Left-hand scene of illus. 55 with the *Sarvamdāda Avādana*.

poet Ksemendra, which survives both in Sanskrit and in Tibetan.[83] In this story, the Bodhisattva in the form of the righteous king comes across a pigeon in terror, fleeing from a hunter, who is Sakka in disguise. The king agrees to ransom the bird from the hunter with his own flesh, cut from his legs and weighed against the weight of the pigeon. Asked if he has any regrets, the king replies: 'I have neither hesitation nor regret for my actions. By the truth of this may my body be restored,' and he is indeed restored to health. The tale is popular in representations in both Andhra Pradesh and elsewhere in early Buddhist Indian art,[84] with a series of other examples depicted in Amarāvatī itself.[85] In the image on the left of our slab, the king is seated on a high-backed throne, probably cradling the bird in his left hand (there is much damage); to the right is a standing figure with scales for weighing the Bodhisattva's flesh, and below the throne, beside the scales, the king is represented again, cutting the flesh from his left leg with a sword.

In this block from the drum frieze a story from the Buddha's life (in the proximate antecedent) is sandwiched by two episodes from previous lives, that is, the remote antecedent, both exemplifying exceptional *dāna* or generosity – the first perfection of the Bodhisattva path in both the Theravāda and Mahāyāna traditions. In both scenes the Buddha-to-be is offering his flesh, even his life, for the sake of other beings. In the centre is a miraculous scene from Buddha's own life that has an interesting thematic link with the two *jātaka* narratives of Sasa and Śibi/Sarvamdāda that flank it. First it is given as the framing story of another *jātaka* tale, the *Cullahamsa Jātaka*. That is, it relates to the *jātaka* tradition by giving the context in the Buddha's last lifetime for when he chose to tell a story of a former incarnation. In this case, the Nālāgiri episode is characterized by the Buddha's attendant, Ānanda, attempting to place himself between his master and the elephant to sacrifice his own life to save the Buddha. Three times the Buddha asks him to move, and three times Ānanda refuses so that the Buddha has to remove him by supernatural power before taming the elephant.[86] In honour of Ānanda's altruism, the Buddha tells the *Cullahamsa Jātaka*, in which he is Cittakūta, the king of the geese, and Ānanda is Sumukha, his chief captain.[87] The king-goose gets caught in a snare but Sumukha refuses to leave him, offering to give up his own life for his master. The fowler who set the trap is so entranced by this altruism that he frees the Bodhisattva. Thus, Buddhologically, all three episodes celebrate the act of *dāna* as the altruistic offer of one's own life or flesh to save another. But, while the acquisition of perfection through generosity by the Bodhisattva is the theme of both the Sasa and Sarvamdāda stories, it is the theme

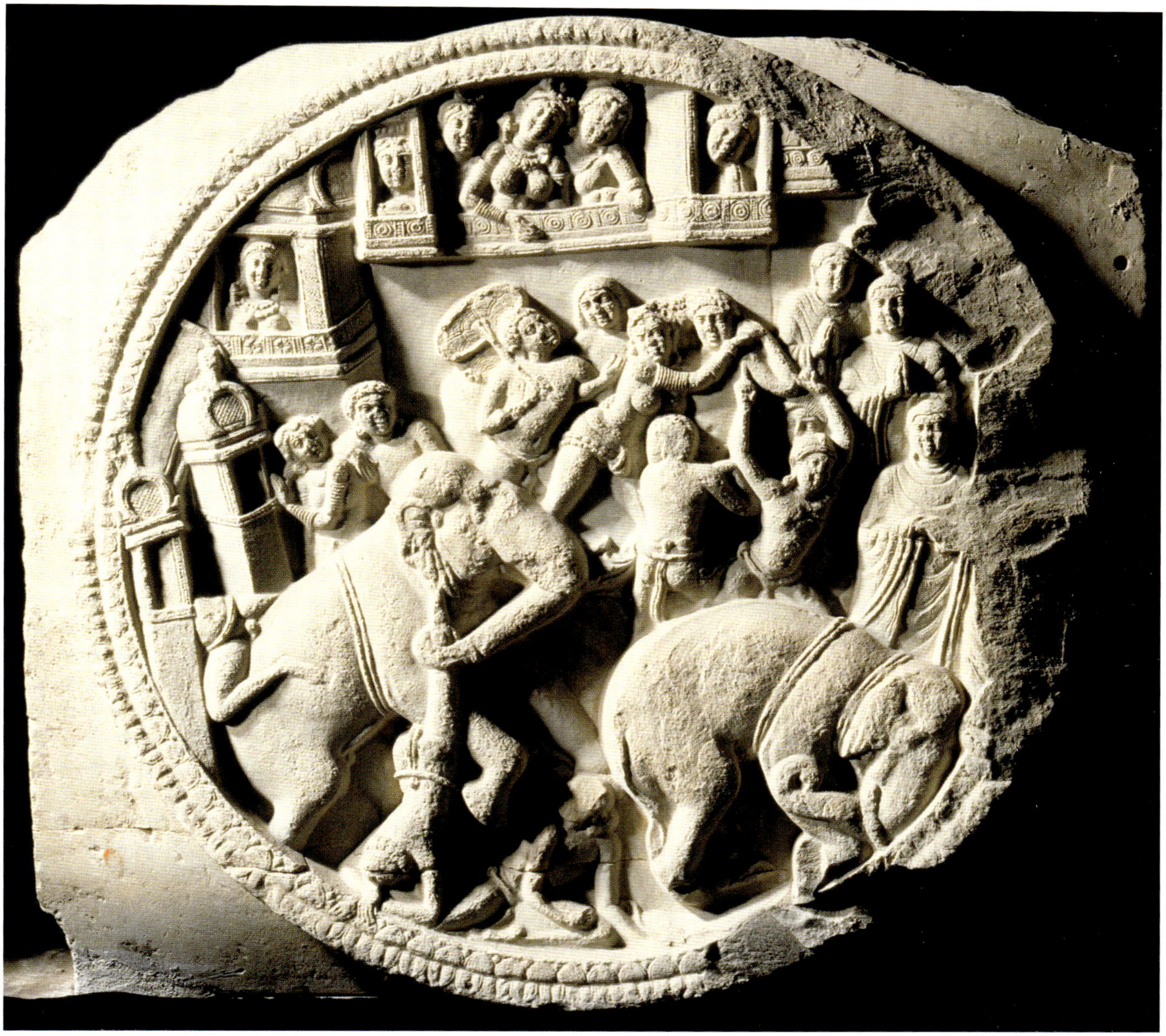

59 Crossbar medallion with the story of the Buddha and the elephant Nālāgiri.

of Ānanda's route to perfection in the Nālāgiri and Cullahamsa stories. In the Nālāgiri episode, the Buddha himself shows mastery of all the perfections in his defeat of the enraged elephant, beyond the compassion of Ānanda's self-sacrifice (which would only have led uselessly to his death). The slab thus uses the episodic model of narrative juxtaposition to illuminate Buddhist teaching about the Bodhisattva path as a process of perfecting that leads to a place beyond even the highest forms of *dāna*. It is also implicitly an image of Ānanda's imitation of the Bodhisattva's path to perfection and hence an encouragement to the viewer to follow these models. This account – achieved through the exegetic move of juxtaposing separate stories, ironically sandwiching a framing narrative between *jātakas* (rather than the other way around, as in the literary culture) – provides a unique spin on the theme. How exactly the doubling of figures in each of the scenes (Sakka as god and brahmin, the elephant twice and the repetition of Sarvamdāda) plays visually into all this is not clear.

It is striking that images of the Nālāgiri story appear again in several different instances in the surviving or attested sculptures from Amarāvatī: in miniature on the inner face of the gateway coping to the right in a relief stūpa from the drum in the British Museum,[88] as well as in several lost slabs attested through Colonel Mackenzie's drawings,[89] and in a railing crossbar medallion now in the Government Museum in Chennai (illus. 59).[90] This latter piece in particular is spectacular, with the elephant twice depicted (as in the drum frieze section just discussed) but this time rampaging towards the right, to be read in the left–right direction in which the pilgrim moved along the inner railing. In several of these cases, the Buddha is shown emblematically at the margin of the image as a flaming pillar crowned by a *trisula* rising from a lotus with *buddhapāda* at the base. (This element has flaked off in the damage to the right-hand side of the Chennai slab, but the flaming pillar can be seen in the miniature images from the British Museum drum slab and on the *āyaka* platform in Mackenzie's folio 35, illus. 60). One difference between these two depictions and the drum frieze panel

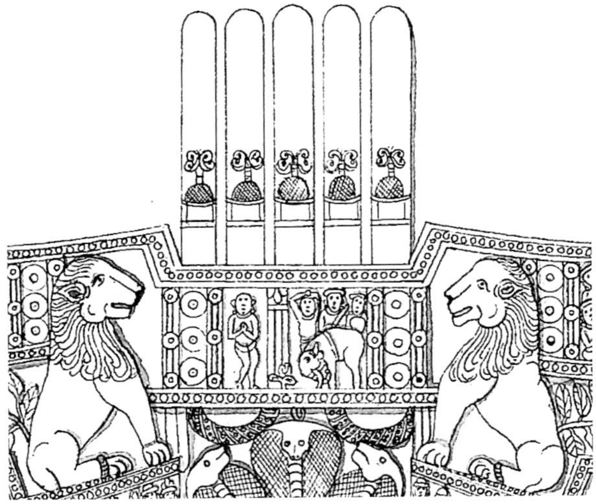

60 Detail of the *ayāka* platform in illus. 70, the drawing of a stūpa in MacKenzie's Album WD1061, folio 35.

is that they are both isolated elements, with no other immediately contiguous images on the same block, as in the frieze, and no possibility for reconstructing their visual context. In them, the emphasis is on the miraculous aspects of the Buddha's elephant-taming, and he is shown in a symbolic way, perhaps implying the *dharmakāya*, or his supra-human truth body, as the agent of the miracle. But in the drum frieze, the Buddha is embodied in the *rūpakāya* of his human form, the embodied form of his repeated incarnations as Bodhisattva (including in his last lifetime before the enlightenment) in which the perfections were worked out. Here the thematic visual thrust is arguably focused on a dialogue of perfection between embodied incarnations within specific lifetimes, rising to his ultimate human rebirth, in which all the perfections have been accomplished.[91] Buddhological issues, in other words, can be seen to determine iconographic choices around the Buddha's form, even in narrative scenes where the same choices are made about what element of the story to depict, as in the doubling of the elephant in the Chennai roundel and the British Museum drum frieze section.

This venture into visual Buddhology through comparative narratives in the context of a single, admittedly highly coherent, slab is unlikely to be based on a prior interpretative text, even if each of the stories is dependent on a folkloric (whether oral or written down) tradition known to the makers. It represents creative thinking with the materials of Buddhist scripture and folklore within the community of artists or their patrons, although it is not impossible that it borrows from traditions like *Nidānakathā* 45–7 or the *Cariyāpiṭaka*,[92] which categorized groups of *jātakas* by virtue of the perfection that their narrative showed its heroes developing. In this case, it is *dāna*: giving or generosity. But the frieze's juxtaposition of biographies is also a subtle merging of times, combining the chronology of the Buddha's own life with lives of the same being aeons ago and with life-forms beyond the human, which include the god Sakka and animals. It represents both the karma of the Bodhisattva's perfected generosity and its fruition in the Buddha's miraculously powerful, loving kindness in dealing with the elephant. That is, even on the relatively minuscule level of a single piece of carved revetment, questions of repetitive time, cosmic time and timelessness,[93] and multiple levels and kinds of beings, in addition to the complexities of causality, are in subtle play. They evoke the universal grandeur of the path to enlightenment across myriad lives that is challenged in the here-and-now of seeing the specific slab and visiting the stūpa in the life of any believing viewer or visiting devotee. That play of time is, of course, immensely magnified beyond any single piece of stone by the richness of the iconographic intermingling between the imagery of the Buddha's final life and the range of images of his many earlier lives. What is created is an interplay of temporalities and causalities much like the uses of typology in early Christian art, which also uses episodic reference to Old or New Testament narratives in contiguity and juxtaposition to make theological claims by visual means.[94]

IMBRICATING THE ANTECEDENTS

Once one grasps the distinction of the antecedents, one can appreciate the thematic function of intermingling images that allude to each of them in a single slab or element of the decoration. The parallel here to the textual traditions is the way the *jātakas* embed the story told (about a past life, in the remote antecedent, in a frame story located during the Buddha's teaching mission, in the proximate antecedent) or in the ways that the Mahāsāṃghika *Mahāvastu* mixes narratives across all three.

Take, for instance, a fine drum slab in the British Museum, which survives in near-complete form despite breakages and abrasion (illus. 61).[95] The miniature images in its decoration represent a microcosm of the ways narrative subjects are juxtaposed and interspersed across the stūpa. In this case (and unlike many others), not only do all the images of narrative reliefs survive, but the majority can be identified iconographically. The coping of the outer railing shows a right-to-left frieze of an elephant trampling human beings, followed by a man who seems to be fighting a beast to his left, on the side to the right of the entrance, and humans riding fantastic animals that are also trampling people on the side to the left. Above this imagery of a mythologized and conflictual *saṃsāra* on the outside of the stūpa's perimeter are the relief panels of the inner monument that can be glimpsed over the railing.

The lower line of reliefs on the drum shows six slabs, two obscured by the lions that sit atop the gateway and one by the summit of the stepped pillar bearing a stūpa topped with umbrellas, which is represented as standing within the precinct behind the railing (illus. 62). It is striking that a real effort has been made to offer an intimation of narrative relief subjects behind images of statuary and the pillar. From right to left (the direction of the coping imagery and of the viewer's approach, if meeting this panel while circumambulating the stūpa) the themes of this frieze are, first and behind the pillar, what has been identified as a scene from the *Vessantara-Jātaka* and a second scene from the same story after it.[96] These refer to the Bodhisattva, in his last human life before the one in which he becomes Buddha, giving away all – both his wife and his children – as acts of supreme generosity. Next, behind the lion facing left and discernible just below the lion's chin, is the First Sermon represented as a *dharmacakra* over a low throne. In the *āyaka*

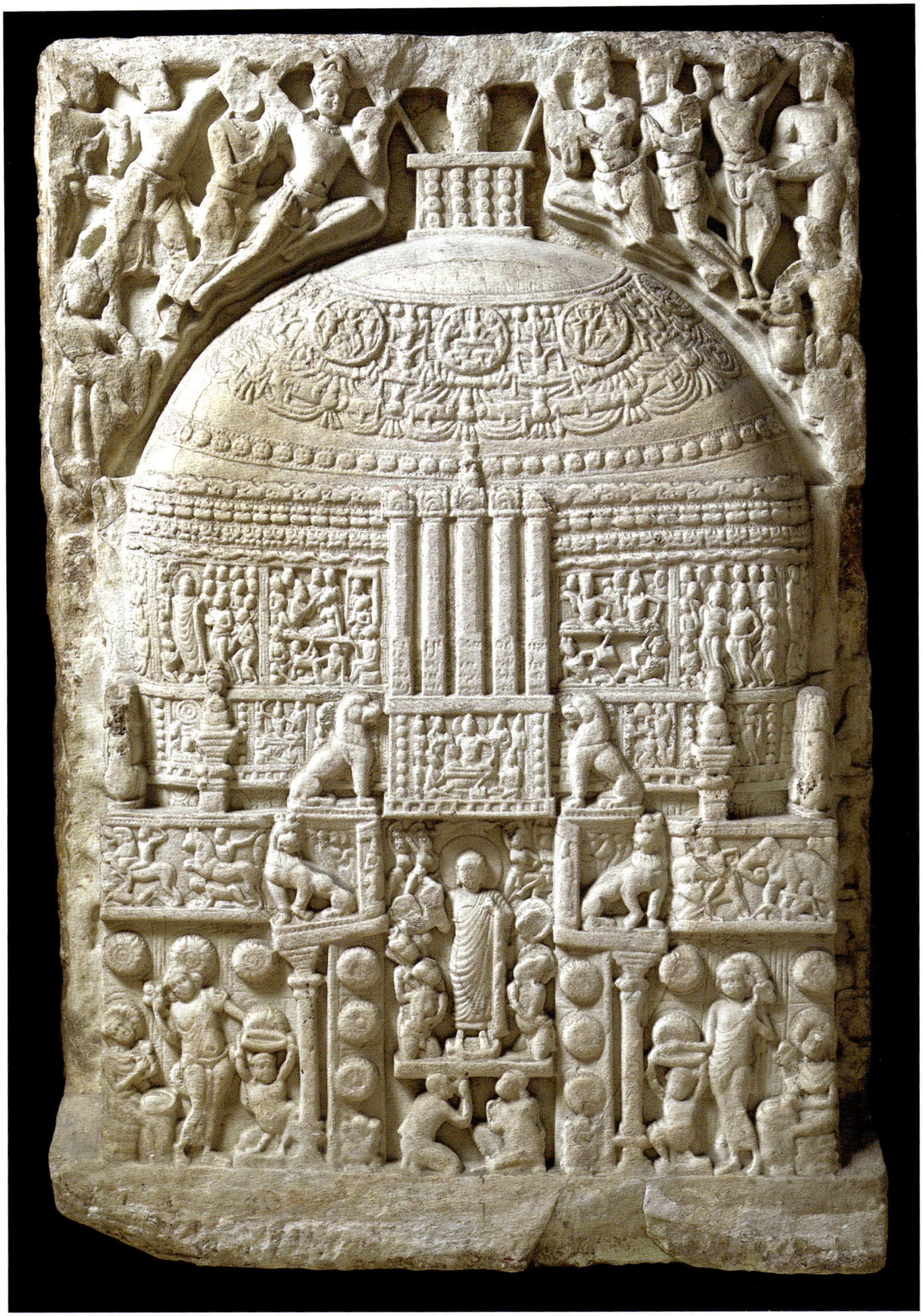

61 Intact but abraded drum slab showing a view of a stūpa through a gateway and from outside its railings (1.37 × 0.86 m).

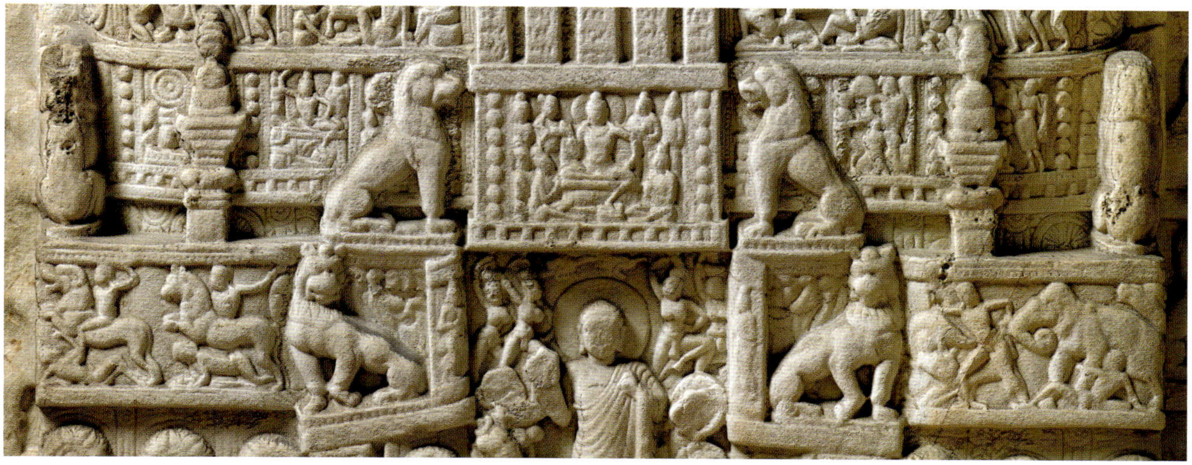

62 Detail of illus. 61 showing the rail coping and lower dome panels including the *ayāka* platform.

platform panel at the same level and above the standing figure in the main entrance, which appears to represent the Bodhisattva (in form identical to the Buddha) as he crosses the Nairañjanā River, is the Bodhisattva in the Tuṣita Heaven in the *abhāya mudrā*, being exhorted by the devas to take his final rebirth. Behind the lion on the left is the enlightenment, in which the edge of the Bodhi treetop is visible. To the left of this is an image of a prince enthroned with his right hand raised, potentially the Bodhisattva in his final birth or perhaps a figure from one of the *jātakas*. On the far left is the First Sermon again, as a *dharmacakra* over an empty throne. This tier of images intersperses all three epochs – the last reincarnation as Vessantara in the remote antecedent, the opening of the not-so-remote antecedent in the Tuṣita Heaven, as well (perhaps) as an image from the Bodhisattva's final human life, imbricated with imagery of the enlightenment and the turning of the Wheel from the proximate antecedent (the two events that determine the attainment of full Buddhahood – when Gautama achieves awakening and when by his own direct teaching of the path he causes the awakening of others).[97]

There are six larger slabs at the top of the drum, the outer two placed on the high-relief curve of the stūpa, almost at a right angle to a head-on viewer, and both damaged (illus. 64, 63, 65). The scene to the far right shows a princely figure on a throne (illus. 65). The scene next to it represents the *Campeyya-Jātaka*, in which the Bodhisattva as the *nāga* Campeyya, the epitome of *sīla* or ethical conduct, hosts King Uggasena (a previous incarnation of the Buddha's great student Sāriputta) in his kingdom.[98] The panel shows the two kings standing side by side facing left and surrounded by attendants, including a dwarf at the lower left (illus. 63). The third scene, to the immediate right of the *āyaka* pillars, depicts two royal figures seated side by side: this is the *Māndhātā Jātaka*, in which the Bodhisattva as the universal monarch Māndhātā is poisoned by greed and even after managing to acquire half of Sakka's Kingdom in the *Tāvatiṃsa* Heaven (the Heaven of the Thirty-Three, the highest of the heavens that maintains a possibility of physical connection with the human world) remains unsatisfied, ultimately falling to his death.[99] To the left of the *āyaka* pillars is a second scene with a royal pair enthroned – this time a prince or king with his consort surrounded by figures. This could represent the Bodhisattva and his consort Yasodharā, mother of Rāhula,[100] or one of the *jātakas* in which the two appear together as prince and princess in previous lifetimes,[101] in any case the royal bliss of fulfilled sexual union prior to renunciation. Next is an image of the standing Buddha in the presence of worshippers, among whom one to his right offers him a bowl. An alternative but likely interpretation of these scenes has

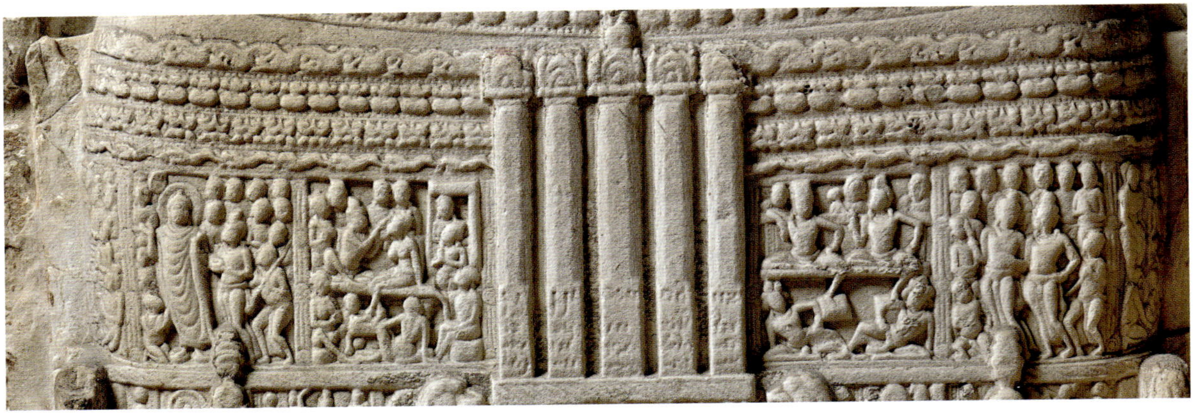

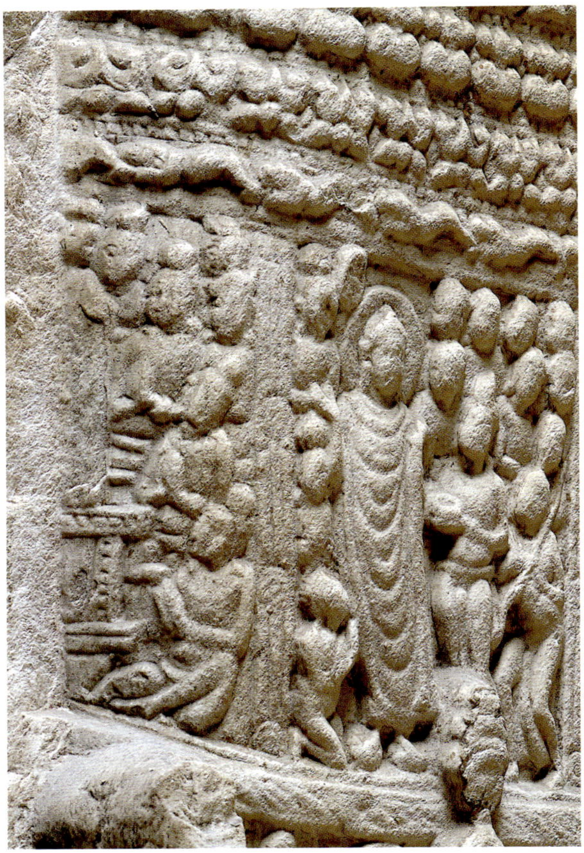

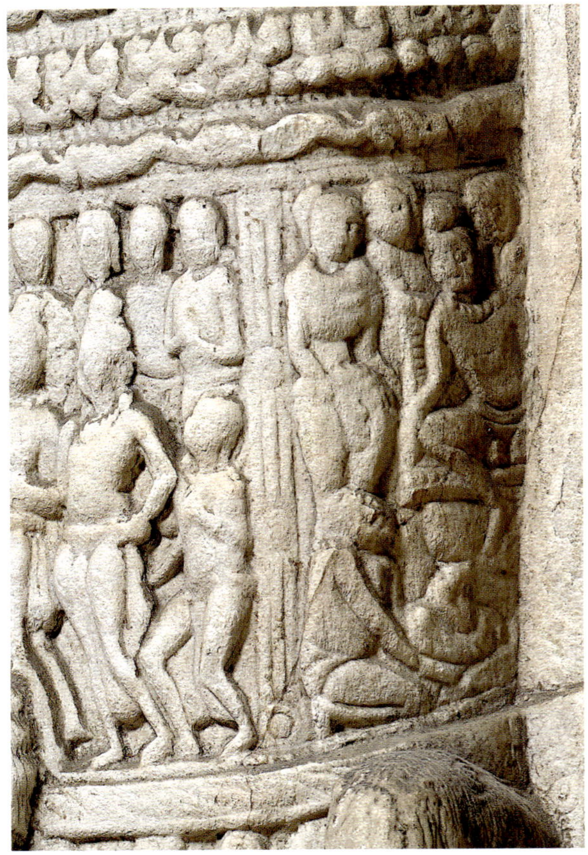

63 Detail of illus. 61 showing the upper dome panels and *ayāka* pillars with inscription.

64 Detail of illus. 61 showing the left-hand section of the upper dome frieze.

65 Detail of illus. 61 showing the right-hand section of the upper dome frieze.

the two together representing the famous story of the Buddha's half-brother Nanda.[102] According to this, on the Buddha's return to his father's palace, seven years after his enlightenment, he went for a meal to Nanda's house. Nanda, however, did not greet him since he was preoccupied making love to his new wife. The Buddha left his bowl and went away. Nanda followed him to return the bowl, and in the ensuing conversation was persuaded to ordain as a monk, despite having just married. He was deeply unhappy, divided between desire for his wife and the wish for enlightenment, but ultimately – after a trip with the Buddha to the *Tāvatiṃsa* Heaven – he triumphed over his desire and attained arahatship, the supreme state of enlightenment for those who follow the Buddha's path.[103] In this case, the scene with the Buddha represents Nanda returning the bowl, while the scene to the right shows Nanda making love with his wife,[104] known as Janapada Kalyani in the Pāli traditions and Sundari in the Sanskrit ones, both subjects attested to elsewhere in the early Buddhist art of India.[105] On the far left, much damaged, is a group of worshippers before a throne, the occupant of which is lost (illus. 64).

Here a series of enthronements (notably the two outer scenes and the two flanking the *āyaka* pillars) move between the remote and the proximate antecedents, with a particular focus on both the opportunities of royal virtue (in the *Campeyya-Jātaka*), its pleasures rooted in the attachment to desire (in the scene of prince and consort) and its risks of excessive greed leading ultimately to downfall (which is the theme of the Māndhātā narrative). If the temporal sequence moves from right to left, then the damaged princely enthronement on the far right (perhaps alluding to a *jātaka*) and two *jātaka* scenes in the remote epoch give way to the scene that represents the Bodhisattva before his renunciation in the not-so-remote epoch, or Nanda and his consort in the proximate epoch, before arriving at the Buddha standing and enthroned in the last two images from the proximate epoch. Certainly, in both these tiers of drum images the *jātaka* narratives are on the right at the beginning of the viewer's engagement. In the lower tier they emphasize the perfection of *dāna*, giving, and in the upper tier the perfection of *sīla*, morality, as a restraint to the unwholesome passions elicited by greed. The karmic pattern of the Bodhisattva's path is thus both to achieve perfection and to be purified of poisons in the mind. In relation to the issue of purification, the greed of Māndhātā – as a defilement in the Bodhisattva himself – has a different status from that of Nanda. Few viewers of the stūpa could reasonably aspire to attaining Buddhahood itself in the course of innumerable future lifetimes, but many could hope that their defilements – like Nanda's desire for sex or, to cite another of the major disciples represented at Amarāvatī, the hatred of the brigand Angulimāla, which led him to commit hundreds of murders before his conversion by the Buddha – could be eliminated, for them to attain arahatship like both Nanda and Angulimāla.[106]

The final tier of historiated narrative images are the five medallions amid the rich decoration of garlands, lotuses and dwarfs in the dome (illus. 66). From right to left, the images are the enlightenment as Bodhi tree over empty throne; the elevation of the Bodhisattva's begging bowl by a trio of flying gods; the Bodhisattva on a low throne in the Tuṣita Heaven surrounded by the devas who beg him to take human rebirth; the elevation of the Bodhisattva's hair-knot by three flying gods; and finally the First Sermon as a *dharmacakra* over an empty throne. Here the two core events of Buddhahood, when the 10,000-world system is said to have shaken,[107] namely enlightenment (the culminating moment of the not-so-remote antecedent) and the First Sermon, which turned the wheel of dharma (towards the beginning of the proximate antecedent), occupy the two outer scenes. They frame three key moments of renunciation in the not-so-remote epoch: when the Bodhisattva decides to give up his abode in the Tuṣita Heaven to take his final rebirth; when he cuts off his topknot as the mark of his renunciation of the princely life after the Great Departure (which the gods immediately elevate to heaven); and when he casts away the bowl in which he takes his last meal before his enlightenment.

We may say that this slab is unique in its narrative choices and configuration of scenes, and indeed none of the relief stūpas is exactly like any other, but most

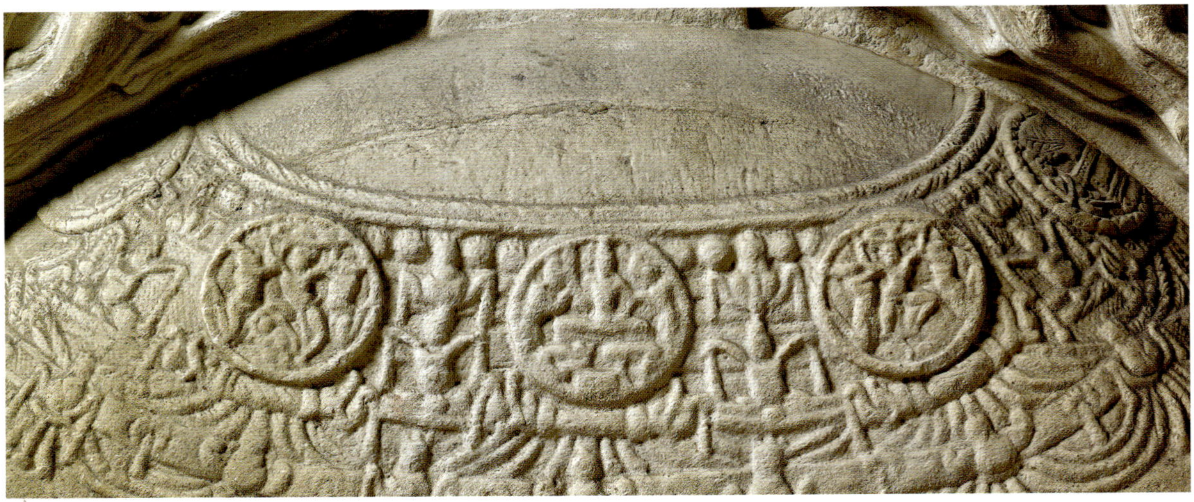

66 Detail of illus. 61 showing the medallions of the upper dome frieze.

were adorned with a similar range of narrative elements in the dome. In many cases, the subjects are less identifiable and, as in the stūpa relief panel in the Chennai Museum discussed in Chapter One, there is sometimes a more directly narrative emphasis in sequential terms in contrast to the imbrication of antecedents in the iconography of this slab. In this case, the central scenes – the dome roundel of the Bodhisattva in the Tuṣita Heaven, the royal scenes flanking the *āyaka* pillars and the *āyaka* platform frieze with the Bodhisattva in the Tuṣita Heaven – systematically represent the Bodhisattva before his final rebirth. They culminate, of course, in the much larger image of the standing figure in the central gateway. This iconography evokes both the numerous three-dimensional statues of the Buddha at the site (see illus. 145–9) and – in the geese flying above the figure as well as the *nāga* figures kneeling to either side – the story of the Bodhisattva crossing the river to go to the Bodhi tree beneath which he will be enlightened.[108] This story (represented with footprints instead of embodied Bodhisattva) appears also in a railing pillar (see illus. 112 and 113), but pertinent to its appearance here in contiguity with the story of Nanda and the begging bowl is the account of Buddhaghosa in *Nidānakathā* 70 that the Bodhisattva ('in the place where many hundreds of thousands of Bodhisattvas go down into the river on the day of their attainment of enlightenment') sent his bowl adrift in the Nairañjanā (Nerañjarā) River where it entered the abode of the *nāga* king Kāla, clanking against the bowls of three previous Buddhas. Imagery evoking the Buddha's enlightenment and teaching largely appears to the edges of the two upper tiers of imagery, so that the dome as a whole may be seen as a celebration of the Bodhisattva process across aeons of lifetimes that has led to Buddhahood, as determined in the standing figure of the Bodhisattva at the centre immediately before he sits beneath the Bodhi tree to enter the meditation session that culminates in liberation, but always in the teleological light of the enlightenment and wheel-turning (the two schematic scenes that directly flank the *āyaka* platform relief).

The narrative imagery is striking in that it can be read both from right to left (which is effectively its most chronologically sequential order, with all the *jātaka* themes on the right, as well as the direction of approach by a viewer and the direction of the coping frieze within the miniature stūpa) and as a convergence from left and right onto the centre. This offers a vertical line of images of the Bodhisattva in the Tuṣita Heaven in the central dome roundel and the *āyaka* platform as well as the standing Bodhisattva in the central gateway, all in the *abhāya mudrā*. A hugely complex play of karmic patterning – not only a chronology across antecedents but a causality of perfections developed and defilements undone – enables multiple ways of reading even a single panel, let alone this slab alongside nearly a hundred others around the drum as well as all the other relief imagery. The directionality is further complicated by the rather eroded donative inscription that is written conspicuously across the lower portions of the five *āyaka* pillars at the centre of the panel and is certainly meant to be read from left to right.[109]

It is worth restating that we cannot reconstruct on the original stūpa the juxtaposition of a single railing pillar or crossbar against any other, and have only very rare cases where we can make joins between two stones of coping. This means we have no certain sense of how the narrative imagery of the railing fitted together. By contrast, the stūpa reliefs give clear programmatic statements of both image and thematic juxtaposition, which makes the failure to exploit them for the study of narrative in Amarāvatī all the more surprising. For instance, arguably there is a visual and thematic logic in the juxtaposition of monarch *jātakas* in the dome friezes of the panel just discussed where two kings appear together, although the thrust of this is obscured by the fact that we cannot identify all the narrative subjects with certainty. Moreover, the miniatures play against versions of the same themes in the large-scale sculptures of the rail. For instance, there is a famous crossbar medallion with Māndhātā and Sakka sharing a joint throne in a heavenly paradise, surrounded by mainly naked ladies, including musicians and dancers (see illus. 77),[110] while there is a much more detailed account of this *Jātaka* narrative in a railing pillar now in Chennai, showing the king as universal monarch with several of his seven treasures in the lower lozenge, enthroned on a lion throne at the central medallion and sharing the throne of heaven with Sakka in the upper (now rather damaged) lozenge.[111] In this case, the square form of the miniature Māndhātā in the drum slab plays off against the circular and lozenge forms of the king's representations in the railing.

The argument of this section has depended on the assumption that the kinds of interconnections of narrative themes and antecedents that can be identified on a single slab with imagery purporting to represent a miniature stūpa can be extended to the larger monument in its full form. The slab – and the others like it – prove that these forms of visual thinking were fundamental to the aesthetics and sculptural arguments of the stūpa's makers.

REPLICATIONS

One issue within the textual traditions, particularly the *Buddhavaṃsa*, which probably dates to the second or first century BCE and is thus contemporary with the earliest images at Amarāvatī and rather earlier than most of the art of the stūpa, is the question of repetitive and non-repetitive time-patterns. That text presents a chronicle of the 24 buddhas preceding Gautama, with each account detailing a third-person narrative of the respective Buddha's life, a first-person account of Gautama's identity at that time, including a prediction of his attainment of future Buddhahood, and a third-person recital of a series of defining details of the given buddha – from the name of his city, clan, family, palaces, disciples and so forth to the kind of tree beneath which he attained enlightenment – before reporting Gautama's own formulaic autobiography as Buddha and foretelling Metteyya (Maitreya) as the next Buddha (at XXVII.19).[112] While, in one sense, this history tells the long diachronic process of the Buddha's path through innumerable lifetimes from taking the Bodhisattva vow as Sumedha to his final enlightenment, in another, it is full of repetitions: the many Buddhas with their parallel enlightenments and repeating patterns of attaining the ten perfections, the repeated prophesies and the formulaic model of recounting this material.[113] In the *Mahāvastu*, multiple former Buddhas, each proclaimed by the last, extend the list.[114] Unlike other stūpa sites, which use epigraphic captions to signal that their imagery draws on these traditions to represent some of the earlier Buddhas (as at Kanaganahalli[115]) or depict the different trees beneath which they became awakened (as at Bharhut[116]), the art of Amarāvatī has no captions to label its themes. This may imply that it dwells only on

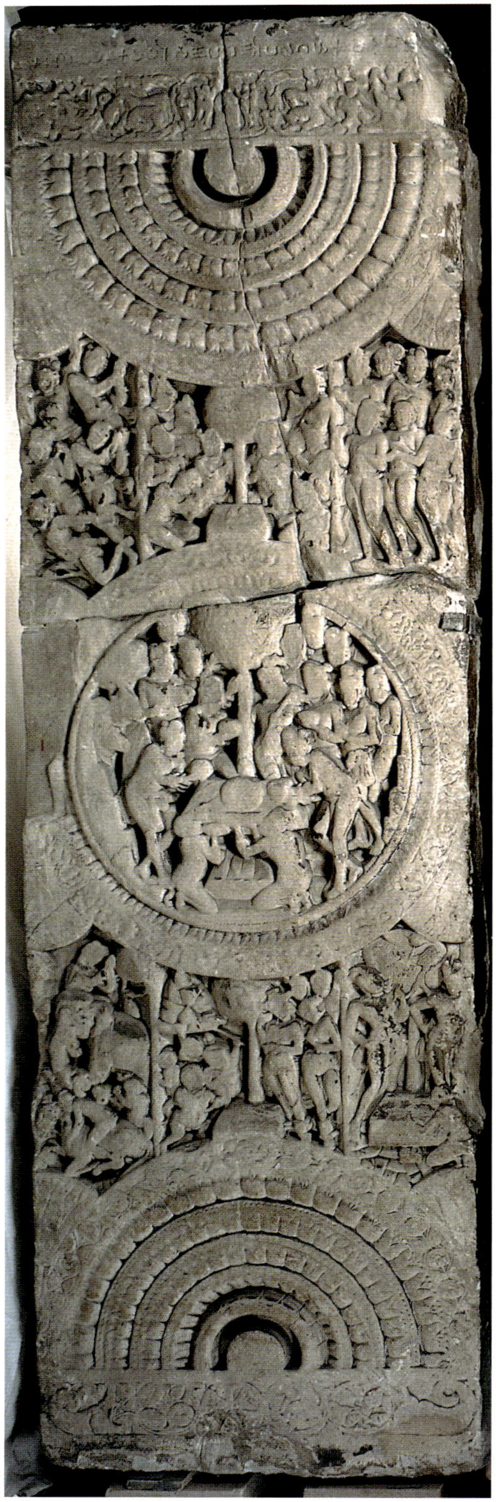

narratives of Gautama Buddha and his previous lives, but it means that the imagery is nonetheless open to be taken to indicate other subjects, such as the lives of different Buddhas.[117] Certainly, the explicit placement of some of the *jātaka* imagery in the lifetimes of other Buddhas implicitly evokes their presence.[118]

At the same time, alongside powerful imagery that evokes sequential narrative, the stūpa's reliefs punctuate their visual argument with repeated iconic images of such themes as the First Sermon or the enlightenment – rarely represented with figures and more frequently shown symbolically as a *dharmacakra* on a column or an empty throne beneath the Bodhi tree. This is especially true of the multiple tall panels on the dome (see Chapter One, and illus. 38 and 39). These kinds of images, symmetrically composed around a centrally focalized depiction of the Buddha, whether figural or emblematic, engage the spectator in a way different from sequential narrative, since they address the viewer directly.[119] These repeated themes are not only images of the Buddha's own key biographical events but effectively those prophesied of him by every one of the 24 Buddhas starting with Dīpaṅkara, and indeed key events in the biographies of those Buddhas. In the absence of caption inscriptions, it is impossible to determine specific meanings for these repeated icons, but in the context of the literary traditions and the visual cultures of other early Buddhist stūpas, it may be that these have a wider resonance in relation to the fulfilment of the Bodhisattva path than sole reference to Gautama. In that case, they extend not only beyond their visual space into the viewers' devotional world, but beyond Gautama's historical trajectory into the timeless and universal replication of infinite Buddhahood. In an abraded railing pillar, the interior side of which survives in entirety in the British Museum, there are three scenes of the empty throne with *buddhapāda* beneath the Bodhi tree (illus. 67).[120] The usual interpretation is that these represent different events in the enlightenment process of Gautama: the enlightenment amid deities in the fluted lozenge at the top, with prior scenes of the temptation by Māra in the lower fluted lozenge and the central medallion. But it is not impossible that these are three different enlightenment scenes for three different Buddhas.

67 Complete surviving railing pillar, interior face, elaborately carved but in poor condition. The three registers each have an empty space beneath the tree of enlightenment; the central one only is a throne (2.60 × 0.80 m).

These resonances and flexibilities at the level of the meanings or referents of any given iconographic type enable the potential for a flexible discursive system in the art of the stūpa. Particular image types (whether repeated symbolic forms, such as the *dharmacakra* column over the empty throne and *buddhapāda*, or narrative subjects) are rendered relationally meaningful through the contiguity.[121] It is not easy to determine the precise effects of this, since the only access to non-speculative conclusions about how juxtapositional narrative configuration was accomplished is in looking at individual slabs (like the Nālāgiri slab or the stūpa relief from the drum discussed earlier, illus. 61). Different contiguities enable subtle differentiations of meaning. Let us take a long and flamboyant drum frieze slab that is currently divided between the British Museum and the Government Museum in Chennai, which appears to read from both ends towards the centre (illus. 68 and 69).[122] The British Museum section has five scenes, separated by a divisional scheme consisting of three roundels arranged vertically (the outer ones in lotus form framing the central one which is historiated); that in Chennai continues the last scene from the London segment at the right end and then offers four more with the same divisional framing scheme.

Starting with the British Museum piece, on the far right is a scene from the *Vidhurapandita-Jātaka* in which the wise sage Vidhura, an incarnation of the Bodhisattva that embodies the perfection of wisdom, portrayed with earrings and elaborate hair and enthroned with his hands together, appears to be addressing a series of *nāga*s and female figures.[123] This *jātaka* is popular in the sculptures of Amarāvatī, appearing (in greater narrative detail) in a coping frieze and several crossbars from the inner railing.[124] Next to this, after the central roundel of the frame that shows a male and female

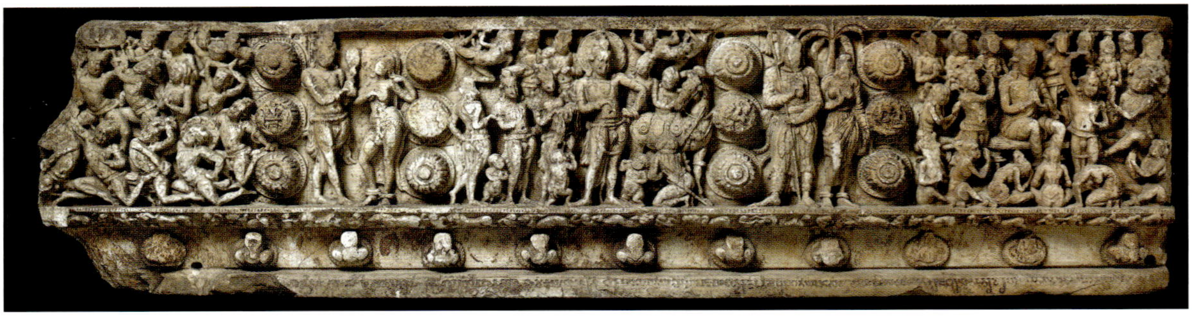

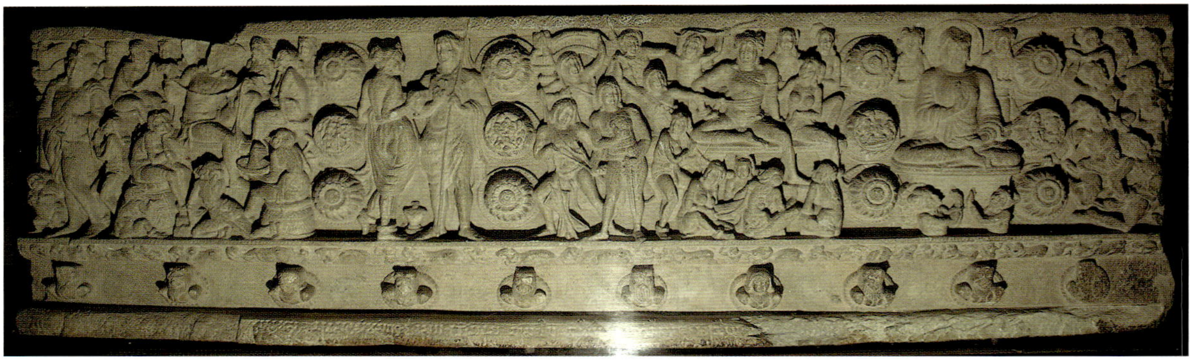

68 Right portion of a drum frieze slab with three principal scenes separated by trios of lotus bosses with two male–female pairs interspersed between them.

69 Left portion of the drum frieze slab in illus. 68 with two further narrative scenes, separated by another male–female couple and the seated Buddha (towards the right). The total length would have been 2.2 metres (7 ft).

couple enthroned, are another male and female in unusual dress who have been identified as the *yakṣa* deities Pañcika and Hārītī, who came to symbolize well-being and wealth in the non-monastic world.[125] The middle roundel of the adjoining frame to the left has the Great Departure as a princely figure on a horse riding towards the left. Next to this, in the central scene of the British Museum's segment of this frieze, is Prince Siddhārtha, with a halo, taking leave of his horse, Kaṁṭhaka, and his groom, Chandaka, with what appear to be a retinue of dwarfs and deities to the left. The central medallion of the frame to the left of this is broken. The next scene to the left has a male and female *mithuna* couple in which he holds up a mirror to her so that she can admire herself. This may be a generalized referent to the theme of lovemaking and adornment in the household sphere, but the mirror might also specifically invoke the mirror episode in the love story of Nanda and his wife Janapada Kalyani.[126] The final scene, broken two thirds across to the left, and at the right end of the Chennai slab, has the elevation by deities of the Bodhisattva's topknot, which he cut off and cast away when he dismounted from Kaṁṭhaka, with the *nāga* king to the lower right. The first full scene on the right of the Chennai section has the Buddha, at a slightly larger scale than the other figures, enthroned in the teaching posture with a standing attendant to either side and two *nāga* worshippers in supplication beneath.[127] This is arguably the concluding scene on which both ends converge. The iconography of the central roundels of the scene division on this side have not been identified, and I cannot make them out from the photographs available to me.[128] To the left of the Buddha is a royal harem scene with a near-naked prince and his nude consort on a high couch, with female attendants below, one playing music, and armed men before a *toraṇa* gateway on the left-hand side, possibly defenders of the prince and possibly attackers.[129] The prince holds a band of three plaits of cord in his right hand, which are being pulled by the figure to his left. To the left of this is a *mithuna* couple in which the woman with falling draperies offers a cup to the man with a spear on her right. The final scene on the left-hand side shows a prince entering the harem through a *toraṇa*, while to the right another figure, or possibly the same person, is seated among attendants holding the three plaits of cord. Clearly there is a connection in the cord imagery of these two scenes, although the meaning is not obvious. The three threads may indeed represent the three fetters of greed, hate and delusion to which the Bodhisattva is still subject before his final liberation, as Sivaramamurti suggests,[130] or more generally the ties that bind one to saṃsāra.

This is a highly sophisticated and complex commentarial take on a familiar narrative, which other friezes tell much more simply.[131] The decision to place the story of Vidhura preaching to the *nāga*s at the right (the first element of the block that a viewer would see as she circumambulated the monument) frames the narrative of renunciation, the supreme example of the perfection of *nekkhamma* (renunciation) according to the *Nidānakathā*,[132] in the context of the development of wisdom. This is both the insight, according to the Buddha's biography, gained by the Bodhisattva's seeing of examples of old age, sickness and death as well as the wisdom of a mendicant who had renounced the world,[133] and the wisdom of the perfections acquired in earlier incarnations. The narrative of the Great Departure is then interspersed with *mithuna* scenes emphasizing the pleasures of the lay life that the Bodhisattva renounces (and if the mirror scene represents Nanda, then the pleasures to which his half-brother is particularly attached and from which he must be converted). These pleasures, as presented in the narrative of his own life, are the principal subject of the scenes on the left of the Chennai panel, expanding on the ties of palatial life. Both sections – the pleasures of the harem and the renunciation of the lay world rooted in wisdom, which is to say seeing the attachments of such pleasures as they lead to old age, sickness and death – converge on the teaching Buddha at the right of the Chennai slab. Given that he teaches *nāga*s both as Buddha and as Vidhura, there is clearly an interplay of the two scenes representing the same individual in different lifetimes. The *nāga* theme is extended by the presence of a *nāga* king in the scene where the Bodhisattva's topknot is taken to heaven. Among the other elements of narrative brilliance is the use of the central framing bosses to extend the commentarial implications (by evoking palace scenes or couples) and to add to the narrative episodes (as in the miniature representation of the Great Departure, which is actually the fundamental subject of the entire frieze here). Effectively, the specific choices in this series of images – to emphasize sense desire in the harem, highlight the wisdom of a former incarnation, interrupt the narrative of palace pleasure and Great Departure with an image of the Buddha teaching and evoke a subplot around *nāgas* – make a unique exegetic argument, a propositional twist unlike any other available interpretation of one of the great events of the Bodhisattva's last life.[134] All three antecedents are intertwined through epitomic imagery to evoke the karmic interrelations of the great being's development across lifetimes and epochs.

COMPENDIA OF NARRATIVES

One of the most interesting aspects of the story traditions of early Buddhism is their role as items within collections: stories by and large exist alongside other stories, brought together by anthologists or commentators for particular purposes. For biographically orientated collections, one might cite the *Jātakatthavaṇṇanā* of the Pāli tradition with its 547 stories of former lifetimes, or the *Mahāvastu* – loosely assembled around an account of the Buddha's final lifetime – with its numerous narratives of previous lives (for example, when this text gets to the introduction of the figure of Yaśodharā, the Bodhisattva's wife,[135] it veers into a series of stories connected by the fact that they link earlier incarnations of Gautama with previous lives of his consort).[136] In the case of the

Jātakatthavaṇṇanā, the rationale for the full collection is as a compendium of the Bodhisattva's earlier lives, itself authorized by the *Nidānakathā*, which was appended to it as a biographical preface that introduced the three antecedents; but each *jātaka* as an account of a former life (in the remote antecedent) is in fact framed in a story from the Buddha's teaching career (in the proximate antecedent), which grounds and explains the didactic value of the particular *jātaka* in relation to an event or the specific needs of the Buddha's audience at that time.[137] That is, the teaching function of these stories – in place of a verse or a sutta or a monastic rule, which might have been alternative teaching pronouncements from the Buddha – is primary. This kind of *Dhamma* framing, without the biographical element that links the stories to the Bodhisattva's own earlier lives, also characterizes the narratives in the Sanskrit *Divyādvadāna*.[138] Other collections of stories are still more explicitly grounded in issues of Buddhist teaching and ethics – so, for instance, the *Dhammapāda* commentary offers narratives that present the occasion on which the Buddha is said to have uttered each of the verses in the *Dhammapāda*;[139] likewise, the *Suttavibhaṅga* of the *Vinaya Piṭaka* in the Pāli tradition gives the rules for the monastic conduct of monks and nuns with an origin story for each one.[140] It is thought that the *Mahāvastu*, although assembled as an account of the Buddha and Bodhisattva, was originally composed to accompany a version of the Mahāsāṃghika *Vinaya*.[141] These kinds of traditions use stories to establish connections of causality, history and biography across varieties of themes and individuals; but together they establish canons of institutionalized lore within (and perhaps across) the varying *Nikāyas* that are simultaneously selective (in choosing stories that fit with the tendentious aims of a given text) and comprehensive in accumulating a large enough number of stories to imply completeness.

The visual culture of early Buddhism – often earlier in its surviving forms than the recensions of the narrative collections that have come down to us – is similarly selective about the narratives it chooses, with the same aim of the appearance of inclusivity and completeness. Whether we think of the cave-painting traditions (from Ajanta to Dunhuang) or of the relief-sculpture traditions of stūpas and other monuments, the patterns of selectivity and collection are similar. The use of radical and creative juxtaposition of stories from the Buddha's life with *jātakas* on the level of the single block of stone has commentarial effects, as we have seen, in relation to chosen themes (generosity, wisdom, greed and so forth), achieved through a contiguity of narratives, something like the embedding of a verse or rule or teaching story in a given origin or cause narrative. What we cannot do, because of the state of the archaeology of Amarāvatī, is analyse beyond speculative hypothesis the effects of this process. But despite the ruined state of so much Buddhist material, it is clear that stūpas function in terms of visual narratives in ways that are parallel to the commentarial compendia of stories. The difference – in part fundamental to the different media – is that most narratives at Amarāvatī are epitomes that allude to a longer story through a single characteristic episode or iconic image-type. They assume oral or written knowledge of the longer sequential narrative, or at least the possibility of it being provided by exegetes and guides at the site. They play similar games of cause and effect or of imbricating histories. In the case of Amarāvatī, at least, these narratives are strongly focused on the Bodhisattva's biography, including his previous lifetimes.

What stūpas can do, more effectively and lightly than textual presentations of narratives, is repeat references to key iconic elements presented as epitomic episodes to make differentiated commentarial points in relation to specific juxtapositions. The placing of the *Vidhurapandita-Jātaka* in relation to the Great Departure places a causal structure of wisdom at the heart of the thematic of the Bodhisattva's renunciation, which is not explicitly emphasized in other versions of this much-repeated subject. Effectively, a meta-thematic of the development of wisdom over lifetimes becomes a pattern that overcomes the temptations of palace life and sensual attraction to culminate in the Buddha image at the right of the Chennai segment of the block. That is by no means the only potential interpretative

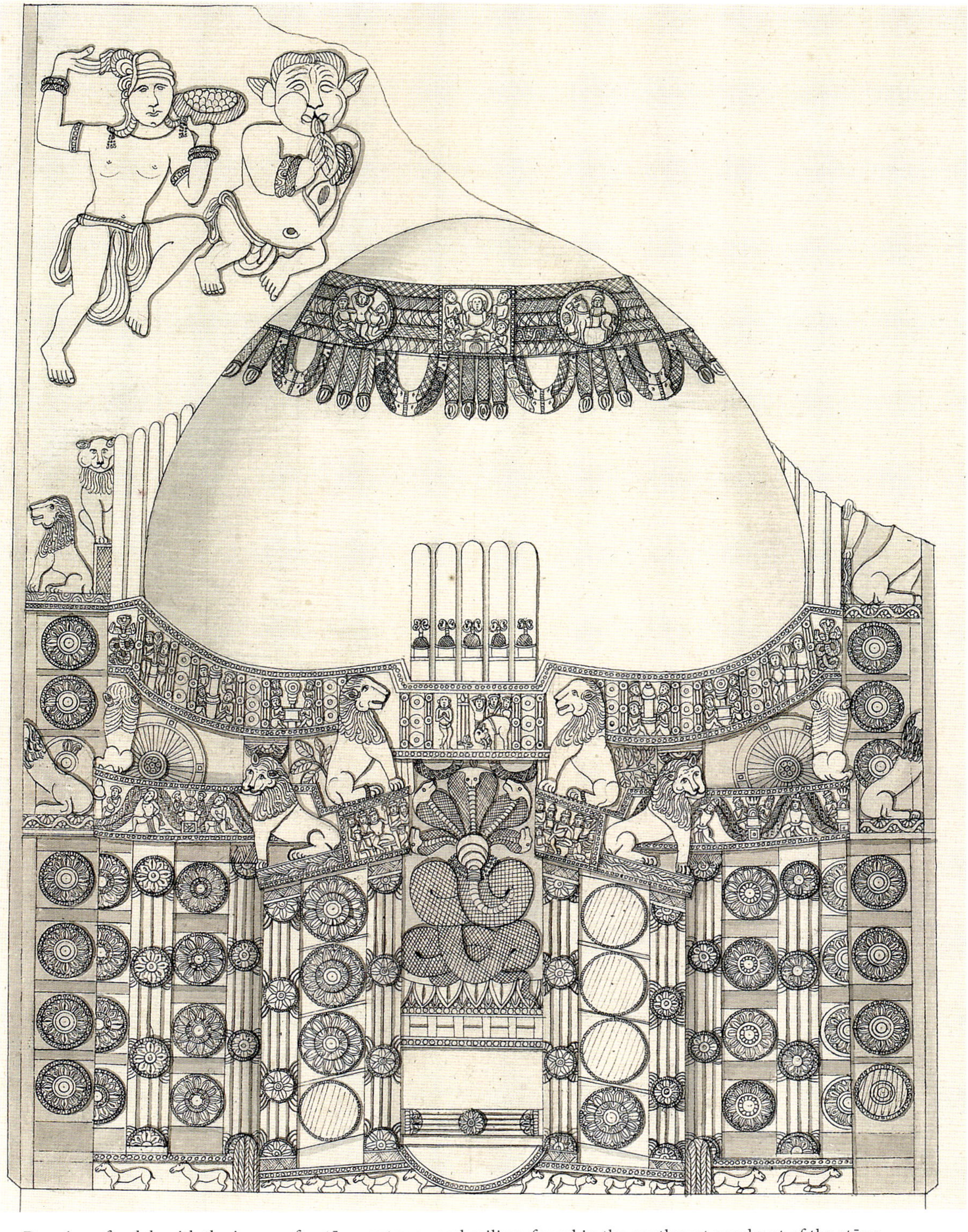

70 Drawing of a slab with the image of a stūpa, gateway and railing, found in the southwest quadrant of the stūpa. Mackenzie's Album, WD1061, fol. 35. Made by Thomas Anderson and Marcellus Burke and dated 15 November 1816.

emphasis for the narrative of the renunciation, but it is the one suggested in the drum relief discussed here. Likewise, the perfection of generosity is effectively made to underlie and frame the Nālāgiri narrative, which determines which aspects of that story (that is, Ānanda's offer to sacrifice his life) are the topic of focalization. That means in the context of the block in the British Museum discussed earlier (illus. 55–8), the exegetic thrust is aligned with the way the story appears in the *jātaka* tradition (in relation to Ānanda's self-sacrificial act of *dāna*) as opposed to, for instance, the way it is told in the *Vinaya* and the *Udāna* commentary where it concerns discord and the wickedness of Devadatta,[142] or in the *Milindapañhā* (a first-century BCE text whose title translates as *Milinda's Questions*) where it is the occasion for a discussion about whether *arahat*s (human beings who have become enlightened by following the Buddha's path) can experience fear,[143] or in Dhammapāla's *Udāna* commentary where the Nālāgiri narrative represents the fruition of the Bodhisattva's negative karma when in a previous lifetime he had the elephant on whom he was riding assail a *paccekabuddha*.[144] However, other representations of the Nālāgiri story at the site may well, in their original context, have offered significations aligned in different commentarial directions. The specific perfection displayed by the Buddha in the act of taming the elephant is *mettā* (loving kindness), the ninth of the ten perfections.[145] This quality plays out in an entirely different series of causal links from the question of schism or the development of generosity, such as stories specifically linked to the Bodhisattva's loving kindness in relation to animals,[146] as well as to the Buddha's teaching of *mettā* for all forms of beings, notably snakes but including 'footless, two-footed, four-footed and many-footed beings'.[147]

Let us take a potent example from a now-lost miniature stūpa from the southwest side of the drum, recorded by Mackenzie's draughtsmen (illus. 70).[148] This has a great *nāga* in the central gateway, with two further rising *nāga*s to the left and right extremities of the frieze across the lower part of the dome. The image of Nālāgiri, bowing to a flaming pillar, is placed in the *āyaka* panel above the central gateway (illus. 60) at the midpoint of a frieze depicting on each side three frontal panels with aniconic columns between worshippers. At the outer edges, these columns appear to be surmounted by a Bodhi tree, implying the enlightenment, to the far left and right; a wheel, or *dharmacakra* (indicating the First Sermon that turned the wheel of the Buddha's dharma, or teaching), on the near left and in the central panel to the right; and a stūpa symbolizing the Buddha's death and interred relics at the middle left and near right. The five *āyaka* pillars arising from the frieze section with Nālāgiri also have relief decoration in the form of stūpas surmounted by umbrellas. Here the Nālāgiri theme, with its emphasis on the loving kindness by which the Buddha tames the tendency to schism and attack, within a visual discourse that is aniconic about the Buddha's own figure, is the central culmination of these columnar representations of the key moments of his mission. This is in counterpoint to the roundels and square panel at the top of the stūpa, the central image of which represents the Buddha in human form amid disciples, with scenes from his path to enlightenment to either side (on the right the great renunciation with the Bodhisattva on his horse Kaṁṭhaka leaving the palace and to the left his throwing away of his begging bowl, which is at once taken up to heaven by deities). The effects of *mettā* on both elephant and, implicitly, snakes (in a context where in the written traditions the same word (*nāga*) is used of both elephants and snakes[149]), as well as a centralizing focus on curing schism within the *saṅgha* of monks, takes the interpretative theme of the teaching of the dharma (in the roundel at the top) into the monastic heritage left by the Buddha.

By contrast, in another richly carved slab drawn by Mackenzie's illustrators, the Nālāgiri theme at the centre of the stūpa's entrance seems to cap a visual interplay of elephant imagery (illus. 71).[150] Elephants move across the coping frieze at the top of the outer railing to left and right of the central opening. In the far-right panel of the drum frieze above this railing, the Bodhisattva himself in the form of a miniature elephant descends upon his mother in the classic iconography of his conception.

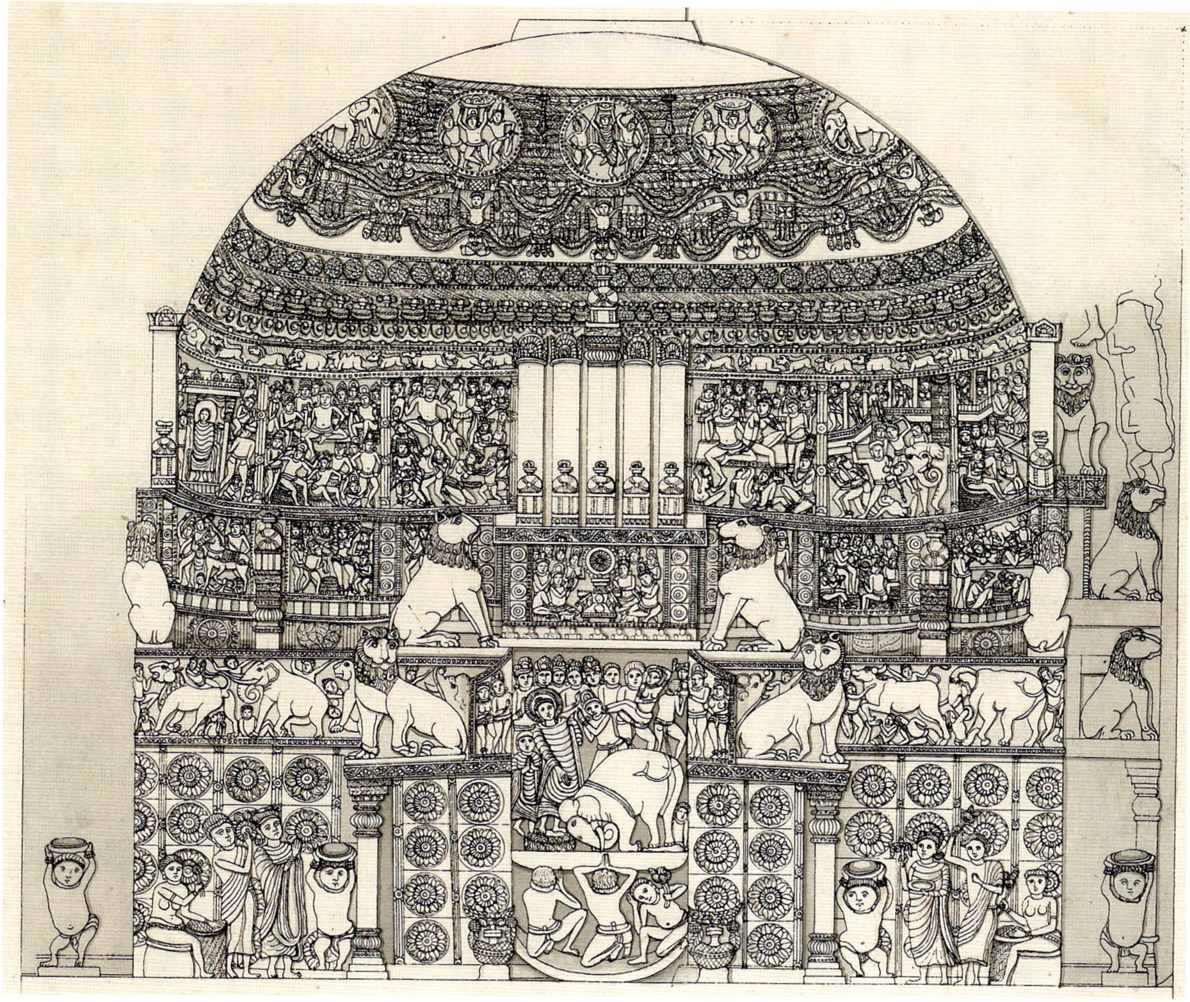

71 Drawing of a slab with the image of a stūpa, gateway and railing, found in the east quadrant of the stūpa. Mackenzie's Album, WD1061, fol. 26. Made by Henry Hamilton and dated 15 October 1816.

Above that, among the larger slabs that decorate the upper drum, an elephant appears in an unidentified military scene. In the two roundels to the extreme left and right of the dome, elephants bow towards the three medallions that show deities carrying relics up to heaven. While the specific interpretative key may elude us, there is no doubt that this imagery plays with and upon elephants and elephant narratives in the tradition.

The karmic force of the imagery of Nālāgiri is that it raises an extraordinarily rich intersection of causations relating to different perfections developed by the Bodhisattva, to his purification of bad karma,[151] and beyond the Buddha himself to the paths across lifetimes of Ānanda and Devadatta. The complexity is vastly reinforced when precisely the same narrative is told at length of the former Buddha Piyadassin in Buddhadatta's fifth-century *Buddhavaṃsa Commentary* with the monk Soṇa replacing Devadatta, the elephant Donamukha replacing Nālāgiri,[152] and Piyadassī replacing the Buddha.[153] The connection of narratives between the two elephant attacks is explicitly drawn at both the opening and close of the story.[154] The emphasis is heavily on the compassion and loving kindness of Piyadassī.[155] Effectively, the presentation of the same narrative in relation to two entirely different Buddhas 1,800 aeons apart,[156] and the absence of labelling in the reliefs, enables the imagery to evoke both Gautama and Piyadassī, with ramifications about schism and loving kindness in both cases. Piyadassī takes the karmic concatenation around the episode out of the patterns of cause-and-effect and multiple lifetimes around Gautama and, implicitly, into an entirely different nexus of karmic interdependence, thereby universalizing the argument. The description in many of these texts of Gautama/Piyadassī as a king elephant adds further edge to the imagery, with a form of mirroring implied between animal and Tathāgata, and the implication of self-mastery of Buddha-elephant (*Buddha-nāga*) over elephant-elephant (*hatthi-nāga*) or animal-elephant (*tiracchāna-nāga*).[157] It is worth noting the effect of the two episodes: in the *Buddhavaṃsa Commentary* as a result of the taming of Donamukha and the teaching offered thereafter, 'eighty hundred thousand people penetrated the *dhamma*'; in the *Cullahaṃsa-Jātaka*, 'eighty-four thousand living beings drank the nectar of immortality'.[158] One may add a final story of bowing elephants, told by Buddhaghosa in the introduction to the *jātakas*, the *Nidānakathā*, where the Bodhisattva's triumph over the forces of Māra immediately before his enlightenment is marked by the moment that Māra's great war elephant, 'Girimekhala, which was one hundred and fifty *yojana*s in height, went down on its knees.'[159]

In formal terms, the drum frieze panel with the Nālāgiri episode from the Buddha's lifetime and a *jātaka* frame story, sandwiched between two *jātakas* – that of Sibi/Sarvamdada and that of Sasa – adopts the classic framing pattern of so many Buddhist texts, although it reverses the model, with a framing story 'of the present' in the centre. This formal model of framing is also a pattern of causality, offering the occasion when particular teachings were given and therefore offering an exegetic understanding of why they were given and aspects of their meanings. It embeds a model of the hermeneutically significant occasion (*nidāna*) into both literary and visual narrative form.[160] This is not only the case with the *jātakas* but with the suttas, which frequently offer episodes, events or questions that then prompt a particular teaching, at the end of which the text refers back to the occasion of origin and the effects on those present. Likewise, in the commentarial tradition, for instance the *Dhammapāda-atthakathā*, verses from the *Dhammapāda* frame the stories told by the commentary to elucidate the occasion when the given saying was pronounced, and hence aspects of its meanings – usually the verse being repeated as both introduction and conclusion to the commentarial story, which may include sub-narratives of past lives and other extensions in addition. The formal structure of the frieze panel (and indeed the stūpa's general obsession with framing its visual elements) is thus a version of the formal framing structure of stories of present and past, or of verses topping and tailing exegetic narratives, or frame-stories that encase any given sutta or *jātaka*, which are fundamental to the conceptual and discursive models underpinning early Buddhism – both its texts and its images. As we have seen, by shifting across different *jātaka* narratives and 'stories from the present', the Nālāgiri frieze panel builds its own specific commentary on the themes of *dāna* and *mettā* in ways that complement both the canonical and the exegetic traditions on a model that may borrow from some lost text, but may equally be original to the visual culture. Beyond the individual block, the range of juxtaposed blocks is precisely parallel to the multiple juxtaposed verses and narratives of such texts as the *Dhammapāda* commentary, making a vast interdependent whole whose rhythms are signalled by frequent visual repetitions and inter-references. That is then further complicated (or its range of potential meanings both elaborated and universalized) by the fact that any one Buddha evokes all the others, and the narratives of their lives and previous lives.

The lengthy story of Piyadassī/Donamukha in the *Buddhavaṃsa Commentary*, with its wonderful description of 'that glorious elephant', is occasioned by a single half-sentence in the *Buddhavaṃsa* itself: 'when the charioteer of men had tamed the elephant Donamukha'.[161] That is, the original text gives what may have been to its early hearers an obscure allusion and is certainly a very concise epitome; to this the commentary adds immense narrative colour and considerable vivid expanse. Did Buddhadatta invent the story, borrowing it from the Nālāgiri episode and changing the names, in order to make sense of an incomprehensible reference in the canon? Did he draw on a rare and unusual older tradition that duplicated the elephant attacks on the two buddhas? Did he retell a narrative so common and frequent that it would have been immediately triggered for many early readers by the very name 'Donamukha', as mentioned in the *Buddhavaṃsa*? We cannot know. But clearly the direction of complexity in textual narratives moves from epitome in the canonical texts to expansion and interpretative elaboration in the commentaries. By contrast, in the visual culture (not only stūpa reliefs but wall paintings), the elaborate diachronicity of stories is reduced to exemplary epitomes, which themselves combine to create garlands of narratives, interconnected by contiguity and placement on the one hand and by the karmic interdependence of their subject-matter on the other. That is, stūpas combine multiple narratives – as do the commentarial traditions (perhaps above all the *Dhammapāda Commentary*) – but they do so through the single episode from which a complete story must be inferred, which is the more common way for the canonical texts to allude to narratives. In this way, by comparison with commentarial practice, they offer a different and complementary visual means for interpretative interaction with the tradition and its fundamental tenets as embodied in its stories.

As we have seen with the Nālāgiri tale, one of the most powerful aspects of the tradition of literary storytelling is the way that narratives are fluid and changing, with small shifts in names and emphases or the addition of episodes. The effect of this is to interconnect stories across epochs and lifetimes, so that patterns of the Bodhisattva's former lives, as well as those of Ānanda and Devadatta, come to a climax in the elephant's attack. Apart from the parallels of Piyadassī's treatment of Donamukha with Gautama's taming of Nālāgiri, the two Buddhas are linked by the Bodhisattva's earlier birth as Kassapa, a brahman youth and donor to Piyadassī who predicts his enlightenment after 1,800 aeons. But this set of connections is different from the karmic interconnection of patterns in the Nālāgiri episode, since it effectively evokes the unknown karmic web of previous lifetimes of Piyadassī and his enemy Soṇa – a move that magnifies and universalizes the devotee's sense of what is at stake in the visual subject.

Part of the compendious exegetic force of the ways narratives are presented, repeated and framed by a stūpa is that numerous levels of meaning can be made to interplay across the totality of the monument. In the case of the parallel of Donamukha/Piyadassī with Nālāgiri/Gautama, there is a vastness of replicative possibilities in which Buddha-lives, enlightenments and karmic actions are repeated across the eras that gives a universalist grandeur to the visual thematics. By such means, the decorative veneer of relief sculpture that adorns the early stūpas – perhaps nowhere more complex and rich than at Amarāvatī – demonstrates an exegetic virtuosity of its own, expressed through images invoking stories told and retold, known and related on-site. They certainly offer a kind of commentarial complementarity through visual narrativity to the forms of commentary offered by the literary collections of the same period and later.[162]

The stūpa at Amarāvatī is a vast visual commentary in its own right, presenting its own interpretative exposition of the Buddha's life and his dharma through relief sculptures and their juxtaposition, and evoking a series of deeper themes that echo through the Buddhist tradition: karma, cosmic time and the epochs, the Bodhisattva path to salvation, the development of the perfections. There is a sense of interconnectedness, or of multiple causes operating in a non-linear and deeply emotional way, which is implied by the very terminology of *nidāna*. The visual culture emphasizes that patterned interconnection between events in different lifetimes that resonate with one another like notes struck in deep time: events in the past, present and future sound together when there is a world-changing event like the Bodhisattva vow, the attainment of Buddhahood or a turning of the wheel of dharma. The art of the stūpa reflects and embodies this sense of complex connectivity, showing how influences and events across different epochs have affinities and karmic, even causal, connections. At the same time, the stūpa is a vast offering, comprising thousands of smaller acts of *dāna* and creating a devotional model for both its pilgrims and visitors of all religious convictions to imitate and emulate.

Part III
The Wider Indian Context

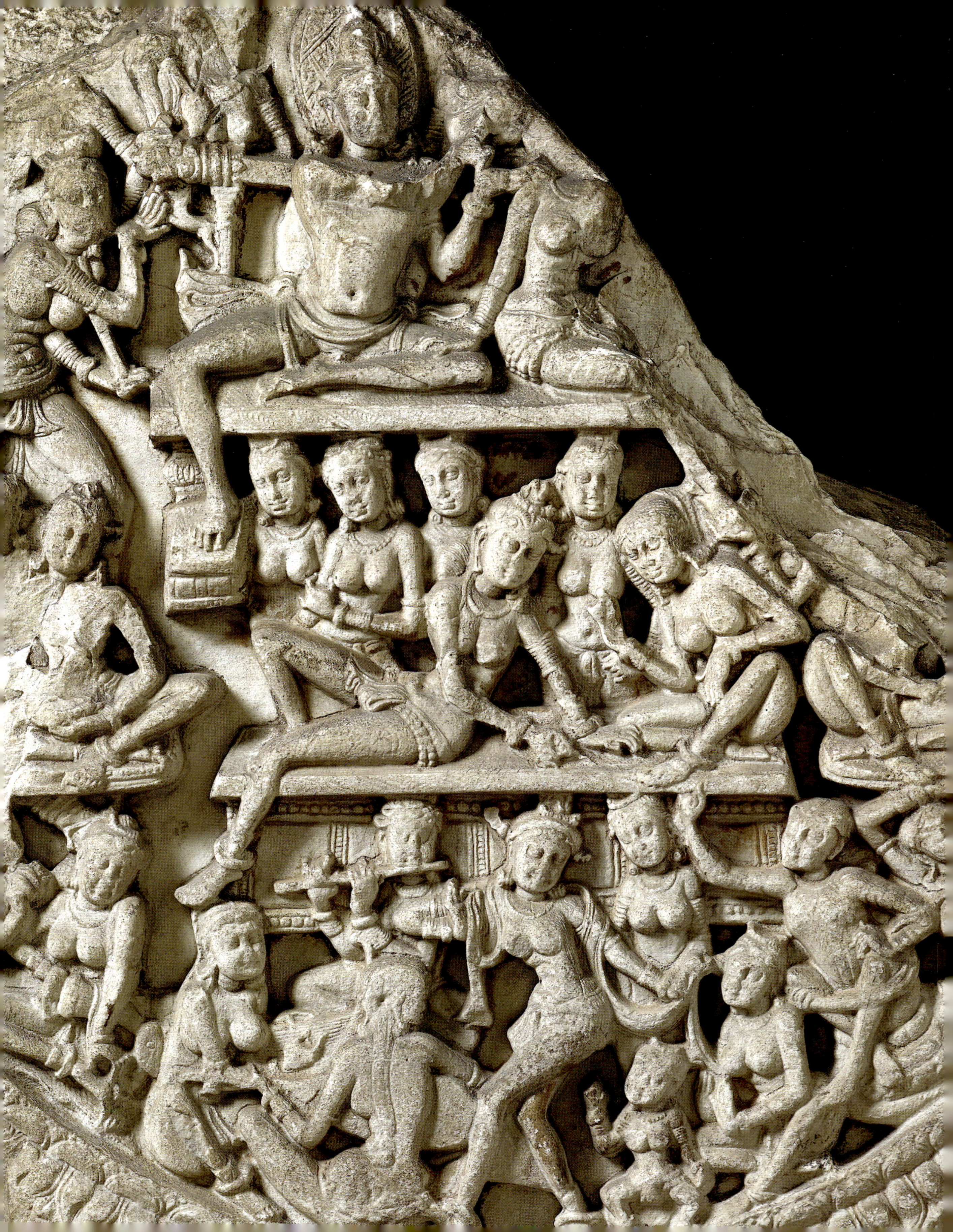

four

Theatricality

It is clear that the art of Amarāvatī shares an intense theatricality with many other artistic traditions of the ancient world, notably both Greek painted pottery and Roman painting.[1] Most of its visual narratives (including what may seem to us highly personal and intimate events, such as lovemaking, the Bodhisattva's moment of conception or the Buddha's enlightenment) are conceived not in terms of isolated intimacy but within a large audience of spectators, comprising human and divine beings of all kinds. Indeed, it is no exaggeration to say that there is hardly a figural or narrative scene in the relief sculpture surviving from the stūpa that is not teeming with observer or worshipper figures, apparently adjunct to the main action. These viewers may be conceived in a number of ways: as witnesses within the time and space of the action depicted, as an external audience in some indefinite time and place watching the action as if it were a play, as listeners to an oral narration or recitation, as worshippers before a sacred act or an act standing in for the sacred site where the original action took place, but in each of these (far from exclusive) options they are figured visually within the art of the stūpa. Whether the placement of the narrative action within so public a space of the gaze is itself related to the early performance of Buddhist stories (the *jātakas*, for instance, but conceivably the Buddha's life, as told in highly literary poems such as Aśvaghoṣa's Sanskrit *Buddhacarita* from the second century CE[2]) in ways similar to those well attested from the anthropology of public performance in the modern period is impossible to determine since we do not have the necessary evidence.[3] But if that were so, then the Buddhist visual arts of early India would be in a dynamic relationship with lost traditions of dramatic and oral arts, each one influencing the other through their shared audiences. In any case, one existential aspect of focalizing narrative action under the gaze of teeming multitudes of beings is

72 The historiated roundel from illus. 74 showing a performance with dance and music before an audience apparently in stacked seating with a royal couple at the top.

to elevate its resonances, rhetorically using theatricality to amplify the power of the stūpa's meanings.

Despite the Buddha's own stated opposition to theatrical performance, at any rate as a pastime for the *saṅgha*,[4] as well as the *Vinaya* prohibitions on singing,[5] by the second century CE monks were themselves composing dramas – notably the great Kāvya poet Aśvaghoṣa in his *Śāriputra-prakaraṇa*, a Sanskrit dramatization of the conversion of the Buddha's chief disciples, Śāriputra and Maudgalyāyana, in nine acts, of which fragments survive.[6] There has been some speculation that Aśvaghoṣa's dramas may have been related to the presence of a theatrical tradition (potentially associated with the cult of Dionysus) in Gandhāra.[7] But in addition to theatre, Buddhist writing included a number of other performative traditions, such as recitation by minstrels and dialogues in both prose and verse.[8] It also included staging numerous dialogues between the Buddha and adherents of other religions, or with monarchs and other lay devotees, before gatherings that might involve monks but might equally consist of members of households where a meal was being offered to the Buddha and his retinue. Thus, performative theatricality (if not stage performance itself) was built into all aspects of early Buddhist scriptural texts, both in form and in content, and certainly into the traditions of their oral delivery in Nikāya and Mahāyāna contexts.[9] In part, in terms of the stūpa's visual argument, this is about the celebration of the pre-Buddhist Brahmanic heritage, out of which and against which Siddhārtha emerged to create a model of ascetic renunciation and ultimately a monastic order.

That relation of the stūpa's visual culture to a spectator- and audience-conceived elaboration of its stories ties it to broader ancient Indian traditions of myth, ritual, performative recitation and theatre.[10] It is the purpose of this chapter to place the stūpa within that context, and thereby to cast light not only on aspects of its artistic resonance beyond Buddhism but on ways in which it reflects as well as extends the resources of its tradition. Culturally speaking, the Buddhism of Andhra Pradesh, which includes its remarkable monuments and artistry as well as the flourishing of religious and philosophical traditions, belongs within the rich mix of religious, literary and linguistic traditions overseen by the ruling dynasties of southern India (none exclusively 'Buddhist' or indeed of any specific religious conviction), especially in the period of the Sātavāhana kings between circa 120 BCE and 230 CE and their successors, the Ikṣvāku dynasty (*c.* 225–315 CE).[11] It was a diverse cultural world, characterized by a pluralism of religious groups (Jain, Ājīvika, Vedic and Brahmanic as well as Buddhist,[12] all of which had distinct local variants as well as claims to universal applicability), multiple local languages outside of Prakrit and Sanskrit – some of which, such as Tamil or Sinhalese, would also be used to produce oral and written literature – and numerous literary forms, including the fluidity with which Buddhist writings shift between prose and verse sections, primary narrative and commentary, didactic teaching and poetic evocation.[13]

A key issue here is that the art of the Buddhist stūpas, as major monumental statements in the religious landscape of India, must be understood as speaking rhetorically in two directions. On one level, they represent – and, in particular, the ways that they tell their visual narratives represent – an artistic formulation within images of the specific kind of Buddhism practised at the site (be it any one of the 'eighteen' Nikāya schools, or a mix of those groups, or a mix of some of those groups with some incipient Mahāyāna thinking). We unfortunately know all too little about the various schools, whose literatures are now lost, and cannot certainly place them in relation to given sites, monasteries or cave complexes. What remains is a visual discourse that works within Buddhism as part of an internal dialogue between changing and evolving positions in a dynamic and deeply learned series of religious and practice traditions. At the same time, stūpas and their art make a statement on behalf of Buddhism, as such, in relation to the plethora of other cults in their context within the pluralism of Indian religious life.[14] These certainly included Jain and Brahmanic religions, and potentially members of other Indian sects. In this discourse, both monuments and texts such as Aśvaghoṣa's *Buddhacarita* plead a kind of apologetic defence as well as a potentially proselytizing claim to salvation on behalf of the range of Buddhist schools taken as a whole.[15] These highly rhetorical uses of visual and literary culture operate under the gaze of multiple spectators, whether Buddhist or of different cultic affiliations – a gaze figured within the arts of Amarāvatī by their 'theatricality', as shall be explored in this chapter. Spectatorship in the imagery of a stūpa is a self-reflexive acknowledgement of the agonistic and public conditions of its monumental expression of identity, both its Buddhist identity in general and that of the specific school of Nikāya practices and scriptural traditions to which it was affiliated.

In Vijayapurī, the Ikṣvāku capital adjoining the Buddhist monastic complex of Nāgārjunakonda on the Krishna River valley in Andhra Pradesh, a square open space largely made of brick, paved and lined with grey stone slabs, was excavated in the 1950s. It consisted of tiered seating in eleven rows all around and more secluded seating in three further rows on the southeastern and southwestern sides.[16] This was moved and reconstructed in the modern site of Anupu when the Nāgārjuna Sagar dam was constructed (between 1955 and 1967), creating a vast lake that submerged the entire archaeological site (illus. 73). It may have been a stadium, or a venue for other kinds of public displays (one wonders about a debating floor, in the manner of later Tibetan monastic culture), but it may also have been or occasionally functioned as a theatre, and it may have had temporary roofing. The excavators assumed it belongs to the period of the major Buddhist monuments of Andhra, since it adjoined a temple thought to have been dedicated to the Buddhist deity Hārītī.[17] Much is uncertain, not least the building's function and date,

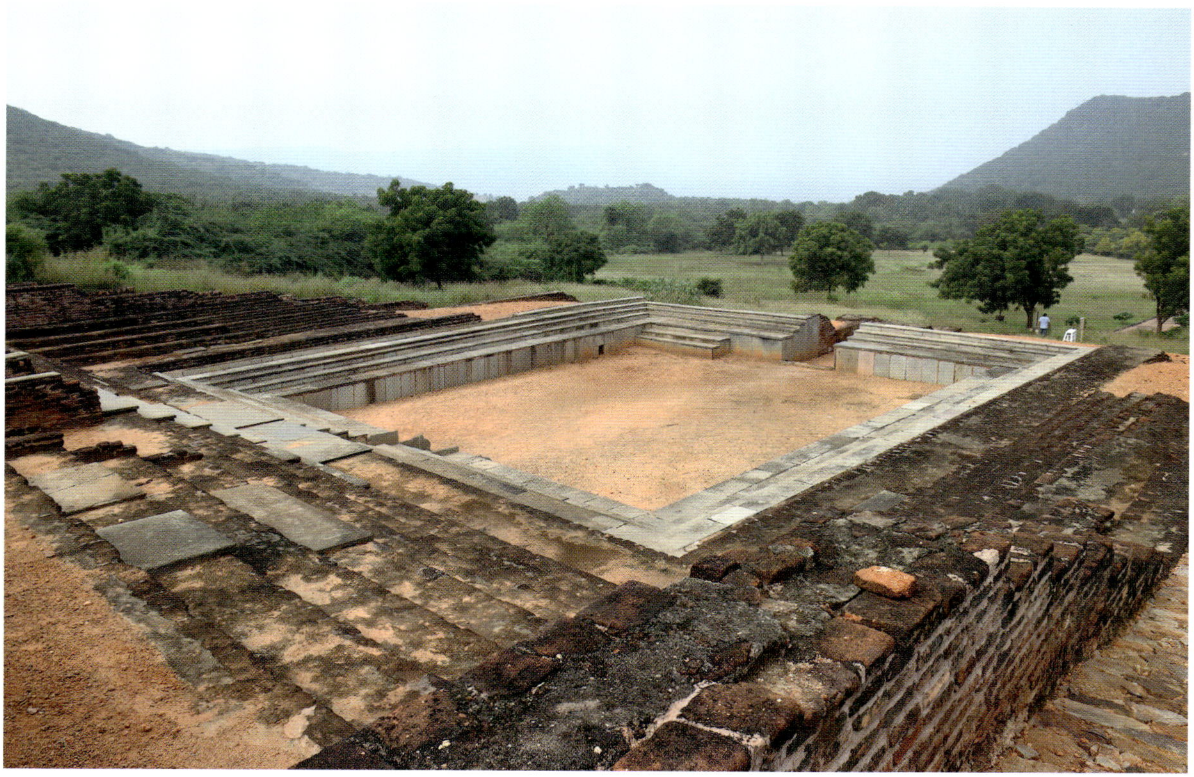

73 Ancient and probably Buddhist public space with stacked seating on four sides which may have been a stadium or a theatre. Excavated in Nāgārjunakonda in the 1950s and moved to modern Anupu outside the lake caused by the dam completed in the later 1960s.

none of this made easier by the fact that the structure is unique and hence incomparable in the Indian context of its likely period, and that its archaeology is now utterly incapable of being revisited.[18] But if it were to have been a theatre, as is at least possible, or even a venue for public display and performance, as is likely, then it would provide archaeological grounding for architectural thinking about theatrical or display space in late ancient Andhra.

ANCIENT INDIAN DRAMATIC AND ARTISTIC THEORY

One way to test the embeddedness of the art of early Buddhist stūpas in the arts of the wider cultural environment in late ancient India is to look at the *Nāṭyaśāstra*, attributed to the sage Bharata. This is an early non-Buddhist Sanskrit treatise on the performing arts, the current form of which seems to have been achieved between 100 and 300 CE, but its origins may lie much earlier.[19] That places it broadly in the same period as the major stūpas and as much of the development of Buddhist scriptural writing, including the rise of the Mahāyāna. Like Buddhist scriptures, this text acquired a rich commentarial tradition over the centuries, and many approaches (admittedly no longer datable or available directly) are incorporated, sometimes with direct quotation, in the surviving commentary of the Saivite Abhinavagupta (950–1020), known as the *Abhinavabhāratī*.[20] The parallels between the theatrical world envisaged by this text and the theatricality of Amarāvatī may be summarized as follows.

First, it has been conclusively established that the *Nāṭyaśāstra* places its model of dramaturgy firmly within a religious context, heavily embedded in concepts of Indian, notably Brahmanic, ritual life.[21] Central to these rites is the placement of the *Brāhma-maṇḍala* at the heart of the consecrated stage, symbolizing the centre of the universe materialized on a symbolic plane with the god present in person: 'Brahmā himself occupied the middle of the stage' (NŚ 1.94), 'the director should offer flowers in the *Brāhma-maṇḍala*, which is another name for the centre of the stage where the deity is supposed to be present and afterwards he should respectfully bow to Brahmā' (NŚ 5.74–5).[22] According to the *Nāṭyaśāstra*, the *maṇḍala* for Brahmā should be made according to detailed instructions during the *pūjā* by which the stage is consecrated, which included placing the god with a lotus at his seat in the centre (NŚ 3.20–32), and a series of other gods around him. If the stūpa is imagined as the living presence of the Buddha, rather than Brahmā in the playhouse, in a great circular *maṇḍala* surrounded by carved floral offerings (as well as real ones from living devotees), then the rich programme of its visual imagery emanates as a series of dramatic narratives performed on the stage of its architectural form. The similarities between theatre and stūpa, both addressing their audience through the agency of a sacred or divine figure with the play of life in the form of images created by human art, is palpable.

Second (although the text is notoriously corrupted[23]), Chapter Two of the *Nāṭyaśāstra* deals with both the rites of theatre foundation,[24] creating a ceremonial setting that was certainly shared with other religious monuments like stūpas or monasteries, and the different physical forms of theatres – of which the second, *caturaśra*, was either square or round with the audience imagined as all around the stage (NŚ 2.7, 91–100).[25] Here the divine theoretics for constructing a playhouse with an audience surrounding the consecrated *Brāhma-maṇḍala* of the stage emulates or anticipates that of the central *maṇḍala* of the Buddha, realized as a circular stūpa, approachable by pilgrims or worshippers from all sides through the gateways at the four cardinal points. The orientation of the stūpa and the playhouse as sacred centres of the world is founded in both cases by a focus on the cardinal directions (for example, NŚ 2.39, 74) and beyond these on the eight directions – that is, the four intermediates, such as northwest (NŚ 2.48–9, 3.23–31), as well as the cardinal points – and the ten directions (including above and below, NŚ 2.38), with precious dedications such as gems in the case of a theatre, and relics in that of a stūpa, to be placed at key points (NŚ 2.73–4). Clearly, although the functions of these buildings are different, as are their religious affiliations, the debt to a shared ritual and conceptual culture with an eye to laying out space so as to create sacred centres, and hence to establish their audiences as devotional, is pronounced.

Third, it has been shown that the *Nāṭyaśāstra*'s obsession with primary colours (which extends beyond offerings associated with orientation in the four directions to the cloths that decorate the stage, the symbolic representation of social classes and the body paint used as make-up on actors) has resonances with the colour symbolism presented in a number of early Buddhist texts, both Nikāya and Mahāyāna.[26] Alongside colour, the *Nāṭyaśāstra* makes some mention of carved sculpture ('in wood rather than stone', NŚ 2.75–9, 94), as well as painting.[27] The playhouse, which explicitly resembles a 'mountain cavern' (like the rock-cut caves of Ajanta), is plastered and whitewashed before being painted with 'creepers, men, women and their amorous exploits' (NŚ 2.81–5). This is close to the decoration of Buddhist stūpas and monastery caves,[28] although the subjects of Buddhist art are more extensive – to include both deities of all types and narratives beyond *mithuna* couples embracing. Given that the stūpa's sculptures were painted, it is likely that their colour schemes would have emulated the kinds of hues emphasized by the *Nāṭyaśāstra*, if only because these represent the most available minerals used for polychromy in the Indian subcontinent at the time.

Given the cultural parallels of the two kinds of monument, the emphasis on spectators in the *Nāṭyaśāstra* offers the potential for intriguing reflections in relation to the visuality of stūpas (especially NŚ 27.49–68, which moves from the ideal spectator to the range of classes and dispositions of different viewers, including assessors and adjudicators of disputes).[29] The fact that our earliest evidence of Indian drama (surviving unfortunately only in fragments) is the Buddhist plays of Aśvaghoṣa,[30] which were probably apologetic arguments for the new faith in response to Brahman audiences,[31] enforces the relevance of spectatorship in the Buddhist context and the sense that public monuments such as stūpas are likely to have received visitors who were not committed or exclusive Buddhists, alongside lay and monastic Buddhist worshippers. The drama of the rich imagery of monuments like Amarāvatī and the qualities of dramatic stagecraft shared with early Hindu cultural practices, such as the theatre, are a fundamental means of communication across the faith divides. In Abhinavagupta's tenth-century commentary on the *Nāṭyaśāstra*, potentially drawing on now lost earlier commentarial traditions, the religious nature of the spectator's concentration in the theatre is emphasized and specifically compared to single-pointed meditative absorption, with the audience constructed as the key active partner to the drama performed for them.[32]

Bharata's claim, put into the mouth of Brahmā himself, that 'drama is a representation of the states of the three worlds' (NŚ 1.106) is a prelude to the offering of moral education by means of artistic mimesis:

> [Theatre] teaches duty to those who go against duty, love to those who are eager for its fulfilment, and it chastises those who are ill-bred or unruly, promotes self-restraint . . . gives courage to cowards, energy to heroic persons, enlightens men of poor intellect and gives wisdom to the learned . . . firmness of mind to persons afflicted with sorrow . . . composure to persons agitated in mind . . . also relief to unlucky persons (NŚ 1.108–14)

This moral purpose, presented, of course, as an apologetic for the theatrical arts (and proposing an entirely different appreciation of the effects of mimesis from its condemnation by the likes of Plato), serves also as a broad justification for the arts in general: 'there is no wise maxim, no learning, no art or craft, no device, no action that is not found in drama' (NŚ 1.116). In the absence of specifically Buddhist forms of aesthetic theorization in the period, these models – shared across the traditions of ancient India – may reflect the theoretical assumptions underlying the artistic practices of the stūpa's artists, with the educational aims suitably adapted to Buddhist teaching.

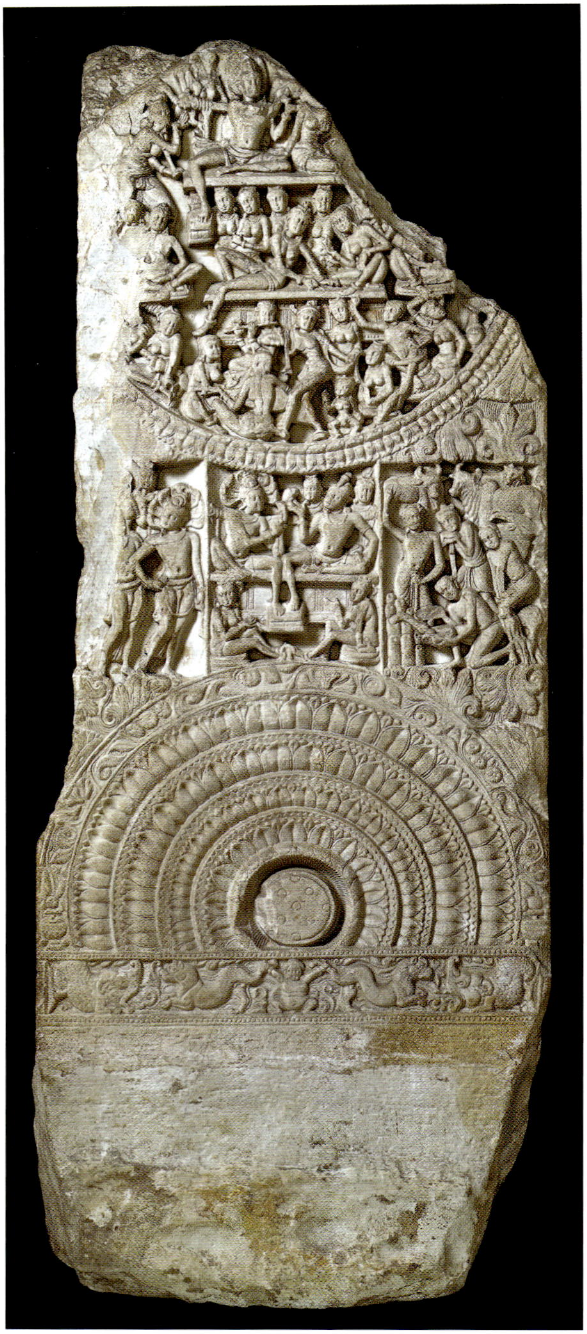

74 Broken fragment of a railing pillar, interior view.

THEATRICALITY AND THE GAZE AT AMARĀVATĪ: COURT SCENES AND PROCESSIONS

Key to the visuality of the stūpa is the central place of the viewer, envisioned as a worshipper whose process of circumambulation is inevitably a ritual practice, even for viewers who were not exclusively 'Buddhists'. The most overtly theatrical of the surviving sculptures – ones that display performances of dance and music in the royal court – make the point powerfully.[33] Take a beautiful, rather badly damaged railing pillar with as yet unidentified subject-matter, now in the British Museum (illus. 74). In the fluting of the base is a series of images that involve *nāga*s, perhaps from one or more *jātakas*, but the precise stories have eluded conclusive identification.[34] The medallion above these images (illus. 75) features another unidentified scene with a king and queen enthroned at the top in a long couch with high backrest, her right hand resting on his knee, although much of her figure is now damaged; a group of court ladies are seated on a bench below them (with no backrest), the two in the foreground focusing on something on the seat between them; at the bottom is an exquisitely rendered dancer (see illus. 4) and a dwarf amid female musicians, with what has been interpreted as a gesturing male jester to the right.[35]

All these elements of performance are found in the *Nāṭyaśāstra*.[36] It may be added that the lotus frame that rimmed the medallion (and is visible at the bottom) as well as the great half-lotuses that flanked the top and bottom of the pillar's decoration, the lower surviving one itself with a lotus-garland frame, evoke the garlands and garland makers celebrated in the *Nāṭyaśāstra*,[37] and represented as flower sellers on so many of the panels that represent stūpas from the drum, whose work casts the entirety as a devotional offering. It is not clear if the image in the roundel represents three separate scenes, separated by the bench-lines of the seated figures, or a single theatrical performance with tiered seating and the royal spectators at the top in larger scale. But clearly the lowest scene offers its representation of dance, music and the jester's humour directly to viewers, roughly at

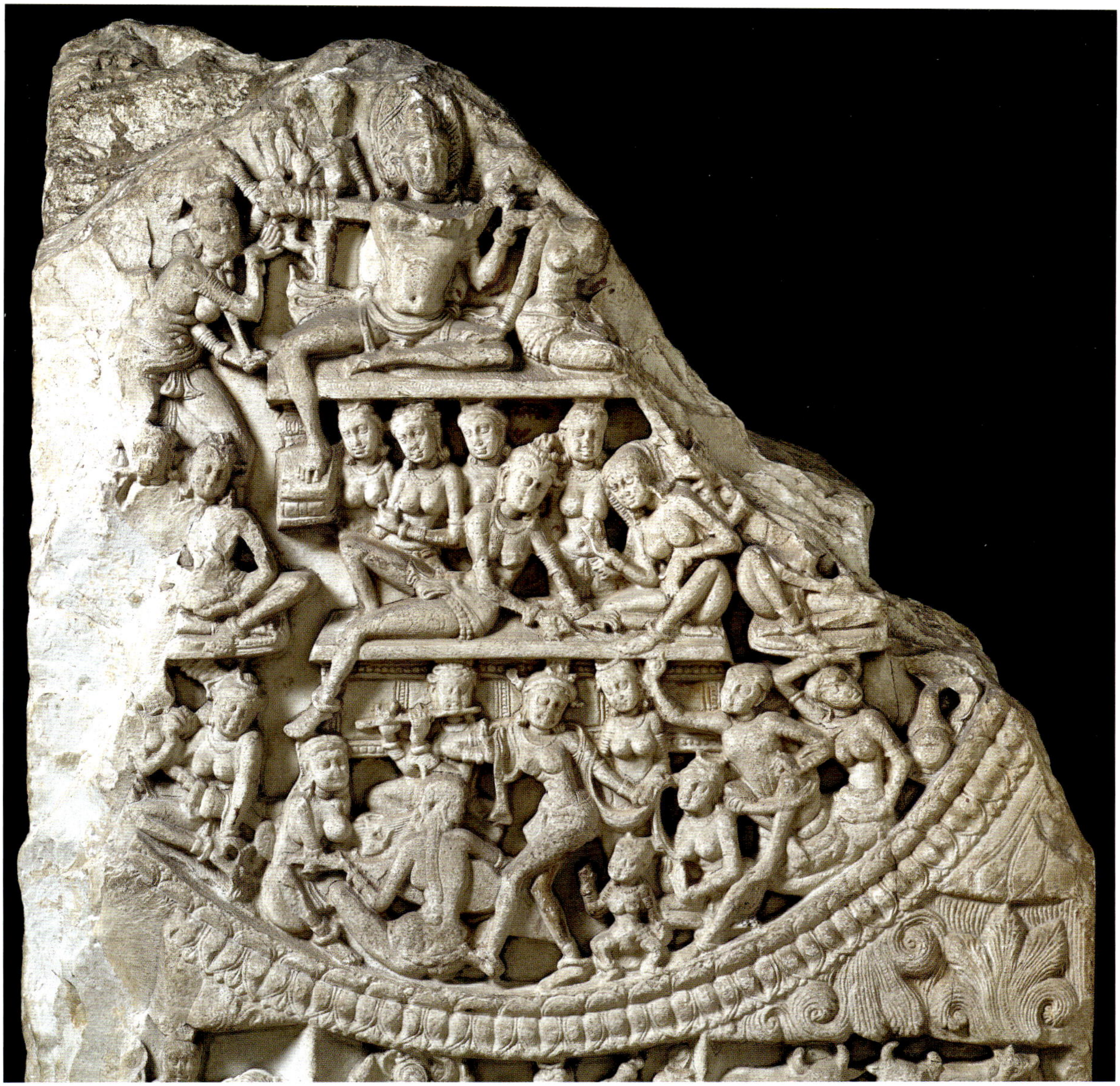

75 The historiated roundel from illus. 74 showing a performance with dance and music before an audience apparently in stacked seating with a royal couple at the top.

eye level, as they walk around the monument. That is, assuming the conceit of the sculpture is a musical dance performance before the harem, despite the vivid realism of the carving, it has been configured to present its subject to the external spectator and not those internal to its form.

In a roundel from what was probably the inner side of a railing crossbar, which survives only in one of the drawings in Mackenzie's album, a group of six dancers performs before what seems to be a youthful monarch in larger scale and with a halo, seated above on a throne with high backrest, flanked by two ladies in high-backed chairs and surrounded by the women of the harem (illus. 76).[38] If the scene is from the Buddha's final life, he is likely to be either the Bodhisattva or his

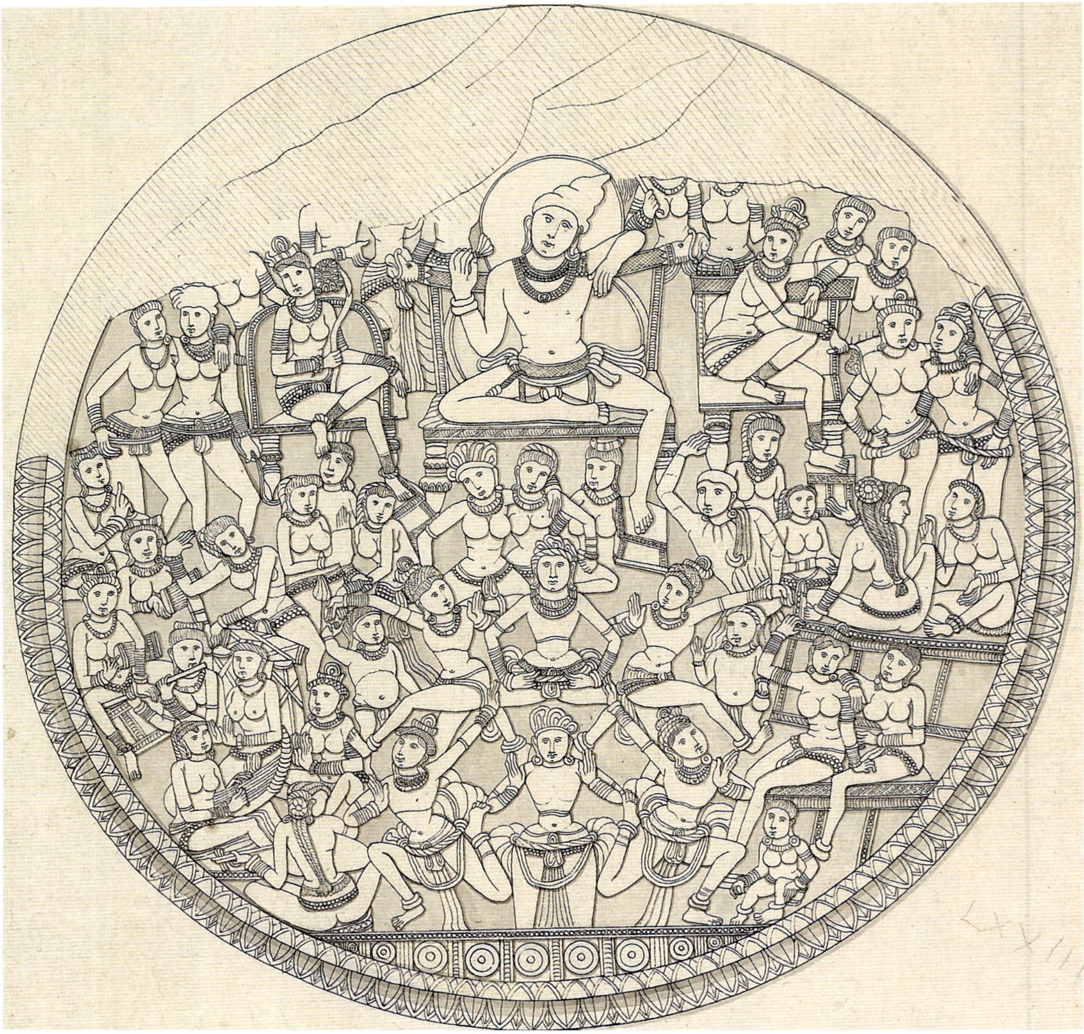

76 Drawing of a crossbar medallion from the inner railing showing a performance by dancers and musicians before a royal male in a halo surrounded by female attendants. MacKenzie's Album, WD1061, folio 66. Made by Thomas Anderson and dated 15 April 1817.

father, but it could also be an episode from a *jātaka*. To the left of the dancers is a group of female musicians in a circle turned towards each other, so that the one closest to the base is shown entirely from behind. As in the British Museum railing roundel, the mainly female spectators sit in tiers around the performers, but the dance is frontally displayed at the lower centre of the sculpture for the viewer of the medallion, who makes up, as it were, the final segment of the audience.

A harem scene as depicted on a crossbar roundel in the British Museum represents the point in the *Māndhātā-Jātaka* where the Bodhisattva, in his incarnation as the universal monarch Māndhātā, acquires an equal share of heaven itself alongside Sakka, the king of the gods (illus. 77).[39] The two kings slouch on a large throne, like a high-backed sofa, surrounded by almost entirely naked women. On the lower left they are entertained by a coterie of female musicians with

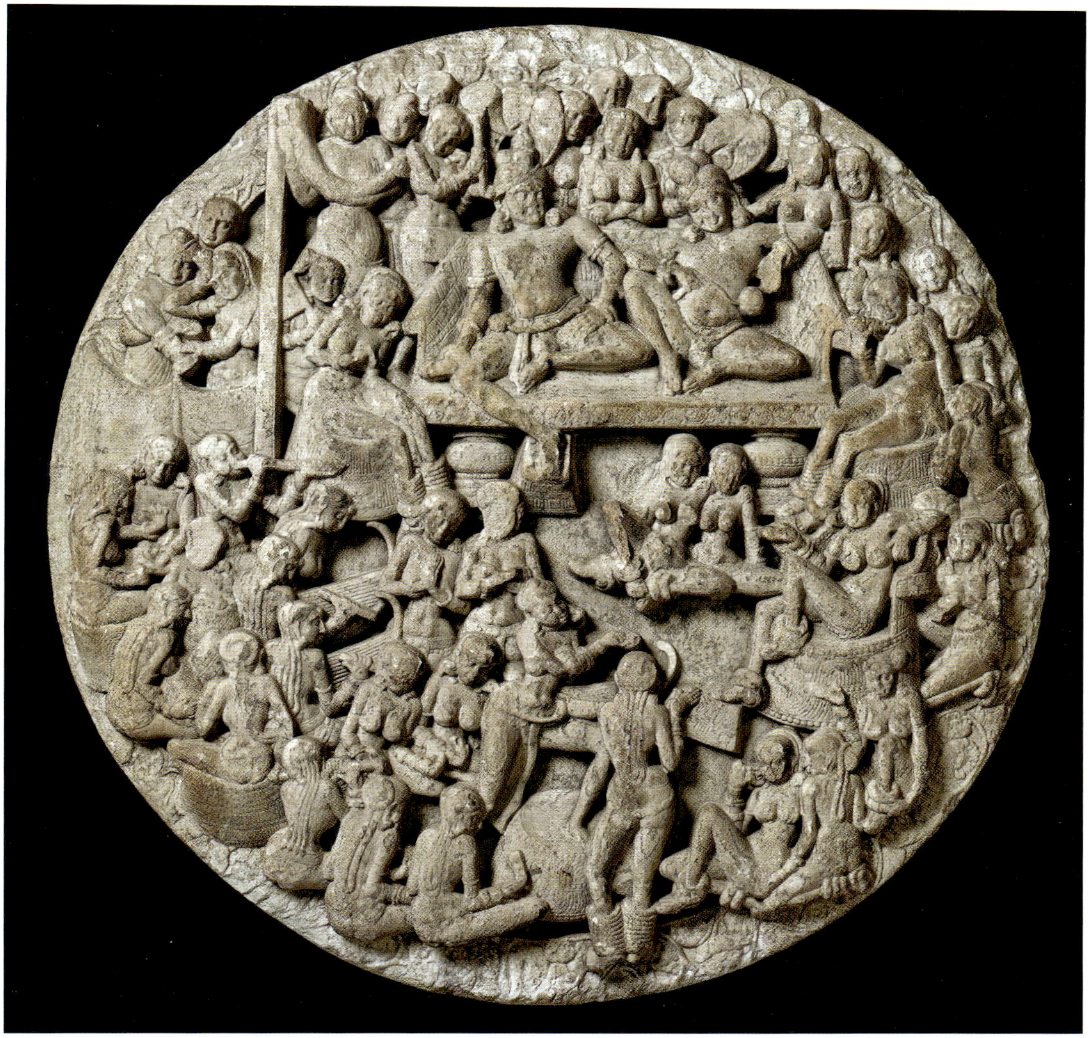

77 Crossbar medallion unfortunately trimmed of its tenons from the interior of the railing with a dance and music performance in the court of heaven before the enthroned pair of Māndhātā (a previous incarnation of the Buddha) and Sakka, the king of the gods.

long flowing hair, while a pair of dancers at the lower centre, one in heavy anklets with her back to the viewer but the other largely turned towards us, perform before the watching court, notably the women arranged to the right. All these images combine the visual staging of spectatorship of theatrical entertainment with a careful calibration of the imagery of performance to the perspective of the reliefs' spectator.[40] We look at not only the representation of dance and music but at its spectacular place at the centre of the panels' internal gaze. All these blocks show courtly performances celebrating non-monastic pleasures in earlier lifetimes or before the Bodhisattva's renunciation – that is, in the royal world of Indian culture from which the Buddha turns away, but which is so deeply celebrated in the *Nāṭyaśāstra*. Theatre, alongside intense sensuality, is the mark of the life that the Bodhisattva in his final incarnation will renounce, but all are necessary and

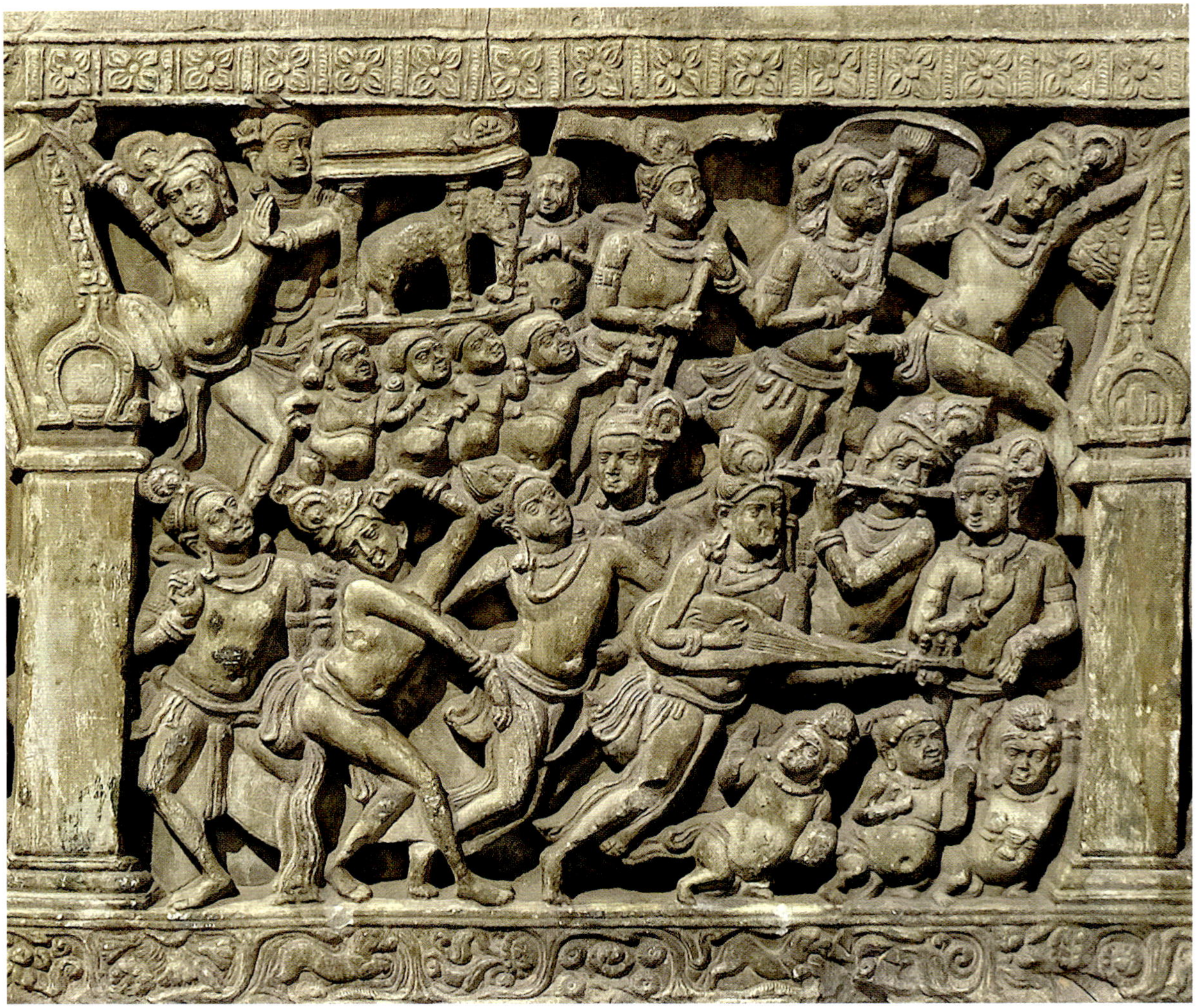

78 Detail of the coping slab, interior face, shown in illus. 52. The image shows a procession of deities with musicians leading the Bodhisattva in the form of a white elephant from the Tuśita Heaven to his last rebirth as Siddhārtha.

celebrated in the stūpa's account of his passage over innumerable lifetimes to the Great Departure.

However, at the same time, all the figures in these scenes – from the king via the chief and other queens to wives, concubines, craftswomen, actresses, dancers, maidservants and errand girls – belong specifically to the *Nāṭyaśāstra*'s careful enumeration of types of character in a play.[41] The model of the visual rhetoric by which these pictorial narratives are expressed in the stūpa overtly celebrates the theatricality of the gaze, as well as enticing a theatre-goer's gaze from its visitors, but it does so through the stock characters, poses and postures of Indian drama. Just as Aśvaghoṣa's plays, so far as we can tell from the fragments, use the characters and traditions of Indian theatre to tell stories taken from Buddhist tradition (as other drama would borrow from the Sanskrit epics, and as Aśvaghoṣa's own narrative poems also repurpose Buddhist legendary material), so the art of the stūpa uses the rhetorical forms of Indian image-making – themselves related to those of the Indian playhouse – to find the means for framing and narrating the Buddhist mythological and didactic tradition. In particular, the iconography of royal leisure is figured – very appropriately to an apologetic for the theatre within Indian culture – as the monarch at rest among the ladies of his harem, being entertained by performers accompanied by musicians.

All the gestural moves within this range of court and harem imagery belong to the rich gestural panoply of 'harmonious representation' (*sāmānyābhinaya*) presented in detail in the *Nāṭyaśāstra*.[42] Examples given by the text include 'feminine graces' (of which there are a number of variations and categories), 'ordinary expression of feeling', 'graceful expression of feeling', 'amorous gestures', 'dishabille' or careless placement of clothing and ornaments, 'confusion', 'affection', 'coldness' and many others.[43] So, for example, the intimate affect of the queen's hand on the king's thigh as she appears to turn back towards him in the British Museum roundel with the dancer and the dwarf just discussed (see illus. 75) is a 'gesture of the major limbs', to which the *Nāṭyaśāstra* devotes an entire chapter (NŚ 9). But it also plays against the categories of 'amorous gestures' (which include the movement of hands, NŚ 24.15) and 'manifestation of affection' (NŚ 24.19), arising from desire (NŚ 24.94–179).[44] It could indeed be argued that this kind of imagery, setting up the sensual context of non-Buddhist, non-ascetic Indian culture, is placed in deliberate and constant opposition to the iconography of numerous teaching scenes showing the Buddha (whether in figural or emblematic form) seated in the midst of large retinues of devotees, whether monks (see illus. 36, 81 to the right, 82, the two figures behind the throne, 123 to the right, 127 medallion to the right and fluting lower right), brahmans (illus. 81 to the left, 115, 125, 127 medallion to the left, 130, 135), women (illus. 82, 114, 116, 123 to the left) or ascetics (127 lower left and centre). Strikingly, canto 4 of Aśvaghoṣa's *Buddhacarita* explicitly and at length depicts the Bodhisattva in terms of resisting the seductive blandishments of courtly women, of the kind to which many earlier Brahman sages are presented as succumbing.[45]

The pageant-like performativity of action to musical accompaniment is celebrated again in those processional scenes where musicians accompany ceremonial cavalcades. A good example is when the gods escort the litter with the Bodhisattva in elephant form, as he leaves the Tuṣita Heaven for his final rebirth, for instance in the central panel of the fine coping slab now in the Kolkata Museum (illus. 78, see also 52 and 53), where the company is led by dwarfs and musicians with male dancers following. Likewise, in a mysterious coping frieze in the British Museum, the subject-matter of which has not been identified (illus. 79),[46] a great procession including horses and elephants riding towards a stūpa is potentially made theatrical by the musicians in the lead (illus. 80). The Kolkata piece depicts flute and lute players, whereas the British Museum block depicts a drummer and a conch-blower, which seems to suggest different types of music to accompany different kinds of contexts. The *Nāṭyaśāstra* explicitly claims:

> In a festival, a royal procession and a Mangala
> ceremony [which I take to mean a marriage],
> in an auspicious and happy occasion, at the time
> of marriage and of birth of sons and so on, in a
> battle where fighters assemble, and during other
> such acts, all the musical instruments should be
> played . . . During expeditionary marches and
> performances of plays, all the instruments
> should be played. (NŚ 33.19–21)

Given the great length of the treatment of music in the *Nāṭyaśāstra*, including discussion of classes of musical instruments, the kinds of sentiments to which different instruments are best applied, and some attention to musicians,[47] it is clear that music is central to Indian conceptions of theatricality. The representation of musical accompaniment in these kinds of processions may frame the depicted activities as if they were performances of the events they show as well as being images of those events. We cannot in the end be clear, for instance, whether the coping frieze now in Kolkata is meant to show the actual descent of the Bodhisattva in the form of an elephant in his last rebirth or to imply a pageant depicting this story, itself reflected at

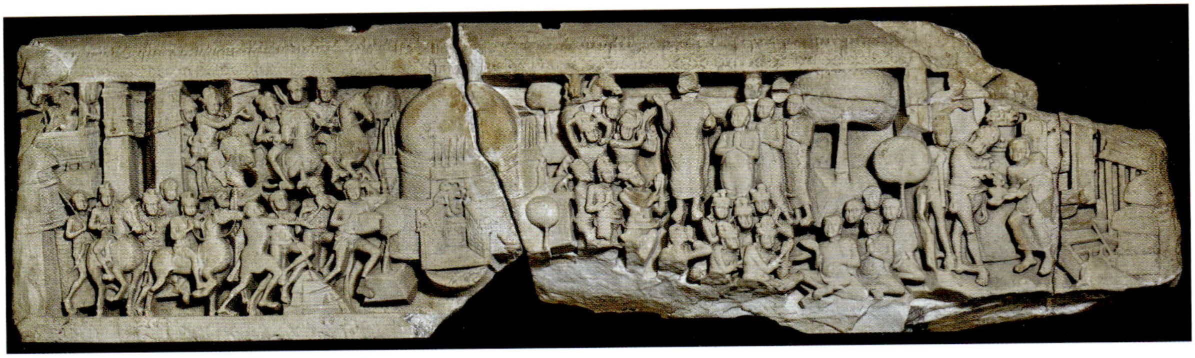

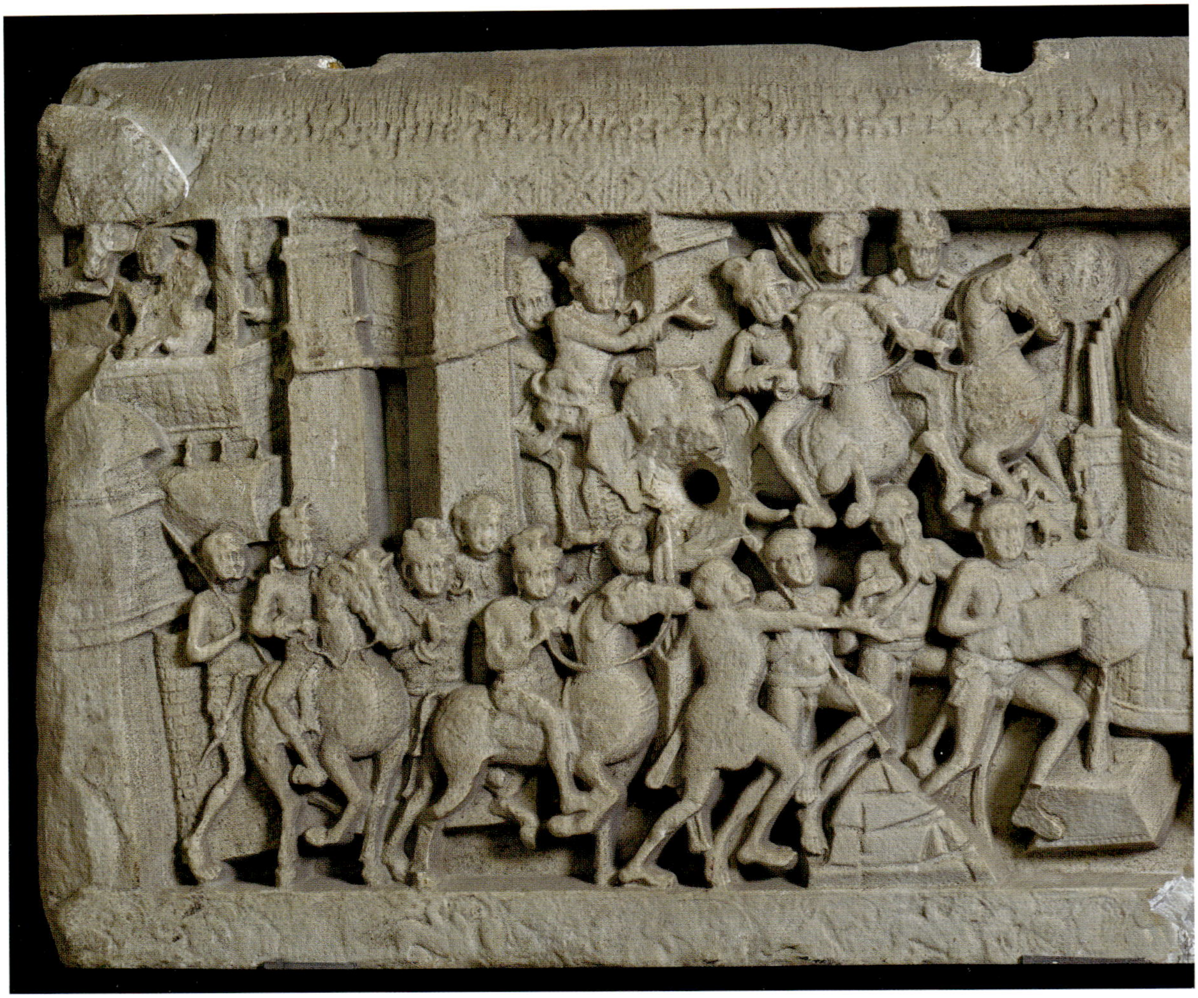

79 Damaged and somewhat abraded but intact coping slab (2.76 m in length), interior face (of illus. 19) showing an unidentified processional scene with music to the left, a stūpa and a scene including a larger-scale figure who appears to be hovering.

80 Detail of illus. 79 showing the procession with musicians at the front.

second hand in sculptural relief. In both these examples from the upper level of the interior decoration of the railing, the viewer moves from left to right along the sculpture, emulating the movement of the people and animals in the processions. Likewise, in the narrow framing friezes at the base, the beasts move in the same direction. The dynamic of processional movement is thus brought into the real time and present moment of any visiting devotee.

What happens in these processional and courtly theatrical scenes, both accompanied by music, is that the stūpa's viewer is afforded a vicarious vision of the celebratory imagery and also the option of participation, given that the performative aspects are always presented for display to the external gaze. The presence of musicians, the stock nature of all the figures represented and the gestural repertoire of their interactions enable a brilliant double perspective, where (in both the theatrical and processional images) it is impossible to be clear as to whether the viewer is meant to be witnessing a real episode of the past, narrated in the normative theatrically influenced visual styles of Indian art, or the image of a theatrical performance of that subject. Theatrical visuality, as inspired by the traditions of the *Nāṭyaśāstra*, thus effectively determines Brahmanic culture in the stūpa's visual discourse (placed in the world of the distant and intermediate epochs, as discussed in Chapter Three) and distances it from the post-enlightenment proximate epoch and thereafter.

NON-THEATRICAL VISUALITY

This range of imagery evoking pre-Buddhist India is set against the rich range of representations showing the Buddha himself, teaching (whether standing or seated, whether in fully human or emblematic form) as the central spectacle surrounded by watching, listening and prostrating devotees. In a host of images, theatrical performance – whether processional or court ceremonial – is replaced by the dharma as object of the gaze. That moves the social level away from monarchs to monastics, from royal status to persons of any social level who take up the Buddhist path. It can also move the attention beyond the Buddha to other enlightened beings in his wake, such as *arahat*s. The figures – the fully enlightened – exist, within the stūpa's discourse, only in the proximate epoch, in the world after the Buddha's awakening and the enlightenments of his numerous *arahat* followers, many of whom belong to our own epoch which succeeds his death. Immediately after the processional scene just discussed, in a coping frieze panel of uncertain subject-matter in the British Museum, there appears an image of a stūpa with *āyaka* platforms and columns surrounded by a railing, with a *nāga* rising in the central gateway, and by four trees, which may all have had a *buddhapāda* beneath them, although the relief is damaged and it survives only in the one to the left foreground (illus. 81).[48]

This appears to mark a point after the Buddha's death. To the right is a scene of a figure larger than the others rising into the air, observed by men in turbans to the left and monks to the right (both adopting the prayerful hands gesture of the *añjali mudrā*, illus. 81). Below this and beside it to the right is a scene of the same turbaned figures seated with their hands in the *añjali mudrā* before a monk who is making a gesture of teaching, with a retinue of other monks behind him. In place of the drama of the procession accompanied by music, here we have a miraculous spectacle of levitation (whether by the Buddha himself or by one of his *arahat*s).[49] Next to it, in place of music, we are offered the oral exposition of the dharma and its hearing by both monks and laypersons. The theatrical visuality of courtly performances and processions is replaced with a visuality of supranormal powers as the demonstration of the dharma alongside the speaking and hearing of the Buddha's teaching.

The supernatural nature of the spectacle afforded by dharma is itself emphasized by the use of emblematic bodies of the Buddha in numerous scenes, especially columns with the wheel at the head rising behind an empty throne with the *buddhapāda* beneath, flaming pillars crowned by the *trisula* above an empty throne and *buddhapāda*, or rising *nāga*s, or the Buddha seated with the *nāga* Mucalinda rising behind him, as in

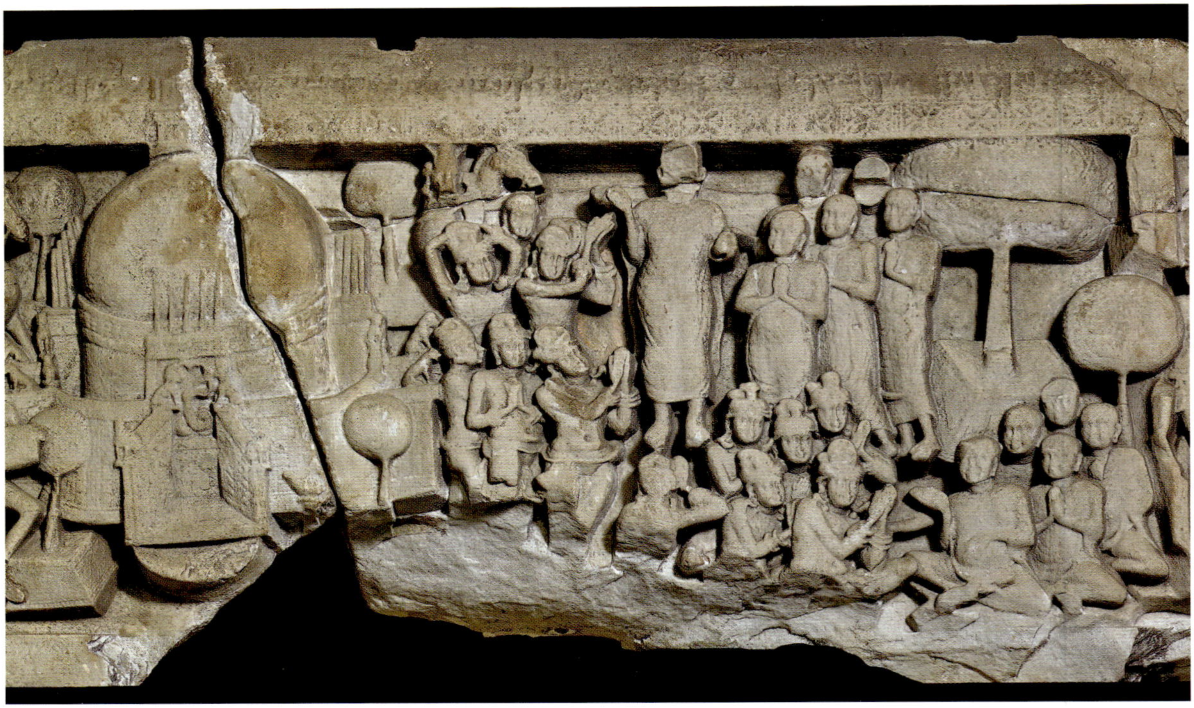

81 Detail of illus. 79 showing the stūpa with trees to either side and a Buddhapāda on a platform beneath the tree to the left, and a scene with the Buddha or another miraculous figure apparently levitating between standing brahman and monastic devotees and seated brahmans and monks to the lower right.

illus. 94 and 95. I will discuss this phenomenon in greater detail in Chapter Seven. But the point is that the supranormal, rather than any kind of theatrical visuality, is effectively the normative spectacle in the monastic world transformed by the Buddha's enlightenment, while the human theatrical universe of mere dramatic imitation as defined by the *Nāṭyaśāstra* is in large part reserved for the society of Brahmanic precursors, or for those who choose a primarily lay life.

DANCE AND MUSIC AS DEVOTION

One aspect of the gestural language of human dance – notably when separated from the representation of musicians – is its use to show devotion, especially in the case of worshipping females. In a fine crossbar medallion from the inner railing, a monarch accompanied by women attendants (all in the *añjali mudrā*) stands to the left of the Buddha's empty throne, with two monks standing behind it (illus. 82). In front of the throne three women are involved in what has been called 'ecstatic worship', utilizing gestures that have been suggested as borrowings from dance movements.[50] The appropriation of dance postures for devotion is different from the representation of dance as a theatrical activity, subject to the human voyeuristic gaze.

In a few of the instances where the upper parts of the miniature stūpas on slabs from the main drum survive, the celebratory deities depicted above the dome play musical instruments. Usually, these deities show devotion in other forms,[51] but in the case of the fine British Museum slab with the Buddha and Mucalinda in the central gateway, musical gods cavort in the air on the upper left, alongside what appears to be a dancing deity (illus. 83, 94 and 95).[52] This motif on the stūpa slabs of the drum, showing the divine celebrations around an entire stūpa, is arguably parallel to the imagery of pot-bellied dwarf-like deities dancing and playing musical instruments, which appear in the fluting of the exterior faces of a series of railing pillars (illus. 84). Usually these are in the form of a central dancer and two musicians on either side.[53] In the conceit of this repeated iconography on the exterior of the stūpa's railing perimeter, deities dancing to music are celebrating the three-dimensional monument, just as the gods above the dome are doing in the drum slabs.

In the mythical origin story of the *Nāṭyaśāstra*, Brahmā instructs Indra, the king of the gods, to dramatize the tales 'composed by me' and have them acted by 'the gods who are skilful, learned, bold in speech and inured to hard work' (NŚ 1.20). But Indra responds that the gods are incapable, and that drama must be handled by the sages, at which point Brahmā commands Bharata (the supposed author of the text) to learn, teach and practise the dramatic and musical arts (NŚ 1.21–5, 41–2). Since music is central to drama, and since it is explicitly denied to the gods in the tradition of the *Nāṭyaśāstra*, it is perhaps strange to see it performed by deities on and around the stūpa. But this is

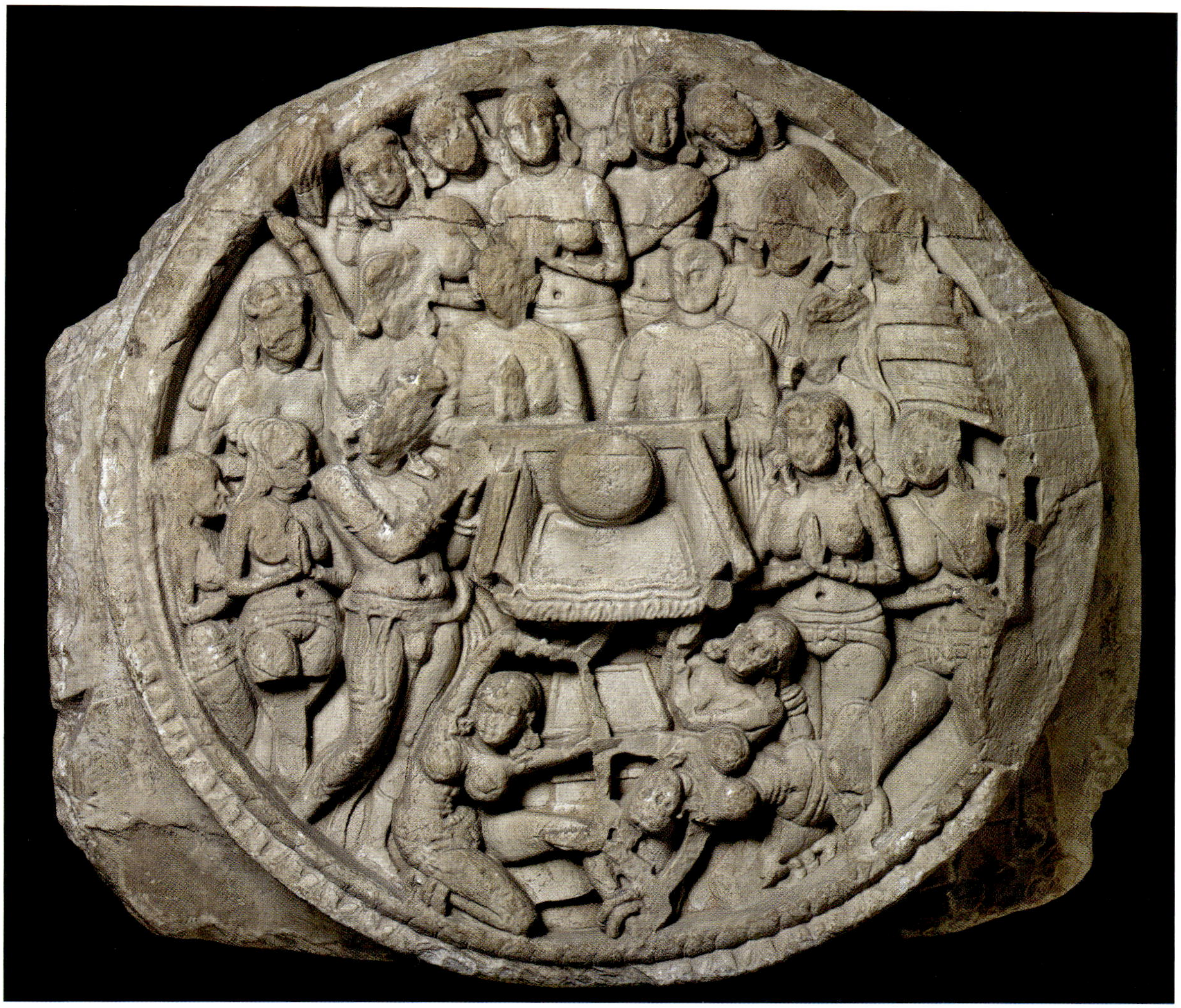

82 Crossbar medallion from the interior of the railing with obeisance paid to the empty throne and ecstatic forms of prostration from the women below.

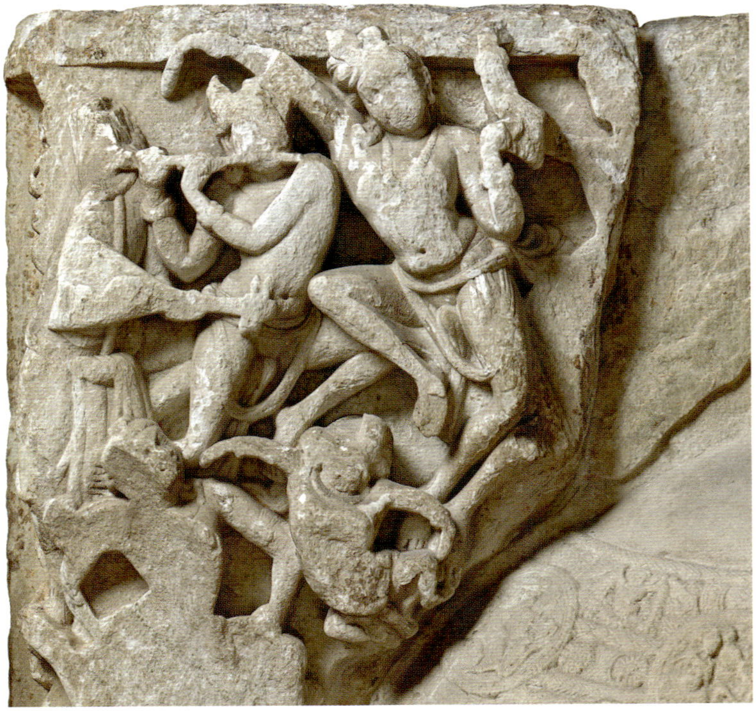

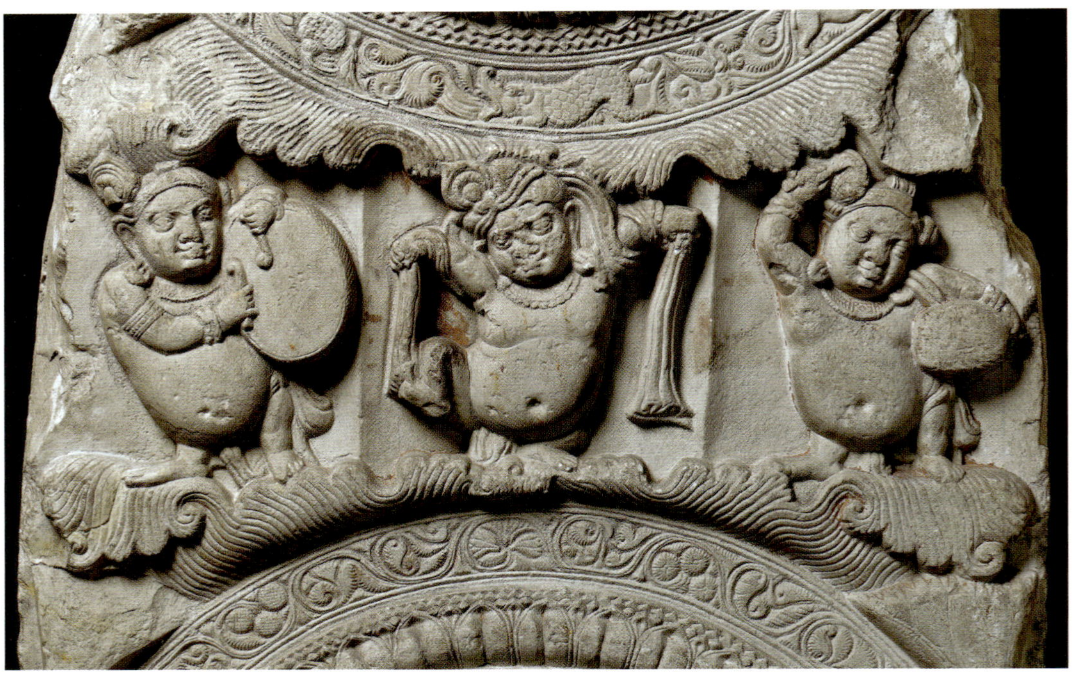

83 Detail of the upper right of a drum slab showing a stūpa (illus. 94 and 95) with divine musicians celebrating.

84 Detail from a fragmentary railing pillar, exterior view, showing a dancing dwarf between two others playing musical instruments.

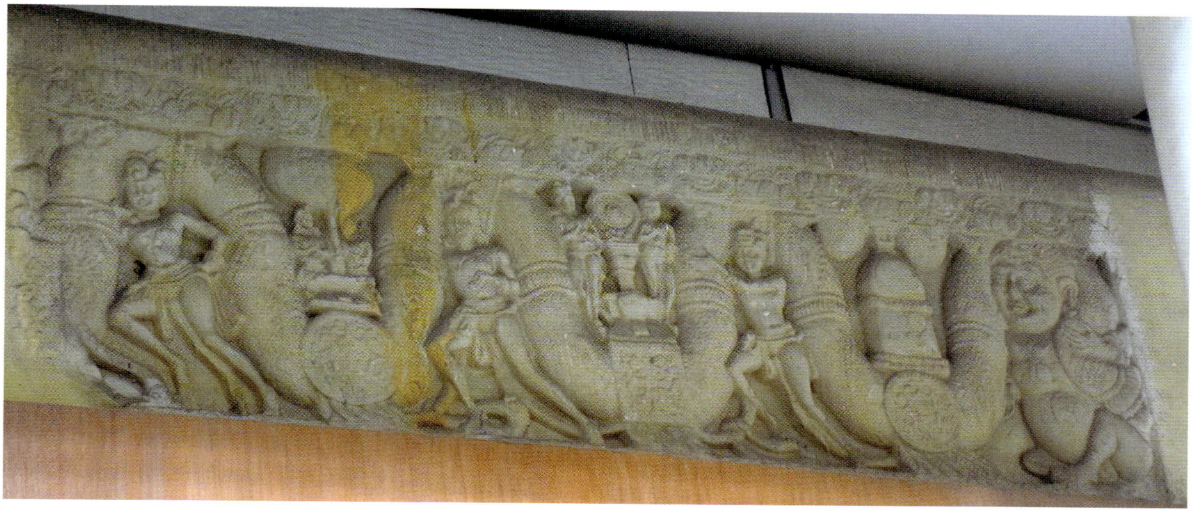

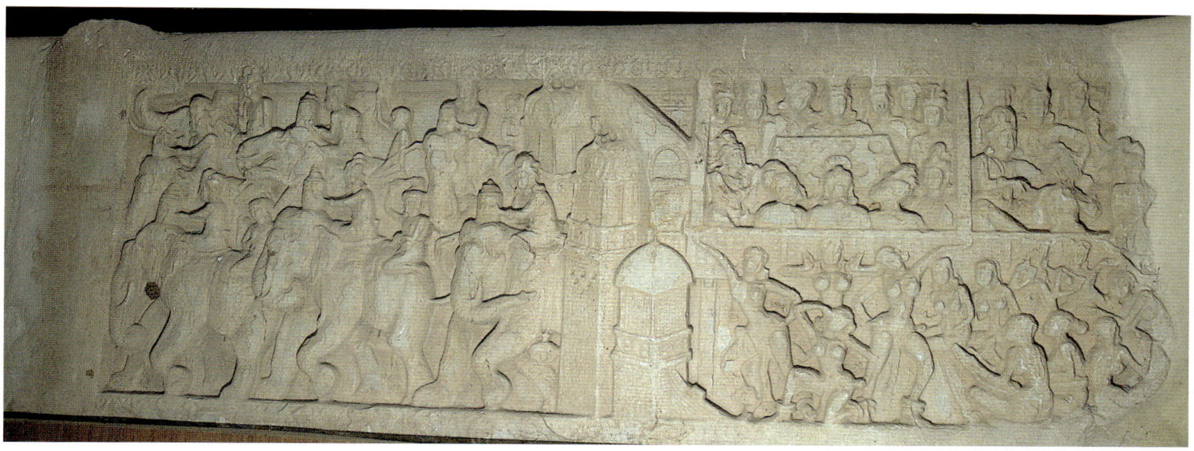

85 Intact coping slab (2.15 m in length) from the end of the railing at a gateway, exterior face with a dwarf holding an undulating garland to the right, garland bearers and imagery of stūpa, *dharmacakra* and Bodhi tree in garland's U-bends.

86 Intact coping slab (2.15 m in length) from the end of the railing at a gateway, interior face of illus. 85, with scenes of the division of relics to the right and their transportation across India to the left.

conceivably a Buddhist riposte to Brahmanic practice, or a fulfilment of the Brahmanic world: these gods do perform (unlike those of the *Nāṭyaśāstra*), and what they celebrate is not a tale composed by Brahmā but the manifestation of a fully enlightened being whose birth, enlightenment, First Sermon and passing away were all events that caused the 10,000-world system to quake. The musician and dancing deities, reversing the *Nāṭyaśāstra*'s origin myth, effectively become part of the visual rhetoric of a Buddhist apologetic, whereby Buddhism completes and fulfils the earlier spiritual life of India by bringing supreme awakening and its possibilities.

At the same time, the employment of the auspicious implications of musical performance and dance may simply mark the sacred-celebratory intimations of the representation of a stūpa. Music – including song – is described as pleasing to the gods (NŚ 36.20–22), as dissipating of evils and as a harbinger of prosperity (NŚ 36.23), including the apotropaic defence against 'ferocious spirits' (NŚ 36.26): 'In places in which there occur instrumental music and dramatic performance, or song and instrumental music, there will surely never be any kinds of inauspicious happening' (NŚ 36. 28). In the scenes including divinities, this means entry into a normally invisible world where the range and variety of gods of the Indian pantheon participate in celebration of the Buddha and his religion, presented as a fulfilment of the Brahmanic world, including the secular and the ascetic cultures within it.

All these themes may be said to converge in the one subject in the Buddha's life story that brings music, dance, laity and monks together, namely the lamentation at the Buddha's passing away. Here, in the text of the *Mahāparinibbāna Sutta*, music and dance by laypersons (the Mallas of Kusinārā, where the Buddha passed away) are repeatedly presented as an aspect of the Buddha's last rites, in relation to both his body before cremation and the relics afterwards.[54] This is explicitly represented in a coping frieze, now in the Government Museum in Chennai, which was probably the endpiece at the opening of one of the four main gateways on the left side of the railing as one walked into the stūpa precinct, since the right-hand edge of the exterior face has a large, fat dwarf seated at the end holding the beginning of the curving roll of garlands that wind their way around the top of the railing (illus. 85).[55] This figure marks an endpoint of the railing before the rising of a pillar with a capital and block base, such as that now in the British Museum (see Chapter Two, and illus. 44), which has a further fat dwarf holding up the image of a stepped base at its upper rim, above which sat one of the monumental lions at the end of the gateway.[56]

The narrative direction on the interior of this slab, unusually for the coping of the rail, proceeds from right to left and shows two scenes divided as often by architectural framing (illus. 86). That is, the imagery is designed to be seen in narrative order as the viewer walks out of the gateway.[57] The section to the right (illus. 87) is itself split into several segments. At the top right (in a rather damaged area) the Buddha's various lay followers disagree about what to do with his remains; in the scene

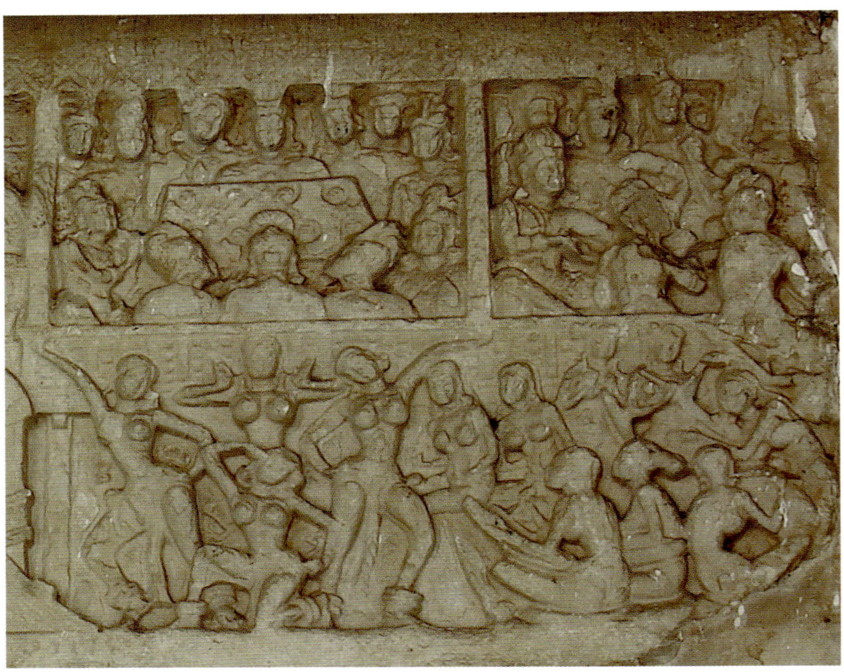

87 Detail of illus. 86: top – division of relics; bottom – mourning ceremonies for the Buddha's cremation, including music and dancing.

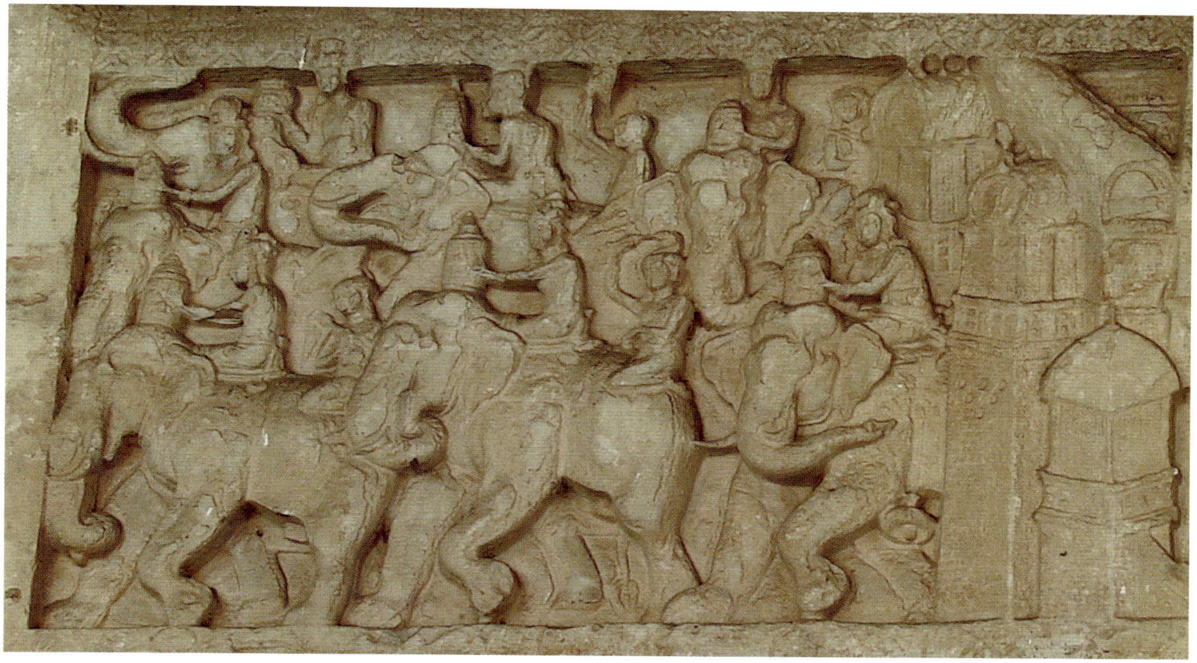

88 Detail of illus. 86: transportation of relics in stūpa-shaped reliquaries by elephant.

next to it, twelve men around an oblong table appear to be dividing the relics into eight portions.[58] All the figures in the upper tier are male. At the bottom is a scene of seated musicians and four dancers. All are female.[59] The four dancers all face out towards the viewer (as usual in dance imagery) in broadly symmetrical formation, with the one in the foreground kneeling. If this scene represents the ceremonies venerating the remains of the Buddha's funeral pyre 'for a week . . . with dancing, singing, garlands and music',[60] then this scene precedes the division of relics. If, however, it represents the festivities of 'singing and dancing' which Buddhaghosa's fifth-century Pāli commentary tells us accompanied the completion of the division of relics and their departure from Kusinārā,[61] then this image immediately follows the two above and precedes the relief to the left side of the slab showing the relics leaving the city. The image to the left shows seven elephants passing through and beyond a grand city gate (illus. 88). Each has two riders who take a domed reliquary in the form of a stūpa to a different location across India, with the eighth casket implicitly remaining in Kusinārā, the site of the *parinirvāṇa*.[62]

Here, in the context of the culminating story of the Buddha's life and the so-called proximate epoch before our own, a story we may presume was told at length along the coping for the viewer to peruse as she walked out of the precinct, the themes of lay and monastic traditions of worship after the Buddha's death are set out. The mourners who celebrate and divide the relics are of both genders, and the division is supervised not by a monk (such as Anuruddha, who determines when the Buddha has actually passed away, or Mahākassapa, who oversees the funeral pyre) but by the brahmin Doṇa. The music and dance performed here – no longer a matter of performance to be observed but of devotional celebration – are the human complement to the gods dancing and playing instruments around the stūpa as monumental reliquary. But the Brahman supervision and ceremonial in relation to the *parinibbāna*, in both the scriptural text and the stūpa's imagery, is a gesture of integrating Buddhism within its Indic context.

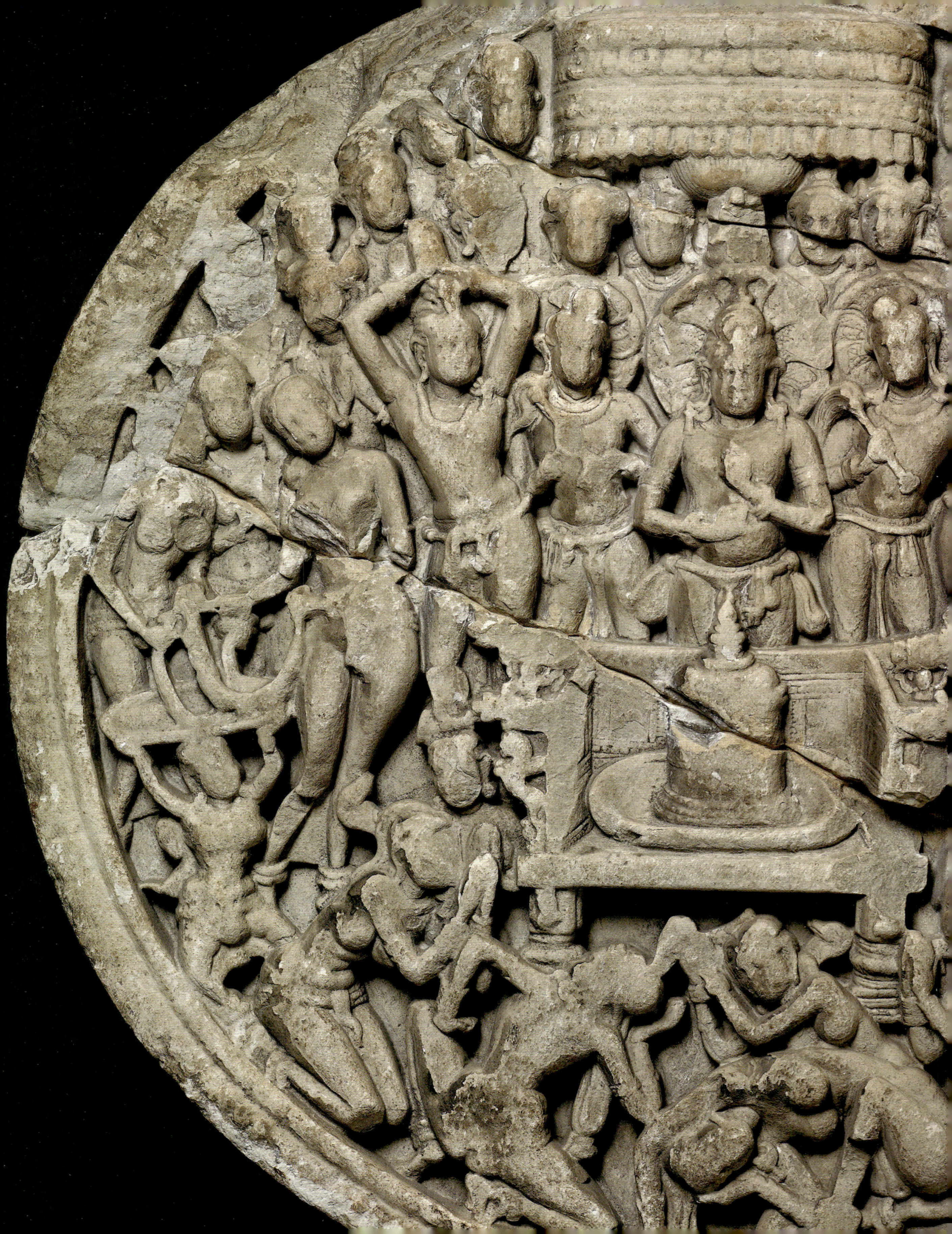

five
Cosmography

Cosmography has recently been defined as 'the rhetoric of cosmology: the art of composing worlds'.[1] More concretely, any example of cosmography is not an instance of a universalist generalization of a given culture's cosmological assumptions,[2] but is rather a particular intervention, a form of 'cosmoplasty'.[3] This is not 'a reflection of . . . culture, the echo of a historical situation or an expression of analogical ontology', but rather 'a standpoint opposed to other standpoints and a transformation of the correspondences that give meaning to things.'[4] 'Cosmography . . . is the composition of possible worlds that coexist on a stage of conflicts and alternatives.'[5] The moment we accept any cosmographic statement as a claim within a bigger world of counterclaims and alternative representations – that is, as a discursive gesture within a larger and continuing cultural conversation – we are liberated from making of it a representative for a larger collective generalization. Thus, what I will attempt to explore here is not ancient Indian Buddhist cosmography in general, or the still more fraught project of placing this within other Indic cosmographies of broadly the same period or earlier (Vedic, Brahmanic, Jain and so forth). Rather, I will focus on how the stūpa at Amarāvatī constructed itself as a cosmography and a cosmological sacred centre.

As we saw in Chapter One, a stūpa is effectively a mound of rubble and earth raised over relics. Because the relics were regarded as living entities, even having rights of property ownership, the stūpa was itself regarded as a living presence – usually, in the case of the Buddhist examples in India, the Buddha's own presence.[6] Unlike the most stunning circular or cylindrical monuments of the contemporary Roman world (such as the Pantheon or the Columns of Trajan and Marcus), a stūpa was not a space to be entered. There was no access to the buried relics, although there was certainly knowledge of their existence, or to the symbolic mapping that constituted

89 Detail of illus. 92: crossbar medallion from the inner railing, showing male and female *nāgas* adoring a stūpa-shaped reliquary.

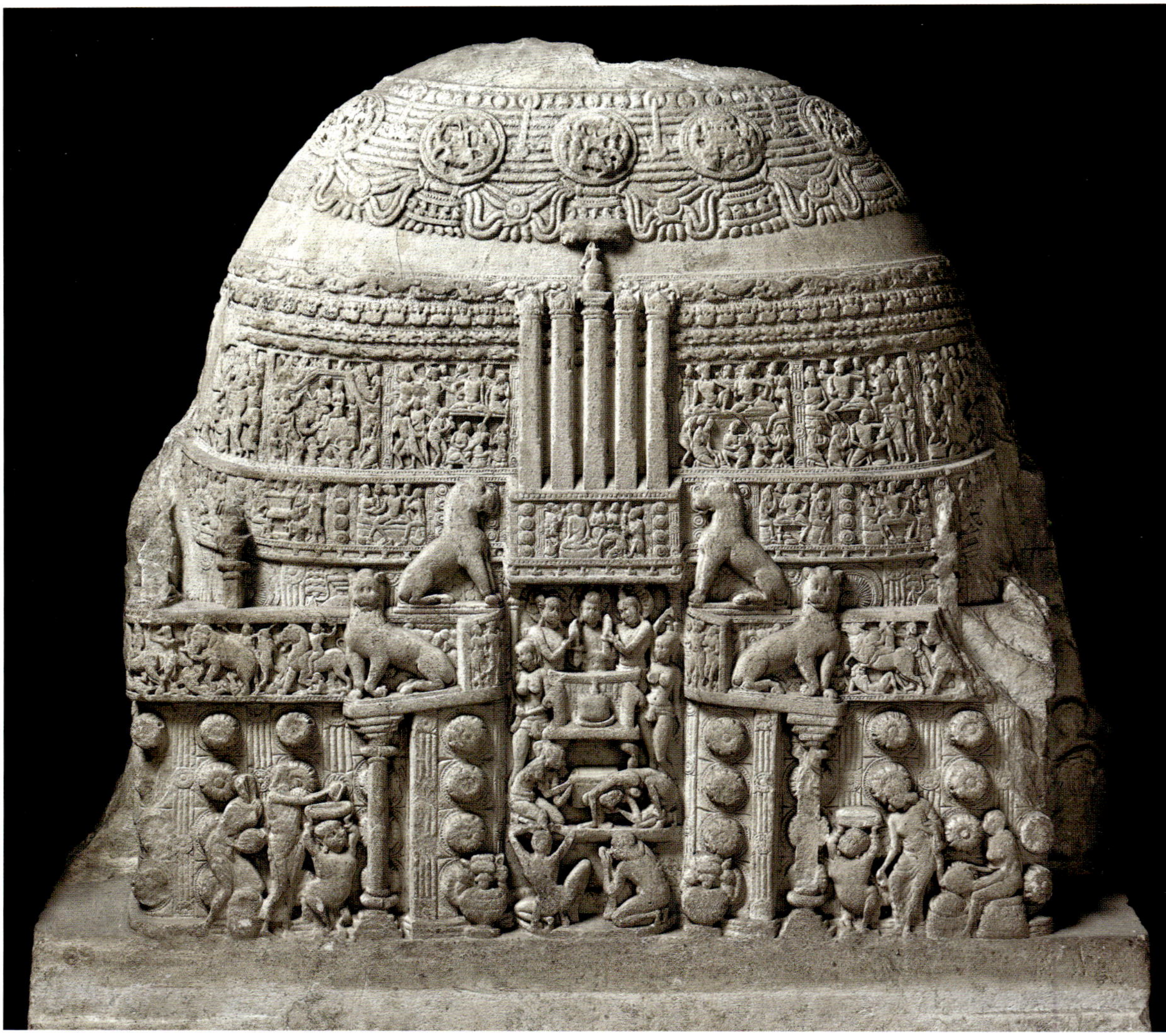

90 Remains of a drum slab showing stūpa, gateway and railing with the image of a stūpa-shaped reliquary adored by *nāgas* in the entrance. Found in the northeast quadrant.

the foundations (which we know from other stūpas but were never properly uncovered at Amarāvatī). However, if we think of cosmography as a form of mapping in space and time, then the very form of the monument in its orientations, hidden structures and relic caskets maps out spatially and monumentally its claim to be a sacred centre.

We may add that relics – usually represented in stūpa-shaped caskets (see illus. 7) – are regularly featured in several of the surviving sculptures (not least in the reliquaries distributed by elephant across India, which were discussed at the end of the last chapter and are seen in illus. 88), thematizing the Buddha's reliquary presence and the stūpa's own sacred centrality as a focus of devotion. One may mention an interesting panel depicting a stūpa that survives from the drum of the main mound (illus. 90).[7] In the central gateway of the depicted stūpa is a reliquary in the form of a stūpa itself enthroned on a fine three-sided and high-backed seat, with three *nāga* kings behind it and worshipping female *nāgas* to

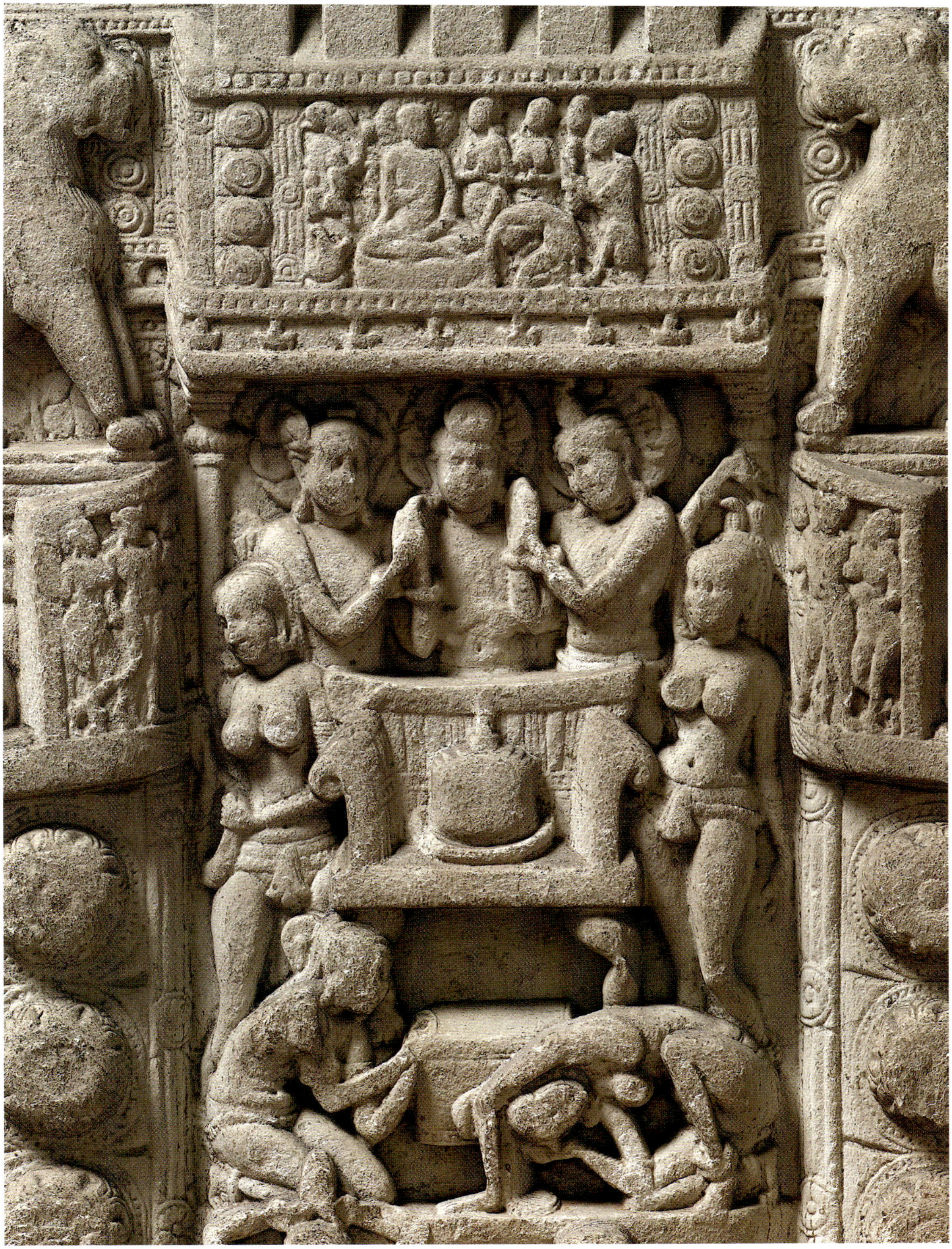
91 Detail of the entrance in illus. 90.

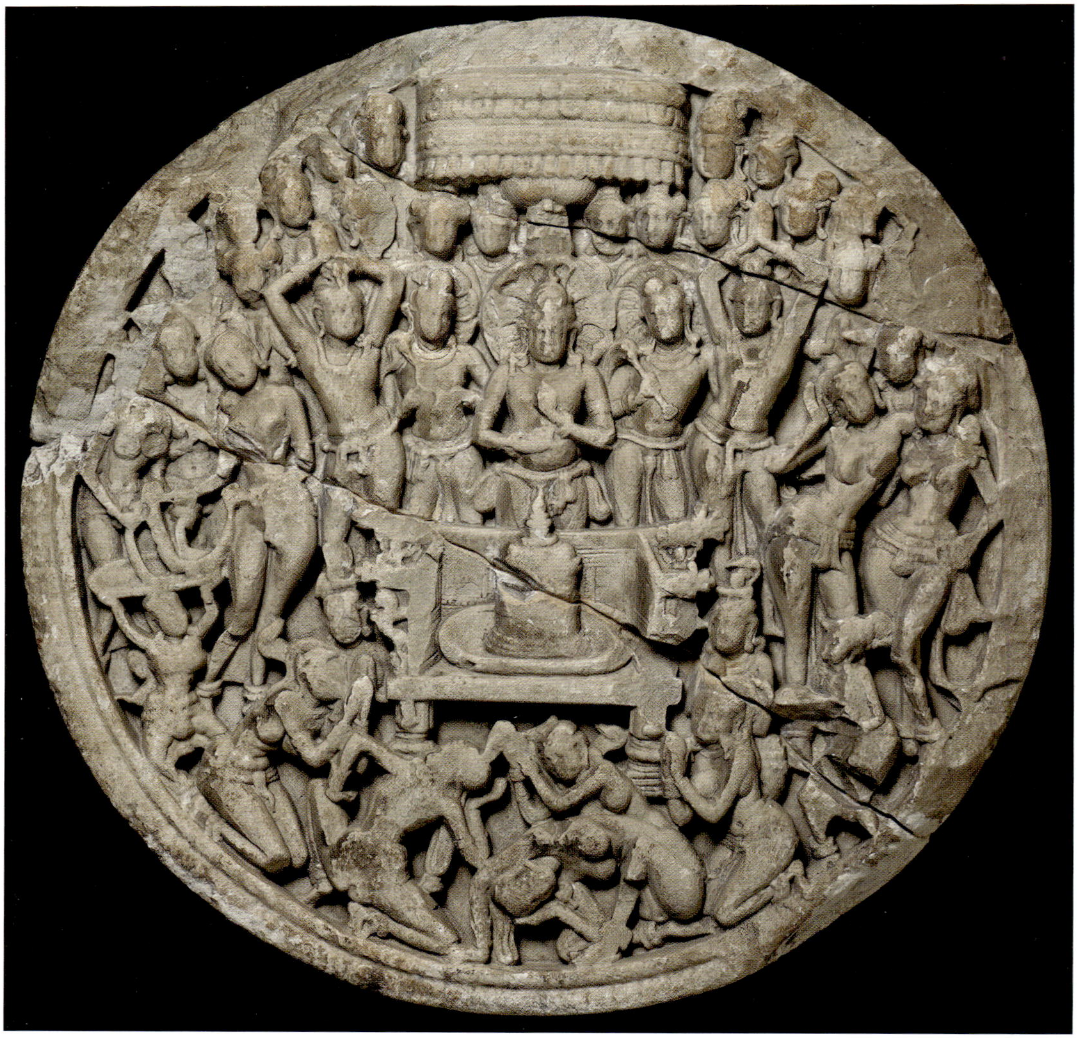

92 Crossbar medallion from the inner railing, trimmed of its tenons, broken and significantly damaged during transport from exhibition in France in 1867, showing male and female *nāgas* adoring a stūpa-shaped reliquary.

the side and below (illus. 91). The kings are defined by the multiple serpents emerging in a kind of halo behind their heads, the females by single serpents rising behind them at the tops of their heads. In the panel depicted immediately above this scene, the figure of the Buddha preaching is represented in the presence of a number of figures, including a prostrating woman in the same posture and effectively the same position, to the right of the object of worship, as the bowing female *nāga* in the central doorway and enthroned casket scene. Effectively, the stūpa-shaped reliquary mirrors the form of the larger stūpa (as so many real reliquaries did), while the worshipping figure not only demonstrates the appropriate form of devotion to a reliquary stūpa but implies that this is precisely the same form of devotion as was appropriate to the living Buddha.[8]

In a fine crossbar from the interior of the great stone railing that surrounded the monument (illus. 92), significantly damaged since it was excavated by Mackenzie, the same subject of male *nāgas* and female *nāga* worshippers

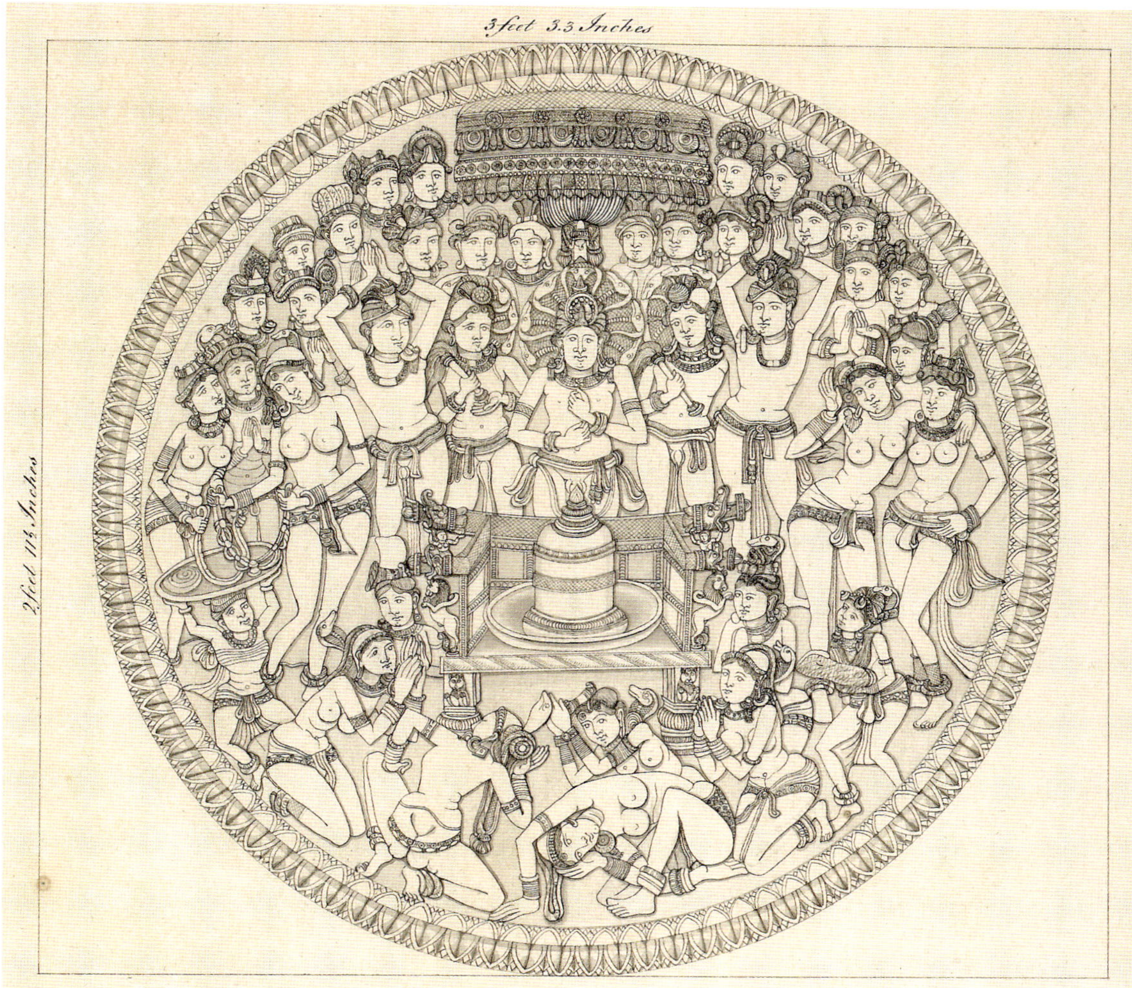

93 Post-excavation drawing of the crossbar medallion from the inner railing shown in illus. 92, MacKenzie's Album WD1061, folio 63. Made by Henry Hamilton, dated April 1817, and inscribed 'The best finished sculpture in Delpadinna'. It shows the excellent state of preservation of the original find.

before the enthroned relic casket is depicted more extensively.[9] Here the stūpa-shaped casket is central, the devotional focus, its finial rising above the throne on which it is placed, while the foreshortened circularity of the basin on which it sits, as well as the foreshortened round tray carried by a serving girl to the left, the flat form of the elaborate umbrella-canopy above (which was probably intended as circular, as can be better seen from the surviving nineteenth-century post-excavation drawing, illus. 93) and the round form of the medallion shape of the sculpture itself are in dialogue with the domed cylindricality of the reliquary's substance. Many details can perhaps be better seen in the drawing, which reveals an object in much better condition than today, with no breaks and the lotus rim of the roundel entirely intact. Quite apart from the impression of worlds within worlds, the divine nature of the participants – notably that of the *nāga*s immediately in the vicinity of the casket – sets up a parallel world to that of the stūpa itself, where divine worshippers circling the casket emulate real human pilgrims circumambulating the stūpa mound.[10] In other sculptures, as we saw in the preceding chapter, the human narrative of the Buddha's own relics – their worship, division and distribution – is told, setting up a historical origin for the specific reliquaries underpinning the monument itself.

TIME AND SPACE

This chapter looks to pursue an account of the cosmography of Amarāvatī by looking at its visual constructions of time and space, as can be ascertained from the surviving sculptural imagery. The extraordinarily rich narrative imagery of the stūpa evokes, above all, a series of events related to the final life of Gautama both before and after his enlightenment, on the one hand, and the rich range of his earlier incarnations as a Bodhisattva, during which he acquired the perfection to become a Buddha, on the other.[11] These need to be understood, as we have seen, according to a tripartite pattern of temporality advanced by a series of early Buddhist texts in terms of a distant epoch (*dūre-nidāna*), which ended with the Bodhisattva's last human incarnation as King Vessantara, an intermediate epoch (*avdūre-nidāna*) from his sojourn in the Tuṣita Heaven via his final rebirth to the moment of enlightenment itself beneath the Bodhi tree, and a proximate epoch (*santike-nidāna*) from the Buddha's enlightenment via his mission and teaching to his death and the partition of relics.[12] Implicitly, the current era, in which the stūpa was constructed and worshipped as a pilgrimage centre, follows from this last. Within this pattern, multiple *jātaka* stories of the Buddha's earlier lives (in which the development of particular perfections are highlighted) are juxtaposed against the full fruition of this process and these perfections in his final incarnation. That patterning of incarnations across aeons is simultaneously a picture of space – the multiple diverse spaces across the subcontinent of India in which the variety of narratives are set, in what we might call horizontal geographic terms, and the great diversity of divine spaces (mainly heavens) in which some parts of the Bodhisattva's story take place.[13] But space here is set within a cosmologically vast vision of multiple lifetimes and immense spans of time, so that space has a similar sense of vastness even if, effectively, it is the world of India that is evoked.

Let us take a fine drum slab in the British Museum, which survives in near-complete form despite breakages and abrasion (illus. 94), as well as being recorded in an early nineteenth-century drawing from Mackenzie's album (illus. 95), when it was clearly in much crisper condition than pertains today.[14] At the top, around the dome, the gods are paying homage to the stūpa (some with music, as we have seen, on the left-hand side), while at the bottom, outside the representation of the outer railing with its four lotus-bosses per pillar in high relief, two standing human figures on either side, now very abraded, are moving towards the centre, probably having purchased flower offerings from the seated figures to the extreme ends, which are probably meant to be placed in the offering trays borne by the two dwarf figures on bases (that is, likely representing statues) that immediately flank the gateway. In other words, the relief representation of the stūpa – with all its rich decorative embellishment – sits cosmographically between an upper and lower framing of divine and human worship.

The miniature representations of its decoration give a microcosm of the ways narrative subjects are juxtaposed and interspersed across the stūpa. In this case, all the images of narrative reliefs have survived but many cannot be definitively identified iconographically. Had we been looking at one of the other better-preserved drum slabs showing a stūpa (such as those discussed at Chapter One, illus. 25–33, or Chapter Three, illus. 61–6), we would have a more precise set of narrative identifications against which to map the biographic history being laid out, but the cosmographic effects are the same. The coping of the outer railing shows a frieze of animals – elephants, bulls and buffaloes fighting human beings, the elephants (to the left side and on the far-right corner at right angles to the main face) trampling human figures, the humans defeating the animals to the right and with fantastic animals on the left near the entrance and at the left corner perpendicular to the main face (illus. 96). Above this imagery of a mythologized and conflictual *saṃsāra* on the outside of the stūpa's perimeter are the relief panels of the inner monument that can be glimpsed over the railing. The lower line of reliefs on the drum shows the tops of slabs with wheels, stūpas and Bodhi trees implying the key events of enlightenment, wheel-turning and the Buddha's passing away. Above these is the platform with the *āyaka* panel jutting forward and six reliefs (three to either side of it) running along the platform's upper rim. Two of these are obscured by the lions that sit atop the gateway and one partially by the top of the (now damaged) stepped pillar bearing a stūpa topped with umbrellas that is represented as standing within the precinct behind the railing on the right. It is striking that a real effort has been made to offer the careful view of an intimation of narrative relief subjects behind images of statuary and the pillar, suggesting the spatial extent and configuration of a three-dimensional monumental mass. This line of reliefs is bordered at the bottom by a row of animal or human busts such as, in fact, appear on the lower borders of a series of drum friezes that survive from the monument (for example, illus. 61, 71, 90[15]), again asserting the evocation of actuality.

The themes of this frieze are impossible to identify precisely. Reading from right to left (the main direction of the coping imagery and of the viewer's approach, if meeting this panel while circumambulating the stūpa, illus. 96), these show a princely standing figure between two women, a princely seated figure on a throne with a lady seated beneath him to the left, a standing male figure with a horse and a dwarf attendant (conceivably an image of the Bodhisattva taking leave of his horse, Kaṁṭhaka, after the Great Departure, somewhat obscured by the lion on the gateway to the right). In the *āyaka* platform is the seated Buddha surrounded by attendants, now almost entirely lost. To the left stands what is probably a universal monarch (cakravartin) with a *cakra* symbol to his left beside his head and an adoring attendant, followed by an unusual scene featuring a woman lounging on a throne surrounded by female attendants and finally three standing female figures to the far left. Apart from the central scene from the proximate epoch of the Buddha's ministry, and the one that may show the Bodhisattva and Kaṁṭhaka from the not-so-remote antecedent, these are likely to refer to *jātaka* narratives from the remote epoch, before the Bodhisattva's final human life.

There are seven larger slabs on the lower dome, the outer two placed on the high-relief curve of the stūpa, almost at a right angle to a head-on viewer, and the central one rather brilliantly intimated behind the *āyaka* columns (illus. 97). The scene to the far right shows the empty throne with the pillar of fire behind it at an oblique and foreshortened angle, surrounded by devotees. This is within an enclosure behind a gateway, which is approached by a male figure with a retinue including two dwarfs. At centre right is a flamboyant battle scene featuring an elephant with three riders on its back, a dying horse and numerous armed men. Next to the *āyaka* pillars at centre right is a prince enthroned in his court, and behind the *āyaka* pillars can be glimpsed the empty throne with a large wheel above it, indicating the First Sermon. To its left are a series of intricate and unidentified scenes. The slab immediately to the left side of the *āyaka* columns shows a party of figures, including riders of an elephant and a horse approaching a very damaged seated figure to the lower right; the slab next to it seems to depict a scene with adults surrounding a child; the slab on the far left appears to show a number of adults with a baby, which is held by the man in the centre.[16] But in all this uncertainty, what is clear is that the two scenes with the Buddha (both in this tier aniconic) point to the proximate epoch, whereas the others most likely belong within the *jātaka* world of the remote epoch.

The final tier of historiated narrative images are the five medallions above and amid the rich decoration of garlands, animals, vases of plenty and dwarfs in the dome (illus. 98). On the far right and left are images of the elevation of the Bodhisattva's begging bowl by a trio of flying gods, effectively echoing the hovering deities around the stūpa's dome and alluding to the monument's reliquary function. The three central scenes in narrative order from right to left show Queen Māyā,

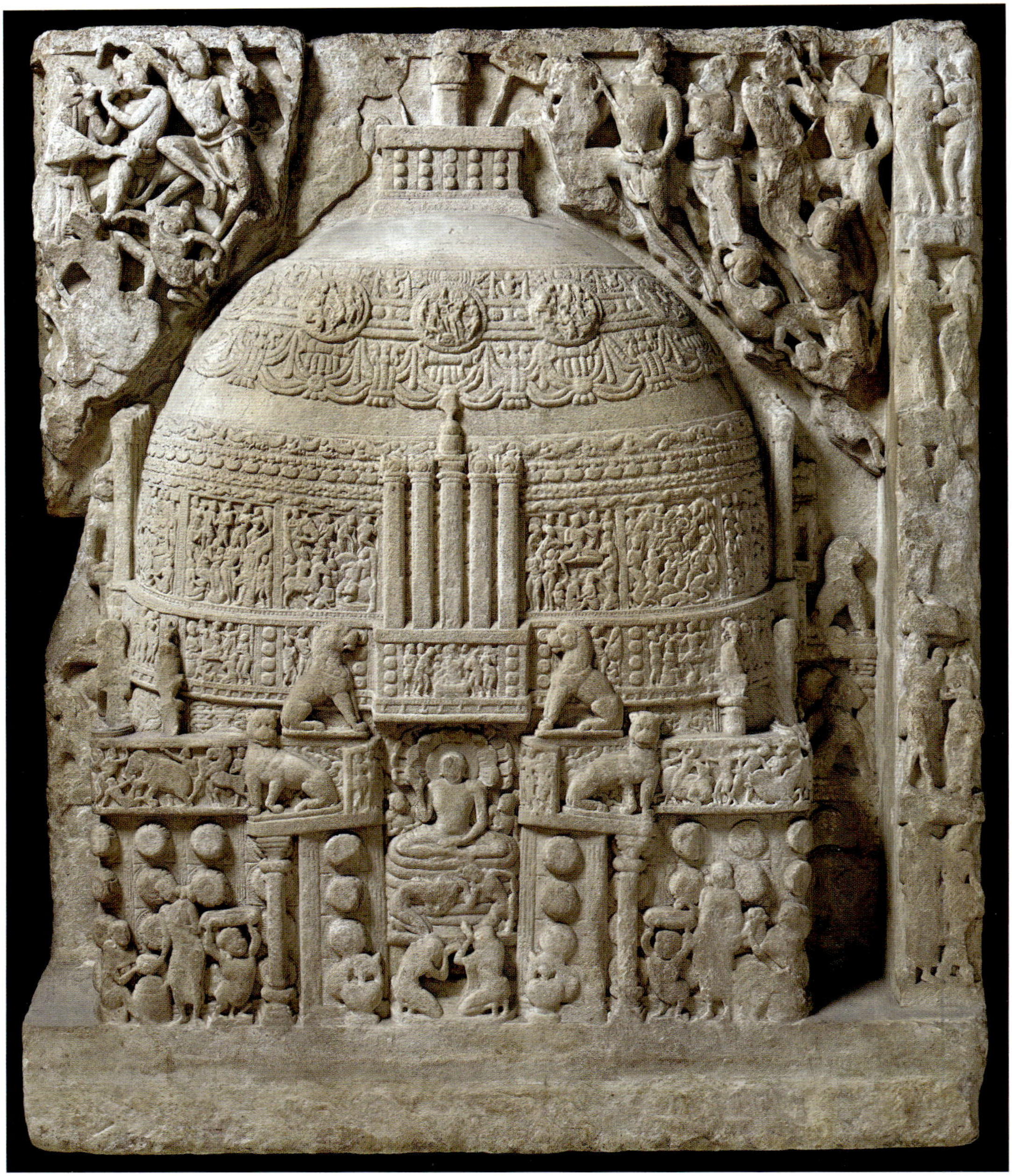

94 Intact, if broken and abraded, drum slab showing a view of a stūpa through a gateway and from outside its railings (1.36 × 1.11 m). Unusually, the slab includes a narrow border to the right (in very poor condition now) with five tiers of male–female couples.

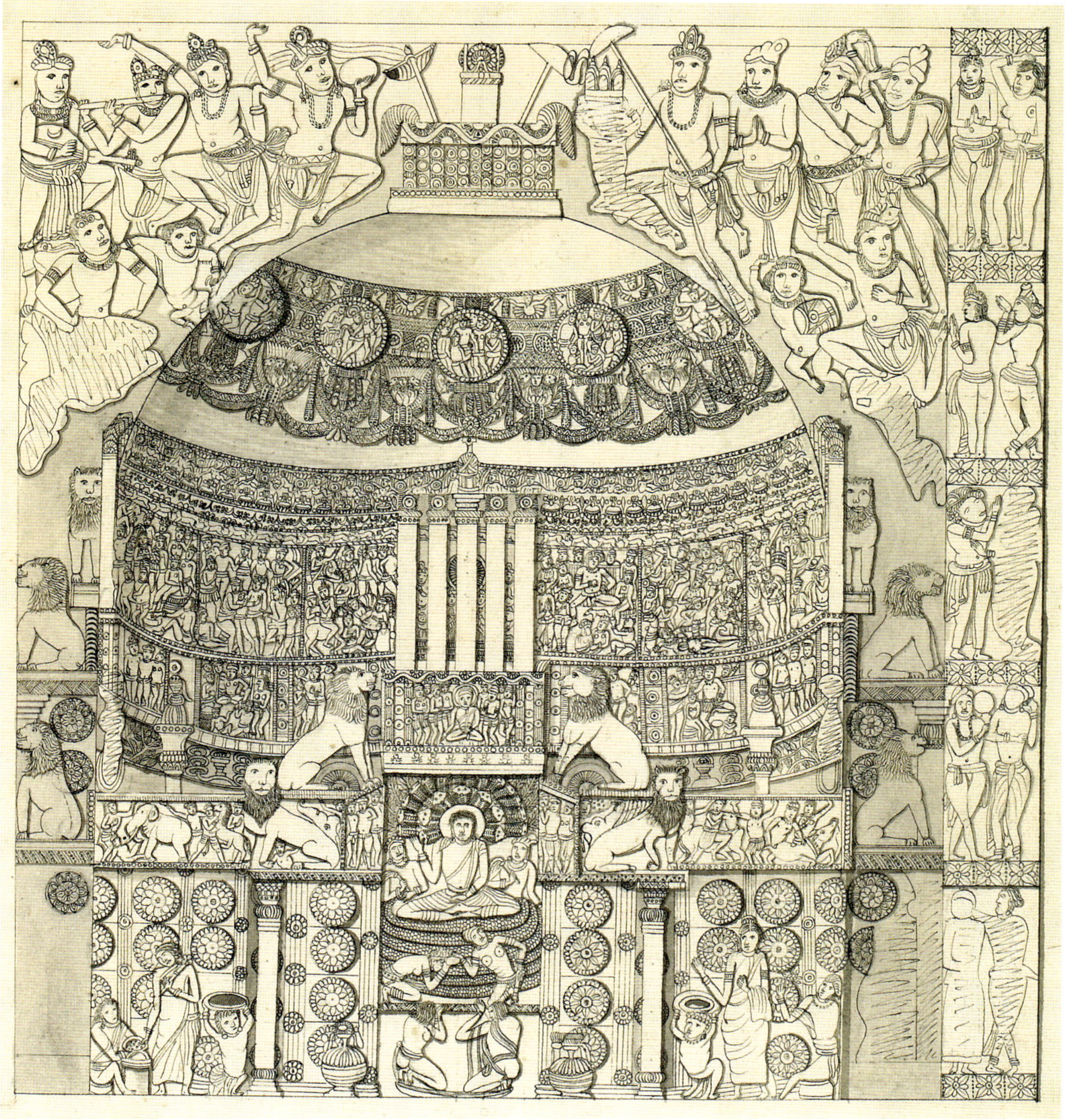

95 The drum slab in illus. 94 as drawn shortly after excavation in MacKenzie's Album, WD1061, folio 24. Made by Marcellus Burke and dated 16 September 1816.

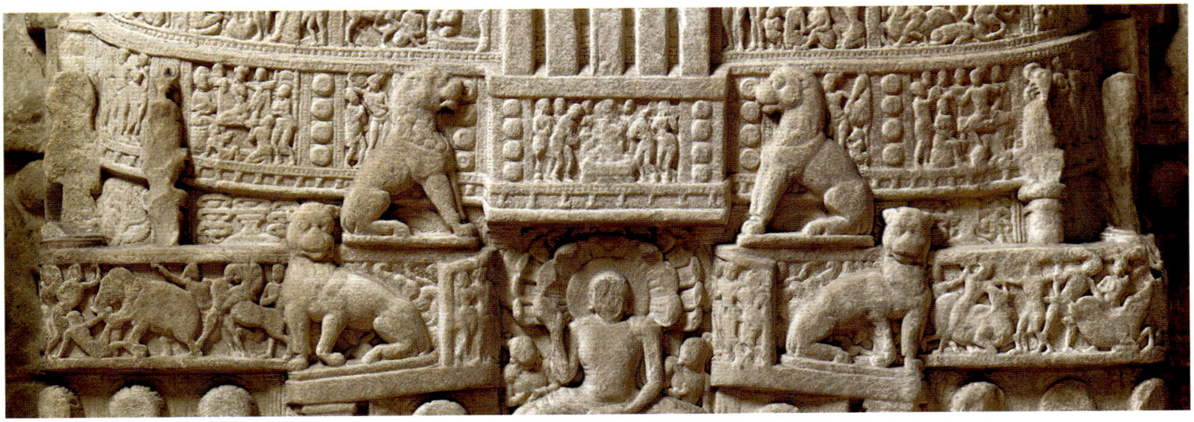

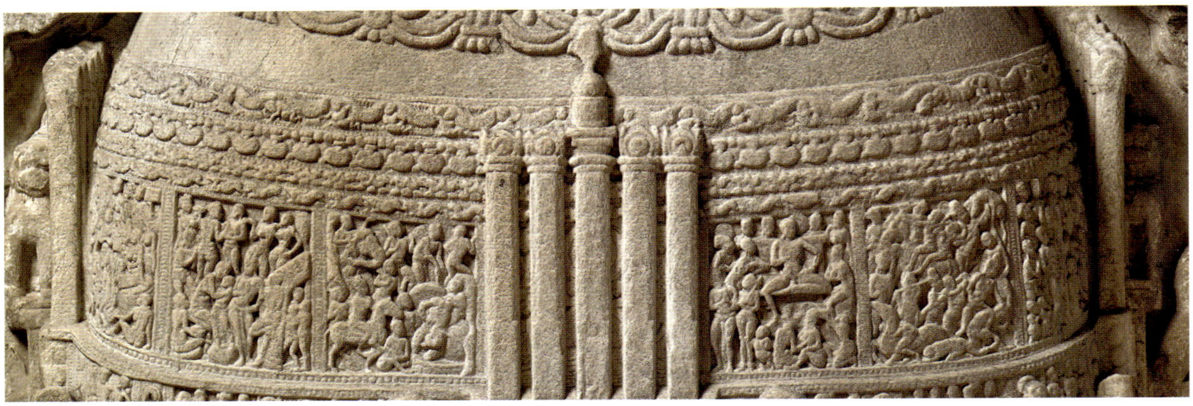

96 Detail of illus. 94 showing the rail coping and lower dome panels including the *āyaka* platform.
97 Detail of illus. 94 showing the upper dome panels and the *āyaka* pillars.

the Bodhisattva's mother, recounting her dream (and the Bodhisattva's conception) to King Śuddhodana; the birth of the baby Siddhārtha from his mother's side beneath the *sāl* tree, against which she leans with her left arm; and the presentation of the baby by his mother to the local tree spirit Śākyavardhana. In both scenes, the baby is represented as a cloth on which we might infer miniature footprints might have been carved or painted, as in the equivalent larger scenes elsewhere in the stūpa's surviving sculpture.[17]

This iconographic programme is incredibly rich and rather exceptional in its narratives, which is why so few can be identified precisely against our knowledge of existing textual or iconographic traditions. It converges on the magnificent image of the Buddha seated in the *abhāya* posture on the seven coils of the great *nāga* king, Mucalinda, whose multiple heads in two tiers rise above that of the Buddha as a double-rimmed protective halo. Two *nāga* maidens (with single serpents rising from behind their heads) stand on either side while four pay homage below, simultaneously to their king and to the blessed one. The line of scenes down the centre is particularly striking, from the birth of the Bodhisattva, via the *dharmacakra* of his wheel-turning First Sermon behind the *āyaka* pillars to the seated Buddha of the *āyaka* platform (very damaged but apparently between approaching human devotees, his posture uncertain) to the Mucalinda image in the gateway. Within the narrative structure, encompassing episodes from all three epochs, a series of thematic repetitions are worth

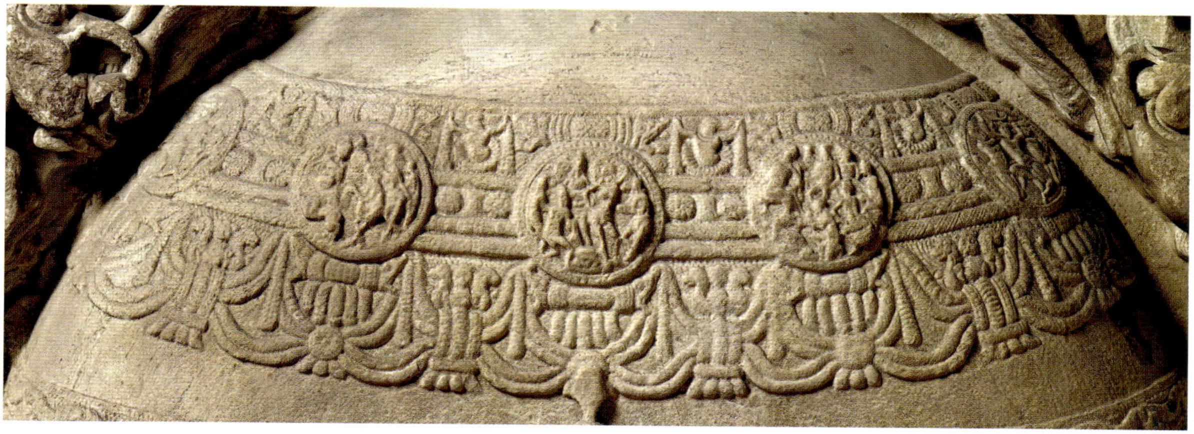

98 Detail of illus. 94 showing the upper dome with medallions.

noting. Scenes of monarchy and peaceful enthronement are mixed with imagery of war and pursuit, with animals – elephants and horses – appearing in several places. There is a repeated thematic of children and parents between the scenes of the Bodhisattva's birth and those with the baby and children on the left of the upper tier in the dome. This imagery – even if we cannot identify the stories – builds intimations of the generations of human beings and the interaction of the human and animal realms into its cosmography.

The Mucalinda episode – the source of one of the most famous iconographic types in Buddhist art – occupies an interesting moment in the Buddha's story between the awakening,[18] when technically he is enlightened but not yet the universal Buddha (*Sammāsambuddha*), which he only becomes when he enables others to become enlightened, and the First Sermon, at which one of the listeners attains the path and hence the certainty of freedom, with the result that the universe shakes as he takes up the role of universal Buddha who can teach the path to liberation.[19] According to the narrative of his mission in the *Mahāvagga* section of the *Vinaya*, in the immediate aftermath of his enlightenment, the Buddha spent a week at 'the foot of the Tree of Awakening, experiencing the bliss of freedom', coming to the formulation of his great teaching on dependent origination, then a week at the foot of the Goatherds' Banyan tree 'in the bliss of freedom' in which he had his first interactions with human beings in the form of a visiting Brahman, and then a week at the foot of the Mucalinda tree 'experiencing the bliss of freedom'.[20] A terrible storm blew up, out of season, for seven days, and 'Mucalinda, the serpent king, having come forth from his own haunt . . . encircled the Lord's body seven times with his coils, having spread a great hood over his head.'[21]

The seven coils are represented in the image, but beneath the Buddha's seat. Dhammapāla's perhaps sixth-century commentary presents the snake's protection in terms of a building (in which case the Buddha would be its reliquary centre).[22] The theme of protection and tempest stresses the depth of the Buddha's meditative concentration, but the carving – in using the *abhāya mudrā* – emphasizes the theme of protection and the gift of fearlessness. The cosmography of the slab's vertical images thus traces the significant movement of the Bodhisattva's transformations from birth via the post-enlightenment passage towards full Buddhahood to the turning of the wheel of dharma and the imagery of him seated amid human devotees.

We may say that this slab is unique in its particular narrative choices and configuration of scenes (and indeed none of the relief stūpas is exactly like any other), but that most were adorned with a similar range of narrative elements in the drum and dome. The imagery offers a hugely complex play of karmic patterning – not only a chronology across epochs but a causality of perfections developed and defilements undone (depending on which specific *jātakas* the narrative scenes represented) – and enables multiple ways of reading even a single panel, let alone this slab alongside nearly a hundred others around the drum as well as all the other relief imagery of the stūpa, some of which repeats these subjects but in different orders, contexts and contiguities.

At the same time, the slab offers a kind of cosmographic diagram of worlds. At the bottom, on the ground and outside the depicted stūpa's perimeter railing, is the world of human beings (male and female). In the line of the railing's coping is a world of animals (some mythical on the left, most real like the elephant, bull and buffalo) and men, punctured by the seated lions on the outer gate. Above are a series of panels carved into the monument's surface that reflect what we may call a sacred-mythological world of the Buddha's life and former lives, which may include references to a number of paradisal worlds, such as that of the *nāga*s, and not least that to which such relics as the Bodhisattva's topknot and bowl are taken.[23] Finally, at the top above the dome, in the 'real time' of the here and now, as is the case for the human baseline on the ground, deities honour the stūpa – deities that are surely meant to be present even if we human visitors cannot see them. In its elegant way, the slab integrates its complex of mythological/hagiographic narratives, which are simultaneously a karmic patterning, into a faux-naturalistic representation of a stūpa like the one on which it is placed that is at the same time a schematic cosmographic sketch of stratified worlds.

The key point in all this is that the visual imagery itself has constructed a highly complex discursive cosmography of cause and effect, of time over innumerable aeons and across spaces both human and divine, of salvation through the person of the multiply reincarnated Bodhisattva as fully enlightened Buddha. Humans, animals, magical beings like *nāga*s and deities of all kinds, such as the gods in the eternal present who worship the stūpa at the top, form the multiple levels of its cosmological vision, all focused through the mood-music of devotional veneration from the human pilgrims outside the stūpa moving towards it, via the bowing *nāga*s around the seated Buddha in the gateway to the deities at the peak. This cosmography, complete in itself in this one image, is nonetheless merely a metonymic instance and two-dimensional reflection of the much vaster monumental cosmography of the stūpa itself, and the multiple parallel reflective cosmographies of the other drum panels like it.

THE MONUMENTAL GESTURE

What is obvious is that neither the stūpa as a whole nor its various slabs carved with intricate relief sculpture provide a careful cosmological map of the 30 (or 31) realms and the three spheres of traditional Buddhist theory.[24] The monument does its own thing within what might be assumed to be a general Indian Buddhist acceptance of this cosmology or one broadly like it in the traditions and scriptures espoused at Amarāvatī itself. Within its particular visual-rhetorical choices – that is, deploying elements of a traditional Buddhist cosmology in its specific articulation of devotional culture and the celebration of the Blessed One – the stūpa avoids a series of gestures or statements that might have been expected within the broad Indian tradition. These silences are rhetorically pointed, potentially polemical, but unstated and hence implicit rather than deliberately aggressive. Among these silences, the stūpa's imagery makes no comment on those cosmological issues about which the Buddha himself said he was refusing to speak since they were not conducive to the holy life; these include whether the world is eternal or not eternal and whether it is finite or infinite.[25] Nor again does the stūpa make any intervention in the question of whether there is an origin to the world, something assumed in the Brahmanic mythologies of creator gods but a subject deliberately avoided by the Buddha,[26] so that the monument neither supports nor denies the cosmogonic views of non-Buddhist visitors to its sacred perimeter.[27] In this avoidance, it makes no comment on the origins of social class, caste and other traditional hierarchies enshrined in the Indian cosmogonic myths,[28] or on the sacrificial implications of the emergence of the cosmic order in Vedic and post-Vedic thought.[29] In other words, its evocation of multiple worlds and spaces (peopled by humans, gods, magical beings and animals), accessible to visitors by means of the living presence of the Buddha through his relics in the stūpa, works both exclusively, through silence, to avoid endorsing a series of traditionalist positions, and inclusively, to enable veneration by any Buddhist or non-Buddhist pilgrims, rather than drawing any explicit doctrinal lines in the sand.

Here the personhood of the stūpa as the Buddha is significant. In a famous passage, the Buddha said:

> I say, friend, that by traveling one cannot know, see or reach that end of the world where one is not born, does not grow old, die, does not pass away and get reborn. Yet I say that without having reached the end of the world there is no making an end of suffering. For it is in this fathom-long carcass, endowed with perception and mind, that I proclaim the world, the origin of the world, the cessation of the world, and the way leading to the cessation of the world.[30]

This is in response to the question from a deity (*deva*) called Rohitassa, who in a previous incarnation as a hermit with psychic powers had attempted to cross the skies to find the end of the world but, despite travelling his whole lifespan of a hundred years, had failed to do so. That kind of cosmography cannot work, but it is within the fathom-long carcass – the body endowed with perception and mind – that the Buddha claims that the origin, cessation and path to the cessation of the world can be discovered.

On the body of the stūpa, as we have seen, Amarāvatī offers panel after panel of microcosmic reflections – variants of its own form, variants of each other, each one distinctively different from any other (at least to judge by the survivals), each one formally similar to the others.[31] While on one level each of the drum slabs representing stūpas replicates the basic structure of the others – similar monuments with sculpted decoration and surrounded by a railing, open gateway, gods above and usually human figures below – at the same time the detailed elaboration of both the narratives chosen for the individual sculpted elements of each relief stūpa and the imagery of the central opening is distinctive and specific. That makes each panel simultaneously unique and broadly replicative. But it means that the stūpa as a whole, incorporating more than a hundred such panels, creates a reflective explosion of options – different entry ways to liberation to suit the needs of multiple kinds of beings on the Buddha's path, as instanced by the multiplicity of subjects placed at the stūpa's gateways. Each individual cosmography sits within a vast pattern of options and alternatives, all with the same intent of offering a map of the terrain encompassed by the stūpa and an opening into the living enlightened presence at its heart.

This remarkable programme, unknown outside Andhra Pradesh but emulated in the smaller stūpas of the Amarāvatī complex itself (to judge from the surviving photographs of one excavated in 1905 and subsequently dismantled, see illus. 24) and apparently also developed in related monuments at Nāgārjunakonda and Gummadidurru,[32] evokes a universe of endless, intimate reflections that are, as it were, internal to the pilgrimage context and complex itself. The reflective visual poetics of the monumental arts of Andhra Buddhism, spinning cosmography into an intimation of universal salvific possibilities, arises directly from the material and iconographic choices made in the decoration of Amarāvatī and the stūpas like it. It need not depend on any specific textual tradition, but – as suggested in an earlier chapter – it has some parallels with the poetics of what are regarded as early Mahāyāna explorations, possibly themselves written in Andhra at the time of the stūpa's making, such as the *Gaṇḍavyūha Sūtra*. I do not claim that its kinds of Mahāyāna cosmology lie behind the conceptual structure of Amarāvatī, but rather that – quite possibly at the same place and the same time – the cosmographic rhetoric of monumental Buddhism through its visual culture was exploring similar metaphoric territory as it riffed on and against Indian cosmological traditions.

Part IV
Icon and Replication

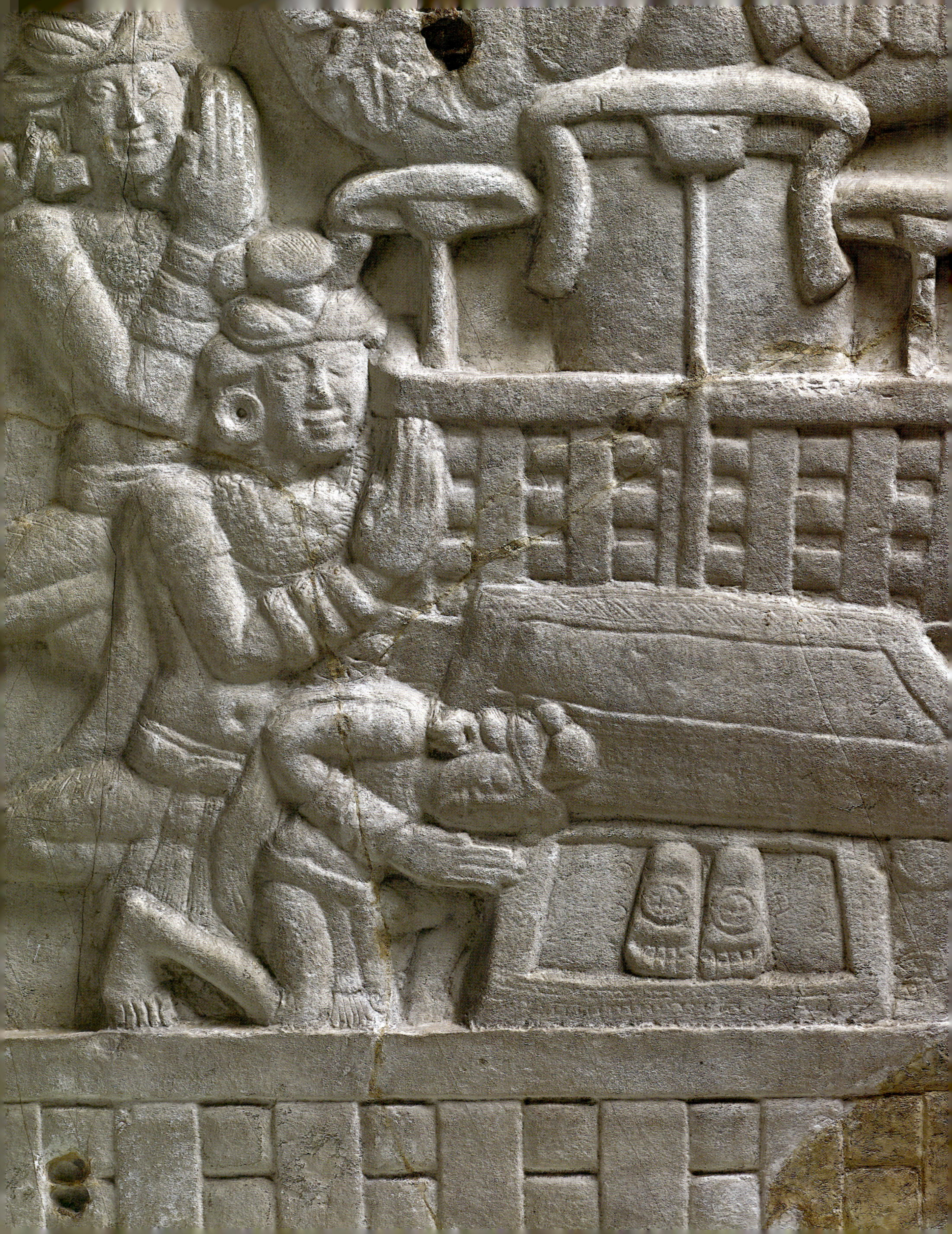

six

Buddhapāda: Symbolism, Visual Epitome and the Creation of Icons

One of the most striking features of the Amarāvatī sculptures is the ways that certain key motifs – essential as aspects of symbolic assemblages such as the trio of Bodhi tree, *dharmacakra* on a column and stūpa, which stood as shorthand symbols for the enlightenment, First Sermon and *parinirvāṇa* (see illus. 38 and 39) – were themselves isolated and developed. That isolation and visual extrapolation leads to extraordinary and detailed elaboration in the directions we have seen in the many representations of stūpas. There is the possibility that the wheel of dharma might have been extracted from its normal form at the site – as a relief atop of a column above an empty throne, with *buddhapāda* beneath – and elaborated in its own right. At any rate, one inscription on a piece of coping stone implies the dedication of a *dharmacakra* at the western gate,[1] which may imply one of the kinds of slabs familiar from the site, but may also indicate something more like the independent limestone sculpture of a wheel with a diameter of over a metre with 28 spokes and *triratna*s around the rim, from roughly the third century, which was discovered in the village of Lingarājupalli in Andhra Pradesh a little way up the coast from Amarāvatī.[2] Similarly, we may wonder if free-standing Buddha images were not themselves iconic extrapolations from the presence of buddhas in narrative reliefs, extracted from narrative, abstracted from contextual elaboration and turned three-dimensional statue instead of being framed in two-dimensional relief, for the purpose of worship.

The most complex extrapolation of a motif in this way at Amarāvatī is the image of the Buddha's feet or footprints, the *buddhapāda*. This visual motif is common to both the enlightenment and Wheel-turning symbols, often appearing beneath the empty throne and always in raised relief, with wheels inscribed at the sole and facing down with the toes towards the viewer (for example, illus. 26, 47, 48, 99, 109, 115, 116, 132).

99 Detail of illus. 109: worshippers before the Bodhi tree, empty throne and *buddhapāda*.

In all cases there is ambivalence as to whether these *buddhapāda*s represent the presence of the Buddha himself by what has been called 'synecdochic' logic (whereby a part stands for the whole[3]), or whether they are intended as *images* of his footprints or feet, and hence signs of his absence.[4] There was a long history of feet and footprints carved in stone and made in clay and mosaic in the religious culture of the ancient Mediterranean, which certainly anticipates and runs concurrently with the *buddhapāda*.[5] This does not mean that the possibility that such things were precursors, even iconographic models, for what ultimately became the *buddhapāda* has any significance for how such imagery was appropriated, reused and made to function in contexts that had nothing to do with Graeco-Roman religion. It is certainly the case, however, that the *buddhapāda* was taken as an iconic theme in its own right, enlarged, given a frame and celebrated at the site – usually in the form of two footprints together but occasionally perhaps as a single footprint (or as a pair of panels where one has now been lost).[6] That process – apparent in Andhra but attested across early Indian Buddhist art – reached beyond Amarāvatī to a series of other key stūpa sites along the Krishna River and the Andhra coast, notably Nāgārjunakonda (which is a site usually dated a little later than Amarāvatī[7]), Thotlakonda, Bavikonda, Phanigiri, Kesanapalli and the recent find in Kanaganahalli,[8] and as far south as the port of Kāverippūmpattinam in Tamil Nadu, where the *buddhapāda* is made from imported Palnad limestone of the same kind as was used to create Amarāvatī.[9]

We know nothing about the function or placement of these objects, although scholars agree that they were probably not part of the main stūpa.[10] That view is in conflict with one piece of visual evidence, namely, the presence of images of *buddhapāda* tablets surmounted by ceremonial umbrellas in the domes of a number of the miniature stūpas that adorned the drum of the main monument. These stūpa panels have, in other respects, been taken (perhaps too much) to be true reflections of its actual appearance, which would imply the likelihood of some *buddhapāda* tablets having been incorporated on the dome (see illus. 34).[11] In any case, the majority of the independent *buddhapāda* slabs from Amarāvatī appear to have been found at the eastern and western gates to the complex in the excavations of 1880 and 1881,[12] and it has been surmised that they were part of the decoration of the processional path between the main stūpa monument and its inner railing, which allowed circumambulation and pauses for veneration or worship.[13] The resemblance of the Amarāvatī *buddhapāda*s to the intriguing fragment of an *āyāgapata* (or tablet of worship) made in the brown sandstone associated with the sculpture of Mathura, and found in excavations in the vicinity of a stūpa at the Ghositārāma Monastery in Kauśāmbī near modern Allahabad, which has been dated on stylistic grounds to circa 75 BCE, may imply some link. The *buddhapāda* on the Kauśāmbī tablet, the inscription on which records its donation by the monk Phagula, is also carved in low relief at the centre of an icon-like slab with a fine floral border.[14] The footprint has a wheel at the sole and auspicious symbols on the toes. It is assumed that *āyāgapata* tablets of this kind – used in Jain as well as Buddhist contexts – were sacred objects of worship,[15] and that may hold true also for the Amarāvatī panels. It is hard to imagine the singling out of *buddhapāda* panels for special treatment through display beneath umbrellas without some element of veneration being intended.[16]

My discussion of the objects in this chapter turns on three issues: panels that deliberately play with the assumptions of naturalism to create the image of an impossible and hence exceptional being; panels that use symbolic pleonasm to create the abstract type of something supramundane; and miniature *buddhapāda*s used within and as part of the narrative imagery of the site. One theme that is germane to all parts of this discussion is the key significance of the wheel-mark on the sole of the footprint as the defining factor of all *buddhapāda*s, notably the miniature examples without space for more elaboration. In the *Buddhavaṃsa*, the late canonical Pāli *Chronicle of the Buddhas*, Gautama recounts in first person the narratives of the 24 buddhas who preceded him, who he himself was during each of their lifetimes and how they prophesied that he would ultimately attain enlightenment. In the remarkable opening to this text, the Buddha performs a great miracle, creating a jewelled walkway that links all the worlds, enabling beings from every sphere to approach him.[17] They collectively sing his praises mentioning the 'Wheel-mark on your feet' (*cakkalakkhaṇa*) and punning on 'setting the wheel of dharma turning' (*dhammacakkappavattana*).[18] The introduction is then marked by a series of worshippers, including the Buddha's most important disciples, paying homage to 'the teacher's Wheel-mark' (*cakkalakkhaṇa*),[19] as if this mark sums up all the auspicious and special characteristics of the Buddha's physical body as well as referring, by visual implication, to the eight-spoked wheel of the path and the Buddha's First Sermon, which turned the wheel of dharma.

ICONS OF THE EXCEPTIONAL BODY

What scholars have thought of as the earliest *buddhapāda* representations from Amarāvatī are now in the British Museum. The largest is carved in low relief on a square slab of limestone, dated to 'the early phase' of Amarāvatī sculpture in the first century BCE or first century CE (illus. 100).[20] The feet point downwards, as is the case in the great majority of examples of this iconography,[21] and they are bordered by a meandering design of large lotus blossoms that appear to emerge from the mouth of a *makara* – a fish-tailed sea monster somewhat like a Graeco-Roman *ketos*, but with an elephant's head – to the lower right.[22] The feet are marked with a series of auspicious signs (as are all *buddhapāda*s) – notably the large, fine-spoked and double-rimmed wheels (*dharmacakra*s) at the central hollow of each foot, and an upside-down ω-motif (whose precise significance is uncertain) topped by a petalled lotus within a beaded rim, which may also be intended as a wheel (identified variously as a *triratna* or *nandyavarta*), that sits between beaded *svastika*s and two pairs of six-petalled flowers at the heel.[23] Beneath the *dharmacakra* on each foot is a further beaded *svastika* between two hourglass-shaped objects. The joints between toes are marked with engraved wrinkles, while their tips are decorated with *svastika*s, except for the big toes, which appear to be marked again with the ω-symbol. The relief of all these symbols, except the wheels at the hollow of the feet, is very light and much abraded, especially on the damaged left-hand side. It is also worth noting that most, but not all, of the *svastika*s turn to the right.

If this image is meant to represent footprints, then it is a very odd representation indeed. Whereas the majority of *buddhapāda*s from Gandhāra are incised into the stone, with the auspicious symbols carved in relief,[24] as are those in the northern gateway at Sāñcī (probably from the first century BCE, illus. 101),[25] this one – indeed like all those in Andhra Pradesh – stands out in relief from the stone behind it.[26] Only the wheels are carved in further relief; the remaining symbols are incised. It is thus a very strange kind of footprint, a monument where a footprint might have been or once was. Moreover, while the image must depict the base of the foot (as indeed a footprint should, and, of course, it makes no reference to any leg emerging from the upper foot), with the wrinkles that appear on the small toes to mark their joints again implying the under part of the foot, the large toes in particular seem to revert to representing the upper foot, since they clearly show nails.[27] Given the extensive visual imagery at the rest of the site, which shows sufficient command of the logic of realism in the representation of figures to prove that the kind of surrealism present here cannot be some kind of mistake or act of incompetence, it is worthwhile to suggest that the disruption of normal expectations in terms of the naturalistic representation of feet in this large iconic image is deliberate and substantive. The 'rules' of what should be normal – an imprint rather than a raised relief for a footprint and the logic of distinction between the upper part of the foot and the bottom – are abandoned to create an icon that evokes the miraculous. In addition to the many auspicious signs, the icon posits the presence of the Buddha and his continuing presence through an image-type that defies the rules of nature.

A second, smaller but thicker slab of the *buddhapāda* from the same site, with very similar iconography and probably a similar date, also survives in the British

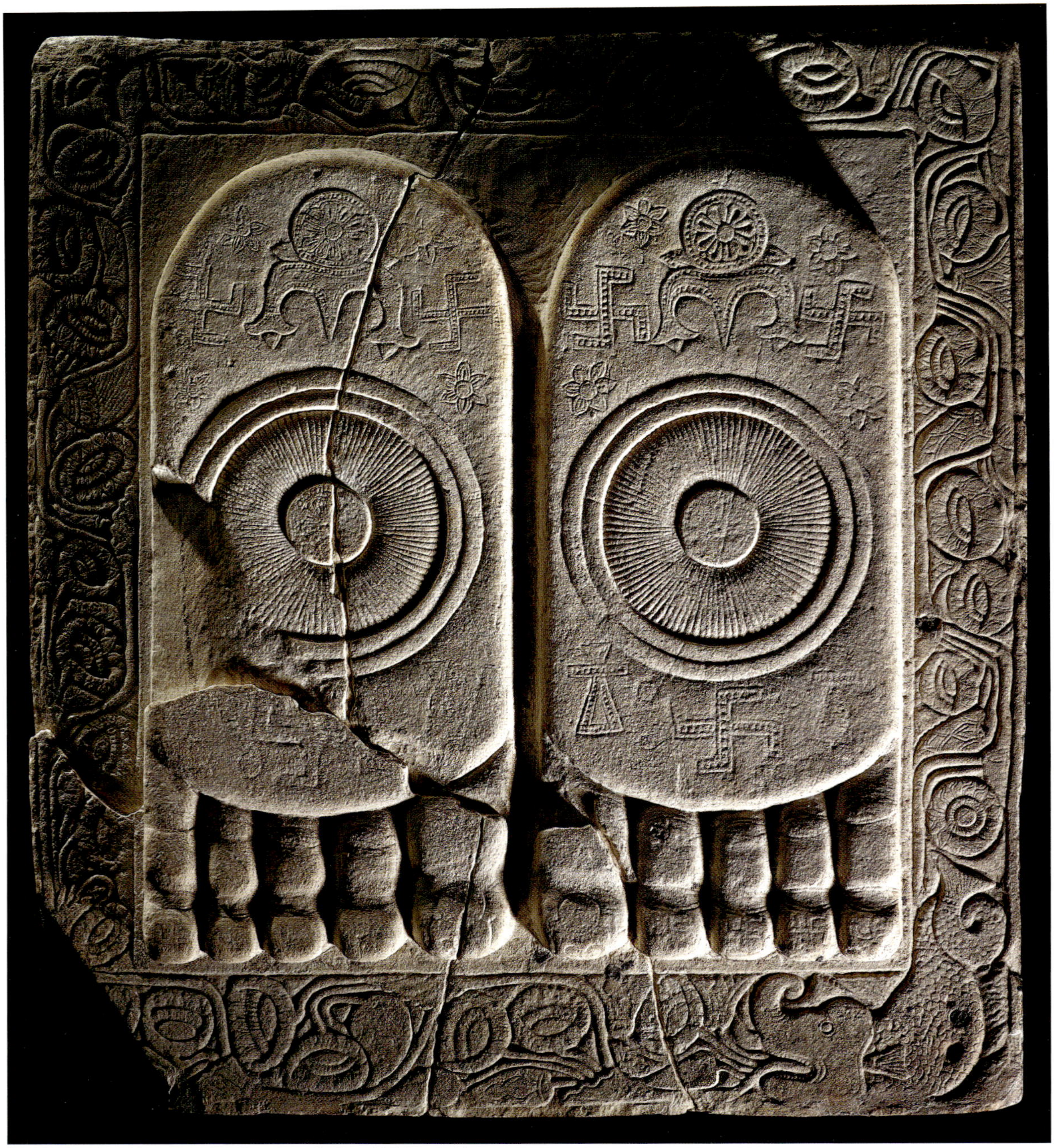

100 *Buddhapāda* slab surrounded with a low-relief lotus frame emanating from the mouth of a fish-tailed *makara*.

Museum collection (illus. 102).[28] Again, the feet are carved in relief, with delicately incised symbols and finely spoked *dharmacakras* with double rims carved at the centre of each foot. The iconography of the symbols is close but not identical to the other panel: ω-motifs and whirl-shaped *cakras* between *svastikas* at the heel, but without beaded rims and with no flowers either alongside the *svastikas* or potentially instead of the *cakras*, elaborately curling *svastikas* between hourglass-shaped symbols beneath the *dharmacakras*, toes with incised wrinkles at the joints, *svastikas* at the tips of the little toes and ω-symbols with wheels at the big toes (illus. 103). The toes are very abraded but look to be marked with faint toenails (most clear on the big toe and the small one next to it on the left foot as you look at the sculpture). Knox concluded that this sculpture, too, shows the upper parts of the toes and indeed the whole foot.[29] The frame is more complex than its sister panel, with elaborate lotus buds to left and right and lotus flowers at the top that seem to emerge from a *makara* at the lower left. At the lower border is a fat *yakśa*, or local deity, on the right-hand side (illus. 103), with a vine that appears to emerge from his navel and become part of a complex design of garlands, lotus heads and intersecting circles; to the far left are a pair of plinths with *nāga* serpents mounted on them. At the lower left of the border are the remains of a largely destroyed inscription that seems to name the donor and define the slab as his or her gift.[30] This panel's representation of the *buddhapāda* defies nature and visual naturalism in exactly the same way as its sister slab, breaking the rules of the normal in the same way.

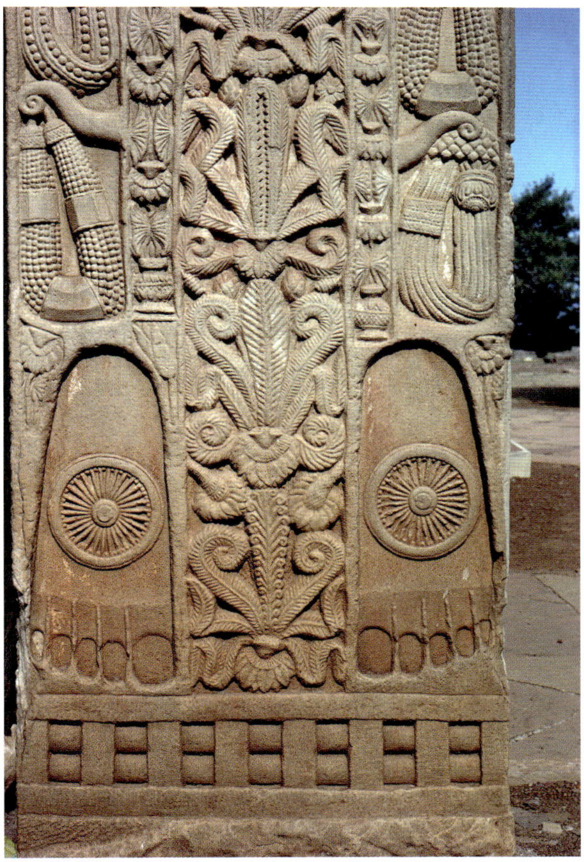

101 *Buddhapāda* from the lower east side pillar of the north *toraṇa* of the Great Stūpa at Sāñcī, traditionally dated to the second century BCE.

A number of other *buddhapādas*, from both the site and elsewhere (such as the slab found at the stūpa at Ghantaśālā[31]), emulate the model of interrogating the impossibilities of naturalistic representation in high relief. These include an interesting (if rather crude) pair of footprints showing *dharmacakras* with single rims, various other symbols (all in relief, and not incised on the foot but rather on the toes and toenails), and, instead of a border, four standing worshippers, two on each side (illus. 104);[32] and a second piece of which only the left foot (on the viewer's right-hand side) survives, also with a pair of standing worshippers to the side.[33] That both objects, as well as the Ghantaśālā panel, which has a lotus scroll behind the feet, appear to show nails, implies that the naturalism-challenging model of the two British Museum panels was replicated not only elsewhere in the site but beyond in Andhra.[34]

Something of how an icon like this resonated is caught by an early Buddhist text, the *Doṇa Sutta*, which begins with the Buddha's footprints. It is preserved in the *Aṅguttara Nikāya* of the Pāli tradition, but it was also found in a series of other recensions, including Kharosthi fragments in Gāndhāri, and several Chinese versions:[35]

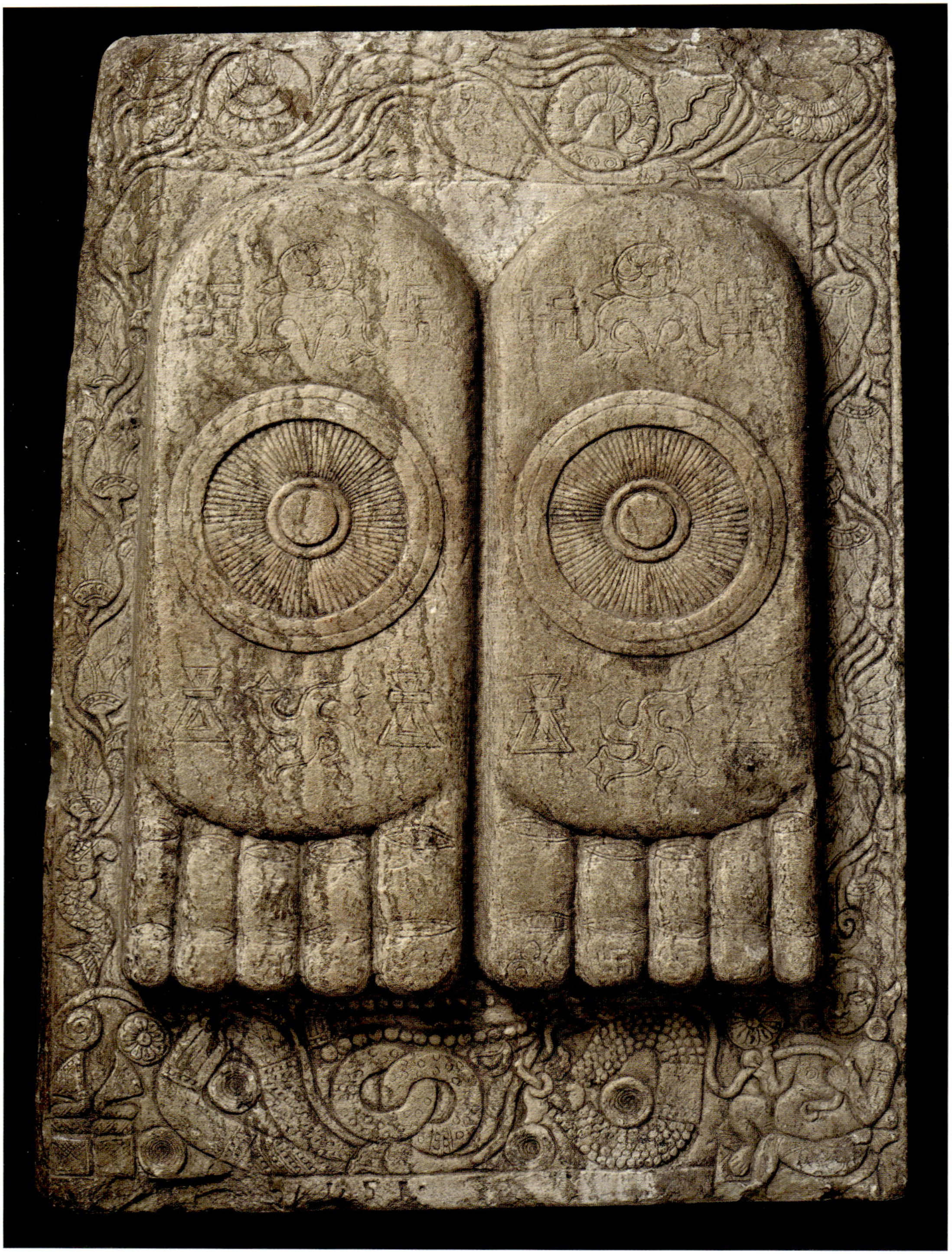

102 *Buddhapāda* slab surrounded on three sides with a low-relief lotus frame emerging from the mouth of a fish-tailed *makara*, and on the bottom with a complex design emanating from the navel of a fat *yakśa*.

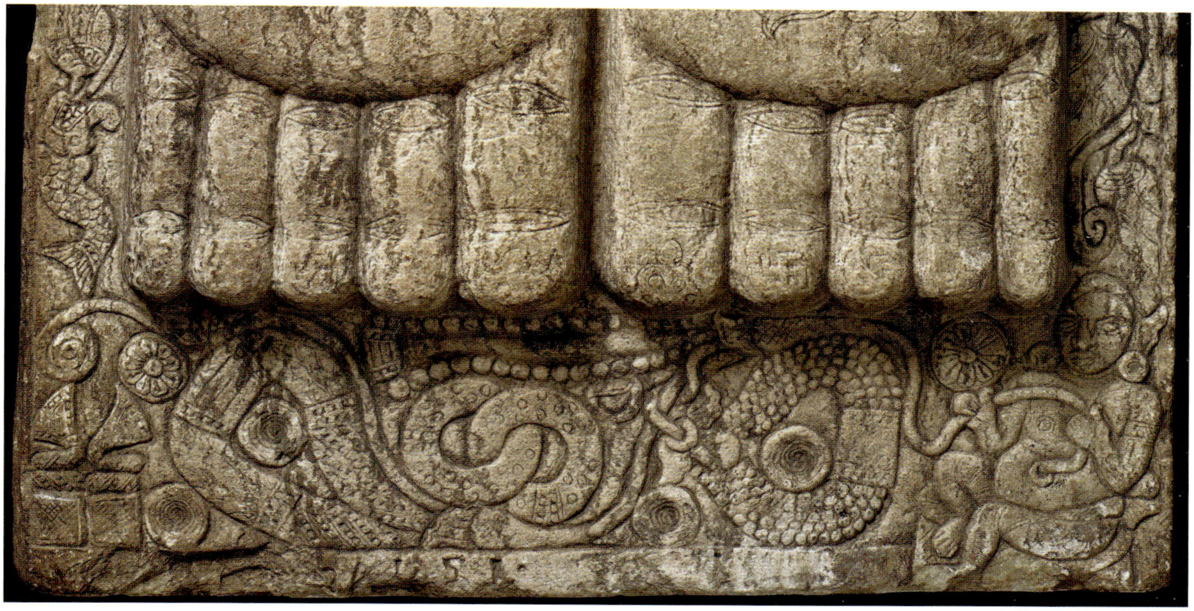

103 Detail of the toes and lower border of illus. 102.

The brahmin Dona was travelling along the highway . . . [and] saw the thousand spoked wheels of the Blessed One's footprints, with their rims and hubs, complete in all respects, and thought: 'It is astounding and amazing! These surely could not be the footprints of a human being!' . . . Tracking Blessed One's footprints, the brahmin Dona saw the Blessed One sitting at the foot of the tree – graceful, inspiring confidence, with peaceful faculties and peaceful mind, one who had attained the highest taming and serenity, [like] a tamed and guarded bull elephant with controlled faculties. He then approached the Blessed One and said to him:

'Could you be a *deva*, sir?'
'I will not be a *deva*, brahmin.'
'Could you be a *gandhabba*, sir?'
'I will not be a *gandhabba*, brahmin.'
'Could you be a *yakkha*, sir?'
'I will not be a *yakkha*, brahmin.'
'Could you be a human being, sir?'
'I will not be a human being, brahmin.'[36]

'When you are asked: "Could you be a *deva*, sir?" you say: "I will not be a *deva*, brahmin." When you are asked: "Could you be a *gandhabba*, sir?" you say: "I will not be a *gandhabba*, brahmin." When you are asked: "Could you be a *yakkha*, sir?" you say: "I will not be a *yakkha*, brahmin." When you are asked: "Could you be a human being, sir?" you say: "I will not be a human being, brahmin." What, then, could you be sir?' 'Brahmin, I have abandoned those taints because of which I might have become a *deva*; I have cut them off at the root, make them like palm stumps, obliterated them so that they are no longer subject to future arising. I have abandoned those taints because of which I might have become a *gandhabba* . . . I have abandoned those taints because of which I might have become a *yakkha* . . . I have abandoned those taints because of which I might have become a human being. I have cut them off at the root, made them like palm stumps, obliterated them so that they are no longer subject to future arising. Just as a blue, red or white lotus flower, though born in the

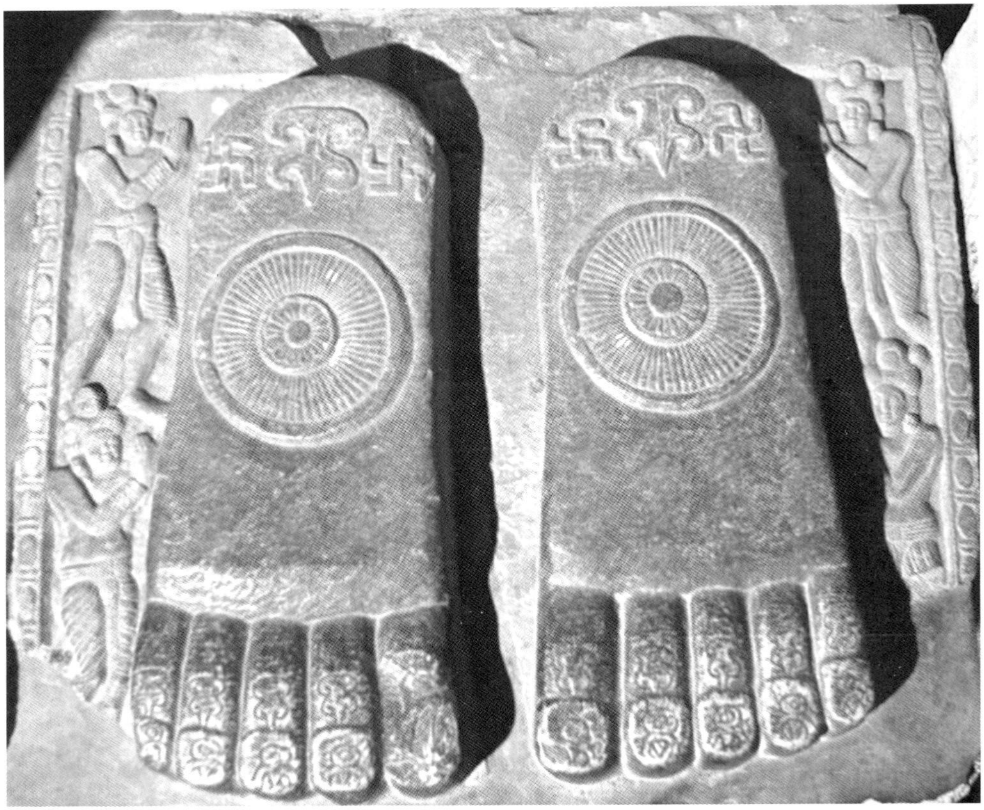

104 *Buddhapāda* slab flanked by two standing worshippers in low relief, the frame broken off by the toes.

water and grown up in the water, rises above the water and stands unsoiled by the water, even so, though born in the world and grown up in the world, I have overcome the world and dwell unsoiled by the world. Remember me, Brahmin, as a Buddha.'[37]

This text – with its focus on defining what kind of being a Buddha is, by virtue of negating the kinds of beings he is not – has strong parallels to the visual negation of the possibilities of naturalistic figural norms in the Amarāvatī *buddhapāda*s. We may say that the *buddhapāda*s develop a form of visual apophaticism, in a different medium but with discursive similarities to the kinds of negation found in the *Doṇa Sutta*. The German scholar-monk Anālayo remarks of the text that this 'episode of the footprints reveals the limitations of the brahmin's reliance on external physical marks', but one might put it another way and argue that the marvellous *buddhapāda*s that Doṇa saw – with their perfect wheels and, in the Gāndhāri version of the first century CE, their 'shining brilliance' – are the spur to his correct intuition that the being who made them was not human, to his search for that being and to the interrogation that will at last bring him to the point of discerning that the being he seeks is a Buddha.[38]

This spur to the path is itself sufficient justification for creating the *buddhapāda* as a distinct icon for veneration across the site as an object of worship. In the case of the Amarāvatī panels, their strange play with naturalism is a means of performing the discourse of negation that characterizes the Buddha's conversation with Doṇa. The framing borders, with their lotuses in both slabs, out of which the feet rise in relief, enact visually the spatial dynamic of the Buddha rising above the world, like a lotus flower rising above the water, to overcome the world, unsoiled by it. The reference within the text to the various beings that the Buddha is not plays out against the beings – *makara*s (including one with an elephant's head), *nāga*s and a *yakṣa* (that is, *yakkha*) – found among the lotuses of the frames. Effectively the panel performs the ending simile of the passage in which – just as the lotus, though born of the water, rises above the water – the Buddha (here symbolized by his feet) rises above the world, including its lotuses and all of its beings. Were the lotuses in the decorative borders ever to have been coloured – blue, red or white (as in the sutta) – then the direct parallel with the sutta would have been stronger still.

Within the context of the many beings shown on the stūpa, the representation of which is subject to the normative rules of realistic depiction, the *buddhapāda*s mark the Buddha's difference. Since he is not subject to those rules, it may be that in their strange impossibility they can simultaneously represent both footprints and feet – both the upper and the lower part of the foot, both the trace of a former presence and its perpetual continuity – precisely through their disruption of literalist or normative visual conventions.

ICONS OF THE ABSTRACT BODY

There are a series of more abstract *buddhapāda* icons that have generally been dated later than the panels so far discussed, but on no grounds more objective than the art-historical eye, and on the assumption that (in this case) more schematic means later.[39] One fragmentary panel now in the Chennai Museum (in which the heels no longer survive) has a lotus border with *makara* (illus. 105).[40] This piece belongs with a group of *buddhapāda*s, which eschew the play with naturalism

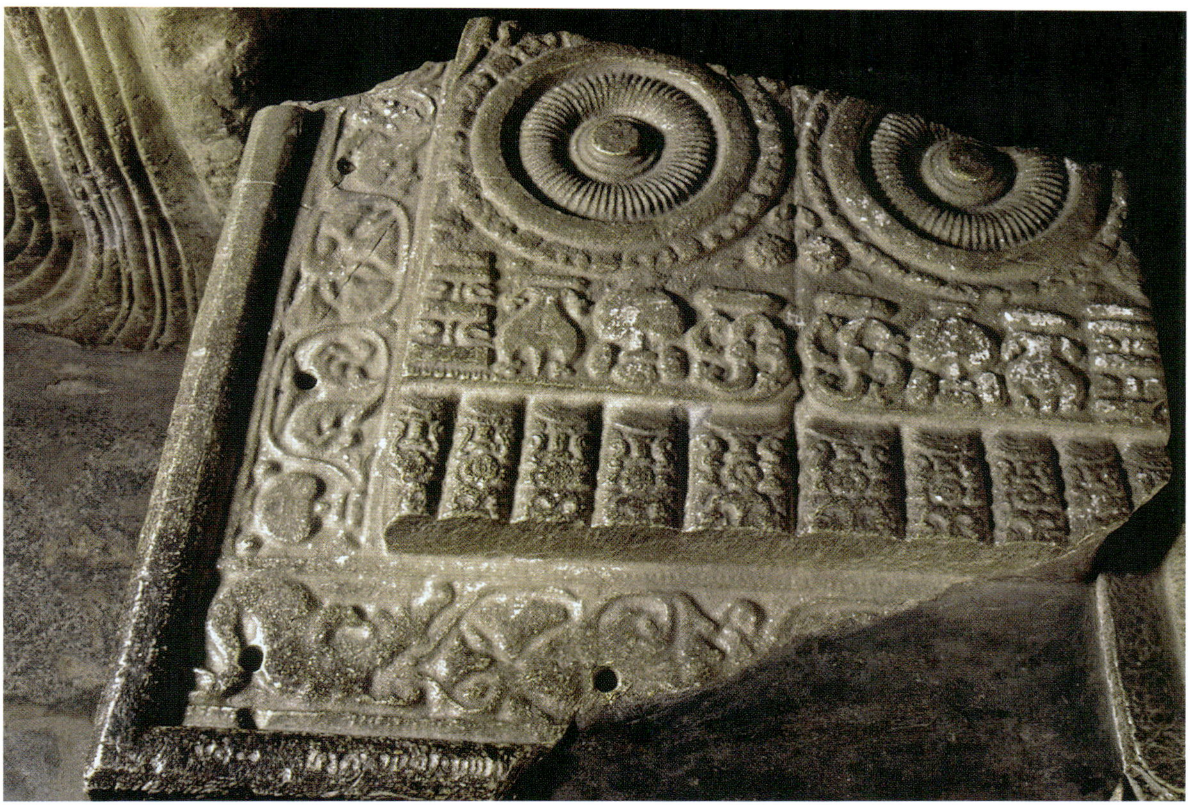

105 Fragmentary *buddhapāda* slab surrounded with a low-relief lotus frame emanating from the mouth of a fish-tailed *makara*.

for a more abstract model whereby the foot is created through a collection of symbols, something like the grouping of symbols that constitute the various kinds of emblematic body of the Buddha at the stūpa.[41] In this case, the *dharmacakras* have a double rim, of which the outer edge is formed by ω-symbols to give a broken effect. The balls of the toes are formed of four symbols – a curved *svastika* turning to the right on a flat base beneath the large toe on each foot, then a *pūrṇaghaṭa*, or vase of plenty, with flowers emerging from the neck, then an ω-shaped shield with swags at the bottom on a flat base and finally a device that appears to be made of two *vajras* with flat lines between them as well as above and below on a flat base (a *vajra* was a club-like symbol implying a thunderbolt associated with Sakka or Indra, the king of the gods). The four symbols do not correspond to the five toes, except perhaps for the *svastika* and the large toe. To this group belongs also a large weather-worn panel (73.66 × 71.12 centimetres, or 29 × 28 in.) without a border also in Chennai (illus. 106).[42] Here the central part of each wheel in the sole is sunk into the surface (emulating in formal terms the underpart of the arch of a foot), with ω-symbols forming the outer rim. Instead of a flat break between the main part of the foot and the toes, as in the example just discussed, this makes that line a curve, which effectively serves as a further outer circumference of the inner *dharmacakra* circle, as if the whole foot were constructed from the wheel as its centre. The curve enables five symbols to be placed before each of the toes (instead of four) and five further symbols in the heel, as if snapshots of a large outer circle that turns around the inner wheel which is cut off by the sides of the feet. The symbols include an ω-shaped shield, *vajra*, square and curling *svastikas* and an ω-shape with wheel, but they are much damaged and difficult to identify precisely. None is replicated within the foot, but each footprint appears to display the same symbols in the same places. The toes are structured as stacks of wrinkles with nails at the ends.

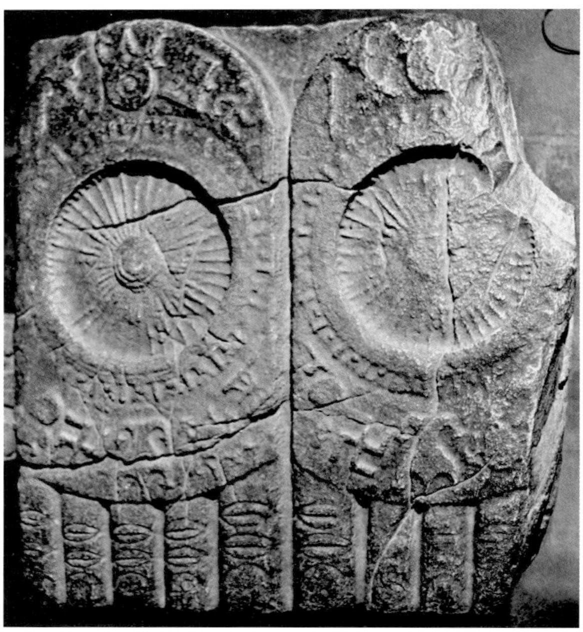

106 Damaged and worn *buddhapāda* slab without border.

Versions of this more abstract kind of footprint are found elsewhere in Andhra, mainly with borders as in the example from the stūpa at Kesanapalli (60 kilometres/37 mi. southwest of Amarāvatī), which has a lotus design,[43] the two from Thotlaconda,[44] or the four found at Nāgārjunakonda with floral frames that include motifs such as the Bodhi tree, the deer from the Deer Park where the First Sermon was delivered, or a stūpa (for example, illus. 107).[45] In the Nāgārjunakonda example with a floral border and an animal at the base, nothing naturalistic remains of the feet except the shape. Even the toe wrinkles have effectively become almond-shaped abstractions. Effectively, we have a particular form, the content of which is constructed by esoteric symbols that eschew any relation to a real foot to the extent that, in this example, for instance, the toes are simply constructed by two or three stacked wrinkles, and up to five in others (many more than the bone joins in actual toes), although the variety of symbols out of which the surface decoration is constructed is elegantly and precisely rendered in crisp relief. Of particular interest, and very different in form, is a further fragmentary slab from Amarāvatī in the British Museum, which has been dated to the first or second century CE and presents only the top of a single foot of the Buddha (illus. 108).

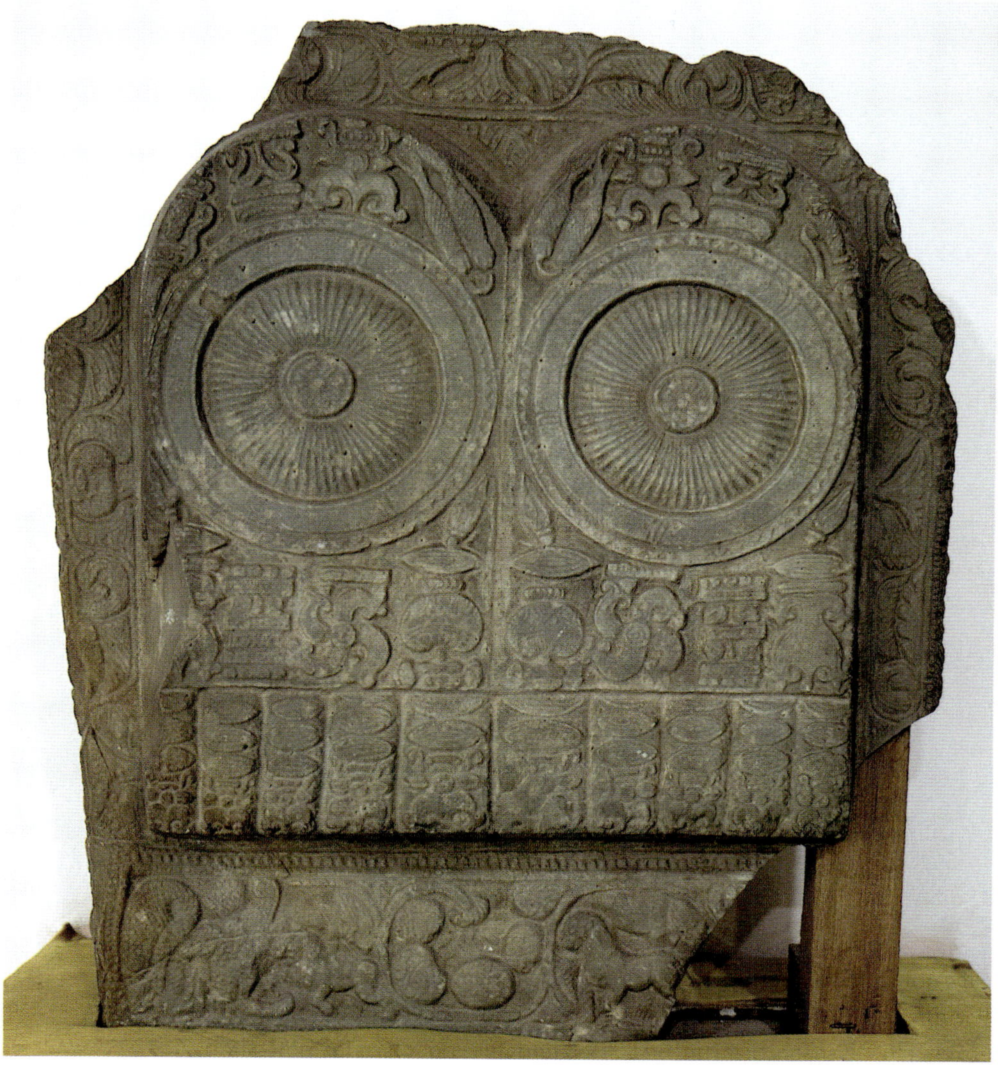

107 *Buddhapāda* slab from Nāgārjunakonda, surrounded with a now damaged low-relief lotus and animal frame emanating from the mouth of a fish-tailed *makara*. National Museum of India, Delhi.

This represents an entirely abstract visualization of the footprint where the central wheel, with many spokes, is rimmed by a double border within which sits a row of broad lotus petals. The outer rim of this border turns into tendrils that become the five toes of the foot depicted in relief as a series of half-open lotus buds, one for each toe, with *svastika*s above the toes on the right and the left.[46] This offers a different, symbolic model for envisaging the *buddhapāda*, although one where the foot seems to grow organically out of the wheel mark in the centre.

The key point in all this is that this site and others in the region offer a variety of iconic models for the footprints, some playing with and against naturalism (as in the two that survive complete in the British Museum), others offering a more schematic accumulation of symbols, within which the British Museum fragment offers exceptional variation. The parallel of the naturalism-challenging tablets with the embodied Buddha alongside the more symbolic panels with his emblematic form is striking. Whether we should really be seeing these images as a chronological progression (from those that interrogate naturalism to those that are largely schematic), as scholarly literature has done previously, or should rather see these icons as co-existing in the art of the stūpa, with different emphases on the *rūpakāya* or *dharmakāya* aspects of the Buddha (as do the different kinds of Buddha images), seems to me an open question given the difficulties of dating anything precisely at the monument.

A key textual tradition related to the Buddha's feet concerns the 32 marks of a great man (either a wheel-turning monarch, *cakravartin*, who is not a Buddha according to the tradition, or a Bodhisattva who will attain enlightenment after renouncing the worldly pleasures in which the *cakravartin* delights, or a fully awakened Buddha).[47] A number of these marks concern the feet.[48] This (perhaps originally pre-Buddhist)

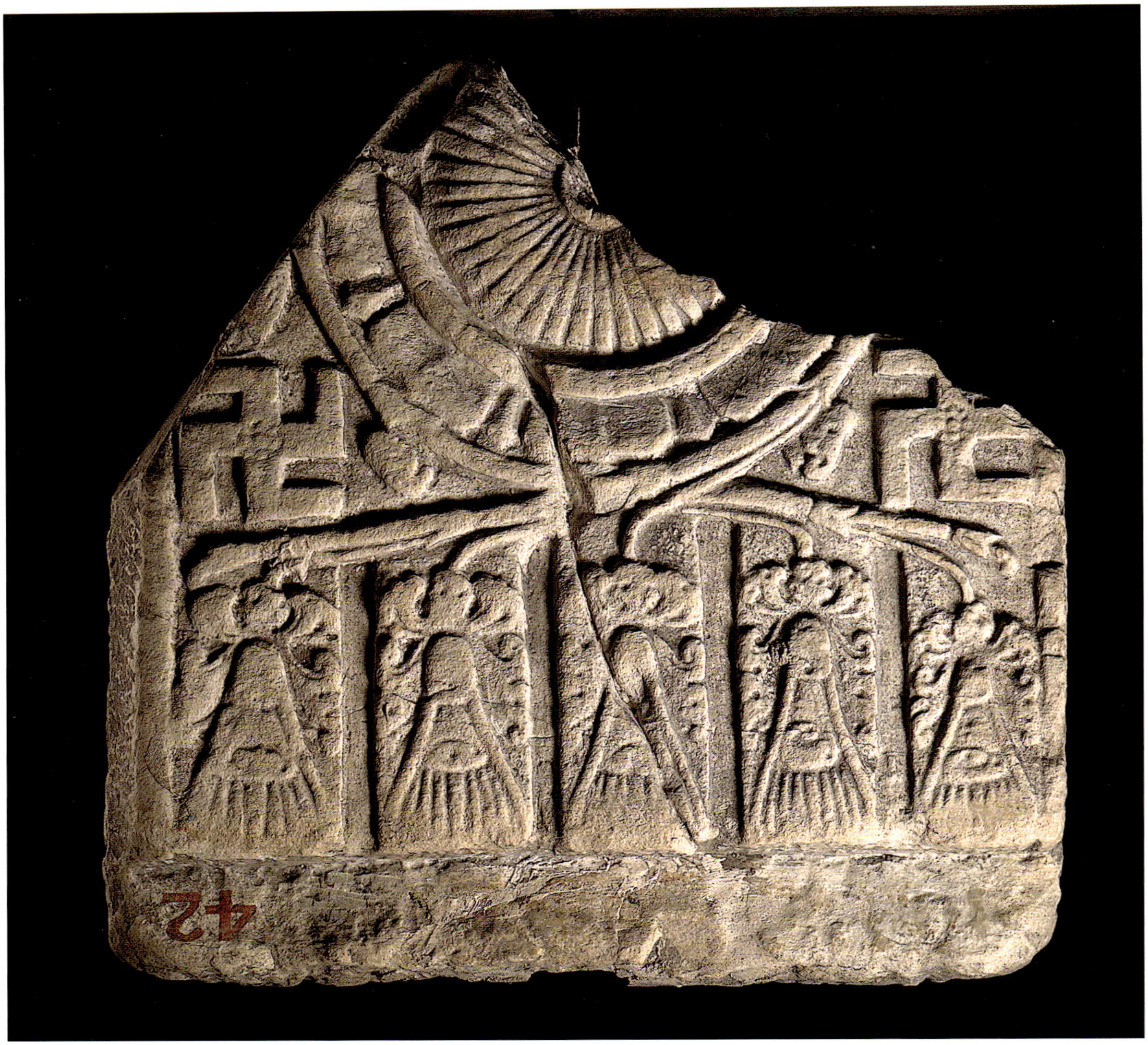

108 Fragment of a single foot from an unusual and abstract *buddhapāda* slab.

tradition of the great man who bears a series of physical marks is presented by a number of suttas in the Pāli canon, by the *Mahāsāṃghika Mahāvastu*,[49] and repeated with much frequency in the Mahāyāna sūtras and commentaries, since it pertains to the physical exceptionalism of a Bodhisattva.[50] The *Mahāvastu* in particular elaborates in visual directions that resonate with the probably *Mahāsāṃghika* imagery of the Amarāvatī *buddhapādas*:

> The feet of those great seers were level of soles, covered with network designs, well formed . . . adorned with the designs of wheels. The soles of their feet were bright with *svastikas*. Lifted with toes ever turning to the right, the feet of the saviours of the world lit up the bright earth as they moved along. Unfettered of feet were these saviours . . . The feet of the saviours of the world who wandered over the bright earth had long toes, copper-coloured nails, network designs and other characteristics.[51]

Take the *Brahmāyu Sutta* of the *Majjhima Nikāya*, which survives in Pāli and in two Chinese versions.[52] Here, the brahmin Brahmayu sends his young student Uttara to visit the recluse Gautama to see if he has indeed been endowed with the 32 marks of the great man. After spending four summer months in company with the Buddha, Uttara returns to give his account to Brahmāyu. The first seven marks concern the feet:

> The report that has been spread about Master Gotama is true, sir, and not otherwise . . . He possesses the thirty-two marks of a Great Man.
> Master Gotama sets his foot down squarely – this is a mark of a Great Man in Master Gotama.
> On the soles of his feet there are wheels with a thousand spokes and ribs and hubs all complete – this is a mark of a Great Man in Master Gotama.
> He has projecting heels – this is a mark of a Great Man in Master Gotama.
> He has long fingers and toes – this is a mark of a Great Man in Master Gotama.
> His hands and feet are soft and tender – this is a mark of a Great Man in Master Gotama.
> He has netted hands and feet – this is a mark of a Great Man in Master Gotama.
> His feet are arched – this is a mark of a Great Man in Master Gotama.[53]

Clearly all visual depictions of the *buddhapāda* make a general reference to this textual tradition – above all the wheels of the second mark with their ribs, spokes and hubs, which as we have seen are taken in the *Buddhavaṃsa* to summarize the Buddha's special nature and implicitly stand for all 32 marks. Arguably in the large icons from Amarāvatī the footprints also reflect the well-placedness of the first mark, the long and slender toes, the marking of the heels with symbols, and perhaps even structure the imagery of the foot through a collection of symbols as an evocation of 'nettedness'. In this sense these images not only are synecdoches for the Buddha by representing him through his feet but, more esoterically, they take seven of the marks to reflect all 32. Placing the foot squarely in the first mark arguably emphasizes the groundedness of the Buddha on the earth – firmly grounded enough to make an imprint.[54] So, in tune with the *Doṇa Sutta*, this tradition supports the visual apophaticism of the *buddhapāda* as taking a particularly human physical feature (the firmly planted foot) and denaturalizing it in order to imply a being that is neither man nor god.

Two further Pāli suttas in the *Dīgha Nikāya*, the *Mahāpadāna Sutta* (the fourteenth in that collection, II.16–19) and the *Lakkhaṇa Sutta* (the thirtieth, III.142–79), which survive also in Chinese versions, include the list of marks and treasures belonging to the great man, whether monarch or Buddha. The *Mahāpadāna Sutta* describes the lineage of the Buddhas, going back to Vipassī, the Buddha 91 aeons before Śakyamuni, and describes the 32 marks as belonging to each Buddha.[55] The *Lakkhaṇa Sutta* proceeds to enumerate the karmic qualities and deeds in previous lives that give rise to each of the signs, and the benefits that the sign confers on its possessor in his new existence.[56] When speaking of the wheels on the soles of his feet, the sutta says: 'how does he benefit? He has a large retinue: he is surrounded by monks, nuns, male and female lay-followers, *deva*s and humans, *asura*s, *nāga*s, and *gandhabba*s. That is his benefit as a Buddha.'[57]

In this case, a range of the kinds of beings negated in the *Doṇa Sutta* are integrated into the Buddha's retinue – constituting his accompaniment both on the low-relief borders of the two Amarāvatī slabs on which I have focused and in the large extent of the imagery at the site, not to speak of the range of human devotees outlined in the many votive inscriptions. Likewise, his projecting heels and long toes are a protection so that no foe 'whether an ascetic or brahmin, a *deva*, *mara*, or Brahma, or anyone in the world can possibly take his life'.[58] Again, here (and repeatedly in its affirmation of the qualities conveyed by the marks), the text reintegrates the miraculous being into the world by means of positive relational qualities to all classes of other beings. And, again, we might see the relations of the footprints to their border imagery in the Amarāvatī *buddhapāda*s as picking up on this.

Beyond these suttas, we find aspects of the contradiction or mutual exclusivity of the Buddha as both within the world and not of the world in the commentarial traditions. The fifth-century scholar Buddhaghosa discussed a number of such 'points of controversy' in his commentary on the *Katthāvatthu* section of the *Abhidhamma Piṭaka* (18.1.1–4), where he discusses whether it is not right to say 'The Exalted Buddha lived in the world of mankind.' Reasoning from all the references to specific places and contexts in the suttas, he argues, 'Surely then the Exalted Buddha lived among men'. But reasoning from the passage in the *Saṃyutta Nikāya* (3.140), which says 'born in the world, enlightened in the world, having overcome the world, undefiled by the world', he argues also 'hence surely it is not right to say "The Exalted Buddha lived in the world of mankind."'[59] Here, without specific reference to the body, the same theoretical issues are aired without clear resolution or doctrinal closure.

The theology of these texts sets out the Buddha as an utterly different kind of being from any other, and yet one with material, if supranormal, manifestations (in his miraculous footprints and physical presence). The marks depict a supranormal body, just as the more abstract of the *buddhapāda*s depict a supranormal foot. The Amarāvatī *buddhapāda* reliefs place their version of this within a vast and rich narrative elaboration of the Buddha's previous lives as the Bodhisattva (the Buddha-to-be, as recounted in the *jātakas* and *avadānas*), the story of his life as the Buddha – from his birth in miraculous circumstances and bearing the 32 marks, to his enlightenment and death – and copious images of the veneration of his monuments, relics and stūpa, as well as many images of supernatural beings.[60] That is, the choice to make and reiterate a large icon of the supreme being through footprints is cast within the larger scope of his many lives as Bodhisattva and the universal context of the salvation that his enlightenment brings.

My claim is not that these panels illustrate specific texts in this rich tradition, or their many commentaries. Rather, in a monastic context where many viewers were steeped in the learnings of the Buddhist tradition, the resonances of these scriptural texts would have been present and available. Moreover, it is in the quality of thinking through a discourse of the miraculous, in relation to a unique being whose transformative coming changed the world of those called to his dharma, that the artistic construction of the *buddhapāda* icons at Amarāvatī reflects the creativity, intelligence and learning of the scriptural tradition in visual terms.

THE *BUDDHAPĀDAS* IN VISUAL NARRATIVES

These large-scale panel icons, which clearly proliferated over the years, coexisted with a series of further miniature representations of the *buddhapāda* within historiated reliefs and hence as elements within narratives.[61] The replication of large icons of the *buddhapāda* as discursive segments – both meaningful in their own right and reflexive of the large panels in the context – within the greater decorative programme of the site has parallels with the frequent representation of stūpas

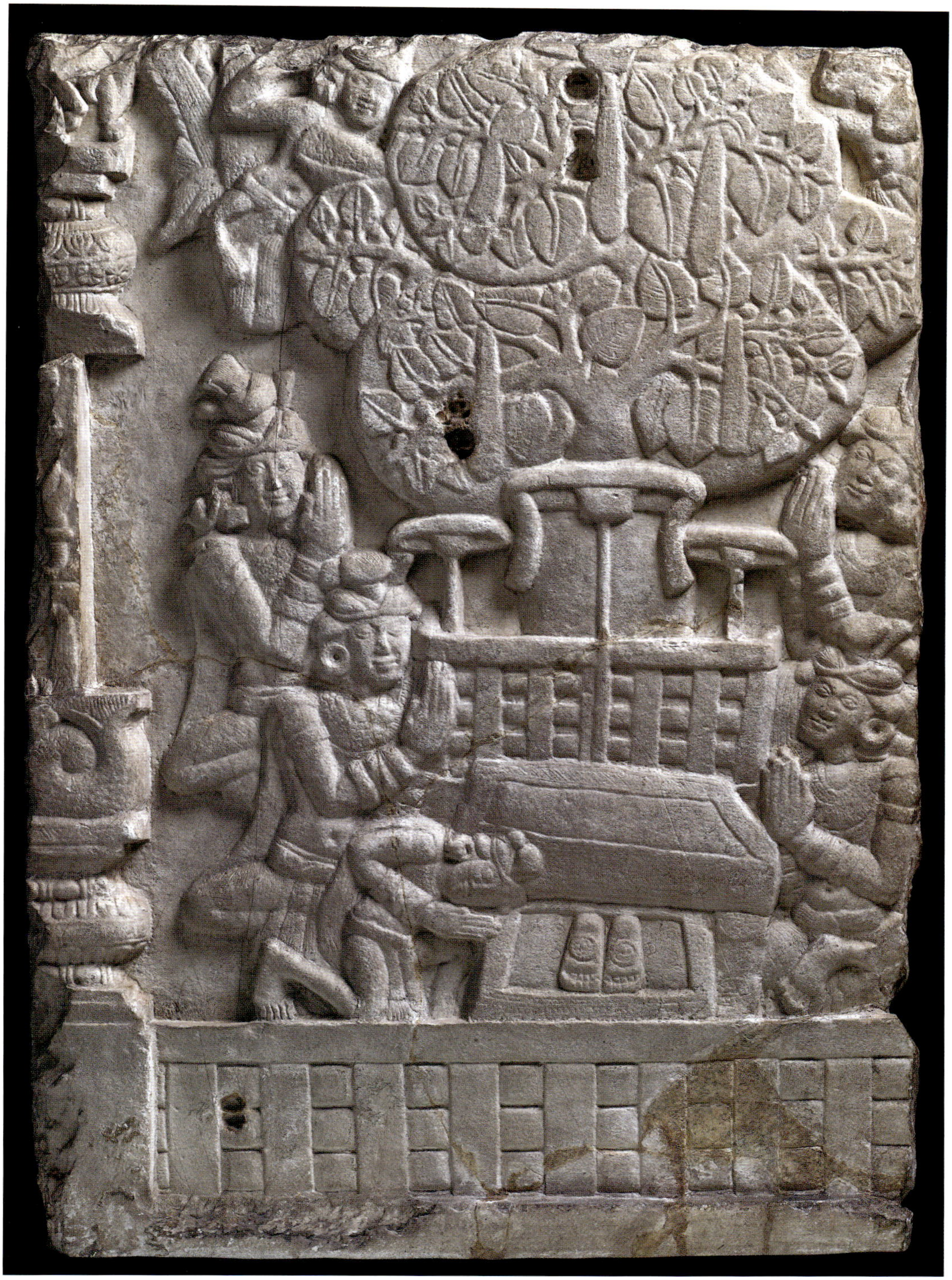

109 Earlier face of a double-sided drum slab, cut down at right, left and top for later reuse with the worshippers before the Bodhi tree, empty throne and *buddhapāda*.

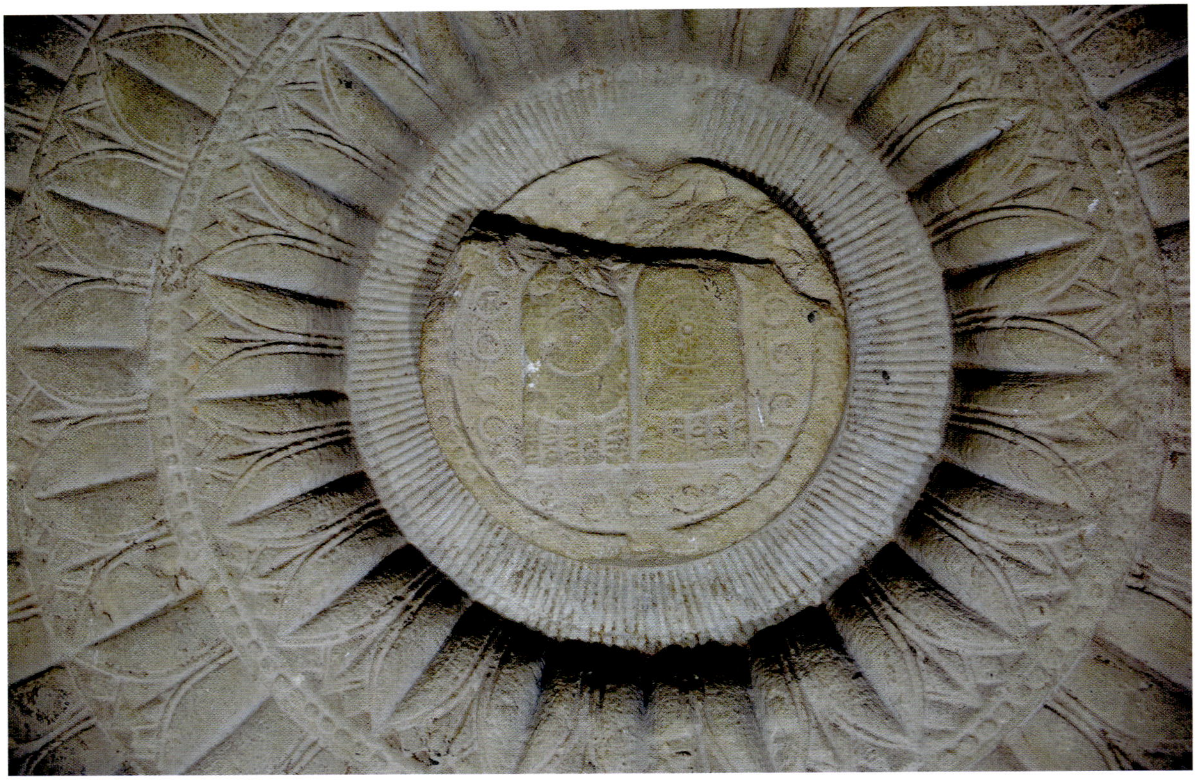

110 *Buddhapāda* engraved in the heart of a lotus crossbar with three rims of petals.

in the relief panels that adorned the drum of the main stūpa.[62] Among the plethora of richly carved slabs around the vast drum that supported the dome, many depict stūpas or the act of worship. Of these, several include the *buddhapāda*. Almost certainly the earliest drum slab in the British Museum (later reversed and re-cut with a fine stūpa relief) shows the Buddha's enlightenment beneath the Bodhi tree with five worshippers around the throne, perhaps representing the five ascetics to whom he later preached the First Sermon (perhaps from the first century BCE, illus. 109). The throne is empty, with just a lotus stem in its centre and the *buddhapāda* beneath, depicted as miniature footprints with rimmed wheels and in a framed footstool, facing out and downwards towards the viewer as if impressed by an invisible person seated on the throne.[63] A fragment of a panel at the Amarāvatī Museum, perhaps of the same date, shows four devotees, two male and female couples, worshipping the throne with a *buddhapāda* beneath and a series of auspicious symbols in the centre.[64] Part of the charm of the British Museum panel is the contiguity of the *buddhapāda* with the foot of the worshipping ascetic to the immediate right (from the viewer's perspective), which is without wheels or the iconic formality of the footprints. In these cases, there is at least a strong possibility that the footprints represent the presence of the Buddha himself in an emblematic body that includes the empty throne and lotus stem. A series of later panels, perhaps from the third century CE, show stūpas whose decoration includes images of *buddhapāda*s – for instance beneath parasols on the dome of the depicted stūpa in a number of examples (see illus. 34, as we have seen),[65] or in the central gateway beneath an empty throne below a column surmounted by a wheel (*dharmacakra*, see illus. 26),[66] or below the Bodhi tree (illus. 115).[67]

Numerous further *buddhapāda*s appear in a variety of other contexts within the decoration of the Amarāvatī stūpa,[68] not least on a lotus crossbar now in the Government Museum in Chennai (illus. 110).[69] Narrative examples include a panel from the inner face of the rail coping, which includes an image perhaps of the Buddha himself and of a stūpa with a platform to the left bearing the Buddha's footprints (illus. 81, although not easy to make out).[70] A dome slab with large-scale relief of a monarch with a horse and a pair of ladies is framed below by a frieze of seated Buddhas over a frieze of horizontal *buddhapāda*s with toes pointing to the left.[71] A fine roundel from a crossbar in the Amarāvatī Museum, damaged horizontally across the centre and upper right rim and rather crudely repaired, has a devotional scene, perhaps showing the Buddha's son, Rāhula, being presented to the empty throne with the *buddhapāda* beneath it (illus. 111).[72] In particular, the *buddhapāda* appears at the bottom of a number of drum pilasters showing a *dharmacakra* on a high pillar over

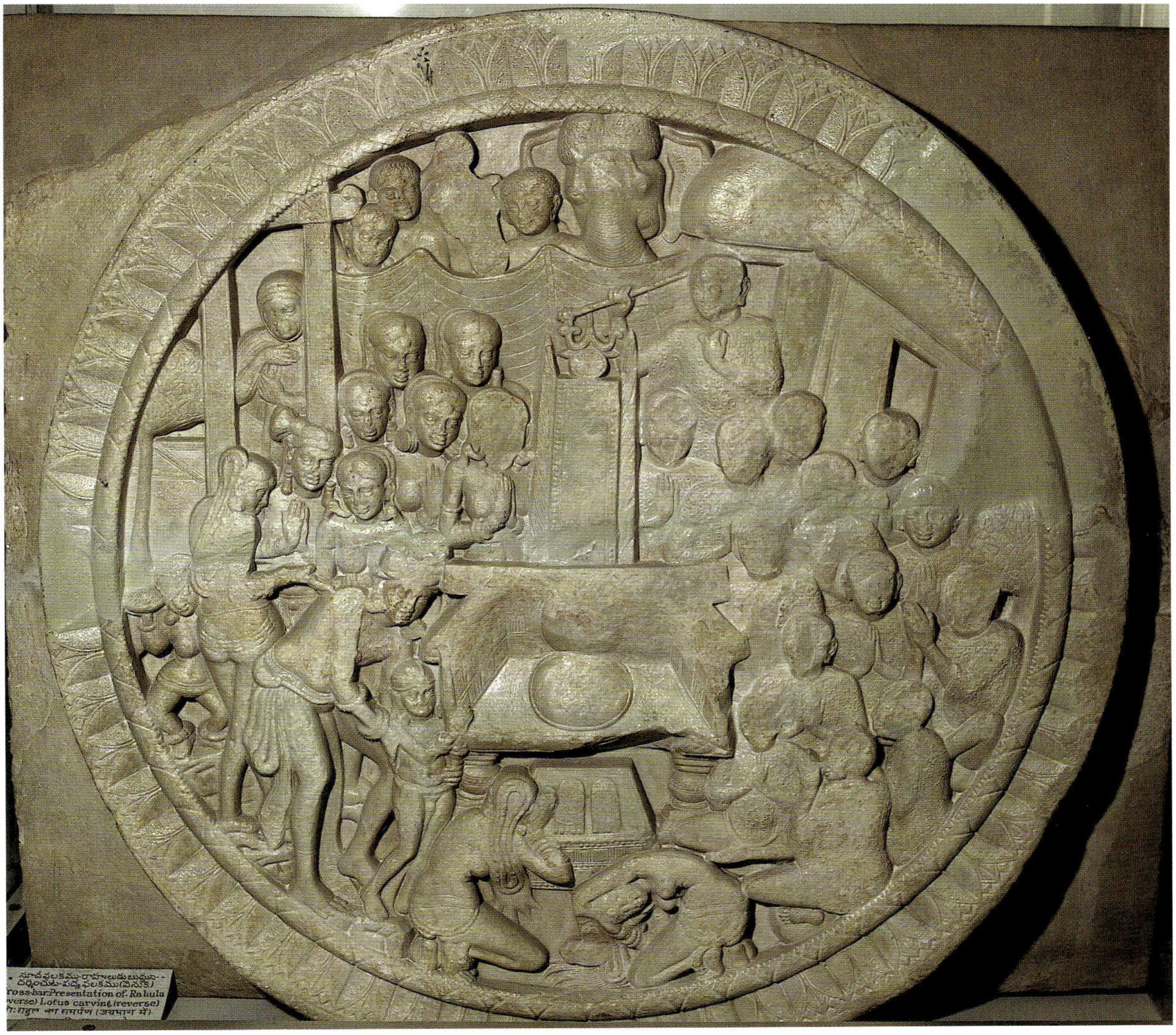

111 Historiated crossbar from the interior of the railing with the presentation of a child, perhaps the Buddha's son Rāhula, to the Buddha represented as a flaming column crowned by a *triratna* over an empty throne with *buddhapāda* beneath.

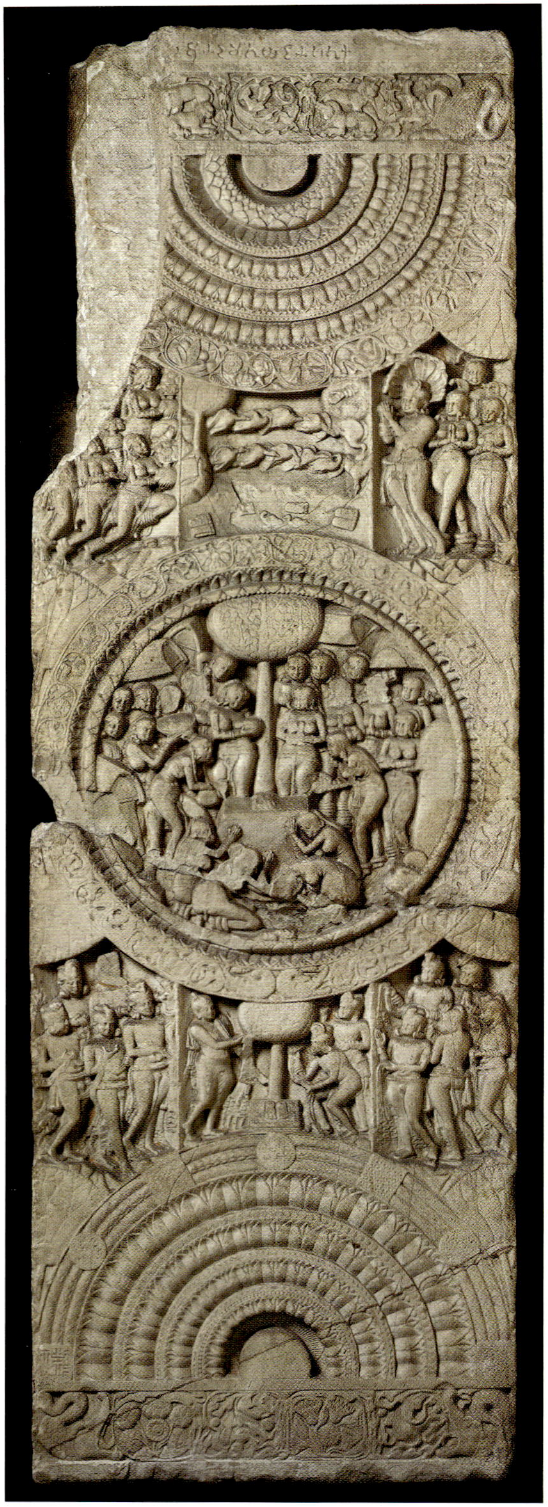

an empty throne with cushions and *buddhapāda* below, surrounded by worshippers, dwarfs and seated deer (see illus. 25 at the sides and 131).[73] This use of the motif places it where the feet might be if the pillar were a person, as is famously the case on the northern gateway at Sāñcī (illus. 101).[74]

The richness in elaboration of the *buddhapāda* motif across the early Buddhist sculpture of the site is rivalled only by the repetition and elaboration of the stūpa theme, in the form of meta-stūpas. The two share a substantive emphasis on representing veneration in numerous forms, both within the mythological or narrative tradition (such as Rāhula before the throne) and in the visualization of perhaps contemporary 'reality', or at least of times after the Buddha's life, as envisaged by some of the sculptures – with numerous worshippers performing different kinds of devotions. Arguably, if the story of the Buddha's previous incarnation Sumedha prostrating himself before the Buddha Dīpaṅkara at the occasion of his taking the Bodhisattva vow is important for the Amarāvatī stūpa, which was built on the legendary site of Sumedha's birth,[75] then the *buddhapāda*'s relationship with devotion evokes this foundational act. To be before the *buddhapāda* is to be called to prostrate, as Sumedha did before the feet of Dīpaṅkara.[76] That act – in the contemporary worshipper – is itself a reminder of the original Boddhisattva vow made aeons ago by the man who would become Gautama Buddha, and potentially (for those with a Mahāyāna vocation) a call to devotees to take the Bodhisattva vow themselves. The visual emphasis on devotion in the historiated images that include the *buddhapāda*, apparent also in the devotional iconography of the meta-stūpas, is arguably a significant cue to understanding the large icons of the *buddhapāda* that are the focus of this chapter.[77]

Let us test what might be called a visual commentary on the meanings of the *buddhapāda* by looking at an

112 Unique example of an intact surviving railing pillar carved on both sides, abraded, broken and damaged at the upper left. The interior side, with scenes from the narrative leading to the Enlightenment, is shown here; the exterior is illus. 14 (2.66 × 0.86 m).

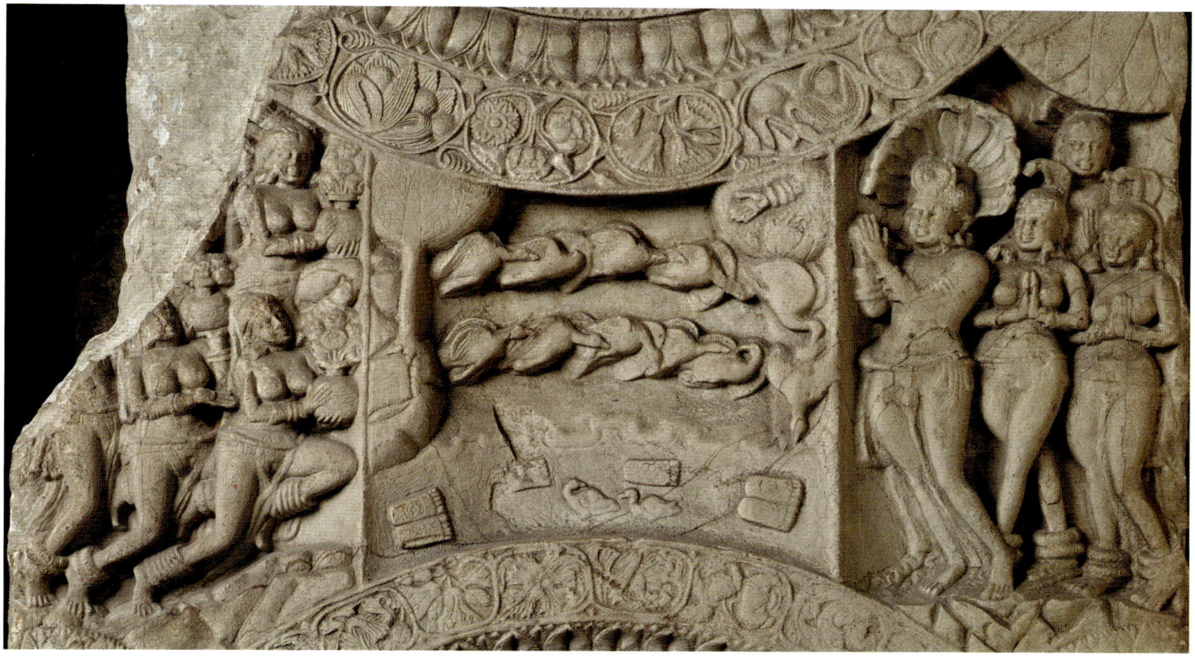

113 The upper lozenge of illus. 112 with the Bodhisattva – rendered aniconically as a series of footprints – crossing the Nairañjanā River.

example of the motif as employed on a small scale in the figurative sculpture of a single pillar from the interior of the railing set up around the stūpa in the second or third century (illus. 112).[78] Sandwiched between two lotus half-roundels with framing borders of floral, vine and lotus motifs with fantastic animals and *makaras* are three historiated scenes. At the top the Bodhisattva – represented only as a series of *buddhapādas*, two together at left and right, two singles in the centre – crosses the Nairañjanā River near Bodh Gaya in an event that took place before his enlightenment (illus. 113).[79] There are two lines of geese above the rendition of the river and a remarkable disembodied hand emerges from what may be a tree on the right; this has been interpreted as a tree god granting aid to the miraculous crossing. The Bodhisattva walks from left to right, in the same direction as the flying geese and as viewers would be walking as they circumambulated the stūpa with the inner railing to their left. To the left are female worshippers, and to the right, the *nāga* king with his wives, and snakes behind his head. In the roundel below (illus. 114), in its lotus border, is the Bodhi tree with a throne on which is placed the *buddhapāda*, now damaged. This is surrounded by figures, including what has been interpreted as the offering of food by the girl Sujātā in what would be the Bodhisattva's last meal before his enlightenment. In the scene at the bottom is the tree again with throne and *buddhapāda* flanked by further figures (illus. 115). In this case, the throne is presented as a square frame with its own incised border around the footprints, making them a version of the large icons we have been examining.

Effectively, the *buddhapāda* is central to every scene in this pillar, whether seen as an element within the narrative (as in the Nairañjanā episode at the top) or potentially within a theme of largely devotional significance, with the footprints depicted as a framed icon in the lowest scene. All may represent events before the enlightenment, but the bottom and central scenes may well be meant to evoke the Buddha after his enlightenment. In terms of vertical thrust, accentuated by the trees one on top of the other in the lower scenes

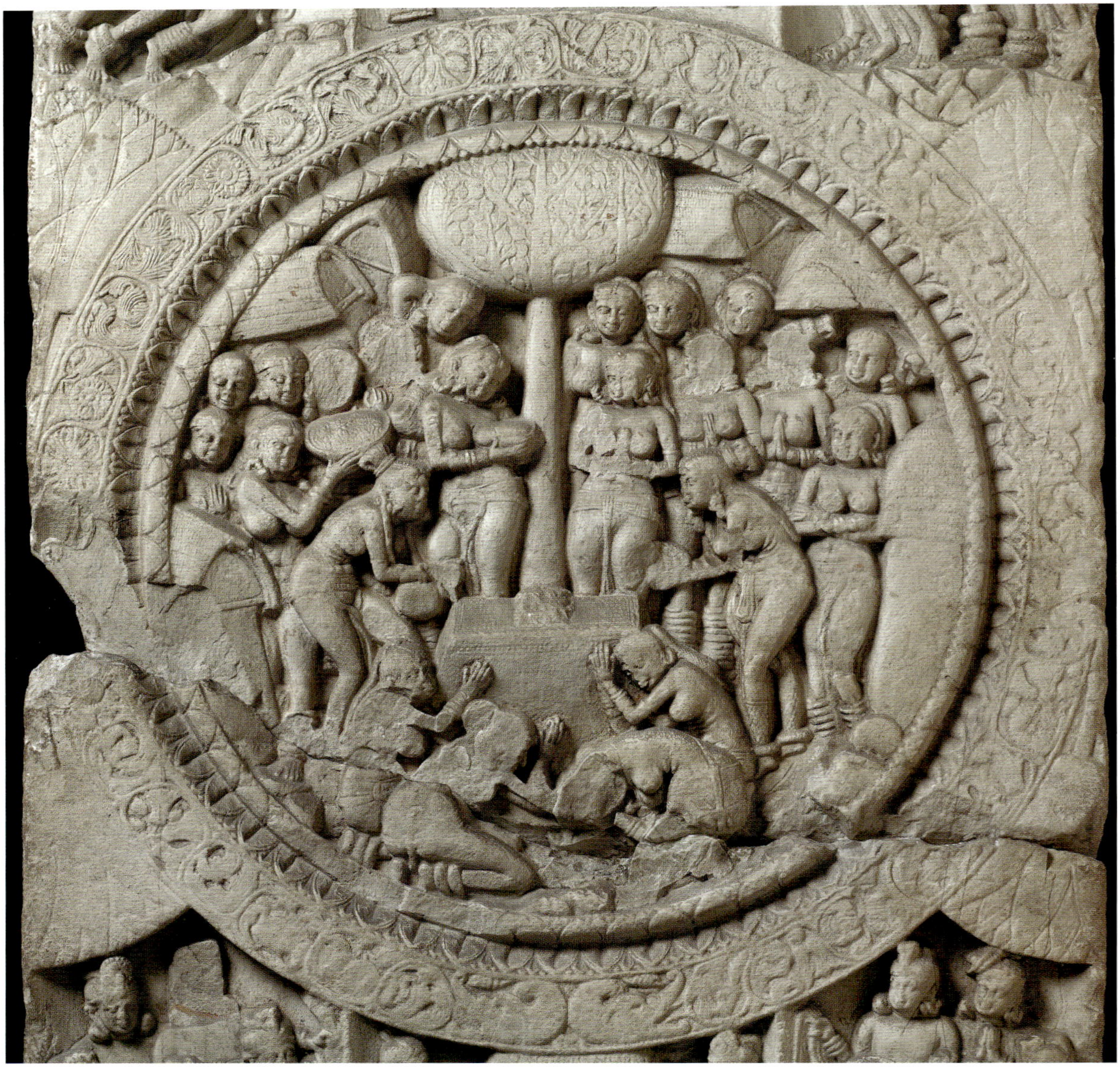

114 The central historiated roundel of illus. 112 with the girl Sujātā surrounded by other females offering milkrice to the Bodhisattva, rendered aniconcially as a platform with *buddhapāda* beneath the tree, before the Enlightenment.

and by the shape of the pillar itself, the *buddhapāda* not only is at the central place of worship in each image, but proliferates across the middle section of the river-crossing at the top. In this collection of images, despite the rich figural iconography, the Buddha himself only appears as the *buddhapāda*, although in many other scenes from the stūpa (including railing pillars probably of the same date) his figure is fully present. As with so many other themes in the Amarāvatī sculptures – from lotus roundels and garlands to the miniature stūpa panel reliefs of the drum, via repeated motifs on all parts of the stūpa's structure – one set of images in the site reflect, replicate, offer variations on, serve as a commentary to other sets of similar imagery in the multiverse pluricosm constructed by the stūpa's creators.

Two general conclusions about the *buddhapāda* motif in Amarāvatī arise. First, it is most often an icon implying the image and presence of the Buddha himself: this is so in the many narrative instances within the decorative reliefs where the motif appears beneath a throne (for example, illus. 111), often under the Bodhi tree (for example, illus. 109, 114, 115), and in narrative images like the crossing of the Nairañjanā (illus. 113) or the Bodhisattva's birth (see illus. 51). It is very likely (if unprovably) the case in the large independent panels that have been my main focus. But, in those drum slabs where it appears twice under a parasol in the dome sculpture to either side of the gateway in a meta-stūpa (for example, illus. 34) and on the railing coping where it stands on a base to either side of the outer railing gate of a mini-stūpa (illus. 81),[80] the motif features as a miniature image of a *buddhapāda* slab. The question whether, in this last set of instances, the small relief image of a slab-icon carries the same weight and presence of the Buddha as the narrative use of *buddhapāda*s to represent the Buddha in other imagery of the same period, carved by the same sculptors at the same site, is not easily soluble. But the phenomenon certainly reflects the way that representations of representations characteristically play on each other at Amarāvatī (as meta-stūpa images play on

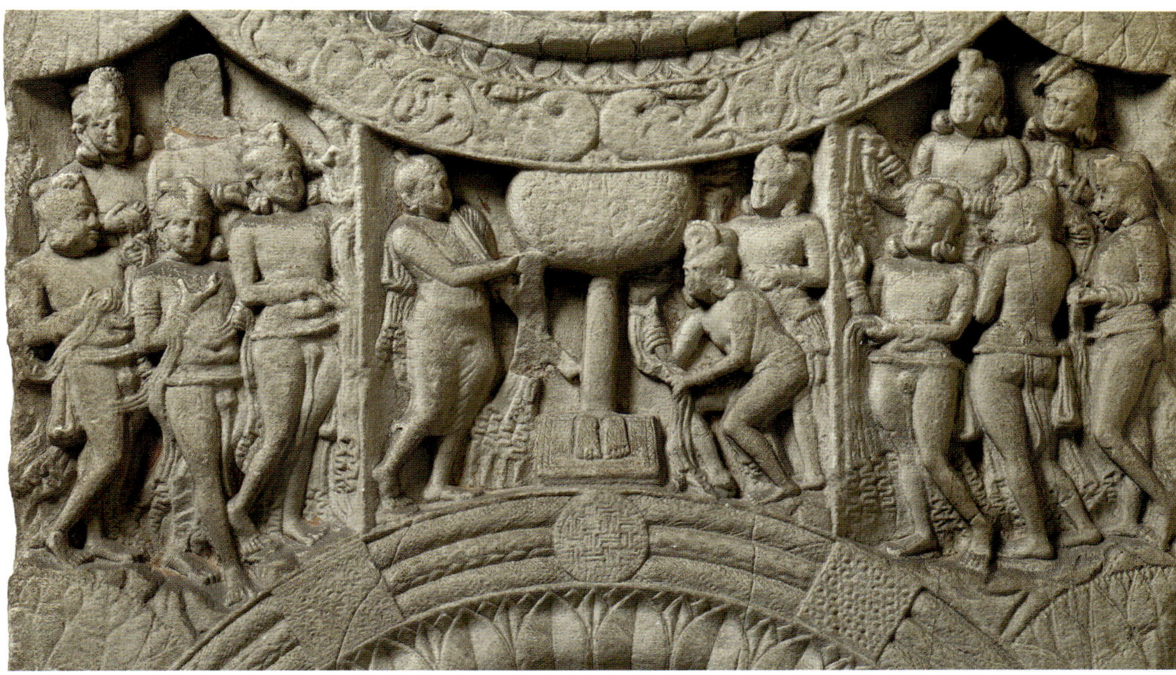

115 The lower lozenge of illus. 112 with males offering clothing to the Bodhisattva, rendered aniconically as platform with *buddhapāda* beneath the Bodhi tree.

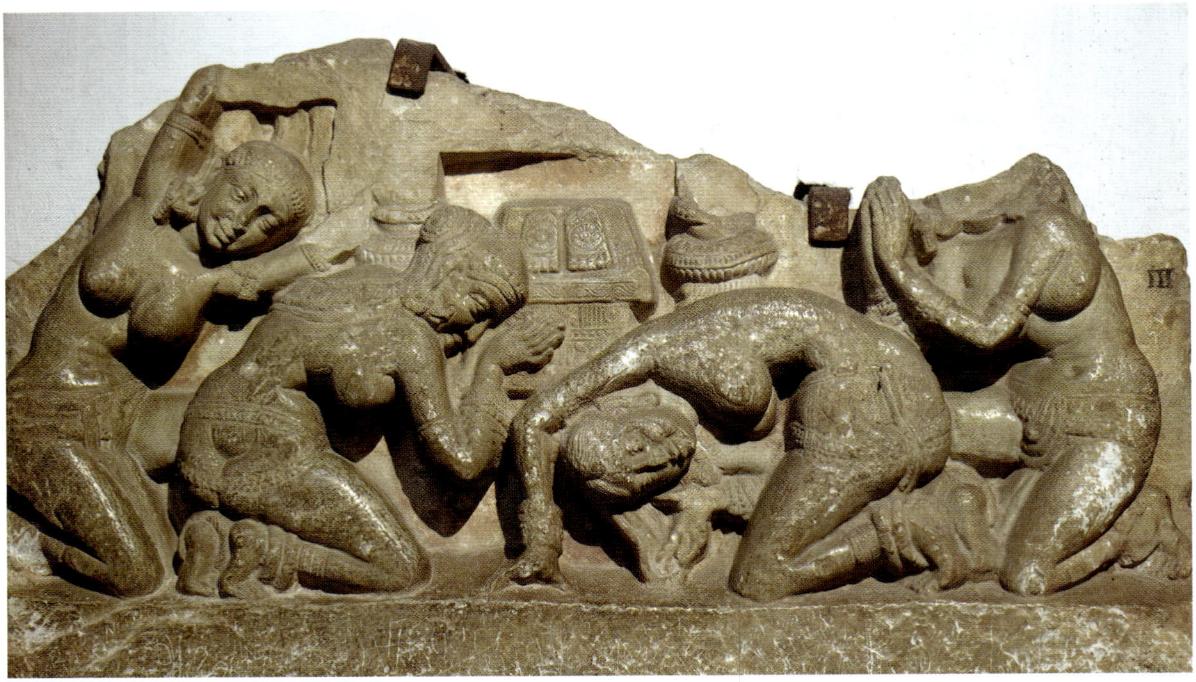

116 Fragment of women adoring the *buddhapāda* beneath the empty throne.

the main stūpa, which they adorn). The issue is parallel to the way in which Byzantine icons may represent their subjects holding miniature icons whose sacred efficacy may be no less powerful because they are copies.

Second, the motif never appears with the toes pointing upwards. This means that it is never perceived from the point of view of a person looking down at her or his own feet but rather as if one were face to face with the holy presence of the *buddhapāda*'s invisible possessor. In those cases, the vast majority, the *buddhapāda* offers a confrontation with a sacred presence – perhaps implying an invitation to obeisance in the way that one might do homage to the feet of a holy person through prostration, as is indeed depicted in a fragmentary relief from a railing pillar, now in the Chennai Museum (illus. 116).[81] In the few instances where *buddhapāda*s are seen from the side (as a framing frieze or in narratives such as the Buddha's birth or the crossing of the Nairañjanā River, illus. 113),[82] it remains the case that the viewer is not in a position to identify with them as potentially his or her own feet, seen as one would see one's own.

There is a remarkable insistence on the *buddhapāda* motif in the sculptural decoration of Amarāvatī – greater than that shown at other stūpas of the same period. In the narrative reliefs, there is a striking emphasis on veneration (illus. 111 and 116). The two complete slabs in the British Museum (illus. 100 and 102) are remarkable and thoughtful gestures in the discourse of visual theology. They take the naturalistic models for representing people and animals in narrative figures or representations and turn them on their head. Instead of being imprints, these footprints emerge from the rock; instead of being footprints, they combine elements of the upper and the lower part of the foot that are impossible in the real world; in addition to being feet, they are medleys of auspicious signs. My contention is that, in a visual culture that insistently emphasizes veneration in connection to a monument designed for devotion, these icons are intended to depict the miraculous nature of the Buddha as one who cannot be defined by the discursive norms of representation. They may also potentially refer to miraculously made and lasting footprint relics of the

Buddha and, by this means, to the Buddha himself.[83] The impossibility of the image – and yet its existence as an image, a trace of the real, realized in reality – is an attempt by visual means to define the supra-normal and supernatural nature of Buddhahood.

ICONS OF EMPTINESS

One final area of exploration, necessarily hypothetical because all issues of dating are so uncertain, is a range of philosophical implications that would later become of central importance to Mahāyāna thinking. It is likely that the Buddhist sect predominant (though by no means exclusively) along the Krishna River, the Mahāsāṃghika school, was open to a number of the philosophical moves that led to the creation of some of the strands of thought that came to be influential in what developed into Mahāyāna Buddhism.[84] In particular, the great philosopher monk Nāgārjuna – whose historical chronology is as obscure as his places of origin and habitation – is, on current analysis, least unlikely among all the other options to have lived and produced his hugely creative development of the philosophy of emptiness in Andhra Pradesh during the second or third century CE.[85] It is hard to overrate the significance of this move in Indian philosophy, since the emptiness of inherent existence would become the fundamental ground on which Mahāyāna understanding of reality and illusion, of the mind's role in creating the real, and hence of the possibilities of salvation through taking up the Bodhisattva path to Buddhahood are founded.[86] There is, however, no certainty that the Nāgārjuna who composed the *Mūlamadhyamakakārikā* need himself have been a Mahāyānist in any form of polemical or apologetic vocation: this philosophical text cites only Nikāya sources and conducts its critique on the foundations of traditional *Abhidharma*.[87] In his philosophy, Nāgārjuna extended the models of negation found in earlier Buddhist writings, such as the *Doṇa Sutta*, discussed earlier. In his great poetic text the *Mūlamadhyamakakārikā*, for instance, he writes:

> Everything is real and is not real;
> Both real and not real;
> Neither real nor not real.
> This is the Lord Buddha's Teaching.[88]

The 'four-cornered logic' (*Catuṣkoṭi*) employed here, borrowed to be sure from earlier Buddhist suttas,[89] is used systematically to open a space around any object of attention (in this case, 'everything') – emptying it of intrinsic, substantive or essentialist identification with anything that can be projected onto it, or attributed to it.[90]

Now certainty is not possible, but the least unlikely best guess at present is that Nāgārjuna formulated this model of thinking in the period when the Amarāvatī stūpa was being decorated with much of the sculpture we have been discussing, and in its vicinity. His philosophical creativity (and that of his interlocutors, whom he taught and with whom he debated) went side by side with that of the stūpa's artists. Since we are equally uncertain about the dates of the sculptures, it is possible that the *buddhapāda*s on which I have focused here are of roughly the same date as the birth of Nāgārjuna's philosophy of emptiness; scholarly consensus puts them a touch earlier on stylistic grounds but without the grounding of external confirmation. Nonetheless, they were certainly available to later viewing in contexts where the fourfold logic of Nāgārjuna was known and applied, and one might argue that their careful formal creation of a kind of object that was not a foot and not a footprint, yet might be thought both, and was not in itself a negative, anticipates or draws on something of the energies of the school of thought around Nāgārjuna.

If we apply the four-cornered logic to the *buddhapāda*, we get something like this:

> The *buddhapāda* is a footprint and is not a footprint.
> It both is and is not a footprint.
> It is neither a footprint nor not a footprint.

Each of these statements is true in itself and in combination with the others; it is also true if we substitute 'foot' for 'footprint'. The *buddhapāda*s of Amarāvatī create something real – as in a series of sculpted works of art – which in some respects refer to the real (to feet and footprints) but in fundamental and deliberate ways refute any possibility of fixing on these icons as things of a mundane or normal kind. They bring to mind a supernatural being, whether in the objects themselves, in the Buddha from whom they emanate or in the actual and venerated footprints of the Buddha elsewhere that they may evoke, yet a being who is by definition empty of any of the normal rules by which the upper and lower parts of a foot are defined, by which what is imprinted and what emerges in relief are differentiated. Arguably the same kind of thinking that in philosophical terms ended up by generating Nāgārjuna's logic of emptiness was in material terms being channelled into the making of the artistic culture of Amarāvatī. In this sense, and in the context of the vibrant intellectual life of the Buddhist communities of the Krishna valley, we may consider the *buddhapāda*s to be icons of emptiness, or rather visual realizations of the kinds of thinking that developed the philosophical expression of emptiness in the *Mūlamadhyamakakārikā*.

Certainly the 32 marks figure in a number of ways in early Mahāyāna literature. In the *Gaṇḍavyūha Sūtra*, one of the sages whom the hero Sudhana is sent to visit is Gopā, a 'girl of the Śakyan clan' dwelling in Kapilavastu (where the Buddha himself was born).[91] He meets Gopā, as is customary in this sūtra, in 'the meeting hall of enlightening beings which shone with the reflections of the cosmos',[92] and after recounting her immense vision of the universe, she describes the kingdom of the Lord of wealth and his son, 'Lord of Glory', who has the 32 marks.[93] In a section that survives only in a Sanskrit version, Gopā describes the 32 marks in detail, including the wheels 'of 1,000 spokes with nave and felly visible, shining and complete in every way'.[94] There is a particular emphasis on the equanimity of tread in the first mark: 'The king's son Lord of Glory stands firm with his hands and feet. He raises the soles of his feet equally and lays them down equally on the earth, and in stepping down completely with the soles of his two feet he touches the earth equally.'[95]

Ultimately the 'Lord of Glory' turns out to be none other than Buddha Śākyamuni in a visionary folktale form that effectively emerges as one of the innumerable reflections of 'sixty decillion Buddhas'.[96] By radical contrast, but closer to Nāgārjuna's model of emptiness, in the *Vajjracchedikā Sūtra*, known as the Diamond Sūtra, the Buddha repeatedly affirms the 32 marks as entirely empty – the Tathāgata 'is truly a no-possession of no-marks'.[97] Arguably, the Amarāvatī *buddhapāda*s, evoking the levelness of the feet and the wheels, have the potential to play to both these models. Their innumerable representations from icon to miniature elements of larger image combinations could be said to evoke the reflective immensity of the vision of the *Gaṇḍavyūha Sūtra*, but their status as simple representations, images rather than the 'real thing' to which they refer, might be thought to speak to the emptiness of the Diamond Sūtra and the famous verses on which it ends:

> As stars, a fault of vision, as a lamp,
> A mock show, dew drops, or a bubble,
> A dream, a lightning flash, or cloud,
> So should one view what is conditioned.[98]

My suggestion is that – in the life of what was a vast sacred and monastic complex in eastern India – the visual theologies of the *buddhapāda*s, which emerge in relief and defy naturalism at Amarāvatī, created an icon-model of real theological complexity in a period of philosophical creativity, and one that certainly had continuing resonance in later centuries than the period of creating the stūpa, when forms of Buddhism more definitely Mahāyānist (rather than mixed or syncretic between varieties of Buddhist positions) began to take hold in the great monasteries of India. The argument here deliberately bypasses, even ignores, the normative model of an aniconic early Buddhism developing towards an anthropomorphic religion. The *buddhapāda* is not aniconic: it is a synecdochic use of certain human features to make an argument about a transcendent and miraculous being.[99] It could certainly sit side by side with fully human versions of the Buddha (just as marks, including wheels, *svastika*s and ω-symbols, appear on the feet of several very early seated buddhas in Mathura[100]), as indeed it did in relation to the rich range of meta-stūpas – some with buddhas and some without – that adorned the drum at the site.[101] Given the precision of the 32 marks in defining a being that is either a wheel-turning monarch or a buddha, we need not resort to aniconism, some kind of abstract symbolism or relatively modern theories of semiotics to explain either the narrative uses of the *buddhapāda* to represent aspects of the birth and life of the Bodhisattva in his final lifetime before and when he became a Buddha, or its functions as a visual declaration of the special status of the being celebrated at Amarāvatī, whose frequent images of devotion prove that this bearer of the marks was a Buddha who had appeared to save the world from suffering.

Two key points are worth emphasizing. First, in its own context at Amarāvatī, the *buddhapāda* is a vibrant and creative visual symbol. Second, it represents a level of theological thinking characteristic of major monastic centres of learning that has found its way into the visual sphere and functions in relation to material forms, using their semiotics and discourses to powerful effect. The limestone icon of the *buddhapāda*, created and much replicated at Amarāvatī, was in all likelihood a powerful think-piece within the liturgical and theological culture of one of Buddhism's greatest Indian sites.

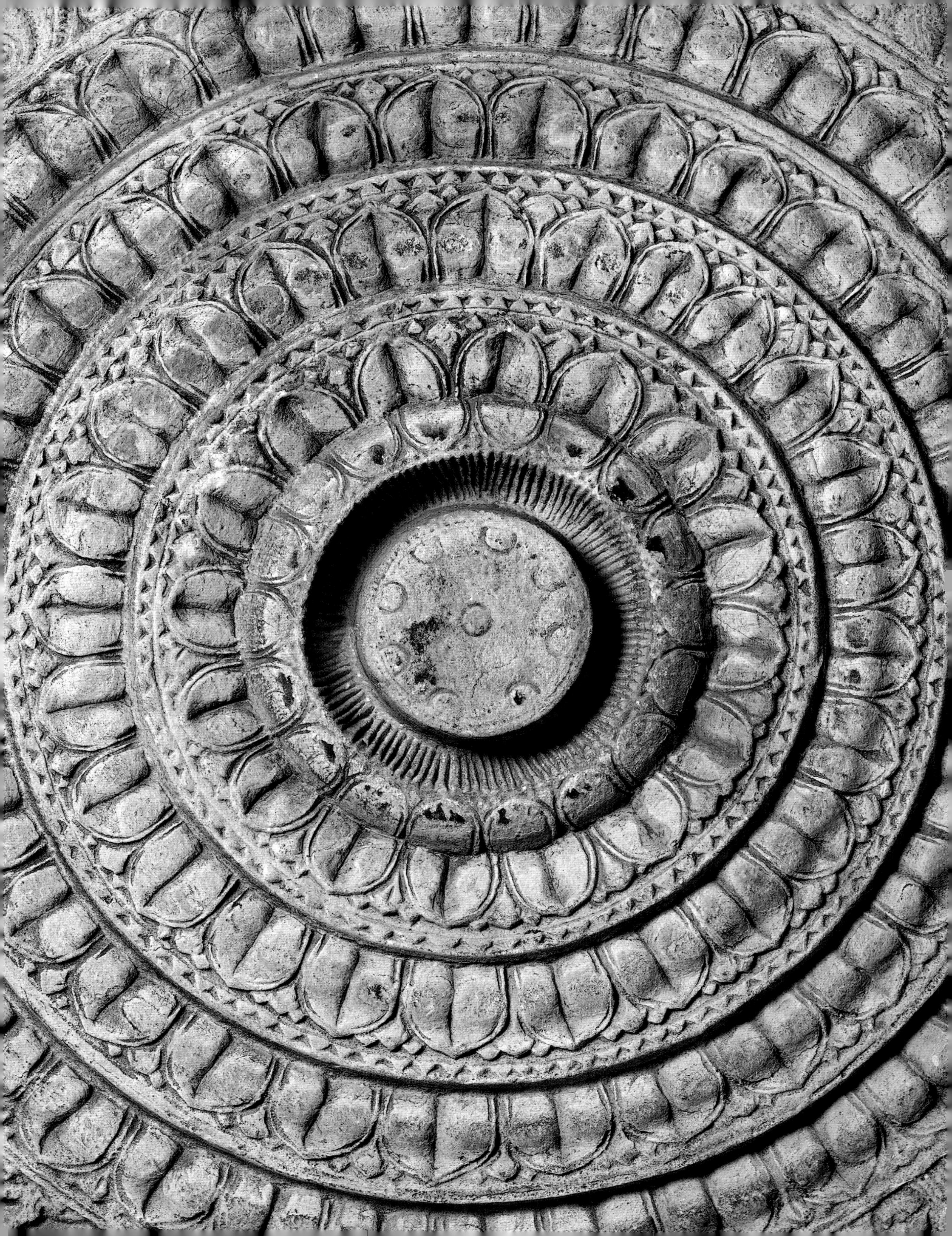

seven

Systems of Representation

The art of Amarāvatī is about representation. It shows an extraordinary flexibility and playfulness with different but also replicative forms of visual discourse that are both semiotically diverse and conceptually open to varieties of theological implication and speculation. This demonstrates exceptional experimentation with a variety of forms (such as the circle) in both two and three dimensions, and with different models of more symbolic and more naturalistic means of depiction. Each image can stand for what it represents and for the absence of that thing (in that it is not that thing, but only a sign for it). For instance, the use of *toraṇa* gateways both adds realistic architectural colour to narratives (implying open-air settings at liminal sites) and points at the same time to the absence of *toraṇas* at the stūpa itself, in contrast to other stūpas elsewhere in India. The endless concern to represent, evoke, and reflect the main monument in its multiverse of stūpa imagery – with different kinds of key centrepieces at the stūpa entrances making parallel but differentiated claims for what is at the heart of the 'Amarāvatī experience' – signals an unusual concern with self-reflexive and commentarial representation itself. The intrinsic incapacity of two-dimensional representations to *be* or to *fully make present* three-dimensional monuments is not only a matter of formal interest and experimentation in the visual arts of the stūpa, but is itself a cipher for, or reflection of, the incapacity of verbal and visual formulations (that is, the canon of Buddhist scriptures and the range of stūpas and their decorative imagery) to transmit the realized entirety of the Buddha's path to his devotees.

This chapter will explore some ramifications of the formal and symbolic creativity of the stūpa's art in relation to issues of replication, of the representation of the Buddha and in relation to the circular plan (which is to say also the domed and cylindrical form) of the stūpa as a whole. One consistent aspect is that these

117 Detail of illus. 118: lotus crossbar with central seed pods, rows of petals, including the incurving petals at the innermost row.

all partake in sophisticated forms of naturalistic representation when it suits them, and at the same time eschew any attempt to imitate reality for schematic or symbolic kinds of depiction. That is, there is no impulse to a fully coherent system of representation (such as the kinds of non-abstractionist naturalism that have predominated at certain times in the arts of Europe), but rather a deliberately ad hoc use of visual evocations to create an artistic language that works flexibly to fulfil the visual needs of the monument's decoration as a commentarial invocation of the Buddha and his path to freedom.

REPLICATIONS

Replication is deep in the art of Amarāvatī. The repetition of motifs (each handmade, so none precisely like any other, but iconographically and formally alike) is essential to all aspects of the stūpa's visual articulation, from the shapes of pillars and crossbars in the railing, and their decoration with elaborately carved lotuses, to the stūpas, *buddhapāda*s and other motifs that create the order of its patterning across the ornamental surface. Each gateway was a version of the others, with its lion statues on stepped capitals and pillars reflections of each other and of the lion pillars of the other gates. Most powerfully, the lotus crossbar bosses and pillar lotus medallions repeated in hundreds across both sides of the railing – each example the same as and yet quite different from any other, with different numbers and sizes of petal rims, and petals pointing both outwards and inwards – offer an extraordinary wealth of varied replication (see illus. 118, 119, 120 and 16). In the dome, the individual oblong blocks stacked with a line of stūpa, *dharmacakra* and Bodhi tree panels and topped with running animals and *trisulas*, when aligned next to one another, become bands of replicated motifs surrounding its circumference, alongside the slabs with *pūrṇaghaṭas* and wreaths (see illus. 38, 39, 41 and 137). Of course, the model of a band across the entire circumference of a dome or cylinder, in which elements are repeated (for example, illus. 25, 61, 70, 71, 90, 94) is only an example of replication if one analyses each element separately and against the others. One might argue that the band is really intended as a coherent whole and a single decorative item; but nonetheless it is constructed from deliberately iterated forms. Likewise, the festoons that appear to wreathe the curve of the dome in many of the miniature relief stūpas emulate not only each other but similar wreaths along the railing copings. In both these cases, the range of replicative slabs (with innumerable small variations) make up horizontal bands that stretch around the building. Beneath the dome, each *āyaka* projection jutting out of the drum platform at the cardinal points had five columns. Each of these columns is a formal replication of the other columns (perhaps differentiated by sculptural embellishment) and the five columns together constitute a collective replication of the other *āyakas* at the other gateways. Insofar as some of them were topped with miniature three-dimensional stūpas, they echoed the same column tops as the free-standing pillars that appear to have been placed within the processional path.

In the drum, the stūpa slabs, repeated in basic form and layout (if very different in individual articulation), are interspersed with *dharmacakra* pilasters in a patterning that implies the rise of complex reflections at the level of the *rūpakāya* or *nirmāṇakāya* (the form and emanation levels of being) in the stūpa reliefs that fall back into the fundamental *dharmakāya* of the eternal body of the Buddha's salvific wheel-turning. I do not mean to imply that the artists or viewers equated these specific forms with the philosophically discursive language of the *kāyas*, but that the replicative variations of the visual culture were a potentially parallel pictorial discourse to the existing and developing philosophical language of Buddhism in the period. The interspersed pattern of replications is thus a rhythmic intimation

118 Well-preserved lotus crossbar whose tenons have been removed, with central seed pods, four rows of petals, including the incurving petals at the innermost row, and a fine outer border of vines, leaves and fruit.

119 Well-preserved lotus crossbar with surviving tenons, central seed pods and five rows of petals with the inner one incurving.

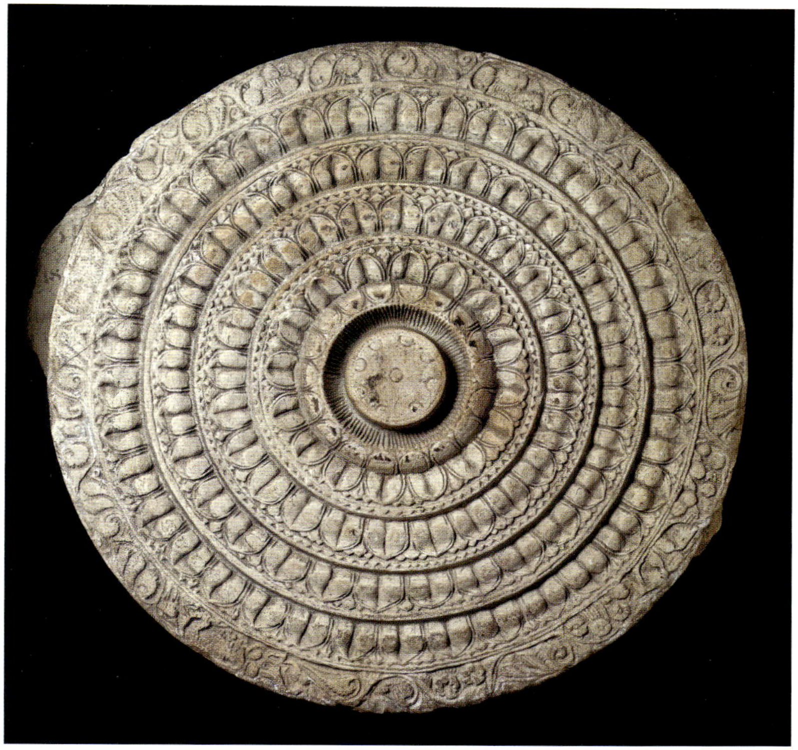

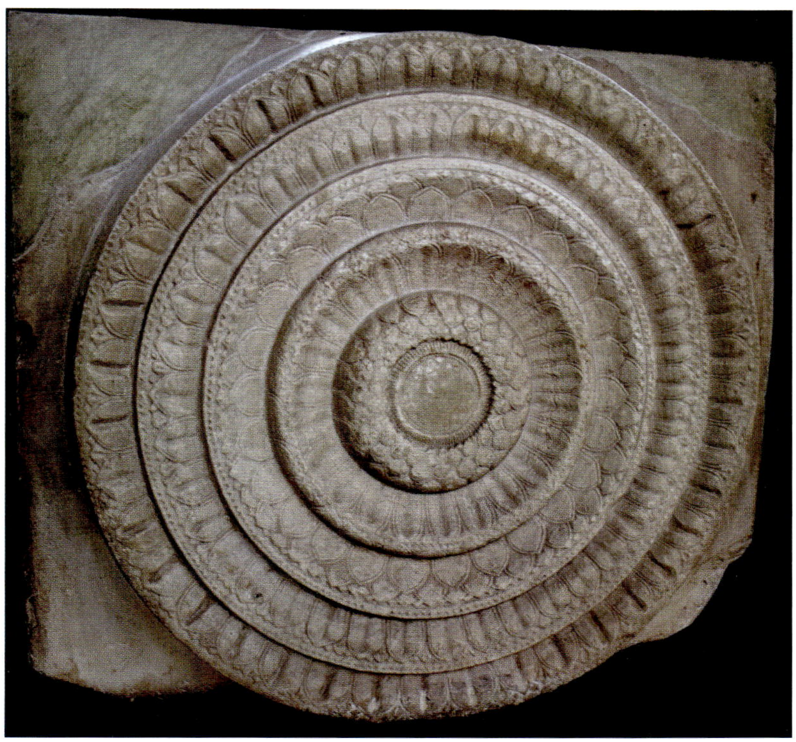

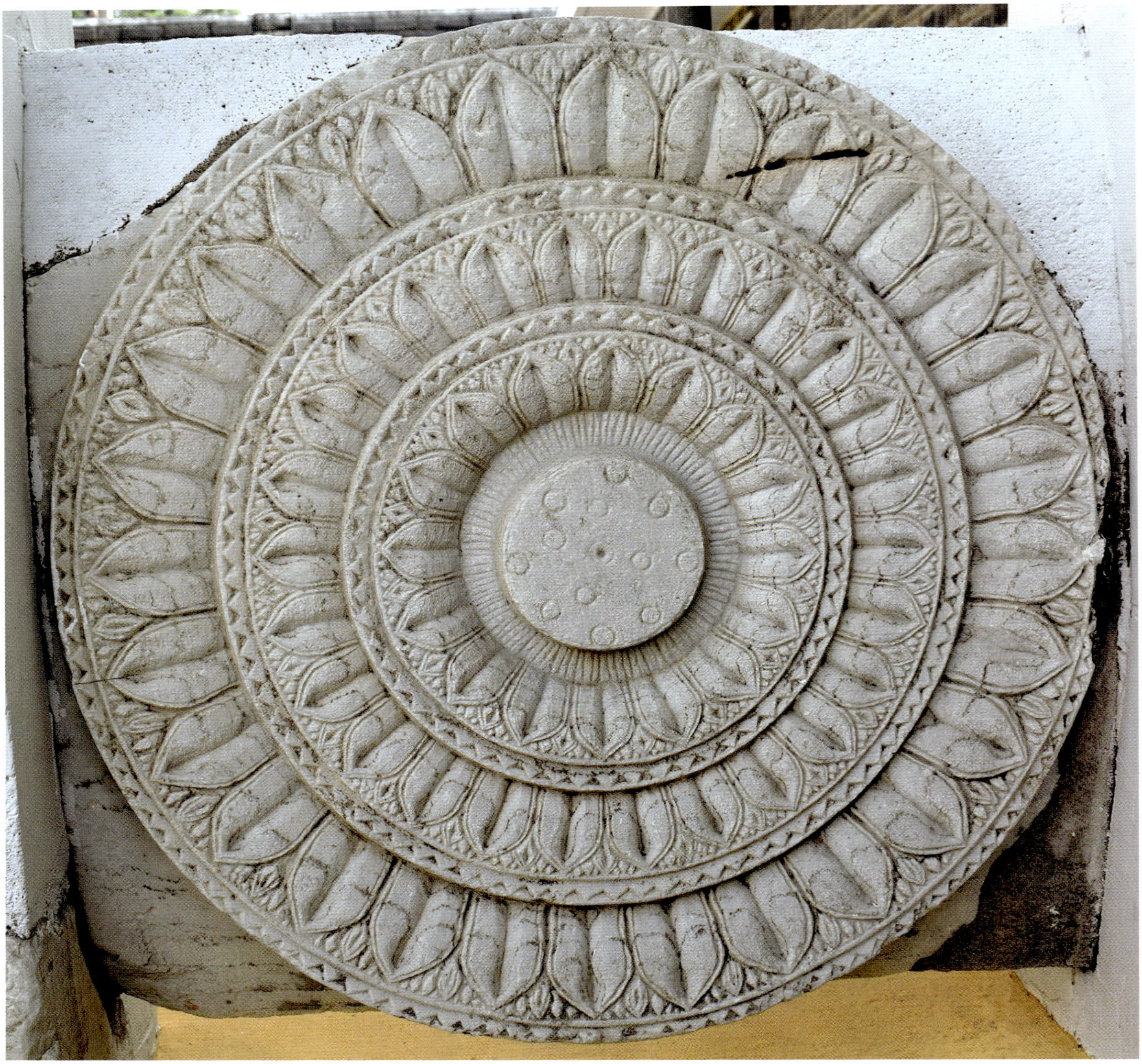

120 Well-preserved lotus crossbar with surviving tenons, central seed pods and three rows of petals from the reconstruction of a segment of railing in the Amarāvatī site museum.

of different manifestations of being, describable as Buddha-bodies, imaging the great presence implied by the mound and relics at different levels of manifestation. The Buddha's form as *dharmacakra* column over empty throne and *buddhapāda* is, in fact, not limited to just the single figure of the historical Buddha Gautama but reflects the wheel-turning of all the Buddhas, the permanent possibility for freedom from the circle of saṃsāra through the discovery of the path. This means not only the list of 28 Buddhas from Dīpaṅkara, whose presence brought Sumedha to the Bodhisattva vow, and his successors enumerated in such texts as the *Buddhavaṃsa* and *Mahāpadāna Sutta*, but all those who will become buddhas, once the beings out of whom they will arise have taken that vow. That is an art-borne cosmological picture of the ever-present *dharmakāya* and its ever-changing emanations in different reflections and forms, different kinds of *rupakāya* or *nirmānakāya*. At the same time, if the miniature stūpas represent a kind of here-and-now of the stūpa's offering of the path to its visitors, the pilasters affirm the future of that path in enlightenment itself (and beyond that the Buddha's teaching of the way to all beings) on the one hand, and the rooting of it all in a basis of a universal Buddha-nature, out of which all the reflections arise, on the other. That basis is the womb out of which the very possibility of freedom and salvation for beings is generated, according to the so-called *Tathāgatagarbha* sūtras, a Mahāyāna tradition apparently first created and taught in Andhra through a series of sūtras composed there.

Within this structure of replication – of forms, simple motifs and complex image-types – the extremely rich variety of one-off narrative subjects setting out the narratives of the *jātakas* is placed. It is clear that just because a story may only be told once and in a single form, this does not make it more 'original', 'creative' or 'artistic' than a rich range of repetitions, as would be the assumptions of post-Renaissance Western art history. On the contrary, the much-replicated narrative subjects – such as those that evoke the great events of the Buddha's life in an epitome of his biography, a range of exemplars that are themselves the patterns for all the Buddha's lives (as described in the *Mahāpadāna Sutta*) – are surely more important when considering the ideology governing the stūpa's making and early Buddhist receptions, as well as being more significant and more recognizable to pilgrims precisely because of their repetition.

The closeness of replications in a complex theme of multiple narratives – clearly dependent on a single visual prototype – may be seen by comparison of the famous drum slab with scenes of the Buddha's birth, now in the British Museum (illus. 121),[1] with the drawing of a lost parallel slab in the Mackenzie album, now in the British Library (illus. 122).[2] The iconography of the four scenes moves right to left, from top to bottom, with the upper right-hand scene showing the dream of Queen Māyā (without the descending elephant in both cases but with one female attendant in the sculpture,[3] and two in the drawing, as well as the guardians of the four quarters, the *lokapālas*). At the upper left panel, seated to the right below her husband, she recounts the dream to King Śuddhodana in his court. At the lower right, the queen has given birth standing beneath the *sāl* tree and grasps it with her left hand, while the newborn Bodhisattva's first steps (taken immediately after birth) are depicted by means of a miniature *buddhapāda* on the long cloth held by the four *lokapālas*. In the scene to the lower left, the queen presents the baby (represented as cloth and footprints) to the local tree-deity, Śākyavardhana, whose gesture recognizes his future Buddhahood (the left-hand part of this scene was damaged before it was drawn by Mackenzie's team).[4]

Clearly there are numerous iconographic differences in fine detail. One might cite in the drawing by contrast to the relief the tree rather than the wall that separates the two scenes at the bottom, the frontal rather than back view of the queen's attendant in the birth scene, the configuration of the *sāl* tree in the two images, the inscription in the drawn panel and its potential differentiation (if the artists observed rightly) of the scene with the standing queen from that of the Bodhisattva's steps, the animal frieze between the upper and lower panels on the right, the two female attendants in the Mackenzie image of Māyā's dream in contrast to the one in the British Museum panel and the slightly different headgear of the *lokapālas* who seem to resemble kings like Śuddhodana in the drawing, the extra attendant at the bottom right of the court scene in the drawing in contrast to the extra attendant at the top right of the relief sculpture, the similarly different placement of the attendants in the two scenes of Māyā with Śākyavardhana, the use of a fly-whisk in the drawing in place of an umbrella in the relief above the newborn in this section.[5] But obviously the closeness is very marked, especially in the disposition of the four panels of the whole, and the similar stances and placements of each of the main figures. How such imagery was displayed or configured in the actual monument (for instance, in potential viewing contiguity) unfortunately cannot be ascertained. But it points to extremely rich options in

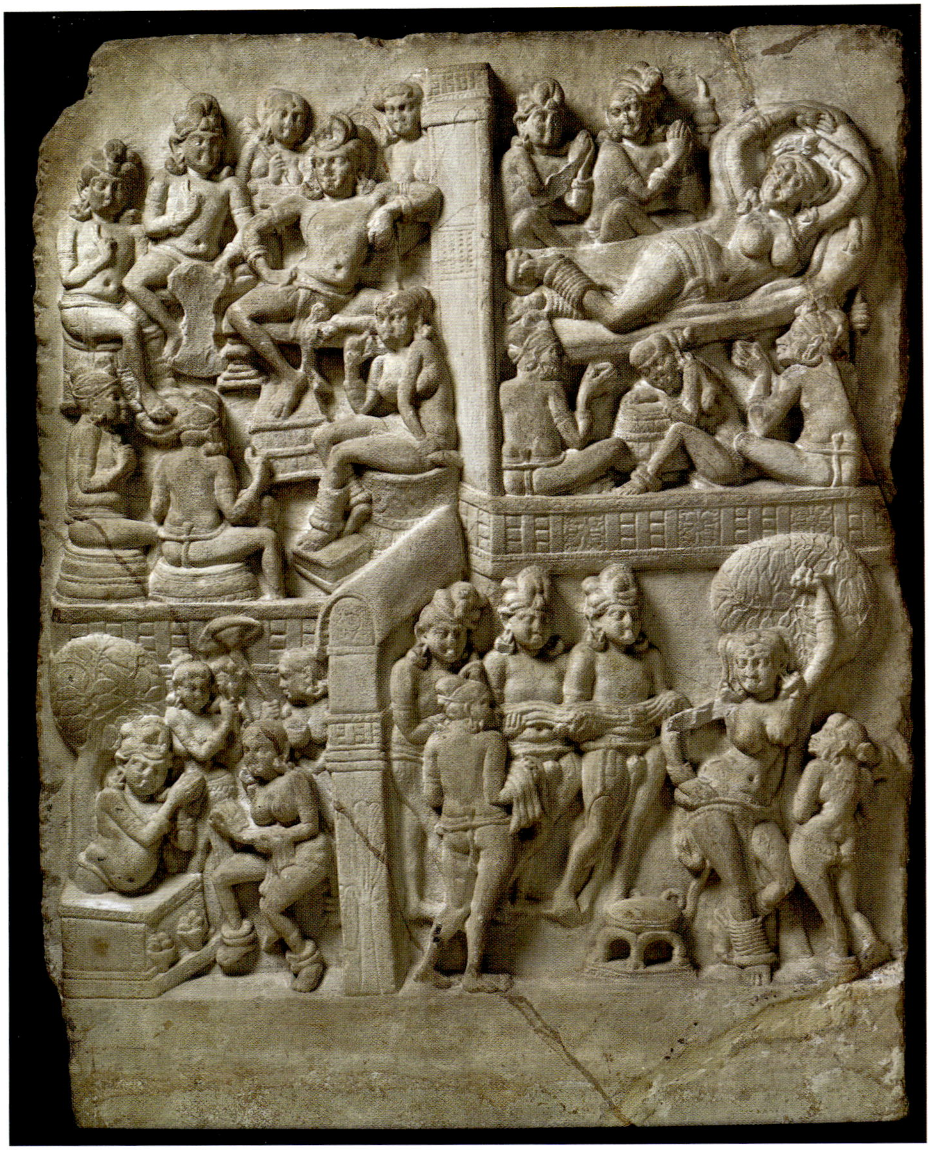

121 Intact drum slab showing four scenes from the Bodhisattva's nativity narrative (1.58 × 0.96 m).

figural repetition as well as variation across the stūpa's art, which go side by side with its inventiveness in different narrative subjects.

In this particular pair of panels, by the by, one may note that a highly complex play of thematic parallels has been created. Sequentially, the narrative moves right to left and top to bottom. But we may add that the two right-hand scenes are key moments of Buddhological action – the conception and the birth of the Bodhisattva, both marked by the presence of the *lokapālas* – while the two left-hand scenes are instances of exegetic interpretation (its representation here highly suggestive for the entire art of the stūpa) and indeed of prophecy, related to the right-hand image on the same tier, when the dream is told to the court and the child is presented to the deity, who prophesies his attainment of Buddhahood. The

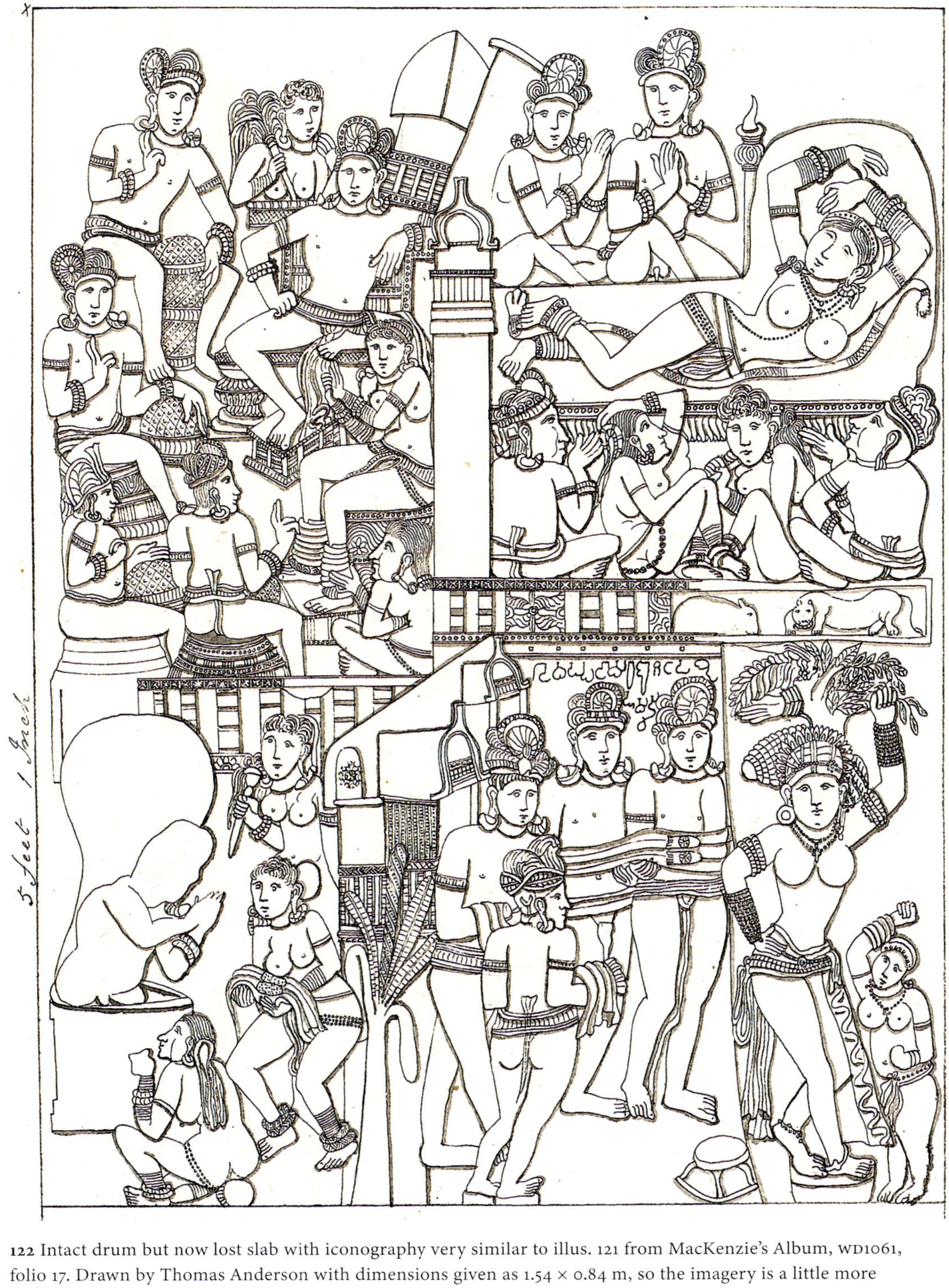

122 Intact drum but now lost slab with iconography very similar to illus. 121 from MacKenzie's Album, WD1061, folio 17. Drawn by Thomas Anderson with dimensions given as 1.54 × 0.84 m, so the imagery is a little more compressed on the left side.

imagery circles around Māyā as the key figure, who appears in all scenes in a series of different postures – lying, standing, bowing and seated. In the two left-hand scenes, the queen is suppliant to a male figure (King Śuddhodana at the top and Śākyavardhana below), while in the scenes on the right she is the principal figure and actor (occupying the right-hand position in all four images). One might go so far as to say that the panels' iconography instantiates the integration of canonical event and interpretation, scriptural text and commentary and narrative moment and exegesis that is fundamental to early Buddhism (writings just as much as visual culture), with the interpretative aspect also tending to the prophetic, which is to say, transcending time and space.

The replicative visual structure of the stūpa's decoration may be thought the material equivalent to the richly replicative nature of early Buddhist texts (both Nikāya and Mahāyāna), which are packed with formulae and formulaic repetitions in both Pāli and Sanskrit versions, themselves often expanded in renditions into Chinese.[6] These are, in part, a result of oral composition and memorization, and of the literary commemoration of oral origins in textual forms.[7] But in part they are the products of a culture given to frequent repetitive replication in its religious life – for instance in meditation practices such as mantra repetition, or repeated visualization, in all kinds of devotion and ritual circumambulation via bowing to the making of offerings, as well as in forms of training and education, well beyond the effects of literary method in Buddhist writings. The key point is that the visual tradition in its use of replications is in close tandem with the textual culture, reflecting its deeper assumptions in material and decorative forms. In rhetorical terms, within what we might call the semantic structure of the monument's interconnected visual programme, the replications enact all the kinds of rhythms, the implications of infinite complexity within a basic clarity and simplicity of the Buddha's teaching,[8] the karmic drama of cause and effect that we find in the textual tradition.

In addition to the semantics of replication, the site created a series of specific icons – complex themes, signalled by large-scale sculptures or panels, perhaps designed for worship – which are not only repeated but developed into complex conceptual images. I turn in the following section to a series of forms of such replication – all concerned with the nature of the Buddha himself: the different kinds of symbolic bodies of the Buddha in which the reliefs of the stūpa's imagery revel; the play in the two-dimensional imagery on reflecting the domed cylinder, which constitutes the monumental reliquary presence of the Buddha at the site; and the grand, three-dimensional statuary of the standing Buddha, which has hardly been discussed but is archaeologically much attested.

EMBLEMATIC AND EMBODIED FORMS FOR REPRESENTING THE BUDDHA

The range of Buddha bodies depicted at Amarāvatī is impressive. They move from the fully human form, through what Vidya Dehejia called 'an emblematic body' made of a variety of signs in combination and in various forms (enthroned or standing, as a pillar of flame or *dharmacakra* column or a tree above an empty throne and *buddhapāda*[9]), and the *pars pro toto* body implied by the elevation of the headdress or especially the *buddhapāda* icon, to the reliquary body entailed by the stūpa itself and the various images of relic worship thereon. All these point to a complex of visually developed theological/philosophical reflections on the nature of Buddhahood, themselves in tune with the varieties of theoretical experiments in the monastic commentarial culture of Andhra Buddhism. It is worth noting also that all these different kinds of bodies are replicated frequently, so as to become expressive or propositional items in the visual discourse of Buddhist theology at the site, just as repeated verbal formulae structure the discursive nature of early Buddhist texts.

The different levels of naturalism and schematism employed with equal panache at the site occupy different positions or propositions within this system. Take, for instance, the iconography of two fine roundels with lotus-leaf rims from the inner railing, one drawn by Mackenzie's draughtsmen and now lost (illus. 123),[10]

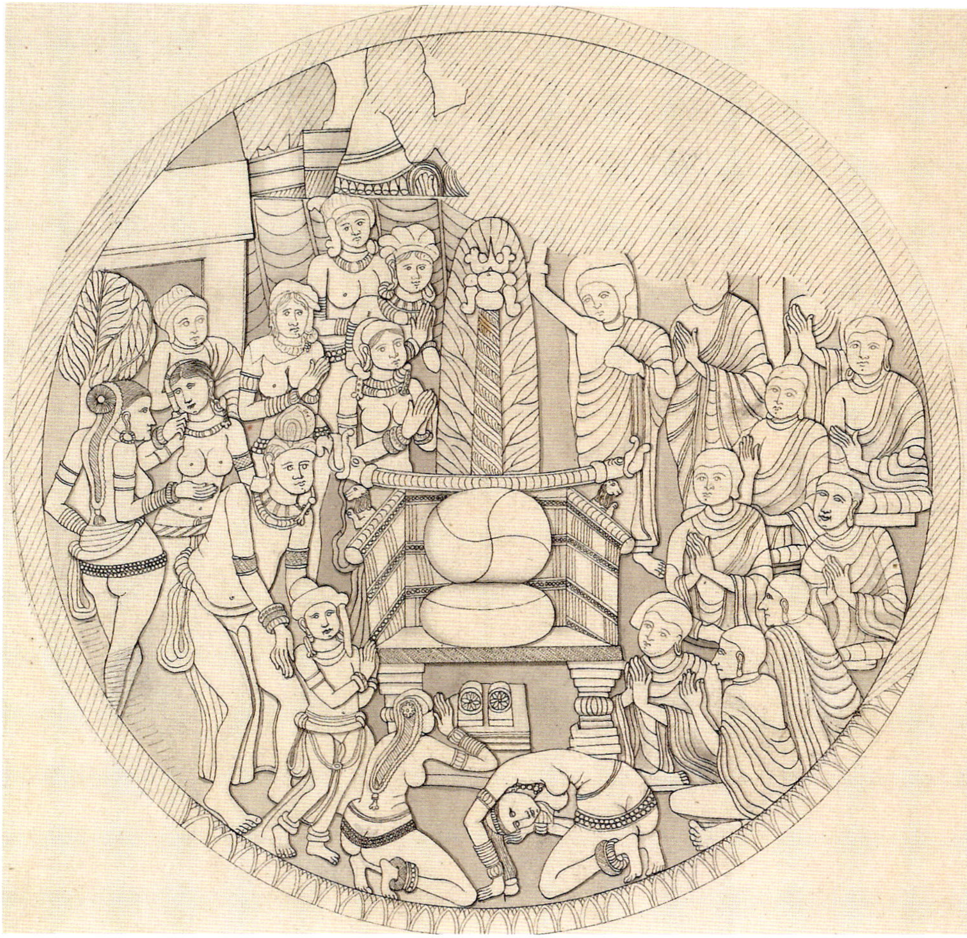

123 Drawing of a lost broken crossbar with the presentation of Rāhula to the Buddha represented as a flaming column over an empty throne with *buddhapāda* beneath. MacKenzie's Album WD1061, folio 45. Made by Henry Hamilton and dated 8 March 1817.

the other now in the Archaeological Museum at the site – this latter certainly a crossbar (see illus. 111).[11] Both show a large gathering around the empty throne and are clearly replicative versions of the same visual prototype. The scene is in the open air, cordoned off at the back but with an elephant and a horse as well as their handlers peeping over (at any rate, in the surviving version, Mackenzie's drawing shows this section broken off in the block his artists drew), a throng of male devotees (with shaven heads and robes, so probably the *saṅgha*) to the right and females with long hair, perhaps the ladies of the court, to the left. Two female figures prostrate themselves at the bottom, the one on the left beautifully rendered with her back turned to the viewer.

The iconography probably captures the moment when, according to the *Vinaya*, the Buddha returned to his paternal home at Kapilavastu and was approached by his son, Rāhula, who asked for his inheritance. In response, the Buddha asks Sāriputta, one of his chief disciples, to admit Rāhula into the order of monks by means of the threefold declaration of refuge to the Buddha, *Dhamma* and *Saṅgha* – thus inventing the model of child monks as novices.[12] The story and its image mark the institution of a significant and continuing

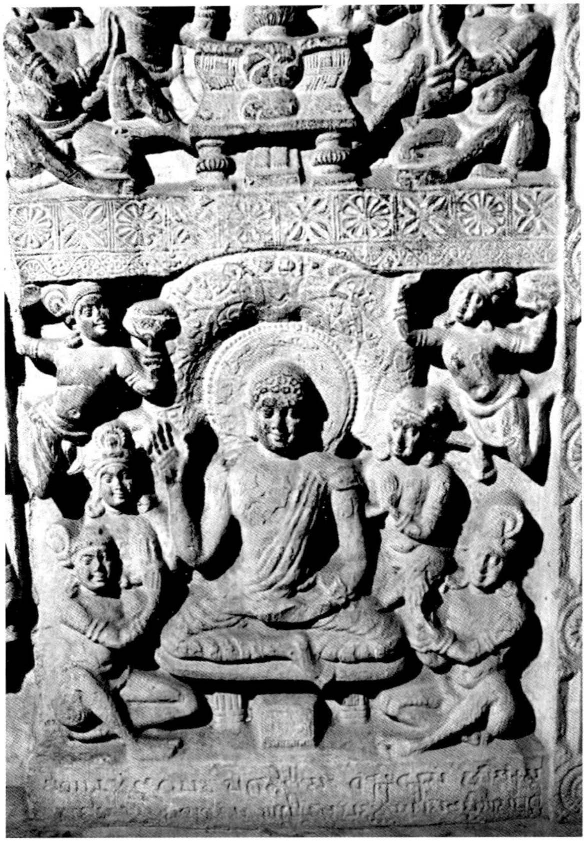

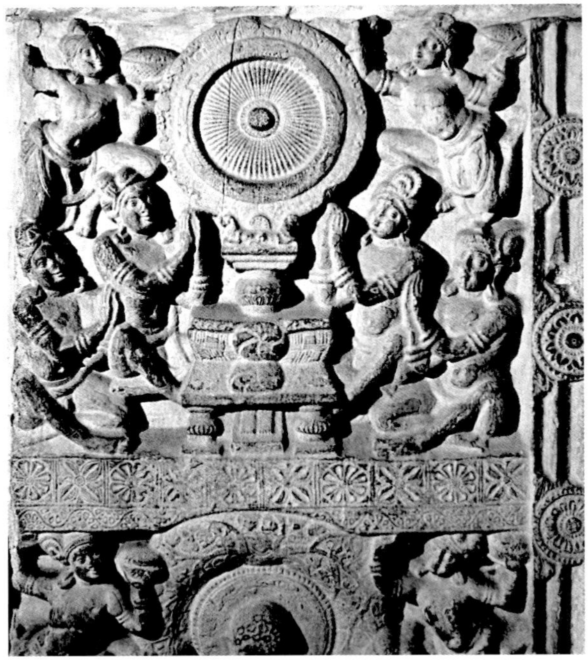

124 Detail of a fragmentary dome slab with four worshippers and two floating deities around the embodied Buddha in the *abhāya* posture with the Bodhi tree behind him.

125 Detail of the fragmentary dome slab shown in illus. 124 with four worshippers and two floating deities around the *dharmacakra* over an empty throne and *buddhapāda* slab.

tradition in the *saṅgha*. To the lower left, an attendant (perhaps a male in a turban) brings the child Rāhula to the throne. So far, all this is a fine example of the narrative arts of Amarāvatī, deployed with playful figural panache and resorting to naturalism when useful. But the Buddha himself appears in emblematic or schematic form – from the bottom up, a raised footstool with *buddhapāda* on which wheels and other symbols are engraved, a cushioned throne (somewhat more elaborate in the Mackenzie drawing, but its low-relief detail abraded in the surviving medallion) behind which rises a pillar of radiance crowned by a *triratna* whose multi-spoked wheel in the surviving crossbar reflects the wheels of the footprints below (see illus. 111).[13] The image is constructed on a dual logic of non-compatible image-systems: figural naturalism for the animals (the frontal elephant in the upper part of illus. 111 is terrific), people and setting and a symbolic form constructed of signs for the enlightened figure. Taking the whole as one, with the two discourses unproblematically intertwined, the roundel evokes a key event in the transmission of the Dharma, as Rāhula would in due course become a monk and an *arahat*, combining the Buddha's heritage as family man (and his inheritance to his son of all that he possessed) with his vocation as one gone from the things of the world (and his new lineage of the monastic *saṅgha*); and a key event in the history of the *saṅgha* through the invention of the novice tradition.

The power of the art of Amarāvatī is that in all its aspects – narrative, iconic, symbolic – its images

126 Drawing of a fragmentary railing pillar in MacKenzie Album, WD1061, folio 48. Made by Henry Hamilton and dated 12 March 1817.

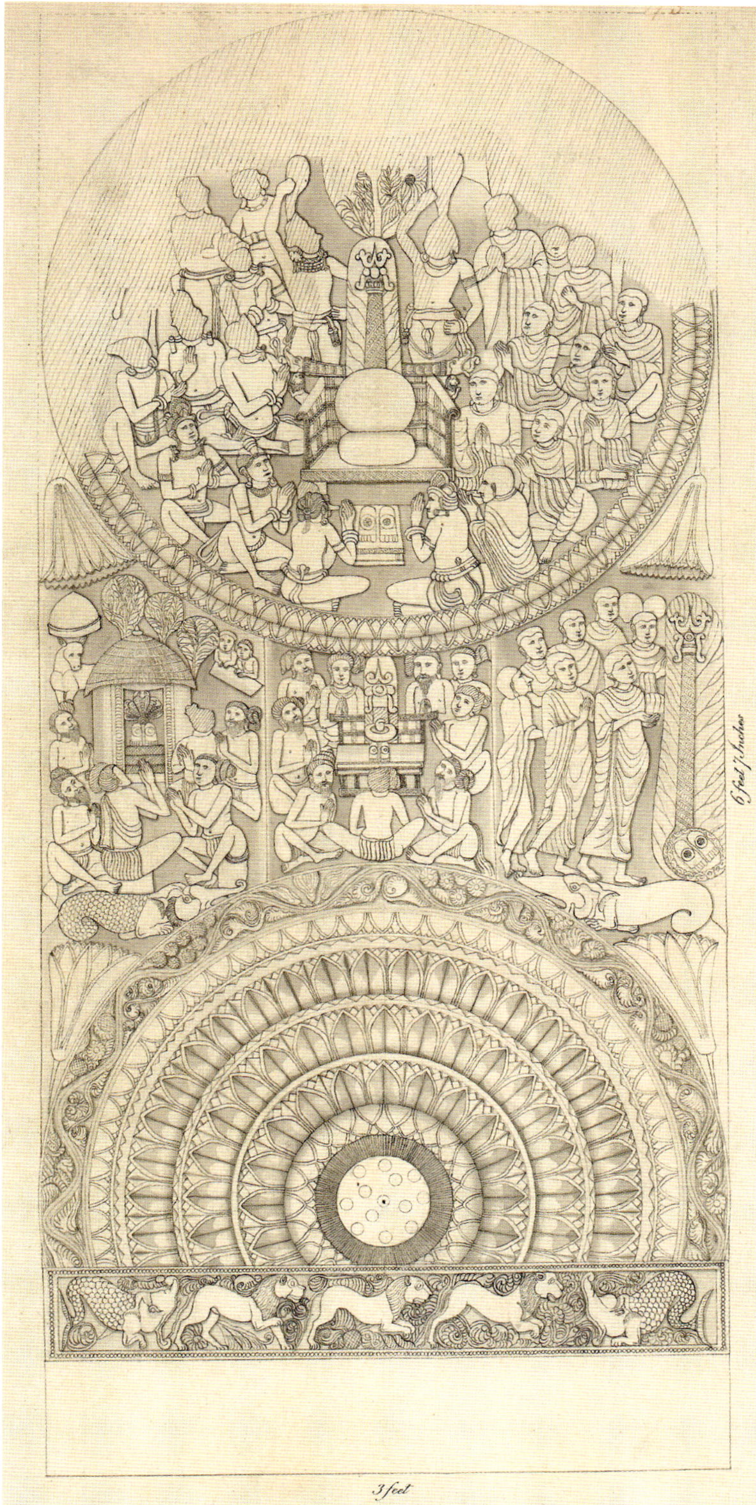
6 feet 7 inches
3 feet

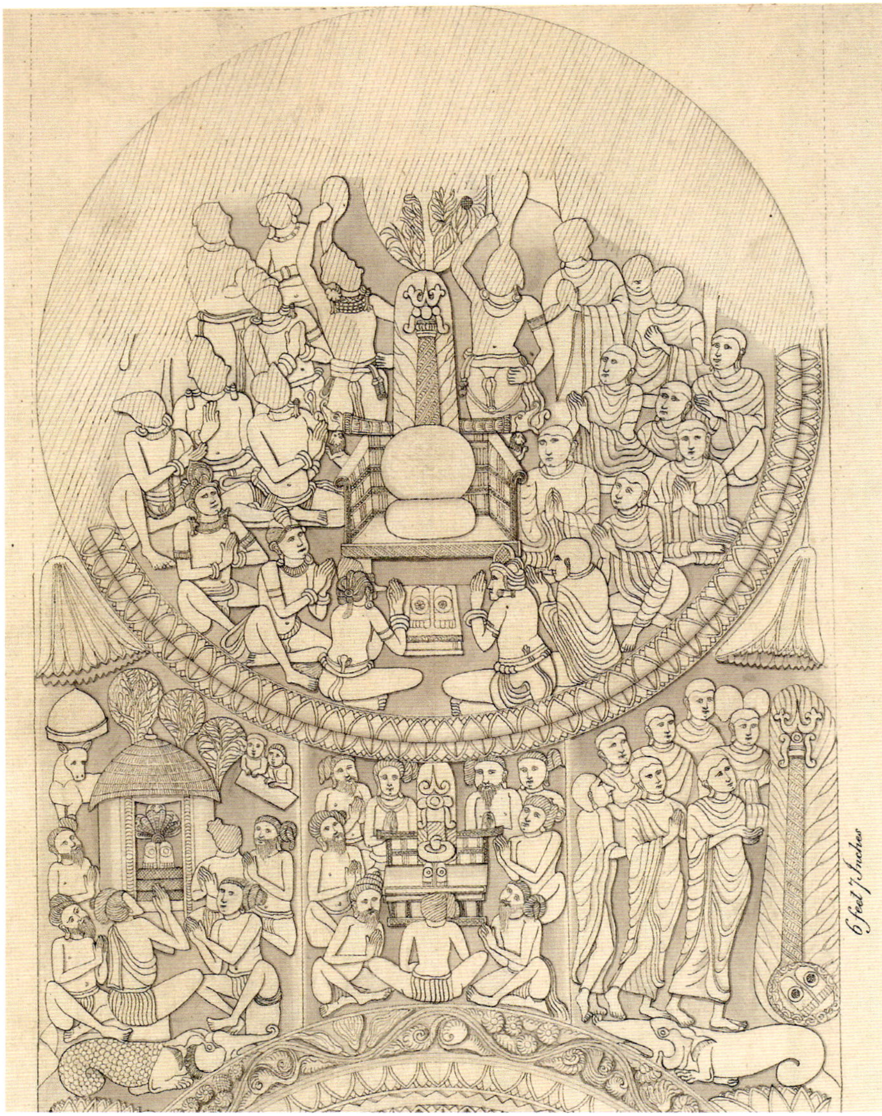

127 Detail of the roundel and lozenge from illus. 50, with narratives of the Buddha's miracles to the fire-worshipping ascetics and their conversion to the *saṅgha*.

function in this sort of propositional, discursive manner. Few surviving single blocks have both an emblematic and figural buddha represented on them in juxtaposition. But one might cite a fine vertical dome slab in the Government Museum in Chennai with the Buddha in the *abhāya* posture beneath the Bodhi tree, flanked by four worshippers and two floating deities in the lower panel, and a scene of devotion to the *dharmacakra* over an empty throne with *buddhapāda* above. Unfortunately, this piece was not on display when I went to the museum, and I can find no single picture of the whole; I can, however, show details of the two panels (illus. 124 and 125).[14] Here the embodied image seems to indicate the enlightenment while the aniconic wheel and column implies the First Sermon. Similarly, the drum frieze that was exceptionally carved from the same well-preserved block as the miniature stūpa that it framed (also in Chennai, see illus. 25) has an enthroned Buddha with both hands raised in the centre, flanked to either side by images of emblematic Buddhas represented by an empty throne beneath the Bodhi tree to the left and an empty throne with cushions to the right.[15] In neither case are these panels with narrative themes. But the point is that slabs with embodied Buddhas and emblematic forms were certainly juxtaposed with free abandon across the surface of the original monument. This is proven by the number of major drum panels with images of stūpas covered in miniature versions of sculptural programmes, which offer both forms of the Buddha-body (examples illustrated in this book include illus. 25 and 143, emblematic; 50, 61, 71, 94, embodied).[16]

Moreover, quite apart from the creative play in many contexts with emblematic and human-embodied forms for the Buddha, there is an interesting penchant for visually interrogating types of emblematic bodies in relation to each other, in ways not at all obvious or parallel to the textual traditions. Take, for example, the lower parts of a striking pillar from the inner railing, no longer extant but recorded by Mackenzie's draughtsmen (illus. 126).[17] In what survived of the central historiated medallion, an empty throne with *buddhapāda* on the footstool beneath, flaming pillar crowned with *triratna* and what appears to be a tree behind the throne, stands in the midst of a crowd of standing and seated male worshippers with their hands in a gesture of veneration – those on the left largely naked with the loincloths and long hair of the Indian ascetic traditions, and those on the right in what may be the robes of the Buddha's *saṅgha*, with their hair cut short (or perhaps represented as shaved, illus. 127). In the fluted area below are three further and differentiated emblematic forms of the Buddha surrounded by devotees: to the left as a *buddhapāda*, surmounted by a serpent in a small hut with ascetics around; at the centre as a different kind of throne, surmounted by a *triratna* with the *buddhapāda* on the seat and an object – perhaps a bowl – above it, again with ascetics; to the right as a radiant column, topped by the *triratna* with the *buddhapāda* below on a lotus base facing right and followed by robed monks who seem to be walking behind this figure. Unlike the other images, which are frontal, like the panels with the presentation of Rāhula, the last scene to the right seems to have the emblematic body fully involved in the narrative action.[18] The direction of movement to the right is of course that of the viewer proceeding along the processional way with the pillars of the inner railing to her left side.

These scenes give a differentiated variety of forms to the emblematic body – in play against each other, against the human figures of the rest of the iconography and in resonance with the theological problematics of how to represent the enlightened being. But they are also a narrative, telling the story of a famous series of miracles concerning fire performed by the Buddha at Uruvelā, itself a name for the site of his awakening,[19] shortly after his enlightenment, as part of the process of gathering monks to create the *saṅgha*.[20] The story is told in rather different versions in the *Mahāvagga*, the second book of the *Vinaya*, in the Pāli Theravāda tradition, at the culminating sequence of the mainly Sanskrit *Mahāvastu*, which was associated with the *Vinaya* of the Mahāsāṃghika school, and in the *Catuṣpariṣatsūtra*, a text from the *Dīrghagāma* or long discourses of the Buddha, as preserved by the Mūlasarvastivādin school, which survives in Sanskrit and Tibetan; it also appears in Chinese versions of the *Vinaya* traditions of the Mahīśasaka and Dharmaguptaka schools.[21] The first two scenes in the fluted lozenge represent the first miracle in the *Mahāvagga*, *Catuṣpariṣatsūtra*, *Mahīśasaka* and *Dharmaguptaka* sequences, but the culminating miracle in the *Mahāvastu*. After requesting of the chief ascetic, Uruvelā Kassapa, that he be allowed to spend the night in the hut where the sacred fire was kept,[22] where it was protected by a fearsome *nāga*, the Buddha entered the hut and duelled with the *nāga*, turning himself into smoke and then fire to overcome the smoke and flames of anger sent by the serpent.[23] It is this duel – represented by the rising *nāga*, a figure that can represent the Buddha himself in other contexts,[24] and the *buddhapāda* in the fire-hut – that appears in the image to the left of the lozenge. In the morning, having defeated the *nāga*, the Buddha put the now-tamed serpent into his alms bowl – presumably the object above the *buddhapāda* (on the enthroned emblematic Buddha's lap) in the central scene of the fluted lozenge. In the final scene, an episode that immediately succeeds the taming of the *nāga* in the *Mahāvastu* but is interrupted by the 3,500 following miracles in the *Mahāvagga*,[25] the three Kassapas (of Uruvelā, Nadī and Gayā) with their thousand ascetics take Buddhist ordination and follow the Buddha along the Nairañjanā River.[26]

In the roundel above, we have an enthronement of the Buddha in his flaming form between ascetics seated to the left and monks seated to the right, both groups with hands together in the *añjali mudrā*. This could represent one of many episodes of teaching in which the Buddha converts the adherents of other sects. In the *Mahāvastu*, two events that immediately follow the conversion of the Kassapas are possible candidates. As they proceed to the river, the Buddha and his retinue come to the hermitage of the Kassapas' nephew Upasena and his three hundred ascetics, and convert this community to the *saṅgha*.[27] From here the Buddha and his company proceed to Dharmāranya and the retreat of seven hundred matted-hair ascetics; to these he preaches a series of verses from the *Dhammapāda*, at which point all are enlightened and pass away.[28] At the same time, the traditions reflected by the *Mahāvagga*, the *Mahīśasaka* and *Dharmaguptaka* accounts and the *Catuṣpariṣatsūtra*, as well as the commentarial discussion of Buddhaghosa in the fifth century, bring the culmination of the process of miraculous conversion of the fire-worshipping ascetics to its climax in the Fire Sermon given at Gayā (the seat of the third of the three Kassapa brothers, Gayā Kassapa) – presented as the third great teaching given by the Buddha – at which point all the thousand monks and ascetics present attain arahatship.[29] It is not inconceivable that the medallion image – and specifically the flaming pillar with *triratna* that represents the Buddha here – is intended to refer to this great teaching, in the context of the narrative imagery below.[30] Support for this might be found in the probably fifth-century CE Chinese version of Aśvaghoṣa's *Buddhacarita* (originally composed in the second century CE and hence contemporary with the stūpa), a high poetic account of the Buddha's life, which survives only to canto 14 (the enlightenment) in the Sanskrit but originally continued through the entirety of his life and mission to his death and the distribution of relics. Canto 16 in the Chinese version tells the story of the Kassapa brothers, including all the episodes in the order illustrated at Amarāvatī, skipping the numerous other miracles in the *Mahāvagga* and *Catuṣpariṣatsūtra* and culminating in the Fire Sermon.[31]

Clearly, however we read the precise referents of the images (which would ultimately depend on the no-longer extant versions of the traditions around the conversion of the Kassapas and the fire miracles dominant in the Amarāvatī region in its *Vinaya*, sutta and commentarial literatures[32]), the broad story is clear. What is exceptional in relation to the discourses of representation and visual theology is the play with the emblematic body and its fiery pillar in the context of repeated miracles and notably miracles focused on fire. Fidelity to the narrative tradition alongside great visual inventiveness in the mixing of figural and 'aniconic' patterns of imagery are here targeted at making a series of Buddhological points. Certainly, apart from the thematic contiguity of all four scenes, the imagery is carefully tied together by repetitions: the *makara*s at the ends of the throne in the medallion, below the left- and right-hand lozenge scenes and bookending the frieze at the very bottom of the pillar beneath the half-lotus; the running lions of the lower frieze and the leaping pair on the two sides of the throne in the medallion, on whose heads the *makara*s rest.

The great roundel from this pillar, like those with the narrative of Rāhula, picks up a frequent topic in the Amarāvatī sculptures – namely the image of the seated Buddha in the act of teaching among a large retinue – sometimes of monks, devas, ascetics, laypersons (from the third, the proximate epoch, that defines the Buddha's ministry after enlightenment rather than the teaching Bodhisattva from the many earlier lifetimes in the distant epoch before his final human rebirth).

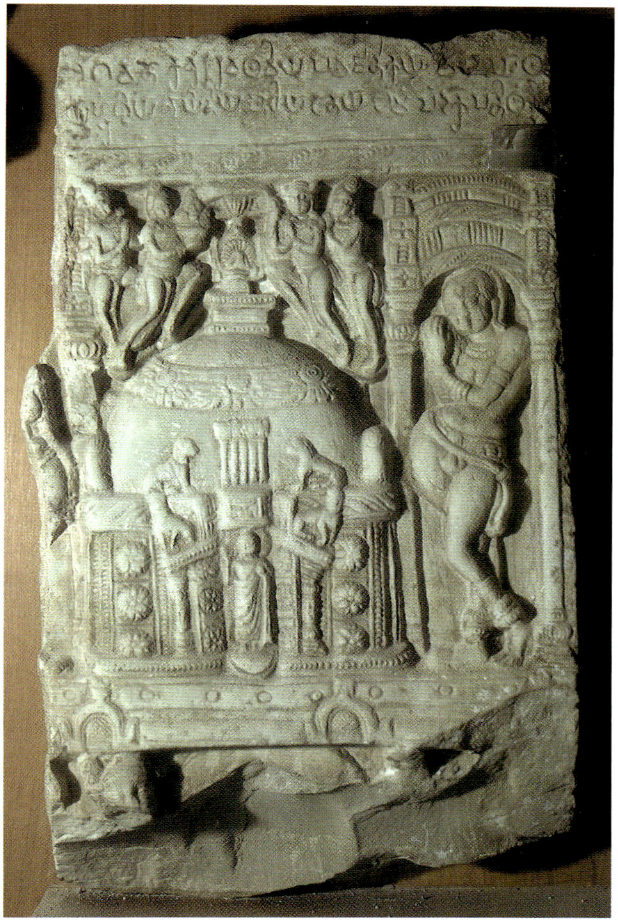

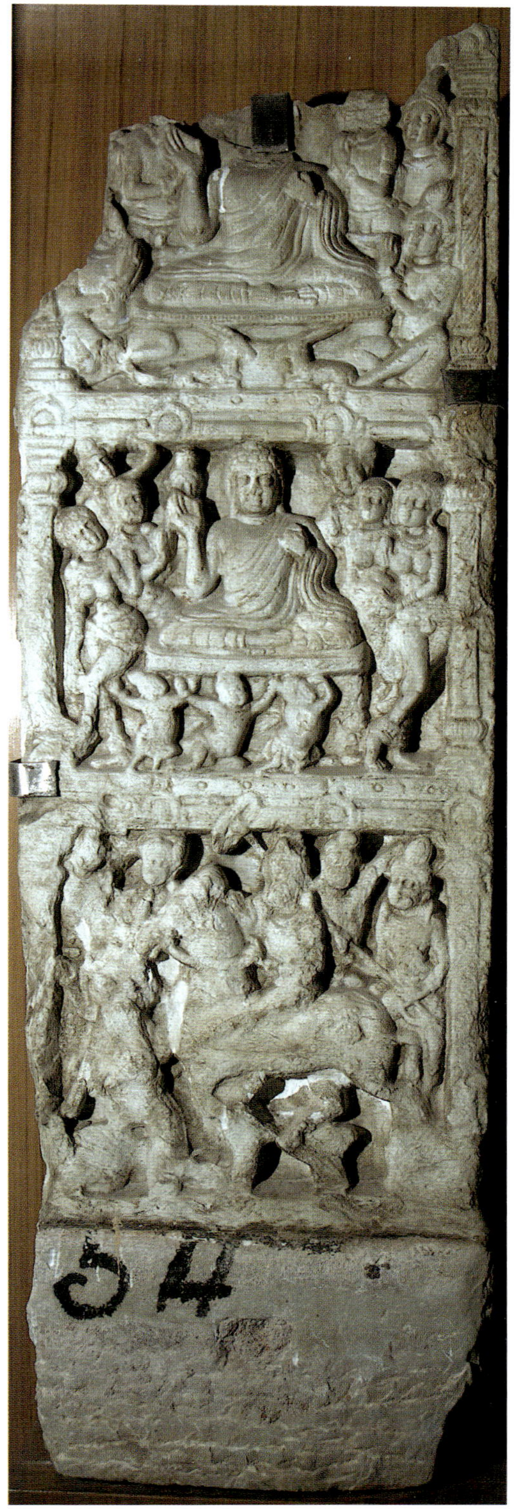

128 Upper panel of a broken pilaster perhaps from the dome with a stūpa and female worshipper in a *toraṇa* to the right.

129 Lower section of the broken pilaster in illus. 128 with the Bodhisattva's departure from the palace and two panels of the seated Buddha in the *abhāya* posture.

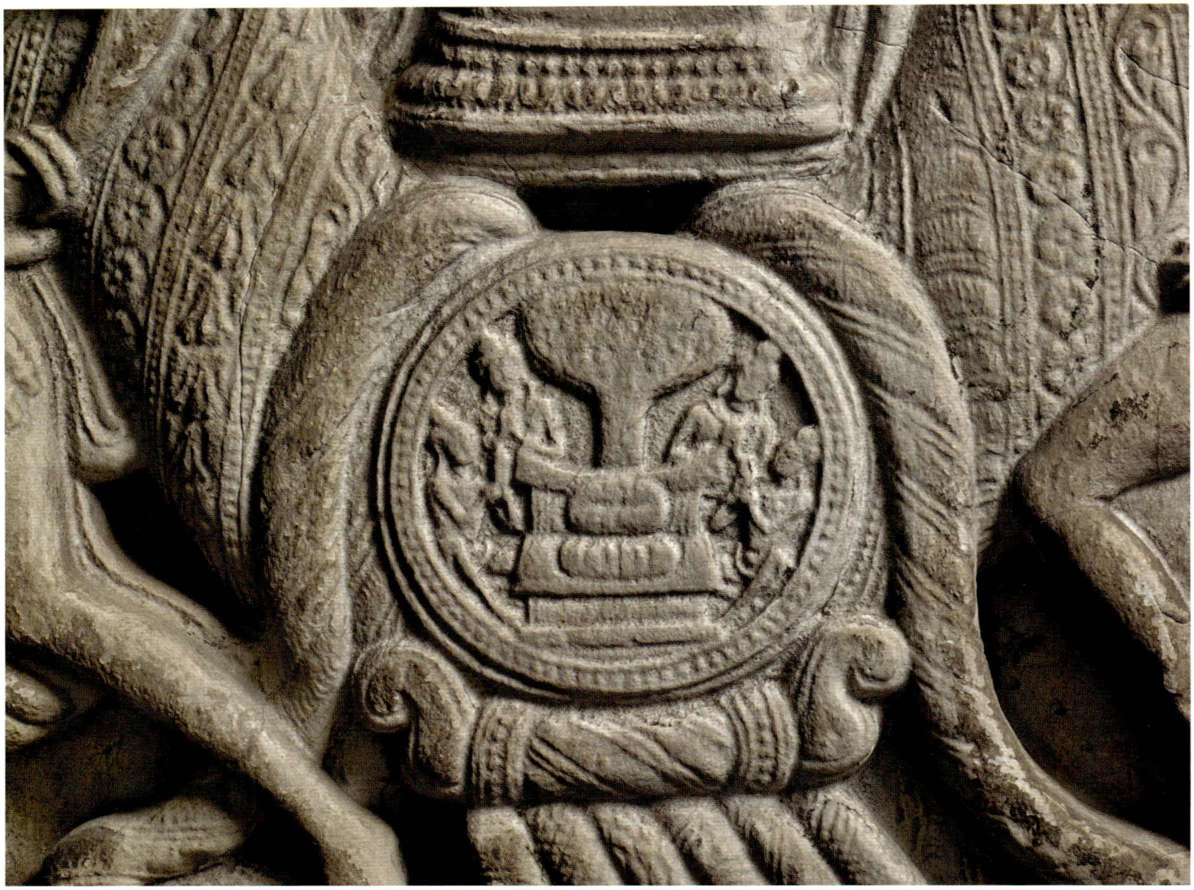

130 Detail of a small roundel in the exterior coping showing the Bodhi tree over an empty throne.

In all the cases discussed so far, that theme has been framed by the Buddha as a column of fire. But this goes side by side with a number of differentiated models, including the embodied Buddha, usually in the *abhāya* posture with his right hand raised. For instance, in a fine upright panel (perhaps a pilaster from the dome) in the Chennai Museum, with four scenes in tiers, two images of the seated Buddha are sandwiched between a fine depiction of a stūpa with standing Buddha at the top and a scene of the Great Departure with the Bodhisattva riding his horse at the bottom (illus. 128 and 129).[33] This has been broken between the stūpa scene at the top and the upper of the two Buddha scenes, and I show both sections. The upper-middle scene, with five figures and the Buddha seated over a pair of deer, appears to be the First Sermon to the five ascetics, given at the Deer Park at Isipatāna.[34] The lower scene has the Buddha in the same posture surrounded by near-naked females. It is usually identified as the Bodhisattva's temptation by the three daughters of Mara after his enlightenment, when they turn themselves into hundreds of alluring maidens.[35] In this case, no direct teaching is involved, but the daughters turn away unsuccessful, swept away 'as a fallen cotton tuft'.[36]

Among the emblematic forms, in addition to the pillar of fire, is the dharma wheel over the empty throne and *buddhapāda*, indicating specifically the First Sermon and the turning of the wheel of dharma (see,

131 Pilaster with *dharmacakra* from the drum.

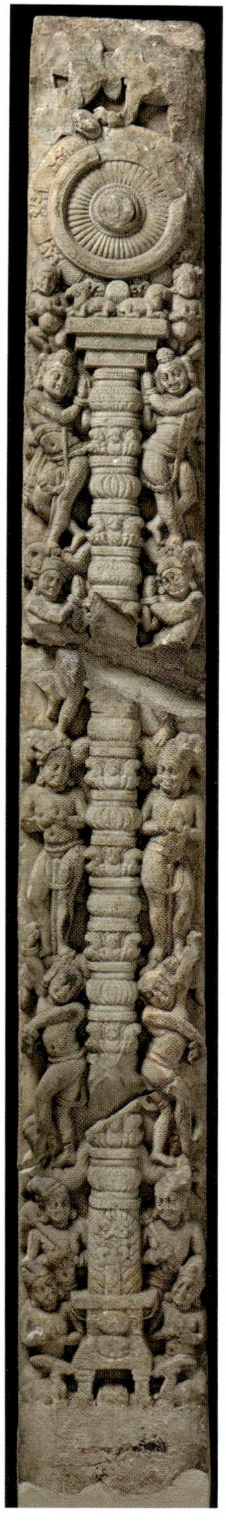

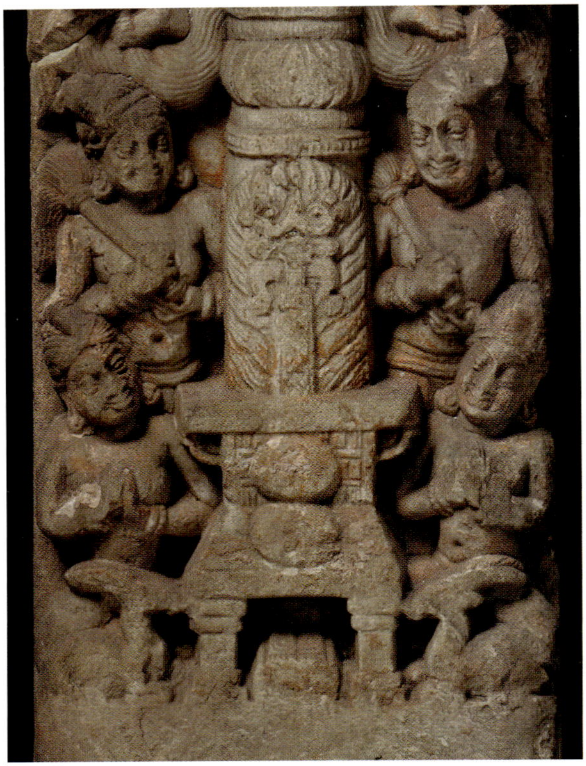

132 Detail of the lower part of illus. 131 with flaming column over an empty throne and *buddhapāda*.

for example, illus. 26 and 125). This is hugely popular, repeated in drum pilasters, at the gateways of miniature stūpas, in the upright dome slabs with tiers of imagery, in friezes and in coping stones. Less popular but still frequent is the image of the empty throne with *buddhapāda* beneath a tree (for example, illus. 130 and 143). This could be the Bodhi tree at the enlightenment, with the multiple figures around being deities and other divine observers, but it could potentially be one of the many other trees beneath which the Buddha conducted his teachings. There are a number of further models, such as the empty throne without *buddhapāda* or attributes like tree or wheel,[37] and some where the specific narratives seem conflated, such as the famous early panel of the empty throne beneath the Bodhi tree whose five devotees may imply also the First Sermon (illus. 109).[38] It is worth emphasizing the remarkable range of resonances enabled by this spectrum of imagery – from the specifically miraculous (as in the Buddha's dealings with Uruvelā Kassapa and his brothers) to the doctrinal, from the humanity of the *rūpakāya* or physically embodied Buddha to the potentially universal implications of the less iconic forms.

Of particular and exceptional interest are the cases where different kinds of Buddha bodies are combined. In at least two cases, imagery showing the dharma wheel, implying both the First Sermon and the Buddha as teacher turning the wheel of dharma, is combined with the pillar of fire.[39] In a finely preserved pilaster from the stūpa's drum, now in the British Museum, the wheel sits on a stepped capital crowned with lions above a pillar of alternating fluted cushions, cushions with lotus leaves and cushions with lion's busts (illus. 131). It is flanked by paired worshippers in postures of devotion. At the base, above the throne with cushions and *buddhapāda* beneath and flanked by the deer that represent the deer park where the First Sermon was given, is a pillar of fire adorned with a *triratna* at its head (illus. 132). It is as if this fire-column is a miniature Buddha body that expands into the hugeness of the column surmounted by the wheel as the dharma is expounded to all beings.[40] The case for a universal Buddha body (in the elongated column and wheel) alongside a more limited one – sized to the dimensions of throne and footrest and deer – but both miraculous and superhuman in form, is here brilliantly made by entirely visual means within the dimensions of the particular panel and within the discursive possibilities evolved by the artistic culture of the site.

Two other examples extend the model. One, from a fragmentary dome slab in the Chennai Museum, shows men and women making offerings to the flaming column capped with *trisula* in front of, indeed arguably engraved into, the Bodhi tree.[41] Here the magical and miraculous manifestations of Buddhahood enhance and explicate the enlightenment. The second, in the frieze above the great stūpa in the famous drum panel now in Chennai (discussed in Chapter One, illus. 25–33), combines the image of the throne and tree with that of the column

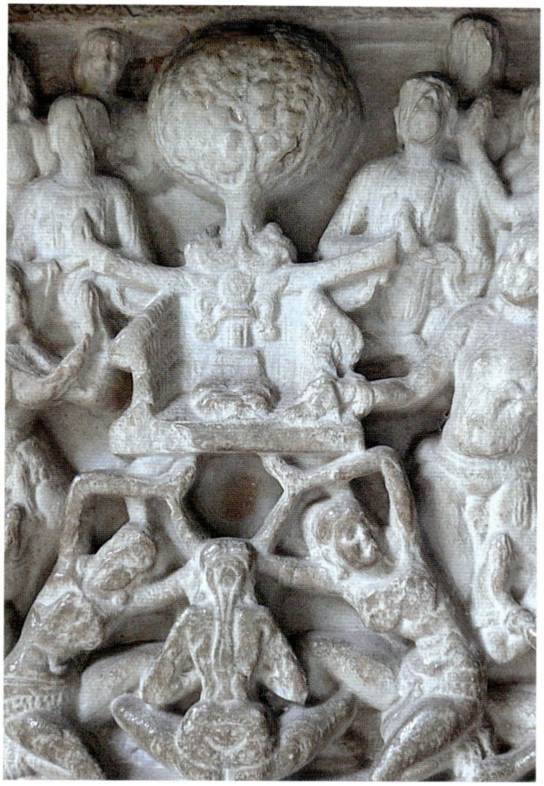

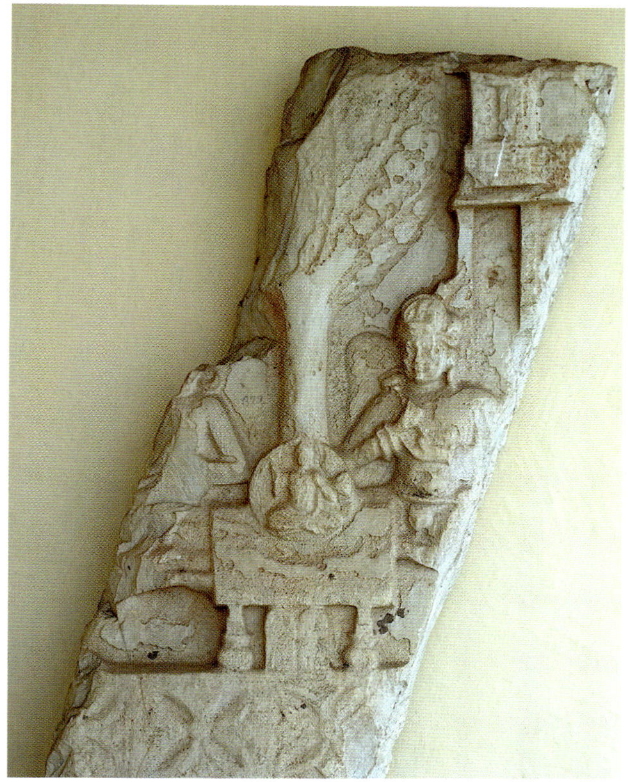

133 Detail of the left scene in the frieze at the top of illus. 25 showing worship of the throne beneath the Bodhi tree on which is placed a *dharmacakra* crowned by a *triratna*.

134 Fragmentary dome slab with the throne and *buddhapāda* beneath the Bodhi tree, but with the cushion carved with an embodied Buddha in the *abhāya* posture.

and wheel. There, the left-hand scene shows a series of devotions before the Buddha's throne beneath the Bodhi tree. In the throne is placed a miniature *dharmacakra* on a column with additional adornments (illus. 133). Not only is the aniconic Buddha replicated in different forms, one within the other, but the celebration of the enlightenment beneath the Bodhi tree is enhanced by its fulfilment in the First Sermon and the turning of the wheel of dharma, which marked the attainment of full and universal Buddhahood in the transmission of awakening to others. Here the transposition of different emblematic bodies underlines a call to universalism.

Fascinating is a very fragmentary and unfortunately abraded image that appears to combine the emblematic and embodied visual discourses for the Buddha (illus. 134).[42] Unfortunately, only a cast was on display at the Amarāvatī site museum when I went to look for this piece, so what is written here depends on photographs. The slab shows devotees around an empty throne with *buddhapāda* beneath and Bodhi tree behind; into the circular cushion of the throne an image of the seated Buddha in the *abhāya* posture has been carved in light but distinct relief. The slab was probably removed from the stūpa and subsequently pared down for later appropriation and reuse; it was originally from a dome panel carved in three tiers, but with somewhat different iconography from those that survive in much better condition.[43] Scholars have attempted to explain (away) the issues by arguing that the relief represents not the Buddha himself but the worship of an image of

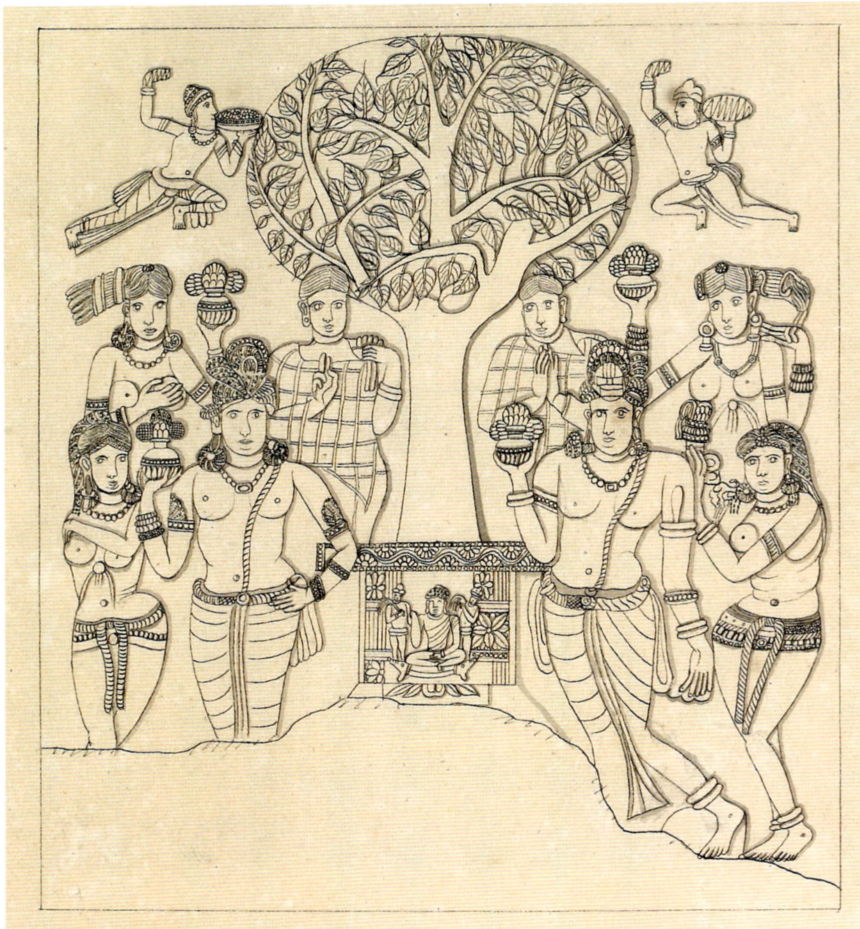

135 Drawing of a lost fragmentary slab found in the southwest quadrant with a miniature Buddha in the *abhāya* posture on the throne beneath the Bodhi tree. Mackenzie's Album, British Library WD1061, folio 25. Made by Marcellus Burke and dated 10 October 1816.

the Buddha, a bas-relief carving placed on a seat,[44] and is effectively the representation of a *site* of cult.[45] If the fragmentary scene below were to represent the descent of the Buddha from the Tāvatiṃsa Heaven, where he had gone for three months to teach the *Abhidhamma* to his mother,[46] then – it has been argued – the image represents the sandalwood statue of the Buddha, whose story is told by Chinese pilgrims from the fourth century onwards in relation to the site of the descent at Sankassa in northern India.[47] Others have suggested that the original sculpture was a classic empty throne beneath the Bodhi tree, into the cushion of which at a later moment (for reasons that cannot be determined) the miniature image of the embodied Buddha was added.[48] But underlying these assumptions is the old discomfort with combining aniconic and anthropomorphic imagery of the Buddha. If we saw this as simply another version of the mixing of dharma column with pillar of fire or Bodhi tree and throne, then this image might have other and more potently theological implications.

Crucial to the discussion is a second piece, no longer surviving except in one of Mackenzie's drawings now in the British Library (illus. 135). This shows the Bodhi tree with a series of male and female figures carrying offerings in their raised right hands. Beneath the tree is what looks like the upper part of the throne with a miniature Buddha or Buddha statue in the *abhāya* posture (not in a roundel) flanked by two attendants and apparently seated on a lotus.[49] The rest of the block was broken off, so the lower part of the throne and *buddhapāda* needs to be surmised to make this iconography strongly parallel to the relief fragment.[50] But whether the original intent when the block was first carved was to make an image of the Buddha, or to combine the embodied with the 'aniconic' discourses for representing the Buddha, or to make an emblematic body to which a later Buddha image was added, the point is that the emblematic model and the figural one are always in dialogue, with the figural theologically implicit in the emblematic and vice versa.

In other words, throughout this discussion of different discourses for representing the Buddha, with the emblematic sometimes preferred for miracles (such as the series of fire-wonders, or many of the images of the quelling of Nālāgiri, or the Bodhisattva's first steps upon his birth) or scenes fundamental to Buddhist doctrine like the enlightenment or turning of the wheel of dharma, at play is the conceptual problem of the Buddha's bodies, known as *kāyas*. This is deep in the tradition, much debated across the different Nikāya schools as well as highly germane to significant strands of Mahāyāna thinking.[51] My point is not that any of the various bodies, still less the specific iconographies,[52] are rigidly or definitively to be identified with specific aspects of *rūpakāya* or *dharmakāya*, as discussed at length by the early schools, let alone later formulations such as *nirmāṇakāya* and *saṃbhogakāya*, which seem to have become prevalent with the rise of Mahāyāna. Rather it is that visual discourse was experimenting with, exploring and debating the same kinds of fundamentally theological issues about what the Buddha was and how he should be best conceived, as were the scholarly monks and textual commentators. The parallels with early Christian visual experimentation for the representation of Christ (from broadly 'aniconic' or symbolic forms like the Chi-Rho to the imagery of a young man, a bearded man or the ancient of days) are striking.

CIRCLES

The Buddha's form as a stūpa is circular and massive. The Amarāvatī stūpa's ground plan was not only circular but doubly so – encompassing both the mound itself and the railing around it. The mound was a low cylinder surmounted by a spherical dome – voluminous circles or portions of circles in space. From a spectator's (that is, a devotee's) point of view, such a monument is impossible to comprehend as a whole but only partially, from perspectives whether at a distance or close by. Once inside the stūpa's railing (probably too close up to see to the top of the dome as it curved away) one would have been overwhelmed with relief images on all sides, as well as free-standing statuary and columns, all articulated within the curving path of the processional way as it fitted itself around the stūpa's own round form. The phenomenological surprises of attempting to comprehend a circling monument much larger than oneself, the shifting of perspectives and angles as one perambulates its forms – which curve away even on approach – and the challenge to imagine a circular ground plan (both abstract, in that its schematic form is not how one experiences it, and absolutely the pragmatic basis of the stūpa's architectural conception) are essential to its experience. But they also become fundamental visual investigations in the rich decorative and formal diversity of the stūpa's articulation of relief sculpture.

One of the most striking aspects of the visual logic that structures the design of Amarāvatī is the choice to play repeatedly with riffs on the circular shape that is its basic form, including visual experiments on how to represent voluminous circles in two dimensions. The circular form is endlessly repeated as a defining shape for the relief decoration. One may list here substantive elements, such as the grand medallions with narrative scenes in the railing pillars and crossbars, and the innumerable flowering lotus bosses on the monumental pillars and crossbars of the outer rail. The remarkable

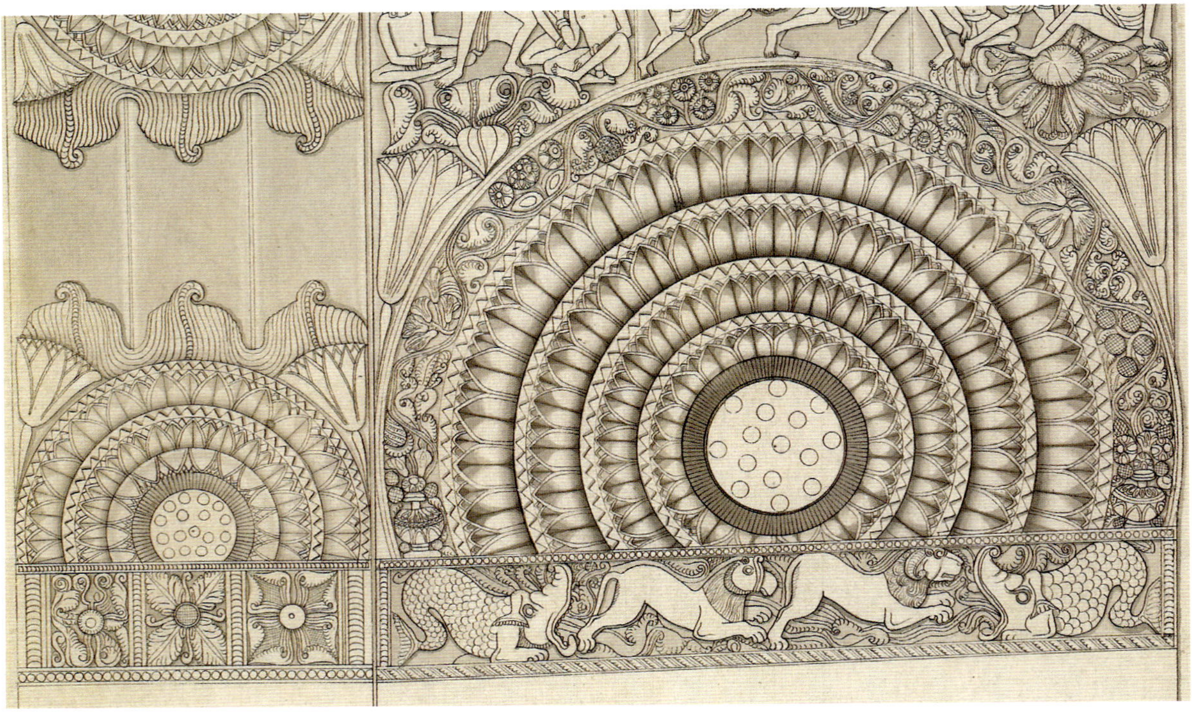

136 Bottom part of a drawing of two pillars from the railing showing lotus medallions, floral ornamentation and animal frieze. Mackenzie's Album WD1061, folio 74. Made by Henry Hamilton and dated August 1817.

series of large-scale relief slabs that made up the principal decoration of the drum displayed the repeated, intensely detailed imagery of stūpas, looking much like the great monument they adorned. As we have seen in Chapter One (illus. 25–33), all these features of the main monument are repeated in microscopic detail in these panels – including lotus roundels in the exquisite miniatures of the mini-railings shown around these relief stūpas and their pinnacles (known as *harmikās*) and the fine sculptural medallions around the upper dome (none of which have survived from the actual dome of the monument). These reliefs also show semi-circular 'moonstones' as the formal initiation of the pavement at the opening of the gateways, defining the boundary between the exterior of the perimeter railing and the stūpa's inner space. Likewise, lines of roundels structure the vertical division markers that separate scenes in the drum friezes. Not least we must mention the circular umbrellas that once rose from the top of the monument like a spectacular layer-cake – some certainly made of stone and some potentially in materials like cloth.

In addition to these structural circular devices, one may add significant iconographic symbols from the innumerable *dharmacakras* or wheels on columns (great and small, incised in minuscule, repeated as pilasters, as iconic statements in the stūpa-gateways of drum panels, in the stacked scenes of dome blocks, in the motifs interspersed in the garlands of the outer railing, from the floral circles at the centres of *triratnas* and *trisulas* to the wheels on the ubiquitous *buddhapādas*, even the cushions on the empty thrones). These are all circles – huge and miniature – seen from the top down as if in two dimensions, perspectives not possible when a human being tries to look at the stūpa itself (although available to the deities who float above it, as in the drum panels with large stūpas carved in relief). These circles are often rimmed with petals (notably the historiated medallions) and lotus garlands, themselves evoking the garland effect of the outer railing and its copings (the main rail showing the lotus heads from above and the coping showing rich wreaths of garlands from the side).

One aspect of the stūpa's own circular nature never being apparent in plan but always perceived partially, from the side, is its decoration's obsession with exploring how to represent the perception of the whole through the partiality of different perspectives. Take an unusual drawing of the lower halves of two railing pillars placed side by side in the Mackenzie album, both blocks now no longer extant (illus. 136).[53] The half-open buds in profile to the sides of the lotus roundels and half-roundels at the lower ends of both these inner and outer railings make up the space for the lozenges that are decorated with historiation in the example to the right and fluting in the one drawn on the left.

Framing each 'open' lotus roundel at the corners, these blossoms show the flower from its sides with its stalk rising from the waters, and also from a perspectival three-quarters view as one might look downwards at an angle towards a flower in bloom. They combine the vision of the same lotus blossom looking very different from different vantage points with a reflection on potential temporal movement – from bud to opening flower to

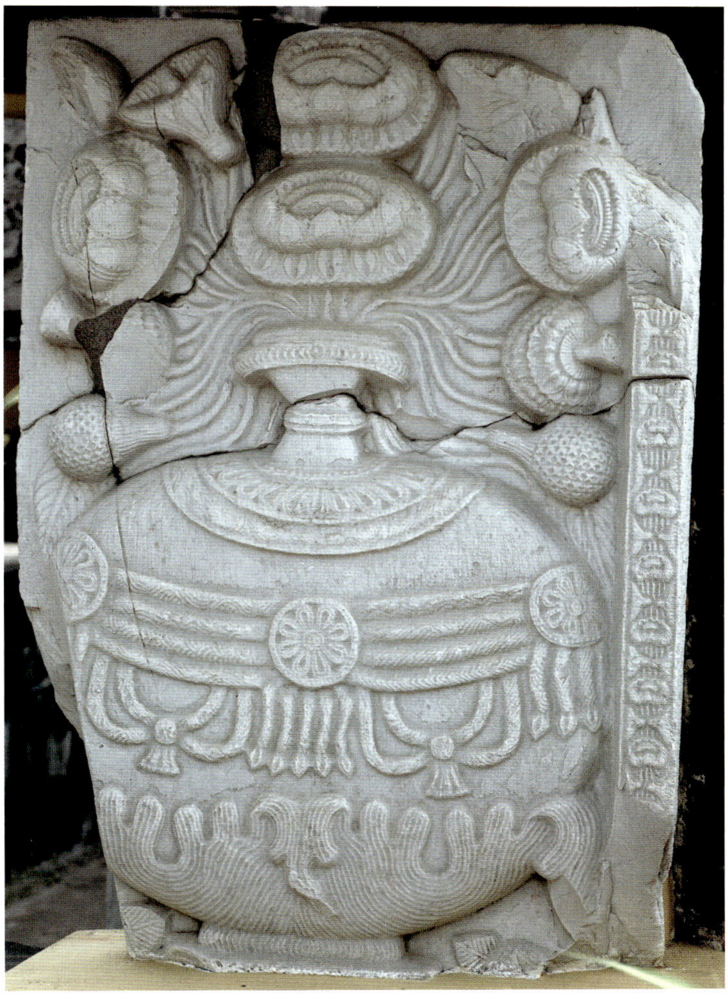

137 Large dome slab (1.21 × 0.85 m) with *pūrṇaghaṭa* vase of plenty and lotus blossoms.

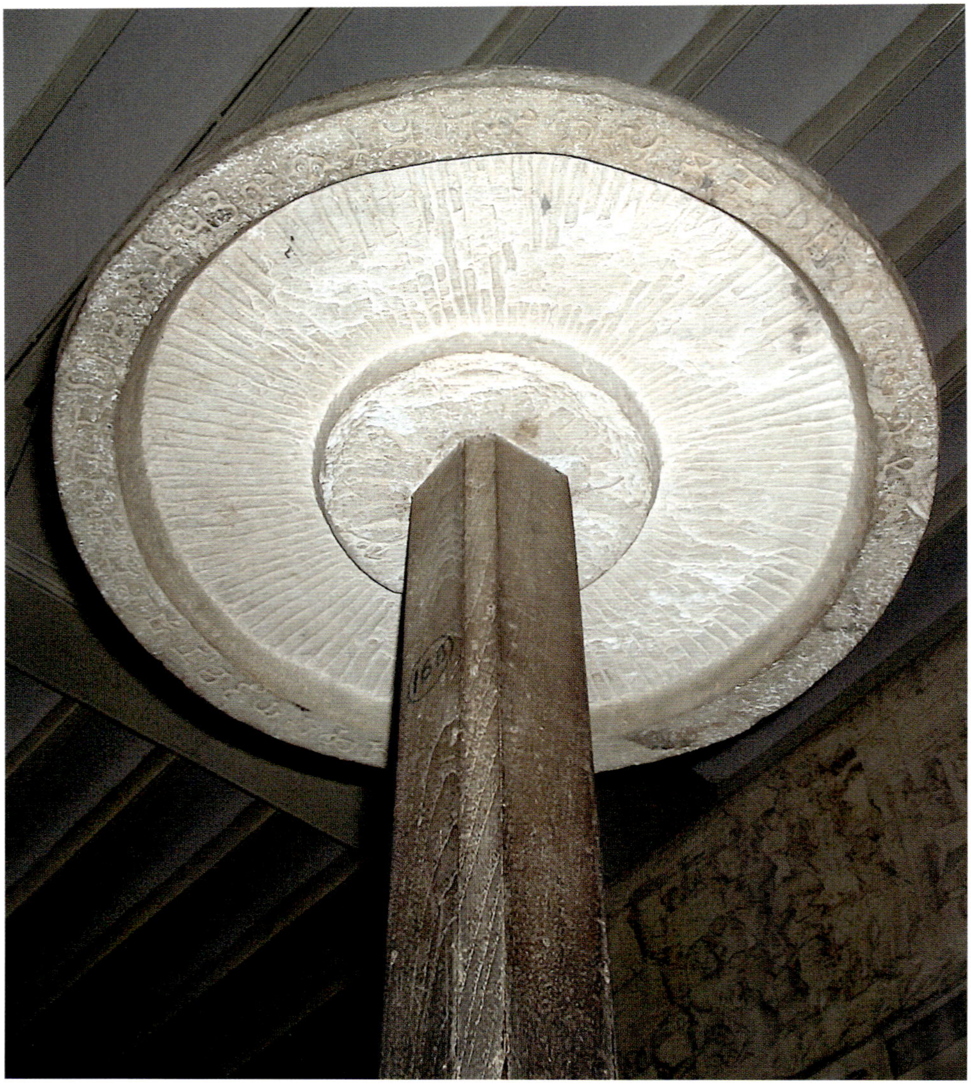

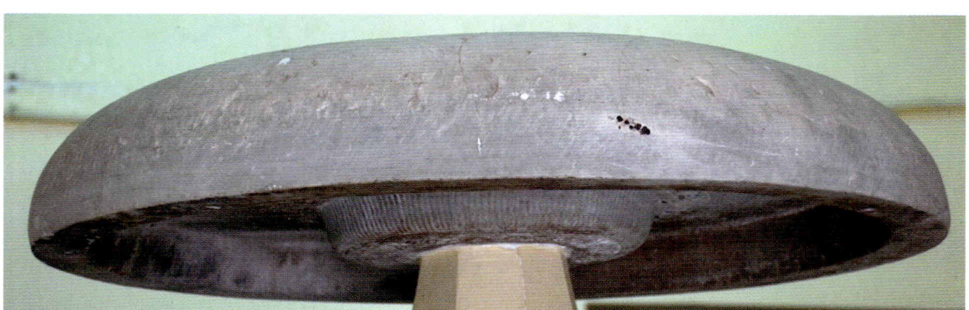

138 Umbrella (*chatta*) seen from below, probably from a small stupa at the site.

139 Umbrella (*chatta*), seen from the side, found at the stūpa at Ghantaśālā, Andhra Pradesh.

mature bloom – as a procession of vantage points in time as well as space. In the bas-relief friezes of so many of the medallion rims (of both lotuses and historiated roundels), also the frames of the British Museum *buddhapāda* panels (illus. 100 and 102) and fine relief moulding at the upper and lower edges of rail pillars (illus. 17), as well as the borders of many drum-frieze panels and railing copings, a number of lotus blossoms, interlinked on tendrils, appear in varieties of three-quarters view, again shifting the perspective and angles in relation to the round flower as a voluminous entity in space. These more spatially and three-dimensionally rendered views of lotus flowers appear in higher relief in the trunks of elephants depicted as approaching stūpas at the upper borders of railing pillars or on the finely rendered lion seat now in the British Museum, which was excavated in the vicinity of the western gate (illus. 44).[54] But they are rendered – as full blossoms seen in three-quarter view, as opening blooms in profile and as buds – in a near-baroque lavishness of naturalistic detail, in high relief emerging from the necks of *pūrṇaghaṭa*s (or vases of plenty), of which a replicative series were placed to create a decorative rim around the dome (illus. 137, see also illus. 41).[55] A characteristic play between schematic and naturalistic (which appears also in the differentiation of emblematic and figural bodies for the Buddha) plays out here in the difference between schematic ideal lotuses, whether seen in profile from the side or from the top down as perfect circles, and 'actual' flowers imagined growing in messy intertwinement within the mud in decorative borders or from vases or as offerings brought by elephants. As with the domed cylinder of the stūpa itself, which can never be appreciated as a whole from a single experiential perspective, these lotuses are rendered in multiple ways and according to multiple models to evoke the struggle to accommodate a totality from the partiality of human experience.

We may say something similar about the depiction of umbrellas (*chattas*), which appear over stūpas on a variety of models from the simple to the flamboyant. The actual umbrellas, to judge from one example that survives intact in the Government Museum at Chennai and may have sat above a small stūpa at the site (illus. 138),[56] were circular with a flattened curve at the top, but with a hollowed-out recession between centre and rim. This example, sadly, has very abraded leaves and foliage carved in the hub, ribs engraved in the surface to mark the stretched cloth extending through the space between hub and rim and an inscription incised in Brahmi script on the rim. Unfortunately, this piece was not on show at Chennai when I went there, but its form with a rim inscription resembles one of the three instances I saw from the stūpa at Ghantaśālā in the site museum there. In this case, the largest example is displayed by being elevated on a pole, so that one can see the convex side of the umbrella (illus. 139). It is perfectly smooth and rounded, creating a powerful material contrast between the incised and inscribed sculpting of the concave interior – which is itself a form of wheel (*chatta* punning on *chakra*) with hub, spokes and rim as well as the umbrella pole as axle – and the pure rounded stone of the outer surface.

It is quite possible several such stone umbrellas were stacked in a tower above each stūpa (the main one and the smaller ones) perhaps of different diameters and potentially some of them made of less durable and heavy materials than stone, such as coloured cloth. Such actual items were rendered frequently in relation to the relief representations of stūpas – from relatively simple and apparently realistic images of what such a parasol and associated banners might have looked like, for example in the well-preserved relief of the *harmikā* with parasol and banners on the great double-sided panel of a meta-stūpa from the drum now in the British Museum (illus. 140),[57] via depictions of stūpas with multiple stacked umbrellas which may indeed be a plausible image of something approaching reality (illus. 141),[58] to much more fantastical displays of an efflorescence of parasols exploding from the stūpa top like lotus blossoms from a vase (illus. 142).[59]

The umbrellas in these last cases – by far the most frequent (see illus. 45 for example) – clearly break out of any attempt to figure the real. Indeed, they become almost organic growths; like the lotus flowers and their tendrils, they attach to twining lines that wrap and knot

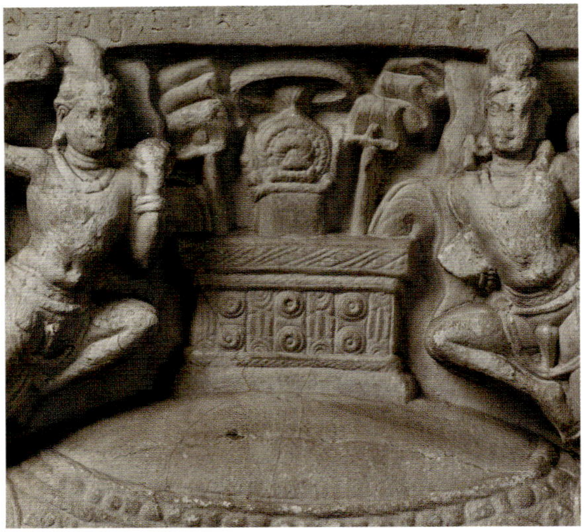

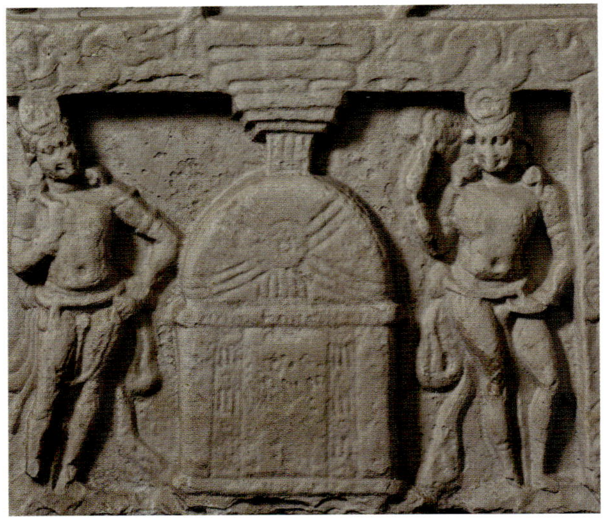

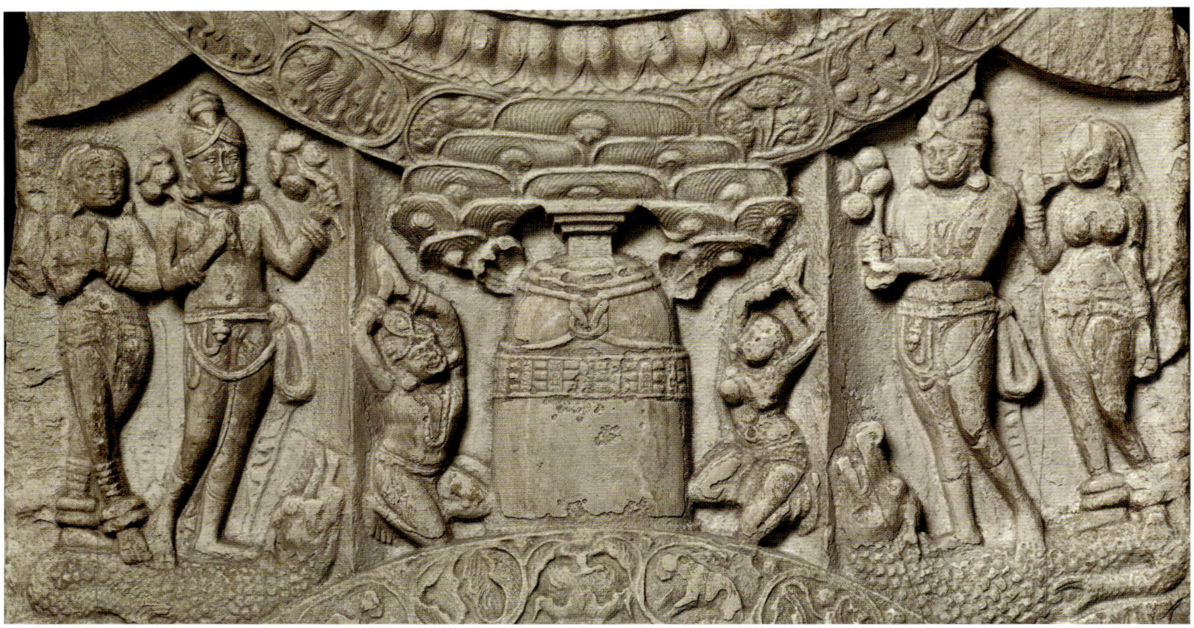

140 Detail of well-preserved *harmikā* with a single small umbrella, from a drum slab depicting a stūpa.

141 Detail of a stūpa with a tidy stack of umbrellas, from a dome slab.

142 Detail of a stūpa with an explosion of umbrellas, from a railing pillar (illus. 14).

themselves around the stūpa. In the case of a fine example of this type from the outer face of a pillar in the British Museum (illus. 142), the umbrellas overlap and ultimately merge into the lotus and tendril border of the medallion above, while the stūpa's dome boasts the protection of two inter-knotted three-headed *nāga* serpents, perhaps protecting the sacred monument, whose bodies and curving heads are themselves riffs on the twirling logic of circling ornament.[60] At the same time, all these umbrellas are configured as circles seen from below, by an angled view approximating with some likelihood the actual way a flat parasol of this kind at the top of a stūpa might be seen from the ground.

The deepest figural exploration of how to render the voluminous circularity of a stūpa takes place on the panels with relief images of stūpas that encircle the drum, reflecting the monument's three-dimensional entirety in miniature detail. These represent the elements largely in two dimensions but with a sophisticated use of depth of carving in the stone block. The great interest in the plastic rendering of circularity through relief is perhaps best examined in the finest preserved panel, now in Chennai, which was discussed earlier as part of the attempt to picture the monument as a whole (illus. 25). The relief layering of the surface is itself cut to imply a circular object, especially at the edges of the dome (and above all in the images of the two external medallions at its upper decorative tier). The different anglings of the decorative tiers, from the flatter curve of the railing at the bottom, via the curves on the drum and the lower dome, to that above the *āyaka* pillars at the upper dome, are designed to evoke a monument that curves away from the viewer at both sides. This is reinforced by the depth of carving towards the edges before the two pilasters that frame the panel, which makes the image of the stūpa stand out at the point closest to the viewer and recede to the sides. The points where the monument's drum and railing extend to right and left on its cylindrical axis perpendicular to the frontal gateway are carved further back to indicate the extending *āyaka* platforms and pillars on the horizontal diameter of the stūpa's cylinder at the left and right cardinal points. The *āyaka* pillars to the sides are seen from behind, the receding view being of their backs, in contrast to the five pillars in the centre. At a further level of depth, and in somewhat lower relief to both sides of the main stūpa, the extension of the railing's entrances to right and left, with the lion statues seated at the ends, are rendered as side-views and stacked so that the railing wall further away appears above that which is nearer. The perspectives of the entrance at the centre of the monument are adjusted to show not only the stūpa mound in the precinct behind the railing but the interior of the railing that is splayed out to either side, in a fundamental denial of realism but a careful insistence on showing the key elements. That is, a variety of schemes, from the relative imitative naturalism of, for example, the lotus bosses in the miniature railing or its miniature sculpture, which certainly evoke with precision the actuality of such decoration in the full-size monument, to the use of false perspectives and stacking (including outsized lions on the sides), are brought together in the panel.

This is a very careful rendering of circularity, both aware of realism and quite happy to ignore it when different kinds of visual conventions deliver the sense of curvature and layered depth that is intended. The emphasis on the curve and the open entrance at the centre evokes the process of circumambulation and hence the spiritual exercise of accessing and progressing around the stūpa. But there are also numerous part-circles – for instance, the 'moonstones' of a number of entrances and the circles (lotuses?) on the threshold stone perpendicular to the moonstone in, for example, the fine surviving slab now in the Amarāvatī Archaeological Museum that once decorated a small stūpa attached to the site (illus. 143).[61] In this case, the play of deliciously articulated miniature stūpa roundels in the railing lotus bosses that flank the entrance and the circles in the railing pillars as well as the threshold, and the round pot being offered by the kneeling worshipper there – all presented in varieties of foreshortening – make an abstract meditation on rendering circularity quite apart from the theme being depicted (illus. 144). That is, the stūpa plays with a remarkable dynamic of circularity across and around

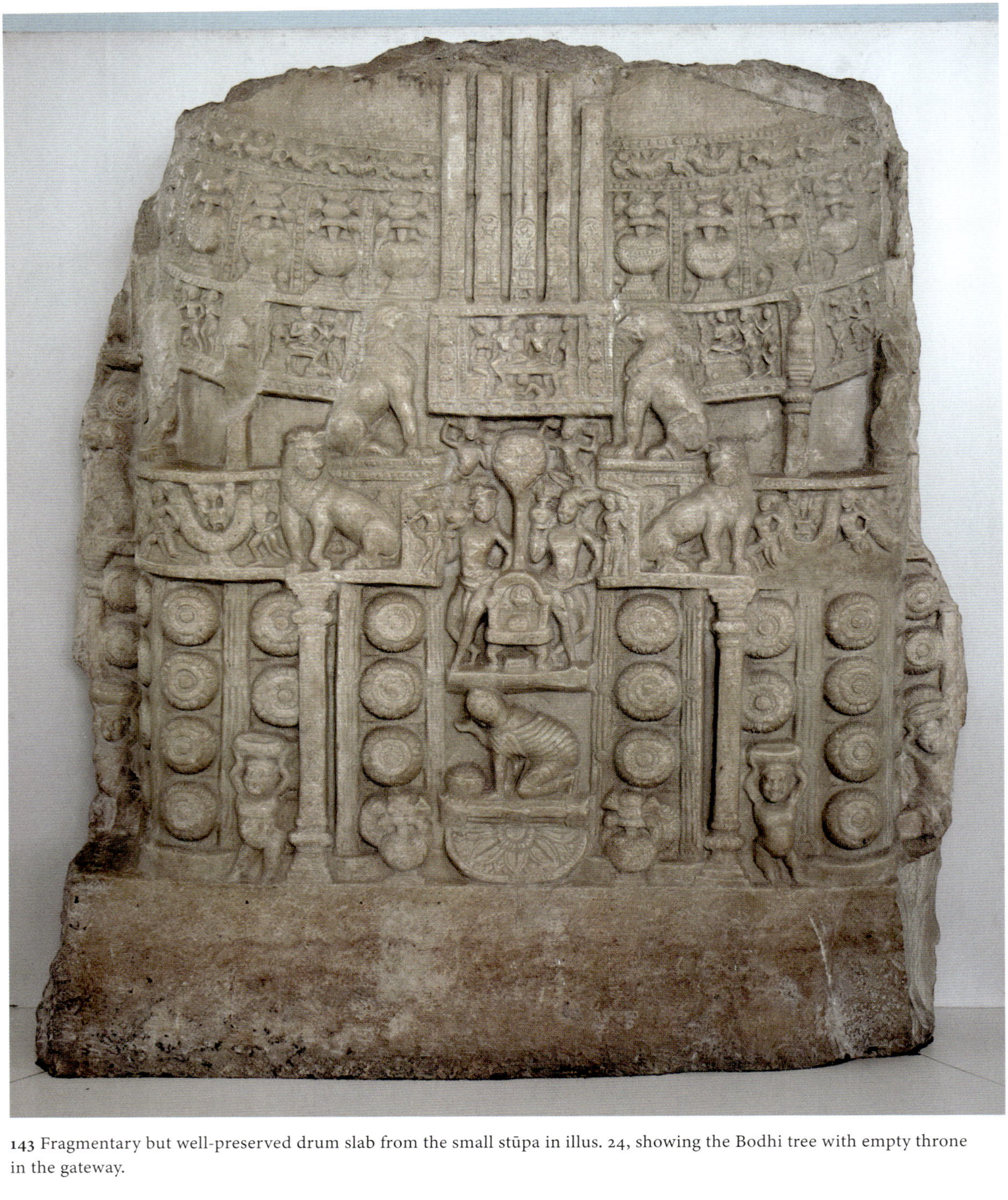

143 Fragmentary but well-preserved drum slab from the small stūpa in illus. 24, showing the Bodhi tree with empty throne in the gateway.

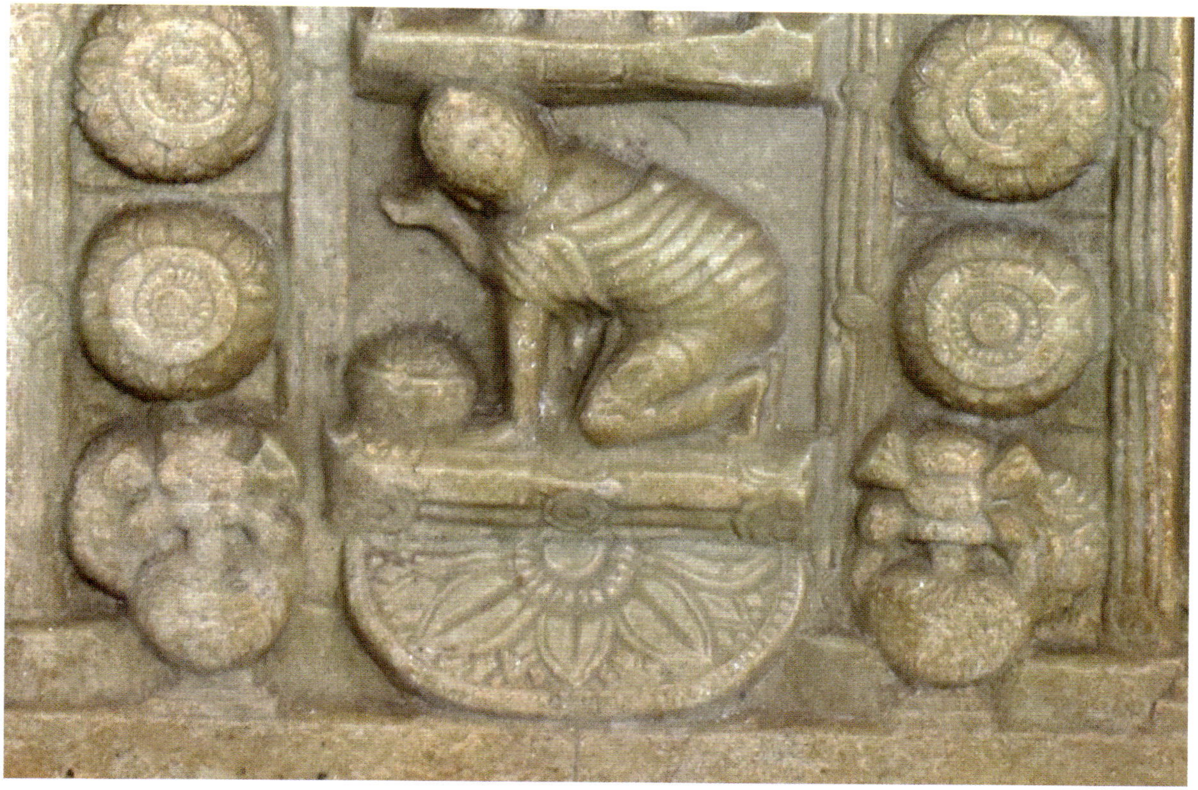

144 Detail of moonstone threshold with kneeling worshipper in illus. 143.

its relief sculpture that both reflects the great circles of Buddhist doctrine (notably the wheel of dharma but perhaps also that of dependent origination[62]) and the specific monumental embodiment of the Buddha as stūpa, that is, as a volumetric circle consisting of a dome on a cylinder. This play between three and two dimensions, between the entire monument and numerous miniatures, itself resembles the play between relief images of the Buddha and other figures and the numerous fully three-dimensional statues discovered at the site that have been hardly discussed but were certainly key to its interior adornment and devotional life.

The same creativity and investigation of the mapping of three-dimensional voluminous forms in the two dimensions of relief is equally apparent in relation to the human figure. We have seen how circles of seated musicians alongside representations of dancers configure the forms of their figures frontally, in three-quarter views to right and left (from both front and back) and fully from behind (see illus. 75, 77, 87), building further circular models of the spatial disposition of people as well as exploring the human body from its many sides.

We have here examined some of the intimate formal ways in which three-dimensional objects in the round are playfully configured and reconfigured in the more relatively two-dimensional schemes of representation available to carvers of reliefs in stone. At the centre of viewing a stūpa lies the embodied movement of circumambulation with one's right side to the monument.[63] All viewing is dependent on the partial perspective of the embodied gaze of such devotees. There is never access to the totality of the monument in a single view, even for the divine beings who hover about the relief panels with stūpas carved on them. Objects and people are constantly distorted or partial in the actual experience of the physical gaze, depending on the viewer's position.

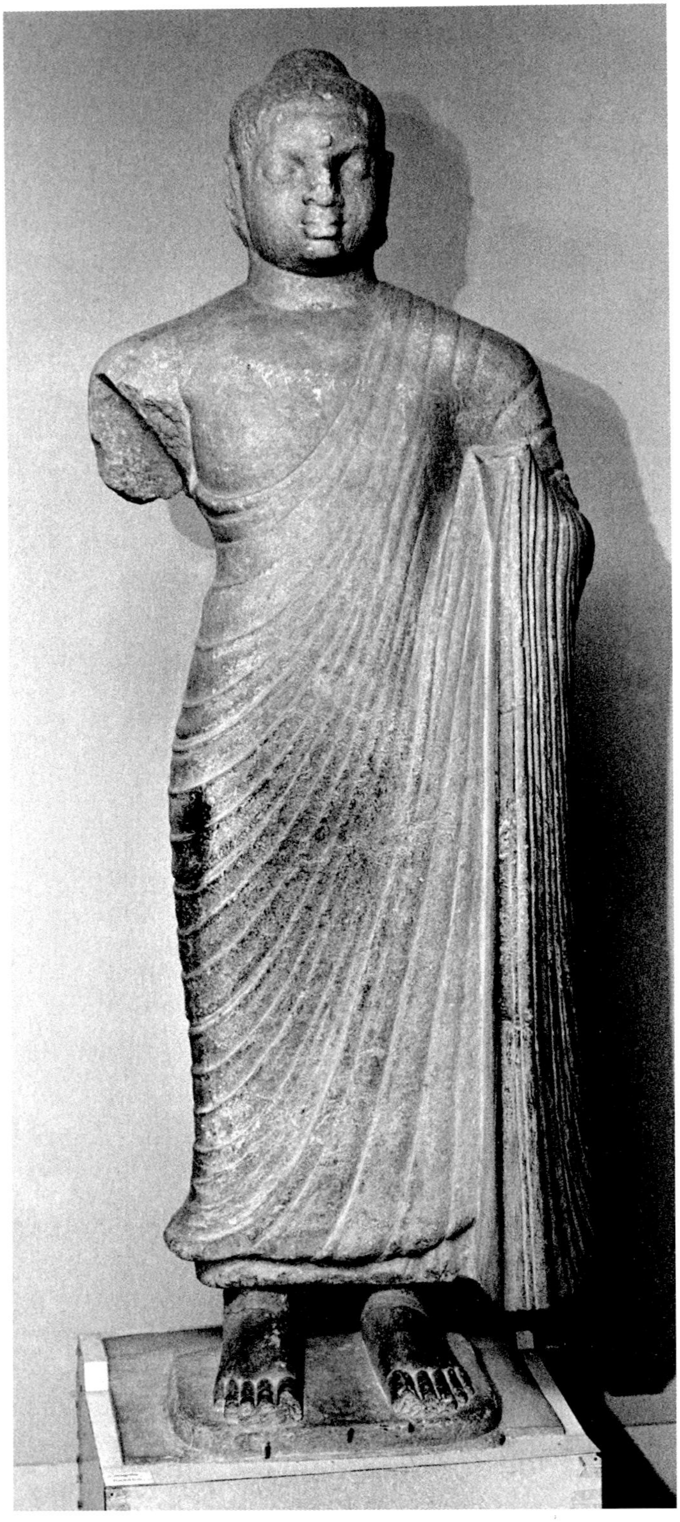

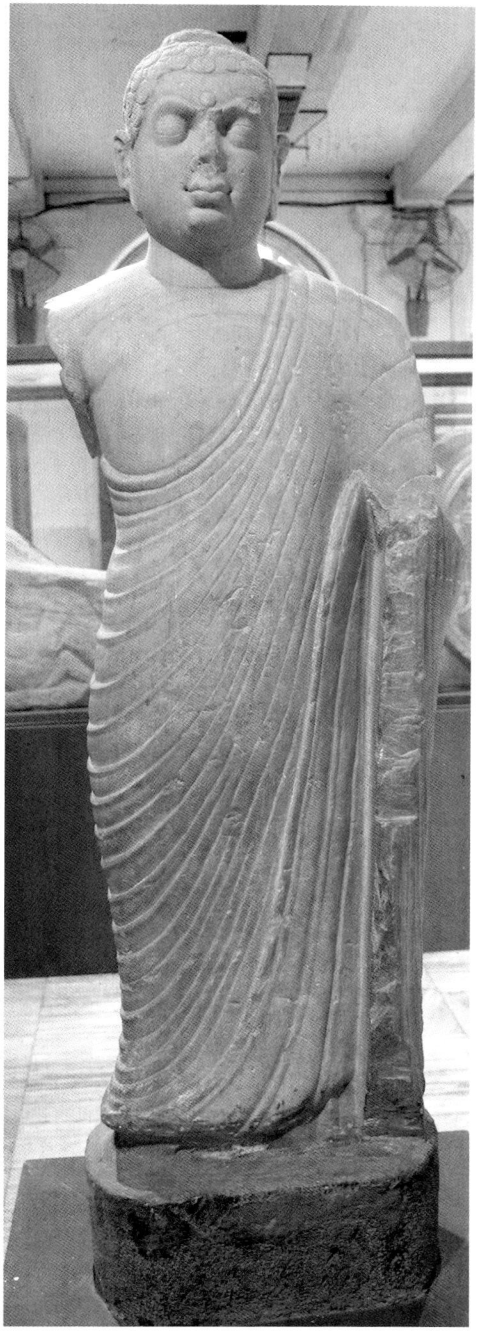

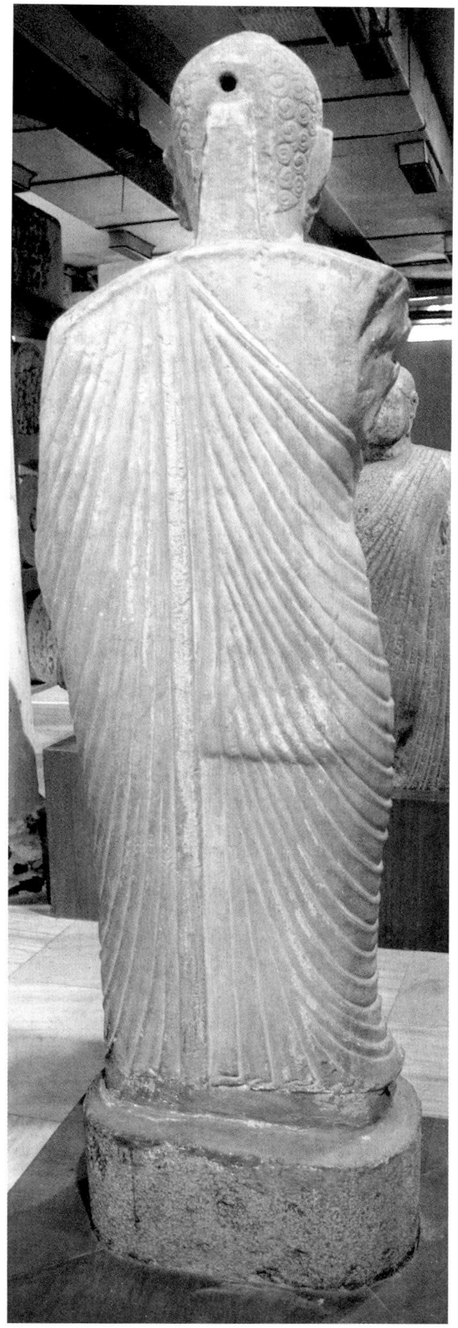

145 Larger-than-life-size standing Buddha statue with broken arms but probably right hand raised in the *abhāya* posture (2 m high).

146 Three-quarter-size standing Buddha statue with broken arms but probably right hand raised in the *abhāya* posture (1.23 m high to the break a little above the feet).

147 Back of illus. 146 showing dowel hole for attachment and strut at the neck.

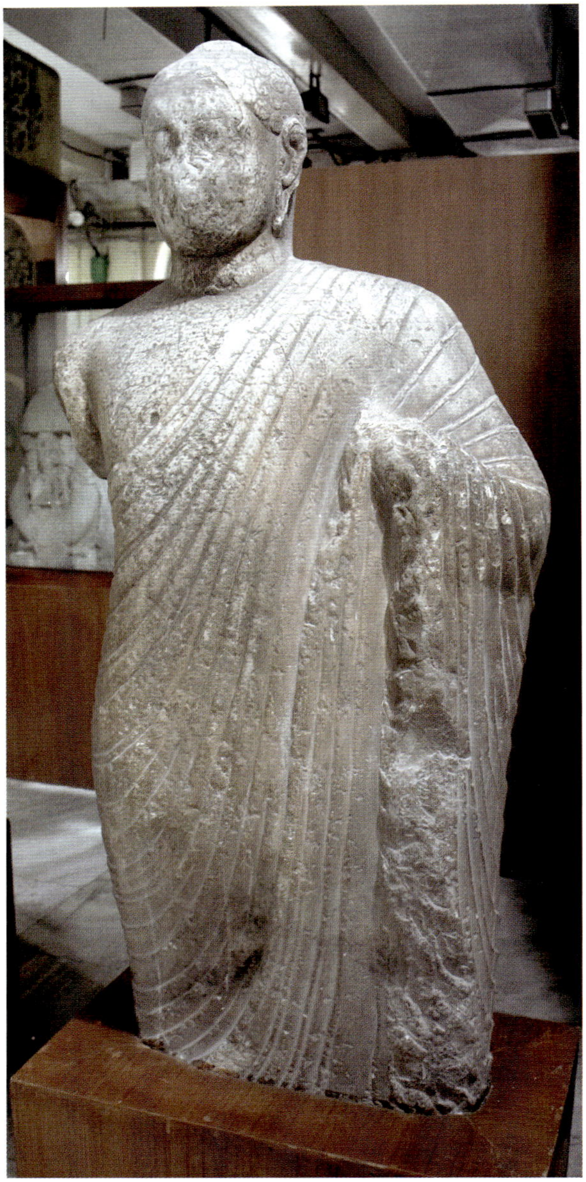

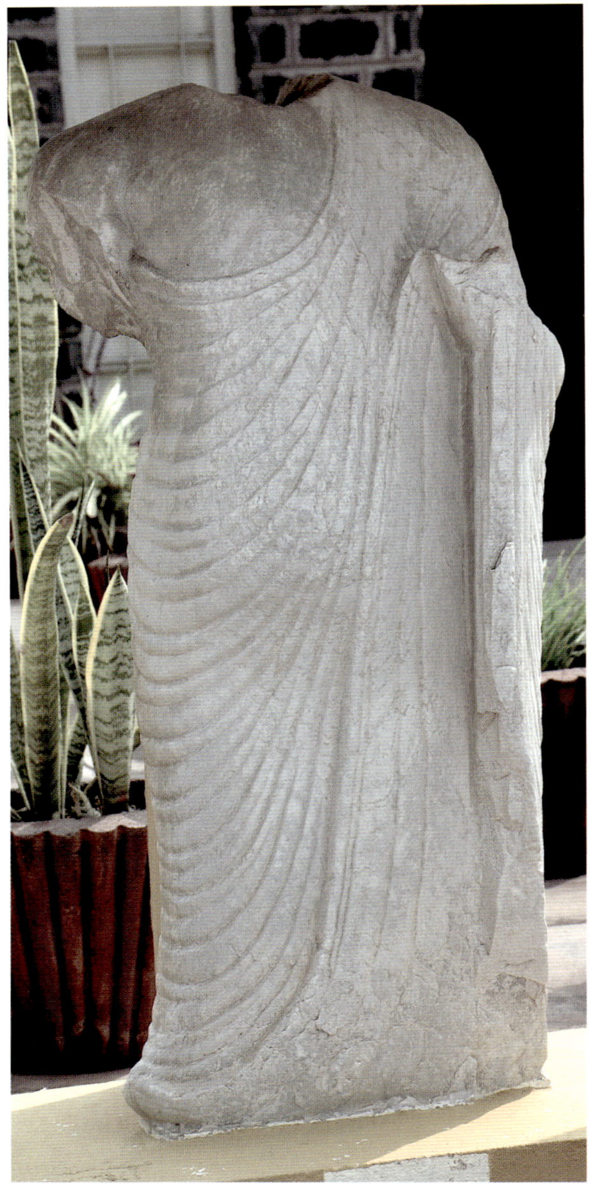

148 Three-quarter-size standing Buddha statue with broken arms but probably right hand raised in the *abhāya* posture (1.39 m high to the break at about the knee).

149 Half-size standing Buddha statue, headless with broken arms but probably right hand raised in the *abhāya* posture (0.97 m high without head).

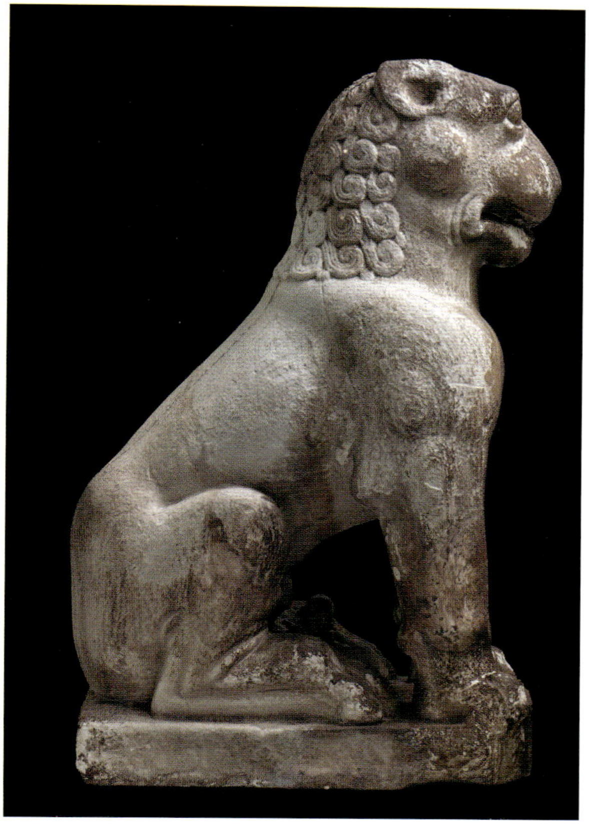

150 Seated lion statue from a gateway (1.05 m high).

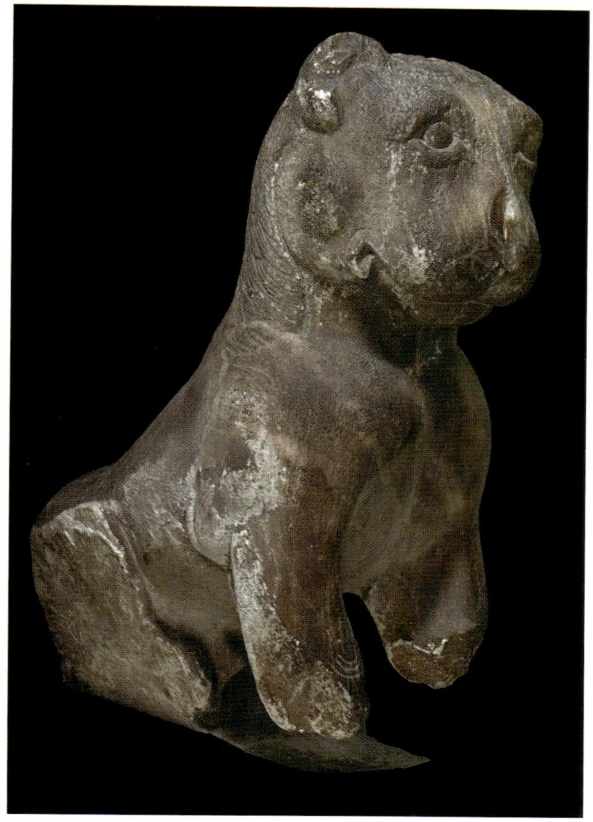

151 Seated lion statue from a gateway (1.13 m high).

The stūpa's sculptures draw repeated and obsessive attention to this problem of partiality, especially in relation to circular objects and forms, like itself.

Philosophically, one is reminded of the famous parable of the blind men and the elephant, probably already ancient in India before it was used by the Buddha in the *Tittha Sutta* in the Pāli canon.[64] After telling the story of how a series of blind men, having touched an elephant on different parts of its body, liken the animal to a series of entirely incompatible things (a water jar, a winnowing basket, a ploughshare and so forth) and come to blows when they disagree, the Buddha comments:

> Some recluses and brahmans, so called,
> Are deeply attached to their own views;
> People who only see one side of things
> Engage in quarrels and disputes.[65]

This is a teaching about views, their partiality and how powerfully they are held,[66] especially when founded on physically embodied engagement with the object of concern, just as the process of circumambulating a stūpa is a physically embodied and inevitably partial view of its substance as a great reliquary containing the Buddha's own relics. The relentless play on circular forms from all kinds of angles and partial perspectives highlights in visual and material terms the problematic of grasping the totality of anything, and above all the fullness of an object endowed with sacred presence. In his perhaps sixth-century commentary Dhammapāla notes that a true *tittha*, or crossing point, is one where beings 'cross over the flood of saṃsāra' on the path to Nirvana, whereas 'the present case . . . is a viewpoint consisting of wrong views as held by those resorting to wrong view by way of perversions consisting of distorted

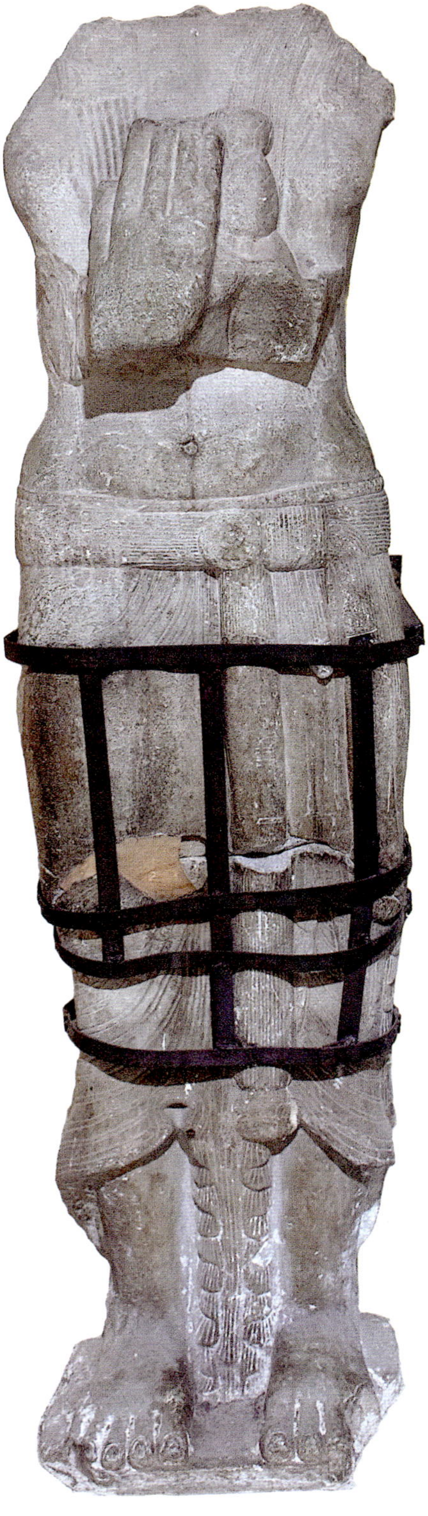

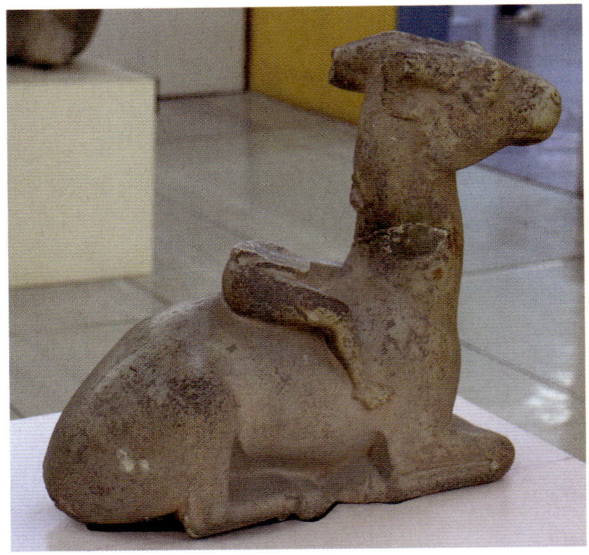

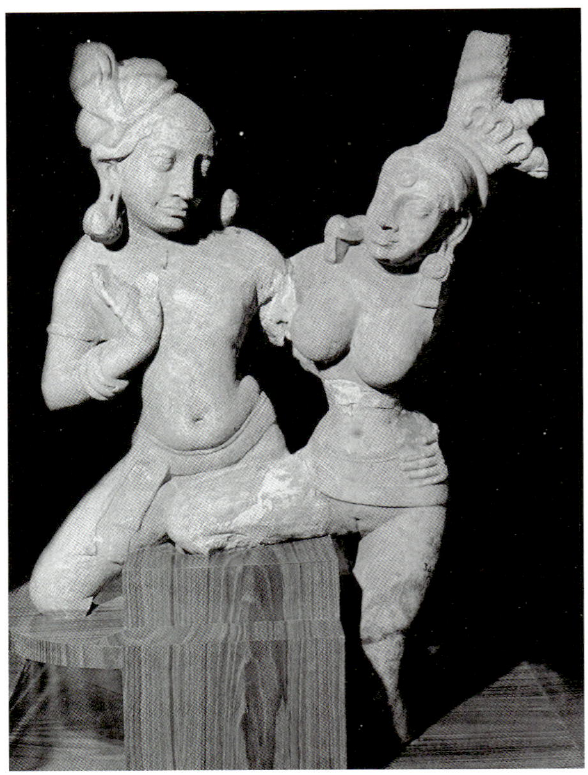

152 Larger-than-life-size statue of a devotee, headless (1.84 m high without head).

153 Small sculpture of a camel and rider (0.45 m high).

154 Small-scale male–female *mithuna* couple, broken at the bottom.

perceptions';[67] in the case of the stūpa, we may argue that the playful juxtaposition of multiple angles and partial perceptions is designed precisely to unravel the problem of wrong views and hence establish the monument, and the pilgrimage to it, as part of the path to crossing the flood of *saṃsāra*. I am not suggesting that the artists and planners responsible for the stūpa's construction over several centuries deliberately planned the monument's decoration to be a conceptual deconstruction of its form, but rather that the cultural context of Indian Buddhist thinking in the early centuries CE permeated into material culture, and that the arts of Amarāvatī were integrally imbricated in the kinds of reflection exemplified by the *Tittha Sutta*.

THREE DIMENSIONS: BUDDHA STATUES AND STŪPAS

The experiments in visualizing cylindrical and spherical forms in two dimensions, and various kinds of Buddha bodies in relief carving, climax in the rich array of replicated three-dimensional monuments at the site – notably small stūpas (one of which survived to be excavated in the early twentieth century and was then tragically dismantled after 1905, illus. 24) and life-size Buddha statues.[68] These statues have been hardly published or properly discussed in any detail, despite the rather original conception within the history of Indian Buddhist sculpture of the typical standing form of the Buddha in Andhra,[69] which parallels the relief iconography of the standing figures in the gateways of stūpas.[70] The form – with very short curls twisting to the right for the hair, a low *uṣṇīṣa* at the top of the head,[71] the right shoulder uncovered with the right arm raised in the *abhāya* posture, and even pleats in the long robe that is gathered at the left while the left hand rises towards the left shoulder (as in the seated and standing examples in relief) – is distinctive, and would prove hugely influential in Southeast Asia and Sri Lanka.[72] In several cases remains of clamps or holes for attachment survive (as in the back in illus. 147).[73]

We do not know how many such statues there once were, or where these free-standing sculptures – some life-size and some smaller – were placed in the stūpa,[74] but the options include around the gateways and along the processional path,[75] which would situate them very close to the worshipper, and on the ridge between the top of the stūpa's drum and the point at which the dome sprang above it, as well as on the *āyaka* platforms that jutted out from this circular space. That would place such statuary just above the pilgrim's head height, if we follow the current consensus that the drum was about 1.8 metres (6 ft) high.[76] In all cases they were therefore visible and accessible to devotees, bringing the stūpa's rich exploration of two-dimensional forms and multiple Buddha-bodies to an embodied three-dimensional fruition, parallel to that afforded by the cylindrical and spherical volume of the smaller stūpas around the site as well as the great stūpa itself in relation to all the relief play with circularity. They were in dialogue with large-scale and nearly in-the-round relief statues of the standing Buddha, which largely survive in poor condition.[77] In almost all surviving cases, the Buddha statues continue the reliefs' insistence on the Buddha's gesture of fearlessness as its act of *dāna* to its multiple visitors, although in almost all cases the right hand raised in blessing has now been lost.

The iconography of this range of statues is entirely within the general frame of the stūpa's sculptural language (and interestingly there are no surviving seated examples). Thematically the presence of what were obviously many Buddha statues in response to the two-dimensional imagery, both figural and emblematic, takes the various visual discourses of embodiment to a new level through material means. Likewise, it mirrors the great stūpa's and numerous smaller stūpas' monumental and volumetric fulfilment of all the discursive play with circles and picturing circles from multiple angles, in three-quarters view, foreshortened, flattened and so forth. Certainly, the fully frontal standing Buddha (in the gateways of certain miniature stūpas carved in relief) is modulated in various closer-to-three-quarters views through the more naturalistic action of numerous narrative scenes,[78] though I know of no surviving rear views. Effectively the perspectival angles on both Buddha figures and circular forms, displayed in the diversity of the stūpa's immensely rich imagery, are fulfilled in the three-dimensional embodiments of those subjects represented by the Buddha statues, the small stūpa mounds and the monument itself. The same may be said of the other surviving statuary, none of it subject to any adequate scholarly discussion or proper stratigraphy to give a sense of where it might have been placed. In addition to the lions that stood at the gateways (illus. 150 and 151),[79] finds include an elephant,[80] a bull,[81] a camel with rider (illus. 153),[82] and various other figures including a three-dimensional life-size statue of a standing devotee (illus. 152)[83] and a *mithuna* couple (illus. 154).[84] Again, these bring into three-dimensional fulfilment the kinds of figures found in the reliefs in two dimensions.

These statues, which offer actual three-dimensional and experiential viewing as voluminous figures confronted in the pilgrim's real space, represent in themselves the complete range of the multiple positions, foreshortenings and perspectives on the Buddha figure (and indeed other human and animal figures) presented by the narrative reliefs. In the same way, the miniature stūpas around the site – as both fully realized cylinders topped by a half-dome in real space and as divine presences through the relics they contained – offered the full reality that encompasses all the circular games of angled views and three-quarter profiles proffered by the representations of circular forms in their decorative carvings. Another way to put this is that the sculpted imagery which is so extensive at Amarāvatī, amounting almost to a *horror vacui*, takes the two most fundamental aspects of the site – that is, the Buddha as physical form and the Buddha as abstract embodiment represented by stūpas and enlivened by their relics – and riffs on them in wildly creative and thoughtful visual play. The Buddha and the world of his many earlier lives, whether presented in human shape or as stūpa, is endlessly ramified in the reflective two dimensions of the monument's visual discourse – as plays with rendering the circular shape, as games with depicting the human body from multiple angles, as manifold options within the rendition of emblematic bodies as well as figural ones. This visual discourse of endless reflectivity and multiplicity echoes the many lives of the Bodhisattva's incarnation, the numerous other buddhas whose life stories map onto that of Gautama, the several levels on which the Buddha's *kāya* may be perceived, the diverse perceptions of his teaching by the many beings to whom he offered salvation. Traditionally, the Buddha was regarded as having offered 84,000 teachings to suit all the varieties of human beings and their perceptions.[85] Traditionally, also, not one of his disciples could offer the fullness of his teaching, or be a refuge in the way he was.[86] Thus, the stūpa's visual discourse presents in artistic form the multiplicity of teachings, lives, bodies and Buddhas that individually offer ways into potential salvation, and that, in the fullness of their many partialities, collectively make up the transformational being that was the Tathāgata.

In particular, these two monumental forms – miniature stūpas and Buddha statues – were themselves replicated across and around the site, and beyond the site to numerous other Buddhist establishments in Andhra. Their three-dimensional multiplicity represents a series of miniatures (like the meta-stūpa slabs in two dimensions) of the great co-ordinating central presence of the *Mahācaitya*, the great stūpa, itself. The great stūpa envelops and encompasses all these forms but offers its presence, embodied with relics and three-dimensional images, as a place of refuge in the still living Buddha for its devotees, while performing many of the narratives, teachings and commentaries that came to constitute Buddhism in its relief sculpture. That sculpture stands at the same time as a multiplicity of perspectival, limited and partial but endlessly reflective evocations of his being, present at the site through its relics, and the path he offered.

Conclusion

This book has attempted to present an interpretation of the remains of the great stūpa at Amarāvatī that is simultaneously embedded in archaeological empiricism, art-historically analytic precision and a range of historical, religious and cultural contexts of which Buddhist theory and ritual are the most central. The first chapter attempted a phenomenological 'circumambulation' around the stūpa, and it is in that spirit – evoking the monument's experiential effects on its likely viewers – that I wish to end.

I have argued in Chapter Three that the stūpa is effectively a vast aid to the meditative practices known as *Buddhānussati* in Pāli and *Buddhānusmṛti* in Sanskrit, that is, the recollection of the Buddha.[1] These contemplations are said in the Pāli suttas to lead to Nirvana:[2]

> Monks, there is one thing that when developed and cultivated, leads exclusively to disenchantment, to dispassion, to cessation, to peace, to direct knowledge, to enlightenment, to *Nibbāna*. What is that one thing? Recollection of the Buddha. This is that one thing, that when developed and cultivated, leads exclusively to disenchantment, to dispassion, to cessation, to peace, to direct knowledge, to enlightenment, to *Nibbāna*.[3]

Likewise, in the Sanskrit canon as translated into Chinese, we find the claim:

> You should practice one dharma, you should propagate one dharma and when you have practiced one dharma, you shall have renown, achieve the great fruit, attain all good, acquire the taste of nectar, and reach the station of the unconditioned; then you shall achieve magic power, eliminate distractions of thought, attain the fruit of the seeker and arrive at *Nirvāna*. What is the one dharma? Namely, *Buddhānusmṛti*.[4]

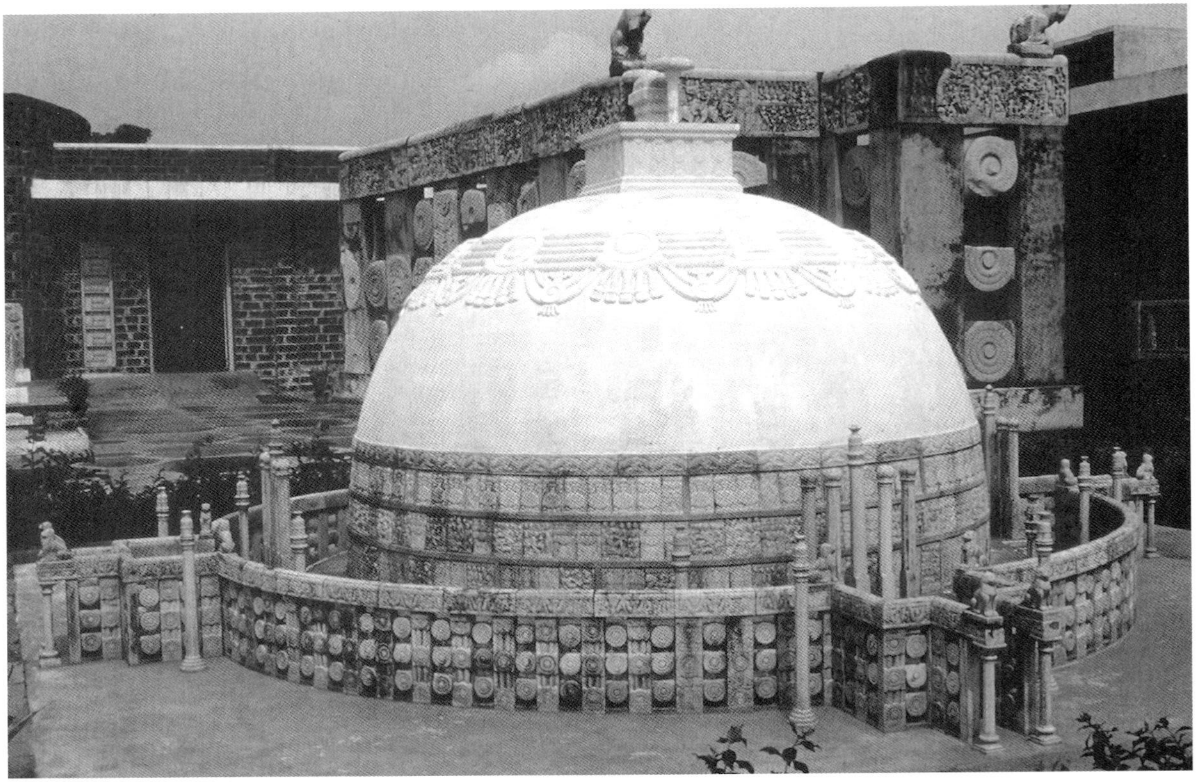

155 Reconstruction of the Great Stūpa, probably with too high a dome, in the Archaeological Museum at the site of Amarāvatī. Maha *caitya* model.

The ritual engagement with a stūpa – namely circumambulation, potentially alongside the recitation of verses such as the ten epithets of the Buddha on which both the major surviving meditation manuals from (probably) the fourth and the fifth centuries CE, the *Vimuttimagga* and the *Visuddhimagga*,[5] base their presentation of *Buddhānussati* – is effectively a form of embodied recollection in response to a sacred monument. The monument is not only the site of the Buddha's living presence in his relics but, as we have seen, a vast visual paean to the innumerable lives, causal interconnections, attainment of perfections and cosmological significances implied in Buddhahood. These are presented in multiple and often repeated narratives relating to the Bodhisattva as well as a series of different embodiments from the human form to varieties of emblematic bodies and symbolic appearances. Indeed, the monument most strikingly replicates itself in a multiplicity of two-dimensional variations in the spectacular panels of miniature stūpas that encircled its main drum. Those multiple embodiments themselves potentially imply not only Gautama Buddha but all and any of the past and future Buddhas, while the Bodhisattva narratives evoke not only the Bodhisattva path to the perfections undertaken by the being who was once Sumedha, but also the Bodhisattva paths of all the other past and future Buddhas, who themselves attained the ten perfections. It is the contemplation and imitation of this as well as the recollection of its full implications – drawn out with such spectacular artistry and no formal or explicit doctrinal lecturing, yet with great exegetic sophistication, by the imagery of the stūpa – that enables *Buddhānussati* to bring the devotee towards Nirvana.

The stūpa was not simply a work of art to be observed, a trigger to recollection or a mnemonic of diverse narratives. It was an immersive physical experience of ritual circumambulation – combined, we may surmise, with recitation, visualizations and bowing or prostration. It drew the pilgrim into the sacred space of its evocation of Buddhahood, which was simultaneously the palatial setting of its relics and a celebration of the immensity of *dāna* by hundreds of individuals, that was itself in imitation of the Buddha's own *dāna* in giving his dharma to the world. The repeated imagery of devotion and worship in so many of the figural scenes invoked the patterns of worship that this great material instantiation of *Buddhānussati* was constructed to enable. The stūpa's concern with theatricality and a regime of the gaze, its narrative events being consistently represented within the scope of public vision, was itself an invocation of collective *Buddhānussati*, performed in public ritual and festival as well as personal devotion.

References

ABBREVIATIONS

AMA: Archaeological Museum, Amarāvatī
BL: British Library, for Mackenzie's Amaravati Album, WD 1061
BM: British Museum
GMC: Government Museum, Chennai
HAABA: Huntington Archive for Ancient Buddhist Art (https://dsal.uchicago.edu/huntington/database.php)

INTRODUCTION

1 Prabha Ray, 2018, p. 1.
2 For a detailed discussion see Shimada, 2013, pp. 59–112, broadly accepted by Becker, 2015, for example, p. 24, n. 3; and Skilling, 2016, p. 24. For some very general accounts of the arts of Amarāvatī in their Andhra context, see Subramanian, 1981; Ray, 1981; Huntington, 1985, pp. 163–83; Sarma, 1988; Ramachandran, 1996, pp. 33–78; and Jithendra Das, 1993.
3 Dehejia, 1997, pp. 150–51.
4 Bachhofer, 1929, pp. 54–5; Dehejia, 1997, p. 150.
5 Mackenzie, 1823, pp. 468–9.
6 See the excellent summary discussion in Rosen Stone, 1994, pp. 21–4; for a synoptic account of styles, see Kramrisch, 1933, pp. 46–53.
7 Rosen Stone, 1994, p. 22.
8 Dehejia, 1997, pp. 150–71; Kumar, 2012, pp. 160–236; Rana, 2013, pp. 76–127; Zin, 2016a, pp. 46–58; Chowdhuri, 2018, pp. 68–148.
9 Gangoly, 1973, pp. 55–8; Rosen Stone, 1994, p. 41; Sudha Piratti, 2002, pp. 13–17, 19–20.
10 On early Buddhism in Andhra, see Lamotte, 1988, pp. 342–9. For an archaeologically inflected summary of the region in roughly the period 300 BCE to 300 CE, see Fogelin, 2006, pp. 11–34. For the environmental context of Andhra archaeology, focusing on the coast to the north of the Krishna River basin, see ibid., pp. 81–5; and, generally, Kumar, 2012, pp. 17–29. For other contemporary stūpa sites in the archaeological context, see Fogelin, 2006, pp. 86–109; and Kumar, 2012, pp. 133–43; Chowdhuri, 2018, pp. 34–56.
11 See Skilling, 2016, p. 25.
12 Burgess, 1882, pp. 4 and 9 (at no. 4b); Rea, 1909, pl. L; Schopen, 1997, pp. 166–7.
13 Schopen, 1997, pp. 166, 169; Shimada, 2013, pp. 171–204 for the most detailed discussion to date. The monastic site of Thotlakonda (also with its own stūpa) about 200 kilometres (125 mi.) to the north on the Andhra coast and of about the same dates is better known archaeologically and provides some sense of what Amarāvatī was like, although it is a much smaller site; see Fogelin, 2006, pp. 85–90, 157–75 (note the absence there of a railing or circumambulatory path, pp. 171–2).
14 In his book on administrative roles in the Indian Buddhist monastic establishment, J. Silk cites several texts in which monks are presented as overseers of stūpa construction and several inscriptions from stūpas that appear to confirm this in practice. See Silk, 2008, pp. 80–81, 83, 90–95 (nn. 92–8 for Amarāvatī). Likewise, some *Vinaya* texts discuss the roles of monastic administrators in managing funds in relation to the repair of stūpas: see Silk, 2008, pp. 153–4.
15 On stūpas as pilgrimage monuments, see Fogelin, 2015, pp. 22–5, 113–24; on physical and virtual pilgrimage to Amarāvatī, see Kinnard, 2008, pp. 97–100.
16 For example, on living presence through both relics and mound, see Schopen, 2005, pp. 44–5, 350–70; Fogelin, 2012, pp. 286–7; for a good review of the issues at stake in the presence or absence of the Buddha in material forms, see Kinnard, 2001, pp. 25–78 (although largely concerned with a somewhat later medieval moment than the arts of Amarāvatī).
17 The classic attack on the 'Protestantism' of the scholarship is Schopen, 1991, taken up effectively by Kinnard, 2001, pp. 13–16, and Appleton, 2010, pp. 16–18. The issue of a 'Protestant' bias towards texts in the data that constitute religion is hardly limited to Buddhism: see the range of discussions in Elsner, 2020. For a brilliant account of how this issue is not only driven by an orientalist perspective on the part of Western scholars but a self-imposed series of restrictions by Indigenous scholars and practitioners in Buddhist countries in response to Westernization and colonial rule since the eighteenth century, see Crosby, 2013a; also Harris, 2006, pp. 161–88. For a number

of issues in the colonial intervention in the archaeologies of Buddhism, see Prabha Ray, 2008b.

18 The literature is immense: see the excellent summary and historiography in Karlsson, 1999, pp. 17–18, 32–40, 48–53. For an attack on the Abrahamic underpinnings of the aniconism model, see Huntington, 2015; and the critical review of Bracey, 2020.

19 For a good material-cultural case for the importance of the object in Buddhism, but related to East Asian material that is later than the Indian origins of the religion and its arts, see Rambelli and Reinders, 2012, pp. 3–43.

20 For example, the notion of the Buddhist Church in Dutt, 1945, vol. II, pp. 5, 12, 44; the universal terms 'relics' and 'reliquaries' or Schopen's own commitments to '*ad sanctos* burial', and other models borrowed both conceptually and terminologically from Christian studies; see Schopen, 1997, pp. 114, 123–5, 131, 167.

21 See for instance, Dutt, 1925, pp. 145–7 ('schism'); Dutt, 1945, pp. 42 ('schism'), 47 ('secession'), 269 ('heretics', 'sect'), 270 ('schism'); Dasgupta, 1969, p. 112 ('seceded', 'split'); Dutt, 1978, pp. 13 ('dissidents'), 30 ('schism'), 31 ('sects'), 39 ('dissensions') and so on; Nakamura, 1980, pp. 61 ('heretical'), 100 ('sects'); Lamotte, 1988, pp. 274 ff. ('heresy'), 279 ('schism'); Hirakawa, 1990, pp. 70 ('split', 'schisms'), 108 ff. ('schism'), 110 ('split'); Bareau, 2013, pp. xxv–vi ('sects', 'schisms', 'heresies') and so on; Silk, 2009, pp. 12–16.

22 See for instance Major Rock Edict 12: 'control of one's speech so as not to extoll one's own sect or disparage another's on unsuitable occasions, or at least do so only mildly on certain occasions. On each occasion one should honour another man's sect, for by doing so one increases the influence of one's own sect and benefits the other man's; while by doing otherwise one diminishes the influence of one's own sect and harms the other man's. Again, whoever honours his own sect or disparages that of another man, wholly out of devotion to his own, harms his own sect even more seriously. Therefore, concord is to be commended, so that men hear one another's principles and obey them.' Translated by Thapar, 1997, p. 255, with discussion at pp. 165–6; see Major Rock Edict 7, with Thapar, 1997, p. 253.

23 The Buddhist *saṅgha* is the subject of the so-called Schism Edict among the Minor Rock Inscriptions; see Thapar, 1997, p. 262, with discussion at pp. 42–5, 159–60, 179–80. For examples of the traction in the *Vinaya* texts, see *Mahāvagga* x in Horner, 1951, pp. 483–513; and *Cullavagga* VII in Horner, 1952, pp. 253–90.

24 For excellent discussions of the problems of the terminology as polemical, apologetic and rhetorical constructs over many centuries, see Fronsdal, 1998, pp. 72–98; Drewes, 2010, pp. 72–3; Gethin, 2012, pp. 1–14 (on Theravāda); Skilling, 2013, pp. 69–162, esp. 75–9, 116–18.

25 For good summaries dealing with many aspects, see, for example, Harvey, 1990, pp. 139–299.

26 See for example Hirakawa, 1990, pp. 105–219; or Bareau, 2013, pp. 3–4, who concludes that 'the existence of some 20 to 30 schools mentioned by the traditions cannot be questioned.'

27 See, for example, Bareau, 2013; Cousins, 2013 and 2017; Westerhoff, 2018, pp. 43–83 on philosophical positions.

28 See Gethin, 2012.

29 See, for example, Hirakawa, 1990, pp. 223–311; Walser, 2005, pp. 16–58; Westerhoff, 2018, pp. 84–9.

30 Schopen, 2005, p. 12. This paper was originally published in 1979.

31 For the extension, see Williams, 2009, pp. 6–7; Tournier, 2018, pp. 26–7; for the refinement, see especially Harrison, 2018, pp. 18–21.

32 Schopen, 2005, p. 11. See also, for example, Cousins, 2003, with riposte from Schopen, 2005, pp. 244–6, admitting that recent finds demand revision; Tournier, 2018 n. 70.

33 On the multifaceted nature of Mahāyāna, see Harrison, 1978, pp. 35–6; Schopen, 2005, p. 52; Bronkhorst, 2018, pp. 119–20.

34 Harrison, 2018, pp. 16–17.

35 For some interesting reflections on the problems of writing Indian chronology, see Trautmann, 2009, pp. 25–52, 255–80.

36 See Schopen, 2005, pp. 11–14 and 223–46; Morrissey, 2009, pp. 1–14. This last, however, is perhaps too committed to a Mahāyāna/non-Mahāyāna model of analysis (for example, pp. 11–14), which may retroject the later precision of differences backwards into a period of much greater doctrinal indeterminacy. For good collections of classic papers on the origins of Mahāyāna, see Williams, ed., 2005; and Harrison, ed., 2018.

37 Dessein, 2009, pp. 34–6, lists the following Mahāsāṃghika sects in the region of Amarāvatī and Nāgārjunakonda (based on inscriptional evidence): Bahuśrutīya, Caitika, Pūrvaśaila, Aparaśaila, Siddhārtika, Rājagiriya. Lamotte, 1988, pp. 347–8, adds Ayiramhamgha and Śaila/Mahāśaila. Further discussion of Śaila, Mahāvinaseliya and Kurukullā activity across Andhra including at the recently discovered site of Kanaganahalli: see Tournier, 2020, p. 892, who argues for 'religious pluralism . . . as the product of historical circumstances facilitating trans-regional exchanges'. For the Rājagiriyas at Amarāvatī, see Tournier, 2021–2, pp. 28–39. For parallel lists, see Shastri, 2001; Krishna Sastry, 2004 and 2008, pp. 105–12. For wise caution about identifying Buddhist schools as predominant in given archaeological sites, see Nakanishi and von Hinüber, 2014, p. 18; and Tournier, 2020, pp. 861–4.

38 Andhra has been thought the dwelling place of Nāgārjuna, perhaps the most significant of all Mahāyāna philosophers, who lived at some point between the first century BCE and the mid-third century CE, the dates of the making of the Amarāvatī stūpa: see Mabbett, 1998, p. 345; Walser, 2002, pp. 258–62; and Walser, 2005, pp. 61–9, 79–88; accepted by Williams, 2009, p. 64; Mitrikeski, 2009, pp. 158–61; and Karashima, 2015, p. 141.

39 See Dutt, 1978, pp. 237–49; Westerhoff, 2018, pp. 45–9.

40 See Walser, 2005, pp. 21, 25–7; Dessein, 2009, pp. 41–3; Drewes, 2010, p. 58; Harrison, 2018, pp. 16–17. But see Cousins, 2012, pp. 45–54, for some interesting exploration of the altruistic emphasis of Mahāsāṃghika thinking in Andhra and its origins. For evidence of Mahāyāna monks and teachers following the Mahāsāṃghika *Vinaya* and being based in Mahāsāṃghika monastic contexts, see, for example, Karashima, 2017b.

41 For some discussion of the issues see Gwynn, 2010; and Ward-Perkins, 2010.

42 For example, Schopen, 2005, pp. 11–12; Skilling, 2013, p. 105. For the difficulties of tying our tentative evidence about Buddhist sects to archaeological information, see, for example, Sarkar, 1966, pp. 97–110.

43 An issue well presented in relation to questions of the Bodhisattva ideal by Fronsdal, 1998. Schopen, 2005, pp. 3–24, 127–8, is too sweeping: it may well be that the evidence for the popularity of Mahāyāna in India (in contrast to China) before

the end of the fifth century is minimal, but his arguments (for example, the absence of imagery of members of the Mahāyāna pantheon like Avalokiteśvara or Amitabha) do not necessarily entail absence of Mahāyāna models of thinking (such as the Bodhisattva ideal or the six perfections), nor do they undermine the creativity of Mahāyāna thought in Nikāya monastic contexts such as those where the great stūpas were built. For a cautious account of potentially early Mahāyāna Bodhisattva imagery, see Rhi, 2018.

44 See the verse *Buddhavaṃsa* ('the lineage of the Buddhas') in the *Khuddaka Nikāya* of the Pāli *Sutta Piṭaka*, IIA, verses 1 and (esp.) 4: 'In the city of Amarāvatī (I was born as) a brahmin named Sumedha' (*Nagare Amaravatiyā Sumedho nāma brāhmano*) with Jayawickrama, 1974, p. 9; and Horner, 1975, pp. 9–10; also the opening of the fifth-century prose *Nidānakathā* ('the story of origins') by Buddhaghosa, seen as an introduction to the *jātakas*, in the *Khuddaka Nikāya* of the Pāli *Sutta Piṭaka*, with Jayawickrama, 1990, pp. 3–4. Buddhaghosa tells the story again in his commentary on the *Dhammapāda*: *Dhammapāda-aṭṭhakathā* I.8, in Burlingame, 1921, pp. 130–31. Interestingly, Buddhadatta's fifth-century CE commentary on the *Buddhavaṃsa*, probably written in South India, not only offers a long discussion of the Sumedha narrative, but opens its exposition of the chronicle of Gautama with a recapitulation of the Sumedha story: see Horner, 1978, pp. 96–170, 387–8 (and p. xxx for Buddhadatta's date and place). For a full list of the Pāli literature on the so-called *Sumedhakathā* or Sumedha story, see Matsumura, 2008. On these late texts as forming the primary material for the Buddha's biography (conceived of course over many lives), see Endo, 1997, pp. 2–4, 25–6. For some critical discussion of the *Buddhavaṃsa* narrative, see Collins, 1998, pp. 260–67. On multiple earlier buddhas, see Tournier, 2019, p. 99, for Sumedha and the Buddha Dīpaṅkara.

45 *Nidānakathā* 63, in Jayawickrama, 1990, pp. 17–18; see *Buddhavaṃsa* IIA verses 52–9, in Jayawickrama, 1974, p. 12; and Horner, 1975, pp. 14–15; with Buddhadatta's commentary in Horner, 1978, pp. 127–34. For the importance of this episode in the *jātaka* tradition of stories of the Bodhisattva's lives, see Appleton, 2010, pp. 87–8, 91–3, 101.

46 *Nidānakathā* 64–8, Jayawickrama, 1990, p. 18.

47 *Buddhavaṃsa* IIA verse 61, Jayawickrama, 1974, p. 13; and Horner, 1975, p. 15, see *Nidāna-kathā*, pp. 69–71, Jayawickrama, 1990, pp. 19–20. On the significance of the Sumedha story within the biographical traditions that make up the Bodhisattva idea, see Fronsdal, 1998, pp. 109–13; and within Theravāda, see Crosby, 2013b, pp. 27–9. For ramifications of the vow and prophecy in Mahāyāna, see Matsumura, 2011 and 2012. This last adds discussion of the gift of lotus blossoms to the Buddha to the spreading of hair on the road (in the Mahāyāna versions), perhaps offering a reflection on the lotuses of the Amarāvatī railing as offerings if the incipient models of such traditions were known in South India at the time of making.

48 For the *jātaka* traditions of previous lives as mythological charters for the validation of place, see Crosby, 2013b, p. 105.

49 On pilgrimage in early Buddhism (and especially to stūpas), see Prabha Ray, 2003, pp. 253–5; Fogelin, 2015, pp. 22–5, 113–24.

50 See Jones, 1949, pp. 1–3.

51 That said, there is an obscure reference to what is a presumably unpublished 'Buddhist sculptural frieze depicting the Dipānkara [*sic*] Buddha' in the Museum in Chennai in Padmanabha Sastry, 2004, p. 164.

52 See Neelis, 2019, pp. 175–7 (with table), who counts 129 examples.

53 See, for example, Longhurst, 1938, pp. 34–5, pl. XXXIVA (= HAABA 0026913 and 0026917, detail, both mistakenly labelled as if from Amarāvatī) for a frieze, and HAABA 0026987 and 0026989 (detail) for a casing slab.

54 *Divyāvadāna* 76.10–80.10 and 465.10–469.18, with Rotman, 2009, pp. 114–26; on the story see also Bareau, 1960, pp. 257–62; and Schopen, 1997, pp. 28–9.

55 See, for example, Lopez, 2016, pp. 21–42.

56 For the speculation that the visual features of this stūpa are based on those from Gandhāra, see Karashima, 2017c. This depends on the assumption that the phrases from the earlier versions of the Sūtra describing the stūpa translated by Karashima as 'it was aglitter, beautiful, nicely decorated with five thousand terraces with railings (*vedika*) attached with flower ornaments, adorned with many thousands of arched niches (*toraṇa*)' accord better with what archaeological evidence offers from Gandhāra than from elsewhere. The point is at least arguable.

57 See, for example, Williams, 2009, p. 156; Lopez and Stone, 2019, pp. 4–5, 136–48. It has recently been argued that the imagery of the two buddhas seated together, popular in East Asia, began in India along the Silk Road: see von Hinüber, 2019.

58 For an overview of Buddhism in its archaeological context in India, see Prabha Ray, 2018. For the history of Indian archaeology, see Chakrabarti, 1988; Prabha Ray and Sinopoli, 2004, esp. pp. 12–152; Singh, 2004; Prabha Ray, 2008a and 2008b. For a potted history of Buddhist archaeology in Andhra, see Subrahmanyam and Reddy, 2012. Good discussions of the excavation history of Amarāvatī include Cohen, 1994, pp. 88–97; Howes, 2002; Singh, 2004, pp. 249–89, 350–51; Howes, 2009, pp. 20–37; Singh, 2010; Shimada, 2013, pp. 1–30; Shimada, 2016; Chowdhuri, 2018, pp. 25–34. For a postcolonial account of the historiography, both 'orientalist' and 'nationalist', see Francis, 2002, pp. 10–50. On some aspects of museology in relation to the transfer of both Amarāvatī and Bharhut to museums, see Guha-Thakurta, 2004, pp. 63–71.

59 Foucher, 1928, p. 9 (the last page of this article carries the date 'March 1914', despite the date of publication).

60 For some of the issues around exhibiting materials from East Asian religions in museums (especially Western museums, but the problems apply more generally), see Sullivan, 2015.

61 For the drawings in the British Library, see http://vll-minos.bl.uk for scans; and on Mackenzie, see Howes, 2002 and 2010, pp. 219–22. For the photographs, see L. Tripe, 'Photographs of the Elliot Marbles and other Subjects in the Central Museum Madras by Captain L. Tripe Government Photographer. 1858'. Scans may be found under shelfmark 958 by searching 'Linnaeus Tripe Elliot Marbles' in the British library online archive, http://searcharchives.bl.uk. On Tripe see Bharath, 2010; Howell, 2016.

62 Similar responses: Singh, 2004, p. 289; and Becker, 2015, pp. 2–4.

63 For a summary of the architectural discussion and how it developed, see Shimada, 2013, pp. 11–14.

64 The pioneering work behind this model was by Jouveau-Dubreuil, 1932; developed by Barrett, 1954, pp. 27–39; and

largely accepted by Knox, 1992, pp. 23–30; and Rana, 2013, p. 16. The drum of the great stūpa at Nāgārjunakonda was 1.5 metres (5 ft) high above the ground and therefore very close in design: see Longhurst, 1938, p. 16.

65 Notably Brown, 1942, pp. 36–8; Kuwayama, 1997, pp. 148–9; Brown's reconstruction (surely wrong) is still occasionally repeated, for example, by Settar, 2020, p. 94, pl. 1.

66 See Brown, 1942, p. 37, for the assumption that the mini-stūpas on the relief panels were 'small duplicate copies' of the monument 'in bas-relief, showing clearly and in full detail exactly what the main structure was like' and thus enabling 'a fairly accurate conjectural restoration of the building', with discussion and critique in Barrett, 1954, pp. 32–6; and Elsner, 2022, pp. 63–6. The issue is still more problematic for Nāgārjunakonda, where the drum slabs showing relief stūpas (mainly excavated from the small stūpas 2 and 3 at the site, *not* from the *mahācaitiya*: Longhurst, 1938, pp. 15, 17), which show a railing (potentially echoing that of the iconographic model for these slabs from Amarāvatī), have been assumed to be a 'faithful portrayal' and used (incorrectly) to deduce the existence of a wooden railing (since no evidence whatever of a stone one survives) around the great stūpa: see Longhurst, 1938, pp. 14–15; followed by Ramachandran, 1953, p. 7.

67 See Barrett, 1954, p. 34: 'four foot thick'; contra Knox, 1992, p. 28, who mistakenly writes 'high' for 'thick'.

68 See Barrett, 1954, p. 36. The equivalent platform at Nāgārjunakonda was 2.13 metres (7 ft) wide: see Longhurst, 1938, p. 16.

69 See Barrett, 1954, p. 34; Knox, 1992, p. 28. The sole evidence for all this, apart from extrapolating from the visual suggestions of the drum slabs, as Barrett admits (1954, 34, n. 42), is in Mackenzie's drawings of the site made in March and particularly June 1817, of which the latter shows the entrance arrangements through the railing and the *āyaka* platform projecting from the main circle of the stūpa on the south side. For the drawings, see, for example, Shimada, 2013, pl. 28 and 29. However, the *mahācaitiya* at Nāgārjunakonda does support this: its *āyaka* platforms were 6.7 metres long by 1.5 metres at the side: Longhurst, 1938, p. 16.

70 Not universal, however. Some stūpas at Nāgārjunakonda, at Salihundam and at Ramatirtham are without *āyakas*: see Sarkar, 1966, p. 84.

71 See Barrett, 1954, pp. 34–5; Knox, 1992, p. 28.

72 In favour of an ambulatory, see, for example, Brown, 1942, p. 37 ('upper processional path') and Kumar, 2003, pp. 97–9: such a drum ambulatory may have had a plain railing, at least at some points in the stūpa's development: see Sarma, 1985, p. 19, no. 4. Against both ambulatory and upper railing, see Barrett, 1954, p. 36. At Nāgārjunakonda, Longhurst proposed the platform was a 'narrow path' but admitted no steps had been found: Longhurst, 1938, p. 16.

73 Barrett, 1954, p. 36.

74 See the discussion of Rea, 1894, pp. 1–4.

75 See Barratt, 1954, pp. 36–8; Knox, 1992, pp. 28–30.

76 For a surviving fragment of the *harmikā* see Sarma, 1985, pl. 28.

77 Potentially the example ibid., pl. 29 (which is large, according to Knox, 1992, p. 30).

78 See Barratt, 1954, pp. 38–9; Knox, 1992, pp. 29–30.

79 See the discussion of Poonacha, 2011, pp. 65–6, figs 11 and 13; Nakanishi and von Hinüber, 2014, pp. 5–9, figs 1 and 3; and Zin, 2018a, pp. 1–3. Interestingly a number of donations at this stūpa are made by patrons from Dhaññakata, which is identified with Amarāvatī: see Nakanishi and von Hinüber, 2014, section II.1, no. 1, pp. 41–2; section II.2, nos 5–6, p. 47, nos 27–9, pp. 52–3; section VI, nos 6–7, pp. 114–15.

80 See Harinarayana, 1990; Dehejia and Rockwell, 2016, p. 118. The same stone was used for the sculptures of Nāgārjunakonda: Misra, 2005, p. 197.

81 For some noble attempts see Zin, 2020, pp. 6–15; and Zin, 2021.

82 British Museum: Barrett, 1954; Knox, 1992; www.britishmuseum.org/collection (with search term: 'Amaravati'). Chennai Museum: Sivaramamurti, 1956; Kannan, 2014. Amarāvatī Archaeological Museum: Gupta, 2008.

83 British Library, Oriental and India Office Collections WD–1061. See Howes, 2002 and 2010, pp. 219–22.

84 For instance, Rana, 2013, pp. 53–6, describes a series of fine drum slabs excavated from the stūpa at Gummadidurru as if they were from Amarāvatī. See her discussion of pls 3.9 and 3.12. In the extremely useful HAABA online photographic archive many items from Nāgārjunakonda are mistakenly classified as if from Amarāvatī.

85 Things have not been improved by the horrible wax-like varnish, presumably in aid of preservation, applied to the fragments in the collections of the Archaeological Survey of India (those from Amarāvatī at the Amarāvatī Archaeological Museum, but also those from Nāgārjunakonda and Ghantaśālā at their respective site museums). It does its best to make the originals look like casts. A sad example, especially clear in the restored sections around the horizontal crack in the centre of the medallion but visible across the 'waxy' surface, is the crossbar roundel with the presentation of Rāhula to the Buddha, illus. 111 in this book.

86 BM 1880,0709.17, in Knox, 1992, no. 14.

87 Mackenzie, 1823, p. 463; Knox, 1992, p. 84 (under no. 28); Middleton, 1992, p. 232, for some scientific discussion of pigments.

88 Dehejia and Rockwell, 2016, p. 25.

89 Principal publications of the inscriptions include Fergusson, 1873, pp. 260–62 (Appendix E by A. Cunningham); Hultzsch 1883 and 1886; Burgess, 1887, pp. 100–106; Lüders, 1912, pp. 1–226, esp. nos 1206–1326, pp. 141–57, and 1205a, p. 179; Chanda, 1919–20; Sivaramamurti, 1956, pp. 273–304; Ghosh and Sarkar, 1964–5; Dehejia, 1969–70; Sarkar, 1970–71; Sarma, 1975; Ghosh, 1979; Sarma, 1980; Roy, 1994, pp. 9–84, 193–218; Hanumantha Rao, 1998, pp. 45–76; Rana, 2013, pp. 128–60; Francis, 2016.

90 See Lüders, Waldschmidt and Mehendale, 1963, pp. XXX–XXXV.

91 See Settar, 2020, pp. 62–91 for an account of the epigraphic evidence on this topic across early Buddhist India.

92 See Francis, 2016, p. 45.

93 This means that the otherwise excellent British Museum website and publications by Barrett in 1954 and by Knox in 1992 are seriously deficient in this regard. On the problem of inscriptions, kings and regnal years see Francis, 2016, p. 48.

94 'Early Inscriptions of Āndhradeśa', http://hisoma.huma-num.fr/exist/apps/EIAD/works, accessed 8 December 2023.

95 See the complaint of van Lohuizen-De Leeuw, 1949, pp. 263–4, about the archaeological and art-historical disregard of the publications of epigraphy, notably Lüders, 1912.

96 Lüders, 1912.
97 For a lively evocation of the larger nightmare across the full range of Andhra Buddhist epigraphy, see Baums, Griffiths, Strauch and Tournier, 2016. Part of the problem is that much of the more recent discussion (by historians like N. Francis) is done in ignorance of both the Brahmi script and the philology of Prakrit and Sanskrit, while the early publications (notably by H. Lüders) are too often summaries, without full transcriptions. Many of the materials collected by Lüders, including, one presumes, his transcriptions and translations of so much of the Brahmi epigraphy which it was his life's work to pursue, were lost in the dispersal that followed the depredation of the documents deposited in a mine in Bernburg by the Berlin Academy on the fall of Germany in 1945. On this last point see Lüders, Waldschmidt and Mehendale, 1963, p. v.
98 As stated explicitly by Sivaramamurti, 1956, p. 26. The current assumptions of styles and dates (essentially following Sivaramamurti) are summarized by Rana, 2013, p. 8.
99 See Barrett, 1954, pp. 43–4, with the word 'historical'. Rana, 2013, pp. 130–46, collects all inscriptions connected to the 'Royal Court' although this includes many that are much later than the Brahmi epigraphy associated with the period of constructing the stūpa and many by people (in their personal rather than official capacities) with positions associated with the court.
100 Sivaramamurti, 1956, p. 173, nos II E 6 and 7 with inscription no. 51 at p. 283 (= Lüders, 1912, p. 147, no. 1248); Hanumantha Rao, 1998, pp. 152–5, no. 21; Rana, 2013, pp. 131–2, no. 2; Francis, 2016, pp. 116–17, no. 160. This is no. 24 in the list of royal Sātavāhana inscriptions in Ollett, 2017, pp. 193–204, Appendix B, p. 196. I cannot find the GMC number nor any listing of the block, despite its significance, in Kannan, 2014, nor any illustration of the block.
101 GMC no. 124, in Sivaramamurti, 1956, pp. 215–16, no. III B 9 with inscription no. 72 at p. 291 (= Lüders, 1912, p. 152, no. 1279); and Kannan, 2014, pp. 169 and 356; Hanumantha Rao, 1998, pp. 159–60, no. 28; Rana, 2013, pp. 132–3, no. 9; Francis, 2016, pp. 115–16, no. 158. This is no. 50, in Ollett, 2017, Appendix B, p. 199.
102 Barrett, 1954, pp. 43–6, followed, for example, by Dehejia, 1972, pp. 67–8.
103 The key numismatic contributions are Cribb, 1992; Cribb, 1998; Cribb, 2000, pp. 39–45; Bhandare, 1999, pp. 168–78 and 305–24; Bhandare, 2011, pp. 63–4; see summary and discussion by Shimada, 2013, pp. 48–58.
104 See Shimada, 2013, pp. 49–54 and esp. 52, with the support of numismatic evidence; most recently Bhandare, 2016, p. 40; Francis, 2016, p. 117, still has 'second half of the second century AD'.
105 Shimada, 2013, pp. 40–42 and 54, 96; Bhandare, 2016, p. 41. Francis, 2016, p. 116, still has 'second half of the second century AD'. For the current consensus on Sātavāhana chronology, see Ollett, 2017, Appendix A, pp. 189–91.
106 For example, Knox, 1992, pp. 31–4 and passim through the catalogue; Gupta, 2008; Kannan, 2014.
107 For example, Sivaramamurti, 1956, pp. 26–43; Barrett, 1954, pp. 40–56; Stern and Bénisti, 1961; Knox, 1992, pp. 31–4; Shimada, 2013, pp. 59–112.
108 A good critical summary is Shimada, 2013, pp. 59–112, with trenchant critique of the unprovable assumption of Aśokan origins at pp. 59–66.
109 For arguments regarding the dates of the Buddha see Bechert, 1991–7; for developments in the Buddhist traditions see, for example, Schopen, 2005, pp. 11–14 and 223–46.
110 For an excellent introduction to the issues see Horner, 1978, pp. vi–xxiv.
111 For example, Hettiarachchy, 1973, p. 20; Zin, 2016, pp. 48–9; Zin, 2020, p. 16.
112 Dessein, 2008, p. 45: 'We do not possess one single work that systematically outlines the complete philosophy of the different Mahāsāṃghika groups'. For attempts to summarize the views of the Mahāsāṃghikas and schools that derived from them, see Dutt, 1925, pp. 225–48; Dutt, 1945, pp. 51–73; Dutt, 1978, pp. 57–97; Bareau, 2013, pp. 55–133.
113 A good discussion of these issues in relation to specific sculptures is Zin, 2004.
114 See, for example, Hettiarachchy, 1973, pp. 126–42; Hanumantha Rao, 1998, p. 10; Dessein, 2008, pp. 41–3. The sects specifically cited for Amarāvatī in the latter are *Mahāsāṃghika*: Lüders, 1912, p. 147, no. 1240 (following the word '*Hanghi*'), whose subsects include *Caitiyaka*: Lüders, 1912, p. 147, no. 1223; Lüders, 1912, p. 147, no. 1248 (= Sivaramamurti, 1956, p. 278, no. 51); Lüders, 1912, p. 148, no. 1250; Lüders, 1912, p. 150, no. 1263 (= Sivaramamurti, 1956, p. 293, no. 79); Chanda, 1919–20, p. 274, no. 55 (= Sivaramamurti, 1956, p. 278, no. 33); and *Aparaśaila*: Lüders, 1912, p. 144, no. 1230 (= Sivaramamurti, 1956, p. 303, no. 124). See also Francis, 2002, pp. 179–83; Kumar, 2012, pp. 364–81 (although the Buddhological and sectarian generalizations here need to be treated with caution as they are largely out of date). I would reiterate the point made in the sentence in the text to which this note is attached: inscriptions may tell us what their inscribers want us to know about them (including sectarian affiliation) but that does not necessarily warrant the generalizing assumption – too often a leap made in scholarly discussions – that a gift from a member of a particular Buddhist school entails large-scale presence of many members of that school.
115 It is thought the Mahāsāṃghika school was predominant, belonging to the Nikāya traditions of early Buddhism: see, for example, Wayman and Rosen Stone, 1990; but for the important Theravāda presence and connections with Sri Lanka see Holt and Padma, 2008; and Tournier, 2018, pp. 49–57. For the rise of Mahāyāna and the provenance of many of its key texts (such as the Prajñāpāramitā tradition) in South India, see, for example, Hirakawa, 1990, pp. 253–4 and 270–74 for the possible connection of Mahāyāna to stūpa worship of the kind particularly popular in the Krishna region.
116 On Mahāyāna and Tantra, see Barber, 2008; on the Theravāda commentator Dhammapāla, see Norman, 1983, pp. 133–7.
117 Generally, on the commentarial tradition, see Norman, 1983, pp. 118–37.
118 See the discussions of Shimada, 2005; and Shimada, 2013, pp. 40–58; following Cribb, 1998; Bhandare, 1999; and Cribb, 2000. For some general pictures of the history (but written before the reassessment of dynastic chronologies), see Prabha Ray, 1986, pp. 13–50; Shastri, 1998; Shastri, 1999.
119 On Sātavāhana patronage of Buddhism see Fynes, 1995; Ollett, 2018; Shimada, 2018 (on cave monasteries); Tournier, 2021–2. On Buddhism in Andhra, for example, Sastry, 2005.
120 Pollock, 2006, pp. 61–2, with references.

121 See Raghunath, 2001, pp. 18–19; Singh, 2016, pp. 50–53 on Nāgārjunakonda.
122 Fynes, 1995, pp. 47–8.
123 As recorded in both image and inscriptions; see Nakanishi and von Hinüber, 2014, nos I.3–14; Ollett, 2018, pp. 449–53; Zin, 2018b, for royal themes in the imagery.
124 Shimada, 2009, pp. 216–34; and Shimada, 2013, pp. 171–96.
125 Turner, 1974, pp. 193–6.
126 On the Jain presence in Andhra in this period see, for example, Seshagiri Rao, 1922; Sastri, 2004; Kranth Choudary and Hema, 2004.
127 For a general picture see, for example, Ramachandran, 1996. It is striking that of 143 early historic sites in Andhra identified by archaeology in Shimada, 2013, pp. 208–35, the vast majority (88) are Buddhist, six are Brahmanical and four both Buddhist and Brahmanical; none appear to be Jain.
128 Fundamental accounts are by Faxian (fourth–fifth century CE), Song Yun (sixth century) Xuanzang (seventh century), Yijing (seventh–eighth century). See, for example, Beal, 1884; Legge, 1886; Takakusu, 1896; Li, 1996. On Amarāvatī in particular, see, for example, Shimada, 2013, pp. 132–5, for 'cultural intercourse as far as Gandhāra or Mathura', Zin, 2016, pp. 47–8, and Rosen Stone, 2016, on borrowings from the Roman world; Becker, 2016 and Bopearachchi, 2016, pp. 13–15, 42–8, on visual connectivity to the South.
129 For an important warning about the difficulties of using Xuanzang's account (not only for issues in the various translations but also because he did not go everywhere and much of what he says is from hearsay, relaying traditions that existed but are not certainly reliable, and expanding on Faxian), see Deeg, 2007.
130 Li, 1996, pp. 271 (10, 929a), 272 (10, 929a), 277 (10, 930b), 278 (10, 930c), 282 (10, 931c).
131 For the stone stūpas, see Beal, 1884, pp. 217–18; Li, 1996, pp. 276–8; for Dhānyakataka, see Beal, 1884, pp. 221–2; Li, 1996, pp. 278–9.
132 Beal, 1884, pp. 222–3; Li, 1996, p. 279. While Xuanzang's impression of the decline of Amarāvatī (indeed its abandonment) by the mid-seventh century clearly has traction, other much later evidence implies some religious life at the site at least to the fourteenth century CE. See Paranavitana, 1934–41, pp. 97–8, for restorations by the Singhalese savant Dharmakīrti in the fourteenth century; and for the travels to India and Sri Lanka by the Thai monk Si Sattha (including a specific trip to and mention of Amarāvatī) in the same century, see Inscription II from Sukhothai, discussed, for example, by Chirapravati, 2008, pp. 20–22.
133 Lüders, 1912, no. 1225 (BM 1880,0709.77, Knox, 1992, p. 55).
134 The 'system' is brilliantly described by Hölscher, 2004, although his account is limited by being focused on Greek models rather than eclectic borrowings also from elsewhere. See Elsner, 2006, for extension and critique. For a thoughtful application of Hölscher's model to Gandhāran art in India (too limited in my view since the issue concerns all Indian art of the period), see Stoye, 2020.
135 For some 'Roman sightings' of India, see Parker, 2015.
136 For the influence of Amarāvatī styles and production across Southeast Asia see Guy, 2005 (especially on bronzes); Bopearachchi, 2015, pp. 201–48. A number of ivory products probably produced in Sātavāhana contexts have been found in the Roman world – notably a female figurine in Pompeii and a comb from Gorsium in Hungary: see, for example, Gupta, 1999, pp. 480–83. The fundamental publications on these objects are Levi D'Ancona, 1950; and Biro, 1985.
137 Contemporary positions on Gandhāra (post the extreme orientalist attitudes of the 1990s when it was politically impossible to assert connections with the West) are well exemplified in, for example, Filigenzi, 2012; Rienjang and Stewart, 2018 and 2019. For a very interesting recent intervention, see Stewart, 2020.
138 On the appropriation of late Roman coins, see Darley, 2015. On trade see, for example, Heitzman, 1984; Ramachandran, 1996, pp. 141–97, for the Krishna valley at the centre of trade routes looking east and west; Prabha Ray, 1994; Prabha Ray, 2003, pp. 165–244, 258–60; Tomber, 2008; Parker, 2008, pp. 147–202 (on commodities); Neelis, 2011, pp. 205–26, for movement between the Ganges valley and the Deccan; McLaughlin, 2014, pp. 172–95; Beaujard, 2019, pp. 385–483. For archaeology, see Nagaswamy, 1981; Nagaswamy, 1995; Krisha Sastry, 1998; Chowdhuri, 2018, pp. 189–220 (with an emphasis on merchants' inscriptions). For architecture of stūpas in relation to Roman art, see Kuwayama, 1997, pp. 119–31, 160–67. For objects moving east and west across the Indian Ocean, see Guy, 2023, pp. 182–9. For art history see Rosen, 1985; Rosen Stone, 1994, pp. 10–11, 29–30, 41, 78–80; Rosen Stone, 2005; Brancaccio, 2005; Rosen Stone, 2006, pp. 54–7; Brancaccio, 2014; Zin, 2015a and the references in n. 1; Rosen Stone, 2016; Zin, 2020, pp. 1–5.
139 See, for instance, Adrych and Dalglish, 2020a and 2020b, with bibliography.
140 See, for example, Osborne, 2011, pp. 185–215; Squire, 2011, pp. 154–201; Platt, 2011, pp. 77–123; Gaifman, 2015 and 2016; Mack, 2018.
141 Skorupski, undated, p. 28.
142 A good summary of the range of positions is Ray, 1999, pp. 404–21, taking in the arguments for southeast versus northwest, non-monastic or lay circles versus 'monasticization', forest renunciant origins versus institutional monastic ones. Further on current thinking about the origins of Mahāyāna, see Boucher, 2008, pp. ci–xvi; Morrissey, 2009, pp. 53–67; Williams, 2009, pp. 21–44; and Drewes, 2010 and Harrison, 2018.
143 See Lamotte, 1988, pp. 348–9.
144 Hoffmann, 1973; Wallace, 2001, p. 3.
145 Osto, 2008, pp. 108–9.
146 Cleary, 1993, pp. 1172–9, assuming the shrine to the east of the city of Dhanyakara is the stūpa of Amarāvatī, to the east of the city of Dhānyakataka.
147 See, for example, Wedemeyer, 2007, pp. 3–62, for discussion (esp. pp. 49–58 on Nāgārjuna and Āryadeva).
148 On Nāgārjuna and Andhra, see Mabbett, 1998, esp. p. 345; Walser, 2002, pp. 212, 250, 258–62; Walser, 2005, pp. 61–9, 79–88; Wayman, 2005; Ichimura, 2005; Yamano, 2008; Westerhoff, 2018, pp. 89–99, esp. 98; Ye, 2019, pp. 336. This (admittedly tentative) proposal is founded on three assumptions: 1. that the text known as the *Ratnāvalī* is correctly attributed to him; 2. that the discussion therein on buddhas on lotuses correctly places this artistic material in the south; 3. that there really was a connection with the Sātavāhana dynasty. All three points are at least contestable. We might add that the immensity of the

uncertainties are highly appropriate for any attempt to pin down the supreme philosopher of emptiness!

149 For example, Walser, 2002, pp. 231–2; Bareau, 2013, p. 422. Ramkumar Ratnam, 2008, pp. 115–16, places him on the Krishna River near Amarāvatī.

150 For Nāgārjuna, see Li, 1996, pp. 272–6 (10, 929a–930a). For Dignāga, see ibid., pp. 277–8 (10, 930bc), Bareau, 2013, p. 422, who places his birth at Kanchipuram in Tamil Nadu 100 kilometres (62 mi.) from Amarāvatī; and Potter, 2003, p. 312. For Bhāviveka, see Li, 1996, pp. 279–81 (10, 930c–931b). See Bareau, 2013, p. 422; Potter, 2003, p. 384; and Ratnam, 2008, pp. 116–18, for his origins in South India, before he went on to found the Svātantrika school of the Mahāyāna in the north. See also Eckel, 2008, pp. 9–11. For Dharmapāla of Nalanda, see Li, 1996, 282 (10, 931c); Bareau, 2013, p. 422; and Eckel, 2008, pp. 10–11.

151 Born in the south according to Ratnam, 2008, pp. 123–5.

152 Buddhaghosa was probably born in South India: see Hikosaka, 1989, p. 25; Malalasekera, 1994, pp. 79–101; Potter, 2003, pp. 110–11; Heim, 2014, pp. 7–8; Nyanatusita, 2021, p. 869. Buddhadatta was perhaps from Uragapura in Tamil Nadu: see Hikosaka, 1989, pp. 22–4; Malalasekera, 1994, pp. 105–12; Potter, 2003, pp. 216–17; Nyanatusita, 2021, p. 869. Dhammapāla was from Kanci in Tamil Nadu: see Hikosaka, 1989, pp. 25–6; Malalasekera, 1994, pp. 112–17. See also Monius, 2001, pp. 5–6.

153 See Wayman, 1978, pp. 42–3; Wayman and Wayman, 1990, pp. viii–ix, 1–4; Wayman and Rosen, 1990; Brown, 1991, p. 3; Rosen Stone, 1994, pp. 12–20; Barber, 2008, pp. 153–4.

154 Barber, 2008, pp. 154–6, although his attempts to locate a number of famous teachers – like Bodhidharma (who brought Chan/Zen to China) in Andhra before his departure, or Padmasambhava who brought important *Tantras* to Tibet, and a number of other named Indian missionaries of forms of Mahāyāna Buddhism, pp. 158–61 – are excessively speculative and largely unconvincing.

155 Hodge, 2006, pp. 3–5; Radich, 2015, pp. 74–5, 82, 202–5; Jones, 2021, pp. 218, 238.

156 See Gomez, 1967, pp. lxviii–lxxii; McMahan, 2002, p. 113; Osto, 2008, pp. 114–16.

157 See Osto, 2009.

158 For example, Kuan, 2013, pp. 163–83; Karashima, 2015, pp. 138–43; Karashima, 2017a, which also supports the likelihood of a particular association with and perhaps promotion of stūpas by the Mahāsāṃghika sect.

159 Xing, 2005, pp. 19–52.

160 See, for example, Endo, 1997, pp. 107–10; Xing, 2005, pp. 66–7. But for hints of an early *trikāya* theory in the Pāli canon, see Harrison, 1992a, p. 46. For the *dharmakāya* in early Buddhism see Jantrasrisalai, 2008, pp. 1–13 and 229–78, on the Pāli texts and early commentators, 13–22 review and critique of current scholarly positions; Appleton, 2010, pp. 132–5; in relation to the Jātaka traditions.

161 See Cousins, 2012, pp. 45–54; Holt and Padma, 2008, pp. 110–13.

162 See Xing, 2005, pp. 53–61, 67–8.

163 On the emblematic body, see Dehejia, 1991, pp. 54–6; and Dehejia, 1997, pp. 48–50.

164 Xing, 2005, pp. 69–181; Williams, 2009, pp. 172–86.

165 Xing, 2005, pp. 19, 111; Williams, 2009, pp. 177–9.

166 See Gomez, 1977; Osto, 2008, pp. 9–10, 23–4, 32–3, 88–9, 98, 102.

167 Skilling, 1996, pp. 159–61 (on Theravāda to about the time of Buddhaghosa in the fifth century) and pp. 168–71 on other schools.

168 Ibid., pp. 173–7; Dutt, 1978, p. 176, drawing on Vasubhandu's *Abhidharmakośa* and its discussion of the Sautrāntika school.

169 Skilling, 1996, p. 180.

170 Ibid., pp. 181–2.

171 *Mahāpadāna Sutta, Dīgha Nikāya* Sutta 14, ii.1–54, trans. M. Walshe.

172 On multiple buddhas, see, for example, Gombrich, 1980 and 1993, pp. 144–68; Collins, 1998, pp. 347–57, 378–83; Collins, 2010, pp. 126–84. On the formulaic lives of the Buddhas as repetitive time in the *Buddhavaṃsa*, see Collins, 1998, p. 261.

one APPROACH AND CIRCUMAMBULATION

1 Quotations translated by Walshe, 1987, pp. 264 and 277.

2 On Buddhist relics, see Strong, 2004; and Stargardt and Willis, 2018. For the fraught question of whether the terminology (utterly Christianizing) is appropriate and in what respects, see Skilling, 2018, p. 10. On reverence to relics in early Buddhist art: Huntington, 2012, pp. 18–29.

3 On stūpas see, for example, Mitra, 1971, pp. 21–30; Dallapiccola, 1980; Harvey, 1984; Jithendra Das, 1993, pp. 24–76 (specifically on Andhra); Benisti, 2003, pp. 1–102; Deeg, 2004; Prabha Ray, 2007, pp. 63–80; Hawkes and Shimada, 2009; Roth, 2009; Skorupski, 2013; Herdman, 2017, pp. 155–69 and 179–206; Skorupski, undated. On the terminology (the word stūpa goes back to Aśoka's inscribed edicts of the mid-third century BCE but the word *caitiya* is also used, for example, in the inscriptions at Amarāvatī), see Skilling, 2016; and Cousins, 2018. The terms for the elements of a stūpa are multiple and not entirely understood: see, for example, Settar, 2020, pp. 94–127; and esp. von Hinüber, 2016b.

4 In excavations of the stūpa at Bavikonda on the coast of Andhra, north of Amarāvatī, relic caskets containing nested reliquaries were found in each of the four cardinal directions: each had a stone urn in the shape of a coconut containing a terracotta jar with a knobbed lid filled with ash, a bone and a silver casket decorated with swastikas and lotuses within which was a gold phial decorated with swastikas and lotuses containing beads of coral, silver and pearls. See Prasad, 1993, pp. 4–7; Prasad, 1994, pp. 53–8; Subrahmanyam, 1998, pp. 71–9; Kedareswami, 2006, pp. 23–41; and Fogelin, 2006, p. 103.

5 See Venkateswara Rao, 1984, 69–70; Subrahmanyam, 1998, pp. 61–71, and Gupta, 2008, nos Q 936–1017 (museum accession numbers: 946–1068); see the gold reliquary in stūpa form found near a small stūpa by the southern gate in the 1908–9 dig in Rea, 1912, pl. xxvii; and Knox, 1992, pp. 41–2, fig. 21.

6 See Gupta, 2008, nos Q. 936, 966, 972, 988, 1005, 1012, 1013. For a list of archaeologically attested early Buddhist reliquaries from sites across India with casket-shapes, contents, materials and contexts see Prabha Ray, 2003, pp. 272–4. Generally for Buddhist reliquaries in India, see Subrahmanyam, 1998; Willis, 2000; Jongeward, Errington, Salomon and Baums, 2012; Stargardt and Willis, 2018.

7 See Schopen, 1997, pp. 126–8. For other reliquaries found in a large number of stūpas in Andhra, see Subrahmanyam, 1998, pp. 60–127.

8 See Marshall, Foucher and Majumdar, 1940, vol. I, p. 342, no. 404; with Schopen, 1997, pp. 128–9.

9 Schopen, 1997, pp. 129–31, with references, and at greater length on 'living presence' and property ownership, pp. 258–78.

10 Schopen, 1997, pp. 131–3, 134–5. Interestingly these attitudes are shared by sources from both the Nikāya and Mahāyāna traditions, and (Schopen, 1997, pp. 179–80, suggests) may have been extended from the Buddha to others over whose remains stūpas were raised. See also Fogelin, 2012, pp. 286–7.

11 See Strong, 2004, pp. 13–16. I agree with Hasan, 2013, pp. 45–6, that suggestions for western origins of the form are 'far-fetched' (not to say orientalist).

12 See generally Gururaja Rao, 1972, and on Andhra, pp. 181–212.

13 Notably the major Jain complex at Kankālī-Tīla, to the southwest of Mathurā, where a brick stūpa was excavated along with significant architectural fragments from railings and *toraṇa*: see, for example, Smith, 1901; Mitra, 1974, pp. 52–61; Cort, 2010, pp. 29–30, 126–30. On the complex issue of whether such Jain stūpas included relics or relic worship, see Bronkhorst, 2011, pp. 225–30.

14 *Nidānakathā* 52: 'The womb in which a Bodhisattva has lain is like the relic chamber of a shrine,' in Jayawickrama, 1990, 69. Compare also *Mahāvastu* 2.16 for the Buddha-embryo as 'a gem of beryl in a crystal casket' in Jones, 1952, p. 15.

15 Strong, 2004, pp. 62–3.

16 See Shimada, 2002; Radich, 2015, pp. 159–68; Jones, 2021, pp. 17–19.

17 Hodge, 2006, pp. 3–5; Radich, 2015, pp. 74–5, 82, 202–5; Jones, 2021, pp. 218, 238.

18 Subrahmanyam, 1998, pp. 69–71, for find-spots.

19 See Sanderson, 2009, pp. 129–32, with discussion of the date at n. 300.

20 See Sivaramamurti, 1956, p. 7. A. H. Longhurst found at least one relic container still intact at the northwest side of the great stūpa at Nāgārjunakonda: he assumes these were the only relics and that their odd placement meant they 'escaped the notice of the treasure-seekers who wrecked the monument': Longhurst, 1938, p. 17; but it may well be there were several reliquaries (for example, at the centre and at various points in the periphery) that the treasure hunters found.

21 For Nāgārjunakonda see Longhurst, 1938, pp. 12, 16, pl. XIIb; and Ramachandran, 1953, 6, with details at 8, 21. Generally in Andhra, see Sarkar, 1966, pp. 84–96; Rao, 1984, p. 18 (but without further documentation); Kumar, 2012, pp. 121–43; Chowdhuri, 2018, pp. 34–55. Wheel-shaped: Adyrru (Chowdhuri, 2018, p. 45), Alluru (Chowdhuri, 2018, p. 37), Bhattiprolu (Sarkar, 1966, pp. 88–9; Sarma, 1988, p. 31; Kumar, 2012, pp. 133–4; Chowdhuri, 2018, pp. 34–5), Ghantaśālā (Sarkar, 1966, pp. 90–91; Kumar, 2012, p. 141; Chowdhuri, 2018, pp. 36–7), Gummadidurru (Kumar, 2012, p. 138), Kodavalli (Kumar, 2012, p. 121), some at Nāgārjunakonda (Rao, 1984, p. 18; Kumar, 2012, p. 121), Nelakondapalli (Chowdhuri, 2018, pp. 51–2), Phanigiri (Chowdhuri, 2018, p. 52), Salihundam (see Subrahmaniyam, 1964, p. 27); *svastika*-centred: some at Nāgārjunakonda and Peddaganjam (Rao, 1984, p. 18; Kumar, 2012, pp. 121–2), also Gummadidurru (Kumar, 2012, p. 138); concentric circles: Vaddamānu (Chowdhuri, 2018, p. 44); the Great Stūpa at Nāgārjunakonda (with three concentric circles, eight spokes in the centre and sixteen in the two outer circles: Longhurst, 1938, p. XIIb).

22 Smith, 1901, pl. III; Mitra, 1974, pp. 53–4.

23 For some aspects of Jain railings and gates for stūpas in Mathura, see Quintanilla, 2007, pp. 37–50, 70–71.

24 Krishna valley stūpas with railings archaeologically attested include Bavikonda (Chowdhuri, 2018, p. 47); Bhattiprolu (Kumar, 2012, pp. 133–4); Ghantaśālā (Kumar, 2012, p. 141); Goli (Chowdhuri, 2018, pp. 37–8, if we believe the two excavated pillars with half-lotuses to imply a lost railing). Stūpas without railings include Nāgārjunakonda, though some have argued for a wooden railing there (Longhurst, 1938, p. 16; Ramachandran, 1953, p. 7; Rosen Stone, 1994, p. 60; Kumar, 2012, p. 123; Chowdhuri, 2018, p. 40), and Jaggayyapeta (Burgess, 1887, p. 107, assuming it existed but is entirely lost: 'The rail had entirely disappeared . . . not a fragment of it could be found').

25 Marshall, 1951, p. 233; Behrendt, 2004, pp. 53–4, 60, 236–7; Hasan, 2003, p. 48.

26 In the words of Strong, 2004, p. 98, the sutta 'ends and culminates in the distribution of the Buddha's relics. Far from being a postscript, these relics are in fact the governing motif that helps determine the shape and format of the Buddha's obsequies.' For Buddhaghosa's fifth-century comments on this passage, see An, 2003, pp. 217–25. For stūpas in the *jātakas*, the narratives of the Bodhisattva's previous lives, see Rana, 2013, p. 12, citing the *Sujātā* and *Mahākapi Jātakas*, in Francis and Neil, 1897, no. 353, pp. 103–4 and no. 406, pp. 225–7. On the complicated issues around the Buddha's funeral and then his relics, see, for example, Schopen, 1996, pp. 99–113; and Silk, 2006.

27 Marshall, Foucher and Majumdar, 1940, pp. 29–30 (main stūpa), 45–6 (stūpas 6 and 7, dressed in masonry but at a later period than the original foundation); Maisey, 1892, p. 10, reports fragments of the exterior coating of plaster '4 inches thick' on the main stūpa, and at p. 67 denies any outer coating to the exterior of stūpa 2.

28 Cunningham, 1879, pp. 4–5.

29 For example, Marshall, 1951, p. 143; Behrendt, 2003, pp. 163–6.

30 Such as the Dharmajarika in Taxila, Manikyala, Jamal Garhi and Butkara-I in Swat: see Marshall, 1960, p. 99; Hasan, 2003, p. 48.

31 See, for example, Benisti, 2003, pp. 121–56, on '*stūpas* with five pillars'.

32 Marshall, Foucher and Majumdar, 1940, p. 30 and pl. 4 (main stūpa), pp. 80–81 and pl. 71 (stūpa 2), pp. 41–2 and pl. 92 (stūpa 3).

33 Cunningham, 1879, 6 and pls II and III; Marshall, Foucher and Majumdar, 1940, pls 71 and 92.

34 See Cunningham, 1879, pp. 6–8 and pls III, VI–IX; Ghosh, 1978, pp. 6–8.

35 Hasan, 2003, p. 48 for the platform.

36 Sānchī: Marshall, Foucher and Majumdar, 1940, pp. 36–7, 43–4, 109–59, 193–237; Bharhut: Cunningham, 1879, pp. 6–8 and pl. III.

37 Coomaraswamy, 1956, p. 18, argues that *toraṇas* mark the boundary between sacred and profane.

38 Exceptions include Phanigiri, where there are the architectural fragments of a *toraṇa*: see Settar, 2020, p. 108 and Guy, 2023, pp. 248–50, as well as a fragment perhaps from Kesanapalli and epigraphic attestation of a *toraṇa* at Ghantaśālā (see Guy, 2023, pp. 246–7).

39 Knox, 1992, p. 28.

40 The evidence for this is not archaeological but that such pillars appear on many of the slabs depicting stūpas from the site: see ibid., p. 28. That depends on expecting a high degree of realism in these reliefs that can be read back into the original monument. The assumptions for this are at best shaky: see Elsner, 2022.

41 See Stern and Bénisti, 1961, pp. 21–5, on the '*torana* figuré' motif at Amarāvatī; also Pandya Dhar, 2009, pp. 18–20.

42 See BM 1880,0709.51, Knox, 1992, no. 103. See also the fragment of a parallel panel (with the gate on the left side and the horse moving to the right) in Chennai: GMC no. 192; Sivaramamurti, 1956, p. 166, no. II A 4–6; Kannan, 2014, p. 192. This latter was drawn in a complete state by Colin Mackenzie's draughtsmen in the early nineteenth century: Album WD1061, folio 28, in Sivaramamurti, 1956, p. 166, fig. 5; and Fergusson, 1873, pp. 217–18, pl. CVIII, 2.

43 Stern and Benisti, 1961: for coping friezes of the inner railing, see figs 18, 19, 22, pls XXIIIa and b, XLVc; medallions of the inner railing crossbars, see fig. 20, pl. XXV b; railing uprights, see fig. 24, pl. LV; dome slabs, see figs 21 and 23, pls XLVI, LIV.

44 On Aśoka and the Buddha's relics, see Strong, 1983, pp. 109–19; Strong, 2004, pp. 124–49; Skilling, 2018, pp. 11–13; Milligan, 2019, pp. 5–9. For a searching account of the meanings of relics in Andhra, focused on Nāgārjunakonda, see Schopen, 1997, pp. 148–61. For some representational traditions of the early relics see Zin, 2016c, pp. 757–76.

45 See Marshall, 1955, p. 32: the 'balustrade . . . of plain design unrelieved by carvings of any kind'. Very little of the railing survives for stūpa 3 at Sāñcī: Marshall, Foucher and Majumdar, 1940, p. 43.

46 For a list of scholars affirming this view see Schopen, 1997, p. 112, n.7; at pp. 30–34, 92–4, 99–111 he provides a compelling series of arguments against it; see also Fogelin, 2006, pp. 47–51; Fogelin, 2012, pp. 278–9.

47 *Mahāparinibbāna Sutta* 5.8, *Dīgha Nikāya* Sutta 16, ii.141. Trans. M. Walshe, pp. 263–4. See also Buddhaghosa's fifth-century commentary from the *Sumangalavilāsinī* in An, 2005, pp. 153–5. The effect of this quality of *samvega* is wonderfully captured in our earliest account of the Chinese pilgrims who came to India, by Faxian in about 400 CE. For instance: 'When Faxian and To-ching arrived at . . . Jetavana, they reflected that this was the spot where the Lord of men has passed 25 years of his life: they themselves at the risk of their lives, were now dwelling among foreigners; of those who with like purpose had travelled through a succession of countries with them, some had returned home, some were dead; and now, gazing on the place where Buddha once dwelt but was no longer to be seen, their hearts were affected with lively regret', *Travels of Faxian* XX, in Beal, 1884, p. xlv. Or 'Faxian, ascending the Gridhrakuta mountain, offered flowers and incense and lit lamps for the night. Being deeply moved, he could scarcely restrain his tears as he said, "Here in bygone days Buddha dwelt and delivered the *Śurangama Sutra*. Faxian, not privileged to be born when the Buddha lived, can but gaze on the traces of his presence and the place which he occupied." Then he recited the *Śurangama* in front of the cave, and remaining there all night, he returned to the new town' (XXIX, in Beal, 1884, p. lx).

48 On Kanaganahalli, see Nakanishi and von Hinüber, 2014, nos V.1.1–4 and V.2.1–18. On Bharhut, see Lüders, Waldschmidt and Mehendale, 1963, nos A 56–80 (monks and nuns), A 5–55 and A 81–128 (laypersons); Dehejia, 1997, pp. 277–80. On Sāñcī, see Marshall, Foucher and Majumdar, 1940, pp. 297–9, for a summary.

49 Chakravarti, 1987, pp. 58–62.

50 I calculate the circumference from the diameter measurement given by Knox, 1992, p. 23. Generally on railings (the ornamental *vedikā*) see Benisti, 2003, pp. 103–18.

51 Knox, 1992, p. 23; Shimada, 2013, pp. 82–3, with more precision on the slightly different sizes at different phases.

52 Knox, 1992, pp. 23–6; Shimada, 2013, p. 83. It should be added that there has been no adequate art-historical account of the incredible virtuosity and versatility of the lotus-theme at Amarāvatī. Stella Kramrisch remarks 'never hitherto has the lotus creeper been so delicately burdened with ingenious flowers': Kramrisch, 1933, p. 35.

53 See, for example, Brown, 1942, pp. 5–6, 14 (in relation to the rail at Sāñcī); Benisti, 2003, p. 104.

54 Burgess, 1887, p. 25; Barrett, 1954, p. 30; Knox, 1992, p. 26; Shimada, 2013, p. 82: these figures were calculated by Burgess and repeated since; no one so far as I know has attempted to review them.

55 I am hesitant to interpret the luxuriant floral imagery of the stūpa in terms of 'nature' or as utopian space, as has recently been suggested by Brown, 2009, since this extends beyond the interpretative frame of the Buddhist builders of such monuments, but he is right that stūpas were open to the plurality of non-Buddhists in India and that we do need to think about the stūpa 'in other than Buddhist terms' (p. 80).

56 Figure 14 (BM 1880,0709.28, Knox, 1992, no. 2) is thought in fact to be the inner face of a relatively early pillar, but no intact examples of outward-facing simple pillars have survived.

57 For discussion of the exterior crossbar lotuses, see Rana, 2013, pp. 31–4.

58 For example, BM 1880,0709.24, BM 1880,0709.28, BM 1880,0709.81, BM 1880,0709.110, respectively Knox, 1992, nos 1, 2, 3 and 4: all of these are inner faces of the stūpa railing with the possible exception of BM 1880,0709.81 (Knox, 1992, no. 3), which was removed at some stage from the railing, recut into a miniature stūpa on the back and reused on the main drum (Knox, 1992, no. 74). For early exterior examples, see also Seattle Art Museum no. 51.95, in Trubner, Rathbun and Kaputa, 1973, 90, no. 3; and Rana, 2013, pp. 20–21, no. 2.9; and the fragment in the India Museum, Calcutta, in Rana, 2013, p. 21, no. 2.11.

59 For example, BM 1880,0709.46 and BM 1880,0709.110, respectively Knox, 1992, nos 5 (outer face) and 4 (outer face); for art-historical discussion, see Stern and Bénisti, 1961, pp. 25–6.

60 For example, BM 1880,0709.4, BM 1880,0709.7, BM 1880,0709.11, BM 1880,0709.14, BM 1880,0709.17, BM 1880,0709.47, respectively Knox, 1992, nos 6 (outer face), 7 (outer face), 10, 12 (outer face), 13 (outer face), 14 (outer face).

61 For discussion see Walser, 2005, pp. 81–7, with examples and bibliography.

62 *Dhammapāda* 4.44–5, trans. Acariya Buddharakkhita.

63 For example, BM 1880,0709.7, BM 1880,0709.81, respectively Knox, 1992, nos 11 (outer face), 3.

64 BM 1880,0709.4, BM 1880,0709.46, BM 1880,0709.110, respectively Knox, 1992, nos 6 (outer face), 5 (outer face), 4 (outer face).

65 For examples with lotus-framing friezes in good condition, see BM 1880,0709.19/20, Knox, 1992, no. 36; Gupta, 2008, no. D 259, fig XIV (ii).

66 BM 1880,0709.81, Knox, 1992, no. 3.

67 Details are not easy to make out, but it looks as if the standing figures outside the railing, in a number of slabs representing stūpas, are holding flowers – possibly purchased from seated vendors at the outer edges of the panel: see BM 1880,0709.70, BM 1880,0709.79, BM 1880,0709.120, BM 1880,0709.121, BM 1880,0709.122, respectively Knox, 1992, nos 69, 72, 78, 79, 80.

68 *Theragāthā* vv. 700–701, trans. A. Olendzki.

69 *Aṅguttara Nikaya*, Book of the Fours, II.38, sutta 36 (Doṇa), trans. Bhikkhu Bodhi, p. 426.

70 *Dhammapāda* vv.58–59, trans. Acariya Buddharakkhita.

71 See *Buddhavaṃsa* IIA, verses 50–51, in Horner, 1975, p. 14, with Buddhadatta's commentary in Horner, 1978, pp. 128–30.

72 See Matsumura, 2012.

73 See GMC nos 136–9, 141–5, in Kannan, 2014, pp. 173–6; Burgess, 1887, p. 67, pl. XXIX, 1–3; Sivaramamurti, 1956, p. 158, nos I B 2–7, pl. XV, 2–3. In BM, see Knox, 1992, p. 39 (types 1 and 2) and 89–91, nos 31–4; Rana, 2013, p. 39, nos 2.42 a–d.

74 See Burgess, 1887, p. 52.

75 See the characteristic triangular shape of the half-open lotuses at the lower right of BM 1880,0709.30, Knox, 1992, no. 44; Rana, 2013, p. 45, no. 2.51 (though she mistakenly claims this fragment is in the Amarāvatī site museum).

76 See BM 1880,0709.19/20, BM 1880,0709.29, BM 1880,0709.30, BM 1880,0709.31, BM 1880,0709.33, respectively Knox, 1992, nos 36 (outer face), 43, 44, 39, 45; GMC nos 63, 64, 72, 134, 153, 160, in Kannan, 2014, pp. 150, 152, 172, 179, 181; also Sivaramamurti, 1956, p. 219, nos III B 11–25 (backs); Burgess, 1887, 55–61, pl. XX–XXVI; see Stern and Bénisti, 1961, pp. 28–30, for some discussion.

77 For instance, in Chennai see GMC no. 134 (outer side) in Kannan, 2014, pp. 172–3, where only the inner frieze is discussed or illustrated with HAABA 27762, 27763; and Burgess, 1887, pl. XX.1.

78 I am not sure why Burgess and Sivaramamurti call these elements 'shields' (for example, Burgess, 1887, pp. 54, 56), but I have avoided the term.

79 For example, BM 1880,0709.31, Knox, 1992, no. 39 – in good condition; GMC nos 134, 153 (outer sides) in Sivaramamurti, 1956, nos III B 20, 21, 23; and Burgess, 1887, pp. 55–61, pl. XX–XXVI (still far and away the best-illustrated and most extensive discussion).

80 For example, BM 1880,0709.29, Knox, 1992, no. 43; Rana, 2013, p. 44, no. 2.50 (in the Amarāvatī Archaeological museum).

81 For example, GMC no. 123, in Sivaramamurti, 1956, no. III B 23; Gupta, 2008, no. D 259, fig. XIV (ii) – in exceptional condition.

82 For example, BM 1880,0709.33, Knox, 1992, no. 45.

83 For example, BM 1880,0709.19–20, BM 1880,0709.29, BM 1880,0709.31, respectively, Knox, 1992, nos 36, 43, 39; Burgess, 1887, pl. XX.1, XXI.1, XXII.1, XXIII.1, XXIV.2, XXV.5–6, XXVI.2.

84 For examples with lotus framing friezes in good condition, see BM 1880,0709.19/20, Knox, 1992, no. 36; Gupta, 2008, no. D 259, fig XIV (ii).

85 GMC nos 160 and 75, respectively Kannan, 2014, pp. 181 and 153.

86 BM 1880,0709.21 exterior, Knox, 1992, no. 35.

87 For instance, BM 1880,0709.83, BM 1880,0709.85, BM 1880,0709.87, BM 1880,0709.121, respectively, Knox, 1992, nos 75, 76, 77, 79.

88 For Kumāralāta, see esp. Loukota Sanclemente, 2019, pp. 35–50 on the author, pp. 85–7 for influence on other collections like the *Divyāvadāna*, 143 as a precedent for Āryaśūra. For Āryaśūra, see, for example, Khoroche, 1989, pp. xi–xix.

89 Slabs with such vendors include: AMA, nos 1 and 235, respectively Gupta, 2008, F 340 (HAABA 0021280), F 347; GMC nos 30–32 at Kannan, 2014, pp. 139; GMC no. 225 at Kannan, 2014, p. 202 (HAABA 0027752); GMC no. 235 at Kannan, 2014, p. 205 (HAABA 0027750); BM 1880,0709.69, BM 1880,0709.70, BM 1880,0709.72, BM 1880,0709.75, BM 1880,0709.79, BM 1880,0709.87, BM 1880,0709.120, BM 1880,0709.121, BM 1880,0709.122, respectively, Knox, 1992, nos 68, 69, 70, 71, 72, 77, 78, 79, 80; Boston 29.151.

90 See Knox, 1992, p. 27.

91 Ibid., 1992, p. 24, figs 9 and 10; Barrett, 1954, p. 28, fig. 2.

92 See Burgess, 1887, p. 28, pl. VI ('between the south and west gates', a pillar fragment in two segments, with historiated medallion, only one of which is illustrated in Kannan, 2014, p. 130 as GMC no. 3), p. 33, pl. IX ('northeast', a pillar fragment with historiated medallion, not in Kannan, 2014 – has it been lost?), p. 46, pl. XVII.2 ('middle of the south-west quadrant', a lotus crossbar boss, perhaps GMC no. 273, in Kannan, 2014, p. 216), p. 46, pl. XVII.4 ('middle of the west quadrant', a historiated crossbar with worship of the flaming column, BM 1880,0709.119, in Knox, 1992, no. 28), p. 47, pl. XVIII.1 ('southwest', a lotus crossbar), p. 48, pl. XVIII.3 ('north-west quadrant', crossbar with worship of the Bodhi tree, GMC no. 157, in Kannan, 2014, pp. 180), p. 48, pl. XVIII.4 ('northeast', crossbar with stūpa worship, GMC no. 150, in Kannan, 2014, p. 178).

93 Notably the crossbar found by Burgess west of the south entrance, which had previously been drawn by Mackenzie's draughtsmen seventy years earlier (Album WD1061, folio 65): Burgess, 1887, p. 45, pl. XVII.1, GMC no. 132, in Kannan, 2014, p. 172.

94 Burgess, 1887, p. 32, pl. VIII and p. 35, pl. XI.3–4 (pillars from the north gateway), p. 46, pl. XVII.3 ('near the west entrance', a crossbar lotus boss), p. 48, pl. XVIII.2 ('near the north gate', historiated crossbar boss,), p. 50, pl. XIX.2 ('east side of the south entrance', historiated crossbar boss), p. 51, pl. XIX.3 (north of the western entrance', lotus crossbar boss with stūpa in the centre), p. 51, pl. XIX.4 ('south of the east entrance', lotus crossbar boss), p. 57, pl. XXIII.4 ('near the south gate', coping frieze), p. 59, fig. 15 ('close to the south gate', coping frieze), p. 62, pl. XXVII.2 ('north gate', coping frieze), p. 62, pl. XXVII.3 (north gate 'near the last', coping frieze).

95 For the *dharmacakra*, see Lüders, 1912, pp. 1–226, no. 1248 (= Sivaramamurti, 1956, pp. 283–4, nos II E 6–7 and no. 51). For the *divathabha*, see Lüders, 1912, no. 1214. For the pillar with a relic, see Burgess, 1887, p. 86, and Sivaramamurti, 1956, pp. 172–3, no. II E 5 and inscription no. 50. For the lost gifts, see Lüders, 1912, no. 1255 (= Sivaramamurti, 1956, pp. 284–5, no. II E 25 and no. 55) recording 'a meritorious gift' (it is not clear of what) 'made at the southern gate'; Chanda, 1919–20, pp. 258–75, no. 56 (a slab of some kind 'at the south side of the main gate' – whatever entrance that is meant to be: there is some evidence that the principal position which the Buddha should face was either south or east, which would imply either of those as the 'main gate; see Nakamura, 1951, p. 352).

96 See Burgess, 1887, pp. 97–9; Barrett, 1954, p. 38; Quagliotti, 1998, p. 119.

97 Measurements in Barrett, 1954, pp. 29, 36; and Knox, 1992, pp. 28–9, with my calculation of the area.

98 For an art-historical discussion, see Stern and Bénisti, 1961, pp. 9–16.

99 For example, BM 1880,0709.10, BM 1880,0709.47, respectively Knox, 1992, nos 7 and 10 (outer face); also AMA no 1023, Gupta, 2008, no. B 6 (HAABA 0012079).

100 For example, BM 1880,0709.19, BM 1880,0709.31, respectively Knox, 1992, nos 36 (outer face), 39; also AMA no. 433, Gupta, 2008, no. D 259, exterior fig XIV (ii); GMC nos 134, 153, 154, 160, in Kannan, 2014, pp. 172 (HAABA 0027764), 179 (HAABA 0027760–1), 179 (HAABA 0027758), 181 (HAABA 0027757), also Sivaramamurti, 1956, nos III E 13, III E 14; Museum of Fine Arts, Boston, no. 21.1516, in Coomaraswami, 1923, p. 56.

101 For example, BM 1880,0709.8, Knox, 1992, no. 27 (where the stūpa is a reliquary casket); GMC no. 150, in Kannan, 2014, pp. 178 (HAABA 0027669, a fine scene of stūpa worship); AMA no. 434, Gupta, 2008, no. C 189. See the unusual incised crossbar with a stūpa and Bodhi tree in the AMA no. 50, Gupta, 2008, no. C 77, pl. 5.

102 For example, BM 1880,0709.19, BM 1880,0709.34, BM 1880,0709.108, respectively Knox, 1992, nos 36 (inner face), 40, 46.

103 For example, BM 1880,0709.91, BM 1880,0709.107, respectively Knox, 1992, nos 53, 51; see GMC nos 226, 227, 230, 236, 239, 242, 256, in Kannan, 2014, pp. 203–12.

104 For example, BM 1880,0709.73, BM 1880,0709.82, BM 1880,0709.85, BM 1880,0709.86, respectively Knox, 1992, nos 83–6.

105 BM 1880,0709.94, BM 1880,0709.95, BM 1880,0709.96, BM 1880,0709.97, BM 1880,0709.114, BM 1880,0709.115, respectively Knox, 1992, nos 88, 90, 91, 92, 94, 95; see AMA nos 12, 25, 27, 163, 177, 209, 221, 222, 240, 243, 268, 310, 311, 312, 374, 385, 394, 502, 876, respectively Gupta, 2008, no. G 393, pl. 29 (HAABA 0021288), G 394, pl. 30 (HAABA 0021290), G 395, pl. 32 (HAABA 0021341), G 410, G 412, G 418, G 421, G 422, G 426, G 429, G 432, G 433, G 434, G 435, G 439, G 442, G 448, G 462, G 489; GMC no. 255, in Kannan, 2014, p. 212, and Sivaramamurti, 1956, p. 258, no. IV A 13 (HAABA 0027740).

106 BM 1880,0709.45, BM 1880,0709.109, respectively Knox, 1992, pp. 116 and 109 (face g): AMA no. 43, Gupta, 2008, no. E 278; GMC nos 174 and 247, in Kannan, 2014, pp. 186 (a fine stūpa at the base of an octagonal pillar) and 209 (octagonal pillar with Buddha images and stūpas).

107 For instance, on Bharhut, see Lüders, 1941, pp. 21–5.

108 See Becker, 2015, pp. 23–77; her terminology follows W.J.T. Mitchell's model of 'meta-pictures': Mitchell, 1994, p. 57.

109 See Casalini, 2021, p. 113.

110 See *Aśokāvadāna* 52–5 in Strong, 1983, pp. 219–21, with discussion at pp. 109–19.

111 One photograph is from Rea, 1909, pl. L. a; reproduced by Knox, 1992, p. 25, fig. 11; a second different view is reproduced by Marshall, 1907, pl. VII.2 facing p. 1006; a third different again is in the archives of the Archaeological Survey of India, reproduced by Rosen Stone, 1994, fig. 72. The votive stūpa in this case had eight relief panels without framing pilasters, one of which represents a stūpa without a railing or as if seen from within the railing. Surviving stūpa panels from this small stūpa are in the AMA: see Gupta, 2008, pp. 53–7 incorrectly presented there as if from the Mahācaitiya, nos F. 339, pl. 19 (without railing, HAABA 21281); F. 341, pl. 21 (HAABA 21301); F. 342, pl. 22 (HAABA 21298); F. 352, fig. XXIV (HAABA 21218).

112 GMC no. 221. For some discussion see Burgess, 1887, pp. 70–73; Sivaramamurti, 1956, pp. 263–4, no. IV C 1; Becker, 2006, pp. 43–51; Rana, 2013, pp. 54–5; Kannan, 2014, p. 201. See also, briefly, Becker, 2015, pp. 38–40.

113 I report the measurements of Kannan, 2014, p. 201. Burgess, 1887, p. 70, gives different figures: 173 centimetres in height and 178 centimetres wide (68 × 70 in.), with the central section representing the stūpa 126 centimetres high and 122 centimetres wide (49 × 48 in.). He may be right. Unfortunately, Sivaramamurti, 1956, pp. 263–4, does not provide measurements.

114 Taken as exemplary also by Shimada, 2013, pp. 106–7.

115 See much of the actual surviving coping, such as the examples in Knox, 1992, nos 36 (outer face), pp. 93–5; 39, p. 98; pp. 43–5, pp. 103–5. On the imagery of garlands in the Amarāvatī sculptures, see Stern and Bénisti, 1961, pp. 26–33.

116 None of the other drum slabs in the Amarāvatī or Chennai Museums extend to this level of detail to show imagery immediately behind and above the railing, but several examples in the British Museum do so. BM 1880,0709.87, Knox, 1992, no. 77, has *dharmacakras* and *nāgas*, and like the Chennai example discussed here, also a *dharmacakra* over the empty throne in the gateway. BM 1880,0709.70, Knox, 1992, no. 69, has *dharmacakras*. BM 1880,0709.75, Knox, 1992, no. 71, have *dharmacakras* and stūpas. BM 1880,0709.69 and BM 1880,0709.72, respectively Knox, 1992, nos 68 and 70, have the Bodhi tree, *dharmacakras* and stūpas. The stūpa images – we see only the upper dome and multiple umbrellas – do not resemble the drum panels of the form being discussed here (with complex railings and greatly detailed sculptural decoration) but a form of stūpa panel without railing and without deities around the drum, replacing these with a profusion of umbrellas. Such panels – usually dated earlier than the stūpas with railings – do survive, for example, BM 1880,0709.39, Knox, 1992, no. 64; AMA nos 2 and 24, Gupta, 2008, nos F 339 (pl. 19) and 338 (pl. 18).

117 See GMC nos 92 and 98, in Kannan, 2014, pp. 158 and 161; Sivaramamurti, 1956, p. 248, nos III F 1–3 (also pls LVIII, 1–2); Knox, 1992, nos 118–19; AMA nos 92, 108, 371, 423, in Gupta, 2008, nos J 691, 693, 706, 711,

118 See, for example, Rea, 1912, pp. 88–9, esp. pl. XXIX a–d, pl. XXX d.; Knox, 1992, pp. 193–208, nos 109–17.

119 The iconographic parallels for this drum decoration are with a fine but much-abraded drum slab now in the British Museum with the same imagery in the central gateway: Knox, 1992, pp. 149–51, no. 77.

120 So at least says Sivaramamurti, 1956, p. 264; followed by Becker, 2006, p. 46, with tentative suggestions. No one has analysed or discussed these in detail in print to my knowledge.

121 The assumption that a stūpa image, especially in the context of tree and Dharma Wheel symbols, signifies the death and *parinibbāna* of the Buddha is ubiquitous in, for example, Knox, 1992; Ebert, 1985, pp. 34–52; or Ebert, 2022, pp. 87–91.

122 For the stories, represented here in visual versions prior to and perhaps belonging to different Buddhist traditions from

the texts best attested in the tradition now, one might site the Pāli account of the 'intermediate epoch' (or 'not-so-remote antecedent') in the *Nidānakathā* introduction to the *jātakas* (sections 47–77), probably written in the fifth century CE in the Theravāda tradition (Jayawickrama, 1990, pp. 63–101); the Sanskrit, Pāli and Prakrit *Mahāvastu*, compiled between the second century BCE and the fourth century CE, from a school in the Mahāsāṃghika tradition (Jones, 1952, vol. II); the Sanskrit *Buddhacarita* of Aśvaghoṣa, probably from the second century CE (see Schotsman, 1995; and Olivelle, 2008). See Tournier and Strong, 2019, for recent discussion.

123 This story – frequent in the visual tradition (for example, the famous panel BM 1880,0709.44, Knox, 1992, no. 61, or Pandya Dhar, 2021, pp. 160–61) – is not told in the texts in the way it appears in the visual culture, although it is cited in an epigraph from Kanaganahalli attached to a scene with this iconography: see Quintanilla, 2017, pp. 126–35. A textual version appears for example in the pilgrimage of King Aśoka within the perhaps second-century *Aśokavādana* 82–3, where the king is brought to meet the tree spirit (female in this text) who witnessed the Buddha's birth and the first steps: see Strong, 1983, pp. 245–7. For the parallel theme of a sage foretelling the child will be a Buddha, see *Nidānakathā* 54–5, in Jayawickrama, 1990, pp. 72–3; *Mahāvastu* 2.30–43, in Jones, 1952, pp. 27–40.

124 *Nidānakathā* 57–8 in Jayawickrama, 1990, pp. 77; *Mahāvastu* 2.45–7, in Jones, 1952, pp. 42–5. On *jhāna*, see, for example, Cousins, 2022, pp. 3–70; and for the scholarly controversy about its meanings in early Buddhism, see Bucknell, 2023, pp. 192–215, 249. For an account in relation to neuroscience, see Dennison, 2022, pp. 29–166.

125 AMA no. 19, Gupta, 2008, pp. 55–6, no. F 341.

126 Further on Kaṁthaka, see Ohnuma, 2017, pp. 101–28.

127 Becker, 2006, p. 45, says it is a seated image of the Buddha, but uses 'Buddha' to mean both the Bodhisattva before his enlightenment and the Buddha afterwards.

128 For some analysis of narrativity at Amarāvatī and elsewhere in the Andhra stūpas, see Dehejia, 1997, pp. 150–82; Rana, 2013, pp. 76–127; Becker, 2015, pp. 78–143; Zin, 2016 (emphasizing how many of the visual narratives cannot be identified).

129 For discussion of the frieze, Becker, 2006, pp. 48–9.

130 See Kannan, 2014, p. 201, following Sivaramamurti, 1956, p. 298, no. 102, revising Burgess, 1887, p. 72, pl. 1 and lvii, no. 17; and Luders, 1912, no. 1281; also Becker, 2006, pp. 65–6.

131 On meta-narratives and meta-meta-narratives in the drum slabs representing stūpas, see Becker, 2015, pp. 137–43.

132 See Barrett, 1956; Stern and Bénisti, 1961, pl. VIIIb; Dehejia, 1997, pp. 152–3 (and figure 129); and Becker, 2015, pp. 38–40.

133 For BM 1880, 0709.79, see Knox, 1992, nos 60 and 72 (for the two sides), pp. 119–20 and 139–41. For Boston 29.151, see Coomaraswamy, 1923, p. 56; Becker, 2015, pp. 36–8.

134 For instance, the dome panel refashioned as a *buddhapāda* slab, Knox, 1992, nos 99 and 120, pp. 178, 211; also Knox, 1992, nos 50 and 113, pp. 110–11 and 200; nos 57 and 65, pp. 116–17, 126–7; no. 101, pp. 180–83.

135 See, for example, Knox, 1992, pp. 9–14; Shimada, 2013, pp. 59–112.

136 Knox, 1992, p. 28.

137 Shimada, 2013, p. 107 and table 7, p. 108, but figures corrected by reference to the measurements of relatively complete slabs in Knox, 1993, for example, nos 68, p. 131; 69, p. 132; 79, p. 136; 72, p. 141; 77, p. 150.

138 For example, Knox, 1992, pp. 119–24, nos 60–63. Knox argues, following Barrett, 1954, p. 48, that these panels may have come not from the drum but from the *āyaka* platforms: p. 41.

139 GMC no. 221, in Kannan, 2014, p. 201 with HAABA 0027624 (detail) and 0027636 (for the stūpa engraved in the central *āyaka* pillar, see also illus. 26 above); BM 1880,0709.79, BM 1880,0709.80, BM 1880,0709.81, BM 1880,0709.83, BM 1880,0709.85, Knox, 1992, nos 72, 73, 74, 75, 76: also among Mackenzie's drawings of now lost slabs BL WD1061, folio 34.

140 GMC no. 229, in Kannan, 2014, p. 203 (HAABA 007751) and BM 1880,0709.107, Knox, 1992, no. 51.

141 For example, Sivaramamurti, 1956, p. 264; Knox, 1992, pp. 129, 138, 144, 146, 147, 149, 152, 152–3, 155; Becker, 2015, p. 66.

142 The fragments of one such statue survive in the Chennai Museum, GMC no. 16, in Kannan, 2014, p. 135. There appear to have been statues of Yakshas outside the railing to the left of the entrances, in the place where the dwarf figures are shown in the Amarāvatī stūpa reliefs, with stone offering bowls over their heads, at the Kanaganahalli stūpa: see Poonacha, 2011, pp. 53, 65 (pls XVIIA–C, XVIIIA).

143 BM 1880,0709.122 in Knox, 1992, no. 80, p. 154.

144 Becker, 2015, p. 67, comes close to this suggestion.

145 In the AMA nos 1, 8, 19, 417, 418, respectively Gupta, 2008, nos F 340, 362, 341, 351 (fig. XXIII), F. 352 (fig. XXIV); BM 1880,0709.87 and BM 1880,0709.121, respectively Knox, 1992, nos 77 and 79.

146 In the AMA nos 1, 19, 418 Gupta, 2008, nos F 340, 341, 352.

147 AMA no. 8, Gupta, 2008, F 362 (HAABA 0021287); BM 1880,0709.87, Knox, 1992, no. 77.

148 GMC no. 241 (HAABA 0027749) in Sivaramamurti, 1956, p. 265, no. IV C 8; and Kannan, 2014, pp. 207; BM 1880,0709.72, Knox, 1992, no. 70; lost slabs among Mackenzie's drawings: BL WD1061, fols 33 and 67. The story of the Buddha's seven-day meditation during a great storm at the foot of the Mucalinda tree, while protected by the serpent king, who encircled his body seven times with his coils and 'spread a great hood over his head', is told in *Mahāvagga* 1.3.1–4, Vin. I.4, in Horner, 1951, pp. 4–5; also in the *Mucalindavagga* of the *Udāna* 2.1, Ud.10, in Masefield, 1994a, 19, with Dhammapāla's commentary (dated any time between the fifth and the tenth century) in Masefield, 1994b, vol. I, pp. 263–5 (section 100 of the commentary).

149 GMC nos 30, 225, 234–5, 254, respectively in Kannan, 2014, pp. 139, 202, 205, 212; Sivaramamurti, 1956, pp. 264–6, nos IV C 5–7, IV C 10, IV C 13 (= HAABA 0027752); BM 1880,0709.75, Knox, 1992, no. 71; Boston no. 29.151; lost slabs among Mackenzie's drawings: BL WD1061, fols 79 (where the Buddha does not adopt the *abhāya* posture) and 80. The seated Buddha also appears in Sivaramamurti, 1956, p. 265, no. IV C 9 (HAABA 0027750), a slab whose inscription implies that it was set up on a small stūpa within the site rather than on the main monument itself – see Sivaramamurti, 1956, p. 299 inscription no. 103 – but which Mackenzie's drawing and note suggests was found on the 'inner circle east side', that is, by the drum of the main stūpa (see BL WD1061, fol. 55).

150 BM 1880,0709.70 and 79, Knox, 1992, nos 69 and 72; also AMA no. 457, Gupta, 2008, F 356; lost slabs among Mackenzie's drawings: BL WD1061, fols 70, 71 and 78.

151 BM 1880,0709.70, 120 and 79, Knox, 1992, nos 69, 78 and 72; from Mackenzie's album: BL WD1061, fol. 33.
152 BM 1880,0709.72, Knox, 1992, no. 70 (very abraded but much clearer in Mackenzie's drawing of 16 September 1816: BL WD1061, fol. 24); GMC nos 32 and 225: Kannan, 2014, pp. 139 and 202; several lost slabs in Mackenzie's album: BL WD1061, fols 33, 34, 69, 71.
153 GMC no. 235, in Sivaramamurti, 1956, p. 265, no. IV. C.9 and Kannan, 2014, p. 205 (HAABA 0027750), which perhaps represents the defeat of Mara (Sivaramamurti, 1956, p. 265; and Becker, 2015, pp. 71–2); BM 1880,0709.75, Knox, 1992, no. 71; one lost slab in the Mackenzie album: BL WD1061, fol. 78.
154 For instance, in Mackenzie's album: BL WD1061, fol. 79 and 80.
155 BM 1880,0709.72, Knox, 1992, no. 70; perhaps in Mackenzie's album, BL WD1061, fol. 67.
156 AMA no. 7, Gupta, 2008, F 361 (HAABA 0021286); GMC no.229: Sivaramamurti, 1956, p. 264, no. IV. C.3; and Kannan, 2014, p. 203 (HAABA 027751); BM 1880,0709.39, 81 and 112, respectively Knox, 1992, nos 64, 74 (= BL WD1061, fol. 46, when there was a good deal more of the object than survives now), and 65; among Mackenzie's drawings in addition, see BL WD1061, fols 20, 23, 32, 35.
157 AMA no 419, Gupta, 2008, no. F 353 (fig XXV) – a finely carved example with miniature stūpas and Bodhi trees incised on the *āyaka* pillars and a scene from the *Mandhatu Jātaka* about the Bodhisattva as a cakravartin in the *āyaka* platform; also AMA. no. 420, Gupta, 2008, F 354 (though I have not seen a photograph nor is the original on display); and from the Mackenzie Album: BL WD1061, fol. 44. The theme appears also on another drum slab from a small stūpa excavated in 1905 adjacent to the main stūpa: see AMA no. 22, Gupta, 2008, no. F 342 (HAABA 0021298) and Becker, 2015, pp. 49–51. This shows the Bodhi tree over the throne, with attendants. It may or may not replicate iconography no longer surviving in the main stūpa relief panels.
158 Burgess, 1882, pp. 74–5, pl. XXXIII.1, reports (after Mackenzie's excavation drawing: BL WD1061, fol. 26) an apparently no longer existent slab with the Buddha and the crazed elephant in the centre.
159 *Nāgas*: BM 1880,0709.69, Knox, 1992, no. 68. Apparently humans: AMA. no. 253, Gupta, 2008, F 348 (but I have not seen an image nor is it on display).
160 BM 1880,0709.120, Knox, 1992, no. 78; among Mackenzie's drawings, BL WD1061, fol. 68. Note that *nāgas* were thought to have special affinity with the Buddha's relics: see Strong, 2004, pp. 676, 120, 126–7 and 135–6; Zin, 2016, 758–9, 760.
161 This scene, on a slab drawn by Mackenzie's draughtsmen but now apparently no longer extant, is reported by Burgess, 1882, p. 74, pl. XXXV.2, as 'quite unusual': see BL WD1061, fol. 81.
162 BM 1880,0709.122, Knox, 1992, no. 80 see Becker, 2015, pp. 66–7.
163 For the Tuṣita Heaven scene, see Amarāvatī Museum: Acc. no. 7, Gupta, 2008, F 361 (HAABA 0021286); BM 1880,0709.120, Knox, 1992, no. 78; Mackenzie album: BL WD1061, fols 20 and 68. For the seated Buddha, see BM 1880,0709.69, Knox, 1992, no. 68; Mackenzie album: BL WD1061, fol. 81. For the imagery from his life, see BM 1880,0709.81, Knox, 1992, no. 74 (where the *āyaka* railing has the raising of the turban between the *dharmacakra* and the Bodhi tree); Mackenzie album: BL WD1061, fols 26 (*dharmacakra* and throne), 35 (the crazed elephant Nālagiri before the Buddha in emblematic form as flaming column crowned by a *trisula*), 44 (Bodhi tree and throne).
164 The examples are BM 1880,0709.80, BM 1880,0709.83 and BM 1880,0709.84, Knox, 1992, nos 73, 75, 76 (this last in roughly the same state but without the diagonal break to the left is probably BL WD1061, fol. 52); also among the Mackenzie drawings, BL WD1061, fol. 34 (now lost, which – unlike others in this group – had no *buddhapāda* with parasols in the dome). A pencil drawing in the BL (WD756) of what is now a lost slab, from the Mackenzie team, has both roundels and *buddhapāda*. For an account of the iconography and its associative force, see Zin, 2019, pp. 371–2.
165 The Tuṣita identification: Knox, 1992, pp. 146, 147; the first meditation: Zin, 2019, p. 372.
166 These two scenes touch on relics associated with the Bodhisattva before his enlightenment. He is said to have completed his renunciation, after fleeing the palace and sending his horse Kaṁṭhaka and groom Chandaka back home to Kapilavastu, by severing his topknot with his sword and flinging it into the air, where it was caught by the gods of the Trāyastrimsa Heaven where it was enshrined in a specially built stūpa; see Strong, 2004, pp. 65–6, with both Sanskrit and Pāli sources, in the Mahāyāna and Theravāda traditions. There are many begging-bowl-as-relic traditions, but the one which seems closest to the imagery here is that the Bodhisattva, seated by the Nairanjana river, after deciding that extreme asceticism is not the right path, accepts milkrice from the laywoman Sujātā (a scene frequently depicted in Amarāvatī); he tosses the bowl in which he has received the rice into the river where it was taken by the *nāga* king; but the king of the gods asks for it and takes it up to the Trāyastriṃśa Heaven, where he enshrines it in a stūpa; see Strong, 2004, pp. 68–9, depending on the Sanskrit *Lalitavistara*. Interestingly both relics are associated with stūpas.
167 See Zin, 2019, p. 372.
168 For instance, AMA nos 19, 194, 235, 270, 417, 419, Gupta, 2008, F 341 (HAABA 0021301), 346, 347, 350, 351, 353; GMC no. 241, in Kannan, 2014, pp. 207 (HAABA 0027749).
169 For instance, AMA nos 1 and 235, respectively Gupta, 2008, F 340 (HAABA 0021280), 347; GMC nos 31–2, 225, 235, 241, respectively Kannan, 2014, pp. 139, 202, 205, 207; BM 1880,0709.69, BM 1880,0709.70, BM 1880,0709.72, BM 1880,0709.75, BM 1880,0709.79, BM 1880,0709.87, BM 1880,0709.120, BM 1880,0709.121, BM 1880,0709.122, respectively, Knox, 1992, nos 68, 69, 70, 71, 72, 77, 78, 79, 80; Boston 29.151. In Mackenzie's album, see BL WD1061, fol. 33, 44, 67, 68, 70, 71, 78, 79 and 81.
170 For example, Kinnard, 2008, pp. 97–100; and Becker, 2015, pp. 48–56, 66–77.
171 For example, AMA. nos 1, 7, 8, 19, Gupta, 2008, nos F 340, 361, 362, 341 (respectively HAABA 0021280, 0021286, 0021287, 0021301), as well as AMA nos 253, 417–20, Gupta, 2008, nos F 348, 351–4; GMC nos 30, 234, 235, 241, 254, respectively Kannan, 2014, pp. 139, 205, 207, 212 (for example, HAABA 0027749, 0027750, 0027752); BM 1880,0709.69, BM 1880,0709.72, BM 1880,0709.75, BM 1880,0709.87, BM 1880,0709.120, BM 1880,0709.122, respectively, Knox, 1992, nos 68, 70, 71, 77, 78, 80; Boston 29.151. In Mackenzie's album, see BL WD1061, fol. 33, 44, 67, 68, 70, 71, 78, 79 and 81.
172 Two extremely interesting cases are the small stūpas at the top of an inscribed dome slab in the Chennai Museum (GMC no. 255,

in Sivaramamurti, 1956, p. 258, no. IV A 13; and Kannan, 2014, p. 212, HAABA 0027740) and on top of a drum pilaster in the British Museum (BM 1880,0709.82, Knox, 1992, no. 84). Both of these seem to copy the drum slabs with lion-topped gateways, but their railings have three lotuses (as in the actual stūpa), with a standing Buddha in the gateway. Whether such representations had the effect of creating *actual* stūpas with more bosses must be moot, but the later stūpa at Kanaganahalli does indeed have railings (1.95 metres above the ground) whose pillars are composed of three full and two half-lotus medallions crowned with a coping and held by four crossbars with lotus roundels: see Poonacha, 2011, pp. 65, 101–8.

173 On the railing, see Knox, 1992, pp. 23–6, 34–40; Shimada, 2013, pp. 82–104. The railing was 59 metres (193 ft) in diameter and 185 metres (606 ft) in circumference. It has been calculated that when complete it contained 136 pillars, 348 crossbars and about 240 metres (787 ft) of coping, all carved on both sides. See Burgess, 1887, p. 25. For discussion of the imagery of railings in the Amarāvatī sculptures, see Stern and Bénisti, 1961, pp. 16–20.

174 For example, BM 1880,0709.80, BM 1880,0709.80, BM 1880,0709.83, BM 1880,0709.112, respectively, Knox, 1992, nos 73, 74, 75, 65.

175 The two instances are BM 1880,0709.72 and BM 1880,0709.75, in Knox, 1992, pp. 136 and 138.

176 *Mahāparinibbāna Sutta* 6.9–11, *Dīgha Nikāya* Sutta 16, II.156–8. At 3.10–20 16, II.107–9 of the same sutta the Buddha gives the eight causes for earthquakes, which include his conception, birth, enlightenment, first turning of the wheel, renunciation of the life principle (when he decides it is time to die) and passing away (or 'attainment of Nibbāna without remainder'). For Buddhaghosa's commentary see An, 2005, pp. 95–102. On earthquakes in the Buddha's biography, see Curtin, 2012.

177 See for an account of this sermon in the *Vinaya*, *Mahāvagga* 1.6.17–29, with the worlds systems quaking at 1.6.30–31; in Rhys Davids and Oldenberg, 1881–5, vol. I, pp. 94–8.

178 For his former life as a Bodhisattva, see BM 1880,0709.122, Knox, 1992, no. 80. For beings venerating his remains, see BM 1880,0709.69, Knox, 1992, no. 68; BM 1880,0709.120, Knox, 1992, no. 78.

179 For example, from Gummadidurru, AMA no 21, Gupta, 2008, F 232 (HAABA 0021299) if the figure in the gateway is a Bodhisattva; from Nāgārjunakonda: HAABA 0026991 and 0027020.

180 For example, from Gummadidurru, AMA no 21, Gupta, 2008, F 232 (HAABA 0021299) if the figure in the gateway is a cakravartin.

181 For discussion, see, for example, Nakamura, 1951; Ray, 1999, p. 334; Huntington, 2012, pp. 10–17; in the context of other rituals; Skilling, 2016, p. 33.

182 In numerous suttas in the *nikāya*s we find the expression *padakkhiṇaṃ karoti* ('he makes to the right', which implies the possibility of circumambulation. As a model of veneration, circumambulation is advocated by the Buddha himself in the *Divyāvadāna* for the arousing of *prasāda* (a skilful state of mental composure, serenity, clarity and trust): see Rotman, 2009, pp. 118–19, 143, 146.

183 For three times, see, for example (from the *Vinaya Piṭaka* I 345) *Mahāvagga* 10.2.11 (the story of Prince Dighavu) for the prince circumambulating his parents' funeral pyre three times or *Dīgha Nikāya Sutta* 16, II. 164 (*Mahāparinibbāna Sutta* 6.22) where Mahākassapa circumambulates the Buddha's funeral pyre three times.

184 Later texts include seven, a hundred or a thousand circumambulations: Nakamura, 1951, pp. 350–51.

185 Barrett, 1954, p. 32; Knox, 1992, p. 28. This requires believing the evidence of the drum slab images as reflecting reality.

186 For instance, BM 1880,0709.24, BM 1880,0709.28, BM 1880,0709.110, respectively Knox, 1992, nos 1, 2, 4 (inner face); perhaps also BM 1880,0709.81, Knox, 1992, no. 3, though it is not clear which face this piece offers – it was later recurved on the other side.

187 For example, BM 1880,0709.46, Knox, 1992, no. 5, with deities elevating the Buddha's turban in the upper lozenge and his begging bowl in the lower one.

188 Examples include, from Mackenzie's Album: BL WD1061, folio 37 (a rising *nāga* in the lowest half-base); BL, WD1061, folio 73 (a Bodhi tree on a base in the lowest half-lotus).

189 For example, BM 1880,0709.1, BM 1880,0709.4, BM 1880,0709.7, BM 1880,0709.11, BM 1880,0709.14, BM 1880,0709.17, BM 1880,0709.48, respectively. Knox, 1992, nos 8, 6, 11, 12, 13, 14, 9. Also AMA nos 23, 405, 1068, respectively Gupta, 2008, no. B 34 (fig. VI), 64 (probably), 76 (fig VIII). Chennai Museum: GMC nos 3, 69, 125, 130, 135, 147, 151, 152, 158, 159, 295–6, in Kannan, 2014, pp. 130, 152, 170, 171, 173, 176–7, 178, 180, 181, 222–3. I cannot find the following in Kannan, 2014: Sivaramamurti, 1956, nos III A 9 (= Burgess, 1887, pl. XIV.1), III A 10 (= Burgess, 1887, pl. X.2), III A 22, III A 25 (= Burgess, 1887, pl. XII.4), III A 26 (= Burgess, 1887, pl. IX.2), III A 27 (= Burgess, 1887, pl. XII.2), III A 31 (= Burgess, 1887, pl. LXIX.3), III B 1, III B 2 (= Burgess, 1887, pl. XIV.3), III B 4 (= Burgess, 1887, pl. XI.2), III B 5 (= Burgess, 1887, pl. VI.2), III B 6, III B 10 (= Burgess, 1887, pl. XIV.2), III B 16 (= Burgess, 1887, pl. VIII.2), III C 5 (= Burgess, 1887, pl. XIII.2), III C 10, III C 11, III C 12, III C 13 III B 16 (= Burgess, 1887, pl. XIV.2).

190 As always in the fertile creativity of Amarāvatī, there are exceptions. One is the unusually narrow railing pillar, perhaps from a gateway, with a large martial procession including spectacular frontal elephant, bigger than the usual lozenge now in the British Museum: see BM 1880,0709.37 in Knox, 1992, no. 15; Burgess, 1887, pp. 37–8. Another is the exceptional top fragment from an inner railing upright in Chennai where even the upper half medallion has been historiated (with the enlightenment figured as Bodhi tree above a throne and *buddhapāda*) while the lozenge below bears the image of the Bodhisattva descending into the Buddha's mother Māyā, for his final birth, in the form of a six-tusked white elephant: see GMC no. 159, in Kannan, 2014, p. 181; Sivaramamurti, 1956, no. IIII A 1; Burgess, 1887, p. 34, pl. XI.1 (HAABA 27674).

191 For example, BM 1880,0709.2, BM 1880,0709.5, BM 1880,0709.8, BM 1880,0709.12, BM 1880,0709.15, BM 1880,0709.16, BM 1880,0709.119, respectively Knox, 1992, nos 26, 25, 27, 23, 24, 21 (his photograph of the barely surviving inner medallion wrongly labelled 'outer face'), 28. Also AMA nos 20, 69, 340, 505, respectively Gupta, 2008, no. C 79 (pl. 8), 84, 169, 203. Chennai Museum: GMC nos 5, 14, 17, 73, 132, 148–50, 155–7, 263, 292, in Kannan, 2014, pp. 131, 134–5, 153, 172, 177–8, 179–80, 214, 222.

192 For example, BM 1880,0709.3, BM 1880,0709.25, BM 1880,0709.26, BM 1880,0709.27, respectively Knox, 1992, nos 20, 16, 17, 18. Also

AMA nos 57, 66, 70, 71, 72, 73, 75, 77, 323, respectively Gupta, 2008, nos C 80, 81, 85, 86, 87, 88, 90, 92, 162. Chennai Museum: Sivaramamurti, 1956, nos. III D 1–15.

193 See Dehejia, 1997, pp. 154–9, for 'sequential networks' of narrative and their patterns in the railing pillars.

194 See ibid., pp. 159–61.

195 Ibid., pp. 162–4.

196 For issues of direction of stories, see ibid., pp. 159–61.

197 Ibid., pp. 161–2.

198 Sivaramamurti constructs the section of his catalogue of the rich holdings of the Chennai Museum that deals with the interior of the railing around the division of stories of the Buddha (Sivaramamurti, 1956, pp. 175–206, nos III B 1–III B 25) and stories of the Bodhisattva's earlier lives (Sivaramamurti, 1956, pp. 206–39, nos III A 1–III A 31).

199 These include many examples in Sivaramamurti, 1956, pp. 239–47 (uprights in his III C category, crossbars in his III D category and coping stones in his III E category).

200 Dehejia, 1997, never discusses the miniature imagery of these in relation to the narrative richness of Amarāvatī.

201 For examples where all these elements survive: Boston Museum of Fine Arts: no. 29.151; British Museum: BM 1880,0709.69, BM 1880,0709.70, BM 1880,0709.72, BM 1880,0709.75, BM 1880,0709.79, BM 1880,0709.83, BM 1880,0709.87, respectively Knox, 1992, nos 68, 69, 70, 71, 72, 75, 77; Chennai: GMC nos 221 and 235, in Kannan, 2014, pp. 201 and 205 respectively; and Sivaramamurti, 1956, nos IV. C 1 and 13; see also the group drawn by Mackenzie's draughtsmen (many of which no longer survive) published by Burgess, 1887, pl. XXXII–XXXIX.

202 See Chapter Two on inscriptions.

203 An apparent exception is AMA no. 56, Gupta, 2008, no. 498, pl. 38, which is described as offering a curved profile. This is one of very few near-complete examples, along with Mackenzie's drawing BL WD1061, folio 29, and BM 1880,0709.93, Knox, 1992, no. 88.

204 See Knox, 1992, pp. 28–30.

205 See Mackenzie's Album BL WD1061, folio 29 (= Sivaramamurti, 1956, p. 166, nos II A 4–6).

206 See ibid.; exceptionally the Bodhi tree is here in the centre of the trio of scenes rather than at the bottom, BM 1880,0709.93, BM 1880,0709.94, respectively Knox, 1992, nos 88, 89; GMC nos 184, 203–6, 253, in Kannan, 2014, pp. 189, 195–6, 211; and Sivaramamurti, 1956, p. 167, nos II A 8–11, 13; AMA nos 56, 241, 242, respectively Gupta, 2008, nos G 498, 427, 428.

207 GMC nos 186–8, in Kannan, 2014, pp. 190–91; and Sivaramamurti, 1956, pp. 165–7 nos II A 2–3, 12.

208 BM 1880,0709.93, BM 1880,0709.94, BM 1880,0709.113, respectively, Knox, 1992, nos 88, 89, 93; GMC nos 184, 187, 204–6, in Kannan, 2014, pp. 189, 190, 196 and Sivaramamurti, 1956, pp. 165, 167–8, nos II A 2, 10, 12, 13, 15; AMA nos 56, 156, 178, 240, 241, 242, 529, respectively Gupta, 2008, nos G 498, 409, 413, 426, 427, 428, 468.

209 BM 1880,0709.93, BM 1880,0709.95, BM 1880,0709.96, BM 1880,0709.97, BM 1880,0709.114, BM 1880,0709.115, respectively Knox, 1992, nos 88, 90, 91, 92, 94, 95; GMC nos 46, 185, 189, 200–202, in Kannan, 2014, pp. 143, 190, 191, 195; and Sivaramamurti, 1956, pp. 168–9, nos II A 14, 16–20; AMA nos 9, 12, 56, 163, 177, 239, 240, 243, 374, 385; Gupta, 2008, nos G 392, 393, 498, 410, 412, 425, 426, 429, 439, 442.

210 For example (examples where the animal and *triratna* friezes survive, rather than fragments of each, of which there are many), BM 1880,0709.96, BM 1880,0709.97, BM 1880,0709.98, BM 1880,0709.114, BM 1880,0709.115, BM 1880,0709.116, respectively Knox, 1992, nos 91, 92, 98, 94, 95, 97; GMC nos 251, 260 and 261, in Kannan, 2014, pp. 211, 213–14; and Sivaramamurti, 1956, p. 169, nos II A 18–20, II B 5; AMA nos 9, 12, 28, in Gupta, 2008, nos G 392, 393, 396.

211 See Kinnard, 2008, pp. 92–4.

212 BM 1880,0709.54, BM 1880,0709.117, BM 1880,0709.118, respectively Knox, 1992, nos 106, 107, 108; GMC nos 190, 191, 197, 198, 199, 207, 208, in Kannan, 2014, pp. 191, 194, 196, 197; and Sivaramamurti, 1956, pp. 170–71, nos II C 1–10; AMA nos 3, 5, 126, 149, 175, 218, 238, 266, 271, 324, 387, 390, 459, 535, 617, 618; Gupta, 2008, nos G 390, 391, 397, 405, 411, 420, 424, 431, 496, 436, 437, 438, 444, 445, 446, 456, 470, 480, 481.

213 For example, BM 1880,0709.69, BM 1880,0709.70, BM 1880,0709.72, BM 1880,0709.75, BM 1880,0709.79, BM 1880,0709.120, respectively Knox, 1992, nos 68, 69, 70, 71, 72, 78.

214 For example, BM 1880,0709.69, BM 1880,0709.70, BM 1880,0709.72, BM 1880,0709.75, BM 1880,0709.79, BM 1880,0709.120, respectively Knox, 1992, nos 68, 69, 70, 71, 72, 78 – see also for this garland frieze, BM 1880,0709.83, BM 1880,0709.85, BM 1880,0709.87, respectively Knox, 1992, nos 75, 76, 77.

215 AMA nos 25 and 27, in Gupta, 2008, nos G 394 and 395; Guy, 2023, pp. 230–31.

216 These are almost entirely depicted as round, but in a few cases the central panel over the *āyaka* pillars is square, for example, BM 1880,0709.74, BM 1880,0709.83, respectively Knox, 1992, nos 63, 75; GMC no. 221, in Kannan, 2014, pp. 201; and Sivaramamurti, 1956, pp. 263–4, no. IV. C. 1. In one case they are alternating square and round: BM 1880,0709.81, Knox, 1992, no. 74.

217 For example, BM 1880,0709.49, BM 1880,0709.50, BM 1880,0709.51, BM 1880,0709.52, BM 1880,0709.53, respectively Knox, 1992, nos 100, 101, 103, 104, 102; Gupta, 2008, nos G 487, 489.

218 A suggestion made by Barrett, 1954, p. 47, tentatively repeated by Knox, 1992, p. 178.

219 BM 1880,0709.19/20, BM 1880,0709.81, BM 1880,0709.112, respectively Knox, 1992, nos 36, 74, 65.

220 Barrett, 1954, p. 38.

221 Mackenzie, 1823, p. 468.

222 Foucher, 1928, p. 10.

223 See Middleton, 1992, p. 232.

224 BM 1880,0709.105, BM 1880,0709.106, respectively Knox, 1992, nos 118–19.

225 BM 1880,0709.29, Knox, 1992, no. 43, with Middleton, 1992, p. 232.

226 Osto, undated, p. 32.

227 Notably the *Mahāsudassana Sutta* in the Pāli tradition: see, for example, Gethin, 2006.

228 See Casalini, 2021, p. 113.

229 We do not know where these statues stood. But at Kanaganahalli colossal three-dimensional standing Buddhas in the *abhāya mudrā* were placed over the southern and western *āyaka* platforms, while seated Buddhas were positioned on the northern and eastern *āyakas*: Poonacha, 2011, pp. 66–7

(pls XIX–XX), 326–8. There only the eastern platform had four *āyaka* pillars, two on each side of the central seated Buddha: ibid., pp. 67, 71–4 and von Hinüber, 2016a, esp. p. 9. There were also eight seated Buddha statues in the cardinal and intra-cardinal directions placed within the circumambulatory passage at Kanaganahalli, all dedicated by a single donor and representing Śākyamuni himself (in the southeast), his six predecessor Buddhas and his successor Maitreya (inscribed Ajita), the Buddha to be: ibid., p. 328, Nakanishi and von Hinüber, 2014, pp. 75–80.

230 See Westerhoff, 2018, pp. 101–4.

231 *Saṃyutta Nikāya* III.142 (*Khandasaṃyutta*) 22, 95 (3) trans. Bikkhu Bodhi, with, for example, Ñāṇananda, 1974, pp. 5–7, where the evocative translation of 'magic-show' is used for 'illusion'.

232 See Buddhaghosa, *Visuddhimagga*, XX.104, in Ñāṇamoli, 1979, p. 738.

233 See, for example, *Pañcaviṃśatisāhasrikā Prajñāpāramitā Sūtra* (The Perfection of Wisdom in Twenty-Five Thousand Lines) I 9, 17a in Conze, 1961, p. 170.

234 For illusion in Nāgārjuna's work, see Westerhoff, 2018, pp. 115–17.

235 See Westerhoff, 2018, pp. 120–38, focusing especially on the *Akuobhayā* (an interpretative text on Nāgārjuna's *Mūlamadhyamakakārikā* that may be by Nāgārjuna himself), and the commentaries by Buddhapālita, Bhāviveka and Candrakīrti, all of whom may have been active in South India.

236 See the *Bodhicittaivarana* 12–13 (ascribed to Nāgārjuna), in Lindtner, 1982, pp. 188–9; and *Mūlamadhyamakakārikā* 17.31–3 (certainly by Nāgārjuna) on magical displays, in which the quotation may be by means of *The Perfection of Wisdom Sūtra in Twenty-Five Thousand Lines* I 9, 17a, where the city of the Gandharvas is mentioned.

237 *Mūlamadhyamakakārikā* 17.31–3, in Garfield, 1995, pp. 47, 243–4.

238 See Gomez, 1967, pp. xxviii–xxxvii; Osto, 2008, pp. 4–7; Hamar, 2015, p. 123.

239 See Gomez, 1967, pp. lxviii–lxxii; McMahan, 2002, p. 113; Osto, 2008, pp. 114–16. For discussion of the history of scholarly approaches see Osto, 2008, pp. 7–12.

240 See Williams, 2009, pp. 128–48. I use the translation of Cleary, 1993, pp. 1135–1518. Note that this is a translation from the Chinese, which has some differences from the surviving Sanskrit versions. For a synopsis and brief introduction, see Cleary, 1993, pp. 1–54.

241 Cleary, 1993, p. 45. For 'literary masterpiece', see Warder, 2000, p. 402.

242 On Vairocana in the *Gaṇḍavyūha Sūtra*, as the same Buddha as Śakyamuni (that is, Gautama, the historical Buddha) but in a different (more celestial) body, see Xing, 2005, pp. 169–71; and Williams, 2009, pp. 134–6; on the complexities of Vairocana and Śakyamuni in the *Avataṃsaka Sūtra* as a whole in its movement from India to China, see Ōtake, 2012.

243 Cleary, 1993, p. 1135. On the opening – its parallels and differences with suttas in the *Nikāya* traditions – see McMahan, 2002, pp. 83–5 (the pavilion and its move to boundlessness being one of the major differences). The 'pavilion' (*kūtāgāra*) may be translated also as 'multi-storied palace or tower' (McMahan, 2002, p. 118) or 'peaked dwelling' (Osto, 2008, p. 49).

244 For this as 'the coming forth of the lion' see Cleary, 1993, p. 1138; for 'yawn' see Osto, 2008, p. 20.

245 Cleary, 1993, pp. 1138–69. McMahan, 2002, pp. 118–21, stresses the difference between the magnificence of this palatial building (with its debt to palace architecture as well as an association with stūpas and viharas) and 'the humble surroundings of the Pāli sutras'. But in contradiction one might cite the *Mahāsudassana Sutta*, which immediately follows the *Mahāparinibbāna Sutta* in the *Dīgha Nikāya* (sutta 17, II.169–99) and quotes it (see Harvey, 1990, p. 119). That portrays a previous life of the Buddha as wheel-turning monarch in a vividly described palace and among a huge retinue. The Buddha, on his deathbed, specifically contrasts Kusinārā, 'the miserable little town of wattle-and-daub, right in the jungle in the back of beyond', where he passes away, with its former glory as Kusāvatī, the capital of king Mahāsudassana. *Mahāparinibbāna Sutta* 5.17–18, sutta 16, II.146–7.

246 Cleary, 1993, p. 1145. The issue is discussed by McMahan, 2002, pp. 104–5.

247 Cleary, 1993, pp. 1146–51.

248 Ibid., p. 1145.

249 Ibid., p. 1170. On Manjushri, see Osto, 2008, pp. 56–9.

250 Cleary, 1993, p. 1172.

251 Shimada, 2013, p. 36, map 3; Sivaramamurti, 1956, p. 7, notes the congruence.

252 Cleary, 1993, p. 1173.

253 Ibid., pp. 1174 and 1179.

254 The *Nidānakathā* and *Buddhavaṃsa* give lists of 24 Buddhas between Dīpaṅkara and Gautama: see Appleton, 2010, pp. 86–8.

255 MacMahan, 2002, p. 124.

256 Cleary, 1993, p. 1474. The actual number in the sūtra as it stands is 53; see, for example, Osto, 2008, pp. 123–4; or Hamar, 2015, p. 111.

257 Cleary, 1993, p. 1463. On Maitreya in the sūtra, see Osto, 2008, pp. 65–9; on the visionary nature of all this see Osto, 2018, pp. 177–205, esp. 183–6 and 192–4.

258 Cleary, 1993, p. 1489. The term used in Sanskrit for the tower is the same as that used for the Buddha's pavilion at the sūtra's opening, *kūtāgāra*; on the tower see, for example, MacMahan, 2002, pp. 127–8; and Osto, 2008, pp. 66–8.

259 Cleary, 1993, p. 1490.

260 Ibid., pp. 1490–93.

261 Ibid., pp. 1495–6.

262 See also the city and palace of the universal monarch in the *Mahāsudassana Sutta*, with Gethin, 2006, pp. 70, 72–102.

263 Cleary, 1993, p. 1209.

264 The quotation (in relation to Maitreya's tower) is from MacMahan, 2002, p. 127.

265 For example, BM 1880,0709.10, BM 1880,0709.47 respectively Knox, 1992, nos 7 and 10.

266 For example, BM 1880,0709.4, Knox, 1992, no. 6 (outer face).

267 For example, BM 1880,0709.19/20, Knox, 1992, no. 36 (outer face).

268 Sivaramamurti, 1956, no. III D 20; Burgess, 1887, pl. xix.3. This object was moved in 2005 from the Government Museum in Chennai to the site museum at Amarāvatī, where I saw it in 2022: see Kannan, 2014, pp. 68–71.

269 BM 1880,0709.108, Knox, 1992, no. 46.

270 For example, BM 1880,0709.8, Knox, 1992, no. 27; AMA no. 434, Gupta, 2008, no. C 189

271 For example, BM 1880,0709.19/20, BM 1880,0709.34, respectively Knox, 1992, nos 36 (inner face) and 40.

272 For example, BM 1880,0709.76, BM 1880,0709.91, BM 1880,0709.107, respectively Knox, 1992, nos 54, 53, 51.
273 For example, BM 1880,0709.73, BM 1880,0709.82, BM 1880,0709.84, BM 1880,0709.86, respectively Knox, 1992, nos 83–6.
274 For example, BM 1880,0709.93, BM 1880,0709.95, BM 1880,0709.96, BM 1880,0709.97, BM 1880,0709.114, BM 1880,0709.115, respectively Knox, 1992, nos 88, 91–2, 94–5.
275 Osto, undated, p. 12.
276 Ibid., p. 18.
277 Ibid., pp. 19–22.
278 For the image of Indra's net in the *Gaṇḍavyūha Sūtra*, see Cleary, 1993, p. 1164. For discussion of reflections and mirrors in the sūtra, see Gomez, 1967, pp. lxxxvii–lxxxviii; on interpenetration, see, for example, MacMahan, 2002, pp. 134–7; and Osto, 2008, pp. 8–9, both emphasizing that this is poetically evoked rather than philosophically grounded or even named. For jewels in the sūtra, see Osto, 2008, pp. 73–87.
279 Cleary, 1993, pp. 1490, 1493, 1494.
280 Ibid., p. 1491.
281 For the Bodhisattva ideal in the Nikāya traditions, see Samuels, 1997; Appleton, 2010, pp. 85–108; Analayo, 2010; Nyanatusita, 2013.
282 See MacMahan, 2002, pp. 143–77, for a discussion.
283 For Nāgārjunakonda, many of the sculptures are preserved in the site museum and several elsewhere; see Rosen Stone, 1994, pp. 60–62, and figs 115, 124, 143–9, 151–2; and Becker, 2015, pp. 57–65. For Gummadidurru, the remains are in the Amarāvatī site museum;' see Gupta, 2008, nos F 363–88; for Alluru, the remains are in the Amarāvatī site museum; see Gupta, 2008, no. F 389; for Ghantaśālā, see Rea, 1894, p. 37 and pl. XXVII. Other sites include Buddham, Dupadu and Uppugundur: see Becker, 2015, p. 49, n. 53 (but with no supporting documentation).
284 See reference no. 112 above.
285 One fine relief of Manjushri was found at the site – but it is a later addition of perhaps the eighth century CE. See BM 1880,0709.125, Knox, 1994, no. 124.
286 See Gifford, 2011, pp. 5–9, 74–146, with earlier bibliography.
287 For 'panoramic art' see ibid., p. 75.
288 Yet it is interesting that Borobudur gives much greater space to the Maitreya episode of the *Gaṇḍavyūha* and Vairocana's tower than to any other (ibid., pp. 76–82): it too focuses, although in a very different mode of visual discourse, on the great hymn to reflective and interpenetrative interdependence with which the *sūtra* culminates and which the stūpa at Amarāvatī tries to enact.

two THE INSCRIPTIONS AND THEIR MESSAGES

1 Key collections and discussions include Fergusson, 1873, pp. 260–62 (Appendix E by A. Cunningham); Hultzsch, 1883 and 1886; Burgess, 1887, pp. 100–106; Lüders, 1912, esp. nos 1206–1326, pp. 141–57, and 1205a, p. 179; Chanda, 1919–20; Sivaramamurti, 1956, pp. 273–304; Ghosh and Sarkar, 1964–5; Dehejia, 1970–71; Hettiarachchy, 1973, 210–17; Sarma, 1975 and 1980; Ghosh, 1979; Roy, 1994, pp. 9–84, 193–218; Hanumantha Rao, 1998, pp. 45–76; Padmanabha Sastry, 2004; Shimada, 2013, Appendix C, pp. 237–42; Rana, 2013, pp. 128–60; Francis, 2016.
2 Francis, 2016, p. 45.
3 Ibid., with a catalogue of 277, including on pottery. This volume has several weaknesses. First, Francis does not cite the objects by museum number, largely ignoring all issues of form, function or visual decoration in relation to the slab on which an inscription occurs (that is, he is concerned with the inscriptions purely as history 'of patronage of Buddhism as a religio-cultural expression', p. 50, as opposed to material culture); second, he fails to give the current museum location for many of the items he lists; third, he arranges the inscriptions by chronological schema supposedly dependent on palaeography, pp. 48–9, despite the significant and unresolved problems around chronology discussed in the Introduction to this book; fourth, he offers no cross-listing index of his own numbers against any earlier collections (notably Lüders and Sivaramamurti), making his text very hard to use; and fifth, he never includes a transcription or translation other than those already published, making it likely that he has no philological or palaeographical command of the primary materials of his analysis. For a historiography of the discovery and study of the Amarāvatī inscriptions, see Francis, 2016, pp. 15–44.
4 Griffiths and Tournier, 2017.
5 On the exemplary donors of the Pāli tradition in canonical and commentarial sources, see Falk, 1990.
6 See Shimada, 2013, pp. 237–42; Francis, 2005. Francis, 2016, pp. 173–242, gives concordances that usefully classify donors through a variety of categories.
7 For example, a railing pillar in the British Museum with a complete inscription at the top announces itself as 'the gift of Sagha, Saghadasi and Kumala, the wives of Lonavalavaka, Sagharakhita and Mariti': Cunningham, 1873, no. 13; Lüders, 1912, no. 1218; BM 1880,0709.37, no. 15, in Knox, 1992.
8 See Francis, 2016, pp. 222–6, for a list of inscriptions that name the object donated. Francis arranges his list by date as inferred principally from palaeography, a dubious procedure given the uncertainties involved in all issues of dating at Amarāvatī and the fact that inscriptions can be archaizing. Since I am concerned here with the relation of epigraphy to the kind of object it is inscribed on, I will use museum catalogues in relation to epigraphic publications.
9 On the epigraphic terminology, see Skilling, 2016. For the vocabularies of early Indian architecture as ascertainable from the inscriptional evidence, see Settar, 2020, pp. 94–127; and von Hinüber, 2016b.
10 For example, free-standing pillars: Lüders, 1912, nos 1208 (*thabha*, BM 1880,0709.104, Knox, 1992, p. 115); 1210 (*chetiyathabha*, BM 1880,0709.109, Knox, 1992, p. 109); 1229 (*chetiyakhaba*, Sivaramamurti, 1956, p. 284, no II E 5 and no. 50); 1244 ('pillar for lamps', *divakhabha*, Sivaramamurti, 1956, pp. 301–2, no IV G 9 and no. 118; Francis, 2016, no. 200); 1260 (*khamba*, Sivaramamurti, 1956, p. 302, no. IV G 10 and no. 120); 1277 (*thabha*, Sivaramamurti, 1956, p. 285, no. II E 29 and no. 59); Dehejia, 1970, p. 42 (two inscriptions on octagonal pillars now in the Amarāvatī Museum labelled 'pillar (*thabha*) of . . .'; Sarkar, 1971, nos 55 (*thamba*), 57 (*thaba*); AMA no. 46, in Gupta, 2008, pp. E 275 (*thabha*). Rail pillars: Lüders, 1912, no. 1266 (*thabha*, Sivaramamurti, 1956, p. 276, no. I F 9 and no. 18); Chanda, 1919–20, nos 3, 6, 7 and 9 (*thabha*, respectively Sivaramamurti, 1956, nos 19, 13–5, 19 (I F 10, I F 4–6); AMA nos 313, 462, 1023, 1031, 1032, respectively in Gupta, 2008, nos B 66 (*thabha*), B 40

(*thabha*), B 6 (*uttaro dasa thabho*, 'the tenth pillar on the north side'), B 3 (*thabha*), B 4 (*thabha*).

11 Crossbars: Chennai Museum: Lüders, 1912, nos 1241 (*suji*, Sivaramamurti, 1956, p. 294, no. III D 24 and no. 84); 1247 (*suci*, Sivaramamurti, 1956, p. 294, no. III D 41 and no. 87); 1254 ('gift of two cross bars (*suciyo*) with circular panels (*paricaka*), Sivaramamurti, 1956, p. 289, no. III A 3 and no. 64); 1263 (*suci*, Sivaramamurti, 1956, p. 292, III D 14 and no. 75); Chanda, 1919–20, nos 13, 16, 17, 18, 19, 20, 32, 44 (*suci*, respectively Sivaramamurti, 1956, nos I G 3, 6, 8, 12, 4, III D 42 and III F 9, whose inscription nos are 20, 23, 25, 29, 21, 88, 95); also Sivaramamurti, 1956, no. 65 (III A 5). Amaravati Museum: AMA nos 166, 167, 223, 296, 460, respectively Gupta, 2008, pp. C 115, 116, 142, 153, 193 (all *suci*). Inscriptions on stones that can no longer be located; Chanda, 1919–20, nos 17, 32 and 33 (all *suci*).

12 Coping: British Museum: Lüders, 1912, no. 1221 (*unisa*, BM 1880-0709–22). Chennai Museum: Lüders, 1912, nos 1231 (*unisa*, Sivaramamurti, 1956, p. 273, no I B 2, and no. 4); 1251 (*unisa*, Sivaramamurti, 1956, p. 291, no. III B 11 and no. 73); 1256 (*unisa*, Sivaramamurti, 1956, p. 295, no. III E 3 and no. 90); 1259 (*unisa*, Sivaramamurti, 1956, p. 292, no. III B 23, and no. 75); 1269 ('6 cubits for the rail enclosure', *vetika*, Chanda, 1919–20, no. 46, and Sivaramamurti, 1956, p. 284, no. II E 24 and no.54); for inscriptions on stones that can no longer be located, Chanda, 1919–20, nos 29 (*vetika chapa*), 42 (*unisa*) and perhaps 53 (although the nature of the stone on which the inscription is carved is unclear); Sarma, 1980, no. 86 (*vedi*), no. 88 (*vetika*). Amaravati Museum: AMA no. 259, in Gupta, 2008, pp. D 243 (*unhisa*).

13 Lüders, 1912, no. 1223 (BM 1880,0709.108, Knox, 1992, p. 46); Francis, 2016, pp. 165–6, n. 257. Dehejia, 1970, pp. 51–2, sees the style of the sculpting of the piece as earlier than the inscription, despite the fact that the inscription describes its function precisely.

14 Dome slabs: Lüders, 1912, nos 1215 (*pata*, BM 1880,0709.50, Knox, 1992, p. 101); 1226 (*pata*, BM 1880,0709.51, Knox, 1992, p. 103); 1262 (*pata*, Burgess, 1887, pl. XLVI.2), 1271 (*udhapata*, Sivaramamurti, 1956, pp. 280–81, no. II A 12 and no. 36); 1272 (*udhapata*, Sivaramamurti, 1956, p. 279, no. II A 10 and no. 34); 1273 (*purnaghatapata*, 'slab with a filled vase', Sivaramamurti, 1956, p. 281, no. II C 3 and no.41); Chanda, 1919–20, nos 47 (*sothikapata*, Sivaramamurti, 1956, p. 282, no. II C 11 and no. 46), and 57 (*udhapata*, Sivaramamurti, 1956, pp. II A 15, no. 39, p. 280–81); Sivaramamurti, 1956, no. 31 (II A 2). Drum slabs: Cunningham in Fergusson, 1873, 262, no. XII (*pata*, BM 1880-0709–72, see illus. 94 and 95 in this book); Lüders, 1912, nos 1213 (*pata* BM 1880,0709.70, Knox, 1992, p. 69); 1243 ('gift of an upright slab (*udampata*) at the foot of the great Caitya').Unidentified slabs (so we cannot be sure if dome or drum): Lüders, 1912, nos 1235 (*udhapata*), 1240 (*pendaka*), 1262 (*upata*), 1287 (*sothikapata*), 1291 (*pata*), 1295 (*pata*); Chanda, 1919–20, nos 56 and 57 (both *udhapata*, the former placed 'at the south side of the main gate', so perhaps not on the stūpa itself).

15 Burgess, 1887, p. 7; Lüders, 1912, no. 1276; Sivaramamurti, 1956, p. 248, no. III F 4, and p. 295, inscription no. 92; Francis, 2016, pp. 114–15, no. 156; discussed in detail by Schopen, 1997, pp. 167–8 and 178–9. The parasol disc was carved with rays or spokes and the inscription was written in a circle around the outer rim: see the photograph in Burgess, 1887, pls XLV.6 and LX.45. See also Sarma, 1980, no. 85; and Francis, 2016, pp. 90–91, no. 103 (*chatta dabho* 'umbrella pillar', on the shaft of the umbrella); Sastry, 2004, no. 4 (*chatta*); Sastry, 2004, no. 5; and Francis, 2016, p. 151, no. 228 (*chatta*).

16 Sāñcī: Majumdar, 1940, pp. 297–384; pillars, nos 397, 402–3, 665, 678, 724, 783, 785, 793 (*tha(m)bho* in all cases, the last two being from temple 40); crossbars, no. 734 (*sūci*). This is a minuscule haul from a site with over eight hundred surviving donative inscriptions. Bharhut: Barua and Simha, 1926, pp. 1–3, gateways: nos 2 and 3 (*toraṇam*); pp. 3–17, rail pillars: nos 1, 3, 8, 11, 13, 17, 18, 20, 21, 23–6, 28, 33–5, 37–41, 43 (*tha(m) bho*); pp. 17–33, railing crossbars: nos 8–9, 11, 15, 27, 29, 32, 40, 45, 52, 57, 63 (*sūci*). Note that Barua and Simha needs to be used with care – see the critique by Lüders, Waldschmidt and Mehendale, 1963, pp. ix–xii.

17 Kanaganahalli: Nakanishi and von Hinüber, 2014, nos II.1.1–4 slabs or columns on the *āyaka* platforms (*āyāga-patta* or *āyāga-thamba*); nos II.2.1–10, 13–14, slabs with flower vases (*puphagahani*, arguably an iconography but potentially the name for a kind of slab carved with such vases); nos II.3.1–8, slabs inscribed 'slab' (*patta*); II.4. A. nos 1–3, railing upright (*pāyaka*); nos II.5.4–7, umbrellas (*chatta*). Nāgārjunakonda: Vogel, 1929–30a, nos A2–4, B 1–5, C 1–5, D 2: pillars (*khamba*); Vogel, 1929–30b: stone slab (*patipadā*); Sircar, 1963–4, nos 1 A, 3, 5, no. 6 A, B.I–`IV, C.I–II: pillars (*tha(m)bo* and *khambo*. All the epigraphy from Nāgārjunakonda published in sporadic articles in *Epigraphia Indica* is collected as published originally but with less full discussion in Soundrarajan, 2006, pp. 539–89. The 84 surviving inscriptions are collected and renumbered in Raghunath, 2001.

18 Sāñcī: Majumdar, 1940, pp. 297–9; Dehejia, 1972, pp. 35–8, 186–8; Dehejia, 1992b, pp. 35–45, esp. 36–9; Schopen, 1996; Singh, 1996. Bharhut: Lüders, Waldschmidt and Mehendale, 1963, pp. 11–65, nos A 1–136.

19 Lüders, 1912, pp. 141–57, esp. nos 1206–1326; Shimada, 2013, pp. 237–42; Francis, 2016, pp. 45–58.

20 See, for example, Willis, 1992.

21 For example, using the numbers in Lüders, 1912: monks and nuns: 1223, 1224, 1237, 1240, 1242, 1246, 1250, 1252, 1257, 1258, 1262, 1264, 1267, 1270, 1272, 1280, 1286, 1289, 1295, 1315 (see also Francis, 2016, pp. 219–22); laypeople: 1206, 1211, 1218, 1222, 1239, 1268, 1276, 1281, 1284, 1303; scribes: 1291; merchants: 1213, 1214, 1229, 1230, 1278, 1281, 1285, 1292; a perfumer: 1210; artisans and artists: 1273, 1298; teachers: 1273; bankers: 1261; officials: 1274, 1279, 1297; generals: 1266; families: 1206, 1209, 1214, 1215, 1216, 1220, 1221, 1222, 1225, 1229, 1230, 1239, 1243, 1244, 1247–52, 1254, 1255, 1256, 1260, 1268, 1269, 1271, 1277, 1278, 1287, 1300–1302.

22 See especially Thapar, 1992; see Francis, 2005, specifically on Amarāvatī.

23 See especially Dehejia, 1992b.

24 At Kanaganahalli, in rare cases an additional donation (a crossbar with a railing upright or a vase slab, *puphagahani*, alongside a railing – *vedika* – slab) are named, but this kind of additional giving is not the sort of transference we find at Amarāvatī): see Nakanishi and von Hinüber, 2014, nos II.2.13–14 and II.4 A. 1–3.

25 Lüders, 1912, no. 1207 (Francis, 2016, pp. 161, no. 246, illustrated by Fergusson, 1873, pl. LXXXIII.1). Others of this kind include Lüders, 1912, no. 1217 (Francis, 2016, pp. 165,

no. 256, a railing pillar, *padukapata*, inscribed on a drum pilaster: BM 1880,0709.73, Knox, 1992, p. 83); Chanda, 1919–20, no. 22 (Francis, 2016, pp. 99–100, no. 125, 'gift of a slab of Lord Buddha, *Budha pamatu pata*', = Sivaramamurti, 1956, p. 283, no. II C 13 and no. 48, inscribed on a dome slab); Chanda, 1919–20, no. 44 ('gift of coping, *unisa*, and foot prints, *pada* . . .', = Sivaramamurti, 1956, p. 296, no. III F 9 and no. 95, inscribed on a slab fragment with a broken half-lotus); Sivaramamurti, 1956, pp. 298–9, no. IV E 2 and no. 104, 'pious gift of a slab (*pata*)' inscribed on a segment of drum frieze.

26 Lüders, 1912, no. 1214 (Francis, 2016, no. 254); other pillar gifts not inscribed on pillars include AMA 599, in Gupta, 2008, p. C 211 (*thabha*) on a crossbar.

27 Lüders, 1912, no. 1216 (BM 1880,0709.60, Knox, 1992, no. 49; Francis, 2016, no. 215); see for other larger gifts recorded on a sculptural fragments: Lüders, 1912, no. 1282, 'gift of four pillars (*khaba*) and slabs (*sapata*)'.

28 Lüders, 1912, no. 1230 (= Sivaramamurti, 1956, p. 303, no. IV G 15 and no. 124; Francis, 2016, no. 224).

29 Lüders, 1912, no. 1248 (= Sivaramamurti, 1956, pp. 283–4, no. II E 6–7 and no. 51, Francis, 2016, no. 160); see Lüders, 1912, no. 1253 'gift of a slab with a wheel (*cakapata*) inscribed on a pillar; Lüders, 1912, no. 1255 (= Sivaramamurti, 1956, pp. 284–5, no. II E 25 and no. 55; Francis, 2016, no. 189) recording 'a meritorious gift' (it is not clear of what) 'made at the southern gate', inscribed on a rail coping stone.

30 Sarkar, 1970–71, no. 56; and Francis, 2016, no. 132.

31 Sastry, 2004, 164, no. 5; and Francis, 2016, pp. 151, no. 228.

32 Lüders, 1912, nos 1283, 1285, 1292 (respectively Sivaramamurti, 1956, p. 299 nos IV E 9, 12 and 8, and respectively nos 109, 111, 108, the last two being Francis, 2016, nos 196 and 221).

33 As suggested by Dehejia, 1970.

34 Lüders, 1912, no. 1225 (BM 1880,0709.77, Knox, 1992, p. 55); Rana, 2013, p. 153, no. 46. The slab is broken at the left but continues from a piece now in the Chennai Museum: Sivaramamurti, 1956, p. 296, no. IV A 3 with inscription no. 97 (= Lüders, 1912, no. 1239), which has been considered as separate but might in fact be the opening, with invocation to the Buddha and the names of the donors.

35 Cunningham in Fergusson, 1873, p. 262, suggests the donors were from Rājgir. For another donation of a pillar perhaps from Rājgir, see Hanumantha Rao, 1998, p. 58, no. 50; Rana, 2013, p. 154, no. 48.

36 See Rana, 2013, pp. 153–5, nos 43–51: most refer to sites on the southeast coast of India, but notable is the inscription on a railing upright by a monk from Pataliputra in northeast India near the Ganges: Sivaramamurti, 1956, p. 276, no. I F 10 with inscription no. 19; Hanumantha Rao, 1998, p. 47, no. 9; Rana, 2013, p. 153, no. 43. For donations from people in Dhañakada, that is, Amarāvatī, to the faraway stūpa at Kanaganahalli in the second century CE, see von Hinüber, 2016a, p. 11.

37 Barua and Simha, 1926, p. 28 no. 50 (= Lüders, Waldschmidt and Mehendale, 1963, p. 54 no. A 106), carved on the railing of the southwest quadrant at Bharhut (see Cunningham, 1879, pp. 140–42, no. 51) may be an exception. It describes the gift of a *Bodhi cakra* or wheel of enlightenment. It is not clear if this was the same as or different from a *dharmacakra*, wheel of the teaching, and whether it was an object in three dimensions or the iconography of a relief.

38 For the gift of a slab of Lord Buddha, see Chanda, 1919–20, p. 22 (*Budha-pamatu pata* = Sivaramamurti, 1956, p. 283, no. II C 13 and no. 48).

39 Lüders, 1912, no. 1248 (*dhamacaka* = Sivaramamurti, 1956, pp. 283–4, no. II E 6–7 and no. 51); Lüders, 1912, no. 1253 (*cakapata*).

40 Lüders, 1912, no. 1273 (*purnaghadakapata* = Sivaramamurti, 1956, p. 281, no. II C 3 and no. 41) and Chanda, 1919–20, no. 48 (*kalasa* = Sivaramamurti, 1956, p. 282, no. II C 10 and no. 45).

41 Lüders, 1912, no. 1287 (Francis, 2016, no. 203: *sothikapatā* and *abātamālā*) and Chanda, 1919–20, no. 47 (*sothikapatā* and *abātamālā* = Sivaramamurti, 1956, p. 282, no. II C 11 and no. 46). Compare Lüders, 1912, no. 1249 (*abātamālā* = Sivaramamurti, 1956, p. 281, no. II C 5 and no. 42; Francis, 2016, no. 187), this last (depending on what *abātamālā* means) is another case of transferred reference since the slab on which it is carved was a *purnaghata*, or vase with overflowing flowers. *Abātamālā* is obscure: Francis, 2016, p. 138, unhelpfully says 'a type of carved slab'; Vincent Tournier (pers. comm.) writes: 'Taking *abāta* as equivalent to Skt. *avāta* (which is unproblematic phonologically), one gets the literal meaning "fresh" (that is, never drying up) "garland" (mālā).' If this is correct, as likely, it implies the interesting issue – especially for a religion so focused on impermanence (*anicca*) – that unlike actual flowers which degenerate swiftly, there is great longevity to the sculpted kind.

42 Sarma, 1980, no. 88, and Francis, 2016, no. 182. See Sarma, 1980, no. 87; and Francis, 2016, no. 181: 'the gift of three elephants for the Buddhist *saṅgha*', presumably meaning three *carved* elephants! Both inscriptions are on fragments of coping.

43 Examples include BM 1880,0709.54, 117 and 118, Knox, 1992, nos 106–8; AMA nos 3, 5, 175, 218, 238, 265–6, 271, 324, 343–4, 387, 390–91, 459, 535, 617–18, respectively Gupta, 2008, nos G. 390, 391, 411, 420, 424, 430–31, 496, 436, 437–8, 444, 445–6, 456, 470, 480–81; GMC nos 190, 191, 197, 198, 199, 207, 208, in Kannan, 2014, pp. 191, 194, 196, 197 and Sivaramamurti, 1956, pp. 170–71, nos II C 1–10.

44 The panels are BM 1880,0709.80, BM 1880,0709.83 and BM 1880,0709.84, Knox, 1992, nos 73, 75, 76.

45 See Burgess, 1887; Barrett, 1954, p. 38; Roy, 1994, p. 120.

46 For the subject labels at Bharhut, see Barua and Simha, 1926, pp. 39–99, nos 135–225; Lüders, Waldschmidt and Mehendale, 1963, pp. 66–181, nos B 1–82. For subject labels at Kanaganahalli see Nakanishi and von Hinüber, 2014, pp. 85–108, nos I.1–2, III.1.1–18, III.2.1–31, III.3.1–6, IV.1, 3–6, 11. For some discussion of both sites, see Dehejia, 2007.

47 These include flower vases (*puphagahani*); the image of a stūpa (*cetiya*), reliefs of *dharmacakras*, *buddhapāda* (*payapata*); see respectively Nakanishi and von Hinüber, 2014, nos II.2.1–10, 13–14; II.5.1; II.5.2–3; II.6.1–4.

48 BM 1880,0709.108, Knox, 1992, p. 46; Guy, 2023, pp. 97–8.

49 Cunningham in Fergusson, 1873, p. 262, no. xxviii; and Lüders, 1912, no. 1223.

50 Dehejia, 1970, pp. 51–2, followed by Knox, 1992, p. 106.

51 Among the sixteen pieces of coping in the British Museum (Knox, 1992, nos 31–46), only one – no. 25, BM 1880,0709.35 – appears to have no carving or inscription on its borders.

52 Examples include BM 1880,0709.1, BM 1880,0709.4, BM 1880,0709.18, BM 1880,0709.22, BM 1880,0709.37, BM 1880,0709.57, BM 1880,0709. 60, BM 1880,0709.70,

BM 1880,0709.77, BM 1880,0709.79, BM 1880,0709.88, BM 1880,0709.91, respectively Knox, 1992, nos 8, 6, 37, 38, 15, 121, 49, 69, 55, 72, 52, 53.

53 BM 1880,0709.24, Knox, 1992, p. 1, with the inscription in Lüders, 1912, no. 1209.

54 BM 1880,0709.28, respectively Knox, 1992, p. 2, with the inscription in Lüders, 1912, no. 1220.

55 See Ahir, 2000, pp. 12–19, for stories in sculptures now in the Chennai and Amaravati Museums; Knox, 1992, pp. 64, 66, 72, 74, 78, 101–2, 115–16, 118, 129, 130, 132, 136, 138, 142, 146, 148, 149, 150, 152 and 154, for stories in slabs collected in the British Museum.

56 See Zin, 2016.

57 See, for example, Becker, 2016, pp. 71–4.

58 Sivaramamurti, 1956, pp. 285–8, no. II E 29 and no. 60; also Rao, 1998, pp. 75–80. See for another late inscription, Sivaramamurti, 1956, p. 285, no. II. E 27 and no. 57.

59 See Sircar, 1965, pp. 127–8. Examples include Sivaramamurti, 1956, nos 7, 8, 31, 33, 34, 36, 37, 39, 41, 44, 50, 51, 55, 99, 103, 110, 111, 117, 118, 124; Sarkar, 1971, nos 60, 61, 63, 65; AMA no. 714, in Gupta, 2008, no. G 485,

60 Examples include Sivaramamurti, 1956, no. 35.

61 Examples include Lüders, 1912, nos 1227 (BM 1880-0709-93), 1234, 1240, 1274; Sivaramamurti, 1956, nos 36, 39, 44, 97 (probably), 100, 102, 103, 110, 111, 124 (probably); Chanda, 1980, no. 86.

62 An unfortunate omission of the most important collection of inscriptions by Heinrich Lüders which gives neither complete transcriptions nor full translations: Lüders, 1912. For a good account of the formulaic nature of the Nāgārjunakonda inscriptions, which are in many ways close to those from nearby Amarāvatī, see Schopen, 1997, pp. 148–9; for some discussion of the formal aspects of the Bharhut inscriptions, see Lüders, Waldschmidt and Mehendale, 1963, p. 1.

63 Burgess, 1887, p. 86; Sivaramamurti, 1956, no. 50; Francis, 2016, no. 145.

64 Burgess, 1887, p. 86.

65 The pillar is GMC no. 177, in Kannan, 2014, pp. 9, 187, with measurements, 366–7; and Sivaramamurti, 1956, pp. 172–3, no. II E 5. See also Burgess, 1887, pp. 86–7.

66 Many inscriptions name more than just the main male, but see Lüders, 1912, nos 1210 (also a *caitya* pillar), 1215, 1303, for named males and no. 1268 for named females.

67 On the economy of merit see Amore, 1971; Spiro, 1970, pp. 92–113 (in relation to the anthropology of Burma); Rotman, 2009, pp. 9–13, 197–9 (focusing on the Sanskrit tradition of the *Divyāvadāna* versions of the *jātakas*).

68 For instance, Cunningham, 1873, nos 5, 13 (= BM 1880,0709.37), 17 and 19; Sivaramamurti, 1956, nos 2 (= Chanda, 1919–20, nos 43, 37 and 38), 4 (= Lüders, 1912, no. 1231), 6 (= Chanda, 1919–20, no. 39), 47 (= Lüders, 1912, no. 1301), 49, 50 (= Lüders, 1912, no. 1229), 59 (= Lüders, 1912, no. 1277), 64 (= Lüders, 1912, no. 1254), 68, 69 (= Lüders, 1912, no. 1250), 70 (= Lüders, 1912, no. 1286), 71 (= Lüders, 1912, no. 1253), 73 (= Lüders, 1912, no. 1251), 74 (= Lüders, 1912, no. 1264), 79 (= Lüders, 1912, no. 1263), 80 (= Lüders, 1912, no. 1315), 83 (= Lüders, 1912, no. 1237), 85, 86 (= Lüders, 1912, no. 1247), 87 (= Lüders, 1912, no. 1261), 88 (= Chanda, 1919–20, nos 32), 93 (= Lüders, 1912, no. 1246), 94, 99 (= Lüders, 1912, no. 1295). Also BM 1880,0709.57 with Knox, 1992, no. 121, p. 212. Unfortunately, Lüders, 1912, does not transliterate all the inscriptions in his corpus, so cannot be used as the basis for making a list.

69 Cunningham, 1873, no. 18 (BM 1880,0709.108); Sivaramamurti, 1956, nos 2 (= Chanda, 1919–20, nos 43, 37 and 38), 48 (= Chanda, 1919–20, nos 22), 52 (= Chanda, 1919–20, nos 24), 54 (= Lüders, 1912, no. 1269).

70 Examples where the stone is named are Sivaramamurti, 1956, nos 4, 59, 64, 73, 79, 85, 86, 87, 88.

71 For instance, AMA nos 1 and 235, respectively Gupta, 2008, F 340 (HAABA 0021280), F 347; Chennai Museum HAABA 0027750, 0027752; BM 1880,0709.69, BM 1880,0709.70, BM 1880,0709.72, BM 1880,0709.75, BM 1880,0709.79, BM 1880,0709.87, BM 1880,0709.120, BM 1880,0709.121, BM 1880,0709.122, respectively Knox, 1992, nos 68, 69, 70, 71, 72, 77, 78, 79, 80; Boston 29.151.

72 AMA nos 7, 8, 19, 22, 417, 418, 419, respectively Gupta, 2008, F 361–2, 341–2, 351–3; Chennai Museum: Sivaramamurti, 1956, pp. 264–6, nos IV C 3–5, 7–10, 13; BM 1880,0709.69, BM 1880,0709.70, BM 1880,0709.72, BM 1880,0709.79, BM 1880,0709.80, BM 1880,0709.83, BM 1880,0709.85, BM 1880,0709.87, BM 1880,0709.120, BM 1880,0709.121, BM 1880,0709.122, respectively Knox, 1992, nos 68, 69, 70, 72, 73, 75, 76, 77, 78, 79, 80; Boston 29.151.

73 Mauss, 1923–4, translated as Mauss, 1954. For rich theoretical discussion about Mauss' model see, for example, Bataille, 1988 (originally in French 1949); Lévi-Strauss, 1950; Firth, 1959; Sahlins, 1974; Hyde, 1983; Davis, 1996; Godbout and Caillé, 1998; Wyschogrod, Goux and Boynton, 2002; Algazi, Groebner and Jussen, 2003; Testart, 2007; Azoulay, 2013; Pyyhtinen, 2014.

74 Of course, this always means from Eurocentric perspective: for an attack on Mauss' occidentalism, see Carrier, 1995; and for the conceptual roots of Mauss' system in Germanic legal concepts see Wagner-Hasel, 2003.

75 These quotations are from Wood, 2011, pp. 223 and 226 ('votive system') and 208, 211 ('bargain struck').

76 This quotation is from Osborne, 2004, p. 2. A recent account of the reciprocity scenario in Greek religious dedications is Smith, 2021, pp. 155–224.

77 On the discussion of *ex votos* see most recently the essays collected in Weinryb, 2016 and 2018; for criticism, see, for example, Godelier, 1999, pp. 108–99.

78 Grace: for St Augustine on grace as a gift given for its own sake and not for a return or reward, see Karfíková, 2012, pp. 75–87, 126–9, 337.

79 See Trautmann, 1981, pp. 279–88; Parry, 1986, pp. 461–3; Hibbets, 1999, pp. 451–6; Heim, 2004, pp. 12–13, 33–55, 144–6, on the denial of both reciprocity and obligation in ancient Indian understandings of the gift; Ohnuma, 2007, pp. 140–66, also 183–93; Appleton, 2014, pp. 75–81. For extended discussion of *dāna* in Brahmanical culture, see Kane, 1941, pp. 837–88 and Nath, 1987. For dāna in the Pāli tradition, see Sizemore and Swearer, 1990, pp. 13–16, 103–5, 224–6; Findly, 2003. On art, see Huntington, 2012, pp. 16–17.

80 See for instance Bailey and Mabbett, 2003, pp. 232–56, on 'exchange'; Rotman, 2009, pp. 7–12, 58–9 on 'market morality'.

81 In particular in matters of religion, gift-giving in Indian culture is 'necessarily unreciprocated' since it is ultimately about

renunciation: Ohnuma, 2007, pp. 164–6; Appleton, 2014, p. 78 (whence the quotation); for what he calls 'heroic generosity' see Egge, 2002, pp. 34–9, 101–4.

82 See, for example, *Majjima Nikāya* 1.379–80 (no. 56, *Upāli Sutta* 18), with Gethin, 1998, p. 83.

83 For the *pāramitā*s, see Dayal, 2004 (first published in 1932), pp. 165–269. For the Theravāda model, see Endo, 1997, pp. 267–99.

84 It is not known how many perfections or in what list and order other Nikāya schools than the Theravāda presented the perfections as the key elements to the Bodhisattva path, but it is not impossible that the usual Mahāyāna six derive from one of these now lost traditions. The two sets of ten and six are reconciled in the Theravāda commentary by Dhammapāla, which may date from any time between the fifth and tenth centuries: Dhammapāla, *Paramatthapadīpanī* XII, in Bodhi, 1978, pp. 243–317, esp. 301–3. In his commentary on the *Itivuttaka*, a collection of discourses in the canonical *Khuddaka Nikāya*, Dhammapāla writes of 'thirty perfections, viz, the ten perfections, the ten higher perfections and the ten ultimate perfections' in *Itivuttaka-aṭṭhakathā* 1.8 and 1.117, in Masefield, 2008, vol. I, pp. 19–20 and 292.

85 See, for example, McCombs, 2014, pp. 1–2, 88; Gaffney, 2003, pp. 99–100, on *dāna* in the *Nidānakathā*. For the place of *dāna* in an early Mahāyāna sūtra, the *Ugraparipṛcchā* (translated into Chinese in the second century CE), see Nattier, 2003, pp. 111–14, 153–4.

86 See Dutt, 1978, p. 228.

87 All three of these texts are found in the *Khuddaka Nikāya*, the last (literally, the 'small') collection of texts in the *Sutta Piṭaka* of Theravāda Buddhism. See Endo, 1997, pp. 219–99, on the Theravāda Bodhisattva tradition (especially in the Pāli commentaries); and Gaffney, 2003, pp. 64–85; also Appleton, 2010, pp. 109–16, with current assumptions about dating and chronology at 114–16. For interesting discussion of Buddhaghosa and the commentarial tradition on these stories, see Heim, 2014, pp. 181–216.

88 See, for example, Pagel, 1995, pp. 1–2 for date, 4–6 for association with (if not origin in) Mahāsāṃghika circles, 145–60 on *dāna* (which he translates as 'liberality'); Nattier, 2003, pp. 41–7, on the likely dates of the *Ugraparipṛcchā* and 240–45, 304–5, for its account of the perfections; Braarvig, 1993, pp. xli–xlix for date and 114–30 for translation of the section on *dāna*.

89 For a brief introduction to these, see Williams, 2009, pp. 45–62. For the complexities of the literary archaeology of the earliest ur-texts, see Walser, 2018, pp. 129–89.

90 *Aṣṭasāhasrikā Prajñāpāramitā* 3.4 (where the first five perfections are effectively subsumed into *prajña*, the sixth); verse summary, Chapters 28–32, with Chapter 31 on giving, although this segment of the text may well be a later addition. See Conze, 1994, pp. x, 69–70, 111–12. See also, for example, *Pañcaviṃśatisāhasrikā Prajñāpāramitā Sūtra* (*The Perfection of Wisdom in Twenty-five Thousand Lines*) I.1e.2, I.7, I.8.2, I.10.7- I.10.8d, V.8.9, VI.1–6, respectively Conze, 1961, pp. 46, 128–31, 132, 198–200, 533–6, 549–51. On the relative dates of the earliest *Prajñāpāramitā* sūtras and developments in India, with a preference for Andhra origins (that remains possible but certainly contestable) see Conze, 1958a, pp. 1–18; and Westerhoff, 2018, pp. 93–5.

91 Mäll, 2003, pp. 96–9; Williams, 2009, pp. 47–9.

92 See Endo, 1997, pp. 237–8, 277–84, 306–7.

93 See Conze, 1958b, pp. 26–7.

94 See Horner, 1978, pp. 388 and 389, referring only to *dāna* out of the ten perfections in relation to the first and last previous lives of the Bodhisattva, that is as Sumedha who took the Bodhisattva vow and Vessantara, his last rebirth.

95 *Pañcaviṃśatisāhasrikā prajñāpāramitā sūtra* I.7a and VIII.5.1 e- VIII.5.3, in Conze, 1979, pp. 128–9, 579–90, with discussion by McCombs, 2014, pp. 36–7. Also *Pañcaviṃśatisāhasrikā prajñāpāramitā sūtra* I.10.8a–d in Conze, 1979, pp. 198–200, where giving and wisdom are discussed in detail to stand for all six perfections.

96 On his location at the Badaratitthavihāra, perhaps near Kanchipuram, see Norman, 1983, p. 134. One interesting aspect of Dhammapāla's work is that he has certainly read the Sanskrit sources and so offers interpretations inflected by engagement with non-Theravāda Nikāya traditions, probably including Mahāyāna texts. See Endo, 1997, pp. 248–9, 271–3, 308.

97 Dhammapāla, *Paramatthapadīpanī* XI, in Bodhi, 1978, pp. 300–301, with Appleton, 2010, pp. 101–3.

98 See Vasubhandu, *Abhidharmakośa*, in Pruden, 1990, pp. 695–706. This represents an approach drawn on the traditions of the Sarvāstavāda and Sautrāntika Nikāya schools. Rupert Gethin tells me he thinks Dhammapāla read and quotes this text.

99 See *Ugraparipṛcchā* 10A–11G, in Nattier, 2003, pp. 240–45.

100 Lamotte, 1970, pp. viii–xliv, on the author and his sources, with xl for the conclusion that the author postdates Nāgārjuna himself.

101 See *Mahāprajñāpāramitāśāstra* II. 750–69, in Lamotte, 1949, pp. 750–69; and Skorupski, 2002, pp. 20–22.

102 *Nidānakathā* 72, in Jayawickrama, 1990, p. 96, with discussion by Gaffney, 2003, p. 118; *Nidānakathā* 74, in Jayawickrama, 1990, p. 97.

103 *Nidānakathā* 74, in Jayawickrama, 1990, p. 98. Compare the much briefer discussion of *dāna* in the Sanskrit *Lalitavistara* 21.188, perhaps from the late second or third century CE. There is no mention either of the perfections nor of calling the earth to witness in our earliest life of the Buddha, Aśvaghoṣa's Sanskrit *Buddhacarita* from the first or second century CE in canto 13 on the defeat of Māra. In the relevant section of the mixed Pāli, Sanskrit and Prakrit *Mahāvastu* 412 (Jones, 1952, vol. II, p. 366), the Bodhisattva strikes the earth to defeat Māra's army but does not call it to witness and there is no reference to the perfections. On the other hand, the imagery of the Bodhisattva touching the earth (the *Bhūmisparśa Mudrā*) is frequent in Gandhāra but largely absent in Mathurā and Andhra. I think we are looking here at multiple early traditions preserved in sources of different date (Buddhaghosa's *Nidānakathā*, like all his commentaries, draws on much earlier now lost material): Spagnoli, 2005, seems to me confused on many of these matters.

104 On the *Nidānakathā*, see Gaffney, 2003 (and esp. pp. 86–120 on the perfections); Appleton, 2010, pp. 61–4; Tournier and Strong, 2019, p. 25. For the text see Jayawickrama, 1990.

105 See *Buddhavaṃsa* II A 117–66, in Horner, 1975, *Chronicle*, 20–23, also Buddhadatta's fifth-century commentary in Horner, 1978, pp. 150–64.

106 *Nidānakathā* 19–25, in Jayawickrama, 1990, pp. 25–32 (with *dāna* described at 25). This in turn borrows from (or perhaps serves as a commentary to) the first-person verse account of Sumedha's

resolution at *Buddhavaṃsa* II A 117–66 in Horner, 1975, 20–23 (with *dāna* at II A 117–20, p. 20). This section of the *Nidānakathā* (that is, the Sumedha story) is reused by Buddhaghosa as part of the introductory setting for the Buddha's attainment of the *Abhidhamma* or higher teaching, in his commentary on the *Dhammasaṅgaṇī*, the first of the seven texts in the canonical *Abhidhamma Piṭaka*; see Heim, 2018, pp. 157–8, where she argues that Buddhaghosa sees the ten perfections as the origin and context of the Buddha's omniscience. See also Heim, 2014, pp. 184–5, for Buddhaghosa's picture of the first glimpse of *Abhidhamma* by Sumedha, the maturity of its command in the *jātakas* and its full mastery under the Bodhi tree.

107 *Jātaka Nidānakathā* §19–25, in Jayawickrama, 1990, pp. 258–69 (with *dāna* described at 58–61).

108 For a rich summary discussion of *dāna*, see Dayal, 2004, pp. 172–93.

109 For an introduction to these, see Appleton, 2010, pp. 1–19. For the Bodhisattva ideal within this literary form, see Fronsdal, 1998, pp. 115–19; Gaffney, 2003, pp. 61–85; Appleton, 2010, pp. 91–108.

110 See Gaffney, 2003, pp. 86–120; Shaw, 2006, pp. xxix–xliv; Appleton, 2010, pp. 12–13, 25–6, 98–103, notwithstanding the comment by Appleton that 'the general association of the *jātaka* genre and the perfections has been overplayed in both Buddhist and scholarly assessments': Appleton, 2020, p. 26.

111 See, for example, Ohnuma, 2007, pp. 26–51 on 'the gift-of-the-body genre'; Appleton, 2014, pp. 94–102. For the problems perceived by some in relation to extreme gift giving as a Bodhisattva practice in the early Mahāyāna, see Boucher, 2008, pp. 27–39.

112 See Horner, 1975, *Basket of Conduct*, pp. xv and 1–17, with discussion by Norman, 1983, pp. 94–5; and Appleton, 2010, pp. 66–8, 98–103.

113 *Jātaka Nidānakathā* 45, in Jayawickrama, 1990, p. 58. See Appleton, 2010, pp. 98–103, on the problem of the mismatch between the lists. For the centrality of gifts and generosity to the Sanskrit Sarvāstivādin *Avadānaśataka* collection of a hundred stories, see Appleton, 2020, pp. 11, 15, 25–6, 38.

114 These are *jātaka* nos 316, 547, in the Pāli collection, respectively Francis and Neil, 1897, pp. 34–7; Cowell and Rouse, 1907, pp. 246–305. Both stories appear in the *dāna* list of the *Nidānakathā*.

115 *Cāriyāpiṭaka* I. 3, 9 and 10; II. 2, 3, 4, 7 and 10.

116 Schlingloff, 1984–6; with Rana, 2013, pp. 115–18 for the relevant slab. See Zin, 2016, pp. 48–9, for the problem.

117 Respectively Rana, 2013, pp. 81–2, *jātaka* no. 40, in Chalmers, 1895, pp. 100–105; and Subrahmanyam, 2005, pp. 53–62 (with comparanda from Goli and Gumadidurru); Rana, 2013, pp. 102–4; *jātaka* no. 514, in Francis, 1905, pp. 20–31.

118 On Mahāyāna models of giving the body, see Ohnuma, 2007, pp. 83–5; and McCombs, 2014, pp. 42–9.

119 The most recent translation is by S. Shaw in Appleton and Shaw, 2015, pp. 534–639, with an introduction at pp. 507–34. See also Cone and Gombrich, 1977, translated with a substantial introduction pp. xv–xlvii; Collins, 1998, pp. 497–554; and Collins, 2015. On *dāna* in this story, see Shaw, 2015, pp. 511–13.

120 For example, at Amarāvatī, BM 1880,0709.35, BM 1880,0709.70, BM 1880,0709.72, BM 1880,0709.83, BM 1880,0709.87, BM 1880,0709.122, respectively Knox, 1992, nos 42, 69, 70, 75, 77, 80; GMC no. 115, in Kannan, 2014, p. 166; and Sivaramamurti, 1956, pp. 260–62, no. IV B 1; AMA no. 1, Gupta, 2008, no. F 340. See Subrahmanyam, 2005, pp. 182–200; for the Amarāvatī examples with rich Andhra comparanda; and Rana, 2013, pp. 107–10.

121 Horner, 1964, pp. 95–109, with discussion by Collins, 2015, pp. 7–11.

122 *Jātaka Nidānakathā* 25, in Jayawickrama, 1990, p. 32; Dhammapāla, *Paramatthapadīpanī* XI, in Bodhi, 1978, p. 299.

123 Dhammapāla, *Paramatthapadīpanī* XI, in Bodhi, 1978, p. 300; see Dhammapāla, *Itivuttaka-aṭṭhakathā* 1.8 and 1.117, in Masefield, 2008, vol. I, pp. 19–20 and 292, for lists of kinds of *dāna* that fulfil the three levels.

124 Dhammapāla, *Paramatthapadīpanī* XI, in Bodhi, 1978, pp. 300–301.

125 See Appleton, 2010, p. 103.

126 Dhammapala, *Paramatthapadīpanī* X, in Bodhi, 1978, pp. 276–88, esp. 277. Mahāyāna examples include *Mahāprajñāpāramitāśāstra* II. 856 in Skorupski, 2002, p. 43 (also II. 700, Skorupski, 2002, p. 10, where the abandonment of defilements is added to abandonment of material goods, the dispensation of Dharma and the bestowal of fearlessness); also the *Bodhisattvabhūmi* I. 9.2.3. in Engle, 2016, p. 224: 'the giving of Dharma, material objects and protection (*dharmāmiṣābhayadāna*)'; and McCombs, 2014, p. 298 (this text is attributed to the fourth-century Gandharan master Asanga but may be earlier; see McCombs, 2014, pp. 252–4); a treatise translated into Chinese by Kumarajiva (344–413) and attributed to Asanga's half-brother the great scholar Vasubandhu entitled *On the Generating the Bodhi Resolve Sūtra* 4. B, with Dahrmamitra, 2009, p. 53. Intriguingly, the order of the list is different in the various commentaries.

127 On *abhayadāna* in medieval Indian thought (Hindu, Buddhist and Jain), see Hibbets, 1999.

128 Dhammapala, *Paramatthapadīpanī* X in Bodhi, 1978, p. 279; *Mahāprajñāpāramitāśāstra* II. 856 with Skorupski, 2002, p. 44.

129 See, for example, Prasad, 2008, pp. 225–6.

130 Just to take the examples in the British Museum. The Buddha or Bodhisattva appears in relief in this posture in BM 1880,0709.11 (a railing pillar, once), BM 1880,0709.40 (miscellaneous slab, once) BM 1880,0709.70 (stūpa relief, four times – standing in the central gateway and in a miniature relief on the left of the dome, and twice seated as Bodhisattva in the Tuṣita Heaven in the *āyaka* platform relief and the central dome roundel), BM 1880,0709.72 (stūpa relief, seated in the central gateway), BM 1880,0709.75 (stūpa relief, three times, seated in the central gateway, seated and standing in two miniature dome slabs to the right), BM 1880,0709.79 (stūpa relief, six times, standing in the central gateway, seated as a Bodhisattva in the *āyaka* platform relief, and four times seated or standing in the dome slabs), BM 1880,0709.83 (stūpa relief, seated as Bodhisattva in the Tuṣita Heaven in the lower roundel in the gateway), BM 1880,0709.120 (stūpa relief, seven times – five at the bases of the *āyaka* pillars, once enthroned as Bodhisattva in the Tuṣita Heaven and once standing in a miniature dome slab to the right), BM 1880,0709.73 (drum pilaster, twice seated), BM 1880,0709. 82 (drum pilaster, once seated), BM 1880,0709.84 (drum pilaster, three times seated), respectively Knox, 1992, nos 12, 69, 70, 71, 72, 75, 78, 83, 84, 85.

131 All these are standing Buddhas who do not have extant hands, but the posture looks correct for the *abhāya mudrā*, especially by comparison with the many reliefs of standing Buddhas. British Museum: BM 1880,0709.128, Knox, 1992, p. 127 (assuming an early date for this piece); Chennai Museum: GMC nos 163, 164, in Kannan, 2014, p. 183; and Sivaramamurti, 1956, nos IV F 3–4, 6–8, in Burgess, 1887, p. 97, pls LII.1–4 and 7; Amarāvatī Archaeological Museum: AMA nos 16, 273, 318, 333, 346, respectively Gupta, 2008, nos J. 690, 838, 839, 840, 842.

132 Sitaramamma, 2004. We may add a number of other sites: the standing Buddhas of the first three decades CE from Guntupalli (ibid., 149) and Alluru (AMA nos 54 and 55, in Gupta, 2008, nos J 827 and 828).

133 Sitaramamma, 2004, p. 150. On the *bhūmisparśa mudrā*, see Spagnoli, 2005.

134 For the *abhāya mudrā* as the main preference at Mathurā and Gandhāra as well as Amarāvatī, see Foucher, 1918, pp. 326–8; also Van Lohuizen-De Leeuw, 1949, pp. 125–30 (on the range of *mudrā*s in Gandhāra with *abhāya mudrā* as the earliest alongside *dhyana mudrā*), 195 (on *abhāya* as the normal *mudrā* in Mathurā); Sharma, 1984, pp. 177, 183, 187–8; Zwalf, 1996, p. 39 (on standing figures); Rhi, 2013, pp. 2–5, for the precedence of the *abhāya mudrā* over the *dhyāna, bhūmisparśa* and *dharmacakra* forms (the meditation, earth-touching and teaching postures). Note that unlike the *dhyana mudrā*, which was shared with the Jains, the *abhāya mudrā* is unique to Buddhism: see Van Lohuizen-De Leeuw, 1949, p. 158.

135 On *pasāda/prasāda*, see the discussions of Gethin, 2001, pp. 112–13; and Rotman, 2009, pp. 66–87.

136 See Rotman, 2008, pp. 1–30, on the text. One of the striking commitments to *dāna* in this text is its inclusion, as the 34th 'story' in the collection, of the *dānādhikarana-mahāyānasūtra*, the Mahāyāna Sūtra on the Topic of Giving: see Rotman, 2017, pp. 197–9. For other *avadāna*s with *dāna* central, see Rotman, 2009, pp. 8–10, 58, 211 n. 23.

137 *Divyāvadāna* 78.6–79.16, in Rotman, 2008, pp. 155–8, with discussion by Rotman, 2009, p. 117.

138 On *prasāda* and sight, see Rotman, 2009, pp. 65, 118, 165–6. On the 'automatic' arousal of *prasāda* in an auspicious context like a shrine of stūpa, see Rotman, 2009, pp. 130–34.

139 On *prasāda*, as cause and agent of *dāna*, both motivating an act of giving and accompanying its performance, see Rotman, 2009, pp. 108–12.

140 *Mahāprajñāpāramitāśāstra* II.724 in Skorupski, 2002, p. 16.

141 Ibid., II.734–50, pp. 17–20.

142 *On the Generating of the Bodhi Resolve Sūtra* 4.G, Dharmamitra, 2009, pp. 59, see 129: 'though he practices giving he does not perceive the existence of anything given' (10.E).

143 *Pañcaviṃśatisāhasrikā prajñāpāramitā sūtra* V.8.9 in Conze, 1979, p. 533.

144 *Mahāprajñāpāramitāśāstra* II. 766–9 in Skorupski, 2002, p. 22.

145 Dhammapāla, *Paramatthapadīpanī* XII, in Bodhi, 1978, p. 308.

146 Ibid., XIII, p. 311.

147 Ibid., XVI, pp. 316–17.

148 Lüders, 1912, no. 1244 (*dhamathāna divakhabhō*, 'a lamp pillar as a seat of merit', Sivaramamurti, 1956, pp. 301–2, no. IV G 8 and no. 118; Francis, 2016, no. 200) on the fragment of an octagonal pillar.

149 Francis, 2016, p. 239, on a slab reused in a later Hindu temple and discovered in the 1930s: 'for the benefit of a *thera* or monk called Chitaka'; Chanda, 1919–20, no. 27 ('for longevity', Sivaramamurti, 1956, p. 304, no. IV G 18 and no. 126; Francis, 2016, no. 242) on the fragment of an octagonal pillar; Lüders, 1912, no. 1207 ('for the benefit of the donors' nephews, sons-in-law, granddaughters and grandsons', Francis, 2016, no. 246) on a drum frieze panel.

150 Sarkar, 1970–71, no. 56 (*savaloka satva hita sukhāya*, Francis, 2016, no. 132) on a pillar from the eastern gate.

151 Lüders, 1912, no. 1281 (*savasa ca lōkasa hitasukhathaya*, Sivaramamurti, 1956, p. 298, no. IV C 1 and no. 102; Francis, 2016, no. 232) on the great drum relief with miniature stūpa in Chennai, discussed at length in Chapter One.

152 Sivaramamurti, 1956, p. 298, no. IV C 9 and no. 103 (*savasatamata a . . .*, Francis, 2016, no. 233) also on a drum slab with a stūpa relief.

153 See Francis, 2002, pp. 241–4.

154 Nakanishi and von Hinüber, 2014, section I, no. 8, pp. 31–2 (120 CE); section I, no. 10, pp. 34–5 (125 CE); section I, no. 12, pp. 36–7 (181 CE); section I, no. 14, pp. 38–40 (225–40 CE); section II.5, nos 4 and 8, pp. 69 and 71; section II.6, nos 1–2, pp. 73–4.

155 See Schopen, 1997, pp. 34–43, for the range from family to 'all beings', also 59–65 emphasizing filial piety.

156 Schopen, 1997, pp. 38–43, insists, surely correctly, that these formulae and the aspiration for the transfer of merit belong to the Nikāya traditions, but he speaks of 'proto-Mahāyāna' in relation to one. We might say that they are entirely compatible with both Nikāya and Mahāyāna, with the latter (certainly during the period of the making of the great Indian stūpas) not a separate tradition but one developing within the local Mahāsāṃghika monastic and scholarly circles at any rate in Andhra.

157 Sāñcī: see Majumdar, 1940, pp. 297–384, esp. stūpa 1: nos 15–22, 24–123, 125–46, 148–55, 157–61, 164–6, 168–206, 209–14, 216–23, 226–31, 237–41, 243–6, 248–54, 256–8, 260–312, 314–42, 344–56, 358–63, 365–6, 368–72, 375–7, 380, 382, 384–8, 390–93, 395, 397–9, 402–3, 405–8, 410–23, 425–6, 428, 430, 436–7, 439–47, 450–79, 481–7, 489–90, 492–5, 498–512, 515–41, 543–7, 549–52, 556–65, 567–9, 581–3, 588, 592–603, 605, 608–12, 614–28; stūpa 2: nos 631–57, 659–89, 691–8, 701–11, 713–16, 718–19; stūpa 3: nos 720–27, 729–35; stūpa 4, pp. 744, 745, 749, 751, 753, 756, 759, 762–3, 765, 768, 770, 772, 774–8, 782, 784–91, 793, 797–8, 800–801, 803, 806–11, 813–15, 817–18, 820–24. This is the vast majority, and of those without *dāna* surviving in the text many are fragmentary. Also now Milligan, 2015, nos 1, 3–5. Bharhut: Barua and Simha, 1926, pillar inscriptions, 3–17, nos 1–45; rail bar inscriptions, 17–33, nos 1–66; coping inscriptions, 35–8, nos 13–15. Again the vast majority, where those without *dāna* surviving in the text are incomplete. For discussion of *dāna(m)* as the formal ending for the majority of Bharhut donative inscriptions, see Lüders, Waldschmidt and Mehendale, 1963, p. 1.

158 Nakanishi and von Hinüber, 2014, pp. section II.2, nos 1–6, 8–14, 24–6, 31–5, 38–40; section II.3, nos 3–8; section II.4, nos 7, 9–11, 13–14, 16, 19, 22; section II.5, nos 1, 10; section III.2, no. 8; section V.1, nos 1–4; section V.2, nos 3, 5–9, 11–14.

159 Kanaganahalli: Nakanishi and von Hinüber, 2014, section I, no. 8, pp. 31–2; section I, no. 10, pp. 34–5; section I, nos 12–14, pp. 36–40; section II.1, nos 3–4, pp. 42–4; section II.2, no. 18, p. 50; section II.5, nos 4 and 7, pp. 69–70; section II.6,

nos 1 and 6, pp. 73 and 75; section II.7. A nos 4–9, pp. 78–80. Nāgārjunakonda: *āyaka* pillar inscriptions with Vogel, 1929–30, nos A 2–4, B 1–5, C 1–5, D 2 and 4, E, F, G, H, J; Vogel, 1929–30; Vogel, 1931–2, nos G1–2, L; Chhabra, 1959–60 (in Sanskrit, late third century CE); Sircar and Krishnan, 1961–2, no. 1; Sircar, 1961–2; Sircar, 1963–4, nos 1 A and B, no. 2 B, no. 3, no. 4, no. 6 A, n. 7 B III; Sarkar, 1965–6; Baums, Griffiths, Strauch and Tournier, 2016, pp. 379–89 and esp. 383.

160 Singh, 2016, pp. 7–28 on Sāñcī, 50–53 on Nāgārjunakonda; Francis, 2002, pp. 98–167 on Amarāvatī; Lüders, Waldschmidt and Mehendale, 1963, pp. 1–10, with examples at 11–65, nos A 1–136 on Bharhut. For commemoration of royal donations at Kanaganahalli, see von Hinüber, 'Buddhist Texts and Buddhist Images', 2016, pp. 13–17.

161 For the subject labels at Bharhut, see Barua and Simha, 1926, pp. 39–99, nos 135–225; Lüders, Waldschmidt and Mehendale, 1963, pp. 66–181, nos B 1–82. For subject labels at Kanaganahalli see Nakanishi and von Hinüber, 2014, pp. 85–108, sections I, nos 1–2, III.1, nos 1–18, III.2, nos 1–31, III.3, nos 1–6, IV, nos 1, 3–6, 11 and Zin, 2018, *ad. loc.* slab by slab. The only Amarāvatī object with label inscriptions (an early pillar) was published by Ghosh and Sarcar, 1964–6, but now Tournier, 2020–21, has argued for a significant label inscription on a coping slab from the inner railing.

three VISUAL STORYTELLING AND THE VISION OF KARMA

1 On Buddhaghosa's fifth-century CE *Dhammapāda-atthakathā*, see, for example, Burlingame, 1910; and her translations of the stories: Burlingame, 1921. Generally on Buddhaghosa as commentator and exegete, see Bond, 1982, pp. 100–192; Norman, 1983, pp. 120–30; and Heim, 2018, pp. 60–106; on the Pāli commentarial tradition see Nyanatusita, 2021, pp. 823–70.

2 For the *Buddhacarita*, see Schotsman, 1995; and Olivelle, 2007; for the *Saundarananda*, see Covill, 2007 and 2009. For some aspects of the poetics of Aśvaghoṣa, see Churn Law, 1946, pp. 23–54; Covill, 2009, pp. 12–17. For the likelihood that Aśvaghoṣa belonged to a proto-Mūlasarvāstivāda doctrinal milieu among the Nikāya schools, see Eltschinger, 2012, 2013 and 2019.

3 Khoroche, 1989, pp. xi–xix; Meiland, 2009, pp. xvii–ixxi.

4 On *Manimēkalai*, see Daniélou, 1993, with discussion by Richman, 1988, pp. 37–9 on the relations of main and branch stories, pp. 123–42 on comparison stories, pp. 157–61 on authorship and dating; Monius, 2001, pp. 41–7 on interdependent stories and causality.

5 For the significance of these Buddhist texts in the bigger picture of Sanskrit poetics, see, for example, Xi He, 2011, pp. 93–6.

6 For karma as key to the *jātaka* and *avadāna* genres, see Strong, 1983, p. 22; Tatelman, 2000, pp. 4–7, 157–63; Egge, 2002, pp. 41–88; Appleton, 2020, pp. 8–9, 28–9, 49–50; Fifleld, 2017, pp. 70–106 on the *Mahāvastu*.

7 *Manimēkalai*, 30.263–4, in Daniélou, 1993, p. 172.

8 Ibid., 21.178–9, p. 92; and discussion by Monius, 2001, pp. 88–100.

9 For the issue of epitomic exemplarity in ancient visual culture, see Elsner, 2023.

10 For similar problems in Gandhāran art (where in certain cases we can begin to attempt reconstructions of sequences between slabs) see Behrendt, 2005.

11 In addition to its exceptional frieze, the narrative issues of this monument have an exceptional literature: see, for example, Brilliant, 1984, pp. 90–123; Settis, 1985, 1988 and 1991; Veyne, 1988 and 2005, pp. 379–418; de Angelis, 2014.

12 I am thinking, for example, here of Sivaramamurti, 1956, pp. 151–7, 164–7, 175–239, 248–62, where the cataloguing effort is done by means of the stories; Kumar, 2012, pp. 160–236; Rana, 2013, pp. 76–127; Chowdhuri, 2018, pp. 68–148. For the same problem in the context of the sculpture of Nāgārjunakonda, see, for example, Rama, 1995, pp. 103–56.

13 Dehejia, 1997, pp. 150–82.

14 Becker, 2015, pp. 78–143. Further accounts of Buddhist narrativity in visual media, concentrating on a wider corpus than just the sites of Āndhra, include, in addition to Dehejia, 1997: Schlinghoff, 1987, pp. 225–71; and Zin, 2019.

15 Dehejia, 1997, pp. 3–35. For a potent critique of some of the Westernizing assumptions about narrativity here and a failure to consider the complexity of the viewer's position vis à vis not always visible images, see Brown, 1997, pp. 64–109, esp. 65–71. For a critique of the simplicity of Dehejia's visual narrative model, in particular in dealing with visualized *jātakas*, see Appleton, 2010, pp. 125–9.

16 Dehejia, 1997, pp. 154–71.

17 Ibid., pp. 55–6.

18 Ibid., pp. 55–72. This is certainly the most extensive discussion to date of the textual canon that relates to the visual tradition. Although Dehejia mentions the *Dhammapāda-atthakatha* (p. 63), she generally underplays the importance of the commentarial tradition for both giving stories and framing them interpretatively, which I discuss below.

19 See Boucher, 2008, pp. 20–39, esp. 22–3.

20 For a brilliant account of Buddhist narrativity (entirely un-visual, it must be said, although images and relics as conceptual issues are discussed), focusing on Nirvana as the ending of narratives, see Collins, 1998, pp. 241–54.

21 See, for example, Zin, 2016.

22 For the definition of *jātaka* in relation to *avadāna* or *pūrvayoga*, a complex issue, see Appleton, 2010, pp. 3–6.

23 For example, Kumar, 2012, pp. 160–236 (life scenes and *jātakas*); Rana, 2013, chapter 4, pp. 76–113 on the *jātakas* and chapter 5, pp. 114–27 on the Buddha's life; Chowdhuri, 2018, pp. 70–114 (*jātakas* and Avadānas), 114–62 (life of the Buddha).

24 For the many complications and a bibliography, see Tournier, 2012 and 2017, pp. 353–5. On the implicit tripartite model of the Buddha's past, echoing the *Nidānakathā*, see Jones, 1949, vol. I, p. xiv; and Jones, 1952, vol. II, p. ix.

25 Current views are that the text as we currently have it was compiled in the fifth century – possibly by one of the famous commentators Buddhaghosa or Buddhadatta – but draws on much older traditions and sources. How far these go back and in particular the tripartite structure is very difficult to judge. See Gaffney, 1996, pp. 85–90.

26 See Frauwallner, 1956, pp. 50, 155, 163–5; Appleton, 2010, pp. 61–4.

27 See *Nidānakathā* 2, in Jayawickrama, 1990, p. 2, with discussion by Collins, 1990, pp. vii–ix.

28 But in her forthcoming translation Sarah Shaw prefers 'Origin'.

29 Cone, 2001, vol. II, pp. 561–2.

30 *Mahānidāna Sutta, Dīgha Nikāya* 15, ii. 55–71, in Walshe, 1987, pp. 223–30.

31 I am very grateful to Sarah Shaw for discussing the issues with me.

32 For Buddhadatta's date and place of activity, see Horner, 1978, p. xxx; and Norman, 1983, pp. 130–32, although at 145–6 he doubts that the *Buddhavaṃsa* commentary is by the same Buddhadatta. On the *Vaṃsa* (chronicle) form of literature, see Collins, 1998, pp. 254–81.

33 Horner, 1978, pp. 6–7.

34 Note that the final section of the *Buddhavaṃsa*, though not discussed in Buddhadatta's commentary (which may mean it was added after the likely fifth-century date of that work), is an account of the distribution of Gautama's relics, including the building of stūpas: *Buddhavaṃsa* XXVIII.1–13. This picks up on the building of stūpas or the distribution of relics for each of the 23 earlier Buddhas discussed in the text: for stūpas see II B 220, III 38, IV 35, V 34, VIII 29, X 33, XI 31 XIII 36, XIV 27, XVI 25, XVII 24, XVIII 28, XX 36, XXI 28, XXIII 27, XXV 52; for relics see VI 29, VII 30, IX 29, XII 31, XV 26, XIX 25, XXII 30, XXIV 29.

35 Text: Fausbøll, 1877–97; English trans. Cowell, ed., 1895–1913, 6 vols (to which I refer by individual volume with its translators as author in the notes) and into German by Dutoit, 1908–21.

36 For an introduction to the issues, see Skilling and Saerji, 2019, pp. 125–7.

37 See especially Zin, 2017.

38 See the discussion of *dāna* above in Chapter Two; Ohnuma, 2007, pp. 40–48; Appleton, 2010, pp. 98–103; Appleton and Shaw, 2015, pp. 4–7.

39 But it is equally the case that they illustrate deep patterns of unskilfulness, such as greed or delusion, that need to be penetrated and purified by the Bodhisattva in his path to perfection. The textual commentaries that focus on the Bodhisattva's perfections are not explicit on this (for example, the *Cāriyāpiṭaka, in* Horner, 1975, the *Nidānathā* 45–7, in Jayawickrama, 1990, pp. 58–61, or the *Madhuratthavilāsinī* 59–61, in Horner, 1978, pp. 89–92); but the stories themselves are (for example, that of Māndhāta, discussed below) and the visual tradition explores this.

40 For an introduction to narrative in the Ajanta murals, see, for example, Dehejia, 1997, pp. 207–37; Schlingloff, 1999.

41 See Heim, 2014, pp. 181–216; Appleton, 2014, pp. 93–102, on moral exemplars.

42 See Heim, 2014, pp. 191–212, for 'causes, reasons and intentions'. For psychology and the complexities of karma see, for example, Appleton, 2010, pp. 3–5, 26–8; and especially Appleton, 2014 (karma); Heim, 2014, pp. 190–91 (psychology).

43 See Ohnuma, 2007, pp. 174–5, on *dāna*.

44 See, for example, Vajirañana, 1975, pp. 185–97; Harrison, 1992b; Shulman, 2021, pp. 6, 84–93, 226.

45 Harrison, 1992b, p. 220; Rotman, 2009, pp. 173–5 and 193–5; Zhao, 2018.

46 *Visuddhimagga* 203, VII.34, in Ñanamoli, 1979, p. 216. The 'thirty perfections' mentioned here refer to the classic ten *parāmīs* of the Pāli tradition, each with three levels of attainment.

47 For discussion of the relations of the two texts see Anālayo, 2009, Nyanatusita, 2021, pp. 6–11. For the translations see Bapat, 1937, pp. xlv–xvii (Chinese), liv–lv (Tibetan); and Nyanatusita, 2021, pp. 14–15 (Tibetan), 89–118 (Chinese). Its original language – possibly Pāli, possibly Sanskrit or a form of Prakrit – cannot be certainly determined: Bapat, 1937, p. lv; though Nyanatusita, 2021, p. 20, is surely right that Pāli is most likely.

48 See *Vimuttimagga* IV.8.3, in Ehara, Soma and Kheminda, 1977, p. 143, = 8.76, in Nyanatusita, 2021, p. 392 (under 'Knower of the world') and Ehara, Soma and Kheminda, 1977, pp. 144–5 (under 'Teacher of divine and human beings') = 8.77–8, in Nyanatusita, 2021, pp. 394–5. Some discussion by Bapat, 1937, pp. 62–6; Harrison, 1992b, p. 219. Note that the order given for the ten perfections in *Vimuttimagga*. 8.78 is not the usual one, but ends with energy and wisdom, the last being the final one in the Mahāyāna tradition.

49 *Vimuttimagga* IV.8.3, in Ehara, Soma and Kheminda, 1977, p. 144, = *Vimuttimagga* 8.78, in Nyanatusita, 2021, p. 394.

50 See Crosby, 1999, pp. 510–12; Nyanatusita, 2021, pp. 44–9: 'between the second and early fifth century CE'.

51 On the other hand, the *jātakas* selected by the *Vimuttimagga* do not for the most part overlap with those chosen for the sculpture at Amarāvatī, and largely focus on animal lives. Other overlaps include the *Chaddanta Jātaka* (Francis, 1905, no. 514; Rana, 2013, pp. 102–4).

52 Translated by Harrison, 1978, p. 38 with discussion pp. 38–9; and Harrison, 1992b, pp. 219–30.

53 *Vimuttimagga* 8.75, in Nyanatusita, 2021, p. 387, with discussion at p. 86. This obscure passage, probably itself originally a mistranslation into the Chinese, is itself mistranslated in Ehara, Soma and Kheminda, 1977, p. 141.

54 *Visuddhimagga* 203, VII.67, in Nyanatusita, 2021, pp. 86 and 387, n. 494 – a phrase repeated also for the recollections of the *Dhamma* and the *Saṅgha* (at VII.88 and VII.100). The word that Nyanatusita translates as 'stūpa shrine-house', *cetiyagharaṃ* (which Ñanamoli, 1979, p. 230 gives as 'shrine room'), certainly implies a stūpa in the root *cetiya*.

55 For some reflections on how images relate to narratives and to imagination in early Buddhist art, with discussion of earlier literature, see Rotman, 2009, pp. 178–85. This does not touch on the issues examined here.

56 *Buddhavaṃsa* XXVIII, in Horner, 1975, *The Chronicle of Buddhas (Buddhavaṃsa)* 98–9; see Collins, 1998, pp. 259–60, on the likelihood that this is a redactor's addition later than the composition of the text and likely later than its fifth-century commentary.

57 There is a parallel here with what Strong, 2004, pp. 229–30 and 232–3, sees as the simultaneously biographical and episodic nature of Buddha relics. Buddhism is far from the only religious culture where image and relic are closely aligned in devotional practice.

58 Dehejia, 1997, pp. 15–19, see 117–20; also Brown, 1997, pp. 67–9.

59 See especially Covill, 2009, esp. pp. 1–30.

60 For example, BM 1880,0709.18 and BM 1880,0709.37, respectively Knox, 1992, nos 37 (with the elephant perhaps part of Mara's demon army) and 15 (an uncertain but exquisitely executed subject on a railing pillar); also within the copings of the railing on the following stūpa reliefs BM 1880,0709.70, BM 1880,0709.72, BM 1880,0709.75, respectively Knox, 1992, nos 69, 70, 71. For the *Chaddanta Jātaka*, see the crossbar medallion in Chennai: GMC no. 149, see Burgess, 1887, p. 50 and pl. XIX.1; Sivaramamurti, 1956, pp. 207–9, nos III B 3; Rana, 2013, pp. 102–4; Kannan, 2014, p. 177; Chowdhuri, 2018, pp. 91–3. For the exquisite rendering of the descent of the Buddha as an elephant from the Tuṣita Heaven into the womb of Queen Māyā, on a coping block now in Calcutta, see HAABA 5073 and 5074, with Mackenzie's drawing

by Nujbulla from 22 April 1819 in the British Library: WD1061, folio 83, illus. 52 and 53 in this volume.

61 For example, BM 1880,0709.4, BM 1880,0709.10, BM 1880,0709.47, BM 1880,0709.108, respectively Knox, 1992, nos 6 (top of the outer face), 7, 10, 46.

62 For the multiple metaphorical meanings of elephants and their training in early Buddhism, see Covill, 2009, pp. 71–98; Ohnuma, 2017, pp. 64–5, 77–8, 129–77. One might add numerous other themes that cut across different storylines – such as *nāgas*, other kinds of magical and divine beings (for example, *yakṣas*) and so forth.

63 Dhammapāla was certainly active in South India (Norman, 1983, p. 134), but unfortunately cannot be dated save that he is after Buddhaghosa, who is most likely early fifth century. Norman, 1983, p. 137, estimates we would 'not be far out if we assume' him to be writing in the mid-sixth century, but recent scholarship has placed him much later.

64 For example, *Paramatthapdīpanī nāma udāna-aṭṭhakathā* 265, 316 (Masefield, 1995, vol. II, pp. 634 and 718, 788 and 844–5). For some discussion of this commentary, see Egge, 2002, pp. 89–100.

65 Dehejia, 1997, pp. 154–62; Becker, 2015, pp. 83–9.

66 Drum friezes that certainly move right to left include: BM 1880,0709.112, Knox, 1992, no. 57, and Becker, 2015, p. 83; GMC nos 114 and 115, in Sivaramamurti, 1956, pp. 251–3, no. IV A 4, pp. 260–62, no. IV B 1; and Kannan, 2014, p. 166. Interior coping friezes that certainly move left to right include: BM 1880,0709.23, BM 1880,0709.35, respectively Knox, 1992, nos 41 and 42; GMC no. 123, in Sivaramamurti, 1956, pp. 235–8, no. III B 23; and Kannan, 2014, p. 169.

67 See Rana, 2013, pp. 121–2, pls 5.6a–c (but mistakenly said to be in the Government Museum Madras); HAABA 0005072–4, with Mackenzie's drawing by Nujbulla from 22 April 1819 in the British Library: WD1061, folio 83.

68 For the texts discussed in this paragraph and the next, see Jayawickrama, 1990, pp. 63–71; and Horner, 1978, pp. 389–400. The *Mahāvastu* offers a Mahāsāṃghika version at Jones, 1952, pp. 1–45. A Mahāyāna version of the story is told in the *Lalitavistara Sūtra*, chapters 5–6, which was translated into Chinese in the fourth century CE (for a translation from the Tibetan version, see Dharmacakra Translation Committee, 2013, pp. 33–59).

69 The quotation is from I. B. Horner's translation in Horner, 1978, p. 291.

70 On Māyā, see Ohnuma, 2012, pp. 66–85.

71 BM 1880,0709.23, Knox, 1992, no. 41.

72 The heights of the two slabs are reported as 82.5 centimetres (83 in.) for the British Museum panel and 83.8 centimetres (33 in.) for the Calcutta panel on Mackenzie's drawing, but with the measurement set against the damaged left-hand side. Both blocks are in excellent condition on the inner side but destroyed on the outer. The similarity of figure execution, border patterns and divisional framing between scenes certainly suggests the same group of artists and date – compare especially the royal figures of the Bodhisattva enthroned and King Śuddhodana in the left-hand scene of each block.

73 GMC no. 159 in Burgess, 1887, pp. 34–5 and pl. xi.1; Sivaramamurti, 1956, pp. 183–6, no. III A 1; Kannan, 2014, p. 181. This is an unusual upright, found near the north gate. Both sides appear to have been historiated (the outer side is Burgess, 1887, pl. x.3). On the inner side the upper half-lotus is most exceptionally carved with a scene of the Bodhi tree and *buddhapāda* beneath it flanked by three worshipping figures to either side, while below two pairs of horizontal figures converge on the centre looking down towards the palanquin with the elephant. It is obvious that this alludes to the enlightenment, but it is possible that it implies the gods' despatch of the Bodhisattva to the Nandana Grove, in expectation of the enlightenment that will result in his final life as Gautama.

74 GMC no. 221 in Kannan, 2014, p. 201, and illustrated at HAABA 0027639. See Chapter One.

75 Striking is the coping slab in Chennai, GMC no. 134, in Sivaramamurti, 1956, pp. 183–6, no. III A 12 (= Burgess, 1887, pl. xx.2) and Kannan, 2014, pp. 172–3, whose narrative moves from far right to far left and culminates in the centre. Likewise, we may see the two fragments NMC no. 105, in Sivaramamurti, 1956, no. IV A 3 and Kannan, 2014, p. 163 (see the photograph in Stern and Bénisti, 1961, pl. XLVa and HAABA nos 12086, 12084, 12082) and BM 1880,0709.77, Knox, 1992, no. 55 – which are the left- and right-hand sides of a single sequence as representing various mainly unidentified scenes around the Bodhisattva's renunciation to either side of the seated Buddha in the *abhāya mudrā* in the centre: see Zin, 2016, pp. 54–7.

76 BM 1880,0709.90, Knox, 1992, no. 56. Beware Knox's text at pp. 115–16, which misrepresents and simplifies the *jātakas* carved on this frieze. For a brief discussion emphasizing the continuity of the scenes and their exemplarity, see Taddei, 2015, pp. 54–5. I discuss this block in Elsner, 2021, pp. 541–9.

77 This famous story is told in the framing narrative of the *Cullahamsa Jātaka*; see Francis, 1905, no. 533, pp. 175–8. It appears also in the Kullavagga section (on dissention within the order of monks) VII.3.11–12 of the *Vinaya* (the Monastic Code of Discipline (see Rhys Davids and Oldenberg, 1881–5, vol. III, pp. 247–50) and *The Questions of King Milinda* IV.9. pp. 207–9 (see Horner, 1964, pp. 300–303), where the elephant is called Dhanapālaka, and is referred to twice in Dhammapāla's *Udāna Commentary* (see Masefield, 1995, vol. II, pp. 634, 788). As early as the first or second century CE it appears in Aśvaghoṣa's Sanskrit *Buddhacarita* 21.36–47, surviving only in the Chinese version in Willemen, 2009, pp. 153–4. The story is popular in both textual and visual culture across ancient Buddhist India: see Zin, 2006, pp. 69–100. For discussion see Ohnuma, 2017, pp. 148–77.

78 Francis, 1905, pp. 176–7.

79 See Covill, 2009, pp. 71–98.

80 See Zin, 2016, p. 48; Zin, 2017. For evidence of a lost Mahāsāṃghika canon, see Dutt, 1978, pp. 58–61.

81 See Francis and Neil, 1897, no. 316, pp. 34–7, and Shaw, 2006, pp. 114–21. For Āryaśūra's fourth-century Sanskrit version see *Jātakamālā* no. 6 in Khoroche, 1989, pp. 32–8. For the frieze slab and story see Subrahmanyam, 2005, pp. 70–75 (with comparanda from Goli and Nāgārjunakonda); Rana, 2013, pp. 92–5; Chowdhuri, 2018, pp. 86–7; for broader comparanda in early Buddhist art, see Schlingloff, 1987, pp. 123–9. The story is mentioned and explicitly quoted in *Nidānakathā* 45 as exemplary of generosity (Jayawickrama, 1990, p. 58), and appears likewise at *Cariyāpiṭaka* I.10 as a model of *dāna* (Horner, 1975, *Basket of Conduct*, pp. 14–16). For discussion see Ohnuma, 2007, pp. 14–17, 126–7, 280–81.

82 Dieter Schlingloff has shown that the narrative in association to Śibi, although not found in Pāli, is represented in a number of Chinese translations from Sanskrit, some from as early as the third century, and is extant in Sanskrit in a fourth-century palm leaf manuscript from Kizil. See Schlingloff, 1984–6; Schlingloff, 1987, pp. 87–8.
83 See Ksemendra, *Bodhisattvāvadānakalpalatā* no. 55, translated by Black, 1997, pp. 269–71; on the story see Handurukande, 1981, and Ohnuma, 2007, pp. 121–2, 169 and 192–3, with reference to the discussion of this narrative in the third- or fourth-century *Mahāprajñāpāramitāśāstra* (see Lamotte, 1944, pp. 255, 275); for the frieze slab and narrative as represented there, see Rana, 2013, pp. 115–18; Chowdhuri, 2018, pp. 70–71. For a range of Andhra comparanda, see Subrahmanyam, 2005, pp. 159–68.
84 Schlingloff, 1987, pp. 86–92; Sugimoto, 2002, pp. 36–8; Zin, 2016, pp. 48–9; Tanabe, 2019, pp. 363–4, on Amarāvatī.
85 For example, BM 1880,0709.14 (a rail pillar), BM 1880,0709.69, BM 1880,0709.87, BM 1880,0709.95 (all miniature decorations with stūpa-relief drum slabs), respectively Knox, 1992, nos 14, 68, 77, 76; GMC nos 238 and 263, in Kannan, 2014, pp. 206, 214; and Sivaramamurti, 1956, nos III B 18 and IV B 2; also from a lost panel recorded among Mackenzie's drawings, BL WD1061, fol. 68, where it appears on a miniature dome slab to the left of the *āyaka* pillars.
86 Francis, 1905, p. 177.
87 Ibid., pp. 178–86; Āryaśūra *Jātakamālā* 22, in Khoroche, 1989, pp. 140–52. Chowdhuri, 2018, pp. 107–8, claims that this narrative is elsewhere depicted at Amarāvatī. For the Ajanta versions, see Schlingloff, 1987, pp. 130–38.
88 BM 1880,0709.81, Knox, 1992, no. 74.
89 BL WD1061, fols 26 (where the episode with the embodied Buddha to the left appears in the gateway at the centre with an unusual *dharmacakra* version of the first sermon in the *āyaka* panel above), 35 (where the elephant bows to the emblematic Buddha as flaming pillar and *trisula* in the *āyaka* frieze), 70 (where the elephant (on the left) bows to the embodied Buddha on a dome slab to the left of the depicted gateway – the panel shows repeated images of the embodied Buddha), 80 (where the narrative appears in the drum frieze with the elephant repeated twice to the right of the *āyaka* panel).
90 GMC no. 14, in Sivaramamurti, 1956, pp. 188–9, no. III A 15; and Kannan, 2014, pp. 134 (HAABA 12015).
91 Another example of a medallion fragment where the Buddha appears in his *rūpakāya* is the piece discovered forty years ago in the Bharat Kala Bhavan Museum in Varanasi: Sivaramamurti, 1981; Zin, 2006, pp. 82, no. 2; Rana, 2013, pp. 35 and pl. 2.35b; HAABA 11595. Both forms of the Buddha in this scene appear in Nāgārjunakonda: see Zin, 2006, pp. 82–4, no. 4–6.
92 For some reflections on the significance of the biographical texts: *Cariyāpiṭaka*, *Buddhvaṃsa* and *Apadāna* in relation to stūpas, see Walters, 1997; and for the *Cariyāpiṭaka* in relation to the perfections see Appleton, 2010, pp. 66–8.
93 On these issues see Appleton, 2010, pp. 63, 86, 117–18 and 148–9.
94 See, for instance, Grabar, 1968, pp. 109–48; Elsner, 1995, pp. 271–87; Schrenk, 1995; Tkacz, 2002, pp. 51–62. One fundamental difference, it might be emphasized, is that no early Christian monument shows anything like the richness and ambition of the early Buddhist stūpas in creating and marshalling complex iconographies across huge surfaces of carved stone. The greatest Byzantine church, Justinian's St Sophia, built in the first half of the sixth century, was essentially uniconic as far as figural or narrative imagery is concerned (at any rate regarding the fabric both inside and outside) although it contained a finely historiated chancel barrier for which the poetic description by Paul the Silentiary from the 560s survives. See, for example, Xydis, 1947; Whitby, 1985; Macrides and Magdalino, 1988; Kostenec and Dark, 2011.
95 See BM 1880,0709.70, Knox, 1992, no. 69, pp. 131–3. My account mostly accepts Knox's identification of the imagery, except where signalled, although I present it from right to left rather than left to right, in accordance with how a worshipper would approach the panel.
96 We have already seen this subject at the centre of one of the stūpa openings (BM 1880,0709.122, Knox, 1992, no. 80). It is certainly the most popular of the reincarnation stories in early Buddhist tradition, demonstrating the perfection of generosity: see *Cariyāpiṭaka* I.9 (in Horner, 1975, *Basket of Conduct*, pp. 9–14) and *Nidānakathā* 45 (in Jayawickrama, 1990, p. 58). The most recent translation is by S. Shaw in Appleton and Shaw, 2015, pp. 534–639, with an introduction at 507–34. See also Cowell and Rouse, 1907, no. 547, pp. 246–305; and Cone and Gombrich, 1977, translated with a substantial introduction pp. xv–xlvii; Collins, 1998, pp. 497–554, and 2015.
97 In *Nidānakatha* 75–7, the enlightenment is the culminating point of the not-so-remote antecedent, although in reality it is the turning point between that and the proximate epoch: see Jayawickrama, 1990, pp. 99–101.
98 The story is given in Rouse, 1901, no. 506, pp. 281–90 and (as the *Campaka Jātaka*) in *Mahāvastu* 2. 177–88; Jones, 1952, vol. II, pp. 171–81. It appears in the *Cariyāpiṭaka* under the group representing the perfection of morality at II.3 (see Horner, 1975, *Basket of Conduct*, pp. 20–21) and in the *Nidānakathā* exemplifying morality at 45 (see Jayawickrama, 1990, p. 58). For this story at Amarāvatī see Rana, 2013, pp. 99–102; and Chowdhuri, 2018, pp. 100–102.
99 See Rouse, 1895, no. 258, pp. 216–18; *Divyādvadāna* 17, in Rotman, 2008, pp. 337–71. For this story at Amarāvatī see Chowdhuri, 2018, pp. 110–12.
100 For the erotic life of the Bodhsattva in the palace, see, for example, Aśvaghoṣa, *Buddhacarita* 2.26–2.34, in Olivelle, 2008, pp. 46–9, with discussion by Regan, 2022.
101 For example, the *Kummāsapinda-Jātaka* or *Āditta-Jātaka* in Francis and Neil, 1897, nos 415, pp. 245–8 and 424, pp. 280–82; the reconciled king and consort at the close of the *Kusa-Jātaka* in Francis, 1905, no. 531, pp. 141–64; King Mahājanaka and his consort Sīvalī before his renunciation in the *Mahājanaka-Jātaka* in Cowell and Rouse, 1907, no. 539, pp. 19–37; or the protagonists at the time of their marriage or when they are reunited and return to the palace at the end of their adventures in the *Vessantara-Jātaka* in Cowell and Rouse, 1907, no. 547, pp. 246–305; Appleton and Shaw, 2015, pp. 544 and 632–7.
102 See Rana, 2013, pp. 115–16.
103 The story is told in the *Dhammapāda-aṭṭhakathā* I. 116–23 by Buddhaghosa, in relation to verses 13 and 14 of the *Dhammapāda*) in Burlingame, 1921, vol. I, pp. 217–23, in Dhammapāla's commentary on the *Nanda Sutta Udāna* 3.2, Ud 21–4 (Masefield, 1994a, pp. 39–43), in *Paramatthapadīpanī nāma Udānatthakathā* 168–79 (in Masefield, 1994b, vol. I,

pp. 449–64) and in *The Questions of King Milinda* III.169 (see Horner, 1964, p. 196). It is famously recounted in Aśvaghoṣa's second-century Sanskrit poem *Saundarananda,* with Covill, 2007 and 2009; see, for example, Shulman, 2018b, for discussion of the variety of versions. For a list of early versions, see Schlingloff, 1987, pp. 49–58; Zin, 2006, pp. 164–73.

104 Aśvaghoṣa *Saundarananda* 4.1–25 (Covill, 2007, pp. 80–87) is entirely explicit about the love-making. For discussion and interpretation of this topic see Salomon, 2009; and Olivelle, 2019, pp. 264–7.

105 Many examples are given by Zin, 2006, pp. 174–90 (with Amarāvatī at 174–5 and 183). Instances of the story from Amarāvatī include BM 1880,0709.11, Knox, 1992, no. 12; while other versions of the iconographies of the two scenes are: (Nanda and his wife) BM 1880,0709.17, BM 1880,0709.34, BM 1880,0709.79, BM 1880,0709.87, respectively Knox, 1992, nos 14, 40, 72, dome slab c (Janapada Kalyani admiring herself in a mirror, as mentioned explicitly in Aśvaghoṣa *Saundarananda* 4.10–20), 77 dome slab f, and (Buddha with Nanda and the bowl) BM 1880,0709.79, BM 1880,0709.120, respectively Knox, 1992, no. 72 dome slab d (misidentified as Buddha and Sujātā), 78 dome slab d, also Sivaramamurti, 1956, nos III A 3 and IV A 8.

106 For images of Aṅgulimāla at Amarāvatī, see Sivaramamurti, 1956, nos I A 3, III A 18 and III A 19, respectively Burgess, 1887, pl. XLVIII.4, XXIII.4 and XI.3–4. For a full account of early Buddhist Aṅgulimāla imagery, see Zin, 2006, pp. 101–24.

107 For the list of causes of earthquakes see *Mahaparinibbana Sutta* 3.10–20, *Dīgha Nikāya* Sutta 16, ii.107–9, alongside for example, *Nidānakathā* 75, in Jayawickrama, 1999, p. 99, on the enlightenment and *Dhammacakkappavattana Sutta, Saṃyutta Nikāya* 56.11 on the turning of the wheel.

108 Other drum slabs with this iconography in the gateway are: BM 1880,0709.79, Knox, 1992, no. 72, and Mackenzie's Album WD1061, folio 71. The episode (very differently presented) appears in Aśvaghoṣa, *Buddhacarita* 12.108–121, in Olivelle, 2008, pp. 366–71; *Nidānakathā* 70, in Jayawickrama, 1999, pp. 92–3; *Mahāvastu* 2.302 (Jones, 1952, vol. II, pp. 283–4); *Lalitavistara Sūtra* 18.26–30, in Goswami, 2001, pp. 252–3. The significance of the iconography of geese in this episode and in general in Buddhist art is uncertain, but see Santoro, 2022, pp. 348–50, on Indian material.

109 The inscription is given by Fergusson, 1873, pl. XCIX.viii and Lüders, 1912, p. 142, no. 1213, as 'The slab of Munasiri son of the Merchant Bodhisamma who lives at Kovurura together with mother . . . and (?) of Dhammasiri, Bapisiri, Saga.' For its placement see Knox, 1992, p. 132.

110 BM 1880,0709.15, Knox, 1992, no. 23.

111 GMC no. 135, in Sivaramamurti, 1956, pp. 223–5, no. III B 14; and Kannan, 2014, p. 173. For discussion of the *CampeyyaJātaka* in the Amarāvatī inner railings, see Parimoo, 2004, pp. 131–4.

112 See especially Collins, 1998, pp. 258–67.

113 In *Mahāvastu* 1.197–227 (Jones, 1949, vol. I, pp. 155–83) and *Mahāvastu* 2.1–26 (Jones, 1952, vol. II, pp. 1–27) the near-identical accounts of the birth narratives of Dīpaṅkara and Gautama make the same replicative point. Further on Dipaṅkara in the *Mahāvastu*, see Tournier, 2017, pp. 106–9, 136–8, 143–62.

114 See *Mahāvastu* 3.224–250, in Jones, 1956, vol. III, pp. 219–39.

115 See Nakanishi and von Hinüber, 2014, pp. 75–80, nos II.7, A, 1–8.

116 See Cunningham, 1879, pp. 45–7; and Lüders, Waldschmidt and Mehendale, 1963, pp. 82–6, nos B 13–17. On the Bodhi trees of the *Buddhavaṃsa*, see Horner, 1975, pp. xxxvi–xlvi.

117 See the discussion above of the princely love scene which may represent Nanda and his consort, but in the absence of a label, may equally be the Bodhisattva and his wife or their appearance in a number of earlier lifetimes as recounted in the *jātakas*, and may indeed use allusion to all these traditions simply to imply both the joys and the fetters of sensual desire.

118 For example, Sivaramamurti, 1956, pp. 219–20; Rana, 2013, pp. 82–5; Chowdhuri, 2018, pp. 77–8: the *Losaka-Jātaka* in Chalmers, 1895, vol. I, no. 41, pp. 105–11, which takes place in the lifetime of the Buddha Kassapa.

119 For discussion this phenomenon in relation to the later Buddhist paintings of Dunhuang, see Wu, 1992, pp. 129–30.

120 BM 1880,0709.1, Knox, 1992, no. 8.

121 On *taxis/ordo* in ancient visual narratives, see Squire, 2014.

122 See BM 1880,0709.77, Knox, 1992, no. 55; GMC no. 105, in Sivaramamurti, 1956, pp. 250–51, no. IV A 3 and Kannan, 2014, p. 163 (HAABA 12080, 12082, 12084, 12086); discussion by Zin, 2016, pp. 54–7. The find-spot was to the west of the northern gate according to Burgess, 1887, p. 81. The BM segment is 158.75 centimetres (62½ in.) long but I can find no record of the length of the Chennai section. The inscription (across both segments) reads left to right, so from the left end of the Chennai slab: '[Adoration] to the best . . ., the foremost of men, the truly Enlightened Sun. [Gift] of Nākhā the wife of the merchant and *upāsaka* (lay follower) Nāgatisa, inhabitant of Nārasala, with her sons, the treasurer Budhi, Mūla . . .' and after a significant lost passage of writing from the left end of the BM section: 'two chaitya slabs, three footprints, a coping stone, a slab with a flower vase and other objects to the great chaitya at Dhanyakata and erection of . . . at Rajagīri at the northern door by . . . together with his relatives.' To my knowledge these have never been read together by an epigrapher as part of one inscription: they are Lüders, 2012, nos 1239 (Chennai) and 1225 (BM) and Francis, 2016, nos 210 (Chennai) and 252 (BM) but neither appears to recognize that the two are from one slab, although the information was certainly available to Francis, who appears to place the inscription on the wrong slab (see Francis, 2016, p. 141).

123 For the subject see N. Appleton in Appleton and Shaw, 2015, pp. 458–505, with an introduction at 455–8; and Cowell and Rouse, 1907, no. 545, pp. 126–56. For the association with *pañña* (wisdom) see *Nidānathā* 46, in Jayawickrama, 1990, p. 59.

124 GMC nos 5, 123, 292, in Sivaramamurti, 1956, pp. 235–9, nos III B 23–5; and Kannan, 2014, pp. 131, 169, 222; Rana, 2013, pp. 105–7; Chowdhuri, 2013, pp. 96–8.

125 On Hārītī, see at length Rowan, 2002, with the key texts translated in the appendix; Ohnuma, 2012, pp. 54–9. On images see Getty, 1928, pp. 84–7, 155–8, for both figures; and Zin, 2006, pp. 35–53.

126 Aśvaghoṣa *Saundarananda* 4.10–20 in Covill, 2007, pp. 83–6.

127 This may represent the *Nāgas* in celebration at the Buddha's enlightenment, as in *Nidānakathā* 75 (Jayawickrama, 1999, pp. 98–9).

128 Zin, 2016, p. 57, concurs.

129 Ibid., p. 53, rightly points out that the same (unidentified) iconography is repeated in a miniature panel on a drum relief of a stūpa (BM 1880.0709.69).
130 Sivaramamurti, 1956, p. 251. But one would want a visual or literary tradition of cords used in this way for this to be convincing.
131 For instance BM 1880,0709.112, Knox, 1992, no. 57, a drum slab which – reading from right to left – offers a *mithuna* couple, the Bodhisattva in his harem (including a sex scene at the lower left), the Great Departure and the Bodhisattva taking leave of his horse Kaṃthaka and his groom Chandaka to the right. For discussion of a parallel breaking of sequential narratives in the Dunhuang cave paintings see Wu, 1992, pp. 136–7.
132 *Nidānathā* 46, in Jayawickrama, 1990, pp. 78–9.
133 For example, *Nidānakathā* 59 (Jayawickrama, 1990, p. 59), *Madhuratthavilāsinī* 279–80 (Horner, 1978, pp. 400–401); *Mahāvastu* 2.150–57 (Jones, 1952, vol. II, pp. 145–52). The same portents are given in *Mahāpadāna Sutta* 2.1–15, *Dīgha Nikāya* 14.ii.22–29, of the former Buddha Vipassī.
134 This adds a further exegetic twist to the issue of the undecipherability of several subjects discussed by Zin, 2016, pp. 53–7: what is missing is not only the specific textual tradition of the monastic community at Amarāvatī but also the commentarial traditions which they used to interpret their scriptures.
135 *Mahāvastu* 2.48 at Jones, 1952, vol. II, p. 45.
136 Ibid., 2.48–115, pp. 45–111, including the *jātakas* of Manjarī, Godhā, the tigress, Dharmapāla, Śaraksepa, Amarā, Śiri and Kinnarī.
137 For example, Appleton, 2010, pp. 6–8.
138 See, for example, Rotman, 2008, p. 2, who identifies three elements – a story in the present (in the Buddha's presence), a story of the past and the closure where the Buddha back in the present as an omniscient narrator identifies the characters across times.
139 See, for example, Burlingame, 1921, vol. I, pp. 30–67, with discussion of the use of *jātakas* at pp. 58–61.
140 See, for example, Heim, 2018, pp. 186–91.
141 See Fifleld, 2017, pp. 7–9, 13–14, 24, 41, 55–60, 67–9, esp. 70–106 on narrative and patterns of causality.
142 In Buddhaghosa's fifth-century exposition of the *Sāmaññaphala Sutta* in the *Dīgha Nikāya aṭṭhakathā*, the Nālāgiri story is cited repeatedly in a list of evil actions that together come to define Devadatta's wickedness and that of his patron King Ajatasattu: see Bodhi, 1989, pp. 62, 71, 73. Crucially, in Dhammapāla's commentary on the brief sutta on schism in the *saṅgha*, *Itivuttaka* 1.2.8 (no. 18), It.10–11, the point is made that only when Nālāgiri is sent to attack the Buddha did Devadatta's intent to murder the Tathāgata become apparent to all: *Itivuttaka-aṭṭhakathā* 67, in Masefield, 2008, vol. I, p. 167. The schism question bleeds into a second elephant story centrally concerned with disputes between monks. According to the *Mahāvagga* section of the Pāli *Vinaya* 10.4.1–10.5.14, Vin. I.337–57, dealing with a quarrel in the *saṅgha* (in Rhys Davids and Oldenberg, 1981–5, vol. II, pp. 312–14), *Nāga Sutta* (*Udāna* 4.5, Ud.41–2 with Dhammapāla's commentary in Masefield, 1995, vol. II, pp. 612–16), and the *Dhammapāda Commentary* 1.5 (in Burlingame, 1921, vol. I, pp. 113–18), disgusted by the conflicts within the *saṅgha* at Kosambī, the Buddha retreats alone to the forest, where he is cared for only by the noble elephant Pārileyakka. In the *Dhammapāda Commentary's* version, when Ānanda is sent to find the Buddha and bring him back, in a fascinating reprise of the Nālāgiri narrative, Pārileyakka charges on him and must be stopped by the Buddha: Burlingame, 1921, vol. I, p. 116. See Ohnuma, 2017, pp. 129–47.
143 Barrett, 1954, p. 36.
144 See Dhammapāla, *Paramatthapadīpanī nāma Udānatthakathā* 265, in Masefield, 1995, vol. II, pp. 634 and 718 (n. 807).
145 This is emphasized in both the Jātaka frame story at Francis, 1905, p. 177 (translated there as 'charity'; for the Pāli see Fausbøll, 1877–97, vol. V, p. 33: *odissakamettāya*) and the *Vinaya* account in Rhys Davids and Oldenberg, 1981–5, vol. III, p. 249 (translated there as 'the sense of his love'; for the Pāli see Oldenberg, 1880, vol. II, p. 195: *mettena cittena*, twice repeated).
146 For instance, the *Suvannasāma-Jātaka* in Cowell and Rouse, 1907, no. 540, pp. 38–52; Appleton and Shaw, 2015, pp. 122–44 – which is occasioned by the issue of appropriate loving kindness for one's parents, and whose hero is associated with love of animals in *Cariyāpiṭaka* III.13 as a model of *mettā* (Horner, 1975, *Basket of Conduct*, p. 46), in *The Questions of King Milinda* IV.6.198–9 (see Horner, 1964, pp. 286–7) and (as the Śyākama *Jātaka*) in, for example, *Mahāvastu* 211 (Jones, 1952, vol. II, p. 201); see briefly Ohnuma, 2012, p. 21 (with 19–20 on the links to *mettā*). For early imagery of this story (which appears not to survive in the extant Amarāvatī relies) see Schlingloff, 1987, pp. 64–72. Significant also, and with a cross-reference to the *Suvannasāma-Jātaka* in its framing tale, is the *Māti-Possaka-Jātaka* in Rouse, 1901, no. 455, pp. 58–61, where the Bodhisattva is a great elephant who cares for his mother with loving kindness.
147 For instance, in the *Ahi Sutta* in the Aṅguttara *Nikāya* 4.7.
148 BL WD1061, fol. 35. It is worth commenting that Mackenzie's draughtsmen had no idea of the stories they were representing when they drew what they saw on the slabs he found. Indeed Mackenzie himself thought the materials he had discovered belonged 'to a place consecrated to religious worship, but by a different sect from the Hindoos of the present day' (Mackenzie 1823, p. 469).
149 See Ohnuma, 2017, pp. 158–9.
150 BL WD1061, fol. 26, Burgess, 1887, pl. XXXIII.1.
151 On this issue see Walters, 1990, p. 77.
152 Nālāgiri is called Dhanapāla in this version.
153 *Madhuratthavilāsinī* 210–12, in Horner, 1978, pp. 303–6 referring to *Buddhvamsa* 14.6, in Horner, 1975, *Chronicle of Buddhas*, p. 61.
154 *Madhuratthavilāsinī* 210, in Horner, 1978, p. 303: 'The Elder Sona who, like Devadatta, was inimical to the Buddha'; *Madhuratthavilāsinī* 212, in Horner, 1978, p. 306: 'So did Lord Piyadassin after he had thus tamed the glorious elephant Donamukha . . . as did our teacher after taming Dhanapāla.'
155 *Madhuratthavilāsinī* 211–12, in Horner, 1978, pp. 305–6, with discussion by Ohnuma, 2017, p. 156. For the great descriptions of the Buddha as elephant (*nāga*) by the Elder Udayin, see *Anguttāra Nijāya* 6.4. (*Nāga Sutta*) and *Theragātha* 15.2
156 See *Buddhvamsa* 27.12, in Horner, 1975, *Chronicle of Buddhas*, 97.
157 See Ohnuma, 2017, pp. 158–61.
158 See ibid., pp. 164–5.
159 *Nidānakathā* 74, in Jayawickrama, 1990, p. 98.

160 See Heim, 2018, pp. 184–217, for the way this works in the commentarial tradition as well as the intrinsically commentarial nature of much of the Pāli canon, notably her discussion of the *Vinaya* and its own internal commentarial analysis (*vibhaṅga*) at 187–91.

161 That is, *Madhuratthavilāsinī* 210–12, in Horner, 1978, pp. 303–6, referring to *Buddhvaṃsa* 14.6, in Horner, 1975, *Chronicle of Buddhas*, p. 61

162 For karmic patterns as generated by the commentaries, see Egge, 2002, pp. 89–118.

four THEATRICALITY

1 For a rich account of the gaze and spectatorship as figures on Greek pottery, Stansbury-O'Donnell, 2006. For the key role of viewer figures in Roman art, see Klein, 1912; Michel, 1982, pp. 537–98; Clarke, 1997, pp. 43–7; Lorenz, 2007; Elsner, 2007, pp. 88–109; Squire, 2009, pp. 332–9.

2 See, for example, Schotsman, 1995; and Olivelle, 2008. The second-century date is reinforced by Falk, 2001 (on the dates of Kaniṣka, the king under whom Aśvaghoṣa wrote).

3 For some discussion of performative traditions of the *jātakas* in contemporary Buddhism, see, for example, Ladwig, 2016; and Bowie, 2016.

4 For instance, in the *Tālapuṭa Sutta* (*Saṃyutta Nikāya* 42.2, IV. 307) and the *Brahmajāla Sutta* (*Dīgha Nikāya* 1, I 5–6) or in the *Vinaya* at *Cullavagga* I.13 1–7, Vin II 9–10 with discussion by for example, Winternitz, 1923, p. 219; and Wijesekera, 1941. But note the narration of theatrical performances in, for example, the *Suruci Jātaka* (no. 489) in Rouse, 1901, no. 489, pp. 198–205.

5 See, for example, Liu, 2018.

6 See Lüders, 1911a and b; Keith, 1924, pp. 80–90; Bhattacharya, 1959; Byrski, 1974, pp. 171–7 (to be used with caution, for example, the certainty that Aśvaghoṣa was Mahāyāna, p. 171, or the implication that Aśvaghoṣa is indebted to the Sanskrit dramatist Kālidāsa, rather than the other way around, p. 174); Sharma, 1987, pp. 105–6; Tieken, 2010; Regan, 2022, doubts the assumption that Aśvaghoṣa was a monk. For discussion of Indian Buddhist drama, see Lévi, 1890, pp. 319–24; Winternitz, 1923; Varadpande, 1981, pp. 29–33; Sharma, 1987, pp. 35–66.

7 See, for example, Brancaccio and Liu, 2009; Galli, 2011, pp. 316–24.

8 See Winternitz, 1923, pp. 219–22.

9 On the monks known as *bhāṇaka*s and *dharmabhāṇaka*s (speakers of dharma), who memorized and then recited all aspects of the teachings, see Drewes, 2011, with earlier literature.

10 For an excellent introduction to orality and performance in relation to the literary genres of the Buddhist sūtras, see Shaw, 2021, pp. 11–62; also Cousins, 1983; Collins, 1992; Wynne, 2004; Shulman, undated; Sujato and Brahmali, 2014, pp. 50–53 and 75–7; Shulman, 2021, pp. 191–9.

11 On this cultural tradition and its politics see Ollett, 2017, pp. 26–49, with dynastic table of monarchs and dates at 189–91. On the mix of Buddhist monasteries and Brahmanic temples in the archaeological record of Vijayapurī, the Ikṣvāku capital attached to Nāgārjunakonda, see Soundararajan, 2006, p. 9; Krishnamurthy, 2006 (Buddhist remains); Subramahnyam, 2006 (Brahmanic remains).

12 For example, Fynes, 1995.

13 A good discussion of much of this is Ollett, 2017, pp. 50–110; see also Ollett, 2019, on literary poetics in the period. For the need to see Buddhist texts as within ancient *Indian* literature as opposed to within some fanciful denominational closet, and thus to be susceptible to the canons of Indian literary criticism, including ancient dramatic theory, see Schopen, 2007, pp. 203–4. For the place of Pāli in this mix, see Gombrich, 2018.

14 On Buddhism and the competitive Brahmanic context in India, see Bailey and Mabbett, 2003, pp. 108–37; Bronkhorst, 2007, esp. pp. 13–54 (on competing spiritual ideologies) and 207–18 (on what Buddhists knew of Vedic texts); esp. Bronkhorst, 2011; Sujato and Brahmali, 2014, pp. 33–8. On the shared mythologies and folklores of Brahmanic, Buddhist and Jain traditions in ancient India, see Appleton, 2017, esp. pp. 170–84; on shared assumptions about karma and reincarnation between Jain and Buddhist culture, see Appleton, 2014. On 'Hindu' and Buddhist patronage see Agrawal, 2005.

15 On Aśvaghoṣa and Brahmanism, see, for example, Hiltebeitel, 2006; Olivelle, 2016 and 2019; Regan, 2022.

16 Anonymous, 1955, p. 22 (a brief excavation report, where the structure is simply described as a 'quadrangle'); Varadpande, 1981, pp. 91–3 (identifying the site as a theatre); Sharma, 1987, pp. 47–9 and 54–5 (insisting on it as a 'theatre'); Soundararajan, 2006, pp. 107–11.

17 Soundararajan, 2006, p. 110, with discussion of the temple (dated there to the fourth century CE) in Krishnamurthy, 2006, pp. 174–8; Sharma, 1987, p. 47, says what he calls 'the theatre' belongs to the 'late 2nd or early 3rd century': but all these dates are guesses.

18 Unique: Sharma, 1987, p. 55.

19 For the text and translation, see Ghosh, 2020. For discussion of the date, see Ghosh, 2020, vol. I, pp. liv–lvii; Gupt, 1994, pp. 1–3; Lidova, 2012, p. 61. For a brief introduction, see, for example, Pollock, 2016, pp. 47–9.

20 On Abhinavagupta's philosophy of aesthetics in *Abhinavabhāratī* and in a broader context, see Masson and Patwardhan, 1969; in his use of earlier commentators, see Masson and Patwardhan, 1970, pp. 5–14; and Gupta, 1987, pp. 26–31 and 220–34.

21 See Lidova, 1994, pp. 7–52; Kintaert, 2017 and 2018; Bansat-Boudon, 2020.

22 See Mehta, 1995, p. 12; Lidova, 1994, pp. 10–11; Kintaert, 2017, pp. 93 and 107 (with n. 88).

23 Kale, 1974, p. 13 ('garbled'); Rangacharya, 1998, pp. 15 ('repetitive, conflicting and confusing'), 17 ('confusion', 'uncertainty'), 19 ('very corrupt'); Mehta, 1995, p. 40 ('obscure').

24 See especially Lidova, 1994, pp. 24–37.

25 Kale, 1974, pp. 13–31; Rangacharya, 1998, pp. 15–23. Most translate *caturaśra* as 'square' but Rangacharya, 1998, pp. 15–16, insists on 'all round' as an option.

26 Kintaert, 2005, pp. 245–74, esp. 270–71.

27 Ibid., pp. 246–7.

28 See Mehta, 1995, p. 67.

29 See, for example, Kale, 1974, pp. 69–74; Mehta, 1995, pp. 23–36; Iravati, 2003, pp. 235–45; Bagad, 2019, pp. 28–34.

30 See Keith, 1924, p. 82; and Churn Law, 1946, pp. 33–5, for the closeness of the *Śāriputra-prakarana* to the tenets and form laid down by the *Nāṭyaśāstra*.

31 For plausible sense of a Sarvāstivāda evangelical mission to

Central Asia about the fragmentary texts found in Xinjiang in the context of these plays, see Sander, 1991.

32 Mehta, 1995, p. 24; see Masson and Patwardhan, 1970, pp. 32–4; and Gupta, 1987, pp. 228–31. Unfortunately, despite its title, Kumar, 2019, only contains a translation of the *Nāṭyaśāstra*. Abhinavagupta's commentary appears never to have been translated into English and I cannot access it directly.

33 For some discussion of musical instruments, musicians and dance in Amarāvatī, see Sivaramamurti, 1956, pp. 144–51. For court culture and theatricality in Gandhāra, see Galli, 2011.

34 BM 1880,0709.17. See Barrett, 1954, p. 70; Sivaramamurti, 1956, p. 150; Knox, 1992, no. 14, pp. 64–6; Parimoo, 2005, pp. 353–5, who suggests all the imagery on this pillar represents the *Campeyya Jātaka*.

35 For discussion see Knox, 1992, p. 66; and Zin, 2016, pp. 50–53.

36 Dance: NŚ 4.1–329, 34.51–3 and 78; music, song and dance: NŚ 5.8–21, 5.148–65; musical instruments: NŚ 4.323–5, 6.27–8, 28.1–31.502, 33.1–301; song: NŚ 32.1–525; jester: NŚ 5.28, 34.21–2, 35.79, 35.92–5; on actors and actresses as musically adept: NŚ 35.100–101. If the dwarf is a hermaphrodite as proposed by Knox, this too is figured among the characters of the harem at NŚ 34.71–3, 79–80. Generally, on music and dance in the stūpa images, see Sivaramamurti, 1956, pp. 144–51. Further on the jester, with direct comparison to the *Nāṭyaśāstra*, see Zin, 2015b.

37 For example, NŚ 3.34, 71–2, 75–6; 5.74; 35.104.

38 *Amaravati Album*, BL WD1061, folio 66. Fergusson, 1873, pl. LXXIII and p. 193 says they are male, Sivaramamamurti, 1956, p. 150, says they are female.

39 BM 1880,0709.15, Knox, 1992, no. 23. For the story, see Rouse, 1895, no. 258, pp. 216–18; *Divyādvadāna* 17, in Rotman, 2008, pp. 337–71; and at Amarāvatī, Chowdhuri, 2018, pp. 110–12.

40 For the *Nāṭyaśāstra*'s account of spectatorship, see NŚ 27.49–81.

41 NŚ 34.21–2 (jesters), 34.31–80 ('the 18 kinds of inmates of the royal harem'), 34.85–8 (the king) with some discussion of how this role is to be impersonated at 35.9–11 and 57–64.

42 NŚ 24.1–79.

43 These examples are at the start of the chapter: NŚ 24.1–20.

44 For literary enactments of this kind of thing in Buddhist contexts, see Aśvaghoṣa's *Saunderananda*, especially canto 4.1–24 for the love of Nanda and Sundari, in Coville, 2007, pp. 80–87.

45 Aśvaghoṣa's *Buddhacarita* 4.1–100, in Olivelle, 2008, pp. 87–124.

46 BM 1880,0709.19/20 in Barrett, 1954, p. 67; Knox, 1992, no. 36; Becker, 2016, pp. 71–4; Tournier, 2021–2, pp. 15–28.

47 For the treatment of the music, see NŚ 28–33. For the discussion of classes of musical instruments, see NŚ 28.1–2. For examples of the kinds of sentiments, see NŚ 29.1–14; 33.19–22. For attention to musicians, see notably NŚ 35.67 for the director needing to be 'expert in playing the four kinds of musical instrument'.

48 See Becker, 2016, pp. 74–5.

49 Ibid., pp. 73–5 has good grounds for contesting the assumption of both Barrett and Knox that this figure is certainly the Buddha, but is on less conclusive territory in suggesting that the scene might represent the Sinhalese narrative of Mahinda's transmission of Buddhism to Sri Lanka (for which he and his retinue are indeed represented as arriving miraculously by means of levitation).

50 BM 1880,0709.2 at Knox, 1992, no. 26, with discussion at pp. 83–4; endorsed by Becker, 2006, pp. 60–61. Knox, 1992, p. 84, makes similar suggestions of the 'athletic dance posture' of the two female worshippers beneath a throne with relic casket in BM 1880,0709.8 (Knox, 1992, no. 27), a crossbar sadly damaged following exhibition in France in 1867, but – as can perhaps be better seen from Mackenzie's drawing of 1817 (Mackenzie Album WD1061, folio) – these females are certainly *nāga*s with single snakes emanating from behind their heads.

51 For example, BM 1880,0709.70, respectively Knox, 1992, no. 69; Boston 29.151; Mackenzie drawings WD1061, folios 20, 23, 32, 35, 46, 71.

52 BM 1880,0709.72, Knox, 1992, no. 70 (= Mackenzie Album WD1061, folio 24); perhaps also BM 1880,0709.79, Knox, 1992, no. 72 (= Mackenzie Album WD1061, folio 69) – here in the upper left dwarf-figures appear to be playing a drum and castanets while a god dances towards the left-hand corner.

53 Examples include BM 1880,0709.4, BM 1880,0709.7, BM 1880,0709.11, BM 1880,0709.14, BM 1880,0709.17, BM 1880,0709.47, respectively Knox, 1992, nos 6, 11, 12, 13, 14, 10.

54 *Mahāparinibbāna Sutta* 6.13–14, 6.16, 6.23, *Dīgha Nikāya Sutta* 16, II.159–60, 161, 164. For discussion of relics in this text (as well as its Sanskrit versions transmitted by Nikāya schools other than Theravāda, as well as their translations into Chinese and Tibetan), see Strong, 2004, pp. 98–123. For song and dance at various stages in the Buddha's funerary rites in other Nikāya traditions, see Bareau, 1971, vol. II, pp. 183–5, 190–91, 199–200, 263.

55 GMC no. 160, in Burgess, 1887, pp. 58–9, pl. XXV; Foucher, 1928, pp. 16–17; Sivaramamurti, 1956, pp. 204–5, no. III A 28; Kannan, 2014, pp. 181–2 illustrated in HAABA 27691, 27692, 27757.

56 BM 1880,0709.108, Knox, 1992, no. 46.

57 Burgess, 1887, p. 58, says the slab is 'from some corner or gate', but if it were at the place where the railing shifts ninety degrees from circling the stūpa monument to lining the entrance passageway, where there was also a seated lion above the rail, then (while the exterior face imagery would be consistent with this assumption), the imagery of the inner face – whose narrative proceeds from right to left and ends finally at the left, dictates that the piece must have been at the end of the gateway, culminating the narrative.

58 *Mahāparinibbāna Sutta* 6.24–5, *Dīgha Nikāya Sutta* 16, II.164–5. For some discussion of this episode, see Buddhaghosa's commentary in An, 2005, pp. 209–17.

59 For the emphasis on women (which some of the Nikāya texts translated into Chinese mark as controversial) see Bareau, 1971, pp. 185–6.

60 *Mahāparinibbāna Sutta* 6.23, *Dīgha Nikāya Sutta* 16, ii.164.

61 See Buddhaghosa on *Mahāparinibbāna Sutta* 6.26, in An, 2005, p. 217, see some of the Chinese versions of these narratives cited by Bareau, 1971, p. 301.

62 *Mahāparinibbāna Sutta* 6.27–8, *Dīgha Nikāya Sutta* 16, ii.166–8. For an explicit account of the seven caskets leaving and one remaining in Kusināra, see, for example, Aśvagosa, *Buddhacarita*, Chinese version, Fascicle 5, 28.55–58, 54a, in Willemen, 2009, pp. 205–6; on relics in the *Buddhacarita*, see Shimoda, 2002, pp. 249–54. For the association of relic caskets with elephants, see Buddhaghosa on *Mahāparinibbāna Sutta* 6.23, in An, 2005, p. 208.

five COSMOGRAPHY

1 Gagné, 2021, pp. 3. Further on narrative, fictional and possible worlds, see Doležel, 1998.

2 Such as has been attempted generally for the Indian context by, for example, Sircar, 1967; Gombrich, 1975; Miller, 1985; or for Buddhism specifically by such as, for example, McGovern, 1923; Masson, 1942; Kloetzli, 1983; Sankarnarayan, Matsuda and Yoritomi, 2002; Huntington, 2018. Particularly useful for an account of pre-Mahāyāna Buddhist cosmology, mainly founded in the Pāli textual tradition of the Theravāda school (so roughly contemporary with the stūpa even if rooted in what was probably not the dominant monastic tradition at Amarāvatī), see Collins, 1998, pp. 297–319.

3 Gagné, 2021, p. 24. Note also the model of 'worlding' borrowed from Philippe Descola and ultimately derived from Martin Heidegger, discussed at ibid. pp. 25 and 60–61 and rightly critiqued at the latter.

4 Gagné, 2021, pp. 25–6.

5 Ibid., p. 27.

6 For having rights of property ownership, see Schopen, 1997, pp. 126–31, with references, and at greater length on 'living presence' and property ownership, pp. 258–78. For the Buddha's own presence, see Schopen, 1997, pp. 131–3, 134–5; also Fogelin, 2012, pp. 286–7.

7 See BM 1880,0709.69, in Knox, 1992, no. 68. This slab, excavated to the northeast of the site, was drawn on 6 March 1817 and the leaf survives in the Mackenzie Album in the British Library as WD1061, folio 47.

8 The scene is exceptionally interesting and has generated a large literature. Knox, 1992, p. 129, says it represents the Buddha receiving worship, but misses the specific references. In the section of the image to the Buddha's left a human figure is trapped between the jaws of a *makara* below him and an elephant facing down towards him. This has been convincingly identified as an unusual and unusually syncopated Andhra version of the famous parable of the Man in the Well, known from many non-Buddhist Indian traditions and reported by a number of Buddhist texts that now survive only in Chinese: see especially Zin, 2011, pp. 33–46, for the iconographic comparanda (especially from Nāgārjunakonda) and the texts; also Becker, 2015, pp. 110–43. The parable is an allegory for saṃsāra, told by the Buddha to the devotees. The story survives in no Pāli source but in a number of translations from Sanskrit into Chinese, from other Nikāya schools than the Theravāda, where it is presented as a teaching given by the Buddha: see, for example, Julien, 1860, vol. II, pp. 131–4, no. 32 and 190–93, no. 53 (with allegory explained); Chavannes, 1910, vol. II, pp. 83–4, no. 205; and Chavannes 1934, vol. IV, pp. 235–8, no. 469. The 'speech-bubble' imagery, whereby what the Buddha says is shown as a narrative scene behind him, is exceptional; but the play of saṃsāra against salvation, as embodied by the Buddha and his relics, is potent.

9 See BM 1880,0709.8, in Knox, 1992, no. 27. This was excavated in the early nineteenth century and drawn by Mackenzie's draughtsmen in April 1817: Mackenzie Album WD1061, folio.

10 For the particular relationship of *nāga*s with relics of the Buddha see Strong, 2004, pp. 6–76, 120, 126–7, 135–6; and Zin, 2016c.

11 For example, Kumar, 2012, pp. 160–236 (life scenes and *jātakas*); Rana, 2013, pp. 76–113 on the *jātakas* and 114–27 on the Buddha's life; Chowdhuri, 2018, pp. 70–114 (*jātakas* and *avadānas*), 114–62 (life of the Buddha).

12 On this tripartite presentation of time, see *Nidānakathā* 2, in Jayawickrama, 1990, p. 2, with discussion by Collins, 1990, pp. vii–ix; Horner, 1978, pp. 6–7 (for a pair of Pāli Theravāda models); Jones, 1949, vol. I, p. xiv and 1952, vol. II, p. ix (for a Sanskrit Mahāsāṃghika model).

13 There are in pre-Mahāyāna Buddhist cosmology three spheres (*avacara*) or levels (*bhūmi*) containing 30 or 31 worlds (*lokā*); these conform to meditational experience (pertaining to the formless, *arūpāvacara*, to subtle form, *rūpāvacara*, and to the senses, *kāmāvacara*). All sixteen of the worlds in the sphere of subtle form as well as six in that of the senses are seen as divine in an ever more refined hierarchy, above the human world; beneath this are four subhuman worlds including the hells. See Kloetzli, 1983, pp. 23–50; and esp. Collins, 1998, pp. 297–304, for lucid summary and scriptural references.

14 For the drum slab, see BM 1880,0709.72, Knox, 1992, no. 70, pp. 132–6 (note the museum number is misprinted there). For the drawing from the Mackenzie album, see British Library Amaravati Album WD1061, folio 24.

15 See also BM 1880,0709.76, BM 1880,0709.77, BM 1880,0709.78, BM 1880,0709.89, BM 1880,0709.90, BM 1880,0709.112, respectively Knox, 1992, nos 54, 55, 58, 56, 59, 57.

16 Knox's suggestions from the *jātakas* for these stories are less than convincing: see Knox, 1992, p. 136.

17 Such as BM 1880,0709.23, BM 1880,0709.44, respectively Knox, 1992, nos 41, 61.

18 The Mucalinda theme appears in two further recorded drum slabs from Amarāvatī – now lost but drawn by Mackenzie's draughtsmen: British Library Amaravati Album WD1061, folios 33 and 67. The subject is repeated in the surviving iconographies of similar miniature stūpa drum slabs from Nāgārjunakonda and Gummadidurru: see respectively Rosen Stone, 1994, pp. 60–61 (but note that pl. 148 is unfortunately printed in reverse), also HAABA 26918–9 and AMA no. 249, in Gupta, 2008, pp. 63, no. F. 388 and fig. xxxii. In all cases the Buddha is in the *abhāya mudrā* except at Gummadidurru, where he is in the meditation posture (*dhyāna mudrā*).

19 See, for example, *Mahāvagga* 1.6.7–47, in Horner, 1951, pp. 13–21.

20 *Mahāvagga* 1.3.1–4, in Horner, 1951, pp. 4–5; this narrative is basically repeated in the Māhiśāsaka and Dhaarmaguptaka *Vinaya* versions originally in Sanskrit that now survive in Chinese, which are probably derived from the same ur-source as the *Mahāvagga*: see Bareau, 1963, pp. 101–5 (including French translations). In other accounts the Mucalinda episode takes place later than the third week after the awakening, but always before the first sermon. See, for example, Buddhaghosa in the *Nidānakathā* 79–80, in Jayawickrama, 1990, pp. 106–7; and Buddhadatta's commentary on the *Buddhavaṃsa* in Horner, 1978, pp. 14 and 416 (both texts – likely fifth century CE but drawing on earlier sources – make it the sixth week); in the Sanskrit *Mahāsāṃghika Mahavastu* 3.300–301, in Jones, 1956, vol. III, pp. 287–8, it is the fifth week; in the Sanskrit *Latitavistara*, a Mahāyāna version of the Buddha's life from the early centuries CE, the episode is presented as during the fifth week after the enlightenment, in Goswami, 2001, pp. 345–6.

21 *Mahāvagga* 1.3.2, Vin. I.4, in Horner, 1951, 4; see *Mucalinda Sutta*, *Udāna* 2.1, Ud.10, with Dhammapāla's commentary 2.100–102, in Masefield, 1994b, pp. 263–5.

22 Masefield, 1994b, p. 264.

23 According to Strong, 2004, pp. 65–8, the hair-knot is taken to the Tāvatiṃsa Heaven while the bowl is venerated in the *nāga* world, but mythological traditions may vary on this kind of thing.

24 As outlined in the *Vibhaṅga*, the canonical second book of the Pāli *Abhidhamma Piṭaka*, at 422.1–2, paragraphs 1021–8, trans.Titthila, 1969, pp. 540–43, which gives the life-limits of the various devas dwelling in the heaven worlds having assumed their correlation with different kinds of consciousness as encompassed within the three spheres. See also the fifth-century CE commentary by Buddhaghosa, *Sammohavinodanī*, pp. 518–22, paragraphs 2575–96, in Ñāṇamoli, revised for publication by Cousins, Nyanaponika and Shaw, 1991, pp. 290–95; this adds some discussion of the hell worlds and human world and stresses the correlation with forms of meditative consciousness, esp. 521–2, paragraphs 2591–5. See the discussion by Collins, 1998, pp. 297–302.

25 See, for example, *Cūlamāluṅkya Sutta*, *Majjima Nikāya* no. 63, I.426–32, in Ñāṇamoli and Bodhi, 1995, pp. 533–6; and *Aggivacchagotta Sutta*, *Majjima Nikāya* no. 72, II.483–9, in Ñāṇamoli and Bodhi, 1995, pp. 590–94.

26 See, for example, *Aggañña Sutta*, *Dīgha Nikāya* 27, III.80–98, in Walshe, 1987, pp. 407–15, for an account of the contraction and expansion of the world and its beings over aeons, delivered to two brahmins, which pointedly avoids creation.

27 For a summary account of Indian cosmogonies, see Bhattacharyya, 1971.

28 For accounts, see, for example, Smith, 1994; Gray, 2017, pp. 105–74.

29 See, for example, Miller, 1985, pp. 203–28.

30 See *Rohitassa Sutta*, *Aṅguttara Nikāya* 4.45 (5) and (6), III.47, in Bodhi, 2012, pp. 434–6, and *Saṃyutta Nikāya* 2.26 (6), I. 61–2, in Bodhi, 2000, pp. 157–8.

31 See especially Becker, 2015, pp. 23–77 (she calls them meta-stūpas) and Casalini, 2021, p. 113 ('multiverse').

32 Nāgārjunakonda: Rosen Stone, 1994, pp. 60–63; Becker, 2015, pp. 57–64. Gummadidurru: Gupta, 2008, pp. 59–63, nos F. 363–88.

six *BUDDHAPĀDA*: SYMBOLISM, VISUAL EPITOME AND THE CREATION OF ICONS

1 Lüders, 1912, no. 1248 (*dhamacaka* = Sivaramamurti, 1956, pp. 283–4, no. II E 6–7 and no. 51). The terminology may imply something different (a wheel in the round) from what is obviously a slab with a wheel in relief at Lüders, 1912, no. 1253 (*cakapata*).

2 See AMA no, 63, Gupta, 2008, no. J. 832 and pl. 58. Sarkar and Nainar, 1992, p. 44, report that it is sandstone.

3 See Petridou, 2015, p. 76.

4 The classic parallel of a *pars pro toto* iconic image in a religious tradition – choosing head rather than foot – is the Mandylion or Veronica icon of Christ, complete with the legends of its miraculous facture. See, for example, Kuryluk, 1991, pp. 28–33; Belting, 1994, pp. 47–77; Kessler and Wolf, 1998; Wolf, 2002, pp. 16–33.

5 The Greek *ichnos* means both foot and footprint. Famous textual discussions include Herodotus, *History* 4.82; and Lucian, *True Histories* 1.7. See, for example, Guarducci, 1942–3; Castiglione, 1968 and 1970; Dunbabin, 1990; Takács, 2005; Petridou, 2009, pp. 81–93; Christodoulou, 2011, pp. 18–21; Platt, 2011, pp. 58–60; Revell, 2016; Krumeich, 2020; and Petridou, 2015, pp. 76–82; for divine footprints as synecdoche and the message of divine bodily presence. For comparative natural footprints across religious cultures, see Monaci Castagno, 2011.

6 An example in the Amarāvati Museum (AMA no. 145) looks as if the slab was certainly conceived as a single left foot: Quagliotti, 1998, p. 27; Gupta, 2008, no. J. 699 and pl. LIII. This has the inscription *pāpumātuyā dānam* cut between the wheel in the hollow of the foot and the circle at the heel. On the phenomenon of 'footprint platforms as separate objects' see Huntington, 2020, pp. 440–44.

7 To the third and fourth centuries CE, see Rosen Stone, 1994, pp. 3–9, 21–4, on style and relations to Amarāvatī.

8 For the Nāgārjunakonda examples, see Krishnamurthy, 1979; Quagliotti, 1998, pp. 36–43, no. I.16–19. For Thotlakonda, see Krishna Sastri, Subrahmanyam and Rama Krishna Rao, 1992, pp. 34 and 94, pls LXIV–LXV. For Bavikonda, see Prasad, 1994, pp. 21, 60. For Phanigiri, see Chenna Reddy, 2008, pp. 8 and 30; Skilling, 2008, pp. 98–100; Skilling, 2021, pp. 47–50. For Kesanapalli, see Quagliotti, 1998, pp. 35–6, nos I.15. For Kanaganahalli, see Poonacha, 2011, pp. 324–5, 462–3, 474; Nakanishi and von Hinüber, 2014, pp. 72–5; Huntington, 2020, p. 442.

9 See Schalk, 1998, pp. 319–25 (323 on the stone, also 325–7 on other aspects of influence from Amarāvatī in Kāverippūmpattinam and the Tamil South); Guy, 2005, p. 495 but with no further bibliography.

10 The evidence of the drum slabs showing *buddhapāda*s beneath parasols in the dome of the stūpas represented in several reliefs might suggest that the large panels could have appeared on the main stūpa itself. See, for example, Gupta, 2008: no. 339, pl. 19; Knox, 1992, pp. 141–9, nos 73, 75 and 76, respectively BM 1880.0709.80, BM 1880.0709.83 and BM 1880.0709.85 (= Quagliotti, 1998, pp. 32–3). The excavators certainly believed that some of the *buddhapāda*s they found were displayed vertically, as opposed to horizontally, 'fixed, perhaps against a wall, by iron bolts'; see Burgess, 1887, p. 98.

11 See Huntington, 2020, pp. 444–9 (with a parallel from Kanaganahalli). Panels with *buddhapāda*s in the dome: AMA no. 2, in Gupta, 2008: no. 339, pl. 19; Knox, 1992, pp. 141–9, nos 73, 75 and 76, respectively BM 1880.0709.80, BM 1880.0709.83 and BM 1880.0709.85 (= Quagliotti, 1998, pp. 32–3).

12 See Burgess, 1887, pp. 97–9; Barrett, 1954, p. 38; Quagliotti, 1998, p. 119.

13 Barrett, 1954, p. 38; Roy, 1994, p. 120; Settar, 2020, p. 109. Fergusson, 1873, p. 209, thought they were not part of the railing; Quagliotti, 1998, p. 28, thinks they were not part of the main stūpa.

14 See Srivastava, 1991, p. 84; Quagliotti, 1998, pp. 17–18 no. I.1; Quintanilla, 2007, pp. 108–9, fig. 130 and appendix II.6; Hegewald, 2020b, pp. 407–9.

15 See Quintanilla, 2007, pp. 97–103. If there is a link between the Ghositārāma *buddhapāda* panel and those in Amarāvatī, it is not at all clear (given the uncertainties of dating based entirely on style) which had the priority and which influenced the other.

Hegewald, 2020b, pp. 407–13, implies the likely priority of Buddhist depictions of footprints over Jain ones.

16 In the scholarly literature it has been assumed that the Prakrit *paduka*, which appears on a number of Amarāvatī inscriptions detailing gifts to the stūpa, meant 'panels with footprints'. However, Vincent Tournier tells me (pers. com.) – following Nakanishi and von Hinüber, 2014, pp. 60–61, nos II.4,1–3 – that it is virtually certain the term means 'upright', as in 'railing pillar'. For the earlier mistaken version, see Lüders, 1912, no.1209 (a gift of two footprints, *patuka*); 1217 (a slab with footprints, *padukapata*); 1219 (a gift of two footprints, *patuka*); 1225 (a gift of three footprints, *patuka*); 1286 (footprints, *paduka*; but here Sivaramamurti, 1956, p. 91, no. A 17 and no. 70 reads 'slab', *pendaka*); Chanda, 1919–20, no. 44 (footprint, *paduko*), with Dehejia, 1970, p. 52; and Elsner, 2021, p. 100 n. 42.

17 *Buddhavaṃsa* I. 1–36, trans. Horner, 1975, pp. 1–5. For Buddhadatta's fifth-century commentary on this, see Horner, 1978, pp. 8–95.

18 *Buddhavaṃsa* I.37–9, in Jayawickrama, 1974, p. 4 (for the Pāli); and Horner, 1975, p. 5. For rich discussion of the layers of meaning see Buddhadatta in Horner, 1978, pp. 61–5.

19 *Buddhavaṃsa* I.56, in Jayawickrama, 1974, p. 5; and Horner, 1975, p. 6.

20 BM 1880,0709.43, in Fergusson 1873, p. 209; Barrett, 1954, pp. 64–5, no. 19; Knox, 1992, pp. 211–12, no. 120; Quagliotti, 1998, pp. 22–6, no. I.6, with more bibliography. The dimensions I report in the caption are after Knox, 1992, p. 212 but the online catalogue records h. 70.2 cm; w. 64.8 cm; d. 10.5 cm. Note that this relief is made from a recycled piece of stone that was itself part of an earlier decorative scheme in the sculptural ornamentation of the site: see Knox, 1992, pp. 177–8, no. 99 (where a photograph of the wrong *buddhapāda* is supplied at p. 178); and Quagliotti, 1998, pp. 25–6.

21 Although not as the object is currently illustrated in the British Museum Collection Online entry, nor how it was displayed on the posters or catalogue cover of the 'Imagining the Divine' exhibition: Elsner and Lenk, 2017.

22 On the *makara* motif at Amarāvatī, see Stern and Bénisti, 1961, pp. 37–42.

23 For *triratna*, see Knox, 1992, p. 211; for *nandyavarta*, Quagliotti, 1998, pp. 83–94.

24 See Kurita, 1988: vol. I, nos 283, 290–91 and vol. II, nos 754–5, 782–9; Quagliotti, 1998, pp. 50–63, also 188–93, nos I.21–33. Note that several of these have worshippers carved in relief to the sides which determine that the foot be aligned upwards and away from the viewer (I.25, I.32 and the example recently purchased by the Yale University Art Gallery, 2015.141.1): are these authentic or modern fakes made for the market? The Roman examples in Dunbabin, 1990, are incised.

25 See Marshall, Foucher and Majumdar, 1940, pp. 37 and 40. A number of fine *buddhapāda*s from the first century BCE inserted in larger narratives appear in scenes on the railing pillars at Bharhut, for example, HAABA, scan nos 4790, 11537 and 4783.

26 Interestingly, *buddhapāda*s are thought to refer to naturally occurring 'footprints' of Buddha, known to have been venerated from very early: see Strong, 2004, pp. 85–97. These are particularly known from the evidence of the Chinese pilgrims, on which see, for example, Quagliotti, 1998, pp. 110–18. Insofar as such 'relics' may be related to fossilized footprints, for instance of dinosaurs, these exist in both imprint and relief form, providing potential natural models for both incised and relief *buddhapāda*s. See, for example, Xing et al. 2011; Xing et al. 2014.

27 The nails of the large toes lead Knox, 1992, p. 211, to see nails in all the toes (not at all clear to me) and to aver that the image shows 'the upper surface of the foot' although this is not possible, not least because there is no leg.

28 BM 1880,0709.57; Barrett, 1954, pp. 65, no. 20; Knox, 1992, pp. 212–13, no. 121; Quagliotti, 1998, pp. 20–22, no. I.5.

29 Knox, 1992, p. 212.

30 The word *dānam* is legible; see ibid.

31 Rea, 1894, p. 33 and pl. XV.

32 GMC no. 169, in Burgess, 1887, pp. 98–9, pl. 53.1; Sivaramamurti, 1956, p. 162, no. I D 3; Quagliotti, 1998, pp. 28–9, no. I.8; Kannan, 2014, p. 185 (see HAABA, scan nos 27696 and 12182). Karlsson, 1999, pp. 115–16 and fig. 24 (contra Roy, 1994, p. 120) dates this earlier than the two British Museum panels, which would simply confirm the formal moves I have analysed but for a somewhat earlier moment.

33 The second example is Quagliotti, 1998, p. 29, no. I.9, apparently also in Chennai but I can find no accession number or mention in Kannan, 2014. Both are discussed by Srivasta, 1991, p. 85.

34 For more nails, see also from the Chennai Museum, see GMC no. 178, in Burgess, 1887, p. 98, p. 52.8; Sivaramamurti, 1956, p. 161, no. I D 2; Quagliotti, 1998, p. 30, no. I.11; and Kannan, 2014, p. 188, who oddly illustrates it upside down (also HAABA. 27701).

35 Anālayo, 2017, pp. 15–17, with full details. For the Gāndhārī version on a birchbark scroll, dated between the first century BCE and the third century CE, see Salomon, 2018, pp. 114–15, with discussion at 108–9. Much information on later *buddhapāda* commentaries and traditions is available in Cicuzza, 2011.

36 In the Chinese version translated by Anālayo, 2017, pp. 17–20, the options of the Buddha being a *naga* and Brahma are added to these.

37 *Aṅguttara Nikāya*, Book of the Fours, II.38, sutta 36 (Dona), trans. Bodhi, 2012. Compare the very early Pāli *Sutta Nipata* 3.4, where the Buddha also presents himself through negation (of caste affiliations): 'I am certainly not a brahman, nor a prince, nor a *vessa* (merchant), nor am I anyone else' (trans. Norman 1984, p. 76).

38 Anālayo, 2017, pp. 20, 23–5.

39 They include the following now in the Chennai (formerly Madras) Museum: Quagliotti, 1998, p. 30, I.10 (= Sivaramamurti, 1956, p. 161, no. I D 1, a fragment for which I cannot find the museum number nor any reference in Kannan, 2014); GMC no. 178, in Quagliotti, 1998, p. 30, I.11; Burgess, 1887, p. 98, pl. 52.8 and Sivaramamurti, 1956, p. 161, no. I D 2; Kannan, 2014, p. 188, an interesting piece without a border, with very large *dharmacakra*s and multiple symbols, clear wrinkles for the toe-joins and clear nails; GMC no. 167, in Quagliotti, 1998, p. 30, I.12; Burgess, 1887, p. 98, pl. 52.6; Sivaramamurti, 1956, p. 162, no. I D 4; Kannan, 2014: 184; GMC no 165, in Quagliotti, 1998, p. 31, I.13; Burgess, 1887, p. 98, pl. 43.1; Sivaramamurti, 1956, p. 162, no. I D 5; Roy, 1994, pl. 30; Kannan, 2014, p. 183. In the Amarāvatī Museum: AMA no. 1039, in Quagliotti, 1998, pp. 31–2, no. I.14 and Gupta, 2008, no. 604, pl. 41 (dated there on epigraphic grounds to the sixth century CE, but the object

could be earlier than the inscription); AMA nos 334, 347, 348, 361, respectively in Gupta, 2008, nos 841, 843, 845 and 846 (all fragmentary and said to be third century CE).

40 GMC no. 165, in Burgess, 1887, p. 98, pl. 43.14; Sivaramamurti, 1956, p. 162, no. I D 5; Kannan, 2014, p. 183, with a fragmentary inscription, no. 8, p. 274 reported also by Lüders, 1912, pp. 155, no. 1308, Quagliotti, 1998, p. 31, no. I.13 and HAABA, scan nos 12179 and 27695). It is unclear why Quagliotti, 1998, p. 31 maintains this piece was found inside the inner railing.

41 On the emblematic body, see Dehejia, 1991, pp. 54–6; Dehejia 1997, pp. 48–50; Huntington, 2020, pp. 506–9.

42 GMC no. 178, in Burgess, 1887, p. 98, pl. 52.8; Sivaramamurti, 1956, p. 161, no. I D 2; Quagliotti, 1998, p. 30, no. I.11; Kannan, 2014, p. 188 (HAABA 27701).

43 See Khan, 1969, p. 1 and pl. 5; Quagliotti, 1998, pp. 35–7, no. I.15.

44 Krishna Sastri, Subrahmanyam and Krishna Rao, 1992, pp. 34 and 94, pls LXIV–LXV.

45 Floral border: Longhurst, 1938, p. 24, pl. 19a; and Quagliotti, 1998, p. 38, no. I.17 (now in Delhi). Bodhi tree: Quagliotti, 1998, pp. 36–7, no. I.16; deer: Quagliotti, 1998, pp. 41–2, no. I.18; stūpa: Quagliotti, 1998, pp. 42–3, no. I.19.

46 BM 1880,0709.42. See Ferguson 1873, p. 209, pl. 87.4; Barrett, 1954, p. 65, no. 21; Knox, 1992, no. 122; Quagliotti, 1998, pp. 27–8, no. I.7.

47 On the 32 marks see Griffiths, 1994, pp. 68, 97–101; Endo, 1997, pp. 45–7, 138–42; Xing, 2005, pp. 25–35; Dehejia, 2009, pp. 60–66.

48 See Endo, 1997, pp. 163–5.

49 For example, *Mahāvastu* 2. 29, 304–7, in Jones, 1952, pp. 26–7, 285–8.

50 See Boucher, 2008, pp. 3–19, on Mahāyāna models and in particular the *Rāstrapālapariprcchā-sūtra*, which was certainly composed before the third century CE.

51 *Mahāvastu* 2.304, in Jones, 1952, p. 286.

52 *Majjhima Nikāya* II.136–7, sutta 91. See Anālayo, 2017, pp. 43–135 for lengthy discussion.

53 Ñāṇamoli and Bodhi, 1995, p. 745. Translations vary – see, for example, Anālayo, 2017, p. 47.

54 According to the *Mahāsāṃghika*, indeed arguably proto-Mahāyāna, *Mahāvastu* 1.163: 'The Supreme of Men always walks without touching the ground for as much as the width of four fingers . . . This earth with its mountains rises and subsides as he walks over it': see Jones, 1949, p. 129. The implication for the *buddhapādas* on this model of interpretation maybe that the earth itself has risen to make a kind of inverse print in emulation of the sacred foot.

55 Anālayo, 2017, pp. 71–94.

56 Ibid., pp. 103–35.

57 *Lakhana Sutta*, 30. 1.8, as translated in Walsh, 1987, p. 444.

58 Ibid., 30. 1.11, p. 445.

59 Ang and Rhys Davids, 1960, pp. 323–4.

60 Note that the *buddhapāda* is used for the scene of Gautama's birth before he become a Buddha, where his first footprints are incised in his swaddling clothes in, for example, Knox, 1992, pp. 119–20, no. 61, BM 1880,0709.44. See also Knox, 1992, pp. 100–101, no. 41, BM 1880,0709.23.

61 For a conspectus of footprints in narrative scenes across early Indian Buddhist art, see Huntington, 2020, pp. 449–509. For the creation and proliferation of Buddhist icons in sixth- to ninth-century CE Dunhuang (in this case based on an image with miraculous powers in human form), including into narrative imagery, see Wu, 2023, pp. 171–237.

62 Becker, 2015, pp. 23–77.

63 BM 1880,0709.79; Barrett, 1954, pp. 15, 64; Knox, 1992, no. 60. Huntington, 2020, p. 457, wants it to represent devotion to the place of enlightenment in the ages after the Buddha's passing away; this is in accordance with her general interpretative emphasis on *buddhapādas* as commemorative ('vestiges left by the Buddha . . . veneration at sacred locations that the Buddha had once visited', p. 509) but that view cannot explain the use of *buddhapādas* in narratives of the Buddha's life or in the iconic panels. I see no reason why polysemic models including all these options should be excluded.

64 AMA no. 24, in Gupta, 2008, p. 55, no. 338, pl. 18; Karlsson, 1999, pp. 112–13, fig. 22. In the British Museum collection, a version appears as a depiction of the first sermon: Knox, 1992: no. 38, BM 1880.0709.22 (see also Knox, 1992: no. 63, BM 1880,0709.74; Knox, 1992: no. 88, BM 1880,0709.93; and Knox, 1992: no. 89, BM 1880,0709.94). Versions of this iconography on drum slabs from the small stūpa of about the third century, excavated at the site by Rea, with a *dharmacakra*, throne and *buddhapādas* within the central gateway of miniature stūpas, are now at the Amarāvatī Museum: AMA nos 418 and 419, in Gupta, 2008: nos 352 and 353, figs xxiv and xxv; and from the main stūpa in the British Museum: Knox, 1992: no. 77, BM 1880,0709,87; Knox, 1992: no. 78, BM 1880,0709,120 – in this case with a *naga* on which the *buddhapāda* is placed.

65 AMA no. 2, in Gupta, 2008: no. 339, pl. 19; Knox, 1992, pp. 141–9, nos 73, 75 and 76, respectively BM 1880.0709.80, BM 1880.0709.83 and BM 1880.0709.85 (= Quagliotti, 1998, pp. 32–3).

66 Such as AMA nos 1, 19, 270, 417, 8, respectively in Gupta, 2008: nos 340–41, 351–2, 362; Knox, 1992, pp. 149–51 and 152–5, nos 77 and 79, BM 1880.0709.87 and BM 1880.0709.121; or the fine slab now in Chennai, GMC no. 221, in Kannan, 2014, p. 201, on which see Burgess, 1887, pp. 70–73; and Sivaramamurti, 1956, pp. 263–4, no. IV C 1.

67 See AMA no. 22, in Gupta, 2008, no. 342 (pl. 22), although this is from a small stūpa at the site, and AMA no. 419, in Gupta, 2008, no. 353 (fig. xxv).

68 Quagliotti, 1998, pp. 173–86, with bibliography.

69 It is not published anywhere I have found, but is available at the Alamy website (www.alamy.com), represented wrongly with the toes upwards, as image AoBCFD. Compare the fine lotus medallion with a stūpa in its centre now in the Amarāvatī site museum: Sivaramamurti, 1956, no. III D 20; and Burgess, 1887, p. xix, fig. 3, and another unpublished so far as I know in Chennai with a *dharmacakra* in the hub.

70 Knox, 1992, pp. 93–5, no. 36, BM 1880,0709.19/20; Quagliotti, 1998, pp. 34–5; the topic of the relief narrative is obscure: see Becker, 2016, pp. 71–4.

71 Knox, 1992, pp. 184–5, no. 102, BM 1880,0709.53; Quagliotti, 1998, pp. 178–80 (no. 15).

72 AMA no. 8, in Gupta, 2008, p. 24, no. 79, pl. 8 (HAABA 0021300).

73 If, as has been suggested by Knox, 1992, pp. 156–7, and on the British Museum website, this iconography represents the first sermon of the Buddha, or the turning of the wheel of dharma (in the absence of any depiction of the five ascetics to whom he preached the sermon), then the imagery of these pilasters may refer to the last part of the *Dhammacakkappavattana Sutta*

(*Sutta Nipata* 56.11), where the entire universe is presented as shaking before the auspicious nature of the event: 'When the Wheel of Truth had thus been set rolling by the Blessed One the earth gods raised the cry: "At Benares, in the Deer Park at Isipatana, the matchless Wheel of Truth has been set rolling by the Blessed One, not to be stopped by monk or divine or god or death-angel or high divinity or anyone in the world." On hearing the earth-gods' cry, all the gods in turn in the six paradises of the sensual sphere took up the cry till it reached beyond the Retinue of High Divinity in the sphere of pure form. And so indeed in that hour, at that moment, the cry soared up to the World of High Divinity, and this ten-thousandfold world-element shook and rocked and quaked, and a great measureless radiance surpassing the very nature of the gods was displayed in the world.' (Trans. Bikkhu Ñāṇamoli.)

74 See BM 1880,0709.71 and BM 1880,0709.123 in Knox, 1992, pp. 156–7, nos 81 and 82. For other examples of similar pilasters with *buddhapāda*s in the same place at the Chennai Museum, see HAABA 0027623, 0027624, 0027626, 0027627, 0027643, 0027644, 0027648, 0027710 (=0027711) and also 0027703 (a pillar relief); and in the Amarāvatī Museum, see HAABA 0021351 and 0021369. On Sānchī, see also Marshall, Foucher and Majumdar, 1940: vol. I, pp. 137–44, and vol. II, pl. 37; for the same motif at Bharhut (now in the Allahabad Museum), see HAABA 1410.

75 On this topic, see the Introduction.

76 The Sanskrit *Divyāvadāna*, an anthology of 38 tales of the karmic results of actions in previous lives, perhaps dating from the second century CE, repeatedly presents proper devotion to the Buddha as 'venerating with one's head the feet of the Blessed One', that is, prostration to the *buddhapāda* and touching the feet with the head: see Rotman, 2009, pp. 115–16, with references.

77 See Fronsdal, 1998, pp. 5–10, on devotion in relation to stūpas and sūtras in the early Mahāyāna; Kinnard, 2008, esp. pp. 97–100; on physical and visual pilgrimage; and esp. Becker, 2015, pp. 31, 33, 36, 48–56, 66–77, on Amarāvatī. On *buddhapāda*s and devotion: Rao, 2005a (though I have no faith in his chronology at p. 348).

78 BM 1880,0709.4, Knox, 1992, no. 6; Quagliotti, 1998, pp. 177–8, no. 10. See Kinnard, 2008, pp. 88–92; on this pillar, with an astute critique of overdetermined readings subject to too much dependence on the assumption of prior texts for images, and 'an image-as-text analysis with the basic assumption of the aniconism thesis' (p. 92).

79 On this image see Huntington, 2020, pp. 469–70.

80 Panels with *buddhapāda*s in the dome: AMA no. 2, in Gupta, 2008, no. 339, pl. 19; Knox, 1992, pp. 141–9, nos 73, 75 and 76, respectively BM 1880.0709.80, BM 1880.0709.83 and BM 1880.0709.85 (= Quagliotti, 1998, pp. 32–3). Railing coping: Knox, 1992, pp. 93–5, no. 36, BM 1880,0709.19/20; Quagliotti, 1998, pp. 34–5.

81 GMC no. 297, in Burgess, 1887, pl. LXIX.3; Sivaramamurti, 1956, no. III A 31; Rao, 2005a, p. 345; Kannan, 2014, p. 223.

82 Frieze: Knox, 1992, pp. 184–5, no. 102, BM 1880,0709.53; Quagliotti, 1998, pp. 178–80, no. 15. Birth narrative: Knox, 1992, pp. 119–20, no. 61, BM 1880,0709.44. Nairañjanā River: the upper relief of Knox, 1992, pp. 50–52, no. 6, BM 1880,0709.4; Quagliotti, 1998, pp. 177–8, no. 10.

83 Strong, 2004, pp. 85–97.

84 Wayman and Stone, 1990, pp. 49–66; Padma and Barber, 2008.

85 Mabbett, 1998, esp. p. 345; Walser, 2005, esp. pp. 61–9, 79–88; Wayman, 2005; a summary of what (little) is known and which texts are most likely to be his: Westerhoff, 2009, pp. 4–9. On the difficulties of Western philosophical approaches to the interpretation of Nāgārjuna's work, see Westerhoff, 2009, pp. 9–12.

86 On emptiness (*sunyata*), see, for example, Harvey, 1990, pp. 99–103; Williams, 2009, pp. 51–5, 68–71, 79–81, 176–9; on Nāgārjuna's model of emptiness specifically, Westerhoff, 2009, pp. 12, 19, 92 and esp. 19–52 on that which emptiness negates.

87 Warder, 1973; Kalupahana, 1986, pp. 7–8, 26; Vélez de Cea, 2005.

88 Garfield, 1995, p. 49.

89 Westerhoff, 2009, p. 74, offers a series of examples from the suttas of the Pāli canon where the 'four-cornered logic' is used by the Buddha himself.

90 For a range of approaches to this complex issue and the large bibliography, see Ruegg, 1977; Priest and Garfield, 2002; Westerhoff, 2009, pp. 53–65 (on the role of negation in Nāgārjuna's thought) and 67–90 (on the *Catuṣkoṭi*); Cotnoir, 2015; Priest, 2018, pp. 51–63. See Kalupahana, 1986, p. 270, for the way in which Nāgārjuna uses his four-cornered logic to *reject* metaphysical assumptions rather than to establish something or some theory.

91 See Cleary, 1993, p. 1397.

92 Ibid., p. 1400.

93 Ibid., pp. 1406–22.

94 See the translation of this section (not in Cleary, 1993, because not in Chinese) in Levman, 2005, p. 34. Levman argues that the Sanskrit word used here (*sanābhi*) meaning 'having the same nave or centre' also means 'of kindred blood' and thus evokes the 'mutual interrelationship of all beings' that is key to this *sūtra*.

95 Levman, 2005, p. 33.

96 Cleary, 1993, p. 1422 for the identity of the Lord of Glory and p. 1423 for sixty decillion.

97 *Vajjracchedikā Sūtra*, 5, 20b, see 26a and 27, in Conze, 1958b, pp. 28, 62–3. On the logical procedure, dependent on Nāgārjuna's four-cornered model, see Nagatomo, 2000, and 2018, pp. 1244–8.

98 *Vajjracchedikā Sūtra* 32a, Conze, 1958, p. 68.

99 Broadly speaking, I agree with Huntington, 1990, pp. 405–7, and 2015, pp. 180–83, on the question of aniconism, though would want to extend the interpretation of Buddhist imagery beyond both narrative and liturgy/ritual to more abstract theology. At the same time her resistance to *pars pro toto* uses of non-figural imagery as potential evocations of the Buddha and to combinations of such imagery to create an 'emblematic body' seems unnecessary (and indeed quite wrong in the context of the repeated visual practices of Amarāvatī: see Chapter Seven on issues of representation).

100 See Quagliotti, 1998, pp. 46–50, nos 1.2–21.

101 See especially Becker, 2015, pp. 38–41.

seven SYSTEMS OF REPRESENTATION

1 BM 1880,0709.44, Knox, 1992, no. 61: 'this may be the finest sculpture in the collection and is certainly one of the most perfectly preserved' (p. 119). It is unclear where this sculpture would have sat – possibly in place of one of the meta-stūpas of the drum, possibly as part of the sculptural decoration of the *āyaka* platforms.

2 Mackenzie Album, WD1061, folio 17.
3 *Pace* Knox, 1992, p. 119, who says two female attendants.
4 For some discussion of the iconography, see Quintanilla, 2017.
5 Both iconographies – fly whisk and umbrella – are attested elsewhere. For some discussion see Quintanilla, 2017, pp. 130–35.
6 On repetition in early Buddhist texts, see Gombrich, 2018, pp. 62–8 and Anālayo, 2022, pp. 101–5 and 127–9; Gethin, 2020, pp. 145–6, on the complex and sophisticated patterns of repetitive method. On expansion in the Chinese, see Harrison, 2003, pp. 121–2. For issues of orality, performance and memorization, see Gethin, 1992; Shulman, 2021, pp. 11–13, 119–25, 191–9; Anālayo, 2022, pp. 167–200; Bucknell, 2023, pp. 35–57; and for formulaic composition Shulman, 2021, pp. 149–99. The fundamental theoretical account of orality and literacy remains Ong, 2012 (3rd edn), although this has nothing on Buddhism (for a little on the Vedas in Indian culture, see pp. 64–6).
7 See, for example, Gombrich, 2018, pp. 49–54; Shaw, 2021, pp. 11–32; Shulman, 2021, pp. 191–9.
8 See Gethin, 2020, p. 157.
9 Dehejia, 1991, pp. 54–6; and Dehejia, 1997, pp. 48–50, endorsed by, for example, Fogelin, 2012, esp. pp. 288–9; and Wenzel, 2011, pp. 270–71. The position was contested especially by Huntington, 1992, esp. 123–4: 'What is the foundation for this interpretation? What is the Buddhological or other evidence?' Dehejia, 1992a, p. 157 responded: 'A wide range of emblems, including a slab of stone, an empty seat, footprints, and empty space topped by a parasol, constitute the Buddha's presence as "absent signifier"'. Huntington appears to have accepted the broad parameters of the model: see Huntington, 2020, pp. 506–9. The idea of a *body* made of a *collection* or *company* of symbols is supported by the meanings of the key term *kāya* in Pāli, which is the base of the *trikāya* or three-body model of Mahāyāna Buddhism and of earlier Nikāya accounts of the Buddha's nature: see Jantrasrisalai, 2008, pp. 137–228. Specifically on iconism and aniconism at Amarāvatī, see Becker, 2006, pp. 49–65; and Kinnard, 2008, pp. 84–97. The strongest support for the emblematic-body theory comes in the appearance of the emblematic body in *narrative* representations (such as the madness of the elephant Nālāgiri) as an alternative to the embodied Buddha: see my discussion above in Chapter Three. There are many parallels in the sculpture of Nāgārjunakonda: see Rao, 2005b.
10 See Fergusson, 1873, 191 and pl. LXXI. 1 and Rana, 2013, pp. 34–5 and pl. 2.34a.
11 AMA no. 20, Gupta, 2008, pp. 24, no. C 79 (HAABA 21300). See also Dehejia, 1997, pp. 48–9; and Rana, 2013, pp. 34–5, pl. 2.34b.
12 The story is told in *Mahāvagga* 1.54.1–3, Vin. I.82, in Rhys Davids and Oldenberg, 1881–5, vol. I, pp. 208–9; and Horner, 1951, pp. 103–4; see also Buddhaghosa's versions in the *Dhammapāda Commentary* 1.116–17, in Burlingame, 1921, vol. I, pp. 155–6; and *Nidānakathā* 91–2, in Jayawickrama, 1990, pp. 123–4. For a much more elaborate version, see *Mahāvastu* 3.254–61, in Jones, 1956, vol. III, pp. 242–61.
13 It is worth stressing that the same subject occurs elsewhere in the site with the Buddha in human form, for instance in a fine railing pillar in the British Museum: see BM 1880,0709.11, Knox, 1992, no. 12.
14 GMC no. 187, in Kannan, 2014, p. 190. See HAABA 27714 and 27714; see for the same iconography but with very damaged *dharmacakra* scene GMC no. 188, in Kannan, 2014, p. 191.
15 GMC no. 221, in Sivaramamurti, 1956, pp. 263–4, no. IV C 1; and Kannan, 2014, p. 201. See Chpater One for detailed discussion of this panel.
16 For example: BM 1880,0709.87 = Knox, 1992, no. 77; also Mackenzie's Album WD1061, folio 16 (*dharmacakra* over empty throne in the entrance, seated Buddha with a halo amid devotees in the dome panels, second from the right); WD1061, folio 26 (Buddha with Nālāgiri in the entrance and *dharmacakra*, over empty throne in the *āyaka* platform); WD1061, folio 67 (Buddha Mucalinda in the entrance, empty throne with Bodhi tree (and elephant) upper drum panel far right).
17 Mackenzie's Album, BL WD1061, folio; Ferguson, 1873, pp. 198–9 and pl. LXX; Dehejia, 1997, pp. 48–50; Zin, 2006, p. 147 (no. 5).
18 Another parallel instance is from the lower lozenge of a now lost railing pillar drawn by Mackenzie's team in March 1817. Here the flaming pillar sits atop an empty throne depicted in three-quarters view facing rightwards and ferried on a boat as part of an unidentified narrative. See Mackenzie's Album, BL WD1061, folio 58.
19 See the discussion of Bareau, 1980.
20 The story is relatively frequent in early Buddhist art: see Zin, 2006, pp. 136–66, but only once more identified (in a very fragmentary piece) in the Amarāvatī 'marbles': see Sivaramamurti, 1956, pp. 155–6, no. I A 2; and Zin, 2006, pp. 146–7 (no. 4). Nowhere does it appear with the sustained 'aniconic' panache of this lost railing pillar from Amarāvatī.
21 *Mahāvagga* 1.15–21, Vin. I.24–35, where the sequence climaxes in the famous Fire Sermon, in Rhys Davids and Oldenberg, 1881–5, vol. I, pp. 118–35; and Horner, 1951, pp. 32–46; *Mahāvastu* 3.424–34, in Jones, 1956, vol. III, pp. 425–35; *Catuṣpariṣatsūtra* 24a.1–27.1, in Kloppenborg, 1977, pp. 50–75; for the *Mahīśasaka* and *Dharmaguptaka* versions in French translation: see Bareau, 1963, pp. 257–330. See also Buddhaghosa's version in *Nidānakathā* 82–3, in Jayawickrama, 1990, p. 111. A variant of the same story with some differences is told by Buddhaghosa in the *Dhammapāda Commentary* 14.6, in Burlingame, 1921, vol. III, pp. 74–7; as the narrative of the conversion of the sage Aggidatta and his retinue of followers by the Buddha's disciple Moggallāna. For some discussion of the surviving range of retellings, see Bareau, 1980, pp. 9–12. On the *Dīrghagāma*, of which early first century CE MS fragments have come to light, see Hartmann, 2004, p. 121, for the place of the *Catuṣpariṣatsūtra*. For an introduction to the complexities of comparing Pāli and Chinese versions of early texts from different schools see Bucknell, 2023, pp. 5–21, and 58–63 on translation traditions to Sanskrit and Chinese, although he believes there is a common ancestor in each case (while it is possible to argue that there were many early Buddhisms rather than one).
22 The Buddha requests three times in *Mahāvagga* 1.15 but only once in *Catuṣpariṣatsūtra* 24a.5–8, *Mahāvastu* 3.428 and the Mahīśasaka and Dharmaguptaka *Vinaya* accounts (Bareau, 1963, p. 259). He receives permission from Uruvelā Kassapa in all versions bar the *Mahāvastu*. For some discussion see Bareau, 1963, pp. 260–66.
23 *Mahāvagga* 1.15.2–7, Vin. I.24–25, in Rhys Davids and Oldenberg, 1881–5, vol. I, pp. 118–22; and Horner, 1951, pp. 33–5 (where in fact there are two duels in two fire-huts, the second with the king of the *nāgas*); *Mahāvastu* 3.428–32, Jones, 1956,

vol. III, pp. 429–34; *Catuṣpariṣatsūtra* 24a.5–22, in Kloppenborg, 1977, pp. 51–3. A version of the same story (in emulation of the Buddha's miracle here) is told of the Elder Sāgata at *Suttavibhaṅga*, 51.1, Vin. IV.107–8, also in the *Vinaya*: see Horner, 1940, pp. 382–3.

24 It is worth noting that the Buddha is called *Nāga* and *nāga*-like in the *Mahāvastu* passage, p. 3.424, in Jones, 1956, vol. III, p. 425, and again at Uruvelā's verse recapitulation of the episode at *Mahāvastu* 3.445, in Jones, 1956, vol. III, 426. In the *Mahīśasaka* version, the *nāga* raises his body to emit fire and the Buddha raises his body and emits fire in return: Bareau, 1963, p. 259. Likewise, Uruvelā's conversion in the *Mahāvastu* is described as a snake casting off its skin: *Mahāvastu* 3.431 and 444, in Jones, 1956, vol. III, pp. 425 and 445. In the image on the left side of the three in the lozenge, therefore, the *nāga* figure may represent the serpent in conflict with the Buddha, or it may represent the Buddha (along with the *buddhapāda*), as *nāga* figures of this kind so often seem to do in the central gateway of many meta-stūpas in the drum slabs, or it may conflate both.

25 Bareau, 1963, p. 316, dismisses the number as part of a naive and late addition to the text.

26 *Mahāvastu* 3.430, in Jones, 1956, vol. III, p. 432; see *Mahāvagga* 1.20.17–19, Vin.I.32–33, in Rhys Davids and Oldenberg, 1881–5, vol. I, pp. 131–3; and Horner, 1951, pp. 42–3; *Catuṣpariṣatsūtra* 25a.1–26.1, Kloppenborg, 1977, pp. 68–73; Mahīśasaka and Dharmaguptaka *Vinaya* accounts: Bareau, 1963, pp. 304–15. The three images of the lozenge thus either follow a source-tradition closer to the *Mahāvastu*, or syncopate the narrative structures of a source-tradition closer to the *Mahāvagga* and *Catuṣpariṣatsūtra* or follow a different tradition altogether such as the literary model in canto 16 of the *Buddhacarita* of Aśvaghoṣa (which only survives in the Chinese and Tibetan translations, see ref. 31 below). Just as none of the surviving narrative accounts – each stemming from a different Nikāya tradition in early Buddhism – are precisely the same, so the pictorial retelling (whether we see it as a primary version or a commentarial exegesis) recalibrates and syncopates the story. Whether this arises from the needs of the monastic community at the site or from a particular version told there (itself belonging either to one of the now lost *Vinaya* traditions within the Nikāya schools or a hybrid version created in Amarāvatī) is not soluble by us now, but reflects the complex range of options within the rich diversity of early Buddhism.

27 *Mahāvastu* 3.431–2, in Jones, 1956, vol. III, pp. 432–3.

28 Ibid., 3.434–6, pp. 436–8.

29 *Mahāvagga* 1. 21.1–4, Vin. I.34–35, in Rhys Davids and Oldenberg, 1881–5, vol. I, pp. 134–5; and Horner, 1951, pp. 45–6; alongside, for example, *Nidānakathā* 82–3, in Jayawickrama, 1990, p. 111; *Catuṣpariṣatsūtra* 26.17–19, in Kloppenborg, 1977, p. 74; Mahīśasaka and Dharmaguptaka *Vinaya:* Bareau, 1963, pp. 317–20. The Fire Sermon (*Ādittapariyāya Sutta*) itself is *Saṃyutta Nikāya* 35.28, IV.19–20. Unfortunately, the Pāli commentaries by Buddhaghosa on this and on the *Mahāvagga* have not yet been translated, so the exegetic traditions which may supply much ancient inflection to these narratives are not available to me.

30 In *Mahāvagga* 1.21.1–4, the enlightenment of the former fire ascetics depends entirely on the Fire Sermon. In the Mahīśasaka and Dharmaguptaka *Vinaya* (Bareau, 1963, p. 318) and the *Catuṣpariṣatsūtra* 26.1–21, the enlightenment follows a teaching of three levels. In the Dharmaguptaka *Vinaya* and the *Catuṣpariṣatsūtra*, these are supernatural power, the supernatural ability of mind-reading and recollection, and finally supernatural *dharma* instruction, this last constituting the Fire Sermon. In the Mahīśasaka *Vinaya*, these are supernatural power, *dharma* instruction and teaching concerning instructions and orders, which may perhaps relate to issues around the *saṅgha*. It is not impossible that the image of the Buddha as a pillar of fire in all these images and especially when delivering the Fire Sermon was meant to evoke some aspect of these teachings of supernatural power, which include the concentration known as the 'fire-element' in which 'various rays came forth from the body of the lord Buddha of blue, yellow, red, white, pink and crystal hue' (*Catuṣpariṣatsūtra* 26.6 and 9).

31 See the Chinese *Buddhacarita*, Fascicle 4, 16.21–48, 31b–32a, in Willemen, 2009, pp. 115–17, with discussion by Eltschinger, 2012, pp. 192–201.

32 In other words, traditions that may be somewhat different in their ordering, emphases and substance from those that survive in the *Mahāvagga*, *Mahāvastu* and *Catuṣpariṣatsūtra*, but depend ultimately on the same narratives and teachings (with variants) within a *Vinaya* context.

33 GMC no. 255, in Burgess, 1887, pp. 77–8, pl. xli.6; Sivaramamurti, 1956, p. 297, no. IV A 13; Kannan, 2014, p. 212. This is either the same object as depicted in Mackenzie's Album WD1061, folio 21 or one almost exactly like it. See also BM 1880,0709.73, Knox, 1992, no. 83 (= Mackenzie's Album WD1061, folio 27). Other fragmentary examples with similar iconography include Mackenzie's Album WD1061, folio 51.

34 The image is damaged, with the Buddha's head damaged and some parts lost on the left. If the Mackenzie drawing is of the same piece or represents its iconography, then there were six rather than five figures around the Buddha in this scene.

35 See, for example, *Māradhītu Sutta*, *Saṃyutta Nikāya* 4.25, I.124–7 in, for example, Bodhi, 2000, pp. 217–20.

36 Bodhi, 2000, p. 220.

37 For instance, BM 1880,0709.2, Knox, 1992, no. 26.

38 BM 1880,0709.79, Knox, 1992, no. 60.

39 Mackenzie's Album WD1061, folio 76 (probably a crossbar medallion) conflates the flaming pillar with the *dharmacakra*; also BM 1880,0709.123, Knox, 1992, no. 82. At the same time, the majority of surviving or attested drum pilasters with *dharmacakra*s do not have the flaming pillar.

40 The iconography is not unique in Andhra: a number of fragments from Gummadidurru (some now in the Amarāvatī site museum, one now in the LA County Museum and one in the Cincinnati Museum of Art, appear to come from drum pilaster slabs with the flaming column and throne with the deer to either side at the bottom of a taller pillar that would likely have been topped with the wheel. See, for example, Rosen Stone, 1994, pp. 83–5, figs 123 and 245; AMA 195, 197–9, 200, 2002, p. 231, in Gupta, 2008, nos I 670–676, with figs XLIX and L.

41 GMC no. 253, in Kannan, 2014, pp. 211; and Sivaramamurti, 1956, p. 168 no II A 14; HAABA 27744: this picture is not sharp enough to be reproduced here; I know of no better one.

42 AMA no. 879, in Gupta, 2008 no. G. 490.

43 See Sitapati and Krishna Sastry, 1980, pp. 12–13 and pl. 4; Dehejia, 1997, pp. 40–41. See also HAABA 21365 and 21366.

44 For example, Dehejia, 1991, pp. 60; Huntington, 1992, pp. 402–3; Karlssen, 1999, pp. 11–12; Becker, 2006, p. 59.
45 Huntington, 1992, p. 403.
46 As implied by Quagliotti, 1994, followed by Dehejia, 1997, p. 41; and Shimada, 2017, p. 184. For some Chinese canonical and Pāli exegetical sources, see Anālayo, 2012.
47 See Quagliotti, 1994, pp. 150–55 (followed by Dehejia, 1997, p. 41); referencing Beal, 1884, pp. xliv–xlv (Faxian) and I. 235–6 and II. 4 (Xuanzang).
48 Shimada, 2017, pp. 183, 207–9. For discussion of instances of likely recutting at Amarāvatī, see Barrett, 1954, p. 58, n. 6.
49 Mackenzie Album, British Library WD1061, folio 25. This is briefly discussed by Dehejia, 1991, p. 61, where it is argued that the piece represents a shrine with Buddha image placed beneath the Bodhi tree; contra Shimada, 2017, p. 208, who writes it is 'presumably the back of a throne'. The frame around the Buddha is not at all out of place among the upper parts of the diverse thrones in other Mackenzie drawings, for example, WD1061, folio 19 (a Bodhi tree with empty throne and *buddhapāda* from a dome slab), folio 76, folio 42 (two very different thrones).
50 The horizontal measurement given by Mackenzie's draughtsmen (81.28 centimetres/2 ft 8 in.) is close to the measurements of the dome slabs surviving in the British Museum (see Knox, 1992, nos 88–97, with measurements for complete horizontals of between 77.5 and 92.5 centimetres/30–36 in.): this makes it likely the piece was once a dome slab like the fragment discussed above.
51 See the extensive discussion in Xing, 2005.
52 For the Buddha's iconography at Amarāvatī, see esp. Shimada, 2017, pp. 215–18.
53 British Library WD1061, folio 74.
54 Lion seat: BM 1880,0709.108, Knox, 1992, no. 46; railing pillars: BM 1880,0709.4, BM 1880,0709.10, BM 1880,0709.47, respectively Knox, 1992, nos 6, 7 and 10.
55 See Knox, 1992, nos 106–8, pp. 188–91.
56 GMC no. 168, in Burgess, 1887, pp. 87; Sivaramamurti, 1956, p. 248, no. III F 4 and inscription p. 295, no. 92; Kannan, 2014, pp. 184.
57 For example, BM 1880,0709.79, Knox, 1992, no. 72.
58 For example, BM 1880,0709.96 and BM 1880,0709.108, Knox, 1992, nos 91 and 46.
59 For example, BM 1880,0709.4 (outer face), BM 1880,0709.39, BM 1880,0709.95, BM 1880,0709.97, BM 1880,0709.107, BM 1880,0709.114, BM 1880,0709.115, respectively Knox, 1992, nos 6, 64, 90, 92, 51, 94, 95.
60 BM 1880,0709.4 (outer face), Knox, 1992, no. 6.
61 AMA no. 22, Gupta, 2008, p. 56, no. F 342.
62 *Mahānidāna Sutta, Dīgha Nikāya* 15, II.55: 'It is through not understanding, not penetrating this doctrine [dependent origination] that this generation has become like a tangled ball of string . . .', trans. Walshe, 1987, p. 223.
63 One striking exception is the slab we have just examined since, unusually for the coping of the rail, its narrative direction proceeds from right to left. Burgess, 1887, p. 58, observed the slab was 'from some corner or gate', implying it was placed at the end of one of the railing's entrance/exit points (rather than along the processional path alongside the drum) with the imagery designed to be seen in narrative order as the viewer walks out of the gateway.
64 *Tittha sutta, Udāna* 6.4 Ud.66–69, in the *Khuddaka Nikāya*. See also Dhammapāla's perhaps sixth-century (or later) commentary, *Paramatthadīpanī nāma Udānatthakathā* 338–43, in Masefield, 1995, pp. 873–81.
65 For example, the version by J. Ireland at www.accesstoinsight.org/tipitaka/kn/ud/ud.6.04.irel.html.
66 See Dhammapāla, *Udānaṭṭhakathā* 338, 342–3, on the parable and the Buddha's verse commentary, in Masefield, 1995, pp. 880–81.
67 Ibid., p. 873.
68 There is no evidence at all for the assertion that these statues are Mahāyāna as supposed by Singh, 2005, p. 393.
69 For example, Coomaraswamy, 1927, p. 71; Srinivasan, 1960, pp. 66–8; Snellgrove, 1978, pp. 76–82; Gangoly, 1973, pp. 51–2; Rao, 1984, pp. 122–3; Verma, 1996, pp. 173–6; Guy, 2023, pp. 267–72. Fine photographs of several examples may be found at HAABA 5065, 12177–9, 21294–5, 21370, 21824, 21844, 26926, 27006, 27012–13, 27032–3, 27043–5, 27056, 27070–71, 27086–7, 27693–4. For pieces in the Amarāvatī site museum (fragmentary, usually without photographs and with brief descriptions that do not always clarify if they are of reliefs or statues), see AMA nos 16, 272, 273, 318, 333, 346, 348, 370, 468?, 474, 476?, 492, 511, 623, 646, 647, 670, 718, 834, respectively Gupta, 2008, nos J 690 (pl. 50), 837, 838 (pl. 59), 839 (fig. LVIII), 840 (fig. LIX), 842, 844 (fig. LX), 705, 716?, 847 (fig. LXI), 718?, 721, 722, 849, 850, 731, 851, 739, 779.
70 Such as BM 1880,0709.70, BM 1880,0709.79, BM 1880,0709.82 (top), respectively Knox, 1992, nos 69, 72, 84; or Mackenzie's Amaravati Album in the British Library: WD1061, folios 71 and 78.
71 *Uṣṇīṣa* is the Sanskrit term (*uṇhīsa* in Pāli) for the turban-like protruberance at the top of a Buddha's head.
72 Snellgrove, 1978, pp. 76–82: 'The so-called Amarāvatī school portrait of the Buddha in the round, as in bas-reliefs, represents a completely original group of characteristics. It was to have strong and lasting influence, not only in Southern India and Sri Lanka but also throughout most of South-East Asia' (p. 76).
73 See Gupta, 2008, p. 100, on AMA no. 16.
74 AMA nos 16, 333 and 348, in Gupta, 2008, pp. 100 and 116 respectively nos J. 690 (pl. 50), 840 (fig. LIX) and 844 (fig. LX) are just larger than life (the first 2m, including low base); GMC nos 163 and 164, in Kannan, 2014, pp. 183 are respectively 123 and 139 centimetres (48 and 54 in.) missing feet, that is, three-quarter size; AMA nos 273, 318, 346, in Gupta, 2008, pp. 115–16 respectively nos J. 838 (pl. 59), 839 (fig. LVIII) and 842 are likewise three-quarter size.
75 Gangoly, 1973, 24, claims two large standing statues were found at the South Gate, but on no traceable evidence.
76 See, for example, Knox, 1992, p. 28.
77 GMC no. 24, in Kannan, 2014, p. 137; BM 1880,0709.128, in Knox, 1992, no. 127 (there dated later than the main stūpa but I suspect this very damaged piece is original); AMA no. 474, in Gupta, 2008, no. J 847 (fig. LXI).
78 Such as BM 1880,0709.70 (upper left of dome), BM 1880,0709.75 (upper right of dome), BM 1880,0709.79 (upper left of dome), BM 1880,0709.120 (upper right of dome), respectively Knox, 1992, nos 69, 71, 72, 78; or Mackenzie's Amaravati Album in the British Library: WD1061, folios 26 (gateway), 55 (upper right of dome), 70 (upper right of dome, twice, and gateway) and 71 (upper right and left of dome).

79 For example, BM 1880,0709.105–106, respectively Knox, 1992, nos 118–19; GMC nos 92 and 98, in Kannan, 2014, pp. 158 and 161; also Sivaramamurti, 1956, p. 248, nos III F 1–3; AMA nos 92, 108, 371, 423, respectively Gupta, 2008, nos 691, 693, 706, 711 (fig. LV).

80 AMA no. 899, Gupta, 2008, no. J 823 (fig. LVI).

81 AMA no 874, Gupta, 2008, no. J 854 (pl. 61). This piece has been significantly restored in recent years.

82 AMA no. 888, in Gupta, 2008, no. J 855 (pl. 62).

83 GMC no. 213, in Kannan, 2014, pp. 198.

84 AMA no. 873, in Gupta, 2008, no. J 853 (pl. 60).

85 Ānanda in *Theragātha* 17.3 (vv. 1024–9), with Buddhaghosa, *Atthasālinī* 27, in Tin and Rhys Davies, 1920, vol. I, p. 34. Technically, these comprise 82,000 teachings given by the Buddha and 2,000 by his chief disciple Sāriputta, during the Buddha's lifetime.

86 See, for example, *Gopakamogallāna Sutta*, *Majjima Nikāya* 108.

CONCLUSION

1 See especially Harrison, 1978 and 1992b; also Herdman, 2017, pp. 50–63 (in relation to stūpas and pilgrimage); Shulman, 2018a, p. 16; and Shulman, 2021, pp. 6, 84–93, 226.

2 By the time of Upatissa's *Vimuttimagga* (say the fourth century CE), *Buddhānussati* is said to enable all four unifications of mind (*jhānas*, see *Vimuttimagga* IV.8.3, in Ehara, Soma and Kheminda, 1977, pp. 148, = 8.83 in Nyanatusita, 2021, p. 403) although Buddhaghosa's fifth-century *Visuddhimagga* 213, VII.66 (Ñanamoli, 1979, pp. 229–30), implies that recollection leads only to the state at which access to these unifications is possible. See, for example, Bapat, 1937, p. 66.

3 *Aṅguttara Nikāya* I.30, in Bodhi, 2012, p. 116 (adapted slightly); for *Nibbāna* as a result of contemplating the Buddha, see *Sutta Nipāta* 5.16, 1131–1155. For injunctions to this practice see also *Aṅguttara Nikāya* III.285, in Bodhi, 2012, pp. 862–3.

4 *Ekottarāgama* III, 1 (Taishō, vol. II, pp. 554a7–b9), translated into Chinese at the end of the fourth century, of uncertain sectarian affiliation within the early schools of Buddhism. Translation into English: Harrison, 1978, p. 37.

5 This is the *Iti pi so* verse: 'The Blessed One is accomplished, fully enlightened, perfect in true knowledge and conduct, sublime, knower of worlds, incomparable leader of persons to be tamed, teacher of gods and humans, enlightened, blessed', from, for example, *Vatthūpama Sutta* 7 of the *Majjhima Nikāya* I. 37, in Ñāṇamoli and Bodhi, 1995, pp. 118–19. Both *Vimuttimagga* IV.8.3 (Ehara, Soma and Kheminda, 1977, pp. 140–48, = 8.76, in Nyanatusita, 2021, pp. 387–93), and *Visuddhimagga* 198–213, VII.2–676 (Ñāṇamoli, 1979, pp. 206–330), are constructed as commentaries on this verse and each of its epithets.

Bibliography

Abe, S., 1995, 'Inside the Wonder House: Buddhist Art and the West', in *Curators of the Buddha: The Study of Buddhism under Colonialism*, ed. D. Lopez Jr (Chicago, IL), pp. 63–106

Adrych, P., and D. Dalglish, 2020a, 'Mystery Cult and Material Culture in the Graeco-Roman World', in Elsner, 2020, pp. 81–109

—, 2020b, 'Writing the Art, Archaeology and Religion of the Roman Mediterranean', in Elsner, 2020, pp. 51–80

Agrawal, A., 2005, 'Buddhism and Hinduism – the Ikshvaku Patronage at Nagarjunakonda', in Kamalakar, 2005, pp. 51–4

Ahir, D., 2000, *The Influence of the Jatakas on Art and Literature* (Delhi)

Algazi, G., V. Groebner and B. Jussen, eds, 2003, *Negotiating the Gift: Pre-Modern Figurations of Exchange* (Göttingen)

Amore, R., 1971, 'The Concept and Practice of Merit in Early Theravada Buddhism', PhD dissertation, Columbia University, New York

An, Y.-G., 2003, *The Buddha's Last Days: Buddhaghhosa's Commentary on the Mahāparinibbāna Sutta* (Oxford)

Anālayo, 2009, 'The Treatise on the Path to Liberation and the Visuddhimagga', *Fuyan Buddhist Studies*, IV, pp. 1–15

—, 2010, *The Genesis of the Bodhisattva Ideal* (Hamburg)

—, 2012, 'Teaching the Abhidharma in the Heaven of the Thirty-Three, the Buddha and His Mother', *Journal of the Oxford Centre for Buddhist Studies*, XII, pp. 9–35

—, 2017, *Buddhapāda and the Bodhisattva Path* (Hamburg)

—, 2022, *Early Buddhist Oral Tradition: Textual Formation and Transmission* (Somerville, MA)

Andrade, N., 2017, 'Drops of Greek in a Multilingual Sea: The Egyptian Network and Its Residential Presences in the Indian Ocean', *Journal of Hellenic Studies*, CXXXVII, pp. 42–66

Ang, A. Z., and C. Rhys Davids, 1960, *Points of Controversy or Subjects of Discourse: Being a Translation of the Kathā-vatthu from the Abhidhamma-Piṭaka* (London)

de Angelis, F., 2014, 'Sublime Histories, Exceptional Viewers: Trajan's Column and Its Visibility', in *Art and Rhetoric in Roman Culture*, ed. J. Elsner and M. Meyer (Cambridge), pp. 89–114

Anonymous, 1955, *Indian Archaeology, 1954–55: A Review*, ed. A. Ghosh (Delhi)

Anonymous, 2016, *Anikonismus in der frühbuddhistischen Kunst am Beispiel der 'Buddhapāda'* (Bonn)

Appleton, N., 2010, *Jātaka Stories in Theravāda Buddhism: Narrating the Bodhisatta Path* (London)

—, 2014, *Narrating Karma and Rebirth: Buddhist and Jain Multi-Life Stories* (Cambridge)

—, 2017, *Shared Characters in Jain, Buddhist and Hindu Narrative: Gods, King's and Other Heroes* (London)

—, 2020, *Many Buddhas, One Buddha: A Study and Translation of Avadānaśataka 1–40* (Sheffield)

Appleton, N., and S. Shaw, 2015, *The Ten Great Birth Stories of the Buddha: The Mahānipāta of the Jātakatthavannanā* (Chiang Mai)

Azoulay, V., 2013, 'Du paradigme du don à une anthropologie pragmatique de la valeur', in *Anthropologie de l'antiquité: Anciens objets, nouvelles approches*, ed. P. Payen and É. Scheid (Turnhout), pp. 17–42

Bachhofer, L., 1929, *Early Indian Sculpture*, vol. I (Paris)

Bagad, P., 2019, 'On the Concept of Divine Success in the *Nātyaśastra*', *Journal of Aesthetic Education*, LIII, pp. 24–39

Bailey, G., and I. Mabbett, 2003, *The Sociology of Early Buddhism* (Cambridge)

Bansat-Boudon, L., 2020, 'Theatre as Ritual Practice', in *Oxford History of Hinduism: Hindu Practice*, ed. G. Flood (Oxford), pp. 311–41

Bapat, B., 1937, *Vimittimagga and Visuddhimagga: A Comparative Study* (Poona)

Bareau, A., 1960, 'La construction et le culte des stūpa d'après le Vinayapitaka', *Bulletin de l'École francaise d'Extrême Orient*, vol. L, pp. 257–62

—, 1963, *Recherches sur la biographie de Buddha dans les sūtrapitaka at des vinayapitaka anciens: De la quête de l'éveil à la conversion de Śāriputra et de Maudgalyāyana* (Paris)

—, 1971, *Recherches sur la biographie de Buddha dans les sūtrapitaka at des vinayapitaka anciens: II. Les derniers mois, le Parinirvana et les funérailles* (Paris)

—, 1980, 'Le Buddha et Uruvilā', in *Indianisme et Bouddhisme: Mélanges offerts à Mgr. Étienne Lamotte* (Louvain), pp. 1–18

—, 2013, *The Buddhist Schools of the Small Vehicle* (Honolulu, HI) (originally published in French, 1955)
Barber, A., 2008, 'Two Mahāyāna Developments along the Krishna River', in Padma and Barber, 2008, pp. 151–67
Barrett, D., 1954, *Sculpture from Amaravati in the British Museum* (London)
—, 1956, 'Two Unpublished Sculptures from Amarāvatī', *British Museum Quarterly*, XX, pp. 70–73
Barua, B., and K. Simha, 1926, *Barhut Inscriptions* (Calcutta)
Bataille, G., 1988, *The Accursed Share* (New York)
Bhattacharya, B., 1959, 'The Co-Ordination among the Fragments of Aśvaghosa's Śāriputra-prakaraṇa and Two other Buddhist Dramas', in *Akten des vierundzwanzigsten Internationalen Orientalisten-Kongresses, München, 28, August bis 4, September 1957, Sektion 10: Indologie*, ed. Herbert Franke (Wiesbaden), pp. 585–8
Baums, S., A. Griffiths, I. Strauch and V. Tournier, 2016, 'Early Inscriptions of Āndhradeśa: Results of Fieldwork in January and February 2016', *Bulletin de l'École française d'Extrême-Orient*, CII, pp. 355–98
Beal, S., 1884, *Si-Yu-Ki: Buddhist Records of the Western World* (London)
Beaujard, P., 2019, *The Worlds of the Indian Ocean*, vol. I (Cambridge)
Bechert, H., ed., 1991–7, *The Dating of the Historical Buddha*, 3 vols (Göttingen)
Becker, C., 2006, 'Artistic Production and Ritual Performance at Amarāvatī and Other Buddhist Stūpas of Andhra Pradesh', PhD dissertation, University of California, Berkeley
—, 2015, *Shifting Stones, Shaping the Past: Sculpture from the Buddhist Stūpas of Andhra Pradesh* (New York)
—, 2016, 'Mahinda's Visit to Amaravati? Narrative Connections between Buddhist Communities in Andhra and Sri Lanka', in Shimada and Willis, 2016, pp. 70–78
Behrendt, K., 2004, *The Buddhist Architecture of Gandhāra* (Leiden)
—, 2005, 'Narrative Sequences in the Buddhist Reliefs from Gandhāra', in *South Indian Archaeology 2001*, vol. II, ed. C. Jarrige and V. Lefèvre (Paris), pp. 283–92
Belting, H., 1994, *Likeness and Presence: A History of the Image before the Era of Art* (Chicago, IL)
Benisti, M., 2003, *Stylistics of Buddhist Art in India* (Delhi)
Bhandare, S., 1999, 'Historical Analysis of the Satavahana Era: A Study of Coins', PhD dissertation, University of Mumbai
—, 2011, 'Linking the Past: Overstruck Coins and the Chronology of the Satavahanas', in *Felicitas: Essays in Numismatics, Epigraphy and History in Honour of Joe Cribb*, ed. S. Bhandare and S. Garg (Mumbai), pp. 53–63
—, 2016, 'Money and the Monuments: Coins of the Sada Dynasty in the Coastal Andhra Region', in Shimada and Willis, 2016, pp. 37–45
Bharath, S., 2010, 'Recording South Indian Architecture: Linnaeus Tripe and Edmund David Lyon', *South Asian Studies*, XXVI/2, pp. 97–118
Bhattacharyya, N., 1971, *History of Indian Cosmogonical Ideas* (New Delhi)
Biro, M., 1985, 'The Indian Ivory Comb from Gorsium', *Acta Archaeologica Academiae Scientiarum Hungariae*, XXXVII, pp. 419–30
Black, D., 1997, *Leaves of the Heaven Tree: The Great Compassion of the Buddha* (Berkeley, CA)
Bodhi, B., 1978, *The Discourse on the All Embracing Net of Views: The Brahmajāla Sutta and Its Commentaries* (Kandy)
—, 1989, *The Discourse on the Fruits of Recluseship: The Sāmaññaphala Sutta and Its Commentaries* (Kandy)
—, 2000, *The Connected Discourses of the Buddha: A Translation of the Saṃyutta Nikāya* (Somerville, MA)
—, 2012, *The Numerical Discourses of the Buddha: A Translation of the Aṅguttara Nikāya* (Bristol)
Bond, G., 1982, *The Word of the Buddha* (Colombo)
Bopearachchi, O., 2015, *From Bactria to Taprobane*, vol. II (Delhi)
—, 2016, *Seven Weeks after the Buddha's Enlightenment: Contradictions in Text, Confusions in Art* (Delhi)
Boucher, D., 2008, *Bodhisattvas of the Forest and the Formation of the Mahāyāna: A Study and Translation of the Rāstrapālapariprcchā-sūtra* (Honolulu, HI)
Bowie, K., 2016, 'Jūjaka as Trickster: The Comedic Monks of Northern Thailand', in Collins, 2016, pp. 100–121
Braarvig, J., 1993, *Akṣayamatirnirdeśasūtra*, vol. II (Oslo)
Bracey, R., 2020, 'The Gandharan Problem', in Elsner, 2020, pp. 27–50
Brancaccio, P., 2005, 'Sātavāhana Terracottas: Connections with the Hellenistic Tradition', *East and West*, LV, pp. 55–69
—, 2014, 'Looking to the West: Stone Molds and Foreign Visual Models in Satavahana Material Culture (First–Second Century CE)', *Archives of Asian Art*, XIV, pp. 33–41
Brancaccio, P., and X. Liu, 2009, 'Dionysus and Drama in the Buddhist Art of Gandhara', *Journal of Global History*, IV, pp. 219–44
Brilliant, R., 1984, *Visual Narratives* (Ithaca, NY)
Bronkhorst, J., 2007, *Greater Magadha: Studies in the Culture of Early India* (Leiden), 2007
—, 2011, *Buddhism in the Shadow of Brahmanism* (Leiden)
—, 2018, 'Abhidharma in Early Mahāyāna', in Harrison, ed., 2018, pp. 119–40
Brown, B., 1991, *The Buddha Nature: A Study of the Tathāgatagharba and Ālayavijñāna* (Delhi)
Brown, P., 1942, *Indian Architecture (Buddhist and Hindu Period)* (Bombay)
Brown, R., 1997, 'Narrative as Icon: The Jātaka Stories in Ancient Indian and Southeast Asian Architecture', in *Sacred Biography in the Buddhist Traditions of South and Southeast Asia*, ed. J. Schober (Honolulu, HI), pp. 64–109
—, 2009, 'Nature as Utopian Space on the Early Stūpas of India', in J. Hawkes and A. Shimada, eds, *Buddhist Stūpas in South Asia* (New Delhi), pp. 63–80
Bucknell, R., 2023, *Reconstructing Early Buddhism* (Cambridge)
Burgess, J., 1882, *Notes on the Amaravati Stūpa* (Madras)
—, 1887, *The Buddhist Stupas of Amaravati and Jaggayyapeta* (London)
Burlingame, E. W., 1910, 'Buddhaghosa's Dhammapada Commentary', *Proceedings of the American Academy of Arts and Sciences*, XLV, pp. 467–550
—, 1921, *Buddhist Legends*, 3 vols (Cambridge, MA)
Byrski, M. C., 1974, *The Concept of Ancient Indian Theatre* (New Delhi)
Casalini, A., 2021, 'Response to J. Elsner, "Buddhapada: The Enlightened Being and the Limits of Representation at Amarāvatī"', in Elsner and Wood, 2021, pp. 112–15
Castiglione, L., 1968, 'Inverted Footprints: A Contribution to the Ancient Popular Religion', *Acta Ethnographica Academiae Scientiarum Hungaricae*, XVII, pp. 121–37 and 187–9

—, 1970, 'Vestigia', *Acta Archaeologica Academiae Scientiarum Hungaricae*, XXII, pp. 95–132

Chakrabarti, D., 1988, *A History of Indian Archaeology from the Beginning to 1947* (Delhi)

Chakravarti, U., 1987, *The Social Dimensions of Early Buddhism* (Delhi)

Chalmers, R., 1895, *The Jātaka; or, Stories of the Buddha's Former Births*, vol. I (Cambridge)

Chanda, R., 1919–20, 'Some Unpublished Amaravati Inscriptions', *Epigraphia Indica*, XV, pp. 258–75

Carrier, J., 1995, 'Maussian Occidentalism: Gifts and Commodity Systems', in *Occidentalism*, ed. J. Carrier (Oxford), pp. 85–109

Chavannes, E., 1910, *Cinq cents contes et apologues: Extraits du Tripiṭaka chinois et traduits en français*, vol. II (Paris)

Chenna Reddy, P., 2008, *Phanigiri: A Buddhist Site in Andhra Pradesh: An Interim Report* (Hyderabad)

Chhabra, B., 1959–60, 'Nāgārjunakonda Inscription of Ehavalasri's Time, Year 11', *Epigraphia Indica*, XXXIII, pp. 147–9

Chirapravati, P., 2008, 'Illustrating the Lives of the Bodhisatta at Wat Si Chum', in *Past Lives of the Buddha: Swat Si Chum – Art, Architecture and Inscription*, ed. Skilling (Bangkok), pp. 13–39

Chowdhuri, S., 2018, 'A Case Study of Amarāvatī Art in the Context of Andhra Archaeology', PhD dissertation, Department of Ancient Indian History and Culture, University of Calcutta, Kolkata, India

Christodoulou, P., 2011, 'Les reliefs votifs du sanctuaire d'Isis à Dion', in L. Bricault and R. Veymiers, eds, *Bibliotheca Isiaca II* (Bordeaux), pp. 11–22

Churn Law, B., 1946, *Aśvaghosa* (Calcutta)

Cicuzza, C., 2011, *A Mirror Reflecting the Entire World: The Pāli Buddhapādamaṅgala or 'Auspicious Signs on the Buddha's Feet'. Critical Edition with English Translation* (Bangkok and Lumbini)

Clarke, J. R., 1997, 'Living Figures within the *Scaenae Frons*: Figuring the Viewer in Liminal Space', in *I temi figurativie nelle pittura parietale antica*, ed. D. Scagliarini Corlàita (Bologna), pp. 43–7

Cleary, T., 1993, *The Flower Ornament Scripture: A Translation of the Avatamsaka Sūtra* (Boston, MA)

Cohen, B., 1994, *Colonialism and Its Forms of Knowledge: The British in India* (Princeton, NJ)

Collins, S., 1990, 'Preface' to Jayawickrama, 1990, pp. ix–xi

—, 1992, 'Notes on Some Oral Aspects of Pali Literature', *Indo-Iranian Journal*, XXXV, pp. 121–35

—, 1998, *Nirvana and Other Buddhist Felicities* (Cambridge)

—, 2010, *Nirvana: Concept, Imagery, Narrative* (Cambridge)

—, ed., 2015, *The Vessantara Jātaka: Columbia Readings of Buddhist Literature* (New York)

Cone, M., 2001, *A Dictionary of Pāli*, 2 vols (Oxford)

Cone, M., and R. Gombrich, 1977, *The Perfect Generosity of Prince Vessantara: A Buddhist Epic* (Oxford)

Conze, E., 1958a, *The Prajñāpāramitā Literature* (London)

—, 1958b, *Buddhist Wisdom Books: The Diamond Sutra and the Heart Sutra* (London)

—, 1961, *The Large Sutra on Perfect Wisdom, with the Divisions of the Abhisamayālaṅkāra* (London)

—, 1994, *The Perfection of Wisdom in Eight Thousand Lines and Its Verse Summary* (Delhi)

Coomaraswamy, A. K., 1923, *Catalogue of the Indian Collections in the Museum of Fine Arts (Boston)* (Cambridge, MA)

—, 1927, *History of Indian and Indonesian Art* (New York)

—, 1956, *La sculpture de Bharhut* (Paris)

Cort, J., 2010, *Framing the Jina: Narratives and Idols in Jain History* (Oxford)

Cotnoir, J., 2015, 'Nāgārjuna's Logic', in *The Moon Points Back*, ed. K. Tanaka, Y. Deguchi, J. Garfield and G. Priest (Oxford), pp. 176–88

Cousins, L. S., 1983, 'Pali Oral Literature', in *Buddhist Studies Ancient and Modern*, ed. P. Denwood and A. Piatigorsky (London), pp. 1–11

—, 2003, '*Sākiyabhikkhu/Sakyanbhikkhu/Śākyabhiksu*: A Mistaken Link to the Mahāyāna?' *Nagoya Studies in Indian Culture and Buddhism: Sambhāsā*, XXIII, pp. 1–27

—, 2012, 'The "Five Points" and the Origins of the Buddhist Schools', in *The Buddhist Forum II (Seminar Papers 1988–90)*, ed. T. Skorupski (Tring), pp. 27–60

—, 2013, 'The Early Development of Buddhist Literature and Language in India', *Journal of the Oxford Centre for Buddhist Studies*, V, pp. 89–135

—, 2017, 'On the Earliest Buddhist Schools', in *Holy Wealth: Accounting for This World and the Next in Religious Belief and Practice. Festschrift for John R. Hinnells*, ed. A. Hintze and A. Williams (Wiesbaden), pp. 21–48

—, 2018, '*Cetiya* and *Thūpa*: The Textual Sources', in Stargardt and Willis, 2018, pp. 18–30

—, 2022, *Meditations of the Pali Tradition*, ed. S. Shaw (Boulder, CO)

Cousins, L. S., Nyanaponika Mahāthera, and C.M.M. Shaw, 1991, *The Dispeller of Delusion (Sammohavinodanī)*, vol. II (London)

Covill, L., 2007, *Handsome Nanda* (New York)

—, 2009, *A Metaphorical Study of Saundarananda* (Delhi)

Cowell, E., ed., 1895–1913, *The Jātaka; or, Stories of the Buddha's Former Births*, 6 vols (Cambridge)

Cowell, E., and W.H.D. Rouse, 1907, *The Jātaka; or, Stories of the Buddha's Former Births*, vol. VI (Cambridge)

Cribb, J., 1992, 'Numismatic Evidence for the Date of the Periplus', in *Indian Numismatics: History, Art, and Culture*, ed. D. MacDowall, S. Shama and S. Garg (Delhi), vol. I, pp. 131–45

—, 1998, 'Western Satraps and Satavahanas: Old and New Ideas of Chronology', in Jha and Garg, 1998, pp. 167–82

—, 2000, 'Early Indian History', in *Buddhist Reliquaries from Ancient India*, ed. M. Willis (London), 39–54

Crosby, K., 1999, 'History versus Modern Myth', *Journal of Indian Philosophy*, XXVII/6, pp. 503–50

—, 2013a, *Traditional Theravada Meditation and Its Modern-Era Suppression* (Hong Kong)

—, 2013b, *Theravada Buddhism: Continuity, Diversity and Identity* (London)

Cunningham, A., 1879, *The Stūpa of Bharhut* (London)

Curtin, E., 2012, '"Thus Have I Quaked": The *Tempo* of the Buddha's Vita and the Earliest Buddhist Fabric of Timelessness', in *Figurations of Time in Asia*, ed. D. Boschung and C. Wessels-Mevissen (Munich), pp. 21–54

Dallapiccola, A., ed., 1980, *The Stūpa: Its Religious, Historical and Architectural Significance* (Wiesbaden)

Daniélou, A., 1993, *Manikmekhalaï* (Delhi)

Darley, R., 2015, 'Self, Other and the Use and Appropriation of Late Roman Coins in Peninsular India (4th to 7th centuries CE)', in Prabha Ray, 2015, pp. 60–84

Dasgupta, S., 1969, *A History of Indian Philosophy*, vol. I (Cambridge)

Davis, J., 1996, 'An Anthopologist's View of Exchange' *Social Anthropology*, IV, pp. 213–26
Dayal, H., 2004, *The Bodhisattva Doctrine in Buddhist Sanskrit Literature* (Delhi)
DeCaroli, R., 2015, *Image Problems: The Origin and Development of the Buddha's Image in Early South Asia* (Seattle, WA)
Deeg, M., 2004, 'Legend and Cult. Contributions to the History of Indian Buddhist Stūpas. Part 1: The "Stūpa of Kaniṣka"', *Buddhist Studies Review*, XXI, pp. 1–34
—, 2007, 'Has Xuanzang Really Been in Mathura? *Interpretatio Sinica* or *Interpretatio Occidentalia* – How to Critically Read the Record of the Chinese Pilgrim', in *Essays on East Asian Religion and Culture*, ed. C. Wittern and S. Lishan (Kyoto), pp. 35–73
Dehejia, V., 1969–70, 'Early Activity at Amaravati', *Archives of Asian Art*, XXIII, pp. 41–54
—, 1972, *Early Buddhist Rock Temples: A Chronology (London)*
—, 1991, 'Aniconism and the Multivalence of Emblems', *Ars Orientalis*, XXI, pp. 45–66
—, 1992a, 'Rejoinder to Susan Huntington', *Ars Orientalis*, XXII, p. 157
—, 1992b, 'The Collective and Popular Basis of Early Buddhist Patronage: Sacred Monuments 100 BC–AD 250', in Miller, 1992, pp. 35–45
—, ed., 1996, *Unseen Presence: The Buddha and Sanchi* (Delhi)
—, 1997, *Discourse in Early Buddhist Art: Visual Narratives of India* (New Delhi)
—, 2007, 'Questioning Narrativity and Inscribed Labels: Buddhist Bharhut, Sannati and Borobudur', in Prabha Ray, 2007, pp. 285–307
—, 2009, *The Body Adorned: Dissolving Boundaries between Sacred and Profane in India's Art* (New York)
Dehejia, V., and P. Rockwell., 2016, *The Unfinished: Stone Carvers at Work on the Indian Subcontinent* (New Delhi)
Dennison, P., 2022, *Jhana Consciousness: Buddhist Meditation in the Age of Neuroscience* (Boulder, CO)
Dessein, B., 2008, 'Of Tempted Arhats and Supramundane Buddhas: Abhidharma in the Krishna Region', in Padma and Barber, 2008, pp. 41–80
––, 2009, 'The Mahāsāmghikas and the Origin of Mahayana Buddhism: Evidence Provided in the *Abhidharmamahavibhasasastra*', *Eastern Buddhist*, XL, pp. 25–61
Dharmacakra Translation Committee, 2013 *The Play in Full: Lalitavistara*, http://resources.84000.co/browser/released/UT22084/046/UT22084-046-001.pdf
Dharmamitra, B., trans., 2009, *Vasubandhu's Treatise on the Bodhisattva Vow* (Seattle, WA)
Doležel, L., 1998, *Heterocosmica: Fiction and Possible Worlds* (Baltimore, MD)
Drewes, D., 2010, 'Early Indian Mahāyāna Buddhism II', *Religion Compass*, IV/2, pp. 66–74
—, 2011, 'Dharmabhāṇakas in Early Mahāyāna', *Indo-Iranian Journal*, LIV, pp. 331–72
Dunbabin, K., 1990, '*Ipsae deae vestigia* . . .: Footprints Divine and Human', *Journal of Roman Archaeology*, III, pp. 85–109
Dutoit, J., 1908–21, *Jātakam: Das Buch der Erzählungen aus früheren Existenzen Buddhas* (Leipzig)
Dutt, N., 1925, *The Early History of the Spread of Buddhism and the Buddhist Schools* (London)
—, 1945, *Early Monastic Buddhism* (Calcutta)
—, 1978, *Buddhist Sects in India*, 2nd edn (Delhi)
Ebert, J., 1985, *Parinirvāna: Untersuchungen zur ikonographischen Entwicklung von den indischen Anfängen bis nach China* (Stuttgart)
—, 2022, 'Some Visual Symbols and Metaphors for the Buddha's *parinirvāṇa*', in Konczak-Nagel, Hiyama and Klein, 2022, pp. 87–104
Eckel, M., 2008, *Bhāviveka and His Buddhist Opponents* (Cambridge, MA)
Egge, J., 2002, *Religious Giving and the Invention of Karma in Theravāda Buddhism* (Abingdon)
Elsner, J., 1994, 'The Viewer and the Vision: The Case of the Sinai Apse', *Art History*, XVII, pp. 81–102
—, 1995, *Art and the Roman Viewer* (Cambridge)
—, 2006, 'Classicism in Roman Art', in *Classical Pasts: The Classical Traditions of Greece and Rome*, ed. J. Porter (Princeton, NJ), pp. 270–97
—, 2007, *Roman Eyes: Visuality and Subjectivity in Art and Text* (Princeton, NJ)
—, ed., 2020, *Empires of Faith: Histories of Image and Religion in Late Antiquity, from India to Ireland* (Cambridge)
—, 2021, 'Buddhapada: The Enlightened Being and the Limits of Representation at Amarāvatī', in Elsner and Wood, 2021, pp. 95–111
—, 2022, 'The Dreamwork of Positivism: Archaeological Art History and the Imaginative Restoration of the Lost', in *Destroyed – Disappeared – Lost – Never Were*, ed. B. Fricke and A. Kumler (University Park, PA), pp. 61–74
—, 2023, 'Visual Epitome in Late Antique Art', in *Epitomic Writing in Late Antiquity and Beyond: Forms of Unabridged Writing*, ed. M. Formisano and P. Sacchi (London), pp. 202–29
Elsner, J., S. Lenk et al., 2017, *Imagining the Divine: Art and the Rise of the World Religions* (Oxford)
Elsner, J., and G. Wolf, 2010. 'The Transfigured Mountain: Icons and Transformations of Pilgrimage at the Monastery of St Catherine at Mount Sinai', in *Approaching the Holy Mountain: Art and Liturgy at St Catherine's Monastery in the Sinai*, ed. S. Gerstel and R. Nelson (Turnhout), pp. 37–71
Elsner, J., and R. Wood, eds, 2021, *Imagining the Divine: Art in Religions of Late Antiquity across Eurasia* (London)
Eltschinger, V., 2012, 'Aśvaghoṣa and His Canonical Sources II: Yaśas, the Kāśyapa Brothers and the Buddha's Arrival in Rājagṛha (Buddhacarita 16,3–71)', *Journal of the International Association of Buddhist Studies*, XXXV, pp. 171–224
—, 2013, 'Aśvaghoṣa and His Canonical Sources I: Preaching Selflessness to King Bimbisāra and the Magadhans (Buddhacarita 16,73–93)', *Journal of Indian Philosophy*, XLI, pp. 167–94
—, 2019, 'Aśvaghoṣa and His Canonical Sources (III): The Night of Awakening (Buddhacarita 14,1–87)', *Journal of Indian Philosophy*, XLVII, pp. 195–233
Endo, T., 1997, *The Buddha in Theravada Buddhism* (Colombo)
Engle, A., 2016, *Arya Asanga, the Bodhisattva Path to Unsurpassed Enlightenment* (Boulder, CO)
Falk, H., 2001, 'The Yuga of Sphujiddhvaja and the Era of the Kuṣāṇas', *Silk Road Art and Archaeology*, vol. VII, pp. 121–36
Falk, N., 1990, 'Exemplary Donors of the Pāli Tradition', in Sizemore and Swearer, 1990, pp. 124–44

Falser, M., 2015, 'The Graeco-Buddhist Style of Gandhara – A 'storia ideologica'; or, How a Discourse Makes a Global History of Art', *Journal of Art Historiography*, XIII, pp. 1–53
Fausbøll, V., 1877–97, *The Jātaka: Together with Its Commentary, Being Tales of the Anterior Births of Gotama Buddha*, 6 vols (London)
Fergusson, J., 1873, *Tree and Serpent Worship* (London)
Fifleld, J., 2017, 'Discipline and Ethical Formation in the Mahāsāṃghika Lokottaravāda Vinayapiṭāka', PhD dissertation, Harvard University, Cambridge, MA
Filigenzi, A., 2012, 'Orientalised Hellenism versus Hellenised Orient: Reversing the Perspective on Gandharan Art', *Ancient Civilizations from Scythia to Siberia*, XVIII, pp. 111–41
Findly, E., 2003, *Dāna: Giving and Getting in Pāli Buddhism* (Delhi)
Firth, R., 1959, *Economics in the New Zealand Maori* (Wellington)
Forsyth, G., and K. Weitzmann, 1973, *The Monastery of St Catherine at Mt Sinai: The Church and Fortress* (Ann Arbor, MI)
Fogelin, L., 2006, *The Archaeology of Early Buddhism* (Lanham, MD)
—, 2012, 'Material Practice and the Metamorphosis of a Sign: Early Buddhist *Stūpas* and the Origins of Mahayana Buddhism', *Asian Perspectives*, LI, pp. 278–310
—, 2015, *An Archaeological History of Indian Buddhism* (Oxford)
Foucher, A., 1918, *L'art gréco-bouddique de Gandhāra*, vol. II (Paris)
—, 1928, 'Les sculptures d'Amaravati', *Revue des arts asiatiques*, vol. V, pp. 9–24
Francis, H. T., 1905, *The Jātaka; or, Stories of the Buddha's Former Births*, vol. V (Cambridge)
Francis, H. T., and R. A. Neil, 1897, *The Jātaka; or, Stories of the Buddha's Former Births*, vol. III (Cambridge)
Francis, N., 2002, 'Buddhist Art, Religion and Society at Amarāvatī and Other Allied Centres BC 300–AD 300', PhD dissertation, University of Calicut, Malappuram, India
—, 2005, 'The Institutional Base of Early Buddhist Art at Amaravati' *Deccan Studies*, vol. III, pp. 47–89
—, 2016, *A Source Book of the Early Buddhist Inscriptions of Amarāvatī* (Shimla)
Frauwallner, E., 1956, *The Earliest Vinaya and the Beginnings of Buddhist Literature* (Rome)
Fronsdal, E., 1998, 'The Dawn of the Bodhisattva Path: Studies in a Religious Ideal of Ancient Indian Buddhists with Particular Emphasis on the Earliest Extant Perfection of Wisdom Sutra', PhD dissertation, Stanford University, CA
Fynes, R., 1995, 'The Religious Patronage of the Sātavāhana Dynasty', *South Asian Studies*, XI, pp. 43–50
Gaifman, M., 2015, 'Visual Evidence', in *Oxford Handbook of Greek Religion*, ed. E. Eidinow and J. Kindt (Oxford), pp. 51–66
—, 2016, 'Theologies of Statues', in *Theologies of Ancient Greek Religion*, ed. E. Eidinow, J. Kindt and R. Osborne (Cambridge), pp. 249–80
—, 2017, 'Aniconism: Definitions, Examples and Comparative Perspectives', *Religion*, XLVII/3, pp. 335–52
Gaffney, S., 1996, 'The Pāli *Nidānakathā* and Its Tibetan Translation: Its Textual Precursors and Associated Literature', in *The Buddhist Forum IV*, ED. T. Skorupski (London), pp. 75–91
—, 2003, 'The "Jatakanidanakatha": A Critical Study, Tibetan Edition and Annotated', PhD dissertation, SOAS, London
Gagné, R., 2021, *Cosmography and the Idea of Hyperborea in Ancient Greece* (Cambridge)
Galli, M., 2011, 'Hellenistic Court Imagery in the Early Buddhist Art of Gandhara', *Ancient Civilizations from Scythia to Siberia*, XVII, pp. 279–329
Gangoly, O., 1973, *Andhra Sculptures* (Hyderabad)
Garfield, J., 1995, *The Fundamental Wisdom of the Middle Way: Nāgārjuna's Mūlamadhyamakakārikā* (Oxford)
Gethin, R., 1992, 'The *Mātikās*: Memorization, Mindfulness and the List', in Gyatso, 1992, pp. 149–72
—, 1998, *The Foundations of Buddhism* (Oxford)
—, 2001, *The Buddhist Path to Awakening*, 2nd edn (Oxford)
—, 2006, 'Mythology as Meditation: From the Mahāsudassana Sutta to the Sukhāvatīvyūha Sūtra', *Journal of the Pali Text Society*, XXVIII, pp. 63–112
—, 2012, 'Was Buddhaghosa a Theravādin? Buddhist Identity in the Pāli Commentaries and Chronicles', in *How Theravāda Is Theravāda? Exploring Buddhist Identities*, ed. P. Skilling (Chiang Mai), pp. 1–63
—, 2020, 'Reading Repetitions in the Saṃyutta-nikāya and Early Abhidhamma: From the Mahā-vagga to the Dhammasaṅgaṇi', in *Research on the Samyukta-āgama*, ed. Dhammadinā (Taiwan), pp. 109–69
Getty, A., 1928, *The Gods of Northern Buddhism* (Oxford)
Ghosh, A., 1978, *The Remains of the Bharhut Stūpa in the Indian Museum* (Calcutta)
—, 1979, The Early Phase of the Stūpa at Amaravati', *Ancient Ceylon*, III, pp. 97–103
Ghosh, A., and H. Sarkar, 1964–5, 'Beginning of Sculptural Art in South-East India: A Stele from Amaravati', *Ancient India*, XX–XXI, pp. 168–77
Ghosh, M., 2020, *Nātyaśastram: A Treatise on Ancient Indian Dramaturgy and Historionics*, 2nd edn, 2 vols (Varanasi)
Gifford, J., 2011, *Buddhist Practice and Visual Culture: The Visual Rhetoric of Borobudur* (London)
Godbout, J., and A. Caillé, 1998, *The World of the Gift* (Montreal)
Godelier, M., 1999, *The Enigma of the Gift* (Cambridge)
Gombrich, R., 1975, 'Ancient Indian Cosmology', in *Ancient Cosmologies*, ed. C. Blacker and M. Loewe (London), pp. 110–42
—1980, 'The Significance of Former Buddhas in Theravådin Tradition', in *Buddhist Studies in Honour of Walpola Rahula*, ed. S. Balasooriya et al. (London), pp. 62–72
—, 1993, 'Buddhist Prediction: How Open Is the Future?', in *Predicting the Future*, ed. L. Howe and A. Wain (Cambridge), pp. 144–68
—, 2018, *Buddhism and Pali* (Oxford)
Gomez, L., 1967, 'Selected Verses from the Gandavyūha: Test, Critical Appratus and Translation', PhD dissertation, Yale University, New Haven, CT
—, 1977, 'The Bodhisattva as Wonder-Worker', in *Prajñāpāramitā and Related Systems: Studies in Honor of Edward Conze*, ed. L. Lancaster and L. Gomez (Berkeley, CA), pp. 221–61
Goswami, B., 2001, *Lalitavistara* (Calcutta)
Grabar, A., 1968, *Christian Iconography: A Study of Its Origins* (Princeton, NJ)
Gray, S., 2017, *A Defence of Rule: Origins of Political Thought in Greece and India* (New York)
Griffiths, A., and V. Tournier, 2017, *Early Inscriptions of Āndhradeśa*, http://epigraphia.efeo.fr/andhra
Griffiths, P., 1994, *On Being Buddha: The Classical Doctrine of Buddhahood* (Albany, NY)
Guarducci, M., 1942–3, 'Le impronte del *Quo Vadis* e monumenti affini, figurati ed epigraifici', *Rendiconti della Pontificia Accademia Romana di Archeologia*, series 3, vol. XIX, pp. 305–44

Gururaja Rao, B., 1972, *Megalithic Culture in South India* (Prasaranga)
Guha-Thakurta, T., 2004, *Museums, Objects, Histories: Institutions of Art in Colonial and Postcolonial India* (New York)
Gupt, B., 1994, *Dramatic Concepts Greek and Indian* (Delhi)
Gupta, M., 1987, *A Study of Abhinavabāaratī on Bharata's Nāṭyaśāstra and Avalo9ka on Dhananjaya's Daśarūpaka* (Delhi)
Gupta, P., 1999, 'A Sātavāhana Ivory Comb Found in Hungary', in Shastri, 1999, pp. 480–83
Gupta, S., 2008, *Sculptures and Antiquities in the Archaeological Museum, Amarāvatī* (New Delhi)
Guy, J., 2005, 'Southern Buddhism: Traces and Transmission', in *South Indian Archaeology*, vol. II, ed. C. Jarrige and V. Lefèvre (Paris), pp. 495–503
—, ed., 2023, *Tree and Serpent: Early Buddhist Art in India* (New York)
Gwynn, D., 2010, 'Archaeology and the "Arian Controversy" in the Fourth Century', in Gwynn and Bangert, 2010, pp. 229–63
Gwynn, D., and S. Bangert, eds, 2010, *Religious Diversity in Late Antiquity* (Leiden)
Gyatso, J., ed., 1992, *In the Mirror of Memory: Reflections on Mindfulness and Remembrance in Indian and Tibetan Buddhism* (Albany, NY)
Hamar, I., 2015, 'Buddhāvataṃsaka', in *Brill's Encyclopedia of Buddhism*, ed. J. Silk, vol. I (Leiden)
Handurukande, R., 1981, 'Sarvamdada, the All-Giver', *Buddhist Studies (BUKKYŌ KENKYŪ)*, X, p. 165–78
Hanumantha Rao, B., 1998, *Buddhist Inscriptions of Andhradesa* (Secunderabad)
Harinarayana, N., 1990, 'The Material of the Amaravati Artist', *Andhra Pradesh Journal of Archaeology*, III, pp. 41–5
Harris, E., 2006, *Theravāda Buddhism and the British Encounter* (London)
Harrison, P., 1978, '*Buddhānusmṛti* in the Pratyutpanna-buddha-sammukhāvasthita-samādhi-sutra', *Journal of Indian Philosophy*, VI, pp. 35–57
—, 1992a, 'Is the Dharma-Kāya the Real "Phantom Body" of the Buddha?', *Journal of the International Association of Buddhist Studies*, XV, pp. 55–94
—, 1992b, 'Commemoration and Identification in *Buddhānusmṛti*', in Gyatso, 1992, pp. 215–38
—, 2003, 'Mediums and Messages: Reflections on the Production of Mahāyāna Sūtras', *Eastern Buddhist*, XXXV, pp. 115–51
—, 2018, 'Early Mahāyāna: Laying Out the Field', in *Setting Out on the Great Way: Essays on Early Mahāyāna Buddhism*, ed. P. Harrison (Sheffield), pp. 7–32
—, ed., 2018, *Setting Out on the Great Way: Essays on Early Mahāyāna Buddhism* (Sheffield)
Hartmann, J.-U., 2004, 'Contents and Structure of the *Dīrghagāma* of the *(Mūla-) Sarvāstavadins*', *Annual Report of the International Research Institute for Advanced Buddhology at Soka University*, vol. VII, pp. 119–37
Harvey, P., 1984, 'The Symbolism of the Early Stūpa', *Journal of the International Association of Buddhist Studies*, VII, pp. 67–94
—, 1990, *An Introduction to Buddhism: Teachings, History and Practices* (Cambridge)
Hasan, S. K., 2013, *Religious Architecture of Gandhara – Pakistan: Buddhist Stupas and Monasteries* (Islamabad)
Hawkes, J., and A. Shimada, ed., 2009, *Buddhist Stūpas in South Asia* (New Delhi)
Hegewald, J., 2020a, *In the Footsteps of the Masters: Footprints, Feet and Shoes as Objects of Veneration in Asian, Islamic and Mediterranean Art* (Berlin)
—, 2020b, 'Foot Stones and Footprints (*Pādukās*): Multivariate Symbols in Jaina Religious Practice in India', in Hegewald, 2020a, pp. 357–423
Heim, M., 2004, *Theories of the Gift in South Asia: Hindu, Buddhist, and Jain Reflections on Dāna* (London)
—, 2014, *The Forerunner of All Things: Buddhaghosa on Mind, Intention and Agency* (Oxford)
—, 2018, *The Voice of the Buddha: Buddhaghosa on Immeasurable Worlds* (Oxford)
Heitzman, J., 1984, 'Early Buddhism, Trade and Empire', in *Studies in the Archaeology and Palaeoanthropology of South Asia*, ed. K. Kennedy and G. Possehl (Delhi), pp. 121–37
Herdman, H., 2017, 'Encircling the Sacred/Pilgrimage: A Comparative Study in the Buddhist and Late Antique Christian Traditions', PhD dissertation, University of Bristol
Hettiarachchy, J., 1973, 'Buddhism in the Northern Deccan under the Satavahana Rulers (*c.* 30 BC–225 AD)', PhD dissertation, SOAS, London
Hibbets, M., 1999, 'Saving Them from Yourself: An Inquiry into the South Asian Gift of Fearlessness (Medieval South Asian Gift Discourses from Jain, Theravada, and Hindu Sources)', *Journal of Religious Ethics*, XXVII, pp. 437–62
Hikosaka, S., 1989, *Buddhism in Tamil Nadu: A New Perspective* (Madras)
Hiltebeitel, A., 2006, 'Aśvaghoṣa's *Buddhacarita*: The First Known Close and Critical Reading of the Brahmanical Sanskrit Epics', *Journal of Indian Philosophy*, XXXIV/3, pp. 229–86
Hinüber, H. von, 2016a, 'Buddhist Texts and Buddhist Images', *Annual Report of the International Research Institute for Advanced Buddhology*, XVIII, pp. 7–20
—, 2016b, 'Some Remarks on the Technical Terms of Stūpa Architecture', *Annual Report of the International Research Institute for Advanced Buddhology*, XIX, pp. 29–46
—, 2019, 'From the Upper Indus to the East Coast of China: On the Origin of the Pictorial Representation of the Lotus Sūtra', *Annual Report of the International Research Institute for Advanced Buddhology at Soka University*, XXII, pp. 377–90
Hirakawa, A., 1990. *A History of Indian Buddhism from Śākyamuni to Early Mahāyāna* (Honolulu, HI) (originally published in Japanese, 1974)
Hodge, S, 2006, 'On the Eschatology of the Mahāparinirvāna Sūtra and Related Matters', www.shabkar.org/download/pdf/On_the_Eschatology_of_the_Mahaparinirvana_Sutra_and_Related_Matters.pdf
Hoffmann, H., 1973, 'Buddha's Preaching of the Kālacakra Tantra at the Stūpa at Dhānyakataka', in *German Scholars on India* (Varanasi), pp. 136–40
Hölscher, T., 2004, *The Language of Images in Roman Art* (Cambridge)
Holt, J., and S. Padma, 2008, 'Buddhism in Andhra and Its Influence on Buddhism in Sri Lanka', in Padma and Barber, 2008, pp. 105–25
Horner, I., 1940, *The Book of Discipline (Vinaya-pitaka)*, vol. II: *Suttavibhanga* (London)
—, 1951, *The Book of Discipline (Vinaya-pitaka)*, vol. IV: *Mahāvagga* (London)
—, 1952, *The Book of Discipline (Vinaya-pitaka)*, vol. V: *Cullavagga* (London)

—, 1964, *Milinda's Questions*, vol. II (London)
—, 1975, *The Minor Anthologies of the Pāli Canon*, vol. III: *The Chronicle of Buddhas (Buddhavamsa) and Basket of Conduct (Cāriyāpitaka)* (Bristol)
—, 1978, *The Clarifier of the Sweet Meaning (Madhurtthavilāinī), Commentary on the Chronicle of Buddhas (Buddhavamsa) by Buddhadatta Thera* (London)
Howell, D., 2016, 'Captain Linnaeus Tripe 1822–1902, 12th Madras Native Infantry. A Soldier and Photographer', *Journal of the Society for Army Historical Research*, XCIV/377, pp. 25–36
Howes, J., 2002, 'Colin MacKenzie and the Stūpa at Amaravati', *South Asian Studies*, XVIII, pp. 53–64
—, 2009, 'The Colonial History of Sculptures from the Amaravati Stūpa', in Hawkes and Shimada, 2009, pp. 20–37
—, 2010. *Illustrating India: The Early Colonial Investigations of Colin MacKenzie (1784–1821)* (Oxford)
Hultzsch, E., 1883, 'Amaràvati-Inschriften', *Zeitschrift der Deutschen morgenländischen Gesellschaft*, XXXVII, pp. 548–64
—, 1886, 'Berichtigungen und Nachträge zu den Amarâvati-Inschriften', *Zeitschrift der Deutschen morgenländischen Gesellschaft*, XL, pp. 343–6
Huntington, E., 2018, *Creating the Universe: Depictions of the Cosmos in Himalayan Buddhism* (Seattle, WA)
Huntington, S., 1985, *The Art of Ancient India* (New York)
—, 1990, 'Early Buddhist Art and the Theory of Aniconism', *Art Journal*, XLIX/4, pp. 401–8
—, 1992, 'Aniconism and the Multivalence of Emblems: Another Look', *Ars Orientalis*, XXII, pp. 111–15
—, 2012, *Lay Ritual in the Early Buddhist Art of India: More Evidence against the Aniconic Theory* (Amsterdam)
—, 2015, 'Shifting the Paradigm: The Aniconic Theory and Its Terminology', *South Asian Studies*, XXXI/2, pp. 163–86
—, 2020. 'Footprints in the Early Buddhist Art of India', in Hegewald, 2020a, pp. 425–516
—, 2022, 'The Agency of Buddhist Images', in *The Oxford Handbook of Buddhist Practice*, ed. K. Trainer and P. Arai (Oxford), pp. 148–73
Hyde, L., 1983, *The Gift: Imagination and the Erotic Life of Property* (New York)
Ichimura, S., 2005, 'Nagarjuna as Author of Suhrullekha and Ratnavali and His Eventual Center of Activity as Southern Kusala', in Kamalakar, 2005, pp. 397–425
Iravati, 2003, *Performing Artistes in Ancient India* (New Delhi)
Jantrasrisalai, C., 2008, 'Early Buddhist Dhammakāya: Its Philosophical and Soteriological Significance', PhD thesis, University of Sydney, Australia
Jayawickrama, N., ed., 1974, *Buddhavamsa and Cariyāpitaka* (London)
—, 1990, *The Story of Gotama Buddha: The Nidāna-kathā of the Jātakaṭṭhakathā* (Oxford)
Jha, A., and S. Garg, eds, 1998, *Ex Moneta: Essays on Numismatics, History and Archaeology in Honour of Dr David W. Mac Dowall* (Delhi)
Jithendra Das, D., 1993, *The Buddhist Architecture in Andhra* (Delhi)
Jones, C. V., 2021, *The Buddhist Self: On Tathāgatagarbha and Ātman* (Honolulu, HI)
Jones, J., 1949, *The Mahavastu*, vol. I (London)
—, 1952, *The Mahavastu*, vol. II (London)
—, 1956, *The Mahavastu*, vol. III (London)
Jongeward, D., E. Errington, R. Salomon and S. Baums, 2012, *Gandharan Buddhist Reliquaries* (Seattle, WA)
Jouveau-Dubreuil, G., 1932, 'L'architecture d'Amarāvatī', *Bulletin de l'Association franćaise des amis de l'Orient*, vol. XII, pp. 5–16
Julien, S., 1860, *Contes et apologues indiens inconnus jusqu'à ce jour: Suivis de fables et de poésies chinoises* (Paris)
Kale, P., 1974, *The Theatric Universe (A Study of the Nātyaśastra)* (Bombay)
Kalupahana, D., 1986, *Nagarjuna: The Philosophy of the Middle Way* (Albany, NY)
Kamalakar G., ed., 2005, *Buddhism: Art, Architecture, Literature and Philosophy*, 2 vols (New Delhi)
Kane, P. V., 1941, *History of Dharmaśāstra (Ancient and Mediaeval Religious and Civil Law)*, vol. II, part 2 (Poona)
Kannan, R., 2014, *Compilation on Amaravati Sculptures and Conservation and Reorganisation of the Amaravati Gallery in the Government Museum, Chennai* (Chennai)
Karashima, S., 2015, 'Who Composed the Mahāyāna Scriptures? The Mahāsāṃghika and Vaitulya Scriptures', *Annual Report of the International Research Institute for Advanced Buddhology at Soka University*, XVIII, pp. 113–62
—, 2017a, 'Ajita and Maitreya: More Evidence of the Early Mahāyāna Scriptures' Origins from the Mahāsāṃghikas and a Clue as to the School-Affiliation of the Kanaganahalli-*Stūpa*', *Annual Report of the International Research Institute of Advanced Buddhology at Soka University*, XXI, pp. 181–96
—, 2017b, 'The Relationship between Mahāsāṃghikas and Māhayana Buddhism Indicated in the Colophon of the Chinese Translation of the Vinaya of the Mahāsāṃghikas', *Annual Report of the International Research Institute of Advanced Buddhology at Soka University*, XXI, pp. 197–207
—, 2017c, 'A Gandharan Stūpa as Depicted in the Lotus Sūtra', *Annual Report of the International Research Institute for Advanced Buddhology at Soka University*, XXI, pp. 471–8
Karfíková, L., 2012, *Grace and the Will According to Augustine* (Leiden)
Karlsson, K., 1999, *Face to Face with the Absent Buddha: The Formation of Buddhist Aniconic Art* (Uppsala)
Kedareswami, J., 2006, *Mahaparinirvana: Sacred Buddhist Relics (with Special Reference to Bavikonda)* (Hyderabad)
Keith, A. B., 1924, *The Sanskrit Drama* (Oxford)
Kessler, H., and Wolf, G., eds, 1998, *The Holy Face and the Paradox of Representation* (Bologna)
Khoroche, P., 1989, *Once the Buddha Was a Monkey: Ārya Śūra's Jātakamālā* (Chicago, IL)
Kinnard, J., 2001, *Imaging Wisdom: Seeing and Knowing in the Art of Indian Buddhism* (Delhi)
—, 2008, 'Amaravati as Lens: Envisioning the Buddha in the Ruins of the Great Stupa', in Padma and Barber, 2008, pp. 81–103
Kintaert, T., 2005, 'Primary Colours in the *Nātyaśastra*', in *Sāmarasya: Studies in Indian Arts, Philosophy and Interreligious Dialogue. In Honour of Bettina Bäumer*, ed. S. Das and E. Fürlinger (New Delhi)
—, 2017, 'Ritual Performances in the *Nāṭyaśāstra* I: Ritual Items', *Cracow Indological Studies*, XIX/1, pp. 83–136
—, 2018, 'Ritual Performances in the *Nāṭyaśāstra* II: Food Offerings', *Cracow Indological Studies*, XX/1, pp. 145–83
Klein, W., 1912, 'Pompejanishe Bildstudien', *Jahreshefte des Österreichischen archäologischen Institutes in Wien*, XV, pp. 143–67

Kloetzli, W. R., 1983, *Buddhist Cosmology: Science and Theology in the Images of Motion and Light* (Delhi)
Kloppenborg, R., 1977, *The Sūtra on the Foundation of the Buddhist Order (Catuṣpariṣatsūtra)* (Leiden)
Knox, R., 1992, *Amaravati: Buddhist Sculpture from the Great Stupa* (London)
Konczak-Nagel, I., S. Hiyama and A. Klein, eds, *Connecting the Art, Literature and Religion of South and Central Asia: Studies in Honour of Monika Zin* (New Delhi)
Kostenec, J., and K. Dark, 2011, 'Paul the Silentiary's Description of Hagia Sophia in the Light of New Archaeological Evidence', *Byzantinoslavica*, LXIX/3, pp. 88–105
Kramrisch, S., 1933, *Indian Sculpture* (Calcutta)
Kranth Choudary, D. K., and P. Hema, 2004, 'Advent of Jainism in Andhra', in Parasher-Sen, 2004, pp. 238–41
Krishna Sastry, V., 1998, 'Indo-Roman Trading Centres in Andhra Pradesh', in Jha and Garg, 1998, pp. 475–99
—, 2004, 'Sects of Buddhism in Andhra', in Parasher-Sen, 2004, pp. 178–83
—, 2005, 'History of Buddhism in Andhra', in Kamalakar, 2005, pp. 145–67
—, 2008, 'Buddhism', in *Early Historic Andhra Pradesh 500 BC–AD 624*, ed. I. Sarma (Delhi), pp. 100–112
Krishna Sastry, V., B. Subrahmanyamand Rama Krishna Rao, N., 1992, *Thotlakonda: A Buddhist Site in Andhra Pradesh* (Hyderbad)
Krishnamurthy, K., 1979, 'The Cult of the Buddha-Pada', *Andhra Pradesh Journal of Archaeology*, I, pp. 81–5
—, 2006, 'Buddhist Remains', in Soundararajan, 2006, pp. 157–99
Krumeich, R., 2020, '"Footprints" and Sculpted Feet: Enduring Marks of Human Presence and Divine Epiphany in Classical Antiquity', in Hegewald, 2020a, pp. 143–220
Kuan, T., 2013, 'Mahāyāna Elements and Mahāsāṃghika Traces in the *Ekottarika-āgama*', in *Research on the Ekottarika-āgama*, ed. Dhammadina (Taipei), pp. 113–94
Kumar, P., ed., 2019, *Nāṭyaśastra of Bharatamuni: Sanskrit Text, Romanised Text, Commentary of Abhinava Bhāratī by Abhinavaguptācārya and English Translation by M. M.Ghosh*, 4 vols (Delhi)
Kumar, R., 2003, *Essays on Indian Art and Architecture* (Delhi)
Kumar, V. D., 2012, 'Early Buddhist Art and Philosophy in the Lower Krishna Valley', PhD dissertation, Department of History and Archaeology, Acharya Nagarjuna University, Namburu, India
Kurita, I., 1988, *Gandhāran Art*, 2 vols (Tokyo)
Kuryluk, E., 1991, *Veronica and Her Cloth* (Oxford), pp. 28–33
Kuwayama, S., 1997, 'A Hidden Import from Imperial Rome Manifest in Stūpas', in *Gandharan Art in Context*, ed. R. Allchin et al. (Cambridge), pp. 119–71
Ladwig, P., 2016, 'Emotions and Narrative: Excessive Giving and Emotional Ambivalence in the Lao *Vessantara Jātaka*', in Collins, 2016, pp. 53–80
Lamotte, E., 1944, *La traité de la grande vertu de sagesse de Nāgārjuna (Mahāprajñāpāramitāśāstra)*, vol. I (Louvain)
—, 1949, *La traité de la grande vertu de sagesse de Nāgārjuna (Mahāprajñāpāramitāśāstra)*, vol. II (Louvain)
—, 1970, *La traité de la grande vertu de sagesse de Nāgārjuna (Mahāprajñāpāramitāśāstra)*, vol. III (Louvain)
—, 1988, *History of Indian Buddhism* (Louvain), originally published in French, 1958
Lang, K., 2008, 'Candakīrti on the Medieval Military Culture of South India', in Padma and Barber, 2008, pp. 127–50
Legge, J., 1886, *A Record of Buddhist Kingdoms* (Oxford)
Levman, B., 2005, 'The Buddhalaksana and the *Gaṇḍavyūha Sūtra*', *Canadian Journal of Buddhist Studies*, I, pp. 31–57
Lévi, S., 1890, *Le théâtre indien* (Paris)
Levi D'Ancona, M., 1950, 'An Indian Statuette from Pompeii', *Artibus Asiae*, XIII, pp. 166–80
Lévi-Strauss, C., 1950, *Introduction to the Work of Marcel Mauss* (London)
Li, R., 1996, *The Great Tang Dynasty Record of the Western Regions* (Berkeley, CA)
Lidova, N., 1994, *Drama and Ritual of Early Hinduism* (Delhi)
—, 2012, 'The Nāṭyaśāstra: The Origin of the Ancient Indian Poetics', *Cracow Indological Studies*, XIV, pp. 61–85
Lindtner, C., 1982, *Nāgarjuniana: Studies in the Writings and Philosophy of Nāgārjuna* (Copenhagen)
Linrothe, R., 1993, 'Inquiries into the Origin of the Buddha Image: A Review', *East and West*, XLIII/4, pp. 241–56
Liu, C., 2018, 'Reciting, Chanting, and Singing: The Codification of Vocal Music in Buddhist Canon Law', *Journal of Indian Philosophy*, XLVI/4, pp. 713–52
Longhurst, A. H., 1938, *The Buddhist Antiquities of Nāgājunakonda (Madras) Presidency, Memoirs of the Archaeological Survey of India*, 54 (Delhi)
Lopez, D., 2016, *The Lotus Sūtra: A Biography* (Princeton, NJ)
Lopez, D., and J. Stone, 2019, *Two Buddhas Seated Side by Side: A Guide to the Lotus Sūtra* (Princeton, NJ)
Lorenz, K., 2007, 'The Ear of the Beholder: Spectator Figures in Pompeian Painting', *Art History*, XXX/5, pp. 665–82
Loukota Sanclemente, D., 2019, 'The Goods that Cannot Be Stolen: Mercantile Faith in Kumāralāta's Garland of Examples Adorned by Poetic Fancy', PhD dissertation, University of California, Los Angeles
Lüders, H., 1911a, 'Das Śāriputraprakaraṇa, ein Drama des Aśvaghosha', *Sitzungsberichte der königlich Preussischen Akademie der Wissenschaften*, XVII, pp. 388–411
—, 1911b, *Bruchstücke Buddhistischer Dramen* (Berlin)
—, 1912, 'A List of Brahmi Inscriptions from the Earliest Times to about 400 AD', *Epigraphia Indica*, X, appendix, pp. 1–226
—, 1941, *Bhārhut und die Buddhistische Literatur* (Leipzig)
Lüders, H., E. Waldschmidt and M. Mehendale, 1963, *Bhārhut Inscriptions* (Ootacamund)
Mabbett, I., 1998, 'The Problem of the Historical Nāgārjuna Revisited', *Journal of the American Oriental Society*, CXVIII/3, pp. 332–46
Mack, W., 2018, 'Vox populi, vox deorum: Athenian Document Reliefs and the Theologies of Public Inscription', *Annual of the British School at Athens*, CXIII, pp. 365–98
Mackenzie, C., 1823, 'Ruins of Amravutty, Depauldina, and Durnacotta', *Asiatic Journal*, XV, pp. 464–78
Macrides, R., and P. Magdalino, 1988, 'The Architecture of Ekphrasis: Construction and Context of Paul the Silentiary's Poem on Hagia Sophia', *Byzantine and Modern Greek Studies*, XII, pp. 47–82
Maisey, C., 1892, *Sānchi and Its Remains* (London)
Majumdar, N., 1940. 'Votive Inscriptions', in Marshall, Foucher and Majumdar, 1940, pp. 297–384
Malalasekera, G., 1994, *The Pāli Literature of Ceylon* (Kandy)

Mäll, L., 2003, *Studies in the Aṣṭasāhasrikā Prajñāpāramitā and Other Essays* (Tartu)
Marshall, J., 1907, 'Archaeological Exploration in India, 1906–7', *Journal of the Royal Asiatic Society*, XXXIX, pp. 993–1011
—, 1951, *Taxila: An Illustrated Account of the Archaeological Excavations, 1913–1934* (Cambridge)
—, 1955, *A Guide to Sāñchī* (Delhi)
—, 1960, *A Guide to Taxila* (Cambridge)
Marshall, J., A. Foucher and N. Majumdar, 1940, *The Monuments of Sanchi*, 2 vols (Calcutta)
Masefield, P., 1994a, *The Udāna* (Oxford)
—, 1994b, *The Udāna Commentary (Paramatthadīpanī nāma Udānatthakathā) by Dhammapāla*, vol. I (Oxford)
—, 1995, *The Udāna Commentary by Dhammapāla*, vol. II (Oxford)
—, 2008, *The Commentary on the Itivuttaka*, vol. I (Oxford)
Masson, J., 1942, *La religion populaire dans la canon bouddhique pâli* (Louvain)
Masson, J. L., and M. V. Patwardhan, 1969, *Śāntarasa: Abhinavagupta's Philosophy of Aesthetics* (Poona)
—, 1970, *Aesthetic Rapture: The Rasādhyāya of the Nāṭyaśāstra*, vol. I (Poona)
Matsumura, J., 2008, 'The *Sumedhakathā* in Pāli Literature', *Journal of Buddhist and Indian Studies*, LVI, pp. 50–58
—, 2011, 'The Story of the Dīpamkara Prophecy in Northern Buddhist Texts: An Attempt at Classification', *Journal of Buddhist and Indian Studies*, LIX, pp. 63–72
—, 2012, 'The Formation and Development of the Dīpamkara Prophecy Story: The *Ārya-Dīpamkaravyākarana-nāma-mahāhānasūtra* and Its Relation to Other Versions', *Journal of Buddhist and Indian Studies*, LX, pp. 80–89
Mauss, M., 1923–4, 'Essai sur le don: Forme et raison de l'échange dans les sociétés archaïques' *L'année sociologique*, I, pp. 30–186
—, 1954, *The Gift: Forms and Functions of Exchange in Archaic Societies* (London)
McCombs, J., 2014, 'Mahāyāna and the Gift: Theories and Practices', PhD dissertation, University of California, Los Angeles
McGovern, W. M., 1923, *A Manual of Buddhist Philosophy*, vol. I: *Cosmology* (London)
McLaughlin, R., 2014, *The Roman Empire and the Indian Ocean* (Barnsley)
McMahan, D., 2002, *Empty Vision: Metaphor and Visionary Imagery in Mahāyāna Buddhism* (London)
Mehta, T., 1995, *Sanskrit Play Production in Ancient India* (Delhi)
Meiland, J., 2009, *Garland of the Buddha's Past Lives by Āryaśūra*, vol. I (New York)
Michel, D., 1982, 'Bemerkungen über Zuschauerfiguren in pompejanischen sogenannten Tafelbildern', in *La regione sotterrata dal Vesuvio: studi e prospettive* (Naples), pp. 537–98
Middleton, A. P., 1992, 'Appendix III: A Note on the Examination of Some Surface Coatings on the Amarāvatī Sculptures', in Knox, 1992, p. 232
Miller, B., ed., 1992, *The Powers of Art: Patronage in Indian Culture* (Delhi)
Miller, J., 1985, *The Vision of Cosmic Order in the Vedas* (London)
Milligan, M., 2015, 'Five Unnoticed Donative Inscriptions and the Relative Chronology of Sanchi Stūpa II', *Annual Report of the International Research Institute for Advanced Buddhology*, XVIII, pp. 11–22
—, 2019, 'Corporate Bodies in Early South Asian Buddhism: Some Relics and Their Sponsors According to Epigraphy', *Religions*, X, pp. 1–22
Misra, N., 2005, 'Buddhist Art of Nāgārjunakonda', in Kamalakar, 2005, pp. 197–206
Mitchell, W.J.T., 1994, *Picture Theory* (Chicago, IL)
Mitra, D., 1971, *Buddhist Monuments* (Calcutta)
Mitra, S., 1974, 'Mathurā', in *Jaina Art and Architecture*, ed. A. Ghosh (Delhi), vol. I, pp. 49–68
Mitrikeski, D., 2009, 'Nāgārjuna and the Tathāgatagarbha: A Closer Look at Some Peculiar Features in the Niraupamyastava', *Journal of Religious History*, XXXIII/2, pp. 149–16
Monaci Castagno, A., ed., 2011, *Sacre impronte e oggetti 'non fatti da mano d'uomo' nelle religioni* (Alessandria)
Monius, A., 2001, *Imagining a Place for Buddhism: Literary Culture and Religious Community in Tamil-Speaking South India* (Oxford)
Morrissey, N., 2009, 'Śākybiksus, Palimpsests and the Art of Apostasy: The Emergence and Decline of Mahāyāna Buddhism in Early Medieval India', PhD dissertation, UCLA
Nagatomo, S., 2000, 'The Logic of the Diamond Sutra: A Is Not A, Therefore It Is A', *Asian Philosophy*, X, pp. 213–44
—, 2018, 'The Logic of Not', *Philosophy East and West*, LXVIII, pp. 1239–64
Nagaswamy, R., 1981, 'Roman sites in Tamil Nadu: Recent Discoveries', in *Madhu: Recent Researches in Indian Archaeology and Art History*, ed. M. S. Nagaraja Rao (New Delhi), pp. 337–9
—, 1995, *Roman Karur: A Peep into Tamils' Past* (Madras)
Nakamura, H., 1980, *Indian Buddhism: A Survey with Bibliographical Notes* (Tokyo)
Nakamura, S., 1951, 'Pradakshinā, A Buddhist Form of Obeisance', in *Semitic and Oriental Studies: A Volume Presented to William Popper*, ed. W. Fischel (Berkeley, CA), pp. 345–54
Nakanishi, M., and O. von Hinüber, 2014, *Kanaganahalli Inscriptions* (Tokyo)
Ñanamoli, 1979, *The Path of Purification: Visuddhi Magga by Bhadantācariya Buddhaghosa* (Kandy)
Ñanamoli, and Bodhi, 1995, *The Middle Length Discourses of the Buddha* (Kandy)
Ñāṇananda, 1974, *The Magic of the Mind in Buddhist Perspective* (Kandy)
Nath, V., 1987, *Dāna Gift System in Ancient India* (Delhi)
Nattier, J., 2003, *A Few Good Men: The Bodhisattva Path According to the Inquiry of Ugra (Ugrapariiprcchā)* (Honolulu, HI)
Neelis, J., 2011, *Early Buddhist Transmission and Trade Networks* (Leiden)
—, 2019, 'Making Places for Buddhism in Gandhāra: Stories of Previous Births in Image and Text', in *The Geography of Gandhāran Art*, ed. W. Rienjang and P. Stewart (Oxford), pp. 175–85
Nelson, R., 2006, 'Where God Walked and Monks Pray', in *Holy Image, Hallowed Ground: Icons from Sinai*, ed. R. Nelson and K. Collins (Los Angeles, CA), pp. 1–37
Norman, K., 1983, *Pali Literature* (Wiesbaden)
—, 1984, *The Group of Discourses (Sutta-nipata)*, vol. I (London)
Nyanatusita, B. N., ed., 2013, *The Bodhisattva Ideal: Essays on the Emergence of Mahayana* (Kandy)
Nyanatusita, B. N., trans., 2021, *The Path to Freedom: Vimuttimagga* (Hong Kong)

Ohnuma, R., 2007, *Head, Eyes, Flesh and Blood: Giving Away the Body in Indian Buddhist Literature* (New York)
—, 2012, *Ties that Bind: Maternal Imagery and Discourse in Indian Buddhism* (Oxford)
—, 2017, *Unfortunate Destiny: Animals in the Indian Buddhist Imagination* (Oxford)
Oldenberg, H., 1880, *The Vinaya Pitakam* (London)
Olivelle, P., 2008, *The Life of the Buddha (Buddhacarita)* (New York)
—, 2016, 'Aśvaghoṣa and the Brahmanical Theology of the Epics and Dharmaśāstras', in *On the Growth and Composition of the Sanskrit Epics and Purāṇas*, ed. I. Andrijanić and S. Sellmer (Zagreb)
—, 2019, 'Aśvaghoṣa's Apologia: Brahmanical Ideology and Female Allure', *Journal of Indian Philosophy*, XLVII/2, pp. 257–68
Ollett, A., 2017, *Language of the Snakes: Prakrit, Sanskrit and the Language Order of Premodern India* (Berkeley, CA)
—, 2018, 'Sātavāhana and Nāgārjuna: Religion and the Sātavāhana State', *Journal of the International Association of Buddhist Studies*, XLI, pp. 421–72
—, 2019, 'Making It Nice: Kavya in the Second Century', *Journal of Indian Philosophy*, XLVII/2, pp. 269–87
Ong, W., 2012, *Orality and Literacy*, 3rd edn (London)
Osborne, R., 2004, 'Hoards, Votives, Offerings: The Archaeology of the Dedicated Object', *World Archaeology*, XXXVI/1, pp. 1–10
—, 2011, *The History Written on the Classical Greek Body* (Cambridge)
Osto, D., 2008, *Power, Wealth and Women in Indian Mahāyāna Buddhism: The Gaṇḍavyūha-sūtra* (London)
—, 2009, '"Proto-Tantric" Elements in the Gandavyuha-sūtra', *Journal of Religious History*, XXXIII/2, pp. 165–77
—, 2018, 'Altered States and the Origins of the Mahāyāna', in Harrison, 2018, pp. 177–205
—, undated, 'The Supreme Array Scripture, Chapter 55: The Vow to Follow the Course of Samantabhadra' (www.academia.edu)
Ōtake, S., 2012, 'Śākyamuni and Vairocana', in *Avakamsaka (Huayan, Kegon, Flower Ornament) Buddhism in South East Asia*, ed. R. Gimelo, F. Girard and I. Hamar (Wiesbaden), pp. 37–52
Padma, S., and A Barber, eds, 2008, *Buddhism in the Krishna River Valley of Andhra* (Albany, NY)
Padmanabha Sastry, C., 2004, 'A Few Prakrit Inscriptions from Amaravati', in Parasher-Sen, 2004, pp. 162–5
Pagel, U., 1995, *The Bodhisattvapiṭaka: Its Doctrines, Practices and Their Position in Mahāyāna Literature* (Tring)
Pandya Dhar, P., 2009, *The Torana in Indian and Southeast Asian Architecture* (New Delhi)
—, 2021, 'Reading Architecture, Constructing Narrative: Visualizing the Phanigiri Torana', in *Phanigiri: Interpreting an Ancient Buddhist Site in Telangana*, ed. N. Ahuja (Mumbai), pp. 152–85
Paranavitana, S., 1934–41, 'Gudaladeniya Rock Inscription of Dharmmakīrtti Sthavira', *Epigraphia Zeylanica*, IV, pp. 90–110
Parasher-Sen A., ed., 2004, *Kevala-bodhi: Buddhist and Jaina History of the Deccan* (Delhi)
Parimoo, R., 2004, 'Narrative Structure and the Significance of the Snake Jātakas in Buddhist Art', in Parasher-Sen, 2004, pp. 129–38
—, 2005, 'Narative Structure and the Significance of Snake Jatakas in Buddhist Art', in Kamalakar, 2005, pp. 351–62
Parker, G., 2008, *The Making of Roman India* (Cambridge)
—, 2015, 'India Cartographical', in Prabha Ray, 2015, pp. 3–29
Parry, J., 1986, 'The Gift, the Indian Gift and the "Indian Gift"', *Man*, XXI, pp. 453–73
Petridou, G., 2009, '*Artemidi to ichnos*: Divine Feet and Hereditary Priesthood in Pisidian Pogla', *Anatolian Studies*, LIX, pp. 81–93
—, 2015, *Divine Epiphany in Greek Literature and Culture* (Oxford)
Platt, V., 2011, *Facing the Gods: Epiphany and Representation in Graeco-Roman Art, Literature and Religion* (Cambridge)
Pollock, S., 2006, *The Language of the Gods in the World of Men: Sanskrit, Culture and Power in Premodern India* (Berkeley, CA)
—, 2016, *A Rasa Reader: Classical Indian Aesthetics* (New York)
Poonacha, K., 2011, *Excavations at Kanaganahalli* (Delhi)
Potter, K., 2003, *Encyclopaedia of Indian Philosophies IX: Buddhist Philosophy from 350–600 AD* (Delhi)
Prabha Ray, H., 1986, *Monastery and Guild: Commerce under the Sātavāhanas*, Oxford
—, 1994, *The Winds of Change: Buddhism and the Maritime Links of Early South Asia* (Delhi)
—, 2003, *The Archaeology of Seafaring in Ancient South Asia* (Cambridge)
—, 2007a, 'The Stūpa: Symbolizing Religious Architecture in Asia', in Prabha Ray, 2007b, pp. 63–80
—, ed., 2007b, *Sacred Landscapes in Asia: Shared Traditions, Multiple Histories* (Delhi), pp. 63–80
—, 2008a, *Colonial Archaeology in South Asia: The Legacy of Sir Mortimer Wheeler* (Oxford)
—, 2008b, 'Archaeology and Empire: Buddhist Monuments in Monsoon Asia', *Indian Economic and Social History Review*, XLV/3, pp. 417–49
—, 2015, *Negotiating Cultural Identity: Landscapes in Early Medieval South Asian History* (Delhi)
—, 2018, *Archaeology and Buddhism in South Asia* (London)
Prabha Ray, H., and C. Sinopoli, eds, 2004, *Archaeology as History in Early South Asia* (Delhi)
Prasad, B. R., 2008, 'Religious Architecture', in *Early Historic Andhra Pradesh 500 BC–AD 624*, ed. I. Sarma (Delhi), pp. 213–30
Prasad, N., 1993, *Recent Buddhist Discoveries in Visakhapatnam District A.P. (Relic Caskets at Bavikonda)* (Hyderabad)
—, 1994, *Bavikonda: A Buddhist Site in North Coastal Andhra Pradesh* (Hyderabad)
Priest, G., and J. Garfield, 2002, 'Nāgārjuna and the Limits of Thought', in *Beyond the Limits of Thought*, ed. G. Priest (Oxford), pp. 249–70
Priest, G., 2018, *The Fifth Corner of Four: An Essay on Buddhist Metaphysics and the Catuṣkoṭi* (Oxford)
Pruden, L., 1990, *Abhidharmakośa Bhāṣyam by Louis de la Vallée Poussin*, vol. II (Berkeley, CA)
Pyyhtinen, O., 2014, *The Gift and Its Paradoxes: Beyond Mauss* (London)
Quagliotti, A. M., 1994, 'Presenting the Images of the Buddha: A Relief from Amaravati', *Annali Istituto Universitario Orientale di Napoli*, LIV, pp. 150–55
—, 1998, *Buddhapādas: An Essay on the Representations of the Footprints of the Buddha with a Descriptive Catalogue of the Indian Specimens from the 2nd Century B.C. to the 4th Century A.D.* (Rome)
Quintanilla, S. R., 2007, *History of Early Stone Sculpture at Mathura, c. 150 BCE–100 CE* (Leiden)
—, 2017, 'Transformations of Identity and the Buddha's Infancy Narratives at Kanaganahalli', *Archives of Asian Art*, LXVII, pp. 111–42

Radich, M., 2015, *The Mahāparinirvāṇa-mahāsūtra and the Emergence of Tathāgatagarbha Doctrine* (Hamburg)
Raghunath, K., 2001, *The Iksvākus of Vijayapuri: A Study of the Nagarjunakonda Inscriptions* (Delhi)
Rama, K., 1995, *Buddhist Art of Nāgārjunakonda* (Delhi)
Ramachandran, A., 1996, *The Cultural History of the Lower Kṛṣṇa Valley: Its Contacts with South East Asia* (Jaipur)
Ramachandran, T., 1953, *Nāgārjunakonda 1938: Memoirs of the Archaeological Survey of India*, 71 (Delhi)
Rambelli, F., and E. Reinders, 2012, *Buddhism and Iconoclasm in East Asia* (London)
Rana, J. R., 2013, *The Sculptural Art of Amarāvatī* (Delhi)
Rangacharya, A., 1998, *Introduction to Bharata's Nātyaśastra* (New Delhi)
Rao, K., 2005a, 'Buddhapada in the Early Art of Andhradesa', in Kamalakar, 2005, pp. 345–9
Rao, M., 2005b, 'Symbolical Representation of the Buddha in the Art of Nagarjunakonda', in Kamalakar, 2005, pp. 207–13
Rao, R., 1984, *Andhra Sculpture* (Hyderabad)
Ratnam, M. R., 2008, 'Contributions of Andhra Thinkers to the Development of Buddhist Thought', in *Early Historic Andhra Pradesh 500 BC–AD 624*, ed. I. Sarma (Delhi), pp. 113–33
Ray, A., 1983, *The Life and Art of Early Andhradesa* (Delhi)
Ray, R., 1999, *Buddhist Saints in India: A Study in Buddhist Values and Orientations* (New York)
Rea, A., 1894, *South Indian Buddhist Antiquities* (Madras)
—, 1909, 'Excavations at Amarāvatī', *Annual Reports, Archaeological Survey of India, 1905–6*, pp. 116–19
—, 1912, 'Excavations at Amarāvatī', *Annual Reports, Archaeological Survey of India, 1908–9*, pp. 88–91
Regan, J., 2022, 'Pleasure and Poetics as Tools for Transformation in Aśvaghoṣa's *Mahākāvya*', *Religions*, XIII, pp. 3–20
Revell, L., 2016, 'Footsteps in Stone: Variability within a Global Culture', in *Beyond Boundaries: Connecting Visual Cultures in the Provinces of Ancient Rome*, ed. S. Alcock et al. (Los Angeles, CA), pp. 206–21
Rhi, J., 1994, 'From Bodhisattva to Buddha: The Beginning of Iconic Representation in Buddhist Art', *Artibus Asiae*, LIV/3–4, pp. 207–25
—, 2013, 'Presenting the Buddha: Images, Conventions and Significance in Early Buddhism', in *Art of Merit: Studies in Buddhist Art and Conservation*, ed. D. Park, K. Wangmo and A. Cather (London), pp. 1–18
—, 2018, 'Looking for Mahāyāna Bodhisattvas: A Reflection on Visual Evidence in Early Indian Buddhism', in Harrison, 2018, pp. 243–73
Rhys Davids, T.W., and H. Oldenberg, 1881–5, *Vinaya Texts*, 3 vols (Oxford)
Richman, P., 1988, *Women, Branch Stories and Religious Rhetoric in a Tamil Buddhist Text* (Syracuse, NY)
Rienjang, W., and P. Stewart, eds, 2018, *The Chronology of Gandhāran Art: Proceedings of the First International Workshop of the Gandhāra Connections Project* (Oxford)
—, 2019, *The Geography of Gandhāran Art* (Oxford)
—, 2020, *The Global Connections of Gandhāran Art* (Oxford)
Rosen, E., 1985, 'A Dated Memorial Pillar from Nagarjunakonda', in *Indian Epigraphy: Its Bearing on the History of Art*, ed. F. Asher and G. Gai (New Delhi), pp. 35–40
Rosen Stone, E., 1994, *The Buddhist Art of Nagarjunakonda* (Delhi)
—, 2005, 'Spatial Conventions in the Art of Andhra Pradesh: Classical Influence?', in Kamalakar, 2005, pp. 67–72
—, 2006, 'The Amarāvatī Master? Spatial Conventions in the Art of Amarāvatī', in *Hari Smriti: Studies in Art, Archaeology and Indology*, ed. A. Banerji, vol. I (New Delhi), pp. 51–60
—, 2016, 'Reflections of Roman Art in Southern India', in Shimada and Willis, 2016, pp. 59–69
Roth, G., 2009, 'Symbolism of the Buddhist Stupa', in *Stupa: Cult and Symbolism*, ed. G. Roth, F. Ehrhard, K. Tanaka and L. Chanda (New Delhi), pp. 9–33
Rotman, A., 2008, *Divine Stories: Divyāvadāna*, Part 1 (Boston)
—, 2009, *Thus Have I Seen: Visualizing Faith in Early Indian Buddhism* (Oxford)
—, 2017, *Divine Stories: Divyāvadāna*, Part 2 (Boston)
Rouse, W.H.D., 1895, *The Jātaka; or, Stories of the Buddha's Former Births*, vol. II (Cambridge)
—, 1901, *The Jātaka; or, Stories of the Buddha's Former Births*, vol. IV (Cambridge)
Rowan, J., 2002, 'Danger and Devotion: Hārītī Mother of Demons in the Stories and Stones of Gandhara', MA thesis, University of Oregon
Roy, A., 1994, *Amarāvatī Stūpa: A Critical Comparison of Epigraphic, Architectural, and Sculptural Evidence* (New Delhi)
Ruegg, D., 1977, 'The Use of the Four Positions of the *Catuṣkoṭi* and the Problem of the Description of Reality in Mahāyāna Buddhism', *Journal of Indian Philosophy*, V/1–2, pp. 1–171
Sahlins, M., 1974, *Stone Age Economics* (London)
Salomon, R., 2009, 'Aśvaghosa's Saundarananda IV–VI: A Study in the Poetic Structure of Buddhist Kāvya', *Indo-Iranian Journal*, LII, pp. 179–96
Samuels, J., 1997, 'The Bodhisattva Ideal in Theravada Buddhist Theory and Practice: A Reevaluation of the Bodhisattva–Sravaka Opposition', *Philosophy East and West*, XLVII, pp. 399–415
—2018, *The Buddhist Literature of Ancient Gandhāra* (Somerville, MA)
Sander, L., 1991, 'The Earliest Manuscripts from Central Asia and the Sarvāstivāda Mission', in *Corolla Iranica*, ed. R. Emmerick and D. Weber (Frankfurt am Main), pp. 133–50.
Sanderson, A., 2009, 'The Śaiva Age: The Rise and Dominance of Śaivism during the Early Medieval Period', in *Genesis and Development of Tantrism*, ed. S. Einoo (Tokyo), pp. 41–350
Sankarnarayan, K., K. Matsuda and M. Yoritomi, 2002, *Lokaprajñapti: A Critical Exposition of Buddhist Cosmology* (Mumbai)
Santoro, A., 2022, '*Haṃsa*: Flying Geese at Kizil', in Konczak-Nagel, Hiyama and Klein, 2022, pp. 343–52
Sarkar, H., 1965–6, 'Nāgārjunakonda Prakrit Inscription of Gautamīputra Vijaya Sātakarni', *Epigraphia Indica*, XXXVI, pp. 273–4
—, 1966, *Studies in the Early Buddhist Architecture of India* (Delhi)
—, 1970–71, 'Some Early Inscriptions in the Amaravati Museum', *Journal of Indian History*, IV/1–2, pp. 1–13
Sarkar, H. and Nainar, S., 1992, *Amarāvati* (Delhi)
Sarma, I. K., 1975, 'Some More Inscriptions from Amarāvatī Excavations and the Chronology of the Mahāstūpa', *Studies in Indian Epigraphy*, I, pp. 60–74
—, 1980, 'More Prakrit Inscriptions from Amaravati', *Journal of the Epigraphical Society of India*, VII, pp. 18–21

—, 1985, ‘Early Sculptures and Epigraphs from South East India: New Evidence from Amarāvatī’, in *Indian Epigraphy: Its Bearing on the History of Art*, ed. F. Asher and G. Gai (Delhi), pp. 15–23
—, 1988, *Studies in Early Buddhist Monuments and Brāhmī Inscriptions of Āndradēśa* (Nagpur)
Sastri, T., 2004, ‘An Unwritten Chapter in the History of Early Deccan’, in Parasher-Sen, 2004, pp. 229–37
Seckel, D., 2004, *Before and beyond the Image: Aniconic Symbolism in Buddhist Art* (Zurich)
Seshagiri Rao, B., 1922, *Studies in South Indian Jainism Part 2: Andhra Karnata Jainism* (Madras)
Schalk, P., 1998, ‘The Oldest Buddhist Artefacts Discovered in Tamilakam’, in *Being Religious and Living through the Eyes*, ed. P. Schalk and M. Strausberg (Uppsala), pp. 307–27
Schlingloff, D., 1984–6, ‘Śibi – Sarvamdada’, *RTAM: Shri Gopal Chandra Sinha Commemoration Volume*, XVI–XVIII, pp. 299–308
—, 1987, *Studies in the Ajanta Paintings* (Delhi)
—, 1999, *Guide to the Ajanta Paintings*, vols I–III: *Narrative Wall Paintings* (Delhi)
Schopen, G., 1991, ‘Archaeology and the Protestant Presuppositions in the Study of Indian Buddhism’, *History of Religions*, XXXI, pp. 1–23
—, 1996, ‘What’s in a Name: The Religious Function of the Early Donative Inscriptions’, in Dehejia, 1996, pp. 58–73
—, 1997, *Bones, Stones, and Buddhist Monks* (Honolulu, HI)
—, 2005, *Figments and Fragments of Mahāyāna Buddhism in India* (Honolulu, HI)
—, 2007, ‘The Learned Monk as a Comic Figure: On Reading a Buddhist Vinaya as Indian Literature’, *Journal of Indian Philosophy*, XXXV/3, pp. 201–26
Schotsman, I., 1995, *Aśvaghosa’s Buddhacarita: The Life of the Buddha* (Varanasi)
Schrenk, S., 1995, *Typos und Antitypos in der frühchristlichen Kunst* (Münster)
Settar, S., 2020, *Early Buddhist Artisans and Their Architectural Vocabulary* (Manipal)
Settis, S., 1985, ‘La colonne Trajane: Invention, composition, disposition’, *Annales ESC*, V, pp. 1151–94
—, 1988, *La Colonna Traiana* (Turin)
—, 1991, ‘La colonne Trajane: L’empereur et son public’, *Revue archéologique*, pp. 186–98
Sharma, H. V., 1987, *The Theatres of the Buddhists* (Delhi)
Sharma, R. C., 1984, *Buddhist Art of Mathurā* (Delhi)
Shastri, A., 1998, *The Sātavāhanas and the Western Kshatrapas* (Nagpur)
—, ed., 1999, *The Age of the Sātavāhanas*, 2 vols (Delhi)
—, 2001, ‘Buddhist Schools in Early Andhra’, *Indian Historical Review*, XXVII, pp. 1–17
Shaw, S., 2006, *The Jātakas: Birth Stories of the Bodhisatta* (London)
—, 2021, *The Art of Listening* (Boulder, CO)
Shimada, A., 2005, ‘The Political Setting of the Amarāvatī Stūpa: Recent Studies’, *Deccan Studies*, vol. III, pp. 33–47
—, 2009, ‘Amarāvatī and Dhānyakataka: Topology of Monastic Spaces in Ancient Indian Cities’, in Hawkes and Shimada, 2009, pp. 216–34
—, 2013, *Early Buddhist Architecture in Context: The Great Stūpa at Amarāvatī (c. 300 BCE–300 CE)* (Leiden)
—, 2017, ‘“A Seated Buddha Image from Amaravati”: A Reinterpretation’ *Artibus Asiae*, LXXVII/2, pp. 183–213
—, 2016, ‘Discovery of the Amaravati Stūpa: Early Excavations and Interpretations’, in Shimada and Willis, 2016, pp. 1–11
—, 2018, ‘Royal and Non-Royal Buddhist Patronage in the Early Deccan’, *Journal of the International Association of Buddhist Studies*, XLI, pp. 473–507
Shimada, A., and Willis, M., eds, 2016, *Amaravati: The Art of an Early Buddhist Monument in Context* (London)
Shimoda, M., 2002, ‘Stūpa Worship as Historical Background to Tathāgatagarbha Theory: As Suggested by Several Seemingly Irrelevant Texts’, in *Buddhist and Indian Studies in Honour of Professor Sodō Mori* (Hamamatsu, Japan), pp. 247–58
Shulman, E., 2018a, ‘Contemplating the Buddha in the *Jātakas*’, *Religions of South Asia*, XXI, pp. 9–33
—, 2018b, ‘Aśvaghoṣa’s Viśeṣaka: The Saundarananda and Its Pāli “Equivalents”’, *Journal of Indian Philosophy*, XLVII/2, pp. 235–56
—, 2021, *Visions of the Buddha: Creative Dimensions of Early Buddhist Scripture* (Oxford)
—, undated. ‘Orality and Creativity in Early Buddhist Discourses’, pp. 1–43 (www.academia.edu)
Silk, J., 2006, *Body Language* (Tokyo)
—, 2008, *Managing Monks: Administrators and Administrative Roles in Indian Buddhist Monasticism* (Oxford)
—, 2009, *Riven by Lust: Incest and Schism in Indian Buddhist Legend and Historiography* (Honolulu, HI)
Singh, S., 2005, ‘Buddhist Art of Amaravati’, in Kamalakar, 2005, pp. 391–5
Singh, U., 1996, ‘Sanchi: The History of the Patronage of an Ancient Buddhist Establishment’, *Indian Economic and Social History Review*, XXXIII, pp. 1–35
—, 2004, *The Discovery of Ancient India: Early Archaeologists and the Beginning of Archaeology* (New Delhi)
—, 2010, ‘Amaravati: The Dismembering of the *Mahācaitya* (1797–1886)’, *South Asian Studies*, XVII, pp. 19–40
—, 2016, *The Idea of Ancient India: Essays on Religion, Politics and Archaeology* (Delhi)
Sircar, D., 1961–2, ‘Nāgārjunakonda Inscription of the Time of Ābhira Vasuhēna, Year 30’, *Epigraphia Indica*, XXXIV, pp. 197–204
—, 1963–4, ‘More Inscriptions from Nāgārjunakonda’ *Epigraphia Indica*, XXXV, pp. 1–36
—, 1965, *Indian Epigraphy* (Delhi)
—, 1967, *Cosmography and Geography in Early Indian Literature* (Calcutta)
Sircar, D., and K. Krishnan, 1961–2, ‘Two Inscriptions from Nāgārjunakonda’, *Epigraphia Indica*, vol. XXXIV, pp. 17–22
Sitapati, P., and V. Krishna Sastry, 1980, *New Satavahana Sculptures from Andhra Amaravathi* (Hyderabad)
Sitaramamma, J., 2004, ‘The Significance of Abhyamudra Buddha from Nagarjunakonda Sculptures’, in Parasher-Sen, 2004, pp. 148–54
Sivaramamurti, C., 1956, *Amaravati Sculptures in the Madras Government Museum* [1942], *Bulletin of the Madras Government Museum*, vol. IV (Madras)
—, 1981, ‘A New Medallion of the Subjugation of Nalagiri’, in *Chhavi-2: Rai Krishnadasa Felicitation Volume* (Varanasi), pp. 239–40
Sizemore, R., and D. Swearer, eds, 1990, *Ethics, Wealth and Salvation: A Study in Buddhist Social Ethics* (Columbia, SC)
Skilling, P., 1996, ‘The Sambuddhe Verses and Later Theravādin Buddhology’, *Journal of the Pali Text Society*, XXII, pp. 151–83

—, 2008, 'New Discoveries from South India: The Life of the Buddha at Phanigiri, Andhra Pradesh', *Arts asiatiques*, LXIII, pp. 96–118
—, 2013, 'Vaidalya, Mahāyāna and Bodhisatva in India: An Essay towards Historical Understanding', in *The Bodhisattva Ideal: Essays on the Emergence of Mahayana*, ed. Bikkhu Nyanatusita (Kandy), pp. 69–162
—, 2016, '*Caitiya, Mahācitiya, Tathagātcaitiya*: Questions of Terminology in the Age of Amaravati', in Shimada and Willis, 2016, pp. 23–36
—, 2018, 'Relics: The Heart of Buddhist Veneration', in Stargardt and Willis, 2018, pp. 4–17
—, 2021, 'Buddhism in Phanigiri', in *Phanigiri: Interpreting an Ancient Buddhist Site in Telangana*, ed. N. Ahuja (Mumbai), pp. 36–65
Skilling, P., and Saerji, 2019, '*Jātakas* in the *Bhadralkalpita-Sūtra* A Provisional Inventory I', *Annual Report of the International Research Institute for Advanced Buddhology*, XXII, pp. 125–70
Skorupski, T., undated, 'The Buddhist Stūpa' (www.academia.edu)
—, 2002, *The Six Perfections: An Abridged Version of E. Lamotte's French Translation of Nāgārjuna's Mahāprajñāpāramitāśāstra, Chapters XVI–XXX*, Buddhica Britannica 9, Tring
—, 2013, 'Buddha's Stūpa and Image: In Search of the Ultimate Icon', in *Art of Merit: Studies in Buddhist Art and Its Conservation*, ed. D. Park, K. Wangmo and S. Cather (London), pp. 19–26
Smith, B., 1994, *Classifying the Universe: The Ancient Indian Varna System and the Origins of Caste* (New York)
Smith, T. J., 2021, *Religion in the Art of Archaic and Classical Greece* (Philadelphia, PA)
Smith, V., 1901, *The Jain Stūpa and Other Antiquities of Mathurā* (Allahabad)
Snellgrove, D., ed., 1978, *The Image of the Buddha* (Paris)
Soundrarajan, K., 2006, *Nāgārjunakonda (1954–60)*, vol. II: *The Historical Period* (Delhi)
Spagnoli, M., 2005, 'Searching for the Origin of the "bhūmisparśa-mudrā"', *East and West*, LV, pp. 329–44
Spiro, M., 1970, *Buddhism and Society: A Great Tradition and Its Burmese Vicissitudes* (New York)
Squire, M., 2009, *Image and Text in Greco-Roman Antiquity* (Cambridge)
—, 2011, *The Art of the Body: Antiquity and Its Legacy* (London)
—, 2014, 'The *Ordo* of Rhetoric and the Rhetoric of Order', in Elsner and Meyer, 2014, pp. 353–417
Srinivasan, P., 1960, 'Buddhist Images of South India', in *The Story of Buddhism with Special Reference to South India*, ed. A. Aiyappan and P. Srinivasan (Chennai), pp. 62–101
Srivastava, A., 1991, *Nandyāvarta: An Auspicious Symbol in Indian Art* (Allahabad)
Stansbury-O'Donnell, M., 2006, *Vase-Painting, Gender and Social Identity in Archaic Athens* (Cambridge)
Stargardt, J., and M. Willis, eds, 2018, *Relics and Relic Worship in Early Buddhism* (London)
Stern, P., and Bénisti, M., 1961, *Évolution du style indien d' Amarāvatī* (Paris)
Stewart. P., 2020, 'Roman Sarcophagi and Gandharan Sculpture', in Rienjang and Stewart, 2020, pp. 50–85
Strong, J., 1983, *The Legend of King Aśoka* (Princeton, NJ)
—, 2004, *Relics of the Buddha* (Princeton, NJ)
Stoye, M., 2020. 'On the Crossroads of Disciplines: Tonio Hölscher's Theory of Understanding Roman Art Images and Its Implications for the Study of Western Influence(s) in Gandhāran Art', in *The Global Connections of Gandhāran Art*, ed. W. Rienjang and P. Stewart (Oxford), pp. 29–49
Subrahmaniyam, R., 1964, *Salihundam: A Buddhist Site in Andhra Pradesh* (Hyderabad)
Subrahmanyam, B., 1998, *Buddhist Relic Caskets of South India* (Delhi)
—, 2005, *Jātakas in South Indian Art* (Delhi)
Subrahmanyam, B., and E. Reddy, 2012, *Buddhist Archaeology in Andhra Pradesh* (Hyderabad)
Subrahmanyam, R., 2006, 'Brāhmanical Remains', in Soundararajan, 2006, pp. 200–234
Subramanian, K., 1981, *Buddhist Remains in South India and Early Andhra History 225 AD to 610 AD* (Delhi)
Sudha Piratti, V., 2002, *Mithuna in Buddhist Art: With Special Reference to Amaravati and Nagarjunakonda* (Delhi)
Sugimoto, T., 2002, 'Gandhāran Jātakas (1)', in *Buddhist and Indian Studies in Honour of Professor Sodō Mori* (Hamamatsu, Japan), pp. 25–42
Sujato and Brahmali, 2014, *The Authenticity of the Early Buddhist Texts*, at http://ocbs.org/wp-content/uploads/2015/09/authenticity.pdf
Sullivan, B., 2015, *Sacred Objects in Secular Spaces: Exhibiting Asian Religions in Museums* (London)
Taddei, M., 2015, 'Narrative Art between India and the Hellenistic World', *Journal of Transcultural Studies*, VI, pp. 34–74
Takács, S., 2005, 'Divine and Human Feet: Records of Pilgrims Honouring Isis', in *Pilgrimage in Graeco-Roman and Early Christian Antiquity: Seeing the Gods*, ed. J. Elsner and I. Rutherford (Oxford), pp. 353–70
Takakusu, J., 1896, *A Record of the Buddhist Religion as Practised in India and the Malay Archipelago (A.D. 671–695)* (Oxford)
Tanabe, T., 2019, 'Gandhāran Śibi Jātaka Imagery: Gandhāra, Kizil and Dunhuang', *Annual Report of the International Research Institute for Advanced Buddhology at Soka University*, XXII, pp. 359–76
Tatelman, J., 2000, *The Glorious Deeds of Pūrna* (London)
Testart, A., 2007, *Critique du don: Études sur la circulation non marchande* (Paris)
Thapar, R., 1992, 'Patronage and Community', in Miller, 1992, pp. 19–34
—, 1997, *Aśoka and the Decline of the Mauryas* (Oxford)
Tieken, H., 2010, 'Aśvaghosa and the History of Allegorical Literature in India, in *From Turfan to Ajanta: Festschrift für Dieter Schlinghoff on the Occasion of His Eightieth Birthday*, ed. E. Franco and M. Zin (Lumbini), pp. 993–7
Titthila, U., 1969, *The Book of Analysis (Vibhaṅga)* (London)
Tkacz, C., 2002, *The Key to the Brescia Casket: Typology and the Early Christian Imagination* (Paris)
Tomber, R., 2008, *Indo-Roman Trade: From Pots to Pepper* (London)
Tournier, V., 2012, 'The Mahāvastu and the Vinayapitaka of the Mahāsāṃghika-Lokattaravādin', *Annual Report of the International Research Institute for Advanced Buddhology at Soka University*, XV, pp. 87–104
—, 2017, *La formation du Mahāvastu et la mise en place des conceptions relatives à la carrière du bodhisattva* (Paris)
—, 2018, 'A Tide of Merit: Royal Donors, Tāmraparnīya Monks and the Buddha's Awakening in 5th–6th Century Āndhradeśa', *Indo-Iranian Journal*, LXI/1, pp. 20–96

—, 2019, 'Buddhas of the Past: South Asia', in *Brill's Encyclopedia of Buddhism*, vol. II: *Lives*, ed. J. Silk (Leiden), pp. 95–108
—, 2020, 'Buddhist Lineages along the Southern Routes: On Two Nikāyas Active at Kanaganahalli under the Sātavāhanas', in *Archaeologies of the Written*, ed. V. Tournier, V. Etschinger and M. Sernesi (Naples), pp. 857–910
—, 2021–2, 'Kings as Patrons of Monasteries and Stupas in Early Andhra: Sada Rulers, the Rajagiriya Fraternity, and the "Great Shrine" at Amaravati', *Buddhism, Law and Society*, vol. VII, pp. 1–58
Tin, M., and C. Rhys Davies, 1920, *The Expositor (Atthasālinī): Buddhaghosa's Commentary on the Dhammasangaṇī, the First Book of the Abhidhamma Piṭaka*, vol. I (London)
Tournier, V., and J. Strong., 2019, 'Śākyamuni: South Asia', in *Brill's Encyclopedia of Buddhism*, vol. II: *Lives*, ed. J. Silk (Leiden), pp. 3–38
Turner, V., 1974, *Dramas, Fields, and Metaphors* (Ithaca, NY)
Trautmann, T., 1981, *Dravidian Kinship* (Cambridge)
—, 2009, *The Clash of Chronologies: Ancient India in the Modern World* (Delhi)
Trubner, H., W. Rathbun and C. A. Kaputa, 1973, *Asiatic Art in the Seattle Art Museum* (Seattle, WA)
Vajiranana, P., 1975, *Buddhist Meditation in Theory and in Practice* (Kuala Lumpur)
van Lohuizen-De Leeuw, J., 1949, *The 'Scythian' Period: An Approach to the History, Art, Epigraphy and Palaeography of North India from the 1st Century* BC *to the 3rd Century* AD (Leiden)
—, 1979, 'New Evidence with Regard to the Origin of the Buddha Image', in *South Asian Archaeology*, ed. H. Härtel (Berlin), pp. 377–400
Varadpande, M., 1981, *Ancient Indian and Indo-Greek Theatre* (New Delhi)
Vélez de Cea, A., 2005, 'Emptiness in the Pāli *Suttas* and the Question of Nāgārjuna's Orthodoxy', *Philosophy East and West*, LV, pp. 507–28
Venkateswara Rao, K., 1984, 'Relic Caskets from the Buddhist Stupas, Andhra Desa', *Andhra Pradesh Journal of Archaeology*, II, pp. 67–72
Verma, S. K., 1996, *Art and Iconography of the Buddha Images* (Delhi)
Veyne, P., 1988, 'Conduites sans croyance et oeuvres d'art sans spectateurs', *Diogène*, CXLIII, pp. 3–22
—, 2005, *L'empire gréco-romain* (Paris), pp. 379–418
Vogel, P., 1919–20a, 'Prakrit Inscriptions from a Buddhist Site at Nāgārjunakonda', *Epigraphia Indica*, XX, pp. 1–36
—, 1919–20b, 'Two Additional Inscriptions from Nāgārjunakonda' *Epigraphia Indica*, XX, p. 37
—, 1931–2, 'Additional Prakrit Inscriptions from Nāgārjunakonda', *Epigraphia Indica*, XXI, pp. 61–7
Wagner-Hasel, B., 2003, 'Egoistic Exchange and Altruistic Gift', in Algazi, Groebner and Jussen, 2003, pp. 141–71
Wallace, V., 2001, *The Inner Kalacakra Tantra: A Buddhist Tantric View of the Individual* (Oxford)
Walser, J., 2002, 'Nāgārjuna and the *Ratnāvalī*: New Ways to Date an Old Philosopher', *Journal of the International Association of Buddhist Studies*, XXV, pp. 210–62
—, 2005, *Nāgārjuna in Context: Mahāyāna Buddhism and Early Indian Culture* (New York)
—, 2018, *Genealogies of Mahāyāna Buddhism* (London)
Walshe, M., 1987, *Thus Have I Heard: The Long Discourses of the Buddha* (Boston, MA)
Walters, J., 1990, 'The Buddha's Bad Karma: A Problem in the History of Theravāda Buddhism', *Numen*, XXXVII, pp. 70–95
—, 1997, 'Stūpa, Story and Empire: Constructions of the Buddha Biography in Early Post-Aśokan India', in *Sacred Biography and Buddhist Traditions of South and Southeast Asia*, ed. J. Schober (Honolulu, HI), pp. 160–92
Ward-Perkins, B., 2010. 'Where Is the Archaeology and Iconography of Germanic Arianism', in Gwynn and Bangert, 2010, pp. 265–89
Warder, A. K., 1973, 'Is Nāgārjuna a Mahāyānist?', in *The Problem of Two Truths in Buddhism and Vedānta*, ed. M. Sprung (Dordrecht), pp. 78–88
—, 2000, *Indian Buddhism*, 3rd edn (Delhi)
Wayman, A., 1978, 'The Mahāsāṃghika and the Tathāgatagarbha (Buddhist Doctrinal History Study 1)', *Journal of the International Association of Indian Studies*, I, pp. 35–50
—, 2005, 'Remarks on Nagarjuna's Dates and Philosophical Position', in Kamalakar, 2005, pp. 15–25
Wayman, A., and E. Rosen Stone, 1990, 'The Rise of Mahayana Buddhism and Inscriptional Evidence at Nagarjunakonda', *Indian Journal of Buddhist Studies*, II/1, pp. 49–66
Wayman, A., and H. Wayman., 1990, *The Lion's Roar of Queen Srimālā* (Delhi)
Wedemeyer, C., 2007, *Āryadeva's Lamp that Integrates the Practices (Caryāmelāpakapradīpa)* (New York)
Weinryb, I., ed., 2016, *Ex voto: Votive Images across Cultures* (New York)
—, 2018, *Agents of Faith: Votive Objects in Time and Place* (New Haven, CT)
Wenzel, C., 2011, 'The Image of the Buddha: Buddha Icons and Aniconic Traditions in India and China', *Transcultural Studies*, I, pp. 263–305
Westerhoff, J., 2009, *Nāgārjuna's Madhyamaka: A Philosophical Introduction* (Oxford)
—, 2018, *The Golden Age of Indian Buddhist Philosophy* (Oxford)
Whitby, M., 1985, 'The Occasion of Paul the Silentiary's Ekphrasis of S. Sophia', *Classical Quarterly*, XXXV, pp. 215–28
Wijesekera, O., 1941, 'Buddhist Evidence for the Early Existence of Drama', *Indian Historical Quarterly*, XVII, pp. 196–206
Willemen, C., 2009, *Buddhacarita: In Praise of the Buddha's Acts*, BDK English Tripitaka Series, Taisho, IV/192 (Berkeley, CA)
Williams, P., ed., 2005, *Buddhism Critical Concepts in Religious Studies*, vol. III: *The Origins and Nature of Mahayana Buddhism: Some Mahayana Religious Topics* (London)
—, 2009, *Mahāyāna Buddhism: The Doctrinal Foundations*, 2nd edn (London)
Willis, J., 1992, 'Female Patronage in Indian Buddhism', in Miller, 1992, 46–53
Willis, M., ed., 2000, *Buddhist Reliquaries from Ancient India* (London)
Winternitz, M., 1923, 'Buddhist Drama', in *Literary History of Sanskrit Buddhism*, ed. G. Nariman (Bombay), pp. 219–23
Wolf, G., 2002, *Schleier und Spiegel. Traditionen des Christusbildes und die Bildkonzepte der Renaissance* (Munich), pp. 16–33
Wood, C., 2011, 'The Votive Scenario', *RES: Anthropology and Aesthetics*, LIX–LX, pp. 207–27

Wu Hung, 1992, 'What Is *Bianxiang*? On the Relationship between Dunhuang Art and Dunhuang Literature', *Harvard Journal of Asiatic Studies*, LII/1, pp. 111–92

—, 2023, *Spatial Dunhuang: Experiencing the Mogao Caves* (Seattle)

Wynne, A., 2004, 'The Oral Transmission of the Early Buddhist Literature', *Journal of the International Association of Buddhist Studies*, XXVII/1, pp. 97–128

Wyschogrod, E., J.-J. Goux and E. Boynton, eds, 2002, *The Enigma of Gift and Sacrifice* (New York)

Xi He, 2011, 'The Prose *Varnaka* in the *Lalitavistara*', in *South Asian Texts in History: Critical Engagements with Sheldon Pollock*, ed. Y. Bronner, W. Cox and L. McCrea (Ann Arbor, MI), pp. 83–102

Xing, G., 2005, *The Concept of the Buddha: Its Evolution from Early Buddhism to the Trikāya Theory* (London)

Xing, L., A. Mayor, Yu Chen, J. Harris and M. Burns, 2011, 'The Folklore of Dinosaur Trackways in China: Impact on Paleontology', *Ichnos*, XVIII/4, pp. 213–20

Xing, L., et al., 2014, 'Upper Cretaceous Dinosaur Track Assemblages and a New Theropod Ichnotaxon from Anhui Province, Eastern China', *Cretaceous Research*, XLIX, pp. 190–204

Xydis, S., 1947, 'The Chancel Barrier, Solea, and Ambo of Hagia Sophia', *Art Bulletin*, XXIX, pp. 1–24

Yamano, C., 2008, 'Nagārjuna and Sātavāhana', *Journal of Indian and Buddhist Studies*, LVI/3, pp. 121–7

Ye, S., 2019, 'Nāgārjuna', in *Brill's Encyclopedia of Buddhism*, vol. II: *Lives* (Leiden), pp. 335–47

Zhao, W., 2018, 'The Conceptions of Seeing the Buddha and Buddha Embodiments in Early Prajñāpāramitā Literature', PhD dissertation, Ludwig-Maximilians-Universität, Munich, Germany

Zin, M., 2004, 'The Mūkapangu Story in the Madras Government Museum: The Problem of the Textual Affiliations of the Narrative Reliefs in Amaravati and Nagarjunakonda', *Annali del' istituto universitario orientale*, LXIV, pp. 157–80

—, 2006, *Mitleid und Wunderkraft: Schwierige Bekehrungen und ihre Ikonographie im indischen Buddhismus* (Wiesbaden)

—, 2011, 'The Parable of the Man in the Well, Its Travels and Its Pictorial Traditions from Amarāvatī to Today', in *Art, Myths and Visual Culture of South Asia*, ed. P. Balcerowicz and J. Malinwoski (Delhi), pp. 33–93

—, 2015a, 'Nur Gandhara? Zu Motiven der klassischen Antike in Andhra', *Tribus: Jahrbuch des Linden-Museums, Stuttgart*, LXIV, pp. 178–205

—, 2015b, 'The Jester and the Viduśāka', in *'In ihrer rechten Hand hielt sie ein silbernes Messer mit Glöckchen . . .': Studien zur indischen Kultur und Literatur. Festschrift Heidun Brückner*, ed. A. Esposito et al. (Wiesbaden), pp. 279–96

—, 2016a, 'Buddhist Narratives and Amaravati', in Shimada and Willis, 2016, pp. 46–58

—, 2016b, 'Nur Gandhara? Zu Motiven der klassischen Antike in Andhra', *Tribus: Jahrbuch des Linden-Museums, Stuttgart*, vol. LXIV, pp. 178–205

—, 2016c, 'The Buddha's Relics and the Nāgas: An Attempt to Throw Light on Some Depictions in the Amaravati School', in *South Asian Religion and Visual Forms in Their Archaeological Context*, vol. II, ed. V. Lefèvre, A. Didier and B. Mutin (Turnhout), pp. 757–76

—, 2017, 'Narrated with Chisel and Paintbrush: On the Importance of Research into Art History for Understanding Buddhism – Some Examples', *Rocznik Orientalistyczny*, LXX, pp. 274–30

—, 2018a, *The Kanaganahalli Stūpa: An Analysis of the 60 Massive Slabs Covering the Dome* (Delhi)

—, 2018b, 'Kanaganahalli in Sātavāhana Art and Buddhism: King Aśoka in Front of the Bodhi Tree', *Journal of the International Association of Buddhist Studies*, XLI, pp. 537–68

—, 2019a, 'Heavenly Relics: The Bodhisattva's Turban and Bowl in the Reliefs of Gandhāra and Andhra (including Kanaganahalli)', in *Arts in Context: Essays Presented to Doris Meth Srivanasan in Admiration of Her Scholarly Research*, ed. C. Wessels-Mevissen and K. Mevissen (Delhi), pp. 365–78

—, 2019b, 'The Techniques of the Narrative Representations in Old India', in *Image – Narration – Context: Visual Narratives in the Cultures and Societies of the Old World*, ed. E. Wagner-Durand, B. Fath and A. Heinemann (Heidelberg), pp. 137–56

—, 2020, 'Traces of Reciprocal Exchange: From Roman Pictorial Models to the World's Earliest Depictions of Some Narrative Motifs in Andhra Reliefs', *Religions*, XI, pp. 1–20

—, 2021, 'Fragments of a Divided Whole: On the Exhibition of Several Narrative Reliefs from the Amaravati School of Sculptures', in *Ratna Dīpaḥ: New Dimensions in Indian Art History and Theory. Essays in Honour of Prof. Ratan Parimoo*, ed. G. Parimoo Krishnan and R. Kulkarni (Delhi), pp. 13–23

Zwalf, W., 1996, *A Catalogue of Gandhāra Sculpture in the British Museum* (London)

Acknowledgements

My interest in Buddhism and Buddhist art has been long in the making, but it was able to find its art-historical scholarly feet during the Empires of Faith research project on the rise of the iconographies of world religions, funded by the Leverhulme Trust, of which I was principal investigator from 2013 to 2018. This coincided with an appointment at the British Museum, which enabled me to spend much time looking at the sculptures in the Amarāvatī galleries as well as in the storerooms, and to conceive the idea of researching and composing a monograph on the monument in its Indian Buddhist context. The courage to range widely and critically across the imagery of the world religions in the period known (from a Eurocentric perspective) as late antiquity owes much to the conversations I had in Empires of Faith, and I thank the participants here: Philippa Adrych, Nadia Ali, Robert Bracey, Belinda Crerar, Katherine Cross, Dominic Dalglish, Stefanie Lenk, Maria Lidova, Georgi Parpulov and Rachel Wood.

By a strange happenstance, the sudden arrival of COVID-19 in the spring of 2020, which put an abrupt stop to any pursuit of my other projects, enabled a period of intense focus and writing. Against all usual art-historical practice and my own normal instincts, I found myself writing about a site I had never visited and many objects that I had not been able to see directly beforehand, since I had planned to visit the key sites in India in the autumn of 2020, prior to writing the book in 2021. But the spread and persistence of the pandemic meant that I was only able to go to the subcontinent and make an intense trip to Chennai and Andhra Pradesh in November 2022. This made the process unusual since I had already written the main draft before seeing many objects directly with my own eyes, but I was able to make final (in some cases extensive) revisions. As an archaeologist and art historian of antiquity, I have always worked on fields in which I had some command of the original languages. That has not been the case here: my Pāli and Sanskrit extend to being able to check the original word (when written in Roman script) that a translation renders, but not beyond. If that is an unforgivable sin in this field, then I am damned. But to ask for a command of not only the ancient Indian literatures but Chinese and Tibetan, the two other key primary languages in this field, alongside Japanese and Korean, many writings in which offer important secondary scholarship, puts the entry bar for the study of ancient Buddhist art extremely high and inevitably excludes anyone who might wish to compare these materials more broadly. It would certainly have excluded me. My major scholarly regret (apart from not having done all this philology in my youth!) is that so much of what one needs to read – for example, of the Pāli commentarial tradition – has not yet been translated. I am, however, incredibly grateful for the immensely valuable help of Indaka Weerasekera with issues of Pāli and Sanskrit, including diacritics and conventions of transliteration.

I wish to offer thanks to a number of institutions: the British Museum (notably for enabling the taking of excellent new photographs of all items on display in the Amarāvatī gallery), the Kunsthistorisches Institut in Florence and the Max Planck Society (for funding the photographic project and a generous subvention towards publication) and Corpus Christi College Oxford (for supporting the India trip), as well as audiences in a number of settings where I have presented some of the material in this volume (notably at Corpus and at the University of Chicago, my two primary bases in the years I have worked on the book). The following have been extremely helpful in responding to queries, reading material, commenting on and improving my work: I offer my thanks and gratitude to Catherine Becker, Marianne Bergmann, Alice Casalini, Wendy Doniger, Rupert Gethin, Richard Gombrich, Peter Harvey, J. D. Hill, Susan Huntington, Sushma Jansari, Thupten Jinpa, Natalia Lidova, Richard Neer, Andrew Ollett, Deven Patel, Hugo Shakeshaft, Charles Shaw, Sarah Shaw, Vincent Tournier, Indaka Weerasekera, Jonathan Williams, Gerhard Wolf and Monika Zin. For help with photographs, my thanks are particularly due to Susan Huntington (again), Gudrun Melzer, Beatriz Waters and Monika Zin (again), to Jonathan Lim for his work on the map and Ella Benson Easton for help with the Index. I am especially grateful to my dear friend Tenzin Choegyal (TC) for organizing my research trip to southern India and for accompanying me there along with our intrepid driver, Tsering Dhonden. I also thank Michael Leaman for his interest in and support of the project, and all the staff at Reaktion Books, especially Amy Salter, for their exemplary professionalism in publication.

Photo Acknowledgements

The author and publishers wish to thank the organizations and individuals listed below for authorizing reproduction of their work.

Agefotostock: 105; AKG Images: 59 (Jean Louis Nou); Alamy: 52 (Zvonimir Atletić), 78 (Zvonimir Atletić), 101 (Robert Harding), 107 (Mirko Kuzmanovic), 155 (ephotocorp); after D. Barratt, *Sculpture from Amaravati in the British Museum* (1954): 2, 9; British Library: 53 (WD1061, folio 83), 60 (WD1061, folio 35), 70 (WD1061, folio 35), 71 (WD1061, folio 26), 76 (WD1061, folio 66), 93 (WD1061, folio 63), 95 (WD1061, folio 24), 122 (WD1061, folio 17), 123 (WD1061, folio 45), 126 (WD1061, folio 48), 127 (WD1061, folio 48), 135 (WD1061, folio 25), 136 (WD1061, folio 74); after A. Cunningham, *The Stūpa of Bharhut* (1879): 10; Jaś Elsner: 1, 3, 20, 21, 22, 30, 33, 40, 42, 73, 85, 110, 116, 119, 120, 137, 139, 143, 144, 145, 146, 147, 148, 149, 152, 153; John C. Huntington (courtesy of the John C. and Susan L. Huntington Photographic Archive of Buddhist and Asian Art): 28, 29, 45, 46, 47, 48, 104, 106, 124, 125, 154; plan based on A. H. Longhurst, *The Buddhist Antiquities of Nāgājunakonda* (1938): 8; after J. Marshall, A. Foucher and N. Majumdar, *The Monuments of Sanchi* (1940): 11; Gudrun Melzer: 25, 26, 27, 31, 32, 87, 88, 133; Wojtek Oczkowski: 39, 41, 69, 86, 111, 128, 129, 134, 138; A. Rea, *Annual Reports, Archaeological Survey of India, 1908–9*: 7, 24; © The Trustees of the British Museum: 4, 5, 6, 12, 13, 14, 15, 16, 17, 18, 19, 23, 34, 35, 36, 37, 38, 43, 44, 49, 50, 51, 54, 55, 56, 57, 58, 61, 62, 63, 64, 65, 66, 67, 68, 72, 74, 75, 77, 79, 80, 81, 82, 83, 84, 89, 90, 91, 92, 94, 96, 97, 98, 99, 100, 102, 103, 108, 109, 112, 113, 114, 115, 117, 118, 121, 130, 131, 132, 140, 141, 142, 150, 151.

Map (p. 6): Jonathan Lim

Index

Illustration numbers are indicated by *italics*